WITHDRAWN

Gold Braid
and
Foreign Relations

Gold Braid
and
Foreign Relations

Diplomatic Activities
of
U.S. Naval Officers,
1798–1883

David F. Long

NAVAL INSTITUTE PRESS
Annapolis, Maryland

Library of Congress Cataloging-in-Publication Data
Long, David Foster, 1917–
Gold braid and foreign relations.
Includes index.
1. United States—Foreign relations. 2. United States. Navy—
Officers—Political activity—History—19th century. 3. Diplomats—United
States—History—19th century. I. Title.

E183.7.L776 1988   327.73   87-34879
ISBN 0-87021-228-1

Book design by Bea Jackson.

To Deborah E. Watson and the other research librarians
at the Dimond Library, University of New Hampshire,
for their intelligence, diligence, and patience

Contents

Illustrations

Portraits

Maps
(circa 1850 unless otherwise stated)

Preface

I feel that it is incumbent upon the author of a historical work to justify the selection of his or her topic; in this case my choice of subject as well as commencement and terminal dates. To some degree I am updating Charles O. Paullin's *Diplomatic Negotiations of American Naval Officers, 1778–1883* (Baltimore, 1912). This was a seminal monograph, and almost anyone describing either the "old" navy (that prior to the "new" navy that began in the mid-1880s) or American foreign relations over the same period has had to dip into it. In my research I have consulted it scores of times. At this writing it is still the only full-length treatment of the subject for the years that it covers. Nor has it lost its usefulness, although I sometimes disagree with Paullin's evaluation of persons and events. Furthermore, I have made no effort to expand the length of his discussions. Since I have so much more ground to cover than he, my coverage of the diplomatic material we both include is usually shorter than his.

Despite its value, Paullin's work is inadequate for the modern scholar. Published in 1912, it perforce omits all the voluminous material about U.S. naval and diplomatic history that has been produced in the last three-quarters of this century. It consists solely of Paullin's 1911 "Albert Shaw Lectures on Diplomatic History," delivered at the Johns Hopkins University, in Baltimore. It has only a short preface and no conclusion whatever. After recounting Commodore Robert W. Shufeldt's treaty with Korea in 1882–1883, and "Early Relations with Africa and the Pacific, 1821–1872," Paullin simply stops writing. His organization is geographical, save for a chapter on the diplomacy of John Paul Jones during the American Revolution. With that I have no basic quarrel, for after much thought and an attempt or two to develop a topical approach, I agree with him that treatment by area is usually the most applicable and useful.

Yet a glance at my table of contents shows that my decision to treat the subject by area has not been a strait-jacket. Diplomatic circumstances for naval officers during the nation's official hostilities are so different from those of peacetime that special segments have been devoted to three of the four wartime periods before 1883. Chapter 1 narrates the U.S. troubles with France, Tripoli, and Algiers to 1816, chapter 2 discusses the War of 1812 inside the framework of the Napoleonic War, and chapter 15 treats the Civil War and its aftermath as a whole. The single exception is the Mexican War, so intimately associated with Mexican-American relations up to that time that it has been included under the geographical heading of Latin America in chapter 4. Moreover, Shufeldt's voyage from Africa to the Far East, 1879–1880, and his Korean treaty, 1880–1883, would be reduced to a meaningless hodgepodge if distributed by area. Chapter 19 links them together in their entirety.

Paullin also ignores the disparity in potency and to some extent in aims between the pre– and post–Civil War navy; national trends after 1865 combined to reduce markedly the instances of U.S. naval diplomacy, which had peaked during the 1850s. A single comparison should suffice: My work contains a mere 34 instances of naval-officer diplomacy during the 14 years from 1870 to 1883, when the American naval decline took full effect. The 11 years from 1850 to 1860 have 135. Furthermore, *Diplomatic Negotiations* came out while many still applauded post-1900 U.S. gunboat diplomacy, permitting Paullin to be considerably more benign about earlier naval aggressions than one writing today would likely be.

Finally, it is unfortunate that Paullin limited himself to "diplomatic negotiations." Granting that they are an integral and meaningful part of the navy's impact upon American foreign policy, there are many others. Nothing that a U.S. naval officer did while in the process of treaty-making came close to the damage caused by Captain Charles Wilkes in 1861 when he removed by force the Confederate emissaries Mason and Slidell from the British ship *Trent* in international waters. Can anyone doubt that his overreaction brought on by far a closer approach to an Anglo-American war than anything else wrought by a naval officer since 1815? But Paullin's self-imposed restriction made him unable even to mention this critical event.

My substitution of the word "activities" for "negotiations" makes possible a much wider coverage than my predecessor's. Instead of one, I have eight categories of naval-officer operations that influenced the foreign relations of the United States:

(1) Throughout, officers' overwhelming major responsibility was the global protection of American merchantmen and citizens, and they simultaneously tried to enlarge commercial opportunities for their fellow-countrymen. (2) They acted as warriors during their nation's declared hostilities. (3) In peacetime they often behaved as actual or potential aggressors, opposing illegal blockades while foreign wars raged, or as policemen on the *qui vive* for pirates and other outlaws. (4) They negotiated or made treaties. (5) As nonbelligerent diplomatic activists, officers spent much time discussing a variety of problems with foreign authorities, not necessarily involving treaty interpretations. (6) They were affiliators, for often an officer was accompanied by, or had to work abroad with, a resident State Department employee; success might depend on how well the two could agree on a course to follow. (7) Under the pleasant heading of humanitarians they rescued those in danger, foreigners as well as Americans. (8) A few officers became expansionists, trying to annex sites for naval depots or even for actual colonies. They were, however, almost invariably overridden by Washington. Except for two tiny uninhabited islands, U.S. overseas territorial acquisitions had to await the late 1890s. The above categories are not hard and fast; often a single activity falls into two or more.

An obvious problem has been that of inclusion. My personal judgment that an officer's activity had some impact upon American external relations has determined selection. The navy's internal operations, such as those during the Seminole Indian War of 1835–1842 or those against outlaws in home waters, have been excluded, unless they had repercussions abroad. Nor does an officer's mere contact with foreign authorities without some degree of diplomatic consequence have a place in this work. For instance, the commander of the U.S. Mediterranean (later the European) Squadron would be sure to have conversations with local officials in fifteen or twenty ports during his short tenure. They deserve no consideration here without the accompaniment of international tensions.

Experts in a particular geographical area may know of naval-diplomatic incidents that they feel should have been discussed. I forecast, however, that they will be few, because I have incorporated in the text roughly 500 cases. Others may complain about some that appear; I can only refer again to my own appraisals. I am sure to receive justifiable objections to my chapters 1 and 2, narrating events from the Quasi-War with France through the War of 1812. They are admittedly episodic and fragmented, lacking the much greater cohesion that commences in chapter 3. Since these earliest activities are bona fide instances of American naval diplomacy, they must be included. I can only point out that they were infrequent and usually disconnected. Another difficulty has been to decide how much background material to present without boring the area specialist or leaving the less knowledgeable in the dark about the local conditions from which events arose. The reader will evaluate the degree of success.

A word of explanation as to why this monograph starts in 1798 rather than 1778, the date Paullin chose. I have decided to omit the naval-diplomatic activities of the American Revolution; Paullin cites only John Paul Jones as an officer worthy of consideration in this context. Moreover, there were two early U.S. navies. The first literally went out of existence (save for a few revenue cutters) when the last Revolutionary warship was turned over to the French ally in 1785. Therefore 1798 appears a better commencement date than any other, for then an independent Navy Department was established and sent its men-of-war to sea. In regard to a terminal date, for two reasons Paullin and I concur that 1882–1883 is correct. First, an expanded and modernized service was on the horizon. Second, when Shufeldt wrote his Korean treaty and oversaw its ratification a year later, it marked the last time that a U.S. naval officer on active duty was given such a responsible diplomatic assignment.

My principal reason for writing this book is the hope that it may have continuing usefulness as a reference work. Paullin's *Diplomatic Negotiations* quickly became passé, but with all its limitations and omissions, for over seven decades it has been required reading for those wishing to burrow beneath generalities in nineteenth-century American naval or diplomatic history. Perhaps *Diplomatic Activities* might provide the same service for a like number of years.

As to those who contributed to this work: Dr. John H. Schroeder, professor of history, University of Wisconsin—Milwaukee, read the entire manuscript with the acute eye of a first-rate naval historian. Commenting helpfully on the parts of it pertaining to their areas of expertise were my colleagues at the University of New Hampshire History Department: Drs. Hans Heilbronner (Europe), Allen Linden (Far East), Frank D. McCann (Latin America), and John O. Voll (Middle East). Similar service was provided by Dr. Pablo Eyzaguirre, Anthropology Department, U.N.H.— now at Yale (Africa); Mr. David Kittelson, Thomas Hale Hamilton Library, University of Hawaii at Manoa (Hawaii and the other Pacific islands); and Commander Tyrone G. Martin (ret.), 57th in command of the USS *Constitution*, Cohasset, Mass. (that famous warship and naval history in general). Dr. Harold D. Langley, curator/director of the Division of Naval History at the Smithsonian Institution; and Dr. William T. Mallison, professor of law and director of the International and Comparative Law Program, George Washington University, both in Washington, D.C., gave me the benefit of their knowledge of international law.

As to the manuscript itself, I owe debts of gratitude for their aid and encouragement to Ms. Laurie Stearns, managing editor, and Dr. Paul W. Wilderson, acquisitions editor, of the Naval Institute Press; and as always to my wife, Susan Robinson Long.

David F. Long
Durham, New Hampshire

Gold Braid
and
Foreign Relations

Introduction

F our questions come to mind in analyzing how "Gold Braid" affected the diplomatic relations of the United States: (1) Under the American constitutional government what right did naval officers have, without specific assignment for that purpose, to write treaties in such areas as West Africa or the South Pacific, where usually no recognized centralized governments existed with which to negotiate? (2) When they acted as diplomats what were their relations with Department of State personnel, who typically had the primary responsibility for conducting foreign affairs? (3) Did the diplomatic activities of officers dovetail with other obligations of their profession, and were they constant or fluctuating during the years covered here? (4) Why may 1882–1883, in addition to being the terminal date for this work, be also deemed a dividing line between the "old" and the "new" navy insofar as they pertained to American external relations?

1. The Right to Sign Treaties

Some diplomacy was carried on by officers who had been granted this particular privilege, thereby becoming in effect agents of the president, empowered to act in his stead. Here would be found, among others, "Special Envoy" Commodore Matthew C. Perry, sent by the Fillmore administration in 1853 to write the first U.S. pact with Japan. Resident ministers abroad (the post of ambassador had to wait until 1893) or civilian appointees dispatched as executive agents acted as treaty-makers more frequently than did naval officers. Nevertheless, a *sine qua non* for all these negotiators was to deal with governments perceived as such under current international law, accepted and imposed upon others by the Western powers. It did not matter whether those regimes were imperial, monarchical, or republican in form, or whether they were long established and potent (as that of Great Britain) or evanescent and feeble (as those of much of Latin America). Those trying to write a treaty usually followed a formal process. After mutual understanding had been reached, the parties concerned would sign their agreement and dispatch copies of it to their respective capitals for ratifications, which, once exchanged, would declare the pact in force. Treaty-signing was only a preliminary. In the American procedure, should the president be dissatisfied with it or the Senate be unable to muster a two-thirds vote in favor, it was dead. Note the lofty status of a treaty; nothing in U.S. law outranks it. According to the Constitution's article VI, "This Constitution, and the Laws of the Land . . . and all Treaties made . . . shall be the supreme Law of the Land."

All this is clear enough and in general takes care of American formal understandings with the countries of Europe, Latin America, and the Middle East. The above ratification process was forced upon the hierarchical and Confucianist governments of the Far East and Southeast Asia. By the outbreak of World War I the relentless march of late-eighteenth- and early-nineteenth-century imperialism had turned almost all of Africa, Southeast Asia, and the Pacific islands into colonies of the Europeans, Japanese, and Americans. This meant that those areas were removed from treaty-making altogether, and agreements applying to them were reached by accords among their colonial possessors.

But prior to that development many independent locales in West Africa and the Pacific (Hawaii excepted until 1898) had no centralized governments at all. They were segmented into tribal units owing allegiance only to their own chieftains. How then could the American commander of a warship or a squadron write what was at least called a treaty with a regime not recognized under international law?

Certainly the language of the commission received by each officer when he entered the navy contained no such power, so that right must be found elsewhere. It has to do rather with how the U.S. Constitution has been interpreted concerning the president's prerogative of delegating his powers, in this instance to appoint presidential or executive agents.

In his *Law among Nations: An Introduction to Public International Law*, Gerhardt von Glahn pinpoints executive agreements as "a uniquely

American practice in conducting relations with other states." Unlike a treaty, with senatorial acceptance mandatory, these agreements are made by the executive branch, either with "prior congressional authorization, or, on occasion, without prior congressional authorization within the powers generally recognized as vested in the presidential office."

Milton Offutt, in *The Protection of Citizens Abroad by the Armed Forces of the United States*, briskly summarizes the matter: Since there is no way that the president can concern himself personally with everything important to the executive department, he " 'speaks and acts through the heads of the several departments in relation to the subjects which appertain to their various duties.' Therefore the act of a departmental head is 'in legal contemplation the act of the President.' Consequently, an order issued by the Secretary of the Navy to the commanding officer of a ship or a squadron has the authority of a direct order from the President and must involve the latter in its consequences."

Von Glahn and Offutt are helpful insofar as they go; their summaries are applicable to most naval diplomatic activities, including the completion of written understandings. But the question of right still remains unclear. Lieutenant Charles Wilkes, commanding the United States Exploration Expedition to the Pacific from 1838 to 1842, wrote treaties with tribal chiefs in the Samoa and Fiji islands. He had received no presidential instructions to do this, passed along to him by the secretary of the navy; he acted independently. What, then, was the basis of his right to sign them?

In grappling with this problem I turned for assistance to two authorities in the field: Dr. William T. Mallison, professor of law and director of the International and Comparative Law Program at George Washington University in Washington; and Dr. Harold T. Langley, curator/director of the Division of Naval History at the Smithsonian Institution. In their letters to me they have combined to explain to my satisfaction how amplifications of the U.S. Constitution relate to this issue. Article II, section 1, says, "The executive power shall be vested in the President of the United States." Section 2 says, "The president shall be commander in chief of the army and navy of the United States. . . . He shall have power . . . to make treaties [and to appoint diplomatic and other personnel] . . . But the congress may by law vest the appointment of such inferior officers, as they think proper, in the President alone."

Professor Mallison focuses upon presidential or executive agreements which include "an independent agreement-making power of the President" . . . "that in the practice of the United States it and it alone is used for certain types of agreements, e.g. armistice agreements." Concerning my doubt about Wilkes's treaties in Fiji and Samoa, he concludes that Wilkes "had the authority to do what was necessary to carry out his responsibilities as . . . [commanding officer]. In the absence of instantaneous communications with Washington, he could not have done his job unless he had entered into agreements which were necessary and ancillary to his primarily naval responsibilities. . . . In my view, Lieutenant Wilkes and those similarly situated would have had authority by necessary implication to enter into appropriate Presidential Agreements."

Dr. Langley notes the similarity between these naval treaties and those concluded by contemporary army officers with American Indian tribes. He quotes Francis Wharton's *Digest of the International Law of the United States* (1886), vol. 1, chapter 4 ("Diplomatic Agents"): "Powers concerning political questions distinguished from naval affairs are entrusted to the care of ministers of the United States; and the President's instructions are communicated through . . . [the Department of State]. Responsibilities of a peculiar character are devolved upon the commander of a squadron; and the President's instructions are conveyed through the Navy Department." Langley concludes his précis: "There being no ministers of the United States in the Pacific to handle the political questions, they were handled by the naval officer . . . so that he could carry out his responsibilities of a peculiar character."

Having managed to discern how U.S. naval officers in out-of-the-way locales could conclude these informal understandings, one must realize that in law they were not treaties at all, no matter if they were designated as such. In 1879 Commodore Robert W. Shufeldt, after signing pacts with tribal chieftains in Madagascar, off lower East Africa, accentuated what they really were: not treaties but "simply agreements in writing, by virtue of which our people can be protected against the violence of a turbulent, savage, and often drunken population which acknowledges no other authority than the chiefs whose signatures we have obtained." Shufeldt might have added that when broken, they gave carte blanche to U.S. commanders to inflict what punishment they wished.

Nevertheless, these "treaties," although never sent by the president to the Senate, or those that failed to receive the two-thirds vote essential for ratification, occasionally worked out as effectively as those satisfying the full constitutional requirements. A case in point is the understanding reached by Commander Thomas a. C. Jones in 1826 with the royal government in Honolulu, upon which the Senate never voted. From then until the first Hawaiian-American treaty was signed in 1849, historians agree that its provisions were regarded as binding upon both peoples and in general obeyed. So, technically inoperative though they may have been, these nontreaties deserve a place in the annals of U.S. naval diplomacy.[1]

2. The Naval-Officer Diplomat vis-à-vis State Department Personnel

Some of the attributes of an excellent officer are conducive to his efficacy as a diplomat, but most are not. The sagacious officer recognized this and shifted his emphases accordingly. But he always knew that the major criterion for climbing the ladder of promotion was his behavior in combat, during declared wars or in hostile peacetime emergencies. Evidence of indecision or the slightest taint of cowardice, even if he escaped a court-martial conviction, would probably result in his being frozen at his current level. Administrative ability in such positions as commandant of a navy yard would help, but any diplomatic triumphs he might have recorded would have little to do with his advancement.

To be ranked high as a warrior, the officer had to have thoroughly mastered seamanship in all its intricate forms. He had to be able to lead into combat a crew used to discipline stern enough to make obedience to orders automatic, without becoming a martinet hated by his men. Before his guns spoke he had to assess the situation intelligently to decide whether to give battle or flee. Once action had commenced he had to be an audacious risk-taker while remaining within the bounds of prudent common sense. In an instant he might have to measure correctly the factors encouraging him to fight on against those urging him to strike his colors.

The diplomat, naval or civilian, used in negotiations the normal procedures of international relations, accepted at least in the West. The officer had a trump card that the civilian negotiator lacked—fire power, or at least the threat of it, to underline his demands. Furthermore, the main reason for the officer's existence was to fight wars, whereas the civilian worked to avoid them. Yet a trait leading toward diplomatic success for both was knowing when to give in and when to stand firm. Perhaps the officer's ability to decide between contending and running away, between continuing the engagement and surrendering, was akin to the civilian's need to evaluate what was vital in negotiations and what was not, and to concede nonvital issues in order to win the big ones. Of course a difference here is that the officer often had to make up his mind quickly, but the civilian might have been able to take a long time in coming to a decision.

Many authors have commented on the qualifications helpful when the sailor turns statesman pro tem. Glenn Tucker, a historian of the early navy, accentuates that "the early commodore had to possess political insight, emotional balance, and understanding of people, and a strong appreciation of the national interest. He was, in fact, the United States on the firing line." Frank M. Harris, a naval officer writing in the 1930s, says: "In days gone by, before the advent of the cable and the radio, the naval commander on foreign station was likewise the diplomat. He embodied both naval and diplomatic policy. He presented his case as diplomatically as might be, and with a force equal to his broadside." Charles O. Paullin considers the officer as "preeminently a 'shirt-sleeve diplomatist' . . . who could best combine force with persuasion." William N. Still, a modern historian, notes, "A naval presence in foreign waters provides a number of advantages. It is available to respond quickly in case of a local threat to its country's interests. It can prevent war or limit it by acting as a passive force. . . . It also acts as an instrument of diplomacy." Naval expert Peter Karsten refers to the service as the cutting edge of diplomacy and calls its warships "floating embassies." As early as the American Revolution, John Paul Jones summarized the heavy responsibilities of the officer-diplomat:

> He should be conversant with the usages of diplomacy, and capable of maintaining, if called upon, a dignified and judicious diplomatic correspondence; because it often happens that sudden emergencies in foreign waters make him the diplomatic as well as the military representative of his country, and in such cases he may have to act without an opportunity of consulting his civic or military superiors at home, and such action may easily involve the portentous issue of peace or war between great powers.

Ideally cooperation between navy and State Department personnel was highly desirable. Often, however, they clashed over the relative status of each. If the commander of a U.S. squadron met the resident American minister in his office to discuss what should be done during a crisis, and they disagreed, which one could command the other? The answer is— neither. Despite the need for collaboration, each had his own special criteria to consider. As to the minister, presumably he knew more than his rival about Washington's policies toward his own area and was more aware of the local political situation. In 1853 Matthew C. Perry spoke for the officer's right to decide matters pertaining to his fleet: "It is the duty of commanders to advise with and act in concert so far as may be practical with those functionaries [ministers, consuls, and special agents], but no one but themselves can properly judge the fitness of their ships for particular service, their supplies, and for steamers of fuel. These are matters rarely considered by those who invoke assistance and whose thoughts are ever engrossed in their business."

This divided responsibility was ably enunciated by Secretary of State William H. Seward in 1869 when Alexander S. Asboth, U.S. minister to Argentina, and Rear Admiral Sylvanus W. Godon, commodore of the South Atlantic Squadron, differed at one point during the war between Paraguay and Argentina, Brazil, and Uruguay. Both sides argued their case, asking for a solution in Washington. Seward's reply was detailed, but was so fundamental to the issue that it merits lengthy quotation:

> There is no subordination of the ministers to the commanders of a squadron, and no subordination of the commander of the squadron to a minister [emphasis added]. It is always unfortunate that agents of the two classes are not able to agree upon a course to be adopted in an unforeseen emergency. But that inconvenience is less than the inconveniences which must result from giving authority to a minister in one state to control the proceedings of a fleet of whose condition he is not necessarily well informed and whose prescribed services are required to be performed not only in the vicinity of the minister, but also in distant fields over which he has no supervision. Nor would it be more expedient to give a general authority to the commanding officer of a squadron to control or supersede the proceedings of political representatives of the United States in the several States which he might have occasion to visit. . . .
>
> It is even now impossible, with all the information of which the Government is possessed, to determine which party, yourself or the admiral, practiced the wisest and soundest discretion in the matter referred to. . . . While, therefore, your own [Asboth's] proceedings are approved, those of Admiral Godon are not disapproved.

The principle that civilian diplomats had no authority over naval officers and vice versa was tailor-made for controversies between them. When the commander visited even a small port, he would be likely to find a resident U.S. consul there. In the capitals of recognized governments he would meet the American minister at his legation. Now and then the officer would be accompanied by a special agent on a specific mission. The nature of these relationships was often determined by the rank of the State Department appointee involved. Especially during the early years, many consuls were Americans absorbed in their own business affairs, impervious to interests beyond their own circumscribed bailiwicks. A few were even foreigners having little knowledge of or regard for the nation they officially represented. The officer's relations with the comparatively low-ranking consul were generally less abrasive and important than those with higher-level diplomats.

Typically U.S. ministers lacked previous diplomatic experience; now and then one would turn out to be of great disservice to his country. A case in point was the rattle-brained Stephen A. Hurlbut, American minister to Peru in the early 1880s, who caused the navy much concern because of his anti-Chilean policies during the War of the Pacific. But some of these cadet diplomats—even such political selectees as unemployed former congressmen—could put to good use the talents they had already demonstrated in other occupations and learn well the niceties of their new profession. The qualifications of special envoys dispatched by the president on particular errands also ranged from the incompetent to the first-rate, and a diplomatic background did not seem to guarantee good performance.

Social status had much to do with how an officer got along with a minister or agent. Peter Karsten has painstakingly confirmed the upper-class origins of most officers. Although he concentrates on the late nineteenth century, there is no reason to think that officers in earlier times were of less aristocratic standing. Nor did the typical minister or envoy emerge from a lower level. Both were members of that little coterie of Americans in politics, business, the law, the professions, and the military who ran the government and most of its institutions; pre–Civil War Southern planters were about the only representatives of agriculture. This social similarity might have operated to produce the kind of affinity due to similar interests, backgrounds, and education.

Often, however, the similarities provoked heat rather than warmth. Both groups called themselves "gentlemen," and many of them justified that appellation by exhibiting the most tender sense of personal honor. Enmity was almost a certainty when two such irascible and opinionated personalities as Humphrey Marshall, U.S. commissioner to China, and Commodore Perry, rapt in his Japanese assignment, were put together in the Far East during 1853, each with his own jurisdiction to protect. Captain James Biddle had to transport Special Agent John B. Prevost to Chile in 1817; by the time they came into Valparaiso they detested each other. The stormy relationship between Commodore Philip Voorhees and presidentially appointed Joseph Balestier in Southeast Asia during 1850–1851 seems in retrospect puerile. Perhaps the wonder is that there was often affinity and accord between the sailor and the civilian.[2]

3. The Major Responsibilities of the Navy, Diplomatic and Otherwise

The officer had many duties to perform beyond his obvious one of keeping his ship and people in fighting trim. In wartime he battled against Frenchmen, North Africans, Britons, Mexicans, and his fellow-American Confederates. Sometimes he was assigned the leadership of exploratory expeditions in which he had to pay careful attention to marine soundings and coastal surveys. The one headed by Wilkes in the South Pacific, 1838–1842, was of enduring importance, and some of its charts were still useful a century later in operations against Japan. The officer occasionally acted as a humanitarian, rescuing castaways of all nationalities and landing at ports to quell fires. Sometimes he had to behave as a policeman, protecting sea lanes from pirates and going ashore to restore order during foreign insurrections or outbreaks of mob violence; now and then he brought refugees on board for transportation to safety. He was known to save missionaries from outraged natives, particularly in the Middle and Far East. While commanding a squadron he continually circulated from port to port throughout his jurisdiction, "showing the flag" to assure Americans living abroad that their country was concerned about their persons and property, in addition to reminding foreigners of U.S. power.

In all these occupations, however, officers followed a single lodestar: the protection and enhancement of the nation's commerce. Almost every navy secretary from 1823 to 1884 alluded to this outstanding responsibility. Abel P. Upshur, in his *Annual Report for 1842*, said that "a commerce such as ours *demands* protection of an adequate naval force. Our people, scattered all over the world, have a right to require the occasional presence of our flag, to give assurance to all nations that their country has both the will and the power to protect them." Secretary Gideon Welles echoed the same theme 23 years later: "The commerce and the navy of a people have a common identity and are inseparable companions. Each is necessary to the other, and both are essential to national prosperity and strength. . . . Following the tracks of commerce, and visiting every navigable portion of the globe, the intelligent officers of the navy are capable, from their position and opportunities, of acquiring and communicating a vast amount of useful information, thereby benefiting commerce, and promoting the welfare of the country and of mankind." The African Squadron was remiss in apprehending slave ships because of the Department's constant reminders to its commodores that first of all they were the advance agents of American enterprise, and their main duty was to open new areas for the country's carrying trade. Interference with the internationally outlawed slaver was a distinctly secondary chore.

The press spoke for commerce. In 1826 the Baltimore paper *Niles' Weekly Register*, writing about the Brazil Squadron, stressed the economic and psychological importance of the navy to the United States:

> It is gratifying to an American to see our national ships in this quarter—their presence, their character, give us confidence, and inspire foreigners with respect for our government, which seems ever ready to watch over our interests and to guard our rights. It is to be hoped that the squadron will be continued on this coast; it has, be assured, a most happy influence on our officers—producing, either directly

or indirectly, benefits cheaply purchased. . . . The time has arrived, when the naval forces of the United States should be kept up and increased, in those seas where our commerce continually displays the swelling canvas of enterprise, beneath the propitiating banner of the "free and the brave."

This central purpose also determined basic American naval strategy. Only Great Britain had the means to keep a powerful fleet in home waters and at the same time maintain squadrons around the world. Washington sagaciously realized that the American people would not stand for the cost of duplicating London's effort. With the Mexican War being the only foreign war from 1815 to 1898, the Atlantic and Pacific provided security against assault from abroad, especially in view of the generally amiable British-American relations. Therefore naval appropriations were required mainly for squadrons located abroad. To be sure, there was a so-called "Home Squadron" from 1842 to 1861, but most of its activities were concentrated in the Gulf of Mexico and the Caribbean, less frequently off eastern Canada.

This naval-commercial alliance made sense in the time before the Civil War, for during the 1840s and 1850s the imports and exports of the United States conveyed in its own vessels skyrocketed, and by 1860 the American merchant marine was approaching the tonnage of its mammoth English counterpart. After Appomattox this momentum began to stall and there occurred a precipitous decline in the percentage of the country's goods carried in its own bottoms. There was nothing haphazard about this development, for the nation deliberately turned its back on the sea in order to focus on opening the West and increasing its industrial potential. The trend was also reflected in a simultaneous weakening of American naval potency for a variety of reasons, commercial and otherwise, until a renaissance of U.S. sea power slowly commenced in the mid-1880s.

Yet the same idea continued to be expressed even after the union between naval officers and merchants had lost much of its former cohesion. When Commodore Robert W. Shufeldt traveled toward the Far East in 1879 and 1880, his official correspondence and private letters revealed his heartfelt intention to create a new "Empire of the Seas" by opening new opportunities for American entrepreneurs in Africa, the Indian Ocean, and Southeast Asia. He labored hard in this quest, but tides moving in other directions frustrated the realization of his master plan. Around the turn of the century new naval requirements imposed by colonial expansion and the need to guard accesses to the prospective Panama Canal, though they did not terminate the formerly potent naval-commercial partnership, certainly weakened it.[3]

4. The Communications Revolution and the Years 1882–1883 as the Dividing Line between the "Old" and "New" Navy

Shufeldt's activities in Korea during the early 1880s were the last independent major treaty-making by a U.S. naval officer. They also coincided with the coming of swift communications, which would soon alter significantly the role of the naval officer as a diplomat. The telegraph, stringing its wires overland and packing them together in the underwater cable at sea, was the great breakthrough. In 1867 Washington was finally connected with London and before and after that a telegraphic network, hastened by rivalry among the powers to outdo one another in the field, stretched through North and South America, Europe, the Middle East, and Africa. As early as 1871 the Far East was reached when wires crossed Siberia to Vladivostok, close to China, Japan, and Korea. The Pacific was the last obstacle to be overcome. Although many of the islands in the southwest ocean were connected by the cable from Singapore to Australia and New Zealand, not until 1903 did Hawaii receive such service. This marked the completion of the global telegraphic web, with radio only a decade away. But it should be stressed that during the time span covered here, in much of the world the American navy had to operate without this time-saving device. Moreover, even when wires were available, departmental economy usually insisted on mail, because of the high costs charged by the cable companies.

Before almost instantaneous exchanges of information were common, transportation dictated the pace of communication. Intelligence could be sent no faster than the means of carrying it, and they were agonizingly slow. Only Mexico, the West Indies, Central America, and the northern coast of South America were close enough to enable Washington to keep in touch with events happening there in terms of weeks. Elsewhere months had to elapse before messages could pass back and forth. A conspicuous instance of the way the snail-like pace of communications affected American history occurred when the British ship carrying the vital tidings that the Treaty of Ghent, signed on 24 December 1814, had ended the War of 1812, met such contrary winds that seven weeks went by before she reached the United States. Had the Atlantic cable been available then, there would have been no Battle of New Orleans on 8 January 1815, and very likely no President Andrew Jackson.

It might be imagined that the better transportation of the mid and late nineteenth century would have considerably speeded up communications, but it was many years before this was accomplished to any significant extent. True, sea-borne conveyance did improve with the coming of the fast clipper ships and the increased number of steamers afloat. Yet the impact of the latter has been overrated. Even in the 1880s the American merchant marine was still mostly wind-propelled, and those of its ships with engines tended to use their sails at sea, relying on steam to enter and leave harbors. So did U.S. warships. They had both steam and sails, but to save money navy secretaries constantly prodded their commanders to use canvas rather than coal.

For some time the revolution in transportation and communication altered little the commander's freedom to make decisions in diplomacy and other endeavors that he had always enjoyed. Once he had lifted anchor for a cruise, he escaped from the direct control of the department. To be sure, he always sailed under orders from his own secretary and occasionally from the secretary of state. But typically these had to be couched in generalities, at least to the extent of recognizing that they might be in large part inapplicable because of changed circumstances abroad. Furthermore, when a squadron was on foreign duty, even the commodore could not supervise one of his subordinates while he was absent on special assignment. As Robert E. Johnson writes, "As soon as the departing warship saw the flagship disappear below the horizon, her captain was almost as independent of his commodore as was the latter of the Navy Department in Washington." This was particularly true once the officer had rounded Cape Horn or the Cape of Good Hope. In the Pacific and Indian oceans he had to estimate that three months or more must pass before his report could reach the secretary, perhaps weeks more while he and the president were digesting his information, another long interval before the officer could read his new instructions. Meanwhile conditions in his area might have changed sufficiently to invalidate anything the secretary told him to do. He was also aware that he must deal with any emergencies with only the force he possessed; requested reinforcements would not arrive before the better part of a year.

Appreciating the problems imposed upon officers in faraway waters by sluggish communications, one newspaper issued an apologia for one of the more bizarre episodes in U.S. naval diplomacy. During 1842 the same T. a. C. Jones who had written the "treaty" with Hawaii in 1826 believed that war had broken out with Mexico and forcibly occupied Monterey in California. Upon realizing his error he evacuated the town within little more than a single day, but his landing naturally widened the breach between Mexico City and Washington. The *Daily National Intelligencer*, while regretting the incident, sprang to Jones's defense:

Naval commanders, it must be considered, serving in remote seas, charged with high and responsible trusts—protectors and defenders of the flag of the Republic—are often constrained to act decisively and promptly, according to their view of facts and circumstances seen only by the lights shed about them at the time; to act, often, indeed, without any certain knowledge of events at home, without orders or despatches from home for perhaps a year or more, when thousands of miles from their native land.

In short, a wide latitude had to be granted to the naval officer's intelligence and common sense in many of the places and during most of the time covered in this work.

The naval officer's freedom to make diplomatic decisions on his own commenced to decline toward the end of the century, when improvements in communication began to take effect. Increasingly the president and the secretary of the navy could hold tighter reins on their commanders. Shortly after World War I, Rear Admiral H. S. Knapp leveled his finger at the difference between naval diplomacy in his day and that of a half-century before: "The ease of modern communications makes the most resolute and self-confident man think twice before adopting a course of action that he would adopt without hesitation if so situated that weeks or months would be necessary for consultation with the home government; while the irresolute or self-distrustful man, or one who fears to take responsibility, has under modern conditions a ready reason for doing nothing until he has been told what to do." Lieutenant Commander G. B. Vroom, writing at about the same time as Knapp, explained how matters had altered to strengthen the role of the professional diplomat and weaken his part-time naval counterpart: "No longer do we commission our naval officers to negotiate treaties with foreign powers, or leave weighty questions of war and peace, or the concluding of alliances to the initiative and judgment of one man. War has become too costly and too serious a calamity to mankind; the swiftness of events, the vast problems of modern war . . . require the almost constant and exclusive concentration of those whose business it is to deal with them." William N. Still cites Rear Admiral Caspar F. Goodrich, who earlier had expressed a sentiment probably common to his colleagues: "The cable spoiled the old Asiatic Station. Before it was laid, one really was somebody out there, but afterwards one simply became a damned errand boy at the end of a telegraph wire."

To some degree Goodrich exaggerates. Naval officers occasionally took independent action after 1883. Perhaps the most extreme example of this was Rear Admiral Henry T. Mayo's highhanded behavior at Tampico in April 1914, which almost brought about a Mexican-American rupture. Henry R. Wriston calls attention to naval officers signing later agreements "relating to wireless telegraphy and to the revision of the Geneva convention, all acting under appointment and by instructions from the Department of State." But such activities conducted by those detached from duty and, in effect, with the secretary looking over their shoulder, can hardly be compared to many one-man, on-the-spot, and vital decisions made by earlier officers. Two mid-nineteenth-century examples: In 1851 Commander Silas Ingraham aimed his guns at an Austrian frigate and took from her a so-called American citizen at Smyrna (modern Izmir), Turkey. Three years later Commander George N. Hollins, on his own volition, risked causing an Anglo-American war by shelling and burning Greytown, a settlement in the British-occupied Mosquito (Miskito) Coast of Nicaragua. In the range and importance of its impact upon its nation's international relations the "old" navy quite outshines the "new."

Taken together, Shufeldt's Korean Treaty and the innovations in communication would appear to make the years 1882–1883 an acceptable terminal date for this account of U.S. naval-officer diplomacy.[4]

CHAPTER ONE

War, Neutrality, and Peace; and the Quasi-, Tripolitan, and Algerian Wars

1798–1816

When the United States was at war—as it was in only 16 of the 85 years covered in this work—the responsibilities of American naval officers were not what they were during periods of neutrality or of general international peace. In wartime, if the U.S. was the stronger maritime power, it could use its navy to transport and cooperate with army landing forces, blockade the enemy coast, and hunt down opposing commerce raiders, as in the Tripolitan, Mexican, and Civil Wars. So overwhelming was the U.S. naval advantage over Algiers in 1815 that a single short strike was sufficient to end the matter. When the contestants were relatively equal, as in the Quasi-War with France, individual ship action became the order of the day. If the United States was clearly the weaker, as in the War of 1812, the Navy Department's primary duty, beyond attempted interference with British invasions, became the harassment of enemy merchant marine, either officially by its men-of-war or semiofficially by privateers. Single-ship victories such as those of the famed USS *Constitution* were much more important in elevating the national morale than in affecting the outcome of the contest.

Wartime strategic considerations often spilled over into the diplomatic. When the duties of U.S. naval officers affected relations with neutrals, all such activities were enhanced during hostilities, with larger rewards and heavier penalties in prospect for the individuals concerned. For instance a wartime situation might permit an officer to gamble that he could get away with a serious violation of a neutral's rights in pursuit of a military objective. Should this illegality promote American aims, as in a case at Bahia, Brazil, in 1864, it could not only be overlooked but even be secretly applauded and rewarded by quick promotions and more desirable assignments, whereas in peacetime it would surely have brought on a court-martial. Yet should an officer's acts have resulted in the entry of another nation into existing U.S. hostilities on the enemy side, the one responsible would have been ruthlessly punished by his government. Luckily for naval officers, that situation never arose, despite many close calls, such as the interception of the steamer *Trent* in 1861, which came within a hair's-breadth of bringing Great Britain into the Civil War against the Union.

There were diplomatic repercussions from naval actions in the Quasi-War with France, 1798–1800; the Tripolitan War, 1801–1805; the War of 1812, 1812–1815; the Algerian War, 1815; the Mexican War, 1846–1848; and the Civil War, 1861–1865. Conflicts with the Indians, such as the Seminole War, 1839–1842, sometimes included naval activities, but these of course had no impact on U.S. foreign relations.

As a rule, very little background will be provided in this book about conflicts in which the United States was a belligerent. Full descriptions would swell the volume to excessive size; a paragraph or two would probably repeat what is common knowledge to many readers. But wars in which the United States was not a belligerent are another matter, because readers may have only the sketchiest knowledge of some of them; hence their backgrounds will be more extensively treated.

As stated earlier, by far the most essential task of the peacetime American navy was to protect the nation's far-flung merchant marine. But this task was much harder to carry out during wars of other nations than when peace prevailed. If one combatant tried to use its supremacy at sea to hamstring the opposition by setting up blockades and sending out privateers to aid its regular navy in cutting enemy supply lines, commanders of American men-of-war might be placed in a most touchy and delicate position. Where should the line be drawn between rescuing illicitly seized American ships and citizens and an unneutral interference with a belligerent legally using its sea arm to win the war? At what point does the behavior of a properly commissioned privateer turn her into a pirate? The U.S. naval officer on the scene had to realize that any laxity in protecting Americans and their property from unlawful belligerent actions could mean his court-martial for disobedience to orders. Yet if he swung too far in the other direction, he might involve his nation in a war, a result that would be sure to bring down upon him Washington's sternest condemnation.

The position of the commander was much less complicated where no war was being waged. There any attacks upon American merchantmen or even interference with their freedom of movement could be labeled piracy, and immediate punishment could be inflicted with relatively little fear of unpleasant military or diplomatic consequences. Under contemporary international law the pirate was recognized as an outlaw, able to call upon no government for assistance.

The Quasi-, Tripolitan, and Algerian Wars, 1798–1816

In the four wars waged by the United States in this period, the state of its navy determined in large part how the country would respond to each crisis. Because of the earlier Barbary assaults upon its merchant marine, followed by more recent similar depredations of French privateers, America finally possessed a fleet of sorts by the late 1790s. The Quasi-War and the Tripolitan War led to a significant increase in the nation's sea power. On the conclusion of the latter in 1805, however, the Jeffersonians opted for inexpensive gunboats rather than the potent larger vessels; by 1809–1810 the Navy Department had only one sizable warship operational. Anticipating an easy conquest of Canada, Washington brashly declared war on London, despite the fact that at the moment the Royal Navy had some sixty-four ships of the line, frigates, and sloops for every one American equivalent. The pendulum commenced swinging the other way with the wartime buildup, which was impressively underlined by the swift evisceration of Algiers in 1815. Its momentum continued, and by the 1830s the Sultan of Turkey actually considered British naval efficacy second to that of America.

The Quasi-War with France, 1798–1800
Lieutenant William Bainbridge at Guadeloupe, 1798–1799

The Napoleonic War became truly worldwide once the struggle spilled beyond its European theater. Among the several distant areas affected were the West Indies, badminton birds hit back and forth by Spain, Britain, France, the Netherlands, Sweden, and Denmark ever since their discovery started by Columbus—Tobago, for example, had changed hands some 20 times. In 1794 the British carried out whirlwind conquests of St. Lucia, Martinique, and Guadeloupe, save for St. Domingue (Haiti) the major

William Bainbridge
(Official U.S. Navy Photo)

French possessions in the Caribbean. But within two years Guadeloupe was retaken, and soon scores of privateers, protected by French warships, swooped out from its shores to fall upon American merchantmen. This was the cockpit in which the first diplomatic activity of a U.S. naval officer took place.

The United States and France, bound together since 1778 in an alliance supposed to last "forever," had grown apart by the 1790s. Milestones along the way to estrangement were American reactions to the bloody excesses of the French Revolution; the outbreak of the Anglo-French war, in which ultra-conservative American Federalists supported London; the touchy issue of America's neutral responsibilities while its ally was at war; and particularly the Anglo-American Jay Treaty of 1794–1795, which Paris viewed as a conspicuously unfriendly act. French privateers soon began apprehending U.S. commercial carriers in the Caribbean and along the southern coasts of the United States, and they took more than 300 by the end of 1797.

The newly independent Navy Department (separated from the War Department in 1798) retaliated under Benjamin Stoddert, its energetic first secretary. Intermittent hostilities of the "Undeclared Naval War with France"—or more succinctly the "Quasi-War"—remained just that, for neither country saw any advantage in escalation. There were three major large-ship encounters: Captain Thomas Truxtun in the *Constellation* captured the French frigate *L'Insurgente* during February 1799 and *Vengeance* twelve months later, and Captain George Little in the *Boston* defeated *Le Berceau* the next October. The fledgling U.S. service did well in its first action, seizing no less than eighty-five French vessels while losing only one. American naval officers contributed significantly to their nation's diplomacy during this contest at Guadeloupe, off Cuba, and in Haiti.

William Bainbridge, after a brief and tumultuous career in the merchant marine, the story of which is spiced by accounts of his physical prowess in quelling mutinies, was commissioned in 1798. That summer his 18-gun sloop *Retaliation* joined Commodore Alexander Murray's little squadron in the Caribbean. He erred by relying on a British report that there were no sizable French men-of-war in the vicinity. Before realizing his error, Bainbridge brought his vessel directly under the guns of the enemy frigates *Voluntaire* and *L'Insurgente*. Down came the American flag without a shot being fired. He had to face the fact that he had just won the sad distinction of being the first to surrender a warship of the U.S. Constitutional Navy. (She would be the only one lost to the French.) Presumably this should have meant his prompt dismissal from the service.

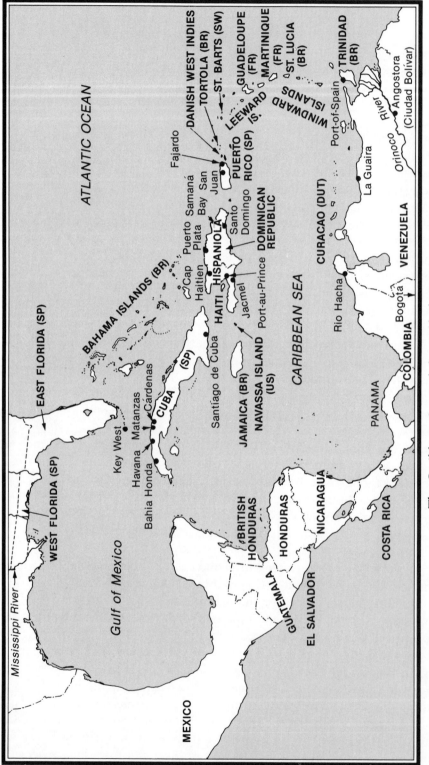

The Caribbean Sea and the Gulf of Mexico

Bainbridge rescued himself, however, by some quick thinking and adroit diplomacy. When he had been brought aboard the *Voluntaire* he lied to the French commodore, grossly exaggerating the guns carried by Murray's two other ships, which were therefore allowed to escape certain capture by *L'Insurgente*. Taken to the French island of Guadeloupe, the young lieutenant successfully countered the machinations of Governor Esmé Etienne Desfourneaux, who was trying to neutralize his island by expressing warm regard for Americans, a stance totally belied by his hostile actions against them. Bainbridge refuted claims by Desfourneaux's agent, who accompanied him back to Philadelphia early in 1799, emerging victorious in a battle of letters between them, published in the local press. The United States continued to view Guadeloupe quite correctly as an enemy outpost, much to the governor's chagrin.

After mulling over the pros and cons of the matter, the Navy Department not only retained Bainbridge on its roster but promoted him to "master commandant" (commander). Later he was occasionally referred to as "Hard Luck Bill," but this nickname could not have been less accurate. To be sure, he would chalk up the unenviable record of pulling down the American flag on the first three national warships ever to endure that indignity—the *Retaliation* in 1798, the *George Washington* at Algiers in 1800, and the *Philadelphia* in Tripoli Harbor during 1803. Yet, each time, compensating factors enabled him to carom off disaster to climb another rung on the naval ladder, until he relished the crowning triumph of his career when his *Constitution* blasted HMS *Java* out of the water off Brazil late in 1812.[1]

Captain Isaac Phillips off Cuba, 1798

In the confusion of sending the navy into its first combat, Isaac Phillips had been given command of the 20-gun converted merchantman *Baltimore* without having officially received his commission. Convoying thirty sail from Charleston to Havana, he was halted off Cuba late in July 1798 by a potent British squadron consisting of three ships of the line and two frigates. Realizing that any resistance would be hopeless, he played for time, going on board the British flagship after signaling his convoy to hasten into Havana, an order that saved the crew of every vessel from forced enlistment in the Royal Navy. The English commodore informed Phillips that any of his men without papers identifying them as bona fide American citizens would be impressed into his service. After protesting this outrage, the captain returned to the *Baltimore*. There he found that his first lieutenant, Joseph Speake—a cousin of Secretary Stoddert—had permitted a British lieutenant to muster everyone on deck and that the visitor was in the process of taking off 55 sailors, about one-third of the ship's complement. Phillips pulled down his flag to signify that he was surrendering to superior hostile forces. The British commodore ignored the move, but perhaps afflicted by second thoughts as to the legality and possible international repercussions of his provocative act, returned all but four of the 55 and departed.

When Phillips reported to the department what had happened, he justified his behavior on two grounds: his instructions had told him that "the vessels of every nation except France are on no account to be molested," and Captain Thomas Truxtun's oral order had told him that he must "keep on good terms with the British by every act of conciliation." Stoddert rejected these explanations, belatedly publishing a statement that no officer should "permit the public vessel of war under your command to be detained or searched, nor any of the officers or men belonging to her to be taken from her by the ships or vessels of any foreign nation." The secretary curtly informed Phillips, "Your services are no longer required."

Stoddert's merciless action may be understandable in light of his conviction that the government had never imagined that orders to maintain amity with the British would be construed to allow such a flagrant insult to the flag. Yet how could Phillips, with a 20-gun former merchantman, be realistically expected to resist forcibly an order from an officer commanding five heavy men-of-war outgunning the *Baltimore* about twenty-five to one? Furthermore, the Navy Department demonstrated no sense of fairness or equity in this matter. Stoddert hounded Phillips out of the service but censored not at all his cousin's craven conduct, which had permitted the British to come on board; indeed, he appointed Speake acting commander of the *Baltimore*. As late as 1820 Phillips tried in vain for reinstatement, even though he was backed by the aged ex-President John Adams, who pointed out that since his commission had never been officially received, he could not be cashiered out of the navy. Nor was the Phillips precedent followed consistently. In mid-1805 a British squadron off Cadiz impressed three men from Lieutenant James Lawrence's *Gunboat No. 6*, but Navy Secretary Jacob Crowninshield took no action against that officer, enabling him to continue his scintillating but short-lived career in the service.[2]

Captain Christopher R. Perry, et al., in the Caribbean, 1799–1800

U.S. naval officers during the Quasi-War contributed much to the formation of what soon became the independent republic of Haiti in western Hispaniola. That former French colony of St. Domingue, rich in tropical exports, had featured probably the most feral form of slavery that existed in the Western Hemisphere. By 1790 some 30,000 whites, 40,000 mulattoes, and 450,000 black slaves inhabited this most opulent and most unhappy European possession in the Caribbean. The French Revolution's winds of freedom drifted across the Atlantic, soon followed by the announcement that slavery had been abolished in the French colonies. Haiti's white rulers were toppled, and most of the planters were either killed or fled into exile. A confusing kaleidoscope of foreign invasions and internal power shifts ensued, out of which emerged André Rigaud as the leader of the mulattoes and Pierre Dominique Toussaint L'Ouverture as the black champion. By early 1800 Rigaud controlled much of the southwest, and his "picaroons" turned the Gulf of Gonave into a piratical lake, sending out armed barges to assail American ships and committing atrocities on their people. Toussaint, controlling the rest of Haiti, seemed aiming at independence, whereas Rigaud accepted the continuation of French rule. The United States saw a clear advantage in backing Toussaint, both to protect its citizens and their property and to weaken the French enemy in the West Indies.

The department sent out Captain Christopher R. Perry (the father of the more famous Oliver Hazard and Matthew Calbraith) in the 28-gun frigate *General Greene* to assist the black leader. When he arrived off Haiti in February he found that Rigaud's army was trapped at the town of Jacmel, and his intervention was decisive. One of Perry's officers described what happened: "We engaged three of Rigaud's forts warmly for 30 or 40 minutes; in which time we obliged the enemy to evacuate the town." Toussaint lavished compliments upon the captain for "signal and important services . . . rendered me. . . . He contributed not a little in the success of his cruise, every effort having been made by him to aid me in the taking of Jacmel."

Eight other U.S. naval commanders were soon emulating Perry's work, among them Bainbridge in the brig *Norfolk*, whose orders were to "cultivate a good understanding with General Toussaint." Somewhere along Haiti's west coast he met that famous black, who regaled him with a sumptuous banquet "served with much taste and elegance," thereby permitting the American to add his bit toward retaining the Haitian's friendship.

Bainbridge then put out to sea and, after sinking the notorious pirate schooner *Beauty*, settled down to cruising off Cuba. This monotonous duty was broken by the information that the Spaniards in Havana were readying a privateer to move against American shipping. Bainbridge reacted peremptorily enough to bring on a Spanish-American confrontation when he notified the governor-general that "*French privateers*, fitted out in *Spanish ports*" would be treated as enemies. If necessary to keep her from sailing, he would blockade Havana. But any potential clash vanished once the vessel in question had been dismantled by her captain.

American naval efforts were successful in both diplomacy and martial action in helping not only to implant Toussaint's rule but also to end the undeclared hostilities with France. Many of Rigaud's corsair ships were picked off and their depredations on American commerce practically eradicated. Such activities climaxed in mid-September when Commander Charles Stewart in the sloop *Enterprise* captured a French schooner with Rigaud aboard; he was imprisoned for the rest of the Quasi-War. All this coincided with a pronounced slackening of French warship and privateer activities in the West Indies. The Quasi-War ended with the Franco-American Convention of 1800, ratified late the next year. It freed the United States from its twenty-two-year alliance, in return for Washington's assumption of monetary claims owed by Paris to American citizens. The U.S. Navy's baptism of fire had been auspicious.[3]

The Tripolitan War, 1801–1805
Captains Henry Geddes and William Bainbridge in the Mediterranean,
1799–1801

The guns of the Quasi-War were still thundering when another conflict loomed, this time in the Mediterranean. Tripoli, Tunis, and Algiers (dependencies of the Turkish sultan, although usually able to act as sovereign states), as well as independent Morocco, had long earned their living by preying upon Christian commerce, seizing ships and enslaving their crews. Even the larger European nations found it cheaper and simpler to pay tribute rather than mount costly naval campaigns against them; their smaller maritime rivals had no choice but to follow suit. Ever since the 1780s American merchantmen had occasionally been pounced upon by North African corsairs. With literally no navy except revenue cutters — the last American Revolutionary warship had been sold in 1785 — the United States signed treaties with all four North African entities between 1786 and 1797. Under these agreements Barbary countries had to be provided with not only cash but naval stores and men-of-war as well. Even so, American shipping was still not safe from harassment by their raiders.

Congress finally appropriated funds for starting the Constitutional Navy in 1794 after Algerian cruisers had snapped up 11 American vessels in the Atlantic. But tribute-paying went on, with Algiers alone receiving during 1798 and 1799 a 36-gun frigate, a 22-gun sloop, and three armed schooners. Ironically, at the same time Americans were exulting in the slogan originating from their refusal to pay bribes to France in 1797: "Millions for defense but not one cent for tribute!"

American naval officers had to perform on a regular basis such degrading errands as delivering tribute to the Barbary potentates. A brief glance at one instance and a more thorough analysis of a second (among many others from the mid-1790s to 1815) will supply examples. In the first, Captain Henry Geddes in the *Sophia* in 1799 had to escort the handsome new brig *Hassan Bashaw* and two schooners to Bobba Mustapha, Dey of Algiers, before going on to deliver presents to Tunis's Bey and Tripoli's Bashaw Yusuf Karamanli. The latter imposed a treaty on the United States that cost $20,000, but as Yusuf would soon show, the more tribute was paid, the more was demanded. Geddes sailed homeward past Gibraltar in July 1799, thankful no doubt that his shameful ordeal was over.

In the second instance, William Bainbridge, in August 1800, was ordered to take the frigate *George Washington*, 32 guns, laden with naval and other supplies, to Algiers. There in mid-September he found that Bobba Mustapha had just realized how deeply he was in trouble with Constantinople. Although Napoleon's army was still in Egypt, he had made a separate peace with France, ignoring the fact that his Turkish overlord remained at war. Only the most lavish gifts to the sultan might spare him and his people from the most condign punishment by the Turkish navy. So Bainbridge, to his utter consternation and disbelief, was informed what he had to do, under the threat of war should he decline. His proud American frigate must take to Constantinople a hundred-man Algerian delegation and a great variety of presents, including a menagerie consisting of 4 horses, 150 sheep, 25 "horned cattle," 4 lions, 4 "Tygers," 4 "antilopes," 12 parrots, and a number of ostriches. Furthermore, he must sail under Algerian colors. Frantic objections by Bainbridge and U.S. Consul Richard O'Brien were unavailing, and according to the *George Washington*'s log, "the pendent [sic] of the United States was struck and the Algerian flag hoisted. . . . some tears fell at this Instance of national Humility," very likely from Bainbridge himself when for the second time he watched his standard descend. Although once his ship was out to sea the American flag was raised, he wrote to the department that never again should he be sent "to Algiers with *tribute* except it be from the *mouth of a cannon*."

His fortunes were about to turn, for his Turkish adventures proved to be as triumphant as those in Algiers had been dismal. As he neared the forts guarding the entrance to the Dardanelles, blocking the way to Constantinople, he was afraid that if he halted for permission to proceed it might be denied. So he decided to befuddle the Turks by lowering his sails as if to halt and then slapping on full canvas, racing up the strait before his subterfuge was realized—he later interceded to save the deluded Turkish commander from execution. The sudden appearance of a foreign warship at the capital understandably caused a furor, but Bainbridge was still welcomed amiably. He landed his Algerian mission and floating zoo; no wonder the log reported that the crew spent three whole days "Washing Decks."

A few days later the main Turkish fleet came in, consisting of fifteen ships of the line and numerous lesser craft. It was commanded by Hussein Kutchuk, a combined secretary of the navy and first admiral, foster brother of the sultan, and recognized as the second highest authority in the empire. Bainbridge's lifelong ability to make new friends on the spot came to the fore, and Hussein was soon showering him with compliments and giving him "every mark of attention." The admiral even suggested that a commercial pact should be signed by the two nations. Bainbridge enthusiastically agreed, forwarding the proposal to his government. The records do not explain why the first Turkish-American treaty would have to wait until 1830, but for some reason the United States during the early 1800s did not follow through on Hussein's suggestion. This was unfortunate, for had it been completed or even under serious discussion, it is most unlikely that Tripoli, the weakest of the Barbary powers, would have dared to declare war.

Although Hussein could not have treated Bainbridge more cordially, his behavior toward the Algerian delegation was totally different. When he read the Dey's letter, with its feeble excuses and craven apologies, he went into "a great rage, first spat, and then stamped upon it." He then assessed the harshest penalties on the hapless Bobba Mustapha. Just before Bainbridge departed for Algiers, the admiral gave him a firman (decree) entitling him to the "greatest respect" everywhere in Turkish territories.

When the *George Washington* anchored at Algiers in January 1801 carrying Hussein's ultimatim, the Dey was plunged into despair by its terms: he must liberate hundreds of Christian slaves with British passports, declare war on France at once, and remit a punitive assessment of $3,240,000. Visualizing what fifteen Turkish battleships could do to his city, he had no option but to comply. He told Bainbridge to ready his ship immediately to transport the necessary funds to Constantinople. For the first time the American had an ace to play and categorically refused, saying that he had already suffered "*every humiliation*," and would do so no longer. At this insolent retort Bobba Mustapha flew into such a frenzy that for a moment it appeared that Bainbridge would be hacked to pieces by Algerian retainers. Just in time he produced his Turkish firman, at the sight of which the Dey was magically transformed "From a furious tyrant . . . into an obedient vassal; his tongue all honey, his face all smiles." Not only was his voyage to Turkey cancelled, but Bainbridge was able to use his new standing to rescue 56 French subjects who had been enslaved when Algiers declared war on Napoleon. A couple of days later, according to the log, he finally escaped the "barbarian's fangs," dropped off the French in Spain (Napoleon later expressed his gratitude), and headed for Delaware Bay, which he reached in mid-April.

Bainbridge's Mediterranean tour must have caused some head-scratching in Washington's administrative circles, akin to that concerning his Caribbean experiences a short time before. Once again he had surrendered an American warship without a shot; he was perhaps a coward, perhaps inept, and certainly ill-starred: he should be cashiered. But second thoughts prevailed. As O'Brien, the U.S. consul at Algiers, had stressed in a report, had Bainbridge denied the Algerians the use of his frigate, a war for which the United States was quite unprepared would inevitably have broken out, permitting Algerian corsairs to engulf the country's unprotected commerce overseas. A conflict with Algeria and Tripoli (with the possible entry of Tunis) would have been a far more difficult fight than one with the Bashaw alone. In addition, Bainbridge had cemented a new friendship between the United States and Turkey, had availed himself of this to cow Bobba Mustapha—thereby ensuring Algerian neutrality in the rapidly approaching Tripolitan War—and had earned French gratitude for saving their nationals from the Dey's vengeance. Once again he escaped punishment. Indeed, he was one of only nine captains retained in the navy's post-Quasi-War reduction in force, praised for his "general good Character," and reassigned to active command.[4]

Commodore Richard Dale at Tripoli, 1801–1802

As for the conflict itself, by the spring of 1801 Yusuf Karamanli, the Bashaw of Tripoli, had confirmed his long-held suspicion that his neighbors, especially the Dey, were receiving from Washington far more than he in warships, commodities, and cash. For many months he had used both cajolery and intimidation in efforts to get more, but to no avail. His patience exhausted, during mid-May he declared war on the United States. Unlike their anti-French activities and their preliminary work in North Africa, adding up to only five partially separated incidents, the diplomatic exertions of American naval officers during Tripolitan hostilities require no similar précis. Naval and diplomatic events were so closely entwined during this conflict that its major salient features may be spotlighted in the forthcoming analyses of what successive commodores could accomplish in both fields.

Commodore Richard Dale's orders were ambiguous, since Washington did not know whether Bashaw Yusuf had actually declared war. The commodore did enjoy one stroke of good fortune when in the *President* he trapped Tripoli's two most potent warships at anchor at Gibraltar during July and immobilized them permanently. He briefly corresponded with the Bashaw off Tripoli but soon broke off negotiations, for he had been granted no treaty-making powers. After blockading the city with some effect, he arrived home in April 1802 and resigned from the service. Considering his lack of specific orders and diplomatic authority, he did about as well as any other commander might have done.[5]

Commodore Richard V. Morris at Tripoli and Tunis, 1802–1803

Commodore Richard V. Morris, who arrived overseas in the *Chesapeake* during May 1802, proved to be the embodiment of indolence, whiling away the time before reaching Tripoli a year later. Unlike Dale, he had been empowered to open peace discussions with the Bashaw, who demanded an immediate $200,000 in cash, an annual payment of $20,000, and compensation for the entire cost of the war. Morris could offer no more than $15,000 in all. In an effort to dispel threats of intervention, he unwisely went ashore at Tunis, where the Bey arrested and held him until he was, in effect, ransomed. This final indignity impelled the department to recall him and dismiss him from the navy, an act that Charles O. Paullin calls "unjust" but from Morris's uninspiring record appears to have been well merited.[6]

Commodore Edward Preble at Morocco and Tunis, 1803–1804

Next in command was Commodore Edward Preble, by far the best Tripolitan War commodore. His fighting abilities operated as exemplars to his officers and men until circumstances beyond his control aborted his diplomatic endeavors to dictate a victor's peace. When he entered the Mediterranean in the *Constitution* during September, he commanded four frigates, five sloops, and sufficient gunboats, apparently a force strong enough to bring the Tripolitans to the conference table.

En route he stopped off at Tangier, for he had discovered that the Emperor of Morocco had authorized attacks upon American merchantmen and had already taken one. His powerful squadron persuaded the Emperor to reaffirm the U.S.-Moroccan Treaty of 1786, thereby keeping that country out of future hostilities. But this diplomatic victory soon

Edward Preble
(Official U.S. Navy Photo)

paled into insignificance beside the appalling news that Captain William Bainbridge and everyone on board the 36-gun frigate *Philadelphia* had been captured in Tripoli harbor late that October, the details of which are well enough known to need no recapitulation here. Not only had Preble lost about one-eighth of his entire force, but now Yusuf held 307 hostages as trumps in any coming negotiations. The entire complexion of Preble's plans to terminate the Tripolitan War had been irrevocably altered.

Making the best of a bad situation, the commodore commenced a policy of the stick and the carrot toward the Tripolitans. He applied the cudgel to the Bashaw with greater élan and efficiency than any other American

Barbary commander until Stephen Decatur in 1815. During August and September 1804 he launched five separate assaults against Tripoli, but the enemy managed to survive. During this period Decatur's small contingent managed to creep into the harbor unseen and incinerate the *Philadelphia* without loss of American lives. This astonishing triumph, however, was offset by a disaster a little later. The little ship *Intrepid*, crammed with combustibles and bombs to wreck the city, detonated while still in the harbor, killing Lieutenant Richard Somers and his volunteer complement. About the same time Preble was recalled, and whether he could have pounded Tripoli into submission has to remain a moot point.

Unfortunately Preble had been able to use his diplomatic carrot less effectively than his naval stick. He and other American officers and diplomats (Bainbridge excepted) never seemed to comprehend that the continued retention of the *Philadelphia*'s people enabled the Bashaw to maintain a practically impregnable position. For instance, after capturing some Tripolitans, Preble thought that this would enable him to force Yusuf to lower his demands significantly, but Bainbridge accurately forecast failure, because the Bashaw would not give "an orange A piece for his subjects." Preble's best offer of $40,000 for the release of the captives was contemptuously spurned. Bonaventure Baussier, the French consul in Tripoli, acted as a go-between during these negotiations, emphasizing to the Americans that they would either have to pay a much larger sum for the hostages or carry the city by fire and sword. Although he was right, for his candor he earned the hostility of both Preble and Bainbridge.[7]

Commodore Samuel Barron at Tripoli, 1804–1805

Samuel Barron, brother of the unfortunate James, who would surrender the *Chesapeake* in 1807, was the next commander. During his entire tenure in the Mediterranean he was ill from a liver complaint, and American blue-water offensives fell into a lethargy that exceeded even that of Commodore Morris. But an electrifying development broke loose ashore. The able and choleric General William Eaton, now naval agent to the Barbary states, was the new factor. After long preparation he formed an alliance in Egypt with Hamet Karamanli, the previous Bashaw of Tripoli, from whom his brother Yusuf had usurped the throne. In March 1805 Hamet, 10 Americans (Eaton, a naval lieutenant, and 8 marines—hence the "Shores of Tripoli" in their hymn), 25 artillerymen, 38 Greek mercenaries, and some 400 Arab cavalrymen marched west. They managed to overcome a host of supply and disciplinary problems while plodding over 500 miles, first to storm and then to hold against counterattacks Derna, the easternmost Tripolitan stronghold.

The possibility of Eaton's advancing on his capital threw Yusuf into a panic. On the one hand it brought him closer to the bargaining table; on the other it apparently menaced the lives of his prisoners. Some modern historians, Glenn Tucker among them, have doubted that they were in peril, arguing that their continued existence was the Bashaw's life-insurance policy, but the evidence to the contrary seems persuasive. Dr. Jonathan Cowdery, who had become the Karamanli family physician and was the captive closest to Yusuf, noted that "the Bashaw declared, that if the Americans [and Hamet] attacked the town he would put every American prisoner to death." Secretary of the Navy Robert Smith later reported, "Many of the officers, late prisoners in Tripoli . . . say positively . . . that the Bashaw had made up his mind to massacre them while our forces were laying waste the town. . . . Having killed his father and a brother, he could not have any scruples in killing a few infidels."

Bainbridge, fearing for his life, grudgingly admired Yusuf and felt only contempt for Hamet, his "poor effeminate fugitive brother." He threw his considerable weight on the side of the American appeasers, Barron and Tobias Lear, consul-general to the Barbary powers. By the spring of 1805 Lear had established a strong domination over Barron, who was suffering from a fever on top of his chronic ailment. The diplomat began acting as de facto commodore, much to the resentment of naval officers.[8]

Commodore John Rodgers at Tripoli and Tunis, 1805

John Rodgers, morosely waiting for Barron either to die or to voluntarily turn over command to him, was much opposed to compromise with the Tripolitans. He claimed that personally he could raise from the fleet's personnel a ransom of $200,000 for the release of the hostages. But by the time he became commodore, negotiations with Yusuf had gone too far to be reversed. Rodgers was able to flex his martial muscles a little later in a different context. During that August he amassed a potent armada of 11 warships, including the *Constitution*, off Tunis, whose Bey had been threatening war unless his blockade runners at Tripoli were returned to him. But after goggling briefly at such concentrated strength, the Bey gave in, granting the United States most-favored-nation standing and sending an "ambassador" to Washington so that future disputes might be settled by on-the-spot diplomacy.

As for Tripoli, the treaty ending its war was signed on 3 June. The Bashaw promised to spare American merchantmen from his cruisers and gave his erstwhile enemy most-favored-nation privileges. The hostages were liberated for $60,000; Eaton's improbable little army was compelled to evacuate Derna, and Hamet was thereby doomed to lifelong exile. On their return to America Bainbridge and his fellows were hailed as conquering heroes, their own and their government's errors of omission and commission that had brought about their imprisonment conveniently forgotten.

Although contemporary commentators and later historians have disagreed about whether the United States should have signed such a disadvantageous pact, the conclusion here is that accepting it was a mistake *if* the nation was willing to pay the high price of the lives of the captives: With the naval forces on hand, soon to be reinforced by additional men-of-war already speeding across the Atlantic to join him, Rodgers would soon have been able to lead into battle "six frigates, four brigs, two schooners, one sloop, two bomb-vessels, and sixteen gunboats"—thirty-one ships and boats in all. Such an irresistible force could have struck together with Eaton's thrust toward the capital. This combination would very likely have toppled Yusuf and avoided the ignominy of ransoming the *Philadelphia*'s complement and ruining Hamet, the former Bashaw. But that probability had to be weighed against the possibility of 307 Americans being murdered in Yusuf's last frenzy, at the cost of arousing intense public outrage and producing a political calamity for the Jefferson Administration. In the last analysis, Bainbridge's loss of his frigate made the terms of the Tripolitan Treaty about as good as could be realistically expected.[9]

The Algerian War, 1815–1816
Commodores Stephen Decatur, William Bainbridge,
and Isaac Chauncey at Algiers, 1815–1816

When hostilities with Great Britain ended in 1815, the United States had the wherewithal to write finis to the humiliations and exasperations heaped upon it since the 1780s by the Ottoman Empire's Barbary dependencies. Consul-General Lear's Tripolitan treaty had impressed the Dey and the Bey little if at all. Algiers remained the most truculent, despite its continued reception of tribute from Washington. Its raiders kept on stalking American vessels, and had not the American Embargo Act of 1807 and further commercial restrictions from 1807 pretty well swept the national commerce from the Mediterranean, Algerian depredations might have been impressive. The Dey treated Tobias Lear, the resident U.S. consul, with contempt, twice requiring him in effect to ransom himself to avoid imprisonment. During the War of 1812 he became a British ally, receiving large amounts of naval stores, but so complete was British naval control that the Dey could take only the *Edwin*, a small Salem merchant-

Stephen Decatur
(Naval Historical Center)

man. In March 1815, after Madison had assured the country that it possessed both the cause and means necessary, Congress declared war on Algiers. Actual hostilities lasted only a few weeks during that summer. No other conflict in American history has had its diplomacy restricted to a single naval officer.

William Bainbridge should have been that man, on the basis of seniority, his triumph over HMS *Java* late in 1812, and his able defense of Boston during 1814, which perhaps spared it from a British invasion. Stephen

Decatur, who had defeated HMS *Macedonian* and brought it into port in 1812, had watched his luck run out later in the war. Trapped during much of 1813 and 1814 in New London, Connecticut, by superior enemy forces, he had lost the frigate *United States* to a four-vessel British squadron early in 1815. Back from British internment, Decatur ached to wipe his escutcheon clean of these stains; as he put it, "I shall satisfy the world that there has been no loss of honor." He would accomplish this by wresting the Algerian command from Bainbridge in a campaign as tactically adroit as it was morally shabby. The relationship between the two officers is important, for it explains why Decatur later threw away some of the fruits of his naval victory.

Secretary of the Navy Benjamin Crowninshield became his minion; the department was soon flooding ships, supplies, and men to Decatur in New York, while withholding them from Bainbridge in Boston. The former was able to sail first with a potent squadron, leaving the latter, frustrated, resentful, and outraged, to tag along with a second. Accompanied by William Shaler, eventual U.S. consul in Algiers, Decatur raced into the Mediterranean, having confided to a friend that he would "whip the cream off the enterprise" before Bainbridge could show up to share in the glory.

Off southern Spain he spotted the *Mashouda*, a 44-gun Algerian frigate, already engaged by the *Constellation*. Decatur knifed his *Guerrière* in between them and polished off the enemy, and in his official report of the engagement did not bother to mention the good work of the other ship. Two days later he drove the smaller Algerian *Estedio* aground on Spanish soil and captured it. The commodore then sailed on to Algiers, resolved to dictate peace, as he complacently said, "at the mouth of a cannon." The Dey, having nothing to match his opponents, quickly gave in and signed what is called the Decatur-Shaler Treaty. A few American prisoners were released, a fine of $10,000 for seizing the *Edwin* was imposed, most-favored-nation status received, and Algiers was compelled to realize that America would never pay tribute again.

Although Shaler deserved some credit for spreading bribes among the Algerian bureaucracy to facilitate the negotiations, it had been basically Decatur's one-man show. But he then threw away much of his accomplishment, impelled by his determination to beat Bainbridge to Tunis and Tripoli. He carelessly promised the Dey that his two lost ships would be returned to him forthwith, ignoring the fact that the *Estedio*, having intruded into their territorial limits, was still being held by the Spaniards. Shaler, as well as other American diplomatic and naval personnel abroad, was infuriated by Decatur's offhand pledge to Algiers (and, later, by his eventual premature departure from the Mediterranean). One of those

Americans cuttingly observed that Decatur would "sacrifice his best friend to aggrandize his own fame—had Bainbridge not been so close at his heels, be assured that the reasons for continuing the war would not have been found wanting." But Decatur, leaving others behind to rectify if they could his unwarranted commitment, sped on to Tunis to collect $46,000 from the Bey for having turned over to the British two wartime prizes brought into Tunis by an American privateer. Before coming home he triumphed again at Tripoli, where the Bashaw was compelled to pay $25,000 and to release European captives.

Meanwhile Bainbridge, also with a powerful squadron, had plowed across the Atlantic, and learned that Decatur had already done everything necessary. He mourned in a personal letter, "I have been deprived of the opportunity of either *Fighting* or *Negotiating*." He went through the required motions, stopping for only a few hours at Algiers, Tunis, and Tripoli before coming into Gibraltar, where he and Decatur held a brief and gelid meeting that cemented their enmity for the next five years.

Decatur then beat Bainbridge back to America and was saluted as the ultimate Christian champion against Islam. Congress appropriated $100,000 for him and his men to compensate for the two Algerian warships that he had taken but that had to be restored to the Dey. The difference in the public receptions given to the rival commanders was summarized in a Philadelphia newspaper: for Decatur—"This is a Glory which has never encircled the brow of a Roman Pontiff; nor blazed from an imperial diadem"; for Bainbridge a small item reading in toto: "We are happy to announce the arrival at Newport of the U.S. Squadron under the command of Com. BAINBRIDGE."

A major breakthrough in European and American relations with Algiers in particular and Barbary in general happened in August 1816. Lord Exmouth, ordered to end North African aggressions once and for all, headed a combined Anglo-Dutch armada, battered down the Dey's fortifications, and compelled him to abolish enslavement of Christians, free his captives, and return Italian ransoms already paid. But Decatur's quick and thoughtless pledge that the *Estedio*, still held in Spain, would be handed back continued to roil American relations with Algiers and enabled the Dey, who was still without his warships, to avoid ratifying the Decatur-Shaler Treaty.

Commodore Isaac Chauncey in the *Washington* joined Shaler in Algiers in July with a six-ship squadron, but lacking treaty-making powers because of an oversight, had to sail back to Gibraltar to get them. A little later the Spaniards released the *Estedio*. By December Chauncey, proper credentials in hand, completed the Decatur-Shaler understanding, modified only slightly. Ratifications were not exchanged for six years, however, probably because of forgetfulness in the Department of State. One must conclude that it was neither Decatur's fighting ability, nor Bainbridge's unnecessary follow-up, nor Chauncey's collaboration with Shaler that eradicated the Barbary menace. It was rather Exmouth's chastisement of the Dey and the takeover of Algiers by the French in 1830 that finally ended the centuries-old North African Moslem harassment of the infidels.

Summary

In the diplomatic performances of the new blue-water constitutional navy, its officers came off reasonably well. If the surrender of Phillips to British press gangs was a national shame, it is hard to see how he could have resisted, and Stoddert perhaps overreacted when he dismissed him. Bainbridge's negotiations with the governor of Guadeloupe and his ensuing war against the governor in the American press were as inspired as his careless behavior leading to the capture of his ship had been negligent. The work of Perry and his colleagues was an important asset to Toussaint L'Ouverture in Toussaint's gaining control of Haiti, thereby aiding in the eventual frustration of Napoleon's aspirations for a new American empire. It is perhaps ironic, however, that the slaveowning United States, through the efforts of its navy, helped to bring about the establishment of the first free black republic.

As to the service's pre–Tripolitan War experiences in North Africa and Turkey, what happened to Geddes in his tributary mission amounted to an American humiliation, but Bainbridge was able to turn his initial abasement by Bobba Mustapha into a diplomatic victory, using his masterful tactics in Constantinople to win a victory over the Dey. In regard to the war itself, the commands of Dale and Morris may be quickly dismissed; the first was hamstrung by his conflicting orders and the second by his natural inertia. There is reason to believe that the dynamic Preble's offshore operations could have coincided with Eaton's assault west from Derna to impose a conqueror's peace on Tripoli. But that becomes only surmise once the Bashaw had Bainbridge and his people as hostages after the *Philadelphia* had been taken. The ailing Samuel Barron could do little save to urge the acceptance of a treaty that fell short of what might have been achieved, and Rodgers came along too late to accomplish much, except with Tunis.

In the Algerian War some success was won by Decatur's helter-skelter naval activities and diplomatic bargaining. But his triumph was diluted by his urgent need to ensure that Bainbridge not share his laurels, a motive dictated by his one glaring character flaw—his overwhelming hubris—a manifestation of which would cause him to fall before James Barron's dueling pistol only five years later. Lauded though he was by his compatriots, it still became necessary for Europeans to terminate the North African threat to their merchant marines.

In evaluating the overall efficacy of the navy's diplomatic contributions, one should recall that it was a brand-new navy, remarkably weak in comparison to the navies of Great Britain, France, and Spain, the European giants. Moreover, its public support, especially during Jefferson's administration, was erratic. The strong pro-navy policy of John Adams was reversed, primarily because a wing of the Jeffersonians considered the fledgling service, in contrast to the army, undemocratic and overly expensive. Hence the government strongly backed it only during times of crisis, such as those of 1798–1800 and 1803–1805, and neglected it until the next international challenge arose. Failures in its record should be judged in this context; so should its accomplishments, which thus become much more praiseworthy.

CHAPTER TWO

The Napoleonic Wars

1807–1815

Peacetime, 1807–1811
Commodore James Barron off the Virginia Capes, 1807

The titanic struggle between Great Britain and France raged, with two brief intermissions, from 1793 to 1815. No matter how ardently the United States might desire to remain neutral, it could not avoid being deeply affected. The belligerents paid little or no attention to American neutral rights, contemptuous of a nation practically without sea power, for the country was paying dearly for the early antinavy policies of the Jeffersonian administration. Britain and France vied with one another in seizing American ships, taking no less than 917 between 1803 and 1812 alone. As one congressman put it, "The Devil himself could not tell which government, England or France, is the most wicked."

But there were special reasons why most contemporary Americans were apt to conclude that the British were particularly culpable. They illegally blockaded the nation's ports, regularly interfering with merchant-ship movements. Faced with thousands of desertions, the Royal Navy impressed into forced service about 9,000 sailors, nearly all of them taken from private vessels, but on three occasions from U.S. warships. On this subject London was obdurate, considering impressment absolutely essential for naval (hence national) survival. Perhaps the most decisive reason why French illegalities were easier to overlook was the proximity of British

Canada, the conquest of which would be about the only way that the United States, without naval strength, could hurt either belligerent militarily. In addition to Canada's value per se, its annexation would have a beneficial twofold result: English-abetted Indian assaults on the frontier would cease and American territorial ambitions (forerunners in attitude of the later "Manifest Destiny" expansionism) would begin to be fulfilled. Moreover, events might work out for the annexation of Spanish East and West Florida. Finally, a severe agricultural depression struck hard at the South and West after 1810, for they depended on exporting American produce. On the other hand, the eastern maritime areas prospered in the perilous but lucrative overseas carrying trade for the British and French. This explains in part why the Northeast, in comparison to other sections, so thoroughly detested the prospect of war with Britain. Efforts of Jefferson and Madison to strike back at the foreign aggressors with commercial warfare signally failed.

Three events involving United States naval officers prior to 1812 had diplomatic consequences. Two of the three, in 1807 and 1811, could have provoked war; all of them fueled the growing American resentment of the arrogant behavior of "the mistress of the seas."

Perhaps one might wonder at the inclusion of the *Chesapeake-Leopard* affair (below) in a work devoted to the diplomatic activities of U.S. naval officers, since James Barron's "activity" in the matter was so passive. Its impact upon Anglo-American relations, however, was so pronounced as to warrant its inclusion. Furthermore, its echoes reverberated through naval circles for the next generation, with its major aftereffect the loss to the service in 1820 of Stephen Decatur, the country's most fervently acclaimed naval paladin.

Barron was ordered to the *Chesapeake*, the early navy's Jonah, to assume command of the Mediterranean Squadron. That frigate had been for some time undergoing refitting at the notoriously slovenly Washington Navy Yard, and she was in sorry condition when Barron took over, with supplies for the squadron scattered helter-skelter throughout the vessel. Within a week he was peremptorily ordered by Secretary of the Navy Robert Smith to depart for Gibraltar. He had no option other than to comply, so he sailed with his decks so littered as to make his 36-gun frigate a travesty of a fighting ship. On 22 June 1807 Captain Salusbury P. Humphreys's potent 56-gun frigate *Leopard* lay in wait for him off the entrance to Chesapeake Bay, acting on instructions from the British high command at Halifax to remove by any means necessary four Royal Navy deserters known to have signed on with Barron.

Humphreys forced the *Chesapeake* to heave to and announced that he

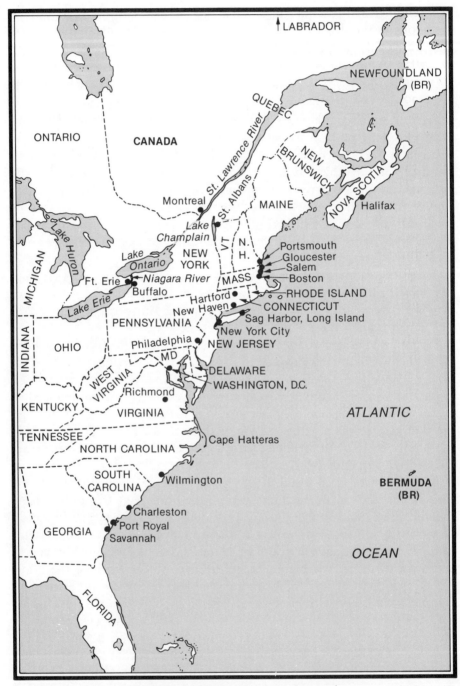

The Eastern United States and Canada

was sending men to board and search her for deserters. Barron was incredulous at the demand, for that indignity had never been imposed on U.S. warships, save for those of Isaac Phillips in 1798 and James Lawrence in 1805. He desperately stalled for time, but Humphreys commenced slamming broadsides into the helpless *Chesapeake*, killing 3 and wounding 18, among them Barron, hit in the leg. In the welter of materiel cluttering the gun deck, the frantic Americans could not even find the matches for their cannon. After Barron had shouted, "Fire one gun for the honor of the flag! I mean to strike!" an officer reportedly carried a live coal up from the galley, which enabled a single shot while the flag fluttered down. The wounded commodore tried to surrender his ship as a prisoner of war but Humphreys ignored him, took off the four deserters, and sailed away. A court-martial later sentenced Barron to a five-year suspension from the service without pay for "neglecting . . . to clear his ship for action."

When the battered frigate limped back into port, a wave of national fury erupted. British officers ashore fled to safety afloat and the Governor of Virginia called out the militia. A Boston paper screamed, "Let us whet the sword! Let us bend the bow!" President Jefferson later avowed, "I had only to open my hand and let havoc loose." But although he temporarily closed American territorial waters to the Royal Navy, he wisely played for time to let the country's rage abate. He knew that his maritime areas were strongly disposed to peace. He also had to recognize that he was totally unprepared for war; in 1807 he had almost no warships in commission, a situation for which he, as head of the economy-minded and weak-navy Democratic-Republican Party, must take the primary responsibility. He turned instead to economic warfare, primarily the ill-fated Embargo Act, about which more later. The admiralty in London realized that Humphreys and his superior had been wrong, but when Jefferson tried to use the *Chesapeake-Leopard* affair as a lever to pry from the British a total disavowal of impressment, they were unwilling to comply, and not until 1811 was an apology received, disavowing the attack and offering to release those taken. By that time the matter of the *Chesapeake* had disappeared into a morass of other issues, and the apology had no effect in slowing the American surge toward war.[1]

Lieutenant John Trippe off the Bahamas, 1810

John Trippe would have been about the last officer to be considered able to commit an act that his fellow countrymen would think cowardly. No one, save Stephen Decatur, had come out of the Tripolitan War with such a reputation for courage in hand-to-hand combat. But six years later his conduct was quite the contrary. On 24 June 1810 Trippe, commanding the sloop *Vixen*, was cruising through the Bahamas when the sloop HMS *Moselle* suddenly opened fire on him, carrying away the *Vixen*'s boom with two shots. Trippe cleared his ship for action, but when the British commander sent over a written apology, claiming that he had mistaken the American for a French privateer, he accepted it and permitted the *Moselle* to depart unscathed.

Public opinion in the United States split in reaction to Trippe's forbearance. Pacifist-minded Federalists applauded him; one New Hampshire paper said, "Like an officer of spirit, he demanded satisfaction of the Captain of the *Moselle*" and after receiving it, "he pursued his voyage." On the other hand, many Americans considered that the lieutenant had let slide a brilliant opportunity to exact vengeance for the *Chesapeake*. As Decatur put it, he had lost his chance "to cancel the blot under which our flag suffers." In Britain the semi-official London *Times* reprinted an account of the affair from a Washington journal written by an American "gentleman of great respectability" who considered such behavior "insolent" and typical of the "meanness" that British naval officers displayed to Americans. Of course the *Times* viewed these circumstances from different windows: "They are proof not of the passivity of Lieutenant Trippe, but of the base malignity of the [Washington] Editor," who was using "every invention and aggravation which may embroil" the Americans against the British so as to "extenuate the foul misdeeds of Buonaparte."

Secretary of the Navy Paul Hamilton was no kinder to Trippe than Decatur. He wrote him about the "extent of his mortification at this affair. I had fondly cherished the hope that our officers needed only an opportunity to vindicate the wounded honor of our flag," and recalled him to face "an inquiry . . . into your conduct." But Trippe died of yellow fever en route home a little over two weeks after his unwillingness to fight the *Moselle*. The American cup of shame, already well filled by Barron in the *Chesapeake*, received a dollop more.[2]

Commodore John Rodgers off the Virginia Capes, 1811

Navy Secretary Hamilton, still seething over the affairs of 1807 and 1810, sent the following directive to his commanders in 1811: "It is therefore our duty . . . to vindicate the injured honor of our navy and revive the drooping spirits of the Nation. It is expected that, while you conduct the force under your command consistently with the principles of . . . neutrality, you are to maintain and support at every risk and cost

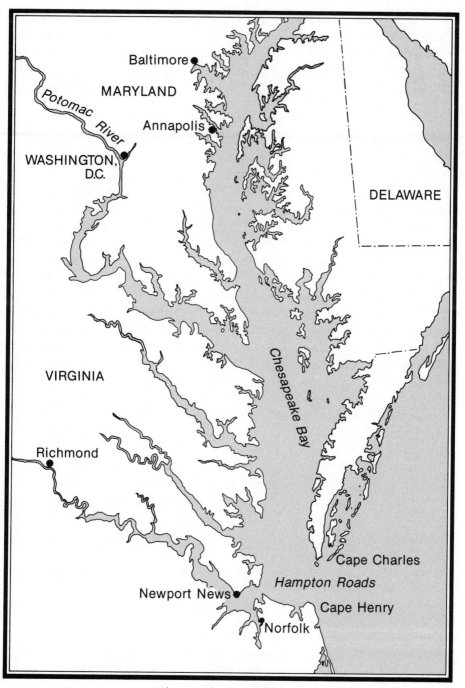

Chesapeake Bay Environs

the dignity of our flag; and that, offering yourself no unjust aggression, you are to submit to none."

In April the *Guerrière*, destined a little over a year later to be the first British frigate to be pounded into surrender by a U.S. frigate, was operating off the New York coast and impressed a sailor from an American merchantman. Rodgers went out through the Virginia Capes to look for her, while a Richmond paper prayed, "May the wounds of the *Chesapeake* and *Vixen* be washed away." On 16 May, some fifty miles offshore, a sail was spotted, from her rigging a naval vessel, and Rodgers assumed that she must be the *Guerrière*. At first the *President* gained on her rapidly, but with failing wind and light it was approximately 8:00 P.M. in the gathering darkness before he closed on the stranger. She turned out to be HMS *Little Belt*, a 20-gun sloop, under Captain Arthur B. Bingham, with despatches for the *Guerrière*, but in the dark Rodgers was unable to see that she was a single-decked sloop, not a double-decked frigate.

Anglo-American accounts varied as to which ship fired first, although the modern consensus holds that it was the *Little Belt*. At least all could agree on the result. One American boy was hurt, as opposed to 9 Britons killed and 23 wounded. Bingham mourned that "His Majesty's ship is much damaged in masts, rigging, and hull . . . many shots still remain inside." Under these circumstances it was remarkable that the Englishman was able to stay afloat and sail off the next morning. Once Rodgers discovered that his "glorious action" had defeated so much weaker an opponent, he was forced to realize that his triumph was tarnished.

London finally decided to respond to the 1811 crisis with diplomacy. When Augustus John Foster, the new British minister to Washington, arrived late that year with a belated apology for the *Chesapeake-Leopard* outrage, he found that the Madison administration was little interested, feeling that the *President-Little Belt* exchange had been ample compensation. But Foster recognized the latter's significance, reporting to his superiors in the foreign office that Americans planned to "make use of it, together with all other topics of irritation, for the purpose of fomenting a spirit of hatred toward England." Indeed they did, and the episodes involving the *Chesapeake*, *Vixen*, and *President* were steppingstones along a path leading to war. They helped to produce a feeling of belligerent nationalism that would eventually overcome the almost hysterical antipathy to hostilities with Great Britain in the maritime areas, and propel the country into a conflict that many Americans opposed.[3]

John Rodgers the Elder, 1773–1838
(U.S. Naval Institute)

The War of 1812 and Aftermath, 1812–1818
Commodore William Bainbridge and Commander James Lawrence at Bahia, Brazil, 1812–1813

The American declaration of war in June 1812 turned out to have been precipitate. The snail-like communications of that day made it impossible for Madison to know that two days later London repealed its obnoxious Orders in Council that had been the legal justification for the apprehension of American merchantmen. So almost from its commencement the War of 1812 became an exercise in futility. Moreover, examples of U.S. naval diplomacy are scanty. Only three officers involved themselves in this activity, two at Brazil and the third in the Pacific Ocean.

During the autumn of 1812 William Bainbridge's squadron, consisting of the flagship *Constitution*; the 32-gun frigate *Essex*, commanded by Captain David Porter; and the 18-gun sloop *Hornet*, under Commander James Lawrence, put out to sea. Departmental orders told Bainbridge to harry British commerce in the South Atlantic, with permission to round Cape Horn should circumstances warrant such an extension of his cruise. The *Constitution* and *Hornet* sailed before the *Essex* was ready, and Porter missed the others off Brazil, proceeding alone to the Pacific. When Bainbridge and Lawrence came into the northern Brazilian port of Bahia (Salvador), they met a chilly reception from the local government. Count dos Arcos, Governor of Bahia State, was reportedly in league with the enemy, sharing in the lucrative profits derived from the annual visits of some fifty British merchantmen.

Bainbridge spotted in port the Royal Navy sloop *Bonne Citoyen* and soon learned that she was carrying no less than $1,200,000 in specie. Despite the temptation, he decided to respect Brazilian neutrality, although he could easily have taken her. Furthermore, Lawrence, following a British packet into the harbor, also spared both enemy vessels. The Commodore was understandably furious when he received a bellicose protest from dos Arcos, calling Lawrence's intrusion "a proceeding decidedly hostile," for which he would seek "satisfaction and vengeance." Bainbridge was also aware that the Brazilians had filed no protest in London about violations of their neutrality, although HMS *Montagu*, a potent ship of the line, had been sojourning at Rio de Janeiro for many weeks beyond the time legally permitted. Outraged at this insolent partiality, he actually threatened a Brazilian-American war, writing the resident U.S. consul, "The Governor of Bahia talks of 'taking vengeance and of hostilities,' pray ask him the question, whether he considers our respective Countries at Enmity—inform me of his answer—and I will act accordingly."

But before any reply could be received, the *Constitution* stood out of the harbor. Lawrence was left to guard against the *Bonne Citoyen*'s departure, although he was soon compelled to sail himself, leaving behind all her appetizing cash. Bainbridge roamed off the coast until 29 December, when he accosted the frigate HMS *Java* and pounded her into surrender in the war's hardest-fought single large-ship action, sinking her the next day. On his return to Bahia, Bainbridge found that his victory had accomplished marvels in improving Brazilian-American relations: dos Arcos now treated him as his warm friend. He hastened home to revel in what he called "the applause of my countrymen [which] has for me greater charms than all the gold that glitters," finally wiping clean the slate of his abasements in the *Retaliation, George Washington,* and *Philadelphia.* His triumph over the *Java* obviated any possibility, remote though it was, that Brazil and its mother country Portugal might be drawn into the war.[4]

Captain David Porter off Peru and at the Galápagos and Marquesas Islands, 1813

Captain David Porter's primary quarry during his extended cruise in the Pacific was the British whaling industry, centered in the Galápagos Islands, well to the west of present-day Ecuador. Proceeding there in March 1813, he took time out to resolve a matter carrying international implications. Learning that the 15-gun Peruvian royalist privateer *Nereyda* had captured two American whalers, he disguised the *Essex* as an Englishman, thereby deceiving the pirate captain, who came aboard the *Essex.* Declaring his true nationality to his terrified visitor, Porter told the Peruvian that he would be hanged as a pirate for assaulting vessels of a country with which Spain was at peace. The *Nereyda*'s captain immediately displayed a commission signed by the royal governor in Lima permitting attacks on American shipping. After the *Nereyda* had been disarmed and partially dismasted, she was sent home, carrying Porter's ironic letter to the governor that he had done this in order to "preserve the good understanding" that existed between Peru and the United States. There were no further Peruvian depredations against American shipping until a heightening of the royalist-patriot war a little later.[5]

Although Porter's campaign in the Galápagos had no immediate diplomatic repercussions, it had considerable wartime and postwar impact, and made some slight contribution toward the agreement at Ghent. For several years London had fostered, through bounties and other economic benefits, the essential whaling business centered in those islands, for the early nineteenth century was dependent upon whale oil for lubrication as well as illumination. Arriving there the *Essex* crisscrossed through them for several months. Her destructive work was simple, because no Royal Navy men-of-war were in the Pacific until after the news of Porter's depredations reached London. From March through September 1813 the *Essex* apprehended ten enemy prizes worth, according to the captain's generous estimate, some $2,500,000, while saving a like number of American whalers from capture by the better-armed British equivalents. His exaggerations aside, Porter's efforts did have short-term and long-lasting consequences. They hit hard the war economy of his opponents; as one contemporary American observed, "the supply of oil was stopped," and London "burnt dark for a year." The squadron dispatched to halt Porter's depredations trapped and captured the *Essex* at Valparaiso, Chile, in March 1814, but the British realized that other American commerce raiders might emulate his work in the China seas and the Indian Ocean. Hence the desire to avert that possibility became one of the many reasons why they were willing to call off hostilities late in 1814. The most far-reaching result of Porter's actions in the Galápagos was that they gave the United States its near-monopoly of whaling in the Pacific for the next half-century, for although London made a brief postwar attempt to rebuild its shattered whaling industry there, it was soon abandoned.[6]

Porter's next diplomatic contribution to his country proved to be amusing rather than meaningful, although from it he won the title "The First American Imperialist." In October he brought the *Essex* for essential repairs into 186-square-mile Nuka Hiva, one of the Marquesas Islands in the south central Pacific. Although small, it was divided into no less than 31 separate tribes, among them the "Tickeymahues" and the "Attakakaheuahs." In November Porter told the Nuka Hivans, unquestionably to their total incomprehension, that he, "on the part of the United States, have taken possession of the island . . . the natives . . . have requested to be admitted into the great American family. . . . I have taken it on myself to promise that they shall be so adopted; that our chief shall be their chief . . . which secures to my country a fruitful and populace [sic] island."

This extraordinary act was the first American imperialistic venture, in the sense of an annexation of a distant area, heavily populated by a people differing from Americans in racial backgrounds, traits, and historical memories. Unfortunately for the captain's expansive vision, his message that he had just extended the nation's boundaries some 7,000 miles to the southwest arrived in Washington during the summer of 1814, coincidentally with the British army. The president's leading biographer writes, "Having trouble nearer at home Chief Madison of the Attakakaheuahs and thirty other tribes did not ask Congress to accept the island." Hence the first U.S. spasm of imperialism has remained a mere curiosity.[7]

To conclude the epic of Porter's cruise to the Pacific: his historical reputation suffered after he fell victim to that consummate hankering for personal fame so characteristic of the early navy's officer corps. Before he left the Marquesas he knew that a British squadron had come into the Pacific in search of him. Panting for glory, he sailed back to Valparaiso, where he was soon blockaded by an enemy frigate and sloop. While trying

David Porter, 1780–1843
(Official U.S. Navy Photo)

to escape, his maneuverability was crippled by a sudden squall that forced him back into the harbor. Cornered there, he was blasted into submission after a brave but futile resistance, which made casualties of some 60 percent of the *Essex*'s people. The diplomatic consequences of his defeat were swift: Chile, heretofore friendly to the United States, became pro-

English. Furthermore, Porter would have served his nation far better had he deliberately avoided combat, sailing instead to attack the unprotected British merchantmen in the western Pacific and Indian oceans. He should have seen that one U.S. frigate harrying enemy commerce in those distant waters would have been worth more to the American war effort than any single-ship triumph.[8]

Summary

Perhaps American naval diplomacy was at its nadir from 1807 to 1818. Granted the existence of compensating factors over which he had no control, Barron's degradation—hence his country's—was especially galling, since the practically navy-less United States could do nothing but commercial warfare to retaliate for the outrage wrought by the *Leopard*. At the very least Trippe should have returned the *Moselle*'s fire with a single gun. Although many Americans cheered Rodgers's hammering of the *Little Belt* as atonement for the behavior of Barron and Trippe, it diplomatically backfired, as Britons chortled over the inability of an American super-frigate to sink at point-blank range a small sloop-of-war.

During the conflict itself, Bainbridge comes off the best. He was able to support his truculence toward the Governor of Bahia State when he shattered HMS *Java*, helping to ensure Brazilian-Portuguese neutrality. Porter's handling of the Peruvian privateer *Nereyda* caused second thoughts among the bureaucracy in Lima about continuing the harassment of American merchantmen and whalers; his annexation of Nuka Hiva Island is comic, but it provides a lively footnote in the history of U.S. imperialism. The growing pains of a new nation were reflected in its deep-water service; as the country waxed in power, its naval diplomacy would be more apt to prosper.

CHAPTER ◆ THREE

The Latin American Wars of Independence

1808–1829

The Latin American struggles for liberation from Spain during the early nineteenth century caused more trouble for U.S. diplomacy and American naval officers responsible for putting such policies into effect than would be encountered at any place or time down to 1883. Spain imposed numerous blockades upon its rebellious colonies but lacked warships enough to enforce them, with the result that they tended to exist in name only, and American commerce suffered from their sporadic enforcement. The insurgents struck back at their former rulers by unleashing scores of privateers to harry the Spanish merchant marine. Most of them, however, soon dropped any pretense of legality to operate in ways indistinguishable from those of outright pirates. Once more American shipping was bled white.

There were also ideological considerations at stake. In the United States public opinion was heartily behind the rebels—after all, they were following a trail toward freedom from European taskmasters blazed by Americans more than a quarter-century before. But successive administrations in Washington saw clearly the folly of risking war with a Spain able to fight on so tenaciously and, moreover, having the solid support after 1815 of the monarchical and reactionary victors over Napoleonic France. This resulted in something of a national dilemma, which compelled American naval officers to edge along a thin line between rebels and the reactionaries.

The United States Navy became diplomatically involved during the Latin American rebellions in four areas: (1) the Spanish Floridas, 1808–1821; (2) the Caribbean, primarily concerning piracy, in Venezuela, the Texas coast, Cuba, and Puerto Rico, 1819–1826; (3) Mexico, 1816–1829; (4) Lower South America, namely Chile and Peru, 1813–1826. In all four of these the flow of events—political, military, and economic—became complicated and confusing.

The Floridas, 1808–1829
Commander David Porter at West Florida, 1808–1809

For economic, security, and strategic reasons, Americans had long looked with avarice upon Spain's West and East Florida. They were natural extensions of Georgia and the northern coast of the Gulf of Mexico, ideal for planting cotton and other tropical produce. The Floridas were havens for escaped slaves, and since Spain lacked the manpower to police them adequately, these escapees sometimes returned to the United States with Indian allies to repay old scores. The mouths of Southern rivers emptied into the sea through those colonies. East Florida lay athwart American trade routes to Havana and other Caribbean ports. West Florida was in such internal chaos as to invite invasion.

David Porter was in command of the naval station at New Orleans, charged primarily with enforcing the U.S. Embargo Act of 1807. This forbade the export of any American commodities; it had been put in by President Jefferson as a coercive economic measure to compel belligerent Britain and France to respect the country's neutral rights.

Porter's troubles stemmed from two sources: the collusion between lawbreakers and Louisiana's public officials, and the attempt to distinguish between American goods, which could not leave the country, and Spanish goods, which could. For instance, Porter nabbed a departing English ship laden with American merchandise in the clearest violation of the Embargo. But the city attorney of New Orleans released ship, cargo, and crew, under the incredible reasoning that her officers had not really meant to break the law. Once one of the commander's gunboats stopped a Spanish schooner carrying wheat, cheese, oil, and clothing. In effect Porter simply threw up his hands, arbitrarily deciding that the wheat was American and subject to confiscation but the rest was not and could be exported.

Porter also had to deal with the machinations of General James Wilkinson, who commanded American forces in the South, one of the shabbiest and most enigmatic military officers in the national history. What the general was up to at this time is not clear (it seldom was with Wilkinson), but probably it was some sort of a foray into Mexico in alliance with the

Governor of West Florida. Certainly Wilkinson knew him and other Spanish officials well; while at the head of the U.S. Army in the area, for twenty years he had been in the pay of the Spanish king. Whatever his plans, he needed Porter's gunboats to put them into effect, and he approached the commander on that subject. Porter played for time and asked Washington if Wilkinson was carrying out some sort of secret orders to move against the Spanish. When assured that no such instructions had been issued, he refused any naval cooperation, thereby aborting the plot.

Shortly after Porter's disapproval his government concluded that although it was bad enough that weak Spain owned the two Floridas, it would be intolerable should either of them fall into the hands of powerful Britain or France. In response to such thinking, Washington staked out its first claim to those colonies in 1810 when, following a pro-annexation uprising of Americans who lived there, it admitted to the United States the part of West Florida between the Mississippi and Pearl Rivers, including the town of Baton Rouge.[1]

Captain Hugh Campbell at Amelia Island, East Florida, 1812

As war with Great Britain edged closer, Congress in 1811 passed a secret act empowering the president to spend as much as $100,000 to take possession of the Floridas, provided that either of two events occurred: a bona fide local rebellion whose leaders asked for American annexation, or a foreign invasion. The Madison administration appointed as its agent George Matthews, an irascible seventy-two-year-old former governor of Georgia, to be the chief negotiator with the Spaniards for such a result. Instead, Matthews decided to foment an uprising from the town of St. Marks in extreme southern Georgia, assembling men to invade East Florida. Throughout, annexation of that colony to the United States was the only prospect that he entertained.

Encouraged by Campbell's agreement to help him with his nine gunboats based on the coast of southern Georgia, Matthews assembled about a hundred volunteers calling themselves "patriots," and led them into East Florida during March 1812. Originally he had contemplated marching directly to St. Augustine, the capital and largest town of East Florida. Had it fallen, probably almost every other Spanish settlement in the colony would have followed suit. But faced with Campbell's reluctance to send his gunboats so far from their Georgia bases, Matthews decided to occupy Amelia Island first. On the 17th his patriots landed at Fernandia, its only village, but the Spanish commandant refused to surrender, even though his entire garrison added up to ten men. According to *Niles' Weekly Register*, the entrance of the navy the next morning decided the matter,

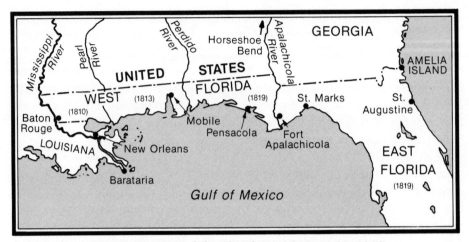

U.S. Acquisition of the Floridas—1810, 1813, 1819

Campbell announcing that he would "aid and assist the *patriots*." Amelia Island was surrendered without an opposing shot and was temporarily annexed to the United States. This, however, was as far as the captain would go. He refused to cooperate in an assault upon St. Augustine. Without sea power, Matthews had no way to seal off the town effectively from being resupplied, and his siege, which lasted into April, failed.

Meanwhile President Madison and Secretary of State Monroe were being acutely embarrassed by northern Federalist opposition to their Florida policy and even more by the spirited protests of the Spanish minister. So Monroe wrote Matthews a letter of dismissal, noting that "the possession of Amelia Island and other parts of East Florida are not authorized." Matthews, livid at such treatment, refused to leave quietly, threatening that he would "be damn'd if he did not blow them all up." Luckily for administrative safety he soon died. The siege of St. Augustine had long since been lifted, and Amelia was evacuated and returned to Spanish occupancy.[2]

Sailing Masters Jared Loomis and James B. Barrett at the Apalachicola River, 1816

Not until the summer of 1814 did the War of 1812 move into the Floridas. Lieutenant Colonel Edward Nicholls (or Nicolls) of the Royal Marines occupied the mouth of the Apalachicola, the boundary between West and East Florida. Some fifteen miles upriver he built a strong fort, in which he stored vast amounts of British munitions. When Nicholls was called home at the end of the war, his Fort Apalachicola was occupied by about 300 blacks and a few of their Indian allies. From then on it was called "the Negro Fort," a haven for escaped slaves and a center for raids to the north.

This development was a matter of deep concern for Washington and Madrid, but since the Spaniards lacked entirely the manpower to cope with it, by default they had to allow the Americans to finish the chore for them. Captain Daniel T. Patterson in New Orleans sent Jared Loomis and James B. Barrett to the Apalachicola with two gunboats to assail the fort in tandem with a U.S. Army detachment. On 27 July, while the army hesitated, the navy gunboats began exchanging shots with the garrison, but the first merely bounced off the thick walls of the parapet. Barrett then had a cannon ball heated red-hot in his gunboat's galley. He raised the muzzle of his gun and lobbed the shell over the walls into the fort. The result could hardly have been more spectacular, for it hit among the hundreds of powder barrels stored in the magazine. A journalistic source claimed that there were 334 in the fort that morning and that 270 were killed right away; all the rest, save three, were wounded, most of them mortally. An American eyewitness added a few details: "You cannot conceive, nor can I describe, the horror of the scene. In an instant hundreds of lifeless bodies were stretched on the plain, buried in the sand and rubbish, or suspended from the top of surrounding pines." Not an American received as much as a scratch. The work of Loomis and Barrett brought about a temporary end of hostilities in the area.[3]

Captain John D. Henley at Amelia Island, 1817

Amelia Island came into the news once more when Gregor McGregor (or MacGregor), a Scottish adventurer acting in the name of the revolutionary Mexican government, captured its town of Fernandia without difficulty that July. He set up his own rule there, illegally selling slaves in Georgia and negotiating with privateers to make Amelia a headquarters for the sale of Spanish prizes. As Secretary of State Adams was well along in his negotiations about acquiring all of the Floridas with Spanish Minister Luis de Onís, this activity was an irksome complication. But worry was needless; McGregor's enterprise soon failed and he sailed away.

His place at Amelia was taken almost immediately by Louis (or Luis) Aury, a Frenchman who had previously worked for both rebel Colombia and Mexico. He arrived at the island in the name of Mexico during

September with 130 black Haitian soldiers and a set of "bloody desperate dogs." Proceeding to outdo McGregor, he sold about a thousand slaves to U.S. Southerners and issued commissions to privateers, who took several prizes valued at a half-million dollars. President Monroe found this interference with American commerce an intolerable violation of American law. Washington's leading newspaper agreed with him that the Frenchman must be ousted, for he had gathered about him at Amelia "British adventurers who had followed in the wake of the English army; Irish and French refugees; Scottish enthusiasts; Mexican and Spanish insurgents; graduates of the Baratarian school [pirates]; . . . privateersmen, slavers, traders, and all manner of scoundrels—in short the nobility of deviltry were all there."

Monroe ordered a naval force under Captain John D. Henley to work with the army. His squadron, consisting of a frigate, two brigs, two schooners, and a gunboat, sailed for Amelia, making rendezvous on 22 December with 250 soldiers under Major James Bankhead. Aury had no choice but to surrender on the next day. By late January 1818 he and his men vacated the island, which was given back to the Spaniards, only in turn to become part of the United States after the ratification of the Adams-Onís Transcontinental Treaty a year later.[4]

The finale of the U.S.'s taking over the Floridas was pretty well settled in 1818 when the Monroe administration took the offensive, tiring of Spain's utter inability to protect the American South from the illicit activities of such foreigners as McGregor and Aury and such illegalities as exporting slaves and commissioning privateers. Worst of all, Spain could not stop the Indians of Florida from raiding across the frontier. Andrew Jackson was sent to remedy the situation. He exploded into both Floridas that spring, capturing every city of importance save St. Augustine, executing two British subjects for intrigues with the Indians, and declaring American laws in force. There was a considerable squabble in Washington about whether Jackson had exceeded his instructions, but it made little difference. Adams used the general's excessive behavior to push home to Onís that Spain had only two choices: to police adequately the borders of the Floridas or to cede both colonies to the United States. Since Jackson's inroads had already demonstrated the impossibility of the first, the second was all that remained. The subsequent Adams-Onís Transcontinental Treaty of 1819, ratified in 1821, gave the nation a satisfactory western boundary with Spain, and more to the point, the United States came into possession of both Floridas in exchange for the assumption of up to $5,000,000 in claims of Americans against that country.

Haiti, 1817–1818

Captain Charles Morris, 1817, and Commander George C. Read, 1818, at Cap Haitien

Unhappy Haiti, where the U.S. Navy had gained one of its earliest diplomatic victories, continued in turmoil after Toussaint L'Ouverture had passed from the scene. In 1810 or 1811 the flamboyant black Henri Cristophe crowned himself King Henri I, ruling northern Haiti from Cap Haitien. He sent coffee and bills of exchange worth over $130,000 to a mercantile house in Baltimore for goods that he wanted, but the Americans reneged on the contract. Understandably furious, Henri resorted to the novel tactic of compelling U.S. citizens doing business in his realm to reimburse him for roughly that amount, telling them to collect from those who had cheated him if they could. The merchants caught in this so-called "great sequestration of 1811" naturally insisted that Washington recover their losses for them.

In 1817 the president sent to Haiti as his personal envoy Septimus Tyler in Captain Charles Morris's *Congress*. Under the technicality that the wording of their letter of introduction was incorrect, the Haitian foreign minister refused to receive them, aborting their mission. A year later William Taylor, former U.S. commercial agent at Port-au-Prince, was dispatched to Haiti in Commander George C. Read's *Hornet*. King Henri sent them away because of the "informal" nature of Taylor's commission. Although Read advised the navy secretary that "nothing but *force* will compel these fellows to do us justice," the Monroe administration saw no reason to go to such extremes; the American businessmen never recovered anything that they had lost in the "great sequestration."

Undoubtedly the major determinant of these embarrassing diplomatic defeats was beyond the control of executive agents or naval officers, namely the long delay in American recognition of Haiti as an independent republic—which did not occur until 1862—thanks in part to the slave-owning Southerners' abhorrence of granting equal relations to a black nation. This resentment, coupled with the unwillingness of Henri to repay such a sizable amount to the American merchants, explains why the civilian and naval diplomats were rebuffed. The historian Henry M. Wriston explains further: "The real fact was that Taylor and Tyler came on missions that were unwelcome. If they had come to do something that Cristophe desired, no difficulties would have been made about credentials."[5]

Piracy in the Caribbean, 1819–1826

Commodore Oliver H. Perry at Venezuela, 1819

Although hostile actions in the Gulf of Mexico and the West Indies were part of the Spanish American wars of independence, so pervasive was the matter of piracy there that it merits separate treatment. Granted that buccaneering had been a way of life in those waters since the days of L'Ollonais, Morgan, and "Blackbeard" Teach, its explosion after 1815 was truly phenomenal. Part of this sharp increase was the fault of Spain, part that of its rebellious colonies. The Spaniards imposed some of the most ludicrous paper blockades in history. One interdicted 1,200 miles of South American shores with only three warships to enforce it, and Secretary of State Adams justifiably called it no blockade at all but rather a "war of extermination against all neutral commerce." Furthermore, Madrid tried to eke out its inadequate naval forces by issuing commissions in wholesale lots to privateers, supposedly to prey upon the shipping of the insurrectionists. Mexico, Colombia, and Venezuela retaliated, emulating the Spaniards by granting licenses to sail against enemy merchantmen to almost anyone requesting them. Once at sea, most of these so-called privateers dropped any pretense of legality by striking at commercial vessels weaker than they sailing under any flag. Finally, the Cuban and Puerto Rican coasts were afflicted with resident pirates who lurked in shoreline hiding places, darting out to snare the unwary. They worked in league with Spanish officials, who fenced their purloined goods and afforded them what protection they could.

The extent of piracy in that time and place was highlighted by a Philadelphian who claimed to have counted such cases in the Caribbean from 1815 to 1822 and found precisely "three thousand and two." This would seem an exaggeration, but if only a third that many occurred, they still amounted to a reign of terror in the southern seas. American newspapers were full of atrocity stories, featuring lurid accounts of torture, rape, and murder. The shipping of New Orleans was particularly hard hit, and the protests of its merchants, coupled with those pouring in from other maritime areas of the country, prompted Congress to respond in March 1819 with "An Act to protect the commerce of the United States, and to punish the crime of piracy." It empowered the navy to convoy American merchantmen and "to subdue, seize, take and send into any port in the United States any armed vessel or boat . . . which shall have attempted any piratical aggression, search, restraint, depredation or seizure upon any vessel of the United States, or the citizens thereof." Since Spain would not accept the independence of its former colonies until the mid-1820s and in some instances long thereafter, this legislation was sure to bring American naval officers into diplomatic confrontations with Spaniards and insurgent Latin Americans alike.

Commodore Oliver Hazard Perry, hero of Lake Erie in 1813, was the first U.S. naval officer to come to grips with the intricacies of privateer-pirates in the Caribbean. Without any legal right to do so, Venezuelan cruisers had fallen upon American shipping with considerable impact, and their government would make no restitution for captured vessels and cargoes. In the late spring of 1819 Perry was ordered south to reach some kind of an accord with "Liberator" Simón Bolivar to stem his privateers and gain compensation for the losses already suffered.

Unfortunately the Venezuelan capital was at Angostora (Ciudad Bolivar), deep in the interior, and Perry had to switch from a comfortable frigate to cramped and airless quarters aboard the little schooner *Nonsuch* for the trip, which took eleven sweltering and mosquito-ridden days during July to navigate three hundred miles up the Orinoco River. At Angostora, Perry found to his dismay that Bolivar was absent on a military campaign and that the only way he might negotiate successfully with Antonio Zea, Venezuelan vice president, was to tell him that the United States was recognizing Venezuelan independence, which, of course, he could not do. With no option but to go back down the Orinoco, Perry began showing the initial stages of yellow fever; the terrifying black vomit appeared, his body chilled, and within a few miles of British Trinidad he died; his body was taken ashore at Port-of-Spain. Perry's funeral featured all the sad majesty that the nineteenth century could devote to its fallen heroes.[6]

Lieutenants John R. Madison and Lawrence Kearny at Galveston, Texas, 1819–1820

The first direct U.S. naval moves against piracy saw warships, acting singly, begin to capture corsair vessels and move against their hiding places. The French-born, gentlemanly buccaneer Jean Lafitte had set up a piratical enterprise at Barataria, only fifteen miles south of New Orleans, from which he had been ousted in 1814 by the American Navy. Although this anti-Lafitte campaign was purely domestic, occurring within U.S. territorial limits, it is of interest because that pirate, despite his loss of Barataria, rebuffed British efforts to make him their ally in the deep South. Instead, he served under Jackson at the Battle of New Orleans in 1815, after which the erstwhile anti-American pirates received presidential pardons. But Lafitte soon became bored with his new respectability and reentered his former occupation, now centered at Galveston, recently evacuated by Louis Aury, who moved to Florida's Amelia Island. Lafitte claimed to be the legal appointee of something called "the republic of Texas." As at Barataria, he unleashed privateer-pirates, who pounced upon vessels sailing from New Orleans in particular.

Late in 1819 the Navy Department ordered Lieutenant John R. Madison in the schooner *Lynx* to investigate the situation at Galveston. He was completely taken in by Lafitte's protestations of amity for the United States and departed, mission unfulfilled. Following further depredations against its merchantmen, the U.S. government decided that it had had enough of Jean Lafitte. Furthermore, the Monroe administration saw in this situation a chance to extend the country's limits by claiming that its boundaries reached through Texas to the Rio Grande and that hence Galveston was within its confines. Commodore Daniel T. Patterson told Lieutenant Lawrence Kearny to sail for Galveston in the brig *Enterprise*. Kearny reported late in February that "Lafitte has burned his house and embarked on board the brig. There is no doubt of his intention to abandon the place immediately, his works of defense razed to the ground." He would "cruise no more in the Bay of Mexico."

The affair ended with the Spanish minister successfully denying the American claim to Texas; not until 1848 would the southwestern boundary of the United States be officially the Rio Grande. As for Lafitte, his life terminated as it began, in obscurity, for he disappears from history; one rumor has it that he was later killed in piratical action and another that he died in the Yucatán in 1826.[7]

Commodore James Biddle at Cuba and Puerto Rico, 1822–1823

Despite these early and somewhat haphazard efforts of Madison and Kearny, the act of 1819 against piracy was not much more effective until the creation of the West India Squadron in 1822. The squadron's responsibilities were impressive—to patrol all the areas within the Gulf of Mexico and the Caribbean Sea; in 1824 its range was extended to cover the west coast of Africa as well. James Biddle became the squadron's first commodore and served in that capacity for two tours during 1822 and 1823. His new command added up, at least on paper, to an extremely impressive armada. He commanded ten ships mounting 208 guns, among them the *Macedonian*, his flagship, and another frigate. But experience would show that his fleet was basically a blue-water operation, for most of his vessels drew too much for shoal-waters. He sailed for the Caribbean in April 1822 under orders from Secretary of the Navy Smith Thompson. He was to capture all the piratical craft he could, convoy American merchantmen throughout the West Indies, and persuade Spanish and other local officials to permit him to chase pirates ashore. The latter privilege would prove to be fundamental: he had the right ships to handle predators afloat, but most of the corsairs hid in sheltered coves, swooping out on their quarry, taking their booty, and dispersing into the interior. Unless they could be followed there, their escape was almost guaranteed.

No sooner had Biddle come into Cuba than his failure was practically preordained in a meeting with Captain General Nicolas Mahé, the island's chief administrator. In response to the American's request that he "sanction the landing upon the coast of Cuba, of our boats and men, when in pursuit of pirates," Mahé replied, "I cannot and must not consent." Thompson and Biddle should have realized that no government able to prevent it would allow its territorial jurisdiction to be violated in such a manner. To be sure, Washington had dispatched Jackson into the Floridas in the face of Spanish inability to police that frontier effectively, but Biddle was given no authority to emulate the general. Furthermore, the situations inside both Cuba and Puerto Rico mitigated against cooperation with the U.S. West India Squadron. Although Mahé himself may have been sincerely against piracy inside his domains, many of his subordinates were not. Obviously illicit activities on such a vast scale could not exist unless local officials worked in collusion with the corsairs, sharing in their profits.

Although it had nothing directly to do with fighting piracy, except as an excuse for Biddle to be in Cuba, he managed to take part in a rather outré plot to wrest Cuba from Spain and annex it to the United States. An envoy from Cuban planters had told a U.S. Senator that "⅔ of the white inhabitants of the island" wanted to be annexed to the United States as a state in the Union. A high-ranking naval officer should be sent to Cuba for negotiations on that subject, he said, and fighting pirates would offer a reasonable explanation of his presence in that area. Biddle went ashore sometime during the early summer of 1822 and made contact with "several respectable and influential Cubans." He learned, however, that many planters feared that uprisings of their black slaves and a possible ending of slavery might ensue in connection with disorders emanating from a pro-American annexation move. Although Biddle's role in this situation was indeed minor, his work helped to cement basic American policy about Cuba for much of the nineteenth century. President Monroe met an emissary from the Cuban planters in Washington in September. But in a cabinet meeting on that subject Secretary of State Adams had little trouble in selling to his colleagues the idea that annexation of the island would be most premature, and that the proper policy for the United States, at least at that time, would be to ensure that Cuba stayed under the rule of weak Spain, resisting to the utmost any British or French efforts to take over the colony. For the next two decades and more, Washington followed Adams's advice about Cuba.

Although Mahé's refusal had crippled him badly, Biddle did the little that remained for him to move against piracy. He had some success; his men-of-war made about thirty captures. He also set up a weekly convoy for American merchantmen over a great loop from Havana to the Leeward and Windward Islands, the northern coast of South America, the shores of Mexico, New Orleans, and back to Havana. But anything that he might have achieved was aborted when his men started falling victim to the scourge of the tropics: yellow fever—the dreaded *vómito negro*.

It is hard today to comprehend how lethal was that disease during the nineteenth century. Its mortality was so high from 1822 to 1825 in the West Indies that Charles L. Lewis, in his *David Glasgow Farragut*, wrote correctly that the U.S. Navy lost "more officers and men, in proportion, than any other service in which they were ever engaged." This generalization is true for the American Revolution, the War of 1812, the Mexican, Civil, and Spanish American Wars, World Wars I and II, the Korean War, and the wars in Indochina.

Starting in May the deadly inroads of the fever began among the *Macedonian*'s complement. Eventually 101 died, about one-third of those in the frigate. Biddle, unaware like everyone else at that time that the fever was caused by the *Aedes aegypti* mosquito, thought that his men had been killed by the "effluvia" from the hatches and bilges of the frigate, caused by inadequate cleaning at the Boston Navy Yard following her return from a long cruise to the Pacific. His theory was, however, rebuffed by the Board of Navy Commissioners, which held him responsible for the disaster by tarrying too long off Cuba "during the sickly season."

Discouraged and resentful about this decision, Biddle nonetheless had to return to the West Indies that November. His new orders from Thompson helped not at all. He was forbidden to escort merchantmen through Spanish blockades, and he must be careful to ascertain that suspect ships were unmistakably pirates before moving against them. It turned out to be a miserable voyage. One of his most efficient officers was lost in action against the buccaneers. His flagship, the frigate *Congress*, barely managed to escape destruction in a hurricane at La Guaira, Venezuela. From November to April 1823, according to one of her midshipmen, the *Congress* cruised for "150 days, 112 of which they had been at sea, we have taken no pirates." Biddle's exploits during this period add up to little, the one clear fiasco in a life otherwise characterized by perceptive, diligent, and successful naval diplomacy.[8]

Commodore David Porter at Cuba and Puerto Rico, 1823–1824

David Porter was Biddle's successor in the unenviable and unhealthy attempt to wipe out piracy in the West Indies. At least the Navy Department aided him considerably by refitting the squadron with ships more appropriate to the tasks they faced. He was permitted to retire the deep-drafted frigates and keep three sloops, one of which he used as his flagship, and three schooners. He implemented his force for shallow-water maneuverings by purchasing eight tiny schooners and five 20-oared barges. In a fascinating historical footnote, he also brought along with him to the Caribbean the little *Sea Gull*, a converted New York ferryboat; she was the first steamer ever to engage in naval hostilities. Beyond question his squadron was much better equipped to meet the responsibilities ahead than Biddle's had been.

Secretary Thompson's instructions to Porter were a masterpiece of bureaucratic equivocation. Some of it was clear enough—he was to convoy American shipping and cooperate with foreign navies, especially that of the British. But he was to seek "the favorite and friendly support" of the Spaniards, all the while realizing that he must not "encroach" upon "their rights." He could only pursue buccaneers ashore in "uninhabited parts"; elsewhere he could do so only "in cooperation with" Spain's local officials. With such ambiguities, Thompson's orders might be cynically summarized as authorizing Porter to do everything he should in order to smash piracy and protect the national merchant marine, except, of course, that he must do nothing that he should not.

No sooner had the commodore arrived in Puerto Rican waters during early March 1822 than he was confronted by an inexplicably brutal act committed by the garrison of that colony's huge fortress at San Juan. Lieutenant William H. Cocke, with American colors prominently displayed on his schooner *Fox*, sailed toward it on the 6th to pick up from Governor Miguel de la Torre a list of commissioned privateers operating out of Puerto Rico. Without warning, the fort's battery opened up on him; one shot shattered Cocke's shoulder, inflicting a mortal wound. Porter wrote to Torre about his astonishment and anger. The governor replied that he had been absent when the event occurred; he attributed the firing to a suspicion of all ships apparently American ever since a vessel flying that flag had tried to land in Puerto Rico on an unfriendly mission, and expressed his "inexpressible sorrow" over the lieutenant's death. Porter forwarded the above exchange to Washington. Secretary of State Adams told his minister in Madrid to protest vigorously this "flagrant, wanton, and unprovoked" murder, but the minister took the better part of a year to present this complaint. So much time had elapsed that Spain was able to ignore it, and Washington allowed the matter to pass into oblivion.

Despite this disheartening beginning, Porter's first cruise, from March through October, was quite auspicious. During April his men crushed the powerful pirate fleet of "Domingo," although the leader managed to escape. In August the well-advertised buccaneer "Diablito" was killed and his establishment broken up. The commodore worked well with the Royal Navy, particularly in turning over pirates for execution by the British. He received from Captain General Mahé in Cuba a circumscribed permission to go ashore in active pursuit of corsairs, but Torre in Puerto Rico was less accommodating. On the whole, Porter was more willing than Biddle to stretch his landing operations to the limit, save where Spanish officials were nearby. Even so, the continued collusion of Mahé's lesser bureaucrats with the freebooters made his job more onerous, for as a rule the pirates carried Spanish "passports," making them legally privateers rather than maritime outlaws.

Despite Porter's troubles, attacks on American shipping, particularly off Cuba, began dramatically declining. The commodore informed the department that by the end of his first summer, the pirates had been largely "driven off the water, with their lurking places invaded, their plunder seized, their occupation afloat gone." Those forced from the sea commenced depredations inside Cuba. This development in turn resulted in a further loss of strength, because Spanish authorities could not countenance such actions and began harassing the pirates ashore.

In August a virulent attack of yellow fever killed 23 of the first 25 U.S. officers afflicted; Porter was among its later victims, although he managed to pull through, ending his first cruise during October. Both Samuel L. Southard, the new secretary of the navy, and the president himself congratulated him that December. Monroe expressed his commendation in a paragraph of a message between two widely separated passages that together make up the doctrine that bears his name.

Porter's second and third sojourns in the West Indies were much less felicitous, and the last resulted in his personal disaster. He returned south and remained there during the winter and spring of 1824. His ships voyaged widely throughout the area but found all quiet. Once again, however, the commodore was felled by "yellow jack" and came close to dying. Shaken by his narrow escape, he came home without permission that June. This unauthorized act formed a watershed in his relations with Monroe, Southard, and Adams, secretary of state soon to be president, all of whom became convinced that they were dealing with an insubordinate troublemaker.

So the ingredients for Porter's downfall were on hand when he showed up for a third Caribbean tour in November. At once he was told a story that infuriated him. Lieutenant Robert Richie had gone to Foxardo (modern Fajardo) in extreme eastern Puerto Rico to investigate the probability that the loot from a robbed American warehouse in the Danish West Indies (Virgin Islands) had been carried there. He was arrested, held for a few hours before being released, and hooted out of town in disgrace. Within two days the choleric commodore led 200 armed men ashore in Puerto Rico, spiked some Spanish guns, lined up Fajardo's officials, and exacted from them an apology to Richie under the threat of the leveling of the settlement. Then Porter departed and complacently awaited the governmental congratulations he was sure to receive. Instead, he was immediately replaced as commodore, recalled, and subjected to a court of inquiry that recommended a court-martial. His trial was held during the summer of 1825 on charges of disobedience to Southard's orders and insubordination in the form of angry letters to the secretary of the navy and President Adams. He was found guilty. Although his sentence was ludicrously gentle for conviction on two such serious charges—a six-month suspension at full pay and allowances—Porter was so incensed by what he considered unfair treatment that he resigned from the U.S. Navy to enter the Mexican service.

Porter's main defense at his court-martial was that what he had done at Fajardo was similar to Jackson's behavior in the Floridas during 1818. But the general had been stoutly upheld by his government, whereas he had been punished and humiliated. This may have been true, but what Porter could not recognize was that Jackson's irruption into Spanish colonies had played perfectly into the hands of the Monroe administration by helping Adams to negotiate a satisfactory treaty with Luis de Onís, the Spanish minister. The situation in 1824, however, was quite different. By that time the reactionary, royalist powers of Europe were striking down nationalism and liberalism wherever they appeared. The possibility could not be overlooked that France, acting for them, might invade the Americas to restore to Spain its rebellious colonies. Such was the reasoning behind the Monroe Doctrine, which contained a quid pro quo: Washington would permit no further European colonies in the Western Hemisphere and would pledge not to interfere with already existing European possessions in the Americas and to keep hands off Europe's internal affairs.

Then, only 11 months after the doctrine's promulgation, Porter invaded a Spanish colony, obviously not in active pursuit of pirates, to dictate an apology at gunpoint from its authorities. This might be just the excuse that the European powers, France in particular, were waiting for to intervene in the Americas. Monroe spelled this out in some private jottings on the subject: he knew that Porter's invasion "would attract the attention, not of Spain alone . . . but of the new governments, our neighbors, to the south, & in certain respects of several of the powers of Europe. . . . [Porter's orders were] dictated by a desire rather to err . . . on the side of moderation, than to risk a variance with any of the nations concerned." Hence, while Jackson could be applauded for his excessive zeal in bursting into Spanish Florida, for roughly the same sort of behavior six years later Porter's condemnation and disgrace were considered essential.[9]

Commodore Lewis Warrington at Cuba and Puerto Rico, 1825–1826

Although he would receive no credit for it, Porter by and large had laid the groundwork for the final eradication of piracy in the seas south of the United States. He had amassed smaller and shallower-drafted ships perfect for their tasks and made the first productive overtures to Spanish officials asking for their cooperation. It was, however, his successor, Lewis Warrington, who would reap the rewards (and they were well deserved) during the mid-1820s. He had already made a name for himself during the War of 1812, and the administration trusted his ability and, in contrast to Porter, his discretion. Therefore he enjoyed stronger governmental support than had his predecessors.

By the summer of 1825 Warrington was spreading his ships like a net throughout the Spanish West Indies. Fleet action against the pirates substantially increased. One of his officers, learning that two corsair vessels were taking captives off eastern Puerto Rico, lured them to their destruction by using two merchantmen as decoys, cramming them full of hidden sailors and marines. In a 45-minute battle he drove ashore a pirate craft and captured "the famous piratical chief Cofrecinas." The chief and 44 others were hanged in Puerto Rico. The bodies of some of them were cut into quarters "and their parts sent to all the small ports around the island to be exhibited," sights that very likely persuaded some of the freebooters to select a means of livelihood somewhat less hazardous.

The changing international situation also helped Warrington. The Latin American wars of liberation were winding down, with the rebels victorious almost everywhere. As hostilities lessened, so too did privateering, the façade behind which so much piracy was able to flourish. Furthermore, Warrington began receiving much-improved cooperation from the Spaniards in Cuba and Puerto Rico. The U.S. and Royal navies worked more closely together than ever before. Lieutenant Isaac McKeever in the *Sea Gull* led three British warships to take two pirate schooners and torch their settlement ashore. Overall, British forces bagged some 13 corsair vessels and 300 men, the Americans about 80 and 1300.

The happy results of Warrington's campaign were soon evident. By the end of the summer he notified the department, "If piracies . . . have been in force on either side of Cuba, they have not only abstained from making captures but they have concealed themselves so effectually as to prevent detection." *Niles' Weekly Register* congratulated the squadron: it has "not made much noise, but silently stopped piracy, by vigilance." Secretary Southard wrote in his annual *Report*, "The duties assigned to it have been signally accomplished" by "Captain Warrington, an active, systematic, and enterprising officer." President Adams agreed in his December 1825 message: "The active, persevering, and unremitted energy of Captain Warrington and the officers and men under his command" is "entitled to the approbation of their country." Matters continued to improve during 1826. In January Warrington wrote Southard that there had been no piracies off Cuba for several months, and in September remarked that throughout his area of command "piracy is unheard of." Although an occasional case of buccaneering cropped up later, organized piracy on anything like its former scale had vanished. Warrington had maneuvered his way to success without arousing Madrid's ill will, while at the same time demonstrating a spirit of friendship and cooperation with the British.[10]

Mexico, 1816–1829
Lieutenant Thomas S. Cunningham at Vera Cruz, 1816

By its late colonial times Mexico had became a seriously divided society. On the one hand a vast chasm yawned between the Spanish whites and the great majority population of Indians and mestizos. On the other, the whites themselves were split. The dominant positions in the government and church were held by the *peninsulares,* born in Spain, who lorded it over the American-born *criollos,* equal to their supposed superiors in education and wealth and considerably greater in number; the *criollos'* resentment had been building for decades. But when it was learned in 1808 that an invading French army had deposed Spain's Bourbon King Ferdinand VII and replaced him on the throne with Napoleon's elder brother Joseph, white Mexicans of almost all persuasions were aghast. As elsewhere in Spanish America, they refused to accept the usurper and formed local juntas to carry on Bourbon royal rule in the name of Ferdinand. Once experienced, de facto independence tended to become habitual in all Spanish colonies in America, save for Cuba and Puerto Rico. This was not accomplished, however, without the most tenacious Spanish opposition, which continued in some areas until the late 1820s.

During August 1816, Thomas S. Cunningham, commanding the 7-gun schooner *Firebrand*, was on routine patrol off Vera Cruz when he was approached by three Spanish men-of-war mounting a total of 60 guns. Without warning, one of them opened fire, mortally wounding one U.S. marine, and Cunningham surrendered. The Americans were sent to the Spanish flagship, where they were slapped into irons, beaten with swords, and told the alarming (and false) news that the new viceroy had declared that the United States had no right "to navigate the Gulf of Mexico," that the entire Mexican coast was under blockade, and that he recognized no difference between the flag of Mexican rebels and that of the United States. After a few hours Cunningham was permitted to depart for New Orleans, where he was later totally acquitted of any wrongdoing by a court-martial.

The news of what had happened to the *Firebrand* naturally became the talk of New Orleans. A letter from that city, published in the *Daily National Intelligencer*, said the act had "grossly outraged the nation. . . . We trust that this will be the last of the long list of our grievances from the miserable bigots who govern Spain. . . . What sensations this outrage may excite at Washington City we know not, but are confident that the public voice will loudly demand *atonement for the past and security for the future—or war!*"

The incident sparked a response from President Madison in his annual message to Congress late in 1816. He stated that "one of our public armed vessels was attacked by an overpowering force under a Spanish commander, and the American flag, with the officers and crew, insulted in a manner calling for prompt reparation." He had just sent additional warships into the Gulf of Mexico. But he then defused a possible explosion by admitting that the Spanish minister in Washington had given him "the strongest assurances that no hostile order could have emanated from his government," and that proper restitution would be made, although documentation does not reveal to what extent this was carried out. A possible explanation of the bizarre behavior of the Spanish commandant is that his squadron was on the lookout for Colombian privateers and that he immediately and erroneously concluded that the *Firebrand* was one of them.[11]

Commodore Charles Ridgely and Commander George Budd and Key West, 1827–1828

Mexican independence actually came into being through what happened in Spain rather than anything that transpired in America. By 1820 most Spaniards had had enough of the devious, capricious, and brutal King Ferdinand VII. They overthrew him and installed a more radical and anticlerical new constitution. This deeply disturbed the *peninsulares* in

Mexico, who decided that they preferred to live in a country separated from a homeland with such liberal sentiments. They joined the *criollos*; enlisted the support of General Vicente Guerrero, a rebel chieftain; and all turned to General Agustín Iturbide, an insurgent leader. Mexico declared itself independent in 1821 and a year later the general became Emperor Agustín I, but he was soon toppled, sent into exile, and shot when he returned in 1824. In that same year the Mexican republic was proclaimed.

But intermittent hostilities between mother and rebellious child lasted for years; Spain did not recognize an independent Mexico until 1836. In the early 1820s Madrid was able to retain possession of the massive fort of San Juan d'Ulua in Vera Cruz harbor, an occupation both irksome and dangerous to the Mexicans. This led to the formation of that country's first navy, and its greatest triumph was the capture of San Juan in 1825, although the Spaniards carried on the naval war from Cuba. A little later David Porter showed up in Mexico, having resigned from the U.S. service after his court-martial and conviction, to accept an appointment as the de facto admiral of the Mexican navy.

By the end of 1827 Porter was able to write with disarming humility, "I have accomplished wonders." He had recruited officers from the United States, trained Indian boys to be sailors, and turned the Mexican navy into a fighting force. By June 1827 he had captured twenty-one prizes. Sometimes basing himself at Key West, he sent out privateers, evoking vehement Spanish protests about the use of American territory to war against them. Commodore Charles Ridgely, commanding the West India Squadron, planned to move against Porter, but much to his bewilderment and anger he was denied permission to oust Mexican warships by force. Probably President Adams, who held two cabinet meetings about the subject, feared that a combination of Porter's continued popularity in the United States and the typical American sympathy for the underdog would operate to the administration's political disadvantage.

The only instance in which Ridgely's frustration was broken took place in the summer of 1828. Commander George Budd in the *Natchez* learned that the Mexican man-of-war *Hermón* and the privateer *Molestare* were anchored at Key West. He complied with the order to avoid violence by using both suggestions and threats to compel their departure, and peace returned to the south Florida environs. Meanwhile, the Mexican government had concluded that whatever Porter might accomplish in the Keys could not compensate for a resultant loss of American popular support, and ordered his withdrawal. The issue quickly became academic, for the

Mexican economy was disintegrating into chaos, and its navy became a casualty, automatically terminating any Mexican-American controversies over Porter's commissioning of privateers or basing himself on United States soil.[12]

Commodore Jesse D. Elliott at Vera Cruz and Commander David Conner off Yucatan, 1829

The last couple of instances involving Mexican-American naval diplomacy were minor. Spain's final effort to reconquer Mexico occurred in the summer of 1829. An expedition of 3,000 men from Cuba moved upon the port of Tampico and took it, holding the city for a few weeks prior to its recapture that September. The American Navy Department, apprehensive that the country's merchant marine might suffer from molestations from either side, sent Commodore Jesse D. Elliott to command the West India Squadron, with the sloop *Peacock* as his flagship. While moored off Vera Cruz that November, Elliott was informed that an American sailor had been impressed into the Mexican navy off the merchantman *Virginia* in that very harbor. He immediately filed a protest with the Mexican general commanding the fortress of San Juan d'Ulua, insisting upon the release of the man, an explanation of the occurrence, and a promise that such would not happen again. The commodore's diplomacy was successful: the sailor was liberated and the Mexican officer combined an apology with a promise of rectitude in the future.

Almost simultaneously Elliott learned that the American ship *Ajax* had been fired upon by two Mexican gunboats near Sisal in the Yucatán. He promptly dispatched Commander David Conner in the sloop *Erie* to that place to investigate the circumstances of the matter. Conner was told by local officials that it had been a case of mistaken identity, they professed their regrets about the incident, and the American expressed his satisfaction.[13]

Lower South America, 1813–1828
Captain David Porter at Chile, 1813, 1814

As in Mexico and northern South America, the tidings of the Napoleonic takeover in Spain resulted in the formation of governments in Argentina and Chile ostensibly loyal to the deposed Bourbon king, but soon gravitating toward secession from the Spanish empire. Argentina had a relatively easier time than the other countries of lower South America, achieving an independence it never lost early in 1813 under the brilliant military leadership of José de San Martín. He decided that the best way to liberate

Chile and Peru was to invade the former across the Andes, and once successful there, to mount a later maritime invasion of the latter, which was the center of royalist strength in South America. San Martín's work was, however, considerably complicated by a deep division among the Chilean rebels, or "patriots." One wing, the more liberal and pro-American, was headed by José Miguel Carrera, who established short-lived dictatorships in 1813 and 1814. The other, more conservative and pro-British, was under Bernardo O'Higgins, for whom San Martín opted. During these events David Porter sailed twice into Valparaiso, starting a chain of circumstances that would have much impact upon his country's Latin-American policy.

The *Essex* remained at Valparaiso for a week in 1813 and for almost two months in February and March 1814, during which Porter embraced most enthusiastically the faction of Carrera. But late in March superior British forces (sent to the Pacific to stop the tremendous damage to their whaling industry) cornered Porter in Valparaiso harbor and hammered him into submission. Eventually he made it back to the United States, but meanwhile Chilean public opinion swung toward Britain and O'Higgins. Carrera soon fled into exile and came to Washington, where Porter welcomed him, provided him with funds for ships and volunteers, and tried to whip up support for him in the highest administrative circles and among the American people. Carrera went back to South America in 1817, only to be arrested by the Argentines, and thereby denied any opportunity to share in the eventual victories of O'Higgins and San Martín over the Peruvian royalists. After escaping and attempting to stir up rebellion in the Argentina back country, Carrera was captured and executed in 1821.

Well before the sad end of his champion, Porter had formed a cabal that argued that the only revolutionary faction in all South America worthy of U.S. support was Carrera's. This brought him into conflict with Henry Clay, the powerful speaker of the House, who was solidly behind O'Higgins and especially San Martín. Although both of these blocs favored quick American recognition of Chile as an independent nation, they split over which leaders to favor, denigrating each other's champions and in this manner reducing the effectiveness of their support. President James Monroe and Secretary of State Adams took advantage of this disarray to put into temporary effect their own policy of neutrality and delay. They feared that premature recognition of Chile and Argentina as independent republics while Spanish royalists were battling them so doggedly might bring about the intervention there of the reactionary Quadruple Alliance ("Holy Alliance" in contemporary documentation) in the form of a French armada

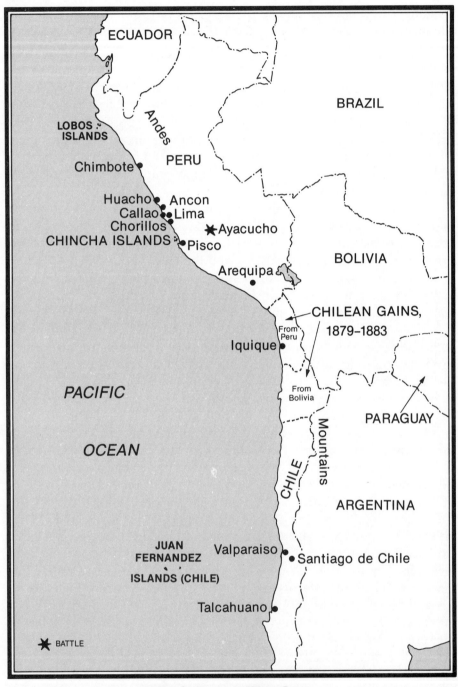

South America, West Coast

invading lower South America to restore Madrid's rule. Furthermore, the administration was committed to procrastination until Adams could complete his important and delicate negotiations with Luis de Onís, Spanish minister in Washington. Not until 1821 was the resultant Adams-Onís Transcontinental Treaty of 1819 ratified, giving the United States the Floridas and a satisfactory Spanish-American boundary from Louisiana to the Oregon country. Once this had been completed and the possibility of European intervention in South America rendered most improbable by the early 1820s, the Monroe administration could recognize Argentine and Chilean independence. Inadvertently Porter's brief sojourns at Valparaiso and their unlikely aftermath had worked to his country's great benefit.[14]

Captain James Biddle at Chile and Peru, 1817–1819

Captain James Biddle had had a noteworthy naval career in the War of 1812, which justified his being selected for the South American command. His orders from Secretary of the Navy Smith Thompson in July 1817 were to sail the 22-gun sloop *Ontario* around Cape Horn to carry to Chile Special Agent John B. Prevost; to plant the American flag at the mouth of the Columbia River, giving the United States a stronger claim in the Oregon controversy with Great Britain; and although not specifically spelled out, to protect American commerce from illicit blockades and seizures by either the royalists or the patriots. On 4 October Biddle and Prevost sailed south.

When the *Ontario* came into Valparaiso on 19 November, Biddle was able to catch up on current events in that quarter. The Peruvian royalists had whipped the patriots at the Battle of Rancagua during October 1814 and for more than the next two years ruled most of Chile under the brutal General Mariano Osorio. In February 1817, however, General José de San Martín, the liberator of Argentina, won the country back to the rebel cause by his victory at Chacabuco. Yet Spanish sea power still dominated in the Pacific. As the patriots had not yet built or bought a navy to compete with the royalists, the latter were able to announce a blockade of the entire Chilean coast just after their defeat at Chacabuco. Not only was it applied without sufficient notification to neutral shipping, but according to American judgment it amounted to no more than a paper blockade. Since the royalists had far too few warships to seal off Chile's 2,600-mile shoreline, ports there would see no enforcing men-of-war for months, but should one suddenly appear, any American vessels would be confiscated for blockade-running, a fate already suffered by some ships before the *Ontario*'s arrival.

James Biddle

During this first stay in Chile, lasting until April 1818, Biddle maintained generally amicable relations with the patriot Bernardo O'Higgins, the nation's "supreme dictator," an ally of San Martín. He joined the Chileans in apprehension during March when Osorio landed south of Valparaiso, marched inland, and at Cancha Rayada put to rout the army of San Martín and O'Higgins. But the defeated forces were quickly reassembled, and in early April San Martín crushed Osorio at Maipú, the decisive battle for Chilean independence. Biddle wrote that this turning point "has given me the most lively joy. . . . The truth is that . . . my

interests as well as my feelings were enlisted on the side of the patriots."
This, however, was to be the high-water mark of American naval cama-
raderie with the rebel cause.

The change in this relationship began as soon as the *Ontario* dropped
anchor at Lima's seaport of Callao, where she remained from late April
into early May. Two consequential events took place in this period. First,
Biddle and Prevost quarreled and parted. The captain insisted upon the
maintenance of as rigid a neutrality as possible, but Prevost, a doctrinaire
liberal, was convinced that American policy must support the patriots.
This division of opinion between American naval and diplomatic persons
would be perpetuated by their successors in Chile and Peru. Second, Biddle
formed a close friendship with the urbane and devious Joaquín de la
Pezuela, Spanish Viceroy of Peru. A bargain was struck between them.
Biddle was able to have the severity of the royalist blockade against his
nation's merchantmen lessened and to achieve the release of some Americans incarcerated in Peru; in return he agreed to carry a mission of
Pezuela's to Valparaiso in the *Ontario*. Ostensibly the emissaries' purpose
was only to discuss an exchange of prisoners with the patriots. But Biddle
had been hoodwinked by the wily viceroy. The Peruvian mission was
actually an exercise in espionage, for two of its members were spies assigned to ascertain rebel weaknesses and strengths. Furthermore, they
carried a letter addressed to "Don José de San Martín," rather than to
"General José de San Martín, commander of the Chilean armies," a sal-
utation sure to be rejected by the patriots.

When Biddle came back to Valparaiso late in May he found that frantic
rebel efforts to raise a navy able to battle the Spaniards, partly with Biddle's
aid, had been partially successful. This compelled the royalist blockade
to be temporarily lifted, so that most of the trapped American merchantmen escaped. But when the letter to San Martín was presented, royalist-
patriot negotiations broke off on the spot, and after Biddle had intervened
to save Pezuela's agents from arrest, Chilean-American relations quickly
nosedived.

Sailing for Oregon in mid-June, Biddle stopped off at Peru for two days,
receiving Pezuela's effusive thanks for his services and accepting from him
a valuable jeweled sword, which he quite properly turned over to the State
Department upon his return home. Back from the Northwest at Callao
late in October, he set about completing the groundwork that he had
already laid for the liberation of American merchantmen, concentrating
especially on the case of John Jacob Astor's *Beaver*. That nabob of fur
had outfitted his ship for $50,000 and crammed into her a cargo valued
at $140,000, a part of it in munitions to be sold to the patriots. The *Beaver*

was unlucky enough to blunder into the only Chilean seaport held by the royalists and was seized. Biddle complied successfully with her captain's appeal for assistance. Counting upon his friendship with Pezuela, and realizing that Peru was now dependent on American shipping for supplies since the surge of Chilean sea power, he delicately called to the viceroy's attention that a refusal to comply with his request for the *Beaver*'s release would have a negative impact on Spanish-American relations. An exultant Astor later congratulated him for rendering "the most important services to your country, by having rescued and protected an immense property belonging to your fellow-citizens of whom I am one." Although Biddle could not bring about the release of all imprisoned Americans, Pezuela as a personal favor did turn over a few.

When the *Ontario* returned to Valparaiso late that December, the Scottish-born Lord Thomas Cochrane commanded the strengthened Chilean navy. This most controversial individual was unquestionably a brilliant naval officer, but he had personal shortcomings of arrogance, ill-temper, and ruthlessness that almost ruined him, and he would clash with every American commander from 1818 to 1822. The Biddle-Cochrane enmity started at once, for the former was already predisposed against the Scotsman because of his reputation, calling him in a personal letter "worse than a beast." They first quarreled over the firing of salutes: Biddle refused to fire any unless assured of an equal number of guns in return. After five long letters had been exchanged, the last of which Biddle called "as ridiculous as it is vulgar," neither saluted the other.

The situation at Valparaiso while the *Ontario* was being readied for departure was potentially much more serious than matters of naval protocol, for Biddle had committed a distinctly unneutral act. In order to ensure that the *Beaver* and others would be released, he had brought from Peru to Chile Pezuela's nephew, a Spanish officer en route to Madrid to get reinforcements for the royalists. Furthermore, the *Ontario* was laden with specie worth $201,000, much of it royalist-owned and subject to confiscation. Finally, the well-known avarice of Cochrane made it all too probable that he might stop, board, and seize the *Ontario*.

Should that happen, Biddle faced impossible odds. His small 17-gun sloop would have to do battle with Cochrane's three frigates and a sloop. He described in his usual unemotional manner the *Ontario*'s embarkation on 31 December, but the tension on board comes through clearly:

> Connecting the reports on shore and the maneuverings of the [Chilean] ships, with the character of Lord Cochrane, which is known to be destitute of principle and

Battles of the Chilean and Peruvian Wars of Independence

regardless of decency, it was quite obvious that there was either the intention to attack us, if we attempted to go to sea, or that the intention was to intimidate us from sailing. I did not choose to be deterred from sailing, whichever was the intention, and therefore at 10 o'clock in the morning, having cleared the ship for action, I weighed and stood out to sea, passing within a half gun shot of the *San Martín* who made sail along with me, when I came abreast of her; and after I had got a few miles out, she & the *Chacaboco* tacked and returned to anchor.

The *Ontario* made an uneventful passage to Annapolis, reaching there on 25 April 1819, but Biddle found that his troubles were by no means over. During the next year he had to write five explanations of his conduct to the administration, four to Secretary Smith Thompson and one to President Monroe himself. Henry Clay mocked him in Congress for accepting Pezuela's sword, although Biddle's giving it to the State Department warded off that assault. More ominous, the *Chileños*, egged on by Prevost and other U.S. diplomats there, protested to Washington about his refusal to exchange salutes with Cochrane, carrying spies to Valparaiso in May 1818, bringing the viceroy's nephew to Chile under the guise of an innocent passenger, and enabling the royalists to export their specie from Peru in his warship. Painstakingly Biddle explained away all of these charges, and his self-defense was accepted by his government. Washington's officialdom harkened to the chorus of approval of Biddle's services from American shipping interests, including Astor, and to the eventual avowal by O'Higgins in Chile and King Ferdinand VII in Spain that Biddle had behaved toward them impeccably. The Navy Department concluded that he "has violated no law or regulations of the Navy," and Secretary Thompson noted "the benefit which has resulted in our trade." Secretary of State Adams spoke the final word when he contrasted the accomplishments of the naval officer against those of the special agent: Biddle had "saved and rescued property to a very large amount. He obtained the release of citizens of the United States who were prisoners. Prevost has never saved a dollar nor obtained the release of a man."

What had Biddle learned from his two years at Chile and Peru? Mulling over his experiences and those of his successors there while testifying at Charles Stewart's court-martial during the summer of 1824, he perceptively commented: "I believe it is impossible for any commanding officer to be in the Pacific without giving offense to one side or the other. The royal party, knowing the general feeling of our countrymen, are jealous of them; the patriots, on the other hand, expecting too much, are dissatisfied."[15]

Captain John Downes at Chile and Peru, 1819–1820

John Downes had earned his meed of fame as David Porter's first lieutenant during the *Essex*'s eventful cruise to the Pacific, in which he had been a mainstay of strength and dependability. In consideration of his experience in the South Seas, he was sent to relieve Biddle in the *Macedonian*. The secretary ordered him to assist American merchantmen and whalers, even to the point of convoying them through illegal blockades, without committing any act that might compromise the neutrality of his country.

The *Macedonian* proceeded south in October 1818, coming into Valparaiso late the following January. He found that Cochrane's Chilean patriot fleet dominated the seas and would eventually move against Peru, the last remaining Spanish bastion in South America. During this interim Downes helped American ships in trouble, cruised to Mexico, quarreled with Prevost almost to the extent of a duel when the agent described the captain's specie-carrying as "disgraceful," and finally arrived at Callao under Cochrane's blockade. In Lima Downes consulted Viceroy Pezuela, who was well aware that he was dependent upon foreign shipping for both supplies and communications; Downes was always able to arrange for the release of captured Americans from Peruvian custody. In June 1820 he had an opportunity to meet the viceroy again, having hurried from Valparaiso to Callao to protect six American merchantmen there from Cochrane's armada of 23 patriot ships, which was transporting San Martín's army to conquer royalist Peru.

While Downes was conferring with Pezuela in Lima, the most serious clashes between the United States and the warring South American factions from 1817 to 1825 broke out during early November. Cochrane, in yet another of his brilliant naval coups, sent his boats into Callao harbor to cut out and successfully storm the Spanish frigate *Esmerelda*. Callao's forts opened up on the captured ship, in the process striking several times the *Macedonian* and one of the merchant vessels she was guarding; luckily no one was hurt. The infuriated Peruvians ashore had concluded that both the Americans and the British had connived with Cochrane to seize the *Esmerelda*. The *Macedonian*'s first lieutenant, in command while the captain was in Lima, stupidly sent into Callao the *Buckskin*, the ship's tender, for supplies. Royalist troops at the dock fired into her at point-blank range, killing 2 and wounding 6; the survivors were taken aboard a nearby British frigate. Coincidentally, some American and English ships in the harbor were looted by mobs, and in Lima several foreigners were assaulted and killed. Fearful of the consequences should the 91 Americans and Britons trapped in the capital also die, Pezuela suggested to Downes that they make their escape, not to Callao, but to Chorillos, a small port a short distance to the south. They did so and on 8 November they were refugees taken aboard the *Macedonian*.

On that same day the American schooner *Rampart* tried to land her cargo in front of Callao's harbor forts, which fired upon her so accurately that she had to be hastily evacuated; then she was ransacked. Downes tied together the outrages perpetrated on the tender and the schooner in a vehement protest to the viceroy, demanding that those who had fired at the *Buckskin* be summarily punished and proper amends made for "the insult offered to the flag." Since it had been Spanish soldiers who had rained shot upon the *Rampart* from the forts, he had to consider such an offense "that of a declared enemy." Pezuela tried to ease the tension by promising to investigate both instances and deal harshly with those responsible, and simultaneously returning the *Rampart* to her captain. Downes considered all this insufficient to redress such atrocities, but stifling his natural truculence he accepted them; he was having trouble enough with the patriots to want no rupture with the royalists. He contented himself with having the *Macedonian* escort safely out to sea the six American and three British vessels that had been caught at Callao.

Downes proceeded north to sniff out any violations that had been committed by patriot blockaders and then returned to Huacho, a port near Callao, on Christmas Day. Cochrane's squadron was at anchor, protecting San Martín's troops camped a few miles inland. While there Downes boldly escorted the American merchant ship *Louisa* safely through the Chilean fleet, even though her case had not yet been decided by Peruvian admiralty courts. He defended his conduct by accusing Cochrane of aiming "to destroy American commerce on this coast" by detaining vessels until their cargoes became worthless and their owners ruined. Chilean "Supreme Dictator" Bernardo O'Higgins was incensed at the *Louisa*'s escape, but resigned himself to it, realistically concluding that he could retaliate in no meaningful way. Downes aimed the *Macedonian* for home in March 1821, arriving at Boston two months later. Although he would err seriously in a later overseas assignment, in this instance the United States was fortunate that Downes had succeeded Biddle.[16]

Captain Charles Ridgely at Chile and Peru, 1821–1822

Charles Ridgely, whose commission dated back to 1799, had made a steady if unspectacular record in the wars against Tripoli and Great Britain, achieving his captaincy in 1815. It did not take him long after the *Constellation*'s arrival at Valparaiso to make the same shift in sympathy as had his predecessors in that quarter. Originally pro-patriot, his preference vanished once he had made contact with the patriots and heard their constant recriminations about the lack of American aid and sympathy that they felt they deserved. He found the royalists in Peru, personified by the courtly and ingratiating Viceroy Pezuela, more to his liking. Yet he never went so far as to disobey his orders by using force to break Cochrane's Chilean blockades of Peru.

During his 15-month stay at Valparaiso and Callao, Ridgely supported American whalers and merchantmen by resupplying and repairing them, hunting in vain for a royalist privateer accused of harassing American shipping, protesting to the proper authorities about Cochrane's illegal blockades, trying to speed up admiralty court decisions when American vessels were snapped up by either side (by which means he liberated four of them), carrying specie with much élan and with profit to himself, and bickering with Prevost as to how much support and understanding should be extended to the patriots. He took one innovative step: late in his tour he transported some Chilean soldiers to their prison colony at remote Juan Fernandez Island so that they could recapture it from mutinous inmates.

Undoubtedly Ridgely's most controversial deed was his part in the escape of Viceroy Pezuela. While Cochrane's fleet was hovering offshore and San Martín's Chilean-Argentine army was closing in on Lima and Callao, Pezuela was overthrown in January 1821 by a cabal, which replaced him as viceroy with José de la Serna. Even though Ridgely promised Serna not to allow the ex-viceroy to sail with him in the *Constellation* through the patriot blockade, he appears to have connived toward that end with the master of the American merchantman *General Brown*. The two ships put to sea in tandem; the *Brown* turned back and picked up Pezuela and his party, who eventually reached Spain unscathed. Ridgely's protestations of innocence in the matter ring hollow, but as usual the outraged patriots could do nothing about it.

More routine duties occupied the captain for the remainder of his tenure; his major problem was to try to stay abreast of the rapidly changing scene in lower South America. San Martín took Lima without difficulty in mid-July, but since the royalists continued to hold Callao for a couple of months, it meant the imposition of a new patriot blockade atop Chile's existing one, both illicit according to Americans. Callao eventually fell that September. Coincidentally Cochrane and San Martín quarreled after the Scots adventurer had seized a large sum of Peruvian money to pay his Chilean sailors. Although most of Peru was now in patriot hands, royalist die-hards still controlled some of the back country.

Ridgely described these events to Commodore Charles Stewart, his replacement, and then set sail for home, coming into New Jersey late the next July. The government was satisfied with his accomplishments, by implication agreeing with the breezy comparison between him and Prevost given by an American whaling captain, as quoted by Edward Billingsley: ". . . I am in hopes that we shall have no mor[e] Frothy Mercantile speculators to assume the garb and name of Consul of the U. States of Amer. who are more capable of Bobbing for EEls [sic] than of supporting the rites [sic] of their Countrymen, or the Dignity and Honor of the Nation." Ridgely, on the other hand, "had been most energetic and decisive, he will do honor to himself and Country."[17]

Commodore Charles Stewart at Chile and Peru, 1822–1824

Charles Stewart had earned his laurels while commanding USS *Constitution* by whipping both HMS *Cyane* and *Levant* in 1815. As he sailed for South America late in 1821, he commanded both the 74-gun ship of the line *Franklin* and the schooner *Dolphin*, thereby becoming the first commodore in the southeast Pacific. Arriving in Chile early the next year, he was soon emulating his earlier counterparts by exchanging snarls with Prevost over which side to favor in the patriot-royalist fracas. He also conveyed large amounts of specie from port to port in his two warships, acting with Eliphalet Smith, his personal friend and de facto business partner. This turned the *Franklin* into what some jealous officers called "a floating bank." He intervened with both sides in repeated efforts to liberate captured American merchantmen and whalers, while always opposing paper blockades. In one critical instance he flatly refused to surrender the *Canton*, Astor's ship, to the Peruvians for allegedly violating their blockade.

Oscillating fortunes of the belligerents kept on plaguing Stewart. San Martín had proclaimed Peruvian independence in July 1821, but the patriot drive soon lessened after he was forced out and sent into a lifelong exile in Europe, being largely forgotten by the time of his death in 1850. Throughout most of the next two years the patriot fleets of Chile and Peru usually maintained sea control, even though Cochrane would depart from Chile in January 1823 amid his typical cloud of controversy. Royalist maritime activities were reduced primarily to dispatching privateers to harry neutral commerce. But ashore it was a different matter. The royalist forces under José de la Serna were able to offer tenacious resistance. They defeated their opponents on several occasions, even after Bolívar and his able subordinate Antonio José de Sucre had marched south to assist the patriots. Meanwhile blockade and counter-blockade succeeded one another with monotonous regularity, none of which the United States recognized, but all of which afflicted the commodore with the need for endless correspondence.

Most of Stewart's difficulties were caused by Admiral George M. Guise, commander of the Peruvian patriot fleet. He announced a blockade that he avowed justified his seizing American vessels. It was ludicrous, for he slapped it on long before its announcement could reach the United States and his squadron was too puny to seal off the interdicted coast effectively. Stewart protested about it in vain until he persuaded Sucre to overrule Guise and free some captured American ships.

Stewart chose an unusual method of coping with the painfully slow communications between Washington and southwestern South America. When an American merchantman entered Valparaiso laden with construction materials for three small schooners, the commodore bought two of the schooners. Not only did they remain his property, to be sold for a profit just before his departure, but they were always manned by U.S.

navy personnel and provided essential service by quickly going back and forth to Panama to speed up communications with Washington. One of them actually rescued an American vessel from a royalist privateer.

After meeting with Commodore Isaac Hull, his successor, Stewart left Chile in the *Franklin* early in May and reached New York late in August. During the summer of 1825 he was tried by a court-martial, especially on charges of constructing and operating the schooners for his own financial advantage, carrying specie for Smith and other Americans, and hampering the patriot war effort by demonstrating extreme partiality to the royalists. The last accusation had been made by both the Peruvian patriot government and John B. Prevost. It was lucky for the accused that the secretary of the navy chose not to turn over to the court a letter in which Stewart called Cochrane and San Martín "two of the greatest rogues ever existing."

The commodore's stout denial of each complaint was buttressed by the testimony of Biddle, Downes, and Ridgely, all of whom swore that they had been confronted by the same problems as Stewart and had responded like him. Further witnesses rebutted the other charges, and Stewart was "fully and honorably" acquitted on all counts. Secretary of State Adams also came down foursquare for the commodore. He had concluded that the division of opinion among American officials in Chile and Peru had been the fault of the diplomat, not the naval officers. He ripped into Prevost, writing him, "I am directed by the President of the United States, to express to you the regret and concern, with which he has been informed of the differences which have occurred between you and the Naval Commanders of the forces of the United States in the Pacific in regard to public duties." Prevost would have unquestionably been recalled and probably sacked, but he died in Peru before he could be. Here is a clear instance in which the navy had outscored the Department of State in diplomacy.[18]

Commodore Isaac Hull at Chile and Peru, 1824–1827

While Stewart was enduring his ordeal in court, Isaac Hull remained in South America, commanding a squadron consisting of the frigate *United States* and two sloops, the *Dolphin*, which had stayed in the Pacific, and the *Peacock*, which had turned Cape Horn somewhat later than the flagship. The portly and affable "Uncle Isaac," as his crew called him, had basked in public acclaim ever since his *Constitution* had blasted HMS *Guerrière* in August 1812, the first American frigate victory. Since then he had preferred commanding navy yards because of the financial rewards, but troubles in Boston impelled him to seek foreign adventure. He arrived at Valparaiso in January 1824. His three-year tour was made enjoyable

Isaac Hull
(U.S. Naval Institute)

by the company of his wife and her attractive sister, who is said to have enchanted no less than Bolívar himself.

For all practical purposes the war for Chilean and Peruvian independence would seem to be over with Bolívar's entrance into Lima and Sucre's decisive victory over Serna at Ayacucho, both during a two-day span in mid-December 1824. By this time the United States had started recognizing as sovereign nations some of the newly independent Latin-American countries, and the Monroe Doctrine had been pronounced. These developments made American public opinion even more favorable to the patriots, a partiality expressed by Hull and his people more than by their predecessors.

Yet the royalists doggedly held out at recaptured Callao until the next September, thereby continuing to pose problems for Hull. Patriot Admiral Guise's blockade was only spasmodically enforced, but tensions were eased when the commodore persuaded Bolívar to order Guise to relax his blockade. The war for Chilean and Peruvian independence ended in January 1826 with the evacuation of the remaining royalist troops from Peru. Hull's last duties before his command ended a year later concerned sending sloops into the central Pacific, especially Hawaii, as lower South America quieted down.[19]

Commodore Jacob Jones at Chile and Peru, 1827–1828

While Peru was in the process of liberating itself from Spain during the late 1820s, circumstances arose that allowed one more brief flareup of unpleasantness between Lima and Washington. Jacob Jones, Hull's successor as squadron commodore, had a tour of duty that was generally placid, save for the impressment question. Over the years American sailors arriving at Callao in their own ships were often enticed to desert by the war-engendered high pay offered by Peruvian captains for risky voyages through blockades. The U.S. consul in Callao reported that "¾ of the Peruvian privateer crews are from the United States." Lima held that anyone who had accepted employment in its vessels automatically became a citizen of Peru, hence subject to conscription into its armed forces. Americans trapped in this manner vehemently protested to Jones and the U.S. chargé d'affaires, who carried these complaints to local authorities but could make little progress. The issue was finally decided, not by American naval and civilian diplomats, but by the waning of the Spanish threat, following which the Peruvians decommissioned most of their fleet, and instead of needing new sailors and soldiers, proceeded to discharge most of those they already had.[20]

Summary

In general the navy contributed effectively to its country's foreign relations during the era of Latin-American rebellions against Spain. In regard to the Floridas, Porter's experiences at New Orleans were dissimilar to those of his three colleagues; only he had to wrestle with the intricacies of enforcing the Embargo. The fruitful naval expeditions of Campbell at Amelia Island in 1812, Loomis at Fort Apalachicola in 1816, and Henley at Amelia in 1817 served well their government's interests. Happily, not one American had even been slightly wounded (save for four at Apalachicola), and two of the three expeditions had been carried through without opposition. Of greater importance, they all gave evidence that Spain, wracked by uprisings against it from the Rio Grande to Cape Horn, was totally impotent in meeting its international responsibility of protecting the American South from hostile incursions of blacks and Indians alike. Although lacking the tremendous impact of Jackson's 1818 incursion into both Florida colonies, the navy's interventions still helped to deliver a pointed message to Madrid—no choice remained but to cede both East and West Florida to the United States.

Little space need be allotted to Morris and Read at Haiti during 1817–1818. The waters there were too muddy and too deep for naval officers, even in league with presidential agents, to recover money expropriated from Americans by Henri Christophe.

The successive commanders operating against piracy from 1819 to 1826 had been ordered to build an impressive diplomatic edifice, but they varied considerably in their accomplishments. Perry could do nothing in Venezuela, and Kearny obviously outdid his fellow-officer Madison at Galveston. Biddle, overall as successful a naval diplomat as any, generally failed in 1822 and 1823, for he had been hampered by conflicting orders, ships ill equipped for their tasks, Spanish refusals to cooperate with him, and the frightful experience of yellow fever aboard his flagship. Porter, victorious in striking hard at Cuban piracies, threw away his opportunity to accomplish more by his overreaction in Puerto Rico, thereby ruining his U.S. naval career. But even so, these two had erected the framework that enabled Warrington to complete the building. Biddle took some thirty corsair ships and commenced the efforts to persuade Spanish authorities to cooperate, which made it easier for his successors to achieve just that. Porter came up with the right vessels and made freebooting in Cuba an occupation replete with premature deaths. His achievements, however, take away nothing from his successor. The merciless work of Warrington's squadron at Cuba and Puerto Rico, linked with his adroit diplomacy with Spaniard and Briton alike, made sure that the disappointments of his predecessors had helped write finis to two-and-a-half centuries of piracy in the Gulf and the Caribbean. It had been a fine moment in American naval history.

It must be admitted that the diplomacy carried on by U.S. naval officers in Mexico from 1816 to 1829 was not exactly masterful. To be sure, none of them behaved rashly or illogically enough to seriously embarrass relations between Washington and Madrid or Mexico City. It is rather that circumstances permitted them to accomplish little. Cunningham cannot be faulted for offering no resistance in the face of such overwhelming odds, but his surrender was, nonetheless, a national humiliation. Ridgely was hamstrung by the Adams administration to such an extent that it had to be American and Mexican diplomats who ousted Porter's warships and privateers from Key West. Finally, Elliott's liberation of an impressed American sailor at Vera Cruz and Conner's acceptance of a tepid Mexican apology at Yucatán were comparatively inconsequential at that time and later.

Seldom in American annals has a sequence of U.S. naval officers accomplished more than in lower South America from 1813 to 1828. Porter was the exception to this generalization, for if his illogical support of the ill-fated Carrera turned out to benefit his country, it was despite, not because of, anything that he was trying to achieve. But the work of Biddle, Downes, Ridgely, Stewart, Hull, and to a lesser extent Jones was triumphant, particularly in view of the obstacles that they faced. The royalists heartily disliked Americans for their antimonarchical and prorebel sentiments, and the patriots resented them for refusing to recognize the former colonies and insisting upon observing a neutrality that seemed to favor the royalists. Nonetheless, these five officers were able to maintain from 1818 to 1828 the non-involvement in the war that their government required. Meanwhile, they were liberating from prison many American citizens and saving American property worth millions of dollars from royalist and patriot expropriations. Their collective accomplishment may be fairly designated as top-drawer.

CHAPTER FOUR

Mexico

1832–1860

During the half-century after winning independence from Spain, Mexico seldom enjoyed anything resembling peace. Politically the nation was dominated by a small wealthy upper class, for its majority Indian and mestizo population was apolitical. The ruling elite, moreover, was divided between the Clericals, usually calling themselves "conservatives," and the Anticlericals, designated as "liberals," although the first appellations are the more accurate. The Clericals, both in Latin Europe and Latin America, favored the continuous intervention of the state-supported Catholic Church into politics, economics, and social operations; their strength was concentrated among the hierarchy, the large landowners, and the upper ranks of the armed forces. The Anticlericals advocated the restriction of the church to matters of faith and morals, and tended to be backed by intellectuals, the more democratically inclined reformers, and the lower echelons of officers whose promotions were blocked by their Clerical superiors.

This division of power and opinion, plus the lack of any democratic tradition, resulted in a recurrent chaos, during which the national instability became chronic. One presumptuous general after another executed a coup d'etat, announced his meaningless new "plan" for the regeneration of his country, and served for a few months before being toppled by another of his ilk. These constant and ruinous shifts in authority at Mexico City are best illustrated by General Antonio Lopez de Santa Anna, who came into and went out of power no less than eleven times from 1833 to 1855. Those years witnessed thirty-six presidents who averaged about seven-and-a-half months in office. During this time internal law and order, as well as its handmaiden of effective governmental protection of foreigners and their possessions, were often conspicuously absent. Mutual provocations between Mexican officials and American naval officers on hand to safeguard the interests of their fellow-countrymen were sometimes characterized by itchy trigger fingers on both sides.

American naval officers' diplomatic negotiations with Mexicans through these years concentrated on these places and wars: Tampico (1832); the Texas Revolution (1836–1837); the California coast (1840–1842); the Mexican War (1846–1848); Mexico's west coast (1854); and the War of the Reform (1858–1861).

Tampico, 1832

Commodore Jesse D. Elliott, June

The Mexican-American disagreement in the spring of 1832 was not the direct product of the Clerical-Anticlerical struggle. It concerned rather the ill-considered act passed by Mexico at the height of its hysteria attending the Spanish invasion of the country in 1829. Under the act all Spaniards born in Spain were expelled from the republic, and Mexico was thus to be deprived of many of its best educated and most prosperous inhabitants.

At Tampico the West Indian Squadron's Commodore Elliott in the *Fairfield* was button-holed in June by three Spaniards in business there who swore that a few years before, they had become American citizens in Florida. Hence, they argued, General Estabán Moctezuma, commanding in Tampico, had no right to order their expulsion. Elliott concurred that such action was illegal under the Mexican-American Treaty of 1831, which specifically provided that neither nation should harass the citizens of the other while they were pursuing legal occupations. He took up the case with Moctezuma, sending him a copy of the treaty, but the Mexican refused to rescind his ouster. Elliott mulled over his options but decided that the situation did not justify the use of force. The Spanish Americans were taken to the United States in the USS *Shark*, leaving the commodore to suffer a diplomatic defeat in a case where he had by far the better legal position.[1]

Lieutenant Josiah Tattnall, September

By the summer of 1832 General Antonio Lopez de Santa Anna, for the moment an Anticlerical, had control of the Gulf of Mexico. He sent the schooner *Montezuma* to blockade the mouth of the Rio Grande. Off Matamoros in August the Mexicans boarded the New York merchantman

William A. Turner, detained the crew for a few hours, robbed them of valuables, and compelled the supercargo, on the threat of being hanged, to sign papers authorizing the larceny. Learning of the outrage, Tattnall in the schooner *Grampus* chased the plunderers into Tampico. Although the city's forts were garrisoned by Santa Anna's troops and one of his warships rode at anchor, Tattnall boldly came alongside the *Montezuma* and took her without resistance from land or sea. He packed her captain and about eighty men into the *Grampus* and landed them in Pensacola for possible prosecution by the town's district attorney.

Back in Tampico, Tattnall found another American vessel, this one laden with some $200,000 in specie, being kept there on what he thought trumped-up charges by local authorities hoping to gain possession of all that tantalizing gold and silver. Although the ship was directly under the guns of the fortress, Tattnall sent the *Grampus*'s boats to escort her safely out to open water, again without Mexican opposition. The insurance companies of New Orleans presented Tattnall with "a beautiful service of silver plate" as a reward for his protection of the nation's commerce in the Gulf of Mexico.[2]

The Texas Revolution against Mexico, 1836–1837
Commodore Alexander J. Dallas at Tampico, May 1836

When Mexicans made the decision during the 1820s that their relatively empty northeastern state of Texas must be populated, in part to stem the raids of Indians further into Mexico, they were poking at a yellow-jackets' nest. The only people available for that purpose were Protestant, slave-owning Americans from the deep South and the Southwest. These new-comers quickly made a joke of the promise they had made to be converted to Catholicism and insisted upon working their cotton lands with slave labor, despite the abolition of slavery in the Mexican constitution. On the other hand, Texans had bona fide complaints against their overlords to the south. As has been noted above, revolution had become a normal part of the Mexican political way of life. As one ineffectual general was succeeded by what amounted to his clone, the national economy went to pieces, and law and order could not be maintained, and property could not be protected. During the mid-1830s Santa Anna came into power as an Anticlerical liberal, but soon betrayed his followers by an about-face to become a strongly Clerical conservative. When he pledged to end slave-owning and to enforce the laws about conversion to Catholicism, the Texans declared their independence in March 1836.

The slaughter of Texan-Americans at the Alamo, the even higher death toll at Goliad, and the astonishingly easy triumph by Sam Houston's army

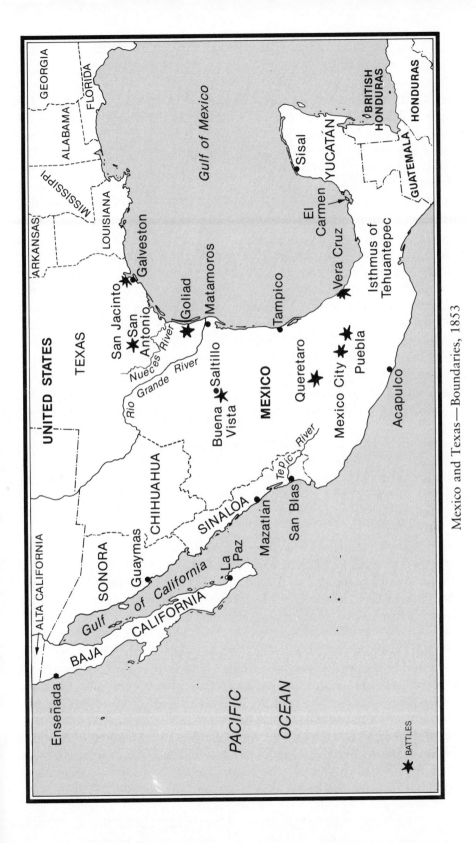

Mexico and Texas—Boundaries, 1853

over Santa Anna's at San Jacinto need no more than a brief mention. This sequence practically ended the Texan rebellion. Although the Mexicans continued to maintain that they still owned that state, after 1836 they never made any real effort to retake it. Relations with Washington, nonetheless, deteriorated further, for the Mexicans were well aware of the extent to which American support and sympathy had contributed to the loss of their province. During 1836 and 1837 their resentment over this loss strongly influenced the five diplomatic incidents concerning the U.S. Navy.

Alexander J. Dallas in the *Constellation*, the new squadron commodore, quickly had his mettle tested. From Pensacola he dispatched Lieutenant Thomas Osborn in the schooner *Jefferson* to Tampico with letters for the resident American consul. On landing, Osborn and his men were arrested and imprisoned by the local commandant, known in contemporary documentation only as "General Gomez," but they were soon released to depart on the *Jefferson*. Dallas still retaliated by sending two men-of-war to menace shipping in the harbor, and his gambit worked. Mexican authorities told the commodore that Gomez had been dismissed and that his conduct would be investigated. Elated, Dallas recalled his ships from Tampico, only to find later that the Foreign Relations Committee of the House sourly noted that Gomez's "punishment" consisted of his being reassigned to "a more important coastal command," where "his hostile feelings might again endanger the security of American citizens or property."[3]

Commander William Mervine at Vera Cruz, October 1836

Events soon confirmed Secretary of State John Forsyth's apprehension that the whitewashing of General Gomez "would be apt to encourage the commission of like indignities thereafter." William Mervine in the *Natchez* came to Vera Cruz late in October 1836 and two weeks later sent a boat ashore. When Passed Midshipman Francis B. Renshaw left the dock to deliver a letter to the local American consul, his sailors with astonishing speed got "more or less intoxicated." They quarreled with a passing fisherman and exchanged blows with him. The guard at the pier rushed to the aid of his fellow-countryman and attacked the sailors with his bayonet. Driving them back to their boat, he left two of them, badly wounded, on the ground. At this juncture Renshaw reappeared, accompanied by Mexican soldiers apparently out for blood. Carnage was averted only when "the port captain," seeing his men leveling their muskets, shouted at them not to fire. Renshaw and the American consul decided that the sailors were too drunk and too battered to go back to the *Natchez*, and had them placed under the custody of the Mexican port captain, who sent the seriously wounded to a hospital and incarcerated the rest in "a humid and loathsome prison on a short allowance of food." Mervine's repeated efforts to secure their release were unavailing at first, but after he left for Pensacola to inform Dallas of the matter, the men were set free.

When President Jackson was informed about Osborn's arrest and the manhandling of the *Natchez*'s boat crew, and heard lurid accounts of violations committed against American merchantmen in the Gulf of Mexico, he reacted with the utmost choler, almost to the point of asking Congress to declare war on Mexico. In a "Proclamation" he requested an act "authorizing reprisals, and the use of the naval forces of the United States . . . against Mexico to enforce them," should that government fail "to come to an amicable settlement" in future controversies involving American warships. Congress was unwilling to go that far, and the administration had to content itself with angry protests from Forsyth to the Mexican Foreign Office.[4]

Commodore Alexander J. Dallas along the Texas Coast, January 1837

When Mexico announced a blockade of the coast of Texas in February 1836, U.S. navy officers were guaranteed headaches, especially when Commodore Alexander J. Dallas made clear where his sympathies lay, issuing a "public notice" that he planned to convoy through the Mexican blockade "every American ship . . . destined for Texas, Matamoros, Tampico, or Vera-Cruz." Furthermore, he was assigning Commander Bladen Dulany in the sloop *Boston* to provide that service. The Mexicans remonstrated that, although the United States had not yet recognized Texas independence, insofar as the blockade was concerned, Dallas was treating illicit rebels in the same manner as an established government with which Washington had maintained official relations for years. The Department of State shrugged off this charge by emphasizing that Dallas's behavior amounted to no more than a declaration of the belligerent rights of both parties in a dispute. This, for instance, had been done in the Latin-American uprisings against Spain well before the insurgent regimes had been recognized. After that, Mexican objections to Dallas's decree amounted to little more than verbiage and were ignored by Washington.[5]

Lieutenant Josiah Tattnall at Vera Cruz, February 1837

When Santa Anna had been found in hiding after his shameful defeat at San Jacinto in April 1836, he had every reason to fear an immediate lynching from those who recalled the Alamo. But Houston, recognizing his value as a hostage, protected him, forcing him to sign two treaties recognizing Texas independence, with the Rio Grande as the boundary of the new republic. Naturally these pacts were declared null and void in Mexico City as having been exacted under duress. Meanwhile Houston permitted Santa Anna to write to President Jackson, who responded by inviting the Mexican to dinner in the White House and then giving him the use of a U.S. warship to take him back to his native land.

This task was allotted to Lieutenant Josiah Tattnall, who headed south from Norfolk during January in the schooner *Pioneer* and dropped anchor at Vera Cruz on 12 February. His passenger was deeply apprehensive about the reception he might receive ashore. As Tattnall's biographer put it: "Defeated in a general engagement which compassed the liberation of a State whose rebellion he was seeking to crush and . . . about to be returned in weakness and misfortune to his country—Santa Anna was under the impression that his rivals and enemies would cause him to be shot down. . . ." The lieutenant clearly considered it his duty to ensure his safety once ashore.

Citizens and soldiers gathered at the mole to await his arrival, and as one eyewitness reported, "matters looked squally." But Tattnall, in full-dress uniform, escorted Santa Anna through the crowd. An American naval officer who was present on the occasion commented, "Tattnall knew the danger of the move, but danger always seemed a welcome guest to him. He was made a lion of in Vera Cruz." He safely deposited the general at his hotel and even stayed with him for an extra week at his hacienda near the city. Perhaps it was typical of the Mexican turncoat that although he had every reason to be grateful to his American naval benefactor, he was not appreciative enough even to mention him in his autobiography.[6]

Commander William Mervine near Matamoros, April 1837

During the late winter of 1836–1837 Commodore Dallas once more dispatched Commander William Mervine in the *Natchez* to Texas, this time to check on the efficacy of the Mexican blockade. Mervine came into a place called "Brazos de Santiago," near Matamoros, at the mouth of the Rio Grande, where he spied the Mexican brig *General Urrea*, commanded by an officer no better identified than "Captain Machin" in the current records, with two merchantmen nearby flying no colors. Correctly surmising that they were captive Americans, Mervine sent boarding parties to them, finding that the *Louisiana* and *Champion* had been "illegally captured and unceremoniously plundered." Since Machin's explanations were evasive, Mervine demanded their release but was told that such an order could come only from the local commander, General Nicolás Bravo, who was absent.

On 17 April 1837 another Mexican warship, the *Bravo*, entered Brazos escorting the American schooner *Julius Caesar*, but Mervine decided to concentrate on the *General Urrea* as the original culprit. One shot from the *Natchez* brought down the Mexican flag, for Machin was heavily outgunned. Mervine took both ships to sea through ineffectual Mexican fire and proceeded up the Texas coast, where, as he put it, he sailed for "ten or twelve days but without seeing or hearing of the Mexican blockading squadron; which . . . demonstrated the total absence of any real blockade." He sent the *Urrea* off to Pensacola and returned south to resume his patrol.

The tidings that an American warship had assailed, captured, and sent into port a Mexican man-of-war detonated a furor in both countries that quickly escalated into a full-fledged war scare. As reprinted in the *Daily National Intelligencer*, a New Orleans paper demanded hostilities: "The bragging Dons have had their way long enough. What they have done is ample cause for war, and one of the most popular measures that Mr. Van Buren [the new president] could now effect would be the declaration of war against the Mexicans. The whole nation would sustain him." The American consul in Mexico City reported that the taking of the *General Urrea* "has produced great excitement . . . and hostile measures were immediately spoken of, and the expulsion of the American citizens from the capital" was discussed "with great warmth in secret sessions of the Congress."

This mutual truculence, however, soon evaporated. The Mexicans realized that they had enough to handle with seceded Texas without adding the United States as an official enemy. The *Intelligencer* in particular hastened to douse the war flames, asking: "Is the captain of a ship of war the proper authority to decide upon the legality of a blockade? And if he be, is he authorized to make war, at his own discretion, to punish what he may consider an infraction of the law of nations by the capture of a vessel for alleged violation of blockade?" Its editors went on to stress that Jackson had recently asked for "authorized reprisals" against Mexico but this had been turned down by both houses "with great unanimity." The pacifistic Van Buren mollified the Mexicans by subjecting Mervine to a court of inquiry about his conduct off Texas. It found him blameless, but returned the *Urrea* to Brazos. This seems to have ended Mexican-American naval clashes in connection with the Texas rebellion.[7]

Along the California Coast, 1840–1842
Commander French Forrest at Monterey, 1840

No sooner had the Mexicans faced the fact that Texas was probably gone forever than they found it necessary to cast nervous glances toward the northwest. Like Texas, California had been ignored by the Spaniards in Mexico, until 1769, when a mission was founded at San Diego. Settlement was extremely slow over the ensuing decades, and by 1840 probably no more than 10,000 Mexicans resided in that huge area. Already some Americans and Englishmen had drifted into the purlieus of Monterey, the early capital of the province, working in various enterprises, among them lumbering and cattle-raising. One of California's major industries of the time was rumor-mongering. Accounts of amorphous plots were bruited about, some that an independent country would be set up, others that either American or British annexation would take place.

Mexican *Californios* and Anglo-American Californians shared a discontent with their rulers in remote Mexico City. Late in 1836 Juan Bautista Alvarado enlisted both communities to overthrow an unpopular Mexican governor, and took that position legally in 1838. Isaac Graham, an irascible distiller, trapper, and trader, was among the Americans who had originally supported him. In 1840 Alvarado, frightened by reports of a Graham-inspired plot to overthrow him, arrested him and 47 other Americans and Englishmen. After being chained and imprisoned in Monterey, they were put in a ship sailing south to Tepic, near San Blas, suffering throughout from "harsh treatment" and a lack of "food, water, and fresh air."

On 13 June Commander French Forrest in the sloop *St. Louis* came into Monterey, where he remained for a little less than a month. He wrote to Alvarado, requesting an explanation of reports that American citizens had been "attacked in their houses, wounded, robbed, imprisoned, and sent away in violation of existing treaties." The Governor replied that "certain foreigners" had been expelled, "according to law, either for offenses against the public peace, or for having entered the country illegally." In his annual report for 1841, Secretary of the Navy Abel Upshur waxed eloquent about Forrest's meager accomplishments: "In the midst of these outrages, Commander Forrest arrived on the coast, and by his prompt and spirited interposition, vindicated and secured the rights, not only of American citizens, but of British subjects. . . . For these services, Commander Forrest received and appears to have well deserved, a formal expression of thanks both of American and British residents."

What Upshur is talking about is hard to fathom, since Forrest's actions at Monterey seem to have added up to nothing even approximating "spirited interposition." Before weighing anchor in July, he did little after writing Alvarado other than "taking testimony from Americans" about their property losses. Some months later Graham and the others were freed at Tepic, because of inflamed publicity about the atrocities committed against them and the spirited efforts of the British consul there, surely not by Forrest's feeble endeavors at Monterey.[8]

Commodore Thomas ap Catesby Jones at Monterey, 1842

During that summer Commodore Thomas ap Catesby Jones in the frigate United States was commanding the Pacific Squadron from Callao, Peru, under the secretary's typical orders that he must protect American commerce but unless "the honor" of the United States was at stake he must not resort to force. But now, in September, Jones faced a quandary. What should he do about a letter from the U.S. consul at Mazatlán, Mexico, stating that a local newspaper had published in June a report that the Mexican foreign minister had used terms so incredibly offensive in a note to Secretary of State Webster that war was "highly probable"? The commodore chose to interpret this as a Mexican "conditional declaration of war." Furthermore, he read in an American newspaper that Mexico had just sold California to Great Britain for $7,000,000. Finally, the movements of the French and British fleets off lower South America were highly suspicious, for they had just hurriedly left for destinations unknown. Imagining that they were heading for Monterey, he could not be aware that the French were in the process of annexing the Society and Marquesas Islands in the South Pacific and the British had tagged along to watch the operations.

He conferred with his subordinate officers, who agreed with him that Mexico and America were probably at war, and that if the British were about to buy California, they would be acting in direct defiance of the Monroe Doctrine. (This is of considerable diplomatic interest, for it is one of the comparatively few references to the doctrine as formulating American policy prior to its resurrection by President Polk in December 1845.) Heartened by his officers' support, Jones set sail for California in his flagship with the Cyane. He tried to cover himself by writing to the department about his plans, promising that "no precipitate steps will be taken, by which aggression will be justly chargeable to me." This was nonsense, for his documentation shows that he had already written his orders for the occupation of Monterey. Contrary winds necessitated a long passage; it was not until 19 October that the two ships reached their destination.

Jones snapped up three Mexican merchantmen in the harbor and later that night sent ashore a demand for Monterey's surrender. Acting Governor Juan Bautista Alvarado, the same man who had been involved with

Thomas ap Catesby Jones
(Official U.S. Navy Portrait)

Graham and Forrest two years before, fell over himself to comply with the American ultimatum. To be sure, he had no choice. His fort's garrison consisted of precisely 29 regular soldiers and 25 recruits who had not yet received "military instruction." As for the "castle's" 11 cannons, they were "nearly useless," and the town's defenses were "of no consequence, as everyone knows." The official surrender would occur the next morning.

That same evening Thomas O. Larkin, a resident American merchant who would soon be the U.S. Consul there, asked Jones to explain who was warring upon whom. He denied Jones's answer that Mexico had declared war "conditionally," avowing that recent Mexican newspapers showed that peace still prevailed. Although Jones asked to see documentary proof of Larkin's assertion, he made no attempt to slow down his occupation plans. He issued a proclamation to Monterey's inhabitants, informing them, "The Stars and Stripes . . . will float triumphantly over you, and, henceforth and forever [,] will give protection and security to you, your children, and to yet unborn countless thousands." Jones's "forever" lasted exactly 28 hours.

At 7:40 the next morning Alvarado and his commander agreed to the commodore's occupation terms. When Larkin came on the scene, he admitted that he could not find the newspapers to which he had alluded the day before. This naturally reassured Jones that they did not exist. At 12:00 the occupation of the town by 150 of the squadron's marines and specially selected sailors was completed without a shot. When the American flag was elevated, the men gave three cheers while the bands from the two warships played "Yankee Doodle" and "The Star-Spangled Banner," after which salutes rang out from the American vessels and the Mexican fort. The night of the 20th passed without incident.

But everything fell to pieces for Jones when he came ashore the next morning. Mexican newspapers that were shown him, dated two months later than the one that he had seen in Callao, proved that, although Mexican-American relations were in their usual state of distrust and dislike, there had been no formal declaration of hostilities. The commodore accomplished an immediate and complete about-face. As one modern commentator has written, "his reputation was transformed from that of a foresighted patriot into an overbold adventurer who had acted too soon, no matter how honest his motives." After returning to his flagship he notified Alvarado that his occupation force would be withdrawn at 4:00 that afternoon, and that everything would revert to what it had been on the 19th. At the word that the Mexican standard was to replace the American, some of the invaders expressed resentment about the decision. One sailor mourned, "So perish all my greatness, adieu all my vision of prise [sic] money," and concluded by calling his commander "a humbugging old fudge." The negative reaction of Midshipman Meriwether Jones, the commodore's son, was considerably more pronounced. When given a direct order to haul down the American flag he refused pointblank to comply. One bystander reported that instead, he stormed off in such a rage that he "immediately drank so much whisky that he fell off a cliff and nearly killed himself." Nevertheless, the American ensign was lowered, that of the Mexicans raised, salutes were exchanged, and what one author has called "The Vest Pocket War of Commodore Jones" was over. Somewhat surprisingly, the two peoples seem to have enjoyed the other's company over the several weeks that the *United States* and *Cyane* remained at Monterey. As one young American officer put it, the men passed their leisure time ashore, "hunting wild deer and dancing with tame Dear," both being prevalent, the one in the surrounding countryside, the other in town.

Press reaction to the conquest of Monterey was relatively bland, although one Mexican paper was convinced that "Commodore Jones had attacked Monterey agreeably to orders from his government, with the object of conquering California." *Niles' Weekly Register* focused upon Jones's fear of British annexation of the area and found it without substance: "The idea that England is desirous to possess herself of California, seems as great a bugbear with the American people, as the designs of Russia on India, are with the English."

Understandably there was a considerable diplomatic ruckus when the news of Monterey's seizure reached Washington and Mexico City. Secretary of State Webster hurried to reassure his Mexican counterpart that "Commodore Jones had no warrant from this Government for his proceeding and that the President exceedingly regrets its occurrence." Meanwhile, General J. N. Almonte, the Mexican minister to Washington, was demanding not only that "the officer committing this unheard-of outrage be punished, in an exemplary manner," but also that the United States should give "immediate reparation for the gross indignity and wrong" that had been inflicted upon his nation.

Nevertheless, the administration changed its mind about Jones, deciding that he had done no more than act imprudently, rather than as a deliberate violator of Mexican honor. All that Washington would admit to Mexico City was that the commodore had erred sufficiently to merit his recall as commander of the Pacific Squadron. Even while notifying him that he would be replaced, Secretary Upshur said that he might come home "in any such mode as may be most comfortable and agreeable to yourself." Jones took advantage of this remarkable leniency, sure that procrastination would work in his behalf. When he finally showed up in the United States late in 1844, he found to his relief that he would not be subjected even to a court of inquiry, to say nothing of a court-martial. Instead, the secretary in a letter the following March lauded rather than condemned him for his occupation of Monterey: President Tyler "has authorized me to say to you . . . that he perceives evidences of an ardent zeal in the service of your Country, and a devotion to what you deemed your duty, regardless of personal consequences, which entitle you to anything but censure from your Government."

Many commentators on this episode seem to have overlooked what turned out to be the most important result of Jones's actions at Monterey in 1842: it had been so flagrant and insulting a violation of Mexico's national sovereignty that thereafter it became impossible for Mexicans to consider American offers to purchase any part of California. Only by armed conquest could the United States take possession of it.[9]

Lieutenant Archibald H. Gillespie, USMC, at Monterey and Klamath Falls, Oregon, 1845–1846

The last pre–Mexican War involvement of the navy (which spilled over into the commencement of hostilities in California) was Lieutenant Archibald H. Gillespie's assignment to Monterey, evidently the only time that a marine officer became a diplomatic agent during the years covered in this work. His selection seems to have been based upon no more than his availability and his fluency in Spanish. He departed from Washington in October carrying a letter from President Polk to Thomas O. Larkin, who had become the U.S. Consul at Monterey. Among his luggage were letters to Army Colonel John Charles Frémont from his wife and the influential Senator Thomas H. Benton of Missouri, his father-in-law. Throughout, this was a murky enterprise about which no certainty exists even today. The president offered little illumination, writing in his diary only that he had held a "confidential conversation" with Gillespie concerning his "secret mission."

It was common knowledge that Polk numbered the acquisition of California among the four major aspirations of his administration, thereby arousing suspicion that the lieutenant's errand was to stir up a Mexican war for that purpose. Yet his message to Larkin was pacifistic. The consul was to bring Californians, both Americans and Mexicans, into cooperation with him to thwart European annexationist intrigues, those of the British in particular. As for the union of California with the United States, that could occur only after a successful rebellion against Mexico and the creation of an independent republic. There seems to be not a word in his instructions justifying American armed intervention in the Far West for either purpose.

Chronology is important here. During 1845 and early 1846 most Americans anticipated a war with Britain over Oregon, as the departmental correspondence of U.S. naval officers demonstrates. But while traveling in Mexico Gillespie learned that the first warlike moves against Mexico had commenced, and he headed for a meeting with Frémont at Klamath Falls, Oregon, just above the California border. That peripatetic officer had been tramping through northern Mexico with 60 soldiers, supposedly engaged in exploration alone. Gillespie poured out his news of probable hostilities in more militant words than those of the president's letter to Frémont, who promptly struck into California. In the town of Sonoma he assisted American settlers in forming the briefly independent "Golden Bear Republic," a precursor of California's becoming part of the United States in 1848.

Gillespie's exact role in these events cannot be evaluated with accuracy, but a reasonable conclusion would seem to be that he helped Frémont ignore Polk's letter. Described as "an energetic, ambitious, egotistical, and rather excitable young officer," he must have used all his efforts to promote aggression rather than preserving the peace. Even so, had he argued otherwise, it probably would have made no difference. Frémont's entire career shows that when presented with a choice between action and inaction, he would choose exertion over lethargy, sometimes to his great personal disadvantage.[10]

The Mexican War, 1846–1848
Commander Alexander Slidell Mackenzie in Cuba, 1846

There is no need to recount the causes and events of the Mexican war, except to point out that it was primarily the U.S. Army that brought the Mexicans to the bargaining table at Guadalupe Hidalgo early in 1848. The navy had relatively little to do with the triumph. Since the enemy hardly had either a navy or privateers, most American officers and men had little to do except to endure the stultifying boredom of blockade duty, usually broken only by the weather or disease. Yet essential blue-water services were provided. In the Caribbean the fleet bottled up Mexican shipping in port, helped to storm Vera Cruz, and furnished both suppliers and transportation for the assault on Mexico City. The navy was considerably more on its own in the Pacific. To be sure, there was an embarrassing oversupply of commanders in that quarter—no less than five—a fact that enabled a leading student of the Mexican War in the Pacific to entitle a chapter "Too Many Commodores." Nevertheless, the navy captured San Francisco and San Diego in Upper (Alta) California, while cooperating with Kearny in establishing American rule there. The conquest of Lower California's few towns was entirely a naval matter, although all of the Baja had to be returned at the end of the war.

Early in the war Polk tried to drop a line in troubled Mexican waters, hoping to gain a relatively bloodless victory. General Santa Anna, of Alamo infamy, had been ousted from power in 1845 and had fled into exile in Cuba. He let Washington know that should he be aided in a comeback, he would make peace on terms most advantageous for the United States. In May the president instructed Commodore David Conner, "If Santa Anna endeavors to enter Mexican ports, you will allow him to pass freely" through the American blockade. The president selected, to make contact with the general, Commander Alexander S. Mackenzie, who had caused a sensation in 1842 by hanging for mutiny Philip Spencer, son of John C. Spencer, at that time secretary of war in Tyler's cabinet, although he was acquitted by a court-martial.

Polk's instructions to Mackenzie were "to ascertain in a prudent way what Santa Anna's views were in regard to peace with the United States and whether if restored in Mexico, there was a reasonable prospect that he would make peace." He should tell the Mexicans that there would be no trouble about a treaty ending the war, provided that parts of Mexico would be ceded in return for "an ample consideration in ready money." When Santa Anna met Mackenzie in Havana during July, he accepted the president's terms and went on to offer the most specific advice about where American armed forces should attack in order to induce Mexican public opinion to choose Santa Anna and peace. It is easy to imagine the Mexican reaction should the news of this monumental treachery have leaked out, so it is little wonder that the general insisted upon "the greatest secrecy," lest his "countrymen [,] not appreciating his benevolent intention to free them from war and other evils [,] might form a doubtful opinion of his patriotism."[!]

Mackenzie hurried back to Washington with this message of duplicity, but it did not matter; everything that Polk had counted on fell to pieces. That August Santa Anna sailed to Mexico in a British steamer to assume power while the U.S. Navy looked the other way. The general dropped at once any overtures for peace and resumed Mexico's war effort, inept though it soon proved to be. At least both Mackenzie and Polk had plenty of company in being victimized by Santa Anna, who throughout his long and shabby career was false to almost any person or cause that he embraced, self-aggrandizement excepted.[11]

Commodore John D. Sloat, et al., at Monterey, etc., 1846–1848

In the spring of 1848 John D. Sloat, old and ailing, remained comparatively inert, not sure that hostilities had officially commenced. Although shortly before his leavetaking his men had captured Monterey and San

Francisco, he was recalled by the department for inactivity. By that time Lieutenant Colonel John C. Frémont, who, as has been narrated above, had helped American settlers in northern California set up an independent republic, calling for American annexation, showed up in the south. He immediately formed an alliance with the equally aggressive and impulsive Commodore Robert F. Stockton, the civil governor and naval commandant. They completed the conquest of the present-day state—Alta or Upper California, as opposed to Baja or Lower California—but Stockton's imperious attitude and antagonistic edicts incensed the Mexican inhabitants. In December General Stephen W. Kearny marched into San Diego, having led his little "Army of the West" all the way from Kansas. Although he carried a letter from Polk appointing him military commander in that area, Stockton and Frémont intrigued against him in order to remain in control. Simultaneously Commodore William B. Shubrick arrived at Monterey, followed a few weeks later by Commodore James Biddle. Now five high-ranking officers, three in the navy and two in the army, were jousting for power.

Luckily for the installation of a proper pecking order in conquered California, senior commodore Biddle, demonstrating his usual ability to cut to the heart of the matter, came down strongly in favor of Kearny and Shubrick. Soon he helped to arrange for the departure of Stockton and Frémont, enabling Kearny to assume full power as military governor. As for Shubrick, he was so unhappy about being junior to Biddle that he asked to be ordered back to Washington. But Biddle handled the situation with admirable generosity. He would remain in the north, occupying himself with paper work, leaving to Shubrick all offensive operations. This arrangement resulted in the capture of all Baja California's towns, although everything in the south had to be returned to Mexico in the Treaty of Guadalupe Hidalgo, which ended the war.

Biddle also rendered excellent service by rescinding Stockton's blockade of Baja; the navy had been trying to police 2,500 miles of shoreline with two sloops, the only warships available for that duty. Detesting paper blockades since his experiences off western and eastern South America and in the Caribbean, he restricted the blockade to only the ports of Mazatlán and Guaymas. He set up a prize court in Monterey for the legal disposal of apprehended Mexican prizes, saving their captors from having to bring them around Cape Horn for adjudication in American cities on the Atlantic coast. Finally, he warned Shubrick to ensure that his men committed no atrocities on Mexican civilians or their belongings, an admonition that was heeded. All this formed a fitting finale to Biddle's generally illustrious career in naval diplomacy. He died in October 1848.[12]

Commodores David Connor and Matthew C. Perry at Yucatán, 1846–1848

The isolated province of Yucatán (composing the modern states of Yucatán, Compeche, and Quintana Roo) became the object of American attention, first because it seemed to offer a means of weakening the Mexican war effort, but by 1848 because it was coveted by Manifest Destiny expansionists in the United States. The racial composition of Yucatán was explosive: a small minority of exploitive white planters lived along the coast and were opposed by the Mayan Indian majority in the interior. White-inspired secessionist tendencies there had been fermenting since Mexico had gained its independence in the early 1820s. Indeed, the *Yucatecos* had briefly allied themselves with the Texans during their rebellion. Early in May 1846 they seceded, but simultaneously a massive Indian uprising broke out, an episode in the long struggle called "the War of the Castes," which flickered off and on in Yucatán until the twentieth century. Fearful that the faction-ridden government in Mexico City could not protect them from the Indians while fighting the United States, early in the war the whites opened negotiations in Washington so that they might at least be neutralized during the conflict.

In 1846–1847 Secretary of the Navy George Bancroft sent Commodore David Conner to learn the strength of the secessionists in Yucatán. He concluded that it was substantial, and his recommendation was adopted that the U.S. blockade of ports there be lifted. By late 1846, however, Mexican loyalists seemed back in control. Commodore Matthew C. Perry, Conner's successor, reimposed the blockade and seized El Carmen, an island that dominated the shoreline. By September 1847 the secessionists once more appeared to be in the saddle. Perry not only ended the blockade and relinquished El Carmen but provided arms for the whites of Yucatán, and occasionally assembled his ships in force, hoping thereby to keep the Indians away from the coast.

Meanwhile the whites sent Don Justo Sierra O'Reilly as their agent to Washington to ensure American protection from the Indians and recognition of Yucatán as an independent nation. But through 1847 the Mayan revolt picked up momentum, and the whites panicked, offering to cede themselves to the United States, Great Britain, or Spain—in short, anyone who would defend them from the Indians.

By early 1848 the faction of land-hungry Democrats called "the All-Mexico Men," now backed by Sierra, began clamoring for the annexation of Yucatán. They warned that annexation was necessary to keep Yucatán from being taken by the British, a fantasy that the expansionists regularly trotted out to justify American land-grabbing. Although his administration was in the process of swallowing the entire Far Southwest, the president was no All-Mexico Man. He was sensible enough to see that Yucatán would be a mare's-nest for any power that might occupy an area so heavily populated with Mexican Indians. Yet the annexationists in his own party were powerful, so he decided to let the Yucatán dust settle, referring that question to Congress without any recommendation whatever. Anti-expansionist Whigs haggled over the matter with Manifest Destiny Democrats until the latter's strength ebbed because of a total lack of evidence that London had any interest there. Finally the civil war in Yucatán took a turn that ended any American opportunity for an acquisition: Mexican loyalists defeated the Mayans, thus effectively quelling any local desire to be attached to the United States. The matter lapsed into oblivion.[13]

Along Mexico's West Coast, 1854
Commander Thomas A. Dornin at Enseñada, Mazatlán, and Acapulco

Mexico, deprived of half of its territory from 1836 to 1848 by the Texas secession and its losses to the United States under the Treaty of Guadalupe Hidalgo, continued to be riven by internal conflicts. This was bad enough in itself, but such compelling evidence of weakness attracted interventions from the outside, namely the activities of filibusters, defined as those mounting an armed attack from one "friendly" (not-at-war) country against another one, illegal under international law. Navy Secretary James C. Dobbin was concerned enough about what was occurring in western Mexico to send Commander Thomas A. Dornin in the sloop *Portsmouth* "to suppress any such unlawful expedition" from the United States in order to prevent this "violation of law and infraction of treaty obligation." Dobbin was referring to William Walker, "the Gray-eyed Man of Destiny," and the chief American filibuster in the nation's history. During late 1853 Walker had left San Francisco with only 45 men and sailed to La Paz in southern Baja California and then to Mexican Enseñada, far to the north near San Diego. Apparently he envisaged some kind of a personal empire carved out in Baja and Sonora State.

During February the *Portsmouth* dropped anchor off Enseñada, where Dornin met Walker. He said that Washington considered Walker no more than an outlaw, although he did not feel empowered to arrest the filibuster on Mexican soil. Secretary of State William L. Marcy tried to use this meeting to prove to the Mexican minister in Washington that the United States was doing its duty to stem "these unlawful attempts against the peace and territorial integrity of a neighboring and friendly nation."

Plagued by shortages in supplies, weakened by desertions, and hounded by Mexican guerrillas, Walker finally recognized the inevitable and in

May surrendered to General John E. Wool. His ensuing trial at San Francisco was sheer farce; the jury took a total of eight minutes to find Walker innocent of filibustering. Understandably a letter from the Mexican Minister to Marcy expressed his fury at this incredible whitewash.

Dornin next heard in San Diego that some 20 Americans had been arrested for passport violations at Guaymas and imprisoned at Mazatlán. Proceeding to that place he persuaded the local governor to liberate the prisoners and took advantage of ships in the harbor to transport them back to San Francisco. He then sailed to Acapulco, where some American steamers needing coal supplies were being subjected to a typical off-again, on-again Mexican blockade. Dornin persuaded the commander there to allow their escape; for this deed he was praised by U.S. Minister to Mexico James Gadsden, and Secretary Dobbin referred to his work as "excellent service."[14]

The War of the Reform, 1858–1860
Lieutenant John J. Almy at Tampico, April 1858

Dornin's chores at Sonora had hardly been completed when Santa Anna's eleventh and final removal from the presidency of Mexico came about in 1855, to be followed shortly by new heights of sanguinary hostilities in that unlucky nation. From 1858 to 1861 Mexico was ripped apart in the War of the Reform; only the Mexican Revolution of 1911–1921 would match it in bloodshed. The Anticlerical liberals under the Indian Benito Juarez had managed to push through an act stripping the Catholic church of much of its land and power, and in 1857 they promulgated a liberal constitution. These, naturally, were anathema to the conservative Clericals, comprising the large landowners, the hierarchy, and most of the armed forces, who struck under the eventual leadership of General Miguel Miramón. The Juaristas fought back. In the War of the Reform, each side systematically massacred its captives and destroyed the villages of the other.

By the spring of 1858 Tampico had come under the control of General Juan José de la Garza and his Anticlerical troops, but they were soon assailed by Clerical forces under an officer no better identified in American correspondence than "General Moreno." When the Navy Department received word that Garza was impounding some American merchantmen and was doubly taxing others, Lieutenant John J. Almy in the sloop *Fulton* was sent to Tampico to size up the situation. He quickly found on his arrival there in mid-April that the allegations against Garza were true: five American vessels were being forcibly detained and two customs houses — each taking its cut from neutral shippers — had been established, the legally authorized one in the port itself and a new one at the mouth of the river running into the harbor.

Almy swung the *Fulton* into position in front of the city with batteries ready to fire. But he had second thoughts immediately. He realized that should he open up he would be directly intervening in the War of the Reform, or, as he put it in a letter to the secretary, it "would be tantamount to taking sides with Gen. Moreno against Gen. Garza." Instead he remonstrated against the seizures and dual taxation. Garza, probably well cognizant of the importance of American sympathy for his cause, quickly complied, releasing the ships and eliminating the customs house by the river. Almy's praiseworthy restraint had chalked up a diplomatic success.[15]

Commander John A. Dahlgren at Vera Cruz, October 1858

Commander John A. Dahlgren in the *Portsmouth* was dispatched to put Almy's off-the-cuff agreements with Garza into a more satisfactory and lasting form. He came into Vera Cruz to meet the Anticlerical leader himself, and with complete success. Juarez promised that such forced "loans" as those to the Tampico customs houses would not be levied in the future, "and those so obtained shall be restored by General Garza." The U.S. consul in Vera Cruz was lavish in his compliments to Dahlgren: "You have done more for the commerce of this place than all the [other American] ships and squadrons." Although it is unstated in the documentation, undoubtedly Dahlgren had been aided by the realization of the Anticlerical Mexicans that they must not quarrel with the United States.[16]

Commander Charles R. Davis at Guaymas and Mazatlán, late 1859—early 1860

The War of the Reform was no easier to bear for Americans residing or trading along Mexico's Pacific Coast than those along the Gulf of Mexico and the Caribbean. Secretary of the Navy Isaac Toucey could not be charged with hyperbole when he described that area as remaining "in a turbulent and revolutionary state." Late in 1858 he sent Commander Charles R. Davis, commanding the sloop *St. Mary's*, to investigate reports of illegal acts against Americans at either Guaymas or Mazatlán or both. These were the firing upon a boat, the stoning of some sailors, an insult offered to a consul, and the theft of property. The records are irritatingly scanty about what Davis actually accomplished. He appears to have looked into at least some of the above matters and did bring about the release of precisely one American captive. He seems rather to have concentrated upon the financial losses suffered by some of his fellow-countrymen. Indeed, some hundred pages of his letters to the secretary concerned the land and belongings taken from an American named John Poloney, all without any conclusion as to the disposal of the affair. When Isaac Toucey, in his *Report* for 1859, said that Davis had "performed most satisfactorily" his duties, it is a conclusion that must be accepted largely on faith.[17]

Captain Joseph R. Jarvis and Commander Thomas Turner at Antón Lizardo, 1860

The murderous Mexican civil war was reaching its crescendo late in the decade. During 1859 the United States finally recognized the government of Juarez's Anticlericals as the legitimate administration in that country. Early the next year, as pressure against the Clericals heightened, their desperate General Miguel Miramón decided to gamble that he could march from Mexico City to capture Vera Cruz. To strengthen himself at sea he leased from the Spanish regime in Cuba two steamers, the *General Miramón* and the *Marquez de Habana*, both under the command of Captain Tomás Marín, a Spanish naval officer. The Juarez government was soon informed of this development and in February issued a circular calling attention to the two ships, announcing that the "aforesaid vessels can be regarded and treated as pirates by the national ships and those of friendly powers." Secretary of the Navy Toucey had already told Captain Joseph R. Jarvis, commanding the frigate *Savannah* off the Mexican Gulf coast, that any Miramón blockade should be ignored, since that would have been imposed by an illegal regime. By implication this meant that any movements of the Clericals' new steamboats should also be regarded as those of outlaws. Jarvis put Commander Thomas Turner of the *Saratoga* in charge of operations against them.

On the morning of 6 March, Turner spotted the two suspect warships passing behind the fortress of San Juan d'Ulua, the major defense of Vera Cruz. Throughout that day neither the *General Miramón* nor the *Marquez de Habana* displayed any colors, although flags went up from the fortress and vessels in the harbor calling upon the intruders to identify themselves. With commendable speed, Turner sent detachments of guns, sailors, and marines to both the *Wave* and the *Indianola*, two small American steamships chartered by the Juarez government. Because the *Saratoga* was a sailer, he ordered the steamers to tow her so that he might keep the strangers under close observation. That evening the suspects were discovered at a place called Antón Lizardo, some 15 miles south of Vera Cruz. The *Wave* and *Indianola*, dropping their towlines, sped forward, enduring some fire from the *Miramón*, which was trying to escape, and harried her so effectively that the *Saratoga* was able to come up, pour in some heavy shot, and drive her ashore. Meanwhile, Captain Marín, offering no resistance, was taken from the *Marquez* and brought before Turner. One American had been mortally wounded and a few others slightly hurt; perhaps 30 from the *Miramón* were casualties. Both captive vessels and their people were sent to New Orleans for judgment by the courts.

According to the *New York Times*, the Antón Lizardo (or Vera Cruz) incident of March 1860 caused "great excitement" and even "a profound sensation" in Washington, appearing for a while as if it might be the precursor of direct American intervention in the Mexican War of the Reform. The *Times* defended Turner's actions; "These steamers appeared on the high seas as pirates, they attacked our ships as pirates, and they will be treated as pirates." Washington brushed aside the protests of the Spanish naval commander in the West Indies and those of a *Miramón* representative, who complained that such "acts of scandalous violence" and "unheard of provocation" had been sealed "with innocent blood." Even though the U.S. district court in New Orleans eventually released Marín and his two ships, the Buchanan administration contented itself with upholding Turner's bellicosity on the grounds that the refusal of Miramón's steamboats to identify themselves made them de facto pirates. Despite the *New York Times*'s editorial excitement, U.S. intervention in behalf of Juarez was, of course, never even considered, nor was it necessary. The siege of Vera Cruz was already being lifted, and soon Miramón and his colleagues would be compelled to flee into a short-lived European exile lasting until they returned under French auspices with the Emperor Maximilian.[18]

Summary

In the two relatively minor instances of naval foreign relations at Tampico in 1832, for obvious reasons the two officers concerned behaved differently. Elliott, despite his strong legal position vis-à-vis Moctezuma, was dealing with no more than three Spanish-born individuals claiming American citizenship, and concluded that the matter was not important enough to warrant a direct clash with Mexico. Tattnall, on the other hand, was faced with a built-in responsibility to be carried out. The *Montezuma* had been a clear-cut pirate in the treatment of the *William A. Turner*'s people. He was also sure that the specie-laden merchantman was being illegally held in port. Had he done nothing to resolve the cases, he would have been recreant to his duty to the department and perhaps would have been subject to court-martial and conviction. Justifiably he was rewarded by the New Orleans insurers.

Of the five diplomatic exchanges between U.S. naval officers and Mexican officials in connection with the Texas uprising, Dallas's eventual favoritism toward the rebels in interpreting blockade rules and Tattnall's errand of mercy for Santa Anna at Vera Cruz, courageous though it was, were relatively insignificant. But the arrest of Osborn's party by General Gomez at Tampico (while Dallas was being hoodwinked about the supposed punishment of that bureaucrat) and Mervine's helplessness in regard to the jailing of the drunken American sailors at Vera Cruz were sufficiently explosive to send President Jackson into a paroxysm of rage so strong as to induce him, in effect, to call for war against Mexico. This was soon coupled with Mervine's atonement for his previous caution by firing upon and seizing the *General Urrea*, in this manner dumping more fuel on the potential conflagration. The bellicose oratory of Jackson and the belligerent (if justified) behavior of Mervine was overruled by more pacifistically inclined diplomats, politicians, and editors both north and south of the Rio Grande.

Forrest and Jones merit no laurels for their conduct along Mexico's California coast during the early 1840s. Why was Forrest so averse to exerting pressure on Governor Alvarez to compel him to speed the release of the Americans languishing in Tepic? Since foreign shipping had been going in and out of Monterey for years, it must have been common knowledge that its defenses were no less than ludicrous and that the town was helpless against the firepower of a U.S. man-of-war, as proven when the fort's garrison fell over themselves in surrendering to Jones. And how could Secretary Upshur possibly view Forrest's inertia in 1840 as anything approximating "spirited interposition"? Since Forrest was promoted to captain four years later, there must have been other aspects of his naval career more praiseworthy than his policy of doing as little as possible at Monterey.

As for Jones, to a large extent he was whitewashed by the Navy Department in his own day and whitewashed by most historians later. To be sure, his actions up to his occupation of the settlement on 20 October were basically sensible and of potential value to his country. From the newspaper he read and the conversations with diplomats he had in Peru, he could have reasonably concluded that a war with Mexico had broken out and that the British were in the process of ingesting California. He had every reason to suspect the designs of the Royal Navy and had to take the reasonable precaution of hurrying to California to block them. But perhaps insufficient attention has been paid to the fatuousness of his precipitate occupation of Monterey. Its nonexistent defenses could be of no use to him against the British, and all he really did was to immobilize his two warships in the harbor, ensuring that they would have been helpless had the British suddenly appeared. Far better had Jones cruised off the port, and taken the time to avail himself of the information Larkin and other Americans there could provide. Indeed, had he delayed as little as 28 hours in raising his flag ashore, he would have known that no war existed. The black mark in the American naval diplomatic record for which he was responsible need never have been made.

Little attention need be paid to evaluating Polk and Mackenzie versus Santa Anna. The wily Mexican imposed his will upon both the instigator and his agent in Havana, for the Americans betrayed themselves in overly roseate expectations. Any ill effects arising from their misapprehensions were obviated, however, by Santa Anna's military ineptitude, which made his return actually beneficial for the United States. But that was fortuitous, rather than the outcome of presidential planning.

The Mexican War operations of Conner and Perry at Yucatán consisted primarily of following departmental orders, since relatively easy and rapid communications with them could be maintained from Washington. Yet they did have some opportunity for individual initiative when they tried to assess the importance of the latest news about the off-again, on-again situations in Yucatán. By not yielding to any temptation to seek personal glory, such as interpreting their instructions to permit them to land in force and participate in the civil war there, they kept Washington's options open. This made it easier for their government to arrive at the astute conclusion that the United States should get out of Yucatán and stay out. In contrast to other occasions in which naval officers complicated their nation's diplomacy by unleashing their desire for self-aggrandizement, the restraint exercised by the two commodores from 1846 to 1848 served their country well.

Dornin's commendable activities along western Mexican shores need no further amplification here, but not so the four instances of American naval operations during the War of the Reform. To be sure, the work of Almy and Dahlgren in the Gulf was more inspired than that of Davis in the Pacific, but the crux of the matter is that all of them managed to avoid bellicosity. Turner, backed by Jarvis, did not. He assaulted and took two vessels belonging to one side in a fraternal conflict. Even though Turner, in so doing, damaged the cause of the party opposed by his own government, his forcible seizure of Miramón's warships might have started a chain of events finally drawing the United States into this civil war. That this did not happen was due to the Department of State rather than officers of the Navy Department.

CHAPTER ◆ FIVE

Central America and the Caribbean

1839–1860

A merican naval diplomacy in Central America and the Caribbean does not fall naturally into a well-organized narrative, as in Mexico. When everything pertains to a single country a cause-and-effect relationship may be quite easily established. In Mexico all was played before a backdrop of Clerical-Conservative versus Anticlerical-Liberal, during which U.S. officers were caught between their innate sympathy for the reformers and their government's insistence upon a strict neutrality in the Mexican civil wars. But with Costa Rica, Nicaragua, El Salvador, Honduras and Guatemala in Central America, British Honduras, Panama (the westernmost province of Colombia), Colombia proper, and Venezuela on South America's north coast, as well as Cuba and the West Indian islands, a shotgun has to replace a rifle. Therefore the chronological pattern that worked so well in Mexico must be discarded in favor of the topical. Better understanding can be achieved if this chapter concentrates upon the two most crucial U.S. relationships during the 1850s in this sphere, those with Spain and Great Britain, leaving to the end less consequential occurrences elsewhere in the area.

As to Spain, U.S. naval diplomacy dealt with cases of some moment concerning Cuba between 1839 and 1855; as to Britain, American interventions in Nicaragua between 1851 and 1857; and in scattered locales between 1846 and 1860, namely in Santo Domingo (Dominican Republic), Colombian Panama, Colombia proper, and Panama again.

Cuba, 1839–1855
Lieutenants Thomas W. Gedney and Richard M. Meade off Long Island, 1839

The involvement of Lieutenants Thomas W. Gedney and Richard M. Meade in the *Amistad* case deserves mention in this work, but just a brief one, since those naval officers were concerned only peripherally. Heavily insured, the *Amistad* was carrying the slaves of a Cuban planter from one of his estates to another. Led by one Cinqué, recently brought in from Africa, the blacks mutinied successfully, killing the ship's owner. But they had to keep alive their master and his friend, for they could not navigate the vessel by themselves to Africa. The whites duped their captors by heading east while being watched during the day, veering north by night. For several weeks they zigzagged up the American east coast before coming into Sag Harbor, Long Island, late in August, desperate for food and water.

Gedney and Meade, surveying nearby in the brig *Washington*, learned of the *Amistad*'s arrival. Pulling into Sag Harbor, they freed the two Cubans and imprisoned Cinqué and his followers. Once they understood that the vessel's owner was dead, making her a derelict, and heard about the insurance she carried, Gedney and Meade became selfishly interested partisans. Should the blacks be convicted of piracy and murder, the officers could not only claim the ship as salvage but share in the insurance, as well as the sale of the cargo and slaves.

The *Amistad* affair promptly became a *cause célèbre* by provoking a clash between American abolitionists and the Spanish government in Cuba. The former argued that the blacks, having been forcibly deprived of their liberty, had the right to use any means to recover their freedom. The latter claimed that under the Spanish-American Treaty of 1795, anything lost through piratical action by the nationals of either country must be restored. In 1840 a Connecticut court held that Gedney and Meade were entitled to "one-third of the salvage," but the records do not reveal how much they actually received. The U.S. Supreme Court, in 1841, found the slaves to be free men, although Spain refused to drop the matter until 1860. Almost every administration from Van Buren's to Buchanan's urged Congress to compensate the owner of the *Amistad*'s blacks, but he never was paid a penny.[1]

Lieutenant John Rodgers, et al., off Key West and Havana

By the end of the Mexican War, American attention became concentrated upon Cuba to an extent unknown since the navy's efforts to end piracy there in the 1820s. Until 1848 Washington's policy had been to ensure that the island remained under the control of relatively impotent

Spain; above all it must not pass into the grasp of Britain or France. But a new American outlook had been created by new developments: the acquisition of California; the establishment of essential transportation routes across Central America to reach the gold fields, threatened by Cuba's position athwart them; and the desires of Southern expansionists either to get that island for new slave territory or at least to make sure that any abolition of slavery there would not spread to their section. In 1848 President Polk offered Madrid the impressive sum of $100,000,000 for Cuba, but prospects for its successful purchase were not exactly strengthened when the Spaniards replied that rather than sell it to the United States they "would prefer seeing it sunk in the ocean."

At this point the diplomat was elbowed aside by the filibuster—previously defined as one who wages unauthorized warfare against a nation with which his own country is at peace. Any such assault is, of course, totally contrary to the responsibility of a nation under international law to police its borders so effectively that such an attack cannot take place. But some leaders, particularly in the U.S. South, aware of the failure of diplomacy to extend slavery's boundaries, backed first Narciso Lopez in Cuba in 1849–1851, and then William Walker in Central America in 1855–1860.

Lopez was a Venezuelan who had fought well for Spain against Simón Bolívar and other Latin-American rebels, services for which he was rewarded with high positions in both Spain and Cuba. But after being ousted from office by a successful rival in Havana, Lopez began devoting himself to bringing about a Cuban rebellion against the mother country, with the end in mind of having the island annexed to the United States. Southern expansionists tended to line up behind him, especially after he attested that he had "ever in view . . . the *ultimate annexation* of the island *to the great confederation of the United States of the North*." Lopez organized his first anti-Spanish escapade in Cuba itself during 1848, but the plot was prematurely exposed and he barely escaped to New Orleans.

There he commenced recruiting for a filibustering expedition, appealing to Southern veterans of the Mexican War, offering land, "plunder, women, drink, and tobacco." In August 1849 he assembled about 800 men at Round Island, near the mouth of the Mississippi, with three ships ready to leave for Cuba. But for once the American government acted decisively to enforce its antifilibustering laws. President Zachary Taylor denounced the expedition, cordoned off Round Island with men-of-war under Commander Victor M. Randolph, and forced Lopez to cancel the endeavor.

Nothing, however, could dissuade the filibuster from pursuing what turned out to be his death wish. During the next year he raised funds for soldiers, supplies, and vessels, primarily the work of Mississippi's Gov-

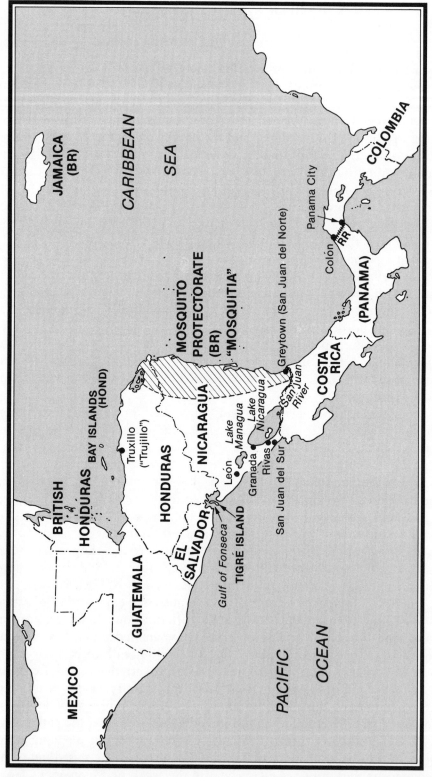

Central America

ernor John A. Quitman. By May 1850 he had brought together about 550 to 600 men (of whom only five were Cubans, the rest Americans) and three ships. Although his plans had been well publicized and the departure of his vessels took place over two weeks, Lopez and his men had little trouble in slipping out of New Orleans and heading for a small island off the coast of Mexican Yucatán. The *Georgiana*, with some 250 aboard, was the first to arrive, then the *Susan Loud* with about 170, and finally the steamer *Creole*, carrying Lopez and the rest of his volunteers, which joined the others on 16 May. Almost at once all the filibusters were crammed into the *Creole* and set out for Cuba, leaving the other two vessels behind. Hardly had Lopez departed than the Spanish warship *Pizarro* and the smaller *Habanero* swooped down upon the *Georgiana* and *Susan Loud* just as they were leaving for New Orleans. All 52 of the Americans on board were arrested. Ten were crew members, but the other 42 truthfully claimed that they were bona fide passengers en route to California and had nothing to do with Lopez. They were transported to Havana for the disposition of their cases, while the *Pizarro* headed out to sea in search of the *Creole*.

Meanwhile Lopez, deciding to avoid fortified Matanzas for Cárdenas, about 50 miles east of Havana, had somehow managed to elude no less than 5 American and 19 Spanish men-of-war on the lookout for him. His followers raced ashore on the 19th, surprising the little Spanish garrison, and easily took Cárdenas. This was the expedition's first and last triumph. The local Cuban populace remained immune to Lopez's call that they join him, and the filibusters soon learned that strong Spanish forces were en route to Cárdenas from the capital. Lopez hoped to continue his project but was voted down by his panicky and mutinous followers. Before they could embark, however, Spanish troops fell upon them, killing and wounding about 70 Americans.

After dark that night the rest managed to pile aboard the *Creole* and aimed her at Key West, about a hundred miles away, and the only neutral port which they could reach with her depleted coal supplies. The next morning they were spotted by the *Pizarro*, which gave chase. It was touch and go for Lopez and his men; they beat their pursuer into Key West just as their coal ran out. Supposedly this made little difference to the Spaniards, for the *Pizarro*'s commander expected that the refugees would be turned over to him. After all, they were pirates, officially designated as such by the U.S. government. But Lieutenant John Rodgers the younger (son of the 1812 commodore) intercepted the *Pizarro* in his little schooner *Petrel* and informed her captain that although the *Creole* was admittedly a corsair, he would deny any Spanish right to seize an American ship in

American territory, no matter what her status. While the thwarted Spaniard sailed away, U.S. officials in Key West freed the fugitives.

American naval officers next concentrated their diplomatic attention to securing the release of the *Georgiana* and *Susan Loud* and, later, the men taken from them to Havana. Actually, they had a strong case under international law for recovering the ships. These American vessels had been captured by the Spaniards, not on the high seas, but within Mexican territorial waters. Commander Victor M. Randolph in the sloop *Albany* and his successor, Captain Josiah Tattnall in the *Saranac*, both told the Spaniards that they would retake the two vessels from any men-of-war convoying them to Europe. Although their gambit temporarily worked, in that the *Georgiana* and *Susan Loud* were kept in Cuba, it eventually made no difference. A Cuban prize court confiscated them, apparently without further American protest.

A happier conclusion attended the case of the Americans captured in the Yucatán. The combined urgings of Commodores Charles Morris and Isaac McKeever, in the *Vixen* and *Congress* respectively, managed to attain the release of the 42 passengers for California. They could not, however, do the same for the ten arrested crew members nor receive any monetary compensation for any of the prisoners. The ten were sentenced to long incarcerations in Spain. But toward the end of the year the queen in Madrid pardoned them, so Morris's and McKeever's efforts were partially if belatedly successful.[2]

Commander Charles T. Platt and Commodore Foxhall A. Parker at Havana, 1851

American juries were unwilling to convict filibusters, no matter what the evidence, so once again Lopez was found innocent in New Orleans and allowed to continue his plotting for the annexation of Cuba to the United States. Despite his recent failure he continued to receive both money and new volunteers from his Southern backers. Early in June the news came that the Cubans themselves had risen against their Spanish masters. The heartened Lopez decided that any further delay in his departure for Cuba would write finis to the opportunity provided by the uprisings. That is why on 3 August he hurriedly collected fewer than 450 men, packed them into the steamer *Pampero*, and put to sea, thereby abandoning many hundreds of eager volunteers, mountains of equipment, and several other ships. Unhappily for Lopez the rebellions in Cuba could not have served his cause worse. At Key West he was informed that all of western Cuba was in arms against its rulers. This was a lie, for the two insignificant revolts were being crushed and their perpetrators executed. There is evidence that the story may have been planted by agents of José de la Concha, captain general of the island, solely to entice the invaders to their doom.

The 435 filibusters dashed ashore on 11 August at Bahia Honda, on Cuba's northwestern coast. This was a tragic miscalculation; the town was the worst spot imaginable, for it was connected to the potent Spanish garrison at Havana by sea lanes and 40 miles of railroad track. After sending the *Pampero* back to Key West for reinforcements, Lopez split his command, leading some 300 into the interior, hoping to join with one or more of the rebel groups. The rest, under Colonel William L. S. Crittenden, a West Pointer and the nephew of the current attorney-general of the United States, remained behind, guarding their supplies. While once again local Cubans ignored American requests that they join them, Spanish fury quickly enveloped both of Lopez's contingents. Crittenden and fifty others, after trying in vain to rejoin the main body, managed to fight their way to the beach and embark in small boats for Key West. They were soon overtaken by a Spanish warship and taken to Havana.

Captain General Concha was determined to make an example of them. After a hurried trial on the 15th, all of the captives were sentenced to die before firing squads, and the verdicts were carried out the next day. Crittenden, allegedly affirming that "A Kentuckian kneels only to his God, and always faces his enemy," was forced to his knees but managed to swing around to confront his executioners before the top of his head was blown off. The rage of slave-state Americans was enhanced by reports, evidently true, that some of the 51 bodies were dismembered to furnish gruesome trophies for the spectators.

As for Lopez and his followers farther inland, they too were being overwhelmed by superior forces. After almost two weeks of searing heat, pouring rain, ravenous insects, and increasing depletions of their food and ammunition, Lopez and the 160 remaining alive were compelled to surrender on the 31st. Concha treated them better than Crittenden's men in that their lives were spared, with but a single exception. Narciso Lopez was publicly garroted in Havana's main plaza on 1 September. All of his filibusters, save four were sentenced to long terms in the quicksilver mines in Spain. When Southern Americans learned the details of the expedition's terrible fate, they took to the streets in New Orleans and Key West for days of anti-Spanish rioting. A mob in Madrid came close to sacking the U.S. legation.

It has to be admitted that the role of the American navy in these proceedings was anything but heroic. Commander Charles T. Platt in his sloop *Albany* was in Havana when first the Crittenden and then the Lopez prisoners were brought ashore for punishment. He made no effort whatsoever to intercede with Concha in behalf of Crittenden's 51, even shrugging off the appeals of Americans in the city to try to have them spared. In this stand Platt agreed with A. F. Owen, the resident U.S. consul, that President Fillmore himself had said that the filibusters "had lost their nationality at the moment of embarking on a piratical expedition." When American merchant-marine captains added their appeals that he speak up for their fellow-nationals, Platt told them "dryly to go back to their own ships and not to meddle with anything." Even if he tried belatedly to aid Lopez's 156 survivors, it would seem that the *Report* of Secretary of the Navy William A. Graham in 1851 was ludicrously over-complimentary when it referred to Platt's "propriety and delicacy . . . his vigilance and industry . . . and his humanity in visiting and interceding for the deluded persons, who . . . had been induced to embark on an adventure of such serious consequence."

Commodore Foxhall A. Parker was appointed "special Commissioner" to Havana to meet Concha, state his regrets about the severity of the punishments inflicted, and procure from him apologies and a pledge of future desistance from such practices as the firing on and boarding of the American steamer *Falcon* by a Spanish warship, which had occurred shortly before. Parker found, however, that the U.S. consul had already performed those chores well. He then asked Concha for mercy toward the 156 destined to toil for years in the hell of Spanish prison mines. It is hard to say to what extent his appeals contributed to the Spanish queen's decision early in 1852 to liberate them, for U.S. diplomats were also working in that sphere, but clearly Parker's arguments could have done no harm. In gratitude for the release of the Americans, Congress soon appropriated $25,000 to recompense Spain for its New Orleans consulate, gutted by a mob the previous September.[3]

Commodore Charles S. McCauley off Cuba, 1855

The finale of Spanish-American difficulties over Cuba during the 1850s was evidently settled easily. In March the Spanish frigate *Ferrolana*, for some reason never explained in the documentation, shot twice at the American mail steamer *El Dorado* near Cuba's coast without harm either to the vessel or her people. After Secretary of the Navy James Dobbin had dispatched a five-ship squadron under McCauley in the *San Jacinto* to that area, some war talk appeared in American newspapers. The little armada patrolled Cuban waters for some weeks, but was recalled during June when fears of Spanish "unfriendly interference" had been allayed. Furthermore, Captain General Concha pledged that no such offense as that committed by the *Ferrolana* would recur. More than two years later,

President Buchanan complained that his nation had as yet received "no satisfaction" in regard to the *El Dorado*. Apparently Madrid never apologized nor paid damages for its breach of international law.[4]

Nicaragua, 1851–1857
Commodore Foxhall A. Parker at Greytown, 1851

Diplomatic responsibilities of U.S. naval officers in the Caribbean markedly lessened after the death of Lopez, but situations in Central America arose to overshadow those in the West Indies. Anglo-American rivalries in the isthmus came to the fore, as did the emergence of a filibuster even more newsworthy and significant than Lopez—William Walker, who was to have an incredible career in Nicaragua.

Guatemala, Honduras, El Salvador, Nicaragua, and Costa Rica became parts of Mexico during the Latin-American wars of independence, but in 1824 formed "The United Provinces of Central America," only to break into its present component parts between 1838 and 1840. This area remained a sleepy international backwater until 1848, when gold was discovered in California. The fastest route from Europe and the eastern United States to Sacramento lay across Central America. Most early migrants to the gold fields crossed the isthmus at Panama (a province of Colombia), its narrowest part. In 1846 Washington established predominance there by its treaty with "New Granada," as Colombia was briefly called. But Nicaragua always existed as an alternative route, and the British concentrated their attention on that country. Much to the annoyance of American popular opinion, in 1848 London declared Nicaragua's Atlantic coast a protectorate, thereby asserting rule over the "Mosquito" (today Miskito) tribe, a mixture primarily of Indians and blacks. Englishmen also seized the little town of San Juan del Norte at the mouth of the San Juan River, renaming it Greytown. To help meet this challenge, "Commodore" Cornelius Vanderbilt and other American entrepreneurs founded the "Accessory Transit Company," using steamships and paved roads through Nicaragua to reach the Pacific.

The competition between Britons and Americans in Central America appeared headed for war unless a diplomatic solution could be found. An agreement occurred in the Clayton-Bulwer Treaty of 1850, the work of Secretary of State John Clayton and the British special envoy, Sir Henry Lytton Bulwer. Since neither nation was willing to sacrifice what it considered its vital interests in Central America, the agreement was couched in ambiguity. It was forthright enough that any future canal cut through the isthmus must be a joint product of Britain and America and must remain unfortified. The deliberate confusion came rather from the provision that neither country would ever "occupy, or fortify, or colonize, or assume, or exercise any dominion over Nicaragua, Costa Rica, the Mosquito Coast, or any part of Central America." The British claimed that this applied only to post-1850 activities, but the United States argued that it was retroactive, calling for an English evacuation of the Mosquito Protectorate. Diplomatic historians have bickered among themselves about whether the Clayton-Bulwer Treaty was an American victory or defeat. One thing is certain, however: because of its self-denying provision against American expansion in that quarter, it quickly became one of the most unpopular agreements ever signed by the United States.

Nor did it quiet the Central American arena; quite the contrary. The first Anglo-American clash occurred in 1851. During that spring the British, to give an air of authenticity to their Mosquito Protectorate, made Greytown a "free port." This permitted the local authorities to collect customs levies and assess port duties. Since the United States never recognized what London called "Mosquitia," Americans announced their unwillingness to be taxed by anyone at Greytown.

That November the Accessory Transit Company's steamboat *Prometheus* came into Greytown, carrying none other than the short-fused Cornelius Vanderbilt himself, who came to oversee the planned expansion of his company in Nicaragua. The port collector attempted to get the captain of the *Prometheus* to pay what American documentation calls "123 dollars" in harbor dues, but apparently the sum requested was that amount in pesos, worth perhaps no more than 11 American dollars. But Vanderbilt obdurately asserted that he would pay nothing "unless I am made [to] by force." The *Prometheus* put out for open water but was twice fired upon by Captain William F. Fead in the sloop HMS *Express* and escorted back to Greytown, where the furious Vanderbilt paid the harbor fee under protest.

Reports that a British man-of-war had shot at the American flag in Nicaragua lit a fuse in the United States, where almost all newspapers described the case as an intolerable outrage. The *New York Times* wondered "why the American flag upon the American coast, is to be dishonored by such treatment." The Fillmore administration mounted an immediate diplomatic and naval offensive. The U.S. minister in London was instructed to demand "an unqualified apology" from the British government. More ominously, Secretary of the Navy Graham sent Commodore Foxhall A. Parker with both the *Saranac* and *Albany* to Greytown, where the *Express* still rode at anchor. An Anglo-American shooting war appeared to be a distinct possibility.

That peace prevailed was due not to the efforts of Parker but primarily to Vice-Admiral George F. Seymour, commanding the Royal Navy in the Caribbean. Upon learning about the incident of the *Prometheus* and the *Express*, Seymour excoriated Fead for what he had done and specifically gave instructions to his commanders that no British warships were to be used to collect port duties. He further soothed American sensitivities by sending Captain Robert S. Robinson in the inappropriately named HMS *Arrogant* to converse with Parker at Greytown. He assured the commodore that Fead's interception of Vanderbilt's ship was completely unauthorized. The crisis ended happily for both countries when London accepted Seymour's recommendation that Fead's "act of violence" be disavowed and that Washington should be sent "an ample apology" for the incident.[5]

Captain George Hollins at Punta Arenas, near Greytown, 1853

Vanderbilt and his fellow-countrymen had little time to relish their diplomatic victory in regard to the *Prometheus*, for soon Greytown once again became the cynosure of international attention. In 1852 the Accessory Transit Company had commenced to transfer its property to Punta Arenas, a vacant island across from the settlement. Warehouses, docks, and a hotel were constructed there, inducing commercial shippers to bypass Greytown altogether and causing it to slump into a depression. That May the British declared that neither they nor their puppet, referred to as "His Mosquito Majesty," would maintain any further jurisdiction over the place. Greytown's inhabitants, some of them Americans, others blacks from Nicaragua or the British West Indies, declared it a free city, with its own constitution. Its council then decided to recoup its fortunes at the Company's expense, and early in 1853 ordered Punta Arenas to be evacuated and its buildings razed; in fact a few of them were torn down. Naturally Transit Accessory complained about its treatment to Washington.

Captain George N. Hollins in the *Cyane* heard about the crisis in Greytown and put in there on 11 March. He discovered that the Greytowners planned to complete the destruction of Punta Arenas on the next day. That morning Hollins told the town council that he was forbidding any "depredations upon the property" of the company; he was answered by the sophistry that "no depredations would be committed, they only intended to pull the buildings down." On the 12th the captain landed marines, who cordoned off the threatened area. According to the *New York Times*, the council met to "*solemnly protest* before the civilized world against the unlawful occupancy of their territory. . . . We therefore submit as a conquered people," and surrendered to the Americans, ending Greytown's brief period of independence. Fearing that Punta Arenas might be razed if he left prematurely, Hollins kept the *Cyane* there for two months, until he was replaced late in May.

The captain had defended his occupation in a letter to Secretary of the Navy James C. Dobbin: "On my arrival here . . . I obeyed strictly the orders from the Navy Department to protect the property of the Accessory Transit Company." Dobbin approved his conduct, remarking that he had been resisting "an unauthorized attempt to disturb the rights of American citizens." In his *Report* for 1853 the secretary said that the *Cyane*'s presence at Greytown "had the desired effect. The conduct of Captain Hollins evinced a gallantry and judgment which entitles him to the commendation of the Department." Hollin's strong-armed activity at Greytown aroused relatively little response along the Anglo-American diplomatic front. The queen's foreign secretary, perhaps recalling his embarrassment over the *Prometheus-Express* affair, did little more than file protests about the occurrence but couched them in conciliatory language, doing no more than to show "sufficient resentment at Hollins's act to preserve the dignity of the government."[6]

Captain George Hollins at Greytown, 1854

If anyone thought that Hollins's short-lived occupation of Punta Arenas would calm the Central American cockpit, he was quickly disappointed. Over the next few months relations between the townspeople and the Accessory Transit Company deteriorated. Robbers broke into the Company's warehouses, and what local authority existed at Greytown could or would do nothing about it. In retaliation, Accessory stopped delivering mail and freight to the settlement. At this point Solon Borland, U.S. Minister to Nicaragua, appeared on the scene to complicate matters. He was an ardent Southern expansionist who had expressed the hope that Nicaragua would eventually become "a bright star in the flag of the United States." He was also strongly Anglophobic. When he urged Secretary of State William L. Marcy to abrogate unilaterally the Clayton-Bulwer Treaty of 1850, he received instead a rebuke, which so infuriated him that he resigned as minister. Naturally the hurt and resentful Borland was in anything but a conciliatory mood while awaiting suitable transportation back to the United States.

On 16 May the former minister was a passenger in Captain T. T. Smith's Accessory steamer *Routh* when she rammed a small boat. Her black captain protested so vehemently about the incident that Smith, turning toward his cabin, casually remarked, "I must shoot this fellow. He has used

George N. Hollins
(Naval Historical Center)

threatening language which shall cost him his life." Coming back on deck, he killed the small boat's captain with a single shot. Borland not only offered no objection, but soon justified the callous murder. Late the same afternoon, while the *Routh* was transferring passengers to the ocean-going steamer *Northern Lights*, a boat carrying about 25 armed blacks arrived. One, claiming to be the town's marshal, tried to arrest Smith for murder, but Borland seized a rifle from a bystander and drove them away. That night he went ashore at Greytown to discuss the situation at the home of Joseph W. Fabens, U.S. commercial agent for Central America. Soon armed men were pounding on the door, this time shouting that they were going to arrest Borland. The latter, who at least possessed an ample supply of courage, was withstanding them when someone threw a broken bottle, cutting him slightly in the face, and the crowd rapidly dispersed. The next morning, stressing that Americans were no longer safe in Greytown, he sailed for home.

In Washington Borland poured out his story and received a sympathetic reception. Navy Secretary Dobbin ordered Hollins, still commanding the *Cyane*, to return to Nicaragua at once and gave him instructions that permitted him the widest leeway:

> It is very desirable that these people should be taught that the United States will not tolerate these outrages, and that they have the power and determination to check them. It is, however, very much to be hoped that you can effect the purposes of your visit without a resort to violence and destruction of property and loss of life. The presence of your vessel will, no doubt, work much good. The department reposes much in your prudence and good sense.

When the bellicose Hollins came into Greytown on 11 July, he closeted himself with Fabens, who told him that he had learned from private sources that the townspeople would neither pay an indemnity for the destruction of the Company's buildings nor apologize for the assault upon Borland. The two decided that they would demand $8,000 for the buildings razed earlier at Punta Arenas, $16,000 for later losses, and "nothing short of an apology, promptly made," for what had happened to Borland. These decisions were announced in placards put up throughout the town, but no sign of compliance could be discerned on the 12th. Later that day Hollins issued a "Proclamation" stating that "if the demands for satisfaction in the matters above-named . . . are not forthwith complied with, I shall, at 9 o'clock A.M., of tomorrow, 13th instant, proceed to bombard the town of San Juan del Norte aforesaid, to the end that the rights of our country and citizens may be vindicated, and as a guarantee for future protection." The *Bermuda*, a tiny British man-of-war, was present at the time, and her commander protested at the top of his voice about what Hollins had in mind, but without enough guns to threaten the American vessel, he was helpless.

Early the next morning Hollins sent a steamer into town to carry to safety those who wished, but few accepted. He was true to his word: at exactly 9:00 A.M. the *Cyane*'s guns opened up at point-blank range, and for three-quarters of an hour they showered Greytown with successive broadsides. A cease-fire occupied the next half-hour, during which, as Hollins said later, he hoped in vain that its inhabitants would accede to his stipulations. For another half-hour the guns again spoke, followed by a three-hour lull. After another twenty minutes of hammering, the *Cyane*'s cannon stopped altogether, and a detachment was sent ashore to set aflame anything that had survived the bombardments. No lives had been lost; the Greytowners had either sailed away in a British vessel or fled into the bush. Hollins wrote to Dobbin that he had behaved as he did to "satisfy the whole world that the United States have the power and determination to enforce that reparation and respect due them as a government in whatever quarter the outrages may be committed." Certainly Hollins had committed one of the more incredible applications in history of U.S. naval diplomacy (to use the word with remarkable inaccuracy).

Realization that an American warship had flattened a settlement under the protection of the Union Jack was bound to detonate vast commotion on both sides of the Atlantic; this it did, if not quite to the extent that might have been expected. American newspapers tended to pillory Hollins, the opposition *New York Times* speaking for many others when it editorially accused the president of war-mongering:

> President Pierce sends a ship of war to Greytown and instructs Captain Hollins to demand an apology and indemnity from the authorities and if they are not granted, to "burn the town." And Captain Hollins does what he is told to do. Not a word of negotiation, not a syllable about the rights of the case, not the faintest recollection, apparently, that there is such a body as Congress in existence. We doubt whether our history can show an instance of more glaring usurpation than that of which President Pierce has here been guilty.

Noting this attack and other, similar comments, the London *Times* observed that what had been committed by Hollins at Greytown "had excited the strongest distrust of an Administration by which such actions so discreditable to the American flag, and so injurious to the positive interests of the country, could be authorized. It is satisfactory to learn that up to the present time no attempt has been made by any parts in the United States to justify that unparalleled attack upon a defenseless town."

For a while it did appear that Hollins might be in trouble with his own government. Marcy admitted that he was taken aback by the extent to which his officer had stretched his instructions. He notified James Buchanan, U.S. minister in London, "The place merited chastisement, but the severity of the one inflicted exceeded all expectations." He informed John Crampton, British minister in Washington, that he regretted the incident. But Pierce and Marcy soon came to the secret conclusion that since Hollins had stretched his orders but not broken them, he must be upheld. Moreover, they thought that any appearance of giving in to the British would make them even more grasping and arrogant in Central America.

Across the Atlantic, British statesmen were enraged by Hollins's deed, and talk of war was definitely in the air. Foreign Secretary Lord Clarendon described what had happened to Greytown as an "outrage without parallel in the annals of modern time." Even though the Crimean War had already broken out, pitting Britain, France, the Ottoman Empire, and later the Italian kingdom of Sardinia against Russia, English sea power was still able to operate at relatively full strength. The anti-American Lord Palmerston, soon to be prime minister, urged Clarendon to stand firm against such "Vulgar minded Bullies," for they have " no navy of which we need be afraid & they might be told that if they were to resort to privateering, we should however reluctantly be obliged to retaliate by burning all their Sea Coast Towns." For a time the foreign secretary followed this belligerent advice, fearing by October that "We are fast 'drifting' into a War with the U. States."

Despite his apprehension, Clarendon told Crampton that he was most disappointed that the American government had not yet disavowed Hollins's evisceration of Greytown. He was, however, even more provoked by the intransigence expressed by the secretary of the navy's *Report* for 1854 and the president's annual message of that December. Dobbin wrote, "I could not reprove this commander for his conduct. Humanity often lends her sympathies to the sufferer, however just the punishment, but patriotism rarely condemns the brave officer who administers that punishment from a sense of justice to his countrymen whose property is destroyed and whose national flag is insulted." Pierce remarked, "It certainly would have been most satisfactory to me if the objects of the *Cyane's* mission could have been consummated without any act of public force, but the arrogant contumacy of the offenders rendered it impossible to avoid the alternative either to break up their establishment or leave them impressed with the idea that they might persevere with impunity in a career of insolence and plunder."

By the turn of the new year, despite his anger at the stiff-necked American refusal to be placatory about the leveling of Greytown, Clarendon was in the process of changing his mind in regard to Central America. He and his fellow-Britons had anticipated a quick victory in the Crimean War, which could release the full power of the Royal Navy to exert pressure on the Americans. But despite allied successes at Alma, Balaclava, and Inkerman, Russian Sevastopol still resisted and would obviously require a long siege. Even more to the point, the British had come to recognize that their title to the Mosquito Protectorate and Greytown itself was "questionable." In this they were finally harkening to the earlier advice given by the *London Globe*. That paper had hoped that if war with the United States became necessary, it "should not be mixed up with the assertion of anything quite so aboriginal as the ill-defined rights, titles, and dominions of the tawny—and to confess the truth—somewhat trumpery majesty of Mosquito." London decided to push the entire Central-American question into the background, at least until the Crimean War was over. Thus the United States was enabled to avoid hostilities with Britain and escape the possibly unpleasant consequences of Hollins's harsh overreaction at Greytown.[7]

Commodore Hiram Paulding at Greytown, 1855

In May, according to Secretary of the Navy Dobbin in his *Report* for 1855, Paulding responded to a story that Britons were illegally arresting Americans at Greytown, that settlement having been reconstructed after Hollins had left it in ashes. The Commodore went there in his flagship, the *Susquehanna*. His ensuing investigation, the secretary concluded, had been marked by "commendable zeal and prudence" and had managed to relieve the "temporary misapprehension" and restore amity between Americans and Englishmen in the Mosquito Protectorate. The only official confirmation was provided by the U.S. Consul at Greytown, who informed the Department of State that Paulding's visit had evoked a "moral effect most useful," adding that his mission had been praised by Nicaragua's foreign minister.[8]

Commander Charles H. Davis at Rivas, February–May 1857

Matters of far greater essence than rumors of arrested Americans in Greytown quickly came to the fore in Nicaragua. It will be recalled that Cornelius Vanderbilt had opened his Transit Accessory Company's route across that country in 1851. While sojourning two years later in Europe, however, he learned that Charles Morgan and Cornelius K. Garrison, two of his corporate associates, were trying to subvert his control of the company. On his return, Vanderbilt sent the two a short note much to the point: "Gentlemen: You have undertaken to cheat me. I won't sue you, for the law is too slow. I'll ruin you." The ensuing clash over Accessory Transit's ownership continued for some years and contributed most meaningfully to the course of Nicaraguan history and the life of William Walker.

No sooner had Walker begun picking up the pieces after his debacle in northwestern Mexico during 1854, caused in part by Commander Thomas A. Dornin, than a new filibustering opportunity beckoned from Nicaragua's chronic civil wars. By 1855 the "Liberals" based at Leon were fast losing ground to the "Conservatives" at Granada, and looked for American aid in restoring their fortunes. After being contacted, Walker leaped at the chance to recoup, and in May 1856 sailed from San Francisco in a leaky old ship, accompanied by 58 men calling themselves "the Immortals." After taking San Juan del Sur on the Pacific, he branched out. Although often outnumbered 10 or 15 to one, he stormed Granada, brought the Conservatives into a temporary alliance with him, and became general of the Liberal army.

Walker had been supplied by the ships of the Transit Accessory Company, but this concern was in the process of being recaptured by Vanderbilt from Morgan and Garrison. The partners, realizing that the filibuster was their one trump to play against their enemy, loaned him $20,000, and sent an emissary to him. Walker was offered a deal: the continuation of adequate provision of men and supplies along both Atlantic and Pacific sea routes in return for the annulment of Accessory Transit's charter and the issuance of a new one to Morgan and Garrison, permitting them to acquire the company's Nicaraguan property. Walker's acceptance of the offer has been excoriated as stupid, for it earned him the lasting enmity of the powerful Vanderbilt, but at the time he was dependent upon the other two.

Nonetheless, by mid-1856 skies looked bright for Walker. That May the Pierce administration recognized his as the legitimate government of Nicaragua, and in July he was elected president of that nation. William Walker thereby became the only American citizen so far in history to rule as a foreign country's head of state. Many in the United States approved of what he was doing in Central America, thinking initially that he was an "advance agent of Manifest Destiny," laboring to make Nicaragua a possession of the United States. This was not so. He rather envisioned a single and potent country, encompassing all the Central American nations, as his personal domain. He reintroduced slavery in Nicaragua, primarily to ensure for himself an adequate labor supply rather than working for secessionists. Even so, Southerners tended to applaud him, for separatists there hoped for a proslavery government friendly to the anticipated independent Southern republic. But Walker's advocacy of slavery lost him much support among Northerners.

The new Nicaraguan strong man's greatest weakness lay in his tenuous supply lines. For a while Morgan and Garrison were able to maintain a small but steady stream of recruits and materiel from San Francisco to San Juan del Sur, and an essential route from New York to Greytown, up the San Juan River to Lake Nicaragua and Walker's headquarters at Rivas on the left bank. It was in the Atlantic that Vanderbilt struck to topple Walker, refusing to carry anything for him in his steamboats and interfering with Morgan and Garrison deliveries. More important, the ruthless Vanderbilt not only urged with success that Juan Rafael Mora, the conservative president of Costa Rica, war upon the intruder, but also sent agents who talked the Hondurans, Salvadorians, and Guatemalans—all of whom feared and hated the filibuster—into joining the Costa Ricans. But until late in 1856 they were crippled by cholera, dissension among themselves, and the spirited defense offered by the few remaining "Immortals" and their newer comrades in arms. At that time, however, the Costa Ricans seized two of Walker's lake steamers, cutting him off altogether from any resources reaching him from the east. This was a devastating blow, from which recovery was impossible.

The worsening plight of Walker and his followers, trapped at Rivas as the weeks of early 1857 dragged by, was naturally watched carefully from Washington. No matter how thoroughly they had shattered their nation's neutrality laws by engaging in such arrant filibustering, they were still American citizens, entitled, to at least some degree, to the protection of the United States. The Navy Department sent Commodore Mervine's *Independence* and Commander Davis's *St. Mary's* around the Horn to the Pacific coast of Central America. The secretary instructed Davis to stop off at Nicaragua to do no more than "to protect the persons and property of American citizens." This clearly gave him no warrant to act as a mediator between Walker and his enemies, but that is precisely what he became.

Early in February the *St. Mary's* arrived at San Juan del Sur, and Walker came over from Rivas to meet Davis, although their discussion was inconclusive. As March passed into April, conditions at the Rivas camp daily worsened, for by this time nothing was being received from Garrison. One of Walker's men complained, "We had neither bread, nor coffee, nor in fact anything to mix with our mule meat, except a little sugar and . . . chocolate." But the Central American allies were still unable to storm Rivas. Costa Rican President Mora, who had previously allowed his troops to murder their prisoners, began offering "protection, food, liquor, and free passage home" to any deserters. This was a disaster for the filibusters. Soon as many as 20 a day were drifting away to accept Mora's proposition. By that time, of the 1,026 men who had joined Walker at Rivas, deaths and desertions had winnowed the number to only 463.

Davis watched the approaching catastrophe with growing apprehension, admitting to the "horror of witnessing the slaughter of my countrymen . . . without the ability to succor them." He visited Mora on 30 April and found that the Costa Rican was eager to end the fighting if Walker was forced to leave Nicaragua. The Americans would be permitted to depart unharmed under the guardianship of the U.S. Navy in exchange for the surrender of their arms and ammunition. When apprised of this agreement, Walker sent two emissaries to Davis for further information, who told them that it was acceptance of Mora's terms or death. When one of them said that the filibusters could always escape on their little ship *Granada*, the commander coldly told them to forget it, that he was going to seize the vessel. Walker at once lost all hope and agreed to quit the fight.

On 1 May the terms, signed only by Walker and Davis, were completed. In place of a farewell speech to his loyal followers, almost half of whom were debilitated by wounds and illness, Walker had a subordinate read a brief message that did no more than to thank them and to place the blame for the debacle on "the cowardice of some, the incapacity of others, and the treachery of many." When his men learned that he and the 16 officers he had been permitted to take with him had already departed for Panama via San Juan del Sur, they were filled with outrage and resentment, although most of them, under U.S. naval protection, were eventually able to come home. The anti-Walker *New York Times* pounced upon the filibuster's treatment of his followers: "He has ingloriously abandoned the field of his operations, after sacrificing a large amount of property and hundreds of lives; he has done a vast deal of mischief, without any compensating benefits to the country he has ravaged, or to those who trusted his courage and sagacity." Meanwhile Davis had seized the *Granada* and turned her over to the Costa Ricans, who, undoubtedly much to Walker's grim satisfaction, promptly rendered her a total loss by running her aground.

When Walker came ashore at New Orleans late in May, he was hailed with almost frantic enthusiasm, an attitude mirrored throughout the South and among some northern expansionists. He proceeded to New York and then to Washington for a prearranged visit with James Buchanan, the new president, who apparently greeted him sympathetically. Totally ignoring that he owed him his life, Walker took this opportunity to lay into Davis, charging that he had been acting "in behalf of the Central American Allies." Indeed, the commander had betrayed him "all along in the surrender negotiations." If this naval interference had not taken place, he claimed, he could have seized the initiative and still won the day, for if his army was suffering from disease, so too were those of his enemies. He also let it be known that Davis had been a tool to gratify Vanderbilt's lust for revenge upon him, working with Secretary of State Marcy and Commodore Mervine to ruin him, accusations that cannot be substantiated. All these charges were bandied about Congress for a time, but without harm to Davis. In his *Report, 1857* Secretary of the Navy Isaac Toucey carefully straddled the question: "The action of Commander Davis, so far as he aided General Walker and his men, by use of the *St. Mary's*, to retreat from Nicaragua and return to the United States, was approved by the Department; but his interference with the *Granada*, and her transfer to the Nicaraguans, was not approved."[9]

Commodore Hiram Paulding, et al., at Punta Arenas, December 1857

While Walker was tying up the strands remaining from his clash with Davis, he was simultaneously busying himself with plans to return to Central America, for his recent disaster had destroyed little of his southern support. He managed to solve his transportation problem by persuading a steamship company to provide him passage there and to keep open to Greytown a conduit for communications, supplies, and men. He also established a company "to send immigrants to Nicaragua," which would operate as a front for the delivery of armed volunteers. When a federal judge at New Orleans ordered his arrest "for preparing to embark on a military mission," Walker turned himself in and was released on a $2,000 bond. He then jumped bail, proceeded to Mobile, boarded his ship *Fashion*, and steamed from that port with 270 men on 14 November after "only token interference from the government."

Ten days later Walker went past Greytown to land a detachment under Colonel Frank Anderson to go up a tributary of the San Juan River and surprise Costa Ricans controlling access into the interior. The *Fashion* returned to Punta Arenas across from Greytown and, by hiding most of the men below deck, thoroughly befuddled Commander Frederick Chatard in the *Saratoga* and dashed past him to land the filibusters. For about two weeks Walker waited in the pouring rain for word from Anderson. On 6 December came the electrifying news that the expedition had been totally triumphant, capturing the Costa Rican headquarters and seizing four steamboats, all without losing a man. But Walker's jubilation lasted for only a few hours. On that very day Commodore Paulding came into Greytown in the *Wabash*, his powerful new 50-gun frigate, and met Chatard in the *Saratoga*; the next day he was joined by Lieutenant John J. Almy in the *Fulton*.

Even more than Davis, Paulding would be Walker's nemesis. When Davis had accepted the filibuster's surrender the previous May, he had at least saved the lives of Walker and his followers. Therefore his probably illegal behavior could be excused on humanitarian grounds. Paulding could expect to benefit from no such rationalization. He was operating under orders from Toucey that were ambiguous, perhaps deliberately so. Certainly, however, there was nothing in them explicitly permitting Paulding to arrest American citizens inside Nicaragua.

The next day, the commodore jockeyed his men-of-war into position with their guns leveled at the filibuster's camp, while sending 300 servicemen to cordon it off. Simultaneously he wrote to Walker, demanding his surrender. This naturally turned the latter's short-lived elation into utter despondency. What made it all the more unbearable was that Paulding's massive intervention had followed so closely upon receipt of the knowledge that Anderson's astonishing victory over the Costa Ricans had evidently opened the way for Walker's return to power in Nicaragua. Hence, when he boarded the *Wabash* on the 8th, for once his iron self-composure, about which so many of his associates had spoken, deserted him. The commodore chortled to his wife that "this lion-hearted devil, who has so often destroyed the lives of other men, came to me, humbled himself, and wept like a child." Walker landed in New York, having been out of his country for only 44 days, and went on to Washington, where Secretary of State Lewis Cass told him that he was a free man, "as the executive department had no right to detain him."

Meanwhile Paulding was telling his wife, "I have taken strong measures in forcing him from a neutral territory. It may make me President or cost me my commission," and the latter was by far the most likely. He tried to ward off any approaching lightning by writing to Toucey that he looked upon the filibusters only as "outlaws who . . . left our shores for the purpose of rapine and murder." The commodore stated later that he would see "whether the pirate who dishonors the country, or the officer of trust who redeems its honor, is to carry the day in the national councils."

Over the next several months Americans divided to support either Paulding or Walker. The *New York Times* upheld the former, avowing that Walker had lost public favor for "bringing our government into reproach—that it was beginning to be universally regarded as either too weak to repress crime, or too dishonest to make the attempt. Commodore PAULDING's action, if directed and sustained by the Administration, will effectually repel this imputation." Walker adherents retorted by stressing three points: once he and his men were at sea, they were outside U.S. jurisdiction until they came home; the president, through his naval officer, needed congressional permission before making any arrest; and Nicaragua had filed no official protest about this occupation of its soil. The division of opinion tended to follow sectional lines, with Walker's support concentrated in the slave states.

In the last analysis, the president pretty well summarized the pros and cons of the argument as early as his special message to the Senate on that subject during January 1857. By that time any original sympathy he may have had for the filibuster was gone: "Disguise it as we may, such a military expedition [as his] is an invitation to reckless and lawless men to enlist under the banner of any adventurer to rob, plunder, and murder the unoffending citizens of neighboring states, who have never done them harm. It is an usurpation of the war-making power, which belongs alone to Congress; and the Government itself . . . becomes an accomplice in the commission of this crime unless it adopts all the means necessary to prevent and punish it." As for Paulding, Buchanan considered that this "gallant officer" had acted from "pure and patriotic motives and in the sincere conviction that he was promoting the interest and vindicating the honor of his country." In regard to Nicaragua, "she has sustained no injury" from him, for he had "relieved her from a dreaded invasion." Had the commodore picked up Walker and his followers at any time and place prior to their landing at Punta Arenas, it would have been "not only a justifiable but a praiseworthy act." In seizing Walker, however, after he had reached Nicaragua, Paulding had made "a grave error." He had exceeded his orders by "landing his sailors and marines in Nicaragua . . . for the purpose of making war upon any military force" there, "no matter from whence they came. That power certainly did not belong to him."

After all the vocal cords had been exercised and all the ink spilled, the upshot of the Paulding-Walker controversy was an ambiguous conclusion. Both sides had to be satisfied with the release of Walker and Paulding's reception of a gentle reprimand from Secretary Toucey and a short suspension from active duty. At least Nicaragua was grateful to the commodore. Early in 1861 that country's chargé d'affaires in Washington asked Attorney General Jeremiah S. Black for permission to give Paulding his legislature's "vote of thanks, a sword, and a tract of its public lands." Since it was unlawful for naval or army officers to accept presents from foreign governments, save under special dispensation, Congress eventually decided that he could welcome the thanks and a "handsome jeweled sword," but not the land, for its potential value might set an unfortunate precedent.[10]

The termination of Walker's dogged quest for glory or death may be quickly told. He kept on plotting to return to authority in Nicaragua, this time via Honduras, where in 1860 he successfully stormed the fortress at Truxillo, but in the process $3,000 worth of British custom receipts disappeared, a loss giving the Royal Navy an excuse to intervene. On 5

September Captain Norvell Salmon in HMS *Icarus* compelled the filibuster to surrender to him "as a representative of Her Majesty's Government." In an act of consummate meanness and duplicity, Salmon then turned him over to his enemies, and a week later Walker was shot by a Honduran firing squad.

Scattered Locales, 1846–1860

Lieutenant David Dixon Porter at Santo Domingo (Dominican Republic), 1846

Santo Domingo, the Spanish-speaking eastern two-thirds of Hispaniola Island, which it shared with French-speaking Haiti, had been conquered in 1821 and ruled by Haiti into the early 1840s. The toppling of a longtime Haitian dictator eventually allowed Santo Domingo to become independent in 1844. It petitioned the United States for recognition (not to be granted until 1866). The Polk administration sent young Lieutenant David Dixon Porter, the son of Commodore David Porter, to survey the Dominican situation. He reached there in the *Porpoise* during May and spent a month on horse-back in the interior; he was struck by its poverty and farcical educational system. He was, however, cognizant of the strategic value of Samaná Bay on the northeastern coast, and thought that potentially rich natural resources could be well developed by American enterprise. Porter's reports about his visit were totally ignored until 1869–1870, when President Grant was trying to annex the Dominican Republic, but their publication in a journal could do nothing to save a failing venture.[11]

Captain Theodorus Bailey and Commodore William Mervine at Panama, 1856

Panama had attracted little attention until the Gold Rush of 1849. After that, this westernmost province of Columbia had rivaled Nicaragua as the fastest route to California. But Nicaragua fell behind with the completion of the Panama Railroad in 1855, connecting Panama City on the Caribbean with Colón on the Pacific. Almost at once this first transcontinental railway proved valuable and immensely profitable, but its construction had featured an appalling death rate among its workers from accidents and a variety of lethal tropical diseases. About 6,000 perished while laying less than 48 miles of track. In a grisly finale, since no one knew even the names of these laborers, their bodies were pickled in barrels of brine and shipped around the world to provide cadavers for medical schools.

The completion of the railroad in 1855 was followed by massive unemployment among the thousands of blacks who had flocked there from

Central America and the West Indies. Necessity forced many of them into extra-legal methods of survival. Their dispositions were not sweetened by the arrant racism displayed by many Americans, either residents or those crossing the isthmus. Panama's effervescent mix was ready to boil over.

The uprising took place at Panama City on 15 April, in the so-called "Watermelon Riot." A drunken American ordered a piece of watermelon from a black fruit-seller and refused to pay ten cents for it. An altercation broke out and shots were exchanged. Inflamed by this event, blacks gathered in the slums, burst out, sacked three hotels and a store, and headed for the Panama Railroad headquarters in the center of town. An ill-starred crowd of 250 to 300 whites who had just debarked from an Atlantic steamer were there, arranging for passage to the Pacific. They were trapped and then besieged by the mob, which was soon joined by the police. According to an eyewitness, the reinforced mob "entered the station . . . and began their work of murder and plunder." Evidently the patrolmen were trying to save themselves, for the blacks had been shouting "*Mueran los blancos!*" A reporter from the Panama City *Star and Herald* described the depot the next morning: ". . . doors and tables of the ticket office were smeared with blood or blackened and torn up by the closely discharged muskets." About 15 Americans were killed and a like number wounded; 2 Panamanians were killed and 13 wounded. The toll would have been much higher except for the mob's penchant for loot rather than homicide.

Naturally the Pierce administration was horrified by the atrocity, and Navy Secretary Dobbin at once sent Captain Theodorus Bailey in the *St. Mary's* and Commodore William Mervine in the *Independence* to Panama. To look ahead, Secretary of State Marcy chose Amos B. Corwine, an American diplomat formerly accredited to Central America, to investigate the affair for his government. Corwine interviewed scores of deponents at Panama, and his massive report (108 handwritten pages) was published in the press during July. He held that the riot had occurred because of the blacks' desire for plunder and to avenge "imagined wrongs." Local officials, he said, had encouraged the uprising, holding Manuel Maria Garrido, the city's police chief, primarily responsible.

Long before, the two U.S. warships had arrived at the isthmus. Bailey told Francisco de Fabrega, Governor of Panama, about his dissatisfaction with the manner in which the local investigation was proceeding; he asked why Garrido was still at large. James B. Bowlin, U.S. minister in Bogotá, lined up with the captain, pointing out that "no arrests have been made, nor any process to recover the stolen goods enforced." A month later Bowlin urged Washington to maintain its naval presence in Panama. He wrote that while he considered Bailey "a most worthy [,] amiable and peacefully inclined gentleman," he inspired "awe" among the Panamanians, and is "awfully feared by those who are restrained only by fear."

While Bailey was attending to this matter, Mervine busied himself in opposing a recently enacted "tonnage tax" on foreign vessels coming into Panama, which he considered illegal under existing U.S.-Columbian treaties. Marcy told him to "resist by force, if necessary," collection of the tax, and Mervine button-holed Fabrega and thought he persuaded him to suspend the measure. When the governor complained loudly about his treatment, the commodore responded that Fabrega was still trying to collect the tax, adding "but probably better faith could not be expected of an official, who could so far outrage humanity as to *order* the massacre of defenseless women and children." Of course Fabrega and his countrymen were beside themselves at this charge, which, after all, was without any definite proof. Yet Mervine's intimidation and outspoken churlishness worked; Colombia eventually rescinded the tonnage tax.

Again trouble loomed ahead in Panama during September 1856. Black and white candidates faced one another in a gubernatorial election and the black was expected to lose. Violence appeared so certain that some whites in Panama City fled to the *St. Mary's* for safety, and Mervine sent ashore 160 men with a cannon to occupy the railroad depot. Three days later the situation was quiet enough for him to withdraw the landing force, after which the white candidate was named governor.

During the greater part of the next two decades, Washington and Bogotá disagreed about responsibility for the Watermelon Riot and how American claims arising from it should be settled. That December President Pierce enunciated his opinion on those subjects: "the perpetrators of the wrongs in question should be punished" and "provision should be made for the families" of Americans killed, "with full indemnity for the property pillaged or destroyed." Nothing, however, happened until 1860, when a treaty appeared to settle the issues. Colombia acknowledged its liability, "especially for damages which were caused by the riot of Panama." Yet the years continued to slip by without payment. No question of Colombian responsibility was ever resolved; nothing ever happened to Fabrega or Garrido. Not until 1874 did Colombia remit $412,393.95, a sum considered excessive by many Latin Americans. Perhaps the unrelenting pressure exerted by Bailey and Mervine 18 years before had finally come into fruition.[12]

Commander Thomas Turner at Navassa Island off Haiti, 1858

The valuable fertilizer guano was found in the Caribbean as well as in the Pacific. The way was opened for Americans to gather it by the U.S. Guano Act of 1856, asserting that any unoccupied island not under recognized foreign jurisdiction "would be considered as appertaining to the United States" if claimed by U.S. citizens. A year later an American started digging on the uninhabited one-mile-square Navassa, about thirty miles west of the Haitian mainland. Port-au-Prince sent gunboats in 1858 to warn the operator to stop work, but left without resorting to force. The American protested to his government, which dispatched Turner with the *Saratoga* and *Plymouth* to Haiti with the warning that there must be no interference with the digging on Navassa. Turner then looked over the island for one hour before coming home.

From 1858 to 1873 the Haitians maintained that they were being robbed of a long-held possession, but their claim was countered by the American assertion that the island was "abandoned and derelict" and always had been. Today Navassa remains uninhabited, and U.S. authority is marked only by an automatic lighthouse, inspected twice a year. As the historian Roy F. Nichols wrote, "In this humble fashion, the American nation took its first step into the path of imperialism; Navassa, a guano island, was the first noncontiguous territory to be announced formally as attached to the republic."[13]

Commander Charles H. Poor at Rio Hacha, Colombia, August– September 1860

On routine patrol through the southernmost West Indies, Commander Charles H. Poor in his sloop *St. Louis* came into the Dutch island of Curaçao, and found there the U.S. consul to Rio Hacha, whose identification in naval correspondence is no more than "Mr. Danies." The consul reported that he had had to flee from his post during a local civil war, when rebel troops had subjected him to "indignities, loss of property, and the flag insulted." The commander, taking Danies along with him, sailed for Rio Hacha. There he demanded of the insurgent general in charge of the town an explanation of the "indignities" endured by the consul, and "required that the flag should be hoisted at the flagstaff of the consulate, and saluted by the troops. It was accordingly done." But Poor took no further action against the Colombians, for he had found out that Danies's troubles had been in large part due to his own unspecified indiscretions. Taking the initiative, the commander simply carried Danies away with him in the *St. Louis*, leaving the Rio Hacha consulate in a successor's hands.[14]

Commodore John B. Montgomery and Commander William D. Porter
at Panama, September–October 1860

Events in Panama in late 1860 were the pre–U.S. Civil War finale of U.S. naval diplomacy in the Caribbean and Central America. While Commodore John B. Montgomery was absent on other business, Commander William D. Porter (yet another son of the prolific Commodore David) anchored the *St. Mary's* at Panama City. On 27 September he became aware that the usual agitation in black-white relations on the isthmus had broken into outright violence. Blacks who had gathered outside the town proceeded to assault it, according to Secretary Toucey "killing six and wounding three of the white inhabitants." The leading Colombian official present begged Porter and Captain Thomas Miller of HMS *Clio*, also moored in the harbor, for assistance in restoring tranquility. Both officers sent ashore landing detachments and cannon and promptly quelled the disorders.

On 7 October Porter withdrew his men, but the British remained. The *New York Times* asserted that this lingering was not approved by the commander, who "made some remonstrance." When English sentries at their consulate arrested some Americans who had ignored their challenges, Montgomery (who had meanwhile come into Panama in the *Lancaster*) picked up the gauntlet. Although Toucey is silent about any such disagreement, historian Robert E. Johnson says that the commodore "entered into an acrimonious exchange of letters" with Miller. "The contretemps was ended by the *Clio's* departure," but American officers believed that the Britons were trying to gain some idea of American reaction if Great Britain took over Panama.[15]

It would appear that such fears were nonsensical. By that time Britain had come to a decision about Central America in general and Nicaragua in particular. As has been stressed before, the importance of Nicaragua's cross-isthmian route, so profitable in Vanderbilt's heyday, had been much reduced by the opening of the Panama Railroad in 1855 and the chaos caused later by Walker. Furthermore, London was becoming increasingly aware, not only of the dubious legality of its claim to the Mosquito Protectorate, but also of the fact that its continued possession was a major source of irritation to the United States. Following the precedent set the year before in returning the Bay Islands to Honduras, in 1860 a treaty was signed with Nicaragua whereby the British withdrew from Mosquitia and Greytown reverted to San Juan del Norte. Although the internal ties of his country may have been unraveling, the treaty permitted President Buchanan in his annual message of 1860 to report that Anglo-American relations were on a footing "eminently satisfactory to this Government."

Summary

American officers behaved with some efficacy in the diplomatic dealings with Spain over Cuba, although there was a conspicuous failure as well. About all that needs to be said about Lieutenants Gedney and Meade is that their apprehension of the *Amistad*'s slaves started a long and inconclusive controversy with Spain. Commander Randolph surrounded Round Island, Louisiana, so well that Lopez was forced to abandon his 1849 invasion plans. Lieutenant Rodger's stout insistence that Spaniards could not seize an American-registered ship in American territorial waters saved Lopez and his followers a year later. Randolph again and Captain Tattnall acted decisively in their endeavors to get back the *Georgiana* and *Susan Loud*, and it was hardly their fault that Spanish maritime courts refused to surrender them. Commodores Morris and McKeever may have helped to persuade the Spanish queen to liberate Americans captured in the Yucatán. Lopez's second and last expedition was attended by U.S. naval ineptitude. Commander Platt made little effort in 1851 to save Crittenden and his men from execution, while refusing to harken to the appeals of other Americans in Cuba that he intercede in their behalf. Commodore Parker found that the U.S. consul in Havana had already received Spanish apologies for their warship's firing on the American steamer *Falcon*, although his appeals for mercy for the filibusters imprisoned in Spain may have helped a little in their release. Commodore McCauley's brief patrol off Cuba in the *Ferrolana–El Dorado* episode in 1855 appears to have had no particular impact.

Perhaps never in U.S. history have naval officers, operating almost on their own, carried on a more aggressive foreign policy than those in Central America during the 1850s. This generalization does not apply to Commodore Parker in the *Express-Prometheus* case at Greytown in 1851, for that complication was settled by the Royal Navy's forthright and honorable admission of guilt, rather than by anything the commodore had done. Nor does it apply to the somewhat placid attempts by Commodore Paulding to aid Americans arrested at the same place four years later. But it certainly does pertain to Captain Hollins at Greytown in 1853 and 1854, and to Commander Davis and Paulding in their reactions to William Walker in Nicaragua during 1857.

Hollins deserves credit for his able defense of the Accessory Transit Company's possessions in his first intervention, but merits only condemnation for the second. Indeed, his overreaction in leveling Greytown in 1854 could well have led to a totally unnecessary war had not outside events dictated otherwise. As to the U.S. Navy and Walker, Davis earns congratulations for his intervention; after all, it saved the lives of the deluded filibusters. Paulding's arrest of Walker is not so simple to evaluate. He did seize American citizens on foreign soil, an act that he had no right to commit. But he still may wear laurels justifiably. His own government had declared Walker an outlaw, and the general's behavior was contrary to whatever Washington hoped to achieve in its foreign policy, convulsing Central America and roiling Anglo-American relations.

In areas other than Cuba and Nicaragua, assessments of U.S. naval diplomacy are harder than those concerning Spain or Britain during the same decades. Lieutenant Porter's errand to Santo Domingo in 1846 amounted to nothing; it would probably have been completely forgotten had he not returned there 20 years later. Commander Poor's rescue of Consul Danies appears to have been no more than saving him from his own folly at Rio Hacha. The troubles of Commodore Montgomery and Commander William Porter with the British at Panama are somewhat perplexing, since details are so murky. But Captain Bailey and Commodore Mervine deserve high marks for their forceful if impolite efforts in getting satisfaction for the atrocities committed during the "Watermelon Riot," in repelling Colombian impositions of new and illegal taxes on American shipping, and in maintaining peace in that September's hotly contested and racially explosive local election.

CHAPTER ◆ SIX

Lower South America

1818–1859

B razil, Argentina, Paraguay, and Uruguay occupy southeastern South America; Chile, Peru, and Bolivia the southwestern part. The naval service's diplomatic impingements in lower South America, except Captain Arthur Sinclair's quarrel at Rio with the local governor in 1818 (see below), came after those countries had become independent. By the early 1820s Brazil had won independence from Portugal, and by 1826 Argentina, Paraguay, Uruguay, Chile, Peru, and Bolivia had liberated themselves from Spain. In general these countries rivaled Mexico, Central America, and the Caribbean in presenting U.S. officers with knotty issues that could be unraveled only with difficulty. These issues and their consequences are set out in this chapter in geographical order, not chronological.

During 1818–1859 naval personnel busied themselves with foreign relations along both coasts of lower South America, but with considerably more activity in the east than the west. In the east there were major confrontations with Brazilians in 1818–1845, Argentines in 1831–1854, and Paraguayans in 1855–1859, but relatively inconsequential law-and-order missions in Argentina and Uruguay in 1833–1858. In the west, naval clashes occurred chiefly in Peru and to a lesser extent in Chile and Bolivia, in 1831–1854. Most of these troubles emanated from civil conflicts in and wars between the Latin-American countries themselves, as well as from their efforts to fend off European interventions.

Brazil, 1818–1846
Captain Arthur Sinclair at Rio, 1818

President Monroe decided in 1818 to send an American fact-finding mission to South America, ostensibly to gather accurate information about the Argentine and Chilean patriots rebelling against Peruvian royalists, although he may also have used the mission to allow the controversy at home over recognizing those revolutionary states to die down. The frigate *Congress*, under the command of Captain Arthur Sinclair, came into Rio de Janeiro during January 1818, carrying the commissioners and letters for Thomas Sumter, U.S. Minister to Portugal-Brazil. A party of American sailors was permitted to go ashore and, as always, proceeded to get drunk, and one of them deserted. A couple of days later two officers from the *Congress* spotted him in the city and started dragging him back toward the dock. But he yelled that he was a Portuguese subject, and hearing his appeal, some soldiers wrested him from his captors and led him away. To keep him in sight, the officers followed him and his rescuers to a room where several Portuguese-Brazilian officers, out of uniform, were sitting. They insulted and threatened the Americans and refused them permission to take the man back to the frigate. As the two officers hastened to their boat, a mob quickly assembled and hissed them as they rowed away to safety.

The local governor sent Sumter a furious letter demanding an abject apology, punishment of the officers, and the surrender of all "Portuguese" sailors on the muster roll of the *Congress*. Sinclair took it upon himself to reply "in a spirited [and negative] manner" that the deserter must be returned to fulfill his enrollment requirements and refused point-blank to surrender any men from his ship, no matter what their alleged nationality. The local authorities responded in turn that should Sinclair attempt to depart without giving satisfaction in this matter, he would be fired upon from the city's main fortifications, mounting a hundred guns. Sumter, worried about the possibility of a serious rupture between Rio and Washington, urged the captain to remain in port until the quarrel could be settled. The naval officer ignored the diplomat and slapped on canvas, and as one of his officers explained to the press, "we went out cleared for action; we even had our matches [al]ready lighted." Happily no resistance was offered, and the *Congress* sailed "unmolested" past the silent guns of the fortress. Nevertheless, the Portuguese-Brazilians were outraged at Sinclair's defiance, and possibly his bold and abrupt departure was responsible, at least in part, for the anti-Americanism that kept cropping up in that country over the subsequent years.[1]

Captain Jesse D. Elliott and Commodore James Biddle off Montevideo and Rio, 1826–1828

Brazil ripped itself away from its centuries-long domination by Portugal and established its independence in 1822. But it quickly came to sword's points with neighboring Argentina, for the latter had expansionistic tendencies, particularly in regard to modern Uruguay, called at the time "Banda Oriental" ("Eastern Bank"). This area had been originally settled by Spaniards from Argentina. Nevertheless, King João VI had annexed it to Brazil in 1821, but was able to control little more than Montevideo and a couple of other ports. Late in 1825 Buenos Aires announced its takeover of Uruguay, and the Emperor Dom Pedro I (João's son) retaliated by declaring war.

Land action brought early Brazilian defeats but soon degenerated into a military stalemate. By and large, Brazil controlled the sea until relatively late in the conflict. When hostilities began, it promptly announced a blockade of the Rio de la Plata's huge mouth in order to cut off supplies to Buenos Aires. It was all too typical of other such interdictions in Latin America during the early nineteenth century: insufficient time had been given to warn neutrals that it had been imposed, and Brazil had too few men-of-war to seal off the blockaded shores effectively. Washington quite properly denounced the subsequent apprehensions of American merchant ships. By 1828 mutual exhaustion was afflicting both belligerents, for neither had the will or the resources in men and money to defeat the other. Under heavy diplomatic pressure from the British, whose commerce had been negatively affected, they signed the Treaty of Rio de Janeiro late in August 1828, "Banda Oriental" became independent Uruguay, as Brazil and Argentina were able to accept the creation of a buffer state between them, rather than having it belong to the other. Both American commanders involved in the conflict turned matters much to their nation's advantage.

When these hostilities started, Captain Jesse D. Elliott in the frigate *Cyane* was already patrolling off Uruguay. According to the American press he performed admirably in behalf of U.S. shipping, which was menaced by Brazilian blockaders. He managed to ensure that before an American vessel could be seized, proof that she had been notified of the blockade's existence had to be presented; a privilege that European ships could not enjoy at that time. Furthermore, he maintained excellent relations with the Austrians by surrendering to them a deserter from one of their warships who had signed on the *Cyane*, while at the same time pleading the man's case so eloquently that he was released. He also upheld American honor. When the commander of a French frigate asked for permission to search a U.S. merchantman for deserters, Elliott replied that under no circumstances would foreigners be allowed to board his country's ships for such purposes. Finally, he appears to have followed Biddle's instructions with precision during the few months that he remained in South America before being ordered home.

The self-assured, perceptive, and patrician Biddle proved during his tenure off southeastern South America that his earlier successful diplomacy on his west coast had been no aberration. His orders were that he should challenge any "illegal exercise of power," especially illicit blockades, that threatened his nation's commerce. He must, however, avoid "collisions" with either Argentina or Brazil, countries with which the United States had maintained and wished to maintain friendly relations. He sailed in the frigate *Macedonian*, of yellow-fever memory off Cuba three years before, and anchored at Rio in August 1826 to assume command of the newly formed "Brazil Squadron," in this instance composed of his flagship, Elliott's *Cyane*, and a sloop.

Since the Brazilians retained maritime control during most of his tour, Biddle's troubles, as Elliott's had been, were primarily with them. Soon he was looking into the case of the Philadelphia brig *Bull*. She had been snapped up by a Brazilian cruiser on the high seas and brought into port, and during the passage her crew had been viciously manhandled. The commodore, working with the U.S. chargé d'affaires in Rio, managed to liberate the prisoners and, it seems, eventually to free the ship. A few months later there was a brief confrontation between Biddle and the Brazilian authorities over the latter's attempt to require that expensive bonds be purchased by all foreign shipping to ensure that they would not "break the blockade of Buenos Ayres." Biddle's strong protest, eventually backed in full by Secretary of the Navy Samuel L. Southard and President John Quincy Adams, proved unnecessary. By the late 1820s the Argentinians, using the talents of the Irish immigrant Admiral Guillielmo (William) Brown, managed to achieve something close to naval equality with the Brazilians. This development, coupled with the winding down of the war, prevented the full imposition of Rio's bond requirement and the question became academic.

The commodore was at his best in defusing a somewhat ridiculous Brazilian-American fracas that just might have wildfired into a crisis. During November 1826 Midshipman John W. Moores was overseeing carpentry work on the *Macedonian*'s spars at the Brazilian government arsenal in Rio. A line of convicts heading for a Brazilian prison passed by and one shouted that he was a kidnaped American sailor. Moores, ac-

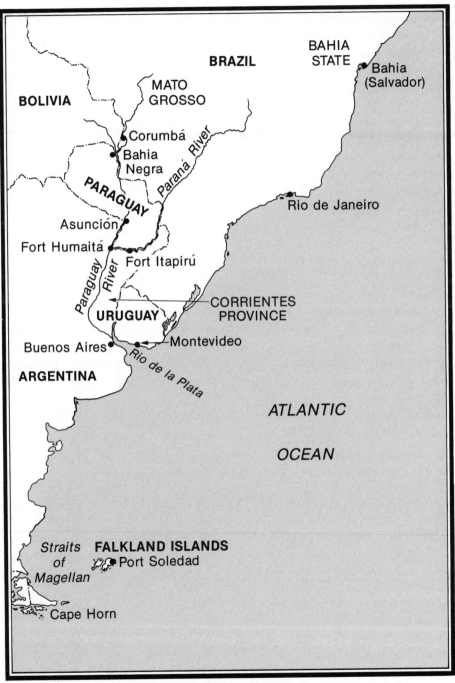

South America, East Coast

cording to one naval colleague, was "a little excited by liquor" and tried a single-handed rescue, for which he was set upon by the guards. The xenophobic and irascible Brazilian Admiral Francisco Antonio de Silva Pacheco appeared at once with a large armed retinue, and after Moores had undiplomatically told him, "You be damned!" he was beaten to the ground under a hail of blows. Not until Pacheco had hit him several more times over the head with his cane was the midshipman permitted to depart. Biddle's disposition of this messy situation was impeccable. He notified Washington that he had decided not to hold a court-martial in the *Macedonian*, implying that very likely his fellow-officers would acquit the culprit. If that occurred the already inflamed Brazilian public would be further outraged by what they would consider a whitewash. So he simply sent Moores home, dumping the matter into the lap of Secretary Southard. Biddle was correct in his assumption; the offender not only escaped a court-martial but was soon promoted. A situation that might possibly have brought about Brazilian-American confrontation had been neatly defused.

Biddle arrived back in the United States late in 1828, bringing the welcome news that the war in lower South America was over and that the American merchant marine would henceforth be spared molestation in that quarter. One must agree with Southard's estimation of Biddle's work there when he expressed the "satisfaction always felt by the department when the duties assigned to our Naval officers are performed with intelligence[,] fidelity and discretion. Accept my compliments on your safe return to your country."[2]

Commander Daniel Turner and Lieutenant Josiah Tattnall at Swedish St. Barts, 1828

About the same time that Biddle was en route home, the finale of U.S. naval concern with the war took place, and although it pertained to an Argentine vessel, it was part of the war between Brazil and Argentina. During December 1828 Commander Daniel Turner in the sloop *Erie* came into St. Barts, where the "Buenos Ayres" privateer *Federal* was anchored. He already knew that the Argentine ship had recently robbed on the high seas the Boston merchantman *Nymph* on the charge of transporting Brazilian goods. Since Turner was convinced that the *Federal*'s captain was well aware that the war had concluded, it was to him a clear case of piracy. In this opinion he was solidly backed by Thomas M. Harrison, the U.S. Consul at St. Barts. But when the commander asked the mayor and other local authorities to turn over that ship to him, much to his astonished fury the Swedes refused to relinquish the vessel, demanding further proof to back his charges. Turner decided to take her anyway, even though she was lying directly under the guns of the Swedish fort. A boat expedition, under the direction of Lieutenant Josiah Tattnall, crept up on the *Federal*, having the luck to enjoy a moonless and rainy night. A contrary wind caused problems for a time, but just as the alerted fortress commenced firing, the breeze shifted, and Tattnall was able to escort the privateer out to sea. Turner sent her off to Pensacola as a "prize of war." Within two months Harrison had built a solid legal case, establishing that if the *Federal* had not been apprehended she would still be assailing U.S. shipping. After that, the Swedes chose to ignore the violation of their sovereignty.[3]

Commander Isaac Mayo off Bahia, 1837–1838

For a decade and more Brazil was in chaos in the wake of its unsatisfactory war with Argentina, and the imperial government was threatened by republican uprisings throughout the country. Late in 1837, while a civil war was raging in the north, Commander Isaac Mayo was cruising in the *Fairfield* off Bahia to protect his country's shipping. He described local affairs to the navy secretary and concluded, "I must confess that my feelings as an individual are with the Republican party and altho' I wish them success shall endeavor not to commit myself in my public capacity." Admirable though his resolve may have been, he allowed his sympathies to overrule both his judgment and Washington's determination that no impetuous naval action should ruffle its relations with Brazil.

The next January Rio's foreign minister wrote U.S. Minister to Argentina William Hunter asking him to order the *Fairfield*'s withdrawal. He charged Mayo with paying no attention to the Brazilian brig performing patrol duty but offering "to engage her in battle." Furthermore, he wrote, Mayo had conveyed into shore an American merchantman laden with supplies for the insurgents and rumored to be carrying the republican leader into Bahia. All this gave credence to the impression that the United States officially favored the rebels. Hunter turned down the request, but admitted to the State Department that there had been "a little too much display of the fervor of republicanism so natural in our citizens." When Mayo learned that his expulsion had been requested, he expressed to Hunter his angry refusal to depart. Soon, however, he was placated by an apology from the foreign minister and the tiff blew over.[4]

Commodore Daniel Turner at Rio, 1845

During January Commodore Turner in the *Raritan* was concerning himself with routine squadron matters when he learned that the reputed American slaver *Porpoise* had come into port. He and U.S. Minister to Brazil Henry A. Wise, an opinionated hothead, decided that the ship should be nabbed and those on board arrested for violating the anti-slave-trade laws of the United States. Turner sent 32 men "with drawn cut-lasses," who swarmed aboard and brought the *Porpoise* under the guns of the *Raritan*. The Brazilian government and its people were incensed by this drastic action and surrounded the slaver while reinforcing the harbor forts. It took a week for Turner and Wise to recognize that they had no legal case whatsoever and release the *Porpoise*.

Washington's official reaction was swift and negative. Turner appears to have come off reasonably well; apparently the Navy Department concluded that he had only been following Wise. But Secretary of State Buchanan castigated the minister, telling him, "The jurisdiction of every independent nation over the merchant vessels of other nations lying within its own harbors" being "absolute and exclusive, nothing but its authority can justify a ship of war belonging to another nation in seizing and de-taining a vessel thus situated for any cause or pretext whatever."[5]

Lieutenant Alonzo B. Davis and Commodore Lawrence Rousseau at Rio, 1846

While ashore in Rio on 31 October 1846, Lieutenant Alonzo B. Davis, attached to the USS *Saranac*, became aware that three sailors from his ship, one of them obviously besotted, were quarreling among themselves. He was taking them to his boat when some policemen and soldiers appeared. Thinking that they had come to aid him, the lieutenant released his men, only to see the Brazilians start beating them "with their swords until they were covered with blood." Ignoring Davis's expostulations, they dragged the sailors away. Having left his sword in a shop, Davis returned for it and raced after the entourage, which by this time was approaching the imperial palace. When he arrived there a Brazilian officer cordially invited him to step inside; he was "immediately seized, disarmed, and imprisoned," and he was held in custody until 2 November. Minister Wise soon filed a protest to the Brazilian foreign office, insisting upon the release of the sailors (which was later done), a disavowal of the arrests, and the prosecution of the policemen and soldiers responsible. Meanwhile the Brazilians were presenting him with a counter-claim, accusing Davis of trying to free his men by force; a little later they asked Washington to recall Wise. Commodore Lawrence Rousseau, in the *Columbia*, com-manding the Brazil Squadron, was in Rio at the time and concluded that the treatment of Davis was an "outrage" and an insult to him, the com-modore, and through him to the American flag. While Wise kept on handing protests and demands to the foreign minister, Rousseau took matters into his own hands by deliberate affronts to his hosts during two public holidays in November and December: the baptism of the emperor's daughter and the ruler's birthday. Rio's houses were fully illuminated on both occasions, but Wise's remained obscured in darkness. All the warships fired salutes, but American batteries were silent. Of course Brazilian public opinion was inflamed.

Secretary of State Buchanan tried to excuse the conduct of Wise and Rousseau to the Brazilian chargé in Washington: "They were both smarting under the recent insult and indignity . . . in the affair of Lieutenant Davis . . . which had just been approved and justified by the Government of His Imperial Majesty, and they embraced these occasions to manifest the sense which they felt of this insult and indignity. But after all, they only omitted to perform acts of courtesy from a deep conviction of what was due to their country."

At this point Rousseau seems to have dropped out of the controversy, leaving the diplomatic battle to the undiplomatic Wise. From then to the end of his tenure as American minister, he was completely ostracized by the imperial court and the Brazilian government. Indeed, Rio recalled its chargé from Washington, in effect unofficially breaking relations with the United States. They were not restored until Rousseau carried Wise home in the *Columbia* in September 1847, shortly after the arrival of the minister's successor.[6]

Argentina, 1831–1854
Commanders Silas Duncan and George W. Rodgers at the Falkland Islands, 1831–1832

Although sighted by an English mariner as early as 1592, the Falkland, or Malvinas, Islands have drawn international attention only in 1982, when the Argentine-British conflict recalled the Argentine-American clash 150 years before. In 1766 Britain occupied the islands but after a short time withdrew its garrison. Subsequent feeble Spanish attempts to colonize them failed, but in 1820 Argentina sent a frigate there to assert its right to the entire archipelago. By the mid-1820s Louis Vernet, a naturalized Argentine, settled at Port Soledad (East Falkland) and prospered, shipping sealskins and other commodities to Buenos Aires. In 1828 he was ceded the islands, told to set up a colony within three years, exempted from taxation, and granted a fishing monopoly for 20 years. A year later he was appointed "political and military governor" of the Falklands. Reportedly concerned by the potential decimation of the seals, his most profitable natural resource, he soon issued a proclamation forbidding foreign vessels, on pain of confiscation, to fish, hunt, or seal anywhere in his domains.

This was a challenge sure to be defied by Americans who had whaled and sealed along those shores for decades. In 1830 Captain Gilbert R. Davison of Stonington, Connecticut, arrived at the Falklands in his schooner, the *Harriet*. In July 1831 he was arrested by Matthew Brisbane, Vernet's British-born second in command, he and his crew imprisoned, his ship seized, and his cargo of sealskins and other items sold to the master of a British merchantman. Within a month the *Breakwater*, another ship out of Stonington, showed up and was apprehended by Vernet's men, although 48 hours later some of her people regained control of the vessel and headed for home with their tale of woe. Almost simultaneously with the *Breakwater*, the *Superior*, a New York City ship, shared the fate of the *Harriet*. Her crew was incarcerated and her cargo of 900 sealskins expropriated by Vernet. Most of the Americans were forced to accompany their captor in a British vessel to Buenos Aires for trial.

Arriving there on 20 November, Davison was able to elude his guards and make his way to the home of George W. Slacum, the resident U.S. consul, who aided him in lodging a protest with Foreign Minister Tomás Manuel de Anchorena, asserting that Argentina was responsible for "all losses" suffered by those in the *Harriet*. Meanwhile, Woodbine Parish, British chargé in Buenos Aires, informed the Americans that Argentina had no valid claim to the Falklands, for Britain had never relinquished its title to them. Undoubtedly this stiffened Slacum's decision that somehow the Argentines must be forced into compliance with his wishes. On 29 November the firepower to accomplish this appeared with Silas Duncan's *Lexington*, the commander having heard about Vernet's actions while cruising off Uruguay.

By this time the *Breakwater* had returned to the United States with the tidings (which Jackson had learned from earlier newspapers) that Argentina was claiming the Falklands and as a result the nation's shipping would probably be threatened. Therefore, months before Americans knew that their sealers were being imprisoned, Secretary of the Navy Levi Woodbury had dispatched Duncan in the *Lexington* to reinforce the Brazil Squadron under orders "to protect the commerce and citizens of the United States and maintain the National character by all lawful and honorable terms." The arrival of the *Breakwater* and information about Vernet impelled the president to take additional measures. In his message of 6 December 1831 he said, "In the course of the present year, one of our vessels engaged in the pursuit of a trade which we have always enjoyed without molestation has been captured by a band acting, as they pretend, under the authority of the Government of Buenos Aires." He added that he was sending south another man-of-war and that he would soon appoint "a minister to enquire into the nature of the circumstances and also the claim, if any, that is set up by that Government [Argentina] to those islands." The ship selected was the sloop *Enterprise*, under Commander George W. Rodgers, and the diplomat chosen was Francis Baylies, a former Massachusetts congress-man.

To return to Buenos Aires: Duncan, Slacum, and Davison met on 3 December to devise a plan that would compel the Argentines to reach an agreement. Their note demanded that all American property seized be returned and that Vernet be instructed to stop the further harassment of American shipping. No satisfactory reply came from Anchorena, so on the 9th the *Lexington* sailed for Port Soledad in the Falklands with hostile intent, arriving there on the 28th. On the morning of 1 January 1832 Duncan arrested Brisbane (Vernet had remained in Buenos Aires) and sent ashore marines to rescue the Americans still imprisoned there, while the *Lexington*'s guns remained leveled at the settlement. The bloodless op-eration went off with precision. The Americans were liberated while six of Vernet's employees were joining Brisbane in chains. Some cannon were spiked, weapons and ammunition either appropriated or destroyed, and looting occurred. Then Duncan informed the colonists that they were all to be evacuated, and that his men would help them in packing up and storing their goods in the *Lexington*. He departed on the 22nd for Uru-guay, "with 20 men, 8 women, 10 children, and 7 prisoners as passengers." Was Duncan ashamed or at least doubtful about the legality of what he had done at Port Soledad? It is possibly significant that the *Lexington*'s log contains not a word about what happened during the three weeks he spent there.

The Argentines were soon aware of what the Americans had done in the Falklands and exploded in collective rage. As reprinted in the *Buenos Aires British Packet*, their government issued a proclamation stating that Duncan had invaded "our new Colony," and some of its inhabitants "fled terrified to the interior of the island; others were violently torn from their homes . . . and others, natives and our fellow-citizens, are conducted as prisoners to the U. States" to be tried there. Since Duncan was beyond their reach, the Argentines had to content themselves with ousting Consul Slacum as *persona non grata*, and in so doing broke diplomatic relations with the United States.

While there was some adverse reaction in the American press about these Falkland events, many newspapers supported the aggression. An American living in Argentina wrote a long letter to the *New York Com-mercial Advertiser*, rejoicing in the eradication of Port Soledad and praising "the course [Duncan] pursued at the Islands, retaking all the American property that could be identified, and seizing upon the persons of those who plundered it." He stressed that Vernet "did not molest the English sealers" and laid into the newly independent South American nations that "look for a forbearance from us that they do not from any other nation."

The essential issue for Duncan was how the administration would regard his activities, which had gone well beyond his instructions. He need not have worried. In his *Report* for 1831 Woodbury endorsed, although unenthusiastically, his occupation of the islands. But the secretary also told Baylies, "It is proper you should . . . know that the President has signified to Captain [sic] Duncan that he entirely approves of his conduct, under the circumstances which he details."

Despite its diplomatic rupture with Buenos Aires, Washington continued efforts to achieve its ends, by this time well hamstrung by Duncan's bellicosity. During April 1832 Commander George W. Rodgers came there in the *Enterprise*, returning as a pacifistic offering the seven men whom Duncan had removed from Port Soledad. It did not matter, for Rodgers could get nowhere, because Argentine public opinion was still too much in arms to permit friendly relations. Nor could the advent of Chargé Baylies in June alter the situation. The letters that passed between him and Manuel Vicente de Maza, acting foreign minister, seem to have been discussing two disparate topics when they passed each other en route without making any meaningful contact. Baylies pounded away on the theme that Americans had sealed, fished, and whaled in the Falklands for generations, while pressing for an Argentine disavowal of Vernet's seizures and compensation for his illegalities. Maza, on the other hand, declared that no other issues could even be contemplated until atonement had been made for Duncan's behavior. The disgusted chargé told the secretary of state that "we have attempted to soothe and conciliate and coax these wayward & petulant fools long enough." He soon added that "no hope of redress and no option but humiliation" remained, and left the country permanently.

The Argentine-American dispute was settled by an unexpected third party. Shortly before he left, Baylies had conversed with the British Minister to Argentina, informing him that the United States had no claim to the Falklands except for the right to fish there, and he asked whether, if Britain took over the archipelago, that right would be granted. In effect the Englishman promised that an authorization to continue the practice would be given. He also predicted that his government would soon do something to put into effect its claim to the islands. He was correct; London had been kept up-to-date as to affairs in lower South America, and responded to a rumor that Washington was considering setting up a naval base in the Falklands to protect its commerce. Over New Year's 1832–1833 the British warships *Clio* and *Tyne* sailed into Port Soledad, and their commanders forced the surrender of a small Argentine warship there, in this manner commencing British rule over the islands, which soon became permanent.

Argentina tried to gain American support in its protest against the British annexation by pointing out that the seizure of the Falklands was contrary to the Monroe Doctrine. But relations between the two nations remained so chilly that Washington responded that the incident did not mean English "occupation" but rather "re-occupation," because Buenos Aires had no creditable claim to them. Nor could the Argentines succeed with Great Britain. Over the years their continual objections to the retention of what they called "Las Islas Malvinas" were either ignored or refuted by a succession of foreign ministers in London. Indeed, the ownership of the Falklands-Malvinas is still legally unresolved, even after the temporary Argentine occupation of the islands in 1982 and the quickly following British reconquest.[7]

Commander William F. Lynch at the Falkland Islands, 1854

There was one later—and very minor—U.S. naval diplomatic event in the archipelago. During 1854 crews from the American whalers *Hudson* and *Washington* landed on the islands and poached for eight months. Their captains were arrested by the British for "killing a large number of [wild] hogs," and their vessels confiscated. The American resident consul notified the navy's Brazil Squadron about this development, and Commander William F. Lynch in the *Germantown* was dispatched to the spot. He sent the governor of the islands a "very discourteous" message, while keeping his guns trained on the courthouse where the American captains were being tried. Understandably, the nervous authorities contented themselves with fines of only £22 for each, under the circumstances little more than slaps on the wrist. London later expressed remorse for the arrests and liberated the two whaling ships, but demanded in return an apology for Lynch's verbal excesses; evidently, however, no regrets were ever sent by the Department of State.[8]

Commodore John B. Nicolson off Montevideo, 1838–1839

As discussed above, the inconclusive war with Brazil that Argentina had fought during 1826 and 1828 had had little effect save to bring about the independence of Uruguay. Shortly thereafter, for the first but most assuredly not the last time, Argentina fell under the sway of a military dictator, in this case Juan Manuel de Rosas, who ruled from 1829 to

1852. He trod the path blazed by Santa Anna and so many other Latin-American "*caudillos*," earning his chevrons as something of a liberal reformer, but becoming more arbitrary and bloodthirsty the longer he remained in power. Rosas set up a secret terroristic society called "*Mazorca*" ("Ear of Maize"), which moved ruthlessly against the dictator's foes, real or imagined. By the time some 5,000 Argentines had been killed, many of them by garroting, the organization became popularly known as "*más horca*" ("more hanging"). Nor was Rosas any more peacefully inclined in his foreign relations. He kept his neighbors in turmoil by attacking in particular Bolivia and Uruguay.

These convulsions naturally interfered with international commerce and aroused antagonism in Europeans and Americans. The French were the most offended, for they were bitter about their inability to receive most-favored-nation status from Argentina, a privilege already won by the English.

Late in March 1838, without a declaration of war, Admiral Leblanc (first names are not given in the documentation) announced a blockade of the entire Argentine littoral along the vast mouth of the Rio de la Plata and extended it far enough east to include Uruguay. That October he struck hard at Rosas by capturing the strategic little island of Martín Garcia, located where the Paraná River joins the Plata near Buenos Aires. Meanwhile the U.S. Consul in the Argentine capital notified the secretary of state, "The blockade is efficiently maintained, and very strictly enforced" by four French warships.

Commodore John B. Nicolson, commanding the Brazil Squadron from the *Independence*, had to be concerned about some of his more trigger-happy younger officers. Lieutenant Hugh Y. Purviance in the *Dolphin* discovered that the commander of a French corvette had trapped the American merchantman *Fleet* in Montevideo harbor and was threatening to move in to take her. Purviance was willing to fight, and his and the French ships cleared for action, but the more cautious Frenchman talked him into turning the case over to Leblanc. Hostilities were averted when the admiral permitted the *Fleet* to leave without challenge. Nicolson and Leblanc themselves clashed in April 1839. The U.S. trading ships *America* and *Eliza Davidson* sailed from Montevideo for a port in extreme southern Argentina. Leblanc had them apprehended at their destination and brought back for confiscation, but released them after Nicolson pointed out that as announced the blockade applied only to the environs of the Rio de la Plata and had no application hundreds of miles to the south.

As Nicolson said to the secretary, "I see no probable termination of this war and blockade which is so injurious to the commerce of all neutrals." He offered his *Fairfield* as a meeting place for the disputants, hoping thereby to mediate their differences. He failed, because as one authority succinctly puts it, "French terms proved unacceptable to the stubborn Rosas; the dictator's counterproposals were inadmissible to the obstinate French." Furthermore, the navy secretary took exception to this diplomatic endeavor, writing Nicolson that "such interferences . . . are delicate matters unless in accordance with express instructions, as they may, sometimes, not accord with the policy of the Government." Conceding that Paulding is correct, it is hard to fault the commodore for trying to end a conflict potentially so destructive to his country's commerce.

Nicolson arrived home in the *Independence* during April 1840 to find that the Van Buren administration showed little interest in what was taking place so far away, even though it applied to the Americas. The United States had nothing to do with the solution of the crisis. But during the next October, partly through the good offices of the British, the French lifted their two-and-a-half-year blockade of Argentina and restored Martín Garcia Island to it. In response, Rosas granted most-favored-nation status to France.[9]

Captain Philip Voorhees off Montevideo, 1844

The lifting of France's blockade of Argentina in 1840 did nothing to ease international tensions along the Rio de la Plata. Dictator Rosas, allying himself with Manuel Oribe, a foe of the Uruguayan president, commenced an intermittent blockade of Montevideo that dragged on for no less than nine years (1843–1852), much to the dismay of European trading interests. In the face of persistent Anglo-French opposition, Rosas expressed a desire for better relations with the United States, in effect broken ever since the Falkland Islands dispute a decade before. This initiative coincided with similar aspirations in Washington, for the Polk administration hoped in this way to pick up a few trumps that might be useful against London or Paris.

These lower-South American troubles spared, relatively speaking, American trade in that area, enabling the U.S. Navy to stay aloof from involvement there until September 1844, when Captain Philip Voorhees spectacularly overreacted to a situation that he should have handled pacifistically. He had sailed in the frigate *Congress* to reinforce Commodore Daniel Turner's Brazil Squadron, and would soon show himself to be quick-tempered and impulsive. Even worse, he was as ready to violate specific orders as thoroughly as any of his naval colleagues. Turner had warned Voorhees that he must be "extremely particular in all your *Official & Private* intercourse with the MonteVidean and Buenos Ayres Govern-

Philip F. Voorhees
(Collection of the Maryland Historical Society, Baltimore)

ments, bearing always in mind that it is not only the policy of our Government, but their earnest desire, to maintain a strict and unqualified neutrality in all things relating to the Belligerents."

While Voorhees was off Montevideo on 29 September, Oribe's one-gun schooner *Sancala*, flying only Uruguayan colors, put out from the city with letters for Juan Fitton, the Argentine commodore. Spotting some fishing vessels, the *Sancala* detoured to pursue one. The panicky fishermen sought safety by ramming and climbing aboard the New York merchantman *Rosalba*, anchored about 300 yards from the *Congress*. As the *Sancala* approached, her crew let loose some musket shots at the escapees that bit into the woodwork of the *Rosalba*. Watching all this, Voorhees concluded at once that since the *Sancala* was not showing both the Uruguayan and Argentine flags, as was customarily done by the blockading squadron, she must be a pirate. Furthermore, since she had committed an act of aggres-

sion against an American vessel, he decided to seize her. He had also
noticed that the *Sancala* was stopping off at Fitton's flagship, actually
only to deliver mail, but to Voorhees it seemed adequate proof of Argentine
complicity in the affair. He sent his boats to chase and take the *Sancala*,
arrest her people, and bring the ship back to the *Congress*. Next he ran
down and captured the little brig *Republicano*, sent a boat to receive the
surrender of the schooner *Nueve de Julio*, and returned to confront Fitton
in the *Vienticinco de Mayo*. He put a cannonball behind the flagship;
Fitton saved his honor by firing one blank shot before pulling down his
colors. Voorhees had bagged the entire Argentine blockading squadron.

When he faced Fitton in the *Congress*, Voorhees demanded to know
the reason why the *Sancala* had acted hostilely toward the United States.
The Argentine claimed that he could not explain her action; that vessel
was Oribe's, he said, and he had no responsibility for her. The American
decided to retain only the *Sancala*, releasing the three Argentine men-of-
war, although they were not able to resume blockading duties until 2
October.

On the 22nd Voorhees continued his feud with Rosas by informing
Fitton's successor as Argentine commodore that the United States would
not respect his reimposed blockade and would not permit his warships to
search American merchantmen, since the British and French were allowed
to have their own men-of-war accomplish that task. Everyone then settled
down to await the U.S. commodore. At Rio on 21 October Turner had
learned what Voorhees had done, and he pulled into Montevideo a week
later in his flagship, the *Raritan*. He promptly set to work trying to repair
as much of the damage inflicted upon Buenos Aires–Washington relations
as possible. On 3 November he notified the Argentines that he was reversing Voorhees and would obey their blockade instructions. Although
he did not actually surrender the vessel until late in November, he told
Buenos Aires that he was returning the *Sancala* solely as an act of friendship—thereby sparing Voorhees from any implication of guilt, although
what he may have said to his subordinate in private may readily be imagined. Turner was eventually rewarded for his endeavors by praise from
Secretary of the Navy George Bancroft.

The U.S. chargé in Buenos Aires wrote that Voorhees had "acted with
rashness" and that the Argentines were "much incensed at his conduct."
Rosas's minister in Washington demanded "complete satisfaction and
reparation" for the *Sancala* and the temporary loss of the blockading
squadron, adding that Voorhees must be recalled. Secretary of State John
C. Calhoun expressed regrets about the incident and informed him that
the captain had already been brought home to face charges. There he was

subjected to three separate courts-martial, at the end of which he was sentenced to dismissal from the navy, although Polk reduced this draconic verdict to a five-year suspension, which would be lifted in 1847. K. Jack Bauer, the recognized authority on this affair, says that Voorhees had wrecked his career. That is not so, for he was given command of the East India Squadron and served in that capacity in 1849–1851. It was what he did then that finished his active duty with the navy.[10]

Captain Garrett J. Pendergast off Buenos Aires, 1845

William Brent, the new American chargé d'affaires in Buenos Aires, arrived there shortly after Voorhees had damaged U.S.-Argentine relations so much. He quickly closed the breach, becoming an enthusiastic advocate of Rosas. By early 1845 the British and French had become infuriated by the long-standing Argentine interference with their trade because of Rosas's blockade of Uruguayan ports not controlled by Manuel Oribe, his ally. Under the leadership of the French admiral, the Europeans announced that they would not obey the tightened blockade just put in force off Buenos Aires. This was anathema to Brent, who protested to the Frenchman "in almost threatening language." He also called upon Captain Garrett J. Pendergast in the USS *Boston*, the highest ranking U.S. naval officer in that quarter, to join him in his objections. Pendergast refused to do more than to ask that the Argentines give American merchantmen the same immunities from blockade regulations that the Europeans were taking for their own carriers. Brent may have been temporarily defeated, but some weeks later Pendergast was overruled by the State Department and informed that he was "obligated to respect the belligerent rights of Buenos Aires."

When relations between Rosas and the Europeans further deteriorated by midsummer, Brent tried to resurrect the Monroe Doctrine by applying it to this controversy. Apparently he had convinced himself that Britain in particular had some sinister empire-building project under way in lower South America. Again he demanded naval backing from Pendergast, writing him that he should tell the European admirals that "the declaration of a blockade by the agencies of a non-belligerent government was contrary to the law of nations."

But the captain remained unconvinced by the chargé's lecture in international law, choosing instead to recall his orders of the previous spring that he must follow a course of the strictest neutrality. To be sure, he was foiled when he tried to reach American mercantile equality with the Europeans, for both foreign admirals summarily rejected his appeal. Nevertheless, Pendergast's unwillingness to join Brent in becoming a mouthpiece for Rosas was mirrored in Washington. The new Polk administration, with a possible Anglo-American war over Oregon in prospect and with aspirations for territorial expansion in the southwest at the expense of Mexico, had no interest in any intensified meddling in distant lower South America. Instead, the president had already promulgated in his annual message of December 1845 the "Polk Corollary to the Monroe Doctrine," asserting that—unlike Monroe's original statement—it applied only to North America, not the entire Western Hemisphere. The conclusion of this disagreement was anticlimactic. Brent was soon recalled in semi-disgrace, and by 1850 the British and French had at least temporarily lost enthusiasm for South American adventure and relaxed their anti-Argentine endeavors.[11]

Paraguay, 1855–1859
Lieutenants Thomas J. Page and William N. Jeffries at Asunción et al., 1855

Paraguay, located amid Brazil, Argentina, and Bolivia hundreds of miles from the sea, was terra incognita for almost all Americans, because its first dictator, who had ruled alone since that country's winning of independence in 1814 to his death in 1840, had isolated it almost completely from the rest of the world. But Paraguay began to inch into the nineteenth century under Carlos Antonio Lopez, *caudillo* from 1840 to 1862, who, inviting foreign assistance, launched a program of economic expansion, especially in digging canals and improving overland transportation. The resultant impact of American penetration into Paraguay began as practically a one-man show. Edward A. Hopkins, adventurer par excellence, resigned his U.S. Navy commission in 1845 and managed to persuade President Polk to appoint him special agent to Paraguay that same year. After walking overland from Brazil to Asunción to examine the country, Hopkins met and at first established warm relations with Lopez. He asked the president for a fifteen-year monopoly on navigation of the Paraguay River, as well as licenses to sell bricks, cigars, lumber, and textiles. He also kept pestering the Department of State for an official diplomatic position, and in 1851 he was named consul to Asunción. At the same time Lopez appointed him Paraguayan Minister to Washington, implying that should Hopkins arrange for American recognition of his country, he would grant his economic requests. This he was able to do, and returning to Asunción he formed "The United States and Paraguay Navigation Company," capitalized at $100,000, which operated through 1853 and 1854.

By that time Lopez was having second thoughts about the extent of the American's control of his economy. Even worse, Hopkins was becoming practically unbearable to him personally. Once, after his brother had been struck by a Paraguayan soldier, Hopkins strode into the dictator's office. When Lopez saw "the stalwart American before him, in top boots and spurs, with his hat on and whip in hand, violently gesticulating and demanding satisfaction, he was both alarmed and angry." Although the soldier was punished, Hopkins was unable to get the public apology upon which he insisted. This permanently soured his friendship with Lopez, who struck back by refusing to relicense Hopkins's factories and revoking his exequator (legal consular authorization).

Enter now Lieutenant Thomas Jefferson Page, bumptiousness personified, although he had some reason for his smug self-satisfaction. His naval and scientific experience in foreign assignments and coastal surveys impelled Navy Secretary John P. Kennedy to send him to Paraguay in the little 375-ton side-wheel steamer *Water Witch* "to explore, for scientific purposes, the various sources of the Rio de la Plata, as far as permission was granted . . . by the governments of those countries." Page was a poor choice for this command; his letters show him to have been impulsive, touchy, and filled with constant irritation if his demands or suggestions were not complied with immediately.

After some travail Page managed to take his *Water Witch* down to lower South America. He found that the Brazilians viewed his mission with distrust and he could get permission to proceed only halfway up the Paraguay River. He did better in Buenos Aires, for the Argentines practically gave him carte blanche to explore its inland waterways. He then went on to Asunción, where he met Lopez. The president cordially allowed him to take his vessel up the Paraguay as far as the town of Bahia Negra, near the point where the borders of Bolivia, Brazil, and Paraguay join. Unfortunately for his future association with the dictator, the lieutenant ignored this restriction and in November 1853 steamed farther north up the Paraguay to the Brazilian settlement of Corumbá. On his return to Asunción he was reproached for his disobedience by Lopez, who asserted that by his action he had set a precedent which the Brazilians could use to roam freely through Paraguay's inland waters. Page responded that since his mission was scientific only, no precedent had been established. The president relented enough to grant permission to explore rivers to the northwest, a feat that Page accomplished over the next few months. But seeds of suspicion about the lieutenant's judgment and trustworthiness had been planted in Lopez's mind.

Some time before, Hopkins had come back to Paraguay and discovered that the dictator's hatred of him had actually increased. Fearing that he might lose possession of some questionable titles to Paraguayan property,

Thomas Jefferson Page
(Naval Historical Center)

he appealed to Page for protection against "the blind vengeance" of the dictator. Page concluded that he must protect American citizens. Back in Asunción the lieutenant fell into a puerile quarrel with Lopez's foreign minister because of his arrogant refusal to have his letters in English put into Spanish, although he had an interpreter present. On 29 September he left the capital, carrying with him Hopkins (dubious titles in hand) and other American employees of the United States and Paraguay Navigation Company. According to a story in the *New York Times*, Page, apprehending some possible perfidy from Lopez, maneuvered the *Water Witch* in front of the presidential palace as if he might open fire. Although the ship departed without incident, it left behind a frightened Lopez, whose hostility was solidified and who four days later issued a proclamation barring all foreign men-of-war from Paraguayan waters.

Within two weeks Washington sent orders to Page for him to arrange the exchange of ratifications of a Paraguayan-American treaty concluded in 1853 but still not formally put into effect. Respecting the ban of Lopez, he kept away the *Water Witch* and communicated with Asunción through one of his lieutenants. But once more Page's high-handed refusal to use Spanish ended any possibility of ratification exchanges. The disgruntled American officer resumed his explorations, concentrating on Argentine rivers. But in January 1855 Page changed his mind and decided to flout the Paraguayan ban against foreign warships; documentation does not satisfactorily explain why. He took off on another expedition with some of his crew in a smaller vessel. Before departure he appointed the newly arrived Lieutenant William N. Jeffers, an officer cut from Page's cloth, to take the *Water Witch* up the Paraná River a hundred or so miles. This, of course, was a deliberate and direct violation of Lopez's restriction and quickly proved to be a serious error in judgment.

On 1 February the *Water Witch* came toward the Paraguayan brick fort called Itapirú, located on a bluff overlooking the two branches of the river, one channel hugging the Argentine side to the north and the other the Paraguayan side to the south. At first Jeffers stayed to the north, but the ship ran aground, so he backed water and steamed up the south channel, above which loomed Itapirú. A Paraguayan in a canoe came out from shore with a copy of Lopez's proclamation against foreign warships, but as it was in Spanish, Jeffers declined accepting it. Nor did he bother to try to understand a Paraguayan officer who shouted to them, in Spanish, of course, to retreat. Two or three blank shots were fired from the fort as warnings, but according to the Paraguayans were greeted with no more than "loud shouts of laughter" from the Americans.

How can one comprehend the thought processes of Jeffers as he neared Itapirú's cannon? The *Water Witch*'s entire armament consisted not of the five heavy guns that men-of-war her size usually bore, but of three small brass howitzers, useful only for frightening away Indian attacks. The lieutenant received what he was asking for when a cannon ball plowed into the helm of the *Water Witch*, mortally wounding Quartermaster Samuel Chaney. Continued salvos from the fort hulled the American ship ten times, although only the first shot did much damage. Jeffers retaliated with his popguns, but without effect. The *Water Witch* went beyond Itapirú but her panic-stricken Argentine pilot warned Jeffers that she would soon go aground, so he had to take the vessel past the Paraguayan fortress once more before sailing down river to report to Page.

When he learned what had happened, Page became almost apoplectic and told the secretary that it had been "a most unprovoked, unwarrantable, and dastardly attack," as well as "a wanton outrage; the act of a Government beyond the pale of civilization." Recognizing that any effort to establish contact with Lopez would be futile, Page turned his attention to the Brazil Squadron's Commodore William D. Salter, sailing to Buenos Aires to enlist his support in avenging the assault upon the *Water Witch*. Much to the lieutenant's "bitter disappointment and mortification," the commodore would do nothing, refusing to send either the *Savannah* or *Germantown* into Paraguayan territory without specific orders from the secretary. Page went over Salter's head by appealing to the department to overrule this do-nothing policy, but in vain.

Secretary Dobbin, in his *Report* for 1855, was remarkably noncommittal, saying only, "Misunderstandings of a very serious nature . . . having occurred between the officers of the *Water Witch* and the President of the Republic of Paraguay, it was deemed expedient . . . to discontinue for the present the completion of the survey of the River Paraná." President Pierce never even mentioned Page or his ship in his annual messages for 1855 and 1856. The reason may be, according to Thomas O. Flickema, the expert on nineteenth-century Paraguayan-American relations, who quotes the secretary of state: "the conduct of the *Water Witch* was wrong, and the attack on her . . . justifiable." Marcy probably persuaded the president that the best way to handle the affair was to ignore it. It would remain for the next administration to do something about Page, the *Water Witch*, and Lopez's Paraguay.[12]

Commodore William B. Shubrick at Asunción, 1859

In sharp contrast to Pierce's hands-off attitude toward Lopez and his nation, President Buchanan became much more militant in his first annual message (1857). Bemoaning Asunción's failure to ratify the treaty of 1853 (a special agent sent for that purpose in 1856 had been rebuffed), he called the assault upon the *Water Witch* "unjustifiable"; charged that American businessmen in Paraguay had had their property expropriated in "an insulting and arbitrary manner"; and concluded by asking Congress to give him "authority to use other means in the event of a refusal." Six months later Congress, while appropriating $10,000 for the expenses of a commissioner to Paraguay, granted the president the authority "to adopt such measures and use such force as, in his judgment, may be necessary" should the Paraguayans be recalcitrant. Many reasons have been given for the sudden shift in administrative attitudes toward Lopez. It seems most likely that Buchanan, by foreign adventure, was trying to arouse latent American nationalism so threatened by burgeoning southern sectionalism, as was his motive in continually urging the annexation of Cuba.

By the summer of 1859 Judge James B. Bowlin, former minister to Colombia, had been named commissioner. He was ordered to meet Lopez in Asunción and demand apologies for the firing on the *Water Witch*; get compensation for the family of Samuel Chaney, killed at Fort Itapirú; either gain the ratification of the 1853 treaty or write a new one; and receive reparations for the losses incurred by Hopkins. Should Lopez refuse, Bowlin was to tell him that a U.S. blockade would shut off his country's access to the sea, followed by his warning of a probable naval attack upriver on Asunción itself.

Bowlin was given a most impressive-looking warship escort. William B. Shubrick, an elderly but extremely competent officer, was appointed commodore and given no less than nineteen men-of-war, mounting some 200 guns and carrying 2,500 sailors and marines. Commanding the flagship *Sabine* under Shubrick was none other than Captain Thomas J. Page, who had concluded his expedition to South America late in 1855. He was delighted that he was in position to help repay Lopez for his treatment of him and his ship. By December the fleet, up to that time the largest aggregation of U.S. Navy warships in history, had rendezvoused off Montevideo.

Yet for Page and other lovers of excitement, tension, and violence, what finally happened was anticlimactic. By January 1859 Bowlin had established contact with López, and remembering the president's ban on foreign war vessels in his nation's rivers, he even offered to come to Asunción overland if necessary. But López permitted him the comfort of water transportation, so leaving behind 17 of his ships, Shubrick took Bowlin to the capital in the USS *Fulton*, accompanied by the *Water Witch*. Within a week in early February the commissioner and the president had reached a relatively satisfactory agreement, appreciated by almost all concerned. A new treaty permitting American merchantmen to visit Paraguay's riverine ports was signed and quickly put into effect. Lopez apologized for the affront to the *Water Witch* and authorized the payment of $10,000 to Chaney's family. Lastly, the two negotiators agreed that the claims of Hopkin's company should be decided by arbitration within a year (although Paraguay never paid a penny). Bowlin and Shubrick left the capital on 10 February, their work done.

How did the United States and Paraguay manage to reach so acceptable an understanding after five straight years of almost total estrangement? Some help came from the Argentines, apprehensive that hostilities in the Rio de la Plata might somehow involve them. But one has to agree with Thomas O. Flickema that the main responsibility for this success rested on Bowlin and Lopez themselves.

The American had decided some time earlier that a conciliatory attitude on his part could allay the suspicions and hatreds of the Paraguayan president, kept at such a high pitch by Hopkins, Page, and Jeffers. Bowlin had not tried to maintain the right to journey to the capital by water, and expressed a willingness to have all his correspondence translated into Spanish. He had insisted upon conducting the negotiations by himself, politely turning down an Argentine offer to mediate, afraid that Latin solidarity would impel the other parties toward an anti-American stand. Most important, after surveying the evidence, he had concluded that the damage demands made by Hopkins and his associates were unwarranted.

The Paraguayan had also been conciliatory. He had permitted the Americans to visit him in two warships, and once the promise of Spanish translation had been given, did not require it. It should be emphasized that the Paraguayan president's decision to settle the disputes amicably was probably not due to the presence of so much American naval fire power. Impressive though Shubrick's armada might have looked on paper, Lopez must have known that it was ill equipped to fight a war in South America a thousand miles from blue water. All Shubrick's ships would have had much difficulty proceeding toward Asunción. Not only would they have been plagued by sandbars and shallows, but they would have been subject to constant attack along the banks of the Paraná and Paraguay. With a mere 2,500 fighting men available, there was no way that the United States could have defeated López's army. Yet even though Paraguay was quite self-sufficient, a tight American blockade at the mouth of the Rio de la Plata could hurt the nation's economy. Furthermore, war with the United States might invite assaults from greedy Latin-American neighbors. So López made the essential compromises: expressing regrets for the *Water Witch* affair, paying compensation for Chaney's death, and signing a treaty favorable to United States interests.

Navy Secretary Isaac Toucey understandably sounded his own horn in his *Report for 1859* in writing that the accomplishment at Asunción had been due to "the zeal, energy, discretion, and courageous and gallant bearing of Flag-officer Shubrick" and his subordinates. Toucey also said that his ships were "in a position to operate against Paraguay." That is nonsense; he admitted that the main fleet had gone only a little above Rosario, Argentina, still hundreds of miles from Asunción.

President Buchanan's emphasis was askew in his report of Paraguayan developments in his 1859 message. To be sure, he did say that Bowlin had "successfully accomplished all the objects of his mission." But he joined Toucey in stressing the navy's contribution a good deal more, also heaping praise on the expedition: "It consisted of 19 armed vessels, great and small . . . all under the command of the veteran and gallant Shubrick. . . . The appearance of so large a force fitted out in such a prompt manner, in the far-distant waters of the La Plata, and the admirable conduct of the officers and men employed in it, have had a happy effect in favor of our country throughout all that remote portion of the world." The president should have accentuated the civilian role. There seems to be no question but that in Paraguay in 1859 Shubrick, the naval officer, although attentive and supportive, was of secondary importance compared to Bowlin, the diplomat.[13]

U.S. Nonbelligerent Naval Landings at Argentina and Uruguay, 1833–1858

Captain M. T. Woolsey, et al., at Buenos Aires and Montevideo

On lower South America's east coast, from the establishment of Latin-American independence to the outbreak of the U.S. Civil War, there were four American naval landings, two in Argentina and two in Uruguay. These occurred when local law and order broke down and there were U.S. and sometimes other warships nearby. The commandant would be asked by those in at least nominal control to send sailors and marines ashore to help stop the disorders. Since that officer would also be protecting American lives and property, he would be glad to comply, either singly or in concert with European detachments. During 1833, amid the confusion attending the advent to power of Juan Manuel de Rosas, Captain M. T. Woolsey landed fighting men from the USS *Lexington* at Buenos Aires to quell the disturbance. In 1852, when the dictatorship of Rosas was disintegrating, Captain Isaac McKeever in the *Jamestown* emulated what Woolsey had done at the same place. The only direct connections that the navy had with Uruguay prior to 1861 were landings at Montevideo by Commander William F. Lynch in the *Germantown* during 1855 and by Commodore French Forrest with the *St. Louis* and *Falmouth* in 1858. So much alike were all four that a description of Forrest's experience fits the others.

During a Uruguayan civil war in 1858, a revolutionary faction was approaching the capital. The government announced its doubt that it could protect foreign persons and possessions in the disorders expected soon to occur. It appealed to the resident European and American consuls to ask their respective naval forces on hand to act in its behalf for that purpose. Forrest, commanding the Brazil Squadron in his flagship, accompanied by the sloop, was in Montevideo harbor, along with a few European warships. He was selected by the other commanders to take ashore a force, primarily American, that occupied the city on 2 January. According to the U.S. Secretary of the Navy, "strict neutrality toward both factions was observed, and the detachment concerned itself with the protection of foreigners." After the surrender of the revolutionaries, Forrest was able to send his men back to their ships on the 12th, "without incident."

Since the four landings briefly described above were examples of American naval interventions abroad, they should be mentioned in a work such as this, but they need no detailed coverage. Like Forrest's landing in 1858 their effects on diplomacy were negligible.[14]

Peru, 1831–1854
Captain John D. Sloat and Commodore Charles C. B. Thompson at Callao, 1831

No sooner had the Spaniards given up, at least for a time, forcible attempts to recover their lost American empire that Peru commenced to follow the trail being blazed by so many other countries from Mexico to Argentina and Chile. Political instability in Lima became chronic during the so-called "Age of the *Caudillos.*"

One general succeeded another only to be toppled by a third. Indeed, there were 40 such coups in less than the first half-century of Peruvian independence. When Simón Bolívar, having helped oust the Spanish, went north in the mid-1820s, the Peruvians soon rose against the officer that the "Liberator" had placed over them. This led to a brief war between Colombia and Peru, in which the latter came off a slight loser. Out of this crisis Agustín Gamarra emerged as the temporary number one in Peru. In 1830 he became president, selecting as his second in command a political chameleon, the "notoriously unreliable" General La Fuente (the records give no first names).

A year or so later Gamarra briefly left the capital, and the vice-president assumed the top position. According to *Niles' Weekly Register* the president himself organized a plot to kill La Fuente, fearful that he might be overthrown by his subordinate, although there is no evidence in that direction. On the night of 16 April La Fuente was in bed, ill with a fever.

Soldiers quietly gathered and cordoned off his house, and a detachment entered to murder him. *Niles'* story has it that he was saved by his wife, who "met the ruffians, and kept them at bay some moments, by heroically seizing their bayonets with her hands, until her husband had time to escape . . . in his night clothes." He was first chased from room to room, then "out of windows," and finally "over roofs." One of his pursuers was shot by mistake, and in the resultant confusion La Fuente was able to flee and make his way the next day to Callao.

At five o'clock in the morning of 18 April, Captain Sloat was wakened in the *St. Louis* and told that La Fuente had reached his ship after hours in a canoe, still clad in his nightshirt. Sloat "provided him with clothes" and reported that he had reached a "perfect understanding" with him "that I am only to afford him asylum against the mob, but, if demanded by the regular government, to be delivered up."

Pacific Squadron Commodore Charles C. B. Thompson, in his flagship, the *Guerrière*, expressed to the American chargé in Lima opinions that may be easily applauded: "I highly appreciate the motives which influenced Captain Sloat to afford protection to the general under the circumstances recited, and commend his conduct as honorable, benevolent, and discreet in all parts." Nonetheless, he warned in regard to La Fuente: "I can, therefore, neither *continue* to afford him protection in the squadron under my orders, or suffer him to *land at any point of Peru*, contrary to the signified wish of the government."

Despite Thompson's directive, La Fuenta remained in the *St. Louis* "for nearly a month," as Sloat said when he presented the secretary of state with a bill for $1,060, of which $960 had been "spent in entertaining" the fugitive. Unfortunately neither he nor the secretary of the navy had any contingency funds for such a purpose. President Jackson recommended that Congress appropriate the necessary funds, and one hopes that it did so.[15]

Commodores Alexander S. Wadsworth and Henry E. Ballard at Callao, 1835–1839

By the mid-1830s relations among the lower Andean nations were worsening. The Chileans had not forgotten old grudges and were now facing a new danger. They recalled that royalists from Peru had smashed their first republic in 1814, that Lima had refused to repay its share of a loan that Santiago had floated to finance San Martín's victorious battles for Peruvian liberation, and that Chile had recently fought a trade war with them. Much more ominous, from Chile's viewpoint, was the emergence of a new power to the north. This had been organized by General

Andrés Santa Cruz, a Bolivian who had considerably strengthened his country since taking control of it in 1829. Late in 1836 he managed, with the assistance of friendly Peruvians, to establish a three-nation confederation, consisting of Bolivia and a divided Peru, with a northern state centered at Lima and a southern counterpart centered at Arequipa.

Even before Santa Cruz had announced this development, the Chileans had dispatched two warships that sneaked into Callao harbor and snapped up three Peruvian men-of-war, practically the confederation's entire navy. The following November Chile declared war. Despite an initial humiliating defeat in 1837, a year later a second Chilean expedition, numbering among its 6,000 men Peruvian exiles Gamarra and La Fuente, dashed ashore to capture Lima. In January 1839 they cornered Santa Cruz and his combined army at the village of Yungay. Chile's victory was total: Santa Cruz fled with a handful of followers, and his confederation collapsed in ruins. This marked the advent of Chile as by far the best organized and most successful military state in the Andes.

Commodore Alexander S. Wadsworth, in the Pacific, seems to have raised inactivity to a fine art; in the single episode during his tenure that deserves mention, he was absent. In 1836—just as the Chileans were attacking the Peruvian navy without warning—Venture Lavalle, Santiago's consul-general in Lima, was arrested and imprisoned for a short time before being released. He went to Wadsworth's flagship *Brandywine* and asked for asylum. Since the commodore was away on an errand at the capital, he was confronted by Captain David Deacon, acting commander, who informed the Chilean that he could not come on board without "an express order from Commodore Wadsworth." The furious Lavalle promptly moved on to the French frigate *Flora*, "where he was instantly admitted, and hospitably entertained." The U.S. chargé at Lima mourned the commodore's absence, for he thought that Deacon's insulting behavior had produced for his country "great mortification, and, consequently, diminution of usefulness."

Henry E. Ballard, the new commodore, came into Callao late in May 1837 in the powerful ship of the line *North Carolina*. Without success he offered his flagship as "neutral premises" for talks between the belligerents, hoping that this might end the conflict. He did arrange for the release in his own custody of 26 American sailors imprisoned and destined "to be tried as pirates" after the Chileans had captured them in a Peruvian warship. But most of the time Ballard apparently kept the *North Carolina* and the four other ships of his fleet idle in Callao harbor, despite a presidential order to disperse as many of his vessels as possible along the coast to "afford the best means of protecting our commerce." His major spasm of activity occurred during the Chilean blockade of the Peruvian and Bolivian coasts, proclaimed in the summer of 1838. As was so often the case, Santiago lacked sufficient warships to make the blockade effective, and Ballard joined the British and French admirals in refusing to obey it until the Chilean force was strong enough to make it relatively airtight. That was that, as far as the commodore's 19-month tour was concerned. The combined work of Wadsworth and Ballard stands in rather sorry contrast to the able diplomacy conducted by Pacific Squadron commodores during 1818–1827.[16]

Commodore Charles S. McCauley at the Lobos Islands, 1852

The Lobos Islands, along Peru's extreme northern coast, and the Chincha Islands, only a few miles off Pisco near Callao, had almost perfect conditions for producing guano; the arid weather permitted layers of it to reach hundreds of feet in depth, especially in the Chinchas. By 1840 it became known that guano was 33 times richer in nitrogenous content than barnyard manure, and the rush was on. In 1860 alone 433 ships sought guano in the Chinchas, and it is estimated that from 1840 to 1875 Peru exported no less than 10,000,000 tons of it.

The initial American-Peruvian disagreement about guano happened during 1852. Secretary of State Daniel Webster argued that the Lobos Archipelago, situated some 25 miles offshore, had been discovered by an American in 1822. Furthermore, Peru had no clear title to it, since the islands were well beyond the three-mile limit that conferred right of possession "by contiguity." Harkening to his opinion, American guano ships set sail for the Lobos, and Webster arranged with President Millard Fillmore to provide naval protection for them. Tremors ran through Lima from apprehension that the United States was about to occupy the islands by force. The Peruvians were most fortunate that J. Randolph Clay, the American chargé in Lima, considered all along that their claim to the Lobos was "perfect and unquestionable." On his own initiative he asked Commodore McCauley in his frigate *Raritan* to sail north from Callao as "the best means of preventing any collision" between American guano ships and "Peruvian troops stationed there."

By that September one Boston vessel had come into the Lobos. "She was immediately *ordered off* by a Peruvian brig which was laying there, but *refused to leave*," preferring to await "the arrival of the American squadron under Commodore McCauley." A month later the commodore appeared and issued a proclamation warning guano-collecting Americans, "I have been instructed by my government . . . to abstain from protecting any vessels of the United States which may visit these islands for purposes forbidden by the decrees of the Peruvian Government, and I am forbid from aiding or abetting any citizens of the United States who may forcibly resist the execution of the laws of Peru." The commodore's pronouncement proved to be decisive, for it was followed up in Washington. Edward Everett, the new secretary of state (Webster had recently died), had restudied the Lobos question and disagreed with his predecessor. He talked Fillmore into reversing his nation's stand on the issue. The President now held that he had "to acknowledge unreservedly her [Peru's] sovereignty over the Guano Islands on her coast and in her possession." The pro-Whig *New York Times* summarized this conclusion with great enthusiasm: " . . . we feel at liberty to congratulate the Government on so speedy an adjustment of a matter which seemed pregnant with difficulty, but which has yielded to the frank and direct manner in which the Administration has met and treated it."[17]

Commander Theodorus Bailey at the Chincha Islands, 1854

Details of the finale of the guano controversy between the United States and Peru are annoyingly vague. The only positive account of Commander Theodorus Bailey's cruise is in Secretary of the Navy James C. Dobbins's *Report, 1854*. During that April Bailey sailed to the Chinchas in the *St. Mary's* and found there "about one hundred and sixteen sail of vessels, two-thirds of which were American. The presence of the *St. Mary's* had a very beneficial effect, and the masters of the large fleet of merchantmen, both English and American, expressed themselves highly gratified at the prompt and energetic action taken by Commander Bailey in regard to their complaints and grievances." The dispatches of neither the U.S. Minister to Peru nor the American Consul in Callao mention Bailey, and the navy's microfilmed letters from commanders are equally devoid of information. So Dobbins's account is all we have about this event.[18]

Summary

U.S. naval relations with Brazil started well. Sinclair, in 1818, was totally correct in ignoring threats from Rio's forts to dictate to him the movements of his own public vessel. In the Brazilian-Argentine War (1826–1828) Elliott not only gained special perquisites from Brazilian blockaders for his nation's merchantmen, but most properly refused to permit the French to search his ship for deserters. Biddle, with his usual cool professionalism, freed some American carriers, rebuffed Brazilian attempts to compel U.S. shipping to purchase bonds, and made sure that there would be no rupture of the relations between the two countries over the somewhat ridiculous Moores-Paceco fracas. Turner and Tattnall amply repaid the

Swedes in the West Indies for their lack of cooperation in the case of the *Federal* by simply capturing the privateer and escorting her into American custody. But during the mid-1840s American diplomacy in regard to Brazil soured. Turner's illicit apprehension of the U.S. slaver *Porpoise* inside Brazil's territorial limits and Rousseau's discourtesy to Rio's royal family—with U.S. Minister Wise egging on both officers in their indiscretions—did little to improve the American image in Latin America.

American naval behavior concerning Argentina was generally successful, with the signal exception of Philip Voorhees in the *Sancala* affair. Silas Duncan's truculence when he occupied the Falkland Islands may be justified by Vernet's and Brisbane's seizure there of American merchantmen, which had engaged in business unmolested for decades by Argentines or anyone else. Nor would Buenos Aires yield to any diplomatic pressure to allow foreign sealing, whaling, and fishing off that distant archipelago, even before its understandable rage following Duncan's annihilation of its "colony" in the Falklands. Having no desire to annex these islands, the United States cared little whether Argentina or Britain would take possession of them, and London had pledged that Americans would be permitted the sealing and other privileges denied by Buenos Aires. Nor did the Argentine attempt to use the Monroe Doctrine to oust the British amount to anything. Despite the language about its application to the entire Western Hemisphere, the doctrine has never been invoked below Central America and the southern shores of the Caribbean. Yet patriotic Argentines who know their own history quite naturally regard Duncan and his work in a different and baleful light. With their national fixation about the recovery of the "Malvinas," they see that that American officer took the first step toward their loss. Duncan unwittingly initiated Argentine-American hostility, which has been more constant than that between the U.S. and any other Latin-American country, having flared as recently as 1982 because of U.S. support of the British in their forceful repossession. Lynch's protection of American poachers in the Falklands during 1854 may be forgotten quickly; it made scarcely a ripple in Anglo-American relations.

John B. Nicolson seems to have proved himself a competent and diplomatic commander during the Anglo-French blockade of Argentina in 1838 and 1839. He tethered his hot-headed subordinates and persuaded the French admiral to release U.S. merchant vessels apprehended by one of his patrollers. Furthermore, it is not easy to condemn him for his attempts to suggest his flagship as the site of negotiations between the Argentines and Europeans, an offer which might have ended a conflict endangering American shipping. Perhaps he deserved better than the somewhat negative response of the Navy Department to his command in waters off the Rio de la Plata, for secretaries of the navy have typically leaned over backwards to avoid condemnation of their officers.

Diplomatically the *Sancala* crisis of 1844 was of little consequence. Rosas and his people were content with American apologies and the retribution visited upon Voorhees. But it does indicate the serious consequences which may be caused by an officer's personal failings. Voorhees had already shown himself to be an impulsive martinet, extremely hard on his underlings, and while at Port Mahon in the Balearics in 1831 had had to be rebuked and overruled by Commodore James Biddle for his impetuosity. Furthermore, he had turned into a rabid anti-Argentine, making no pretense of conducting the neutral course upon which Turner and the State Department insisted. As K. Jack Bauer wisely comments, "A more judicious officer would have detained *Sancala* pending an investigation of the attack on the *Rosalba*; demanded an explanation from Fitton before moving against his squadron; and if necessary referred the whole case to Watterson [U.S. chargé] in Buenos Aires in default of a satisfactory local solution." He concludes that during the entire nineteenth century there was "no better example of the dangers to American interests resulting from incompetent or injudicious naval officers."

The fact that Pendergast, rather than Brent, spoke for his government during the bickerings between Rosas and the Europeans is not the paramount significance of the controversy between the two Americans. It is of greater consequence as an example of the difficulty of formulating a consistent foreign program for areas located many weeks away in both transportation and communications when the diplomatic and naval arms of the government are at sword's points.

As for relations with Paraguay (1855–1859), the navy's officers unfortunately ranged from the arrogantly incompetent to the able but nonessential. The behavior of Thomas J. Page and William N. Jeffries practically defies comprehension. Page's touchy sense of his personal honor, his defiance of Lopez's restrictions, and his efforts to resort to naval violence after the *Water Witch* had been understandably fired upon demonstrate the threat to a nation's amicable foreign relations that may be inflicted by the wrong person in the wrong place. Jeffries could hardly have been more inept in defying a fort while lacking the power to subdue it; he was fortunate that his ship was not shot to pieces and his people made either casualties or prisoners. And both officers were incredibly witless in sparking a crisis by their unwillingness to use the language of their host country, even though interpreters were available. Four years later Shubrick comes off much better. His performance as both a commodore and a diplomat seems to have been impeccable. Furthermore, he was an experienced enough officer to realize that his fleet, powerful though it may have appeared, had no chance in operations so far inland. Finally, his efforts were overshadowed by the skillful negotiating of James B. Bowlin, which might well have achieved the same results even without Shubrick's presence. Enough has already been said about the temporary U.S. naval occupations of Buenos Aires and Montevideo.

American naval diplomacy along South America's west coast primarily affected Peruvians. In that area John D. Sloat was able to show the humanitarian impulses sometimes felt by his colleagues. He gave sanctuary to the fugitive Peruvian vice-president, while agreeing with Commodore Charles C. B. Thompson that he was merely protecting him temporarily from mob violence; in no way must his errand of mercy be permitted to give offense to the legal authorities in Lima. Alexander S. Wadsworth, in command during the early days of the war between Chile and the Bolivian-Peruvian Confederation in the late 1830s, appears entirely passive. Moreover, his record was sullied when a subordinate refused asylum in his flagship to the Chilean consul-general, behavior quite contrary to that of Sloat. While Henry E. Ballard, Wadsworth's successor, did make a brief attempt to mediate the war, arranged for the release of some imprisoned American sailors, and objected tepidly to some Chilean blockading rules, these were only the short-lived exceptions to the inertia of a year and a half.

In the case of Peru's guano-rich offshore possessions, Charles S. McCauley, in 1852, when he warned off American ships from collecting guano at the Lobos Islands without permission from Lima, was accentuating his government's praiseworthy recognition that Peru's claim to them was watertight. Two years later Theodorus Bailey evidently upheld the rights Americans enjoyed in working the deposits on the Chincha Islands.

CHAPTER SEVEN

Europe

1816–1861

During the years before the Civil War, in no way could the United States avoid entanglements in Europe or elsewhere whenever its interests clashed with foreign nations. A distinction is being made in this work between confrontations that arose from situations in other areas and those native to Europe itself. For instance, activities in China in which U.S. naval officers became involved during the 1840s and 1850s emerged from Far Eastern conditions and merit treatment in that context. Similarly, when the navies of Washington and Madrid glowered at one another in the Caribbean and lower South America during the early and mid-nineteenth century, rancor emanated from the Latin-American Wars of Independence and their lengthy aftermath, and have been discussed in relation to Mexico, Central America, the West Indies, and South America. But some European-American disputes lacked external linkage, and they are taken up here. In addition, this chapter is being used as something of a catchall. Throughout the period 1816–1861 Britons and Americans warily eyed each other across the Canadian border. Events concerning the U.S. Navy, however, were so few in number and so scattered in time and location—one occurred 34 years earlier than and 3,000 miles away from the other two—that it would seem unreasonable to devote to them a separate segment necessarily so much shorter than any of the others.

Hence this chapter narrates the navy's impact on foreign relations concerning the Kingdom of the Two Sicilies (1816 and 1832); the Oregon Country (1818); the French at Toulon (1834); and two situations arising from the Revolutions of 1848, the first related to Italy (1848–1849), and the second to the Austro-Russian crackdown on the Hungarian uprising (1851–1853). Great Britain was involved in two controversies with the United States, one concerning American rights to fish along eastern Canada throughout most of the 1850s, and the second about British searches and visitations of possible slave-carriers displaying American colors off Cuba late in that decade. Finally, there were some minor U.S. naval actions in connection with Italian unification in 1860.

The Kingdom of the Two Sicilies, 1816, 1832
Commodore Isaac Chauncey at Naples, 1816

In 1809 Napoleon I ousted the Bourbon monarch in Naples and replaced him as king with his brother-in-law, General Joachim Murat. In obedience to his master's instructions, Murat commenced apprehending any American merchantmen that encroached upon his territorial limits. The total rose to 47, according to President Madison's message to the House in 1812. When Napoleon was toppled for the second and last time after Waterloo, Murat's brief reign also ended, and by 1815 the Bourbons were again ruling the Kingdom of the Two Sicilies (southern Italy and Sicily). By then the plundered American shipowners were hammering at the door of the White House, demanding that their government move to procure them proper compensation for their losses. Madison responded by telling the Marylander William Pinkney, en route to Russia as U.S. minister, to stop off at Naples to discuss the spoliation matter. Commodore Isaac Chauncey, in the new ship of the line *Washington*, was to transport him there and to provide him with a show of naval bravado that might induce the Italians to harken closely to Pinkney's arguments. In addition, the commodore was to see if the United States could gain a naval base in the Two Sicilies, because its present station at Mahon on the Spanish island of Minorca was a shaky tenure, in view of tensions between Madrid and Washington over the Floridas in particular.

The two pulled into Naples during that summer. Chauncey had called the other ships of the Mediterranean Squadon to join him in the harbor. This caused the local populace to fear an American bombardment, for they recalled what Decatur had done to the Algerians the year before. London feared that the Americans might simplify their Mediterranean-base problem by seizing some port in the Two Sicilies, but once the Neapolitans rejected any naval concessions to the United States, its concern evaporated. Chauncey remained quietly at Naples, aware that he lacked orders to move belligerently. Pinkney toiled hard for the two months that he was there to reach an accord, but by mid-October had to leave for Russia. The Neapolitan spoliation issue slumbered for the next decade and a half.[1]

Commodore Daniel T. Patterson and Commander Matthew C. Perry at Naples, 1832

During the summer of 1832 John Nelson, U.S. chargé in the Two Sicilies, notified Washington that his endeavors to talk the Neapolitans into meeting their spoliation responsibilities were being thwarted by deliberate procrastination and that an American naval flourish would be advisable. Commodore Daniel T. Patterson complied, dispatching the frigates *Brandywine*, his flagship, and *Constellation* to that harbor. Because the commodore was too busy juggling his personal life at Mahon—he had a wife aboard his command and a mistress ashore—he sent Commander Matthew C. Perry to execute his official responsibilities. When this massed firepower showed up, the city's frightened inhabitants prepared for what feeble resistance they might be able to offer, but relaxed when both warships departed. Perry, however, had concluded that on-again, off-again pressure would be the most productive course open to him. The *Brandywine* returned a few weeks later and joined two other U.S. men-of-war already there. Neapolitans had been able to expect British armed support in 1816, but in this case London was adopting a hands-off attitude. Neapolitan nerves cracked. By October a treaty was signed and by June it was ratified, in which Naples agreed to pay roughly $2,000,000 to compensate Americans for the vessels they had lost over twenty years before. The installments were spread over nine years and were paid in full.

Unlike Chauncey's naval efforts, those of Patterson and Perry were decisive. The commodore informed the Secretary, "It is admitted by Mr. Nelson that the appearance of the squadron . . . has had great effect in producing so favorable a result." Senator Thomas H. Benton agreed that "the indemnity from Naples . . . may be looked upon as the most remarkable of Jackson's diplomatic successes."[2]

Great Britain and the Oregon Country, 1818

Captain James Biddle at Fort Astoria on the Columbia River, 1818

Biddle's cruise to South America in the *Ontario* from 1817 to 1819 was primarily aimed at protecting American commerce while the United States remained neutral in the struggles of Chile and Peru to liberate themselves from Spain. But at the urgings of President Monroe and Secretary of State John Quincy Adams, the Navy Department ordered him to interrupt these more pressing duties to make a quick visit to the Oregon Country. This sprawling half-million-square-mile tract was the source of a sluggish controversy among Spain, Russia, Great Britain and the United States, all of which had some sort of claim to it on the grounds of exploration, propinquity, treaty rights, or settlement. Eventually, however, Britain and America became the leading contenders. During the War of 1812 Captain David Porter in the *Essex* broke loose into the Pacific, compelling London to send a three-ship squadron around Cape Horn. Two of them fulfilled their chief responsibility by cornering and capturing the *Essex* at Valparaiso. The third arrived at the Columbia's mouth to claim the area for the Canadian-based North West Company, a fur enterprise soon to merge with Hudson's Bay Company. But this occupation might have to be voided when the Treaty of Ghent restored all conquests to their prewar status.

Biddle's instructions read, "You will . . . then proceed to the Columbia River, with a view to assert, on the part of the United States, the claim to the sovereignty, by some symbolic or appropriate mode adapted to the occasion," but do so without resorting to violence. During mid-August 1818 Biddle reached his destination, and without needing her guns, anchored his sloop and went ashore in a boat. Landing at the ill-omened Cape Disappointment on the river's north shore, he raised the American flag before a small group of bewildered Indians and, as he himself told it, "I turned up a sod of soil, and giving three cheers, I nailed against a tree a leaden plate in which were cut the following words: "TAKEN POSSESSION OF IN THE NAME AND ON THE BEHALF OF THE UNITED STATES BY CAPTAIN JAMES BIDDLE COMMANDING THE UNITED STATES SHIP ONTARIO, COLUMBIA RIVER, AUGUST 1818." He proceeded to the nearby village of Fort Astoria, founded in 1811 by employees of John Jacob Astor's American Fur Company who, in 1814, had sold it to the North West Company just before the arrival of the British warship. Biddle chatted briefly with the agent of that concern and put up the same announcement on the Columbia's south bank. Business done, he departed for Peru on the next day.

Biddle had left a question for future settlement: had the British gained Astoria through legal purchase and made thereby a permanent acquisition or was it returnable property through Royal Navy conquest? In London, Foreign Secretary Lord Castlereagh, to placate the Americans, sent a man-of-war to tell the North Westers that they must vacate the place.

Of course the Anglo-American negotiators of the Convention of 1818 knew nothing about Biddle's work when they put Oregon on the shelf for the next ten years, opening the country to access by either people (the

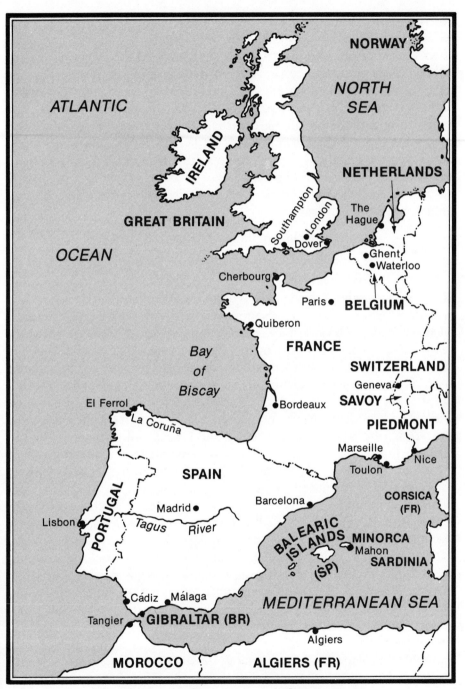

The Western Mediterranean and Western Europe

oft-used term "joint occupancy" is incorrect), and saying nothing about its eventual disposition. Nonetheless, the *Ontario*'s stopover had some effect on the future of this disputed area. It enabled those who wrote the Oregon Treaty of 1846 to proceed on the a priori assumption that the territory north of the 49th parallel (the boundary set by the convention of 1818) was British, and most of that to the south was American. The treaty permitted the remaining controversy over tracts to the north and west of the Columbia to be more easily settled in 1846 by simply extending the 49th to the Pacific, with a jog south so that Britain's Vancouver Island would not be severed. Biddle lived long enough to reflect that eventually his two-day sojourn in Oregon had advanced his nation's interests, to some small degree at least.[3]

France and the Spoliation Claims, 1831–1836
Captain Henry C. Ballard at Toulon, 1834

As they had felt about Neapolitans for a like tardiness, Americans had long smoldered about the delayed redress for illicit French seizures of their maritime carriers during the Napoleonic Wars. Eventually, in an agreement reached in 1831, France promised to pay 25,000,000 francs in six yearly installments, commencing in 1833. But when that date arrived, the French Chamber of Deputies refused to appropriate the needed sum, partly because of monarchical dislike of the upstart republicans and partly because of local political infighting, and the next year refused to pay anything. The president, in his annual message to Congress that December, struck back by recommending that if the French did not meet their obligations in their next legislative session, he wanted Congress to give him the authority to "seize" enough of their property in the United States to equal in value the amount owed.

The reaction in Paris was explosive, and for many months war loomed as a distinct possibility, especially after each side recalled its envoy from the other's capital. Several U.S. naval officers, James Biddle among them, asked for combat commands, sure that their services would soon be required. Outraged by the wording of Jackson's message, the deputies, while agreeing to provide the required amount, voted that the Americans would not receive any part of it until the president had apologized for his statements. This he stoutly averred he would never do, although he did offer, late in 1835, an "explanation" of them. The French proclaimed that Jackson's "explanation" was apology enough, but the president could deny that he had given any apology whatever. The entire sum due was eventually paid.

While anger in both Washington and Paris was commencing to boil over, on 1 May 1834 an accident occurred that just might have been considered a *casus belli* had not Americans moved precipitately to avert any potential damage. The *United States*, Ballard's command, while at the French naval base at Toulon, had joined in celebrating King Louis Philippe's birthday with salutes from her cannon. The man in charge of one battery "through negligence" fired three live shots that slammed into the French warship *Suffren*, killing two and wounding four French seamen. Both the captain and the president took immediate steps to avoid any fallout from the incident. Ballard profusely apologized to Toulon's admiral, expressing his "profound sorrow" about the occurrence, promising to court-martial the offender, and telling him that the officers and men of the *United States* had collected on the spot 5,000 francs for the families of the victims. Jackson went even further. In June he asked Congress to pay the French casualties the same pensions that would be given to families of Americans who had been wounded in battle. His request was quickly granted, and between 1835 and 1837 a total of $9,600 went to the proper recipients. Surely Americans could have done no more to compensate for this unfortunate and unforgivable laxity, thereby providing no fuel for the Franco-American crisis, hot enough without it.[4]

The Revolutions of 1848; Italy, 1848–1849
Captain John Gwinn, Commodore George C. Read, et al.,
at Italian ports, 1848–1849

Americans exulted in the success of their Manifest Destiny expansionism, which they believed proved the supremacy of the liberal democratic principles. Hence they reacted with delight to the European revolutions of 1848 as finally imitating their 1776 example. It appeared that European reaction had at last been put to flight. Starting in France, the liberal surge had flashed across the continent, Britain and Russia being the major exceptions. But these high hopes had been quashed by the end of 1849, as the conservatives fought back, driving revolutionary regimes out of office. Monarchy once again was in the saddle.

Although U.S. warships made a couple of visits to Germany during this European turbulence, the only naval activities of any consequence centered on Italy. That peninsula was an olio of states: with its larger units, Austrian-owned Lombardy and Venetia, to the northeast; to the northwest the Kingdom of Sardinia (that island and mainland Piedmont, with its great port of Genoa); in the middle Tuscany and three smaller duchies, as well as the Papal States, ruled from the Vatican in Rome; and the entire south under Naples in the Kingdom of the Two Sicilies. Almost everywhere the Italian uprisings were triumphant in early 1848, but then victories and defeats began oscillating between revolutionaries and reactionaries. By mid-1849 abject discouragement permeated the rapidly declining rebel cause. Further complications arose from the on-again, off-again war between Austria and Piedmont, with Vienna eventually establishing complete domination. Finally there was the matter of Pope Pius IX. He had started off as an ardent reformer, but changed his mind after Roman radicals had set up a republic, driving him into a temporary Neapolitan exile. From that time on he was an implacable foe of liberalism in any form.

It would serve little purpose to follow all the movements of Commanders Samuel Mercer in the *Jamestown* and Frederick Engle in the *Princeton*, Captain John Gwinn in the *Constitution*, or Commodore George C. Read in the *United States*. They sporadically darted from Italian port to port, protecting Americans and their belongings. Gwinn and Read, however, merit brief scrutiny. At first U.S. officers were hailed by the victorious rebels as the progenitors of democratic and nationalistic enlightenment. They tended to respond in kind, but this partisanship commenced to wane in the face of the counterrevolutionary comeback. More to the point, most officers recognized that Washington was determined to remain at peace with all factions.

Commodore Charles W. Morgan made sure that his subordinate commanders realized this situation, only to find that Gwinn had deliberately disobeyed his orders. At Gaeta he welcomed aboard the *Constitution* with full honors the despotic King of Naples and Pius IX. This was the first time that a Roman pontiff had stepped on American territory and the last until Pope Paul VI visited the United States in 1965. Morgan was so infuriated by this championship of reaction that he recommended to Washington that Gwinn and his frigate be posted immediately to the Brazil Squadron, and unquestionably the full weight of departmental displeasure would have fallen upon him. But Gwinn, who had turned the cruise of that famous ship into a hell at sea by his pitiless application of the whip for the most insignificant delinquencies, died before paying the price for his disobedience. To show their opinion of him, his resentful men made a drunken shambles out of his funeral ceremonies at Palermo.

At least the navy gained something of value from its experiences in revolutionary Italy. Spain had recently withdrawn its permission to have Mahon in the Balearic Islands as an American naval station, and a replacement in the Mediterranean had to be found. When Read brought the *United States* into Genoa in March 1848, he was offered the nearby port of La Spezia for that purpose, and it remained the navy's Mediterranean depot for the next few years.[5]

Austria and the Hungarian Revolution's Aftermath, 1851–1853
Captain John C. Long in the Mediterranean, 1851

More than by Italian occurrences, the American national imagination had been captured by the Hungarians' uprising against their Austrian masters, led by the flamboyant and passionate Louis Kossuth. When a massive Russian intervention crushed the rebellion in mid-1849, if anything it created further admiration for the exiled Hungarian. So extreme became pro-Kossuth enthusiasm in the United States that Chevalier Johann G. Hülsemann, the Austrian chargé in Washington, strongly protested against such interference in the internal concerns of a friendly power. Although Americans cheered, Austro-American relations froze when Secretary of State Daniel Webster sneeringly replied late in 1850 that his country had nothing to fear from Vienna, for its territorial possessions made those of Austria "but a patch on the earth's surface." Hülsemann's superiors told him to have nothing to do with Webster. He obeyed, and there followed a de facto break in diplomatic relations that lasted until Webster's death in 1852.

Long before, Kossuth, despite his public promise to resist the Russians in Hungary as long as he lived, fled into exile in Turkey, but the danger to him remained acute, for the Sultan was besieged by Austrian demands for his extradition, which would undoubtedly have meant his speedy execution. The U.S. Navy came to the rescue of Kossuth and his fellow-fugitives (among them Martin Koszta, about whom more below) by offering them passage to the United States in the *Mississippi*, commanded by Captain John C. Long. By this time, however, most Americans who had come in contact with the touchy Hungarian had grown to dislike and distrust him. The U.S. minister to Constantinople had paid for his support there without receiving either recompense or thanks. He warned Long and Mediterranean Commodore Charles W. Morgan that should Kossuth be permitted to go ashore, particularly in France, he would try to rekindle his snuffed-out revolution, thereby in all probability compromising American neutrality. Long agreed that he must curb the exile as much as possible. Once aboard, Kossuth concluded that he was in a prison ship, and commenced quarreling with the captain. At Marseille he demanded to leave the *Mississippi* so that he might travel overland to the English Channel. When Paris refused that permission, he was livid, sure that the Amer-

The Eastern Mediterranean and Eastern Europe

ican had surreptitiously influenced the decision. By the time the Hungarian disembarked at Gibraltar, he and Long were barely on speaking terms.

Kossuth went on to Britain for a few weeks, basking in adulation, before sailing for New York. If Englishmen had welcomed him uproariously, it was mild compared to the homage paid to him in the United States; poet Henry Wadsworth Longfellow claimed that his country had gone "*clean daft*" over him. The Kossuth craze, however, endured for only a few months. Funds for a renewed Hungarian rebellion were frittered away on entertainment expenses; disillusioned, he soon returned to Europe. But during the time of his popularity, Kossuth could do little wrong in the eyes of the American public. Although a few newspapers dissented, the *New York Times* spoke for the majority when it leveled a barrage against Long that continued for several months, accusing him of baiting the Hungarian "from day to day with little discourtesies," which added up to treating his passenger "*with the utmost contempt and insolence*." Despite this editorial hammering, Long escaped any official censure, for Morgan and the Navy Department lined up behind him on the ground that he had done no more than obey his instructions. He earns plaudits for his refusal to be stampeded by the public mania for Kossuth and his forlorn cause, keeping American neutrality from being compromised.[6]

Commander Duncan N. Ingraham at Smyrna, Turkey, 1853

Austro-American relations, strained after Kossuth's passage from Europe in a U.S. warship and his hysterical welcome in New York City, received another fillip two years later. The Martin Koszta incident is one of the very few in the history of American naval diplomacy to have had an entire book devoted to it: Andor Klay, *Daring Diplomacy: The Case of the First American Ultimatum*. Koszta, a Hungarian-born Austrian subject, had fought side by side with Kossuth and escaped into exile with him, and had come along with him in the *Mississippi*. In the United States he announced his intention to become an American citizen, but before the essential waiting period had expired, sailed to Turkey on personal business. Aware of his presence in Symrna (Izmir), the Austrian resident consul sent "hired ruffians" to seize him in a coffee house. Pouncing upon him, they threw him into the harbor and with a boat dragged him through the water to the Austrian man-of-war *Hussar*, where he was carried below and put in chains. These outrageous deeds so inflamed public opinion in the city that its prostitutes, "being full of indignation, vowed vengeance against the Austrian officers and refused to have anything to do with them." A few days later, two of the *Hussar*'s officers, stupid enough to drop into a cafe, were set upon by a mob, which killed one and wounded the other.

The Koszta case was full of complications for U.S. Consul Edward S. Offley. Austrians had apprehended inside Turkish territorial limits one who claimed American protection on the ground of his intention to become a citizen of the United States. At this juncture Commander Duncan N. Ingraham in the *St. Louis* dropped anchor at Smyrna. To both men the central issue was that Koszta's life was at stake; diplomatic niceties had to be secondary. Their determination was reinforced by a letter from John B. Brown, the U.S. chargé in Constantinople, asking that their "intervention in behalf of Martin Koszta" be continued. Ingraham and Offley rowed over to the *Hussar*, where her Captain Von Schwartz (documentation omits his first names) told them that he could do nothing without further instructions. Coincidentally, Caleb Lyon, a junketing U.S. congressman, bolstered Ingraham's resolve by calling to his attention that "The eyes of nations are upon the little *St. Louis* and her Commander. . . . For God's sake and for the sake of humanity, stand for the right!"

Early in the morning of 2 July, Ingraham sent Von Schwartz a note: "Sir: I have been directed by the American chargé at Constantinople to demand the person of Martin Koszta, a citizen of the United States, taken by force on Turkish soil and now confined on board the brig *Hussar*, and if a refusal is given to take him by force. An answer to this demand must be returned by 4 o'clock P.M." Klay says of this note, "An American ultimatum, written, first of its kind, is on its way into history."

Ingraham had calculated the odds should battle ensue. His *St. Louis*, mounting 18 guns, would face the *Hussar* (16 guns) and the schooner *Artemisia* (12 guns), plus "a steamer of four guns," although the American cannon were of slightly larger caliber than those of the Austrians. Tension rose to fever pitch as the ultimatum's limit approached until a mere ten minutes was left. At that point a boat was lowered from the *Hussar* with Koszta aboard. An explosion of cheers greeted the sight, and cries of "*Vive l'Amérique*" rang from the waterfront. In October the Hungarian finally sailed for the United States, there to slip into oblivion.

Despite his successful display of martial ardor, Ingraham had based his activity on the argument that Koszta was an American citizen. Of course he was not, for the law in force at that time was specific about residence requirements for naturalization. Worried, the commander wrote to George P. Marsh, the U.S. minister in Constantinople: "And now, you Gentlemen of the pen must uphold my act as it was done in accordance with Mr. Brown's instructions backed by Mr. Lyon's advice." He need not have been concerned. Austria naturally protested loudly, but the Turks complained only about Koszta's original abduction, and the European press

Duncan N. Ingraham
(Naval Historical Center)

in general applauded Ingraham's daring. At home newspapers joined their government in standing foursquare behind the commander. Secretary of the Navy Dobbin characterized his behavior thus: "With prudence and discretion, yet with promptness and spirit, and marked determination, Commander Ingraham gave the protection, and the man is free." Noting the objections of the emperor in Vienna, President Pierce rejected them, concluding that "the acts of our officers . . . were justifiable, and their conduct has been fully approved by me." In 1854 Congress, "for his judicious and gallant conduct," awarded him a gold medal, and he was soon promoted to captain.[7]

Great Britain and the Right of Search, 1852–1858
The Fisheries, 1852–1853;
Commodore Matthew C. Perry off Eastern Canada, 1852

The lengthy dispute between Washington and London over the British peacetime claim to the right to stop and investigate American merchant-men and fishing vessels rose to a climax during the 1850s. They strongly disagreed concerning Americans fishing in Canadian waters early in the decade and slavers flying the U.S. flag off Cuba a few years later. In the first case the British dispatched the Royal Navy to prohibit Americans from exceeding their treaty privileges; in the second it acted to ascertain whether suspected slavers had any legal right to display that emblem. If bona fide Americans, they would be spared English naval interference. Washington's stand was absolute in both instances. Successive adminis-trations recalled how mercilessly British cruisers had harried their mer-chant marine prior to the War of 1812, and were positive that such provocations were really designed to cripple the maritime commerce of their leading rival. Americans insisted that any peacetime interference with their maritime right to pass where they wished without let must be resisted. The U.S. Navy was naturally the country's arm that would bear the brunt of any foreign defiance.

The Anglo-American dispute over the fisheries composed the longest, and to many historians, the dullest and most odoriferous in U.S. diplomatic annals. The trouble commenced with an ambiguity in the Treaty of Paris, which ended the American Revolution in 1783; the British delegation to the treaty negotiations argued that when Americans seceded from the British empire, they gave up their opportunities to fish and land within the domains of Canada and Newfoundland. John Adams, spokesman for the Massachusetts fishing ports, successfully argued that since combined Anglo-American operations had driven the French from Canada, Amer-icans had won equal rights in the fishing grounds. During 1817–1818 the Royal Navy, acting upon the principle that the American declaration of war in 1812 had automatically terminated such privileges, briefly har-assed New England fishermen. But except for an occasional bickering about this subject, matters remained quiet until 1851, when a Hudson's Bay Company agent wailed, "For God's sake send a man of War here, for the Americans are Masters of the place, one hundred sail are now lying in this Harbour." Vice-Admiral Sir George F. Seymour responded by leading a fleet into the troubled waters, where his ensuing crackdowns led to angry calls in Congress for the navy to protect American citizens there.

The department dispatched the well-traveled Commodore Matthew C. Perry in the *Mississippi* to do what he could to allay the unrest on both sides. During the summer of 1852 he met Sir George and they mutually agreed on conciliation. The admiral promised to ensure that his underlings conduct no overly rigorous visitations and searches; the commodore pledged to warn his fishermen that they must respect British requirements about where they could land and must refrain from illicit purchases. If they did not, he said, they could expect no naval support. Back in Washington Perry reported to the secretary that tales of British outrages were much inflated; a mere four fishing ships had been taken between 1848 and 1851.[8]

Commodore William B. Shubrick off Eastern Canada, 1853

Despite Perry's encouraging conclusions, the department felt it necessary the next year to dispatch Commodore William B. Shubrick in the *Princeton* to lead three other warships off Newfoundland, Nova Scotia, and New Brunswick to review the fishery situation. After the three smaller vessels had looked into the shores in question, Shubrick was able to tell the secretary that the British squadron was behaving with commendable restraint. Only one American fishing master had been seized, and he was released after paying no more than the costs of the admiralty court, despite his admission that he had committed acts clearly illegal. The secretary was pleased with Shubrick's accomplishments, applauding his "fidelity and zeal."

The controversy went into cold storage in 1854 when the Anglo-American Reciprocity Treaty permitted the agricultural produce of Canadians and Americans to pass freely over both borders without tariff impositions. More to the point, it removed almost all restrictions upon Americans fishing to the north, in exchange for a somewhat meaningless permission for Canadian fishermen to work along the U.S. coast a thousand miles to the south. The fisheries confrontation then lapsed until the post–Civil War era, and even then its renewal was handled by diplomats rather than naval officers. The combined efforts of Perry and Shubrick, with the cooperation of Seymour, taught that when the two services could collaborate, they could allay a threatening situation that might otherwise escalate into the critical.[9]

Great Britain and Suspected Slavers, 1858
Commodores Elie A. F. Lavallette and James M. McIntosh off Cuba, 1858

During 1858 questions arising from the old problem of the illicit slave trade from West Africa across the Atlantic roiled Anglo-American relations to an even greater extent than had the matter of the Canadian fisheries. Having ended slavery in the empire during the 1830s, an aroused British government, solidly backed by public opinion, sent its Royal Navy patrols against apparent slavers, determined to eradicate this loathsome traffic. Americans, however, with 15 slave states in the Union, demonstrated no such enthusiasm. The basic controversy pertained to the right of search, blazing hotter than in the Canadian fisheries. This became a matter of extreme touchiness to Washington. London admitted that it had no right to board and investigate ships under true American registry. But Spanish, Portuguese, and Brazilian carriers of "black gold" (whose governments had been compelled to grant the right of search to the Royal Navy) discovered that running the Stars and Stripes up the mast rendered them immune from English seizure and punishment.

London hoped that there had been something of a breakthrough in the Webster-Ashburton Treaty of 1842, in which the United States agreed to maintain a permanent squadron along the West African coast to inspect vessels flying American colors, leaving others to British inspection. Yet apparently this new arrangement made relatively little difference. U.S. men-of-war assigned there were too few and too deep-drafted for essential shallow-water operations, the distances they had to patrol were too great, and sometimes secretaries of the navy from the slave states were less than zealous in executing their responsibilities.

By the 1850s the British began changing their tune a little by asserting that they did not really want the "right to search" but merely the "right of visitation," simply to find out if an American-flag carrier was authentically American or a foreigner using it as a subterfuge. The United States maintained that search and "visitation" were one and the same and would not be tolerated. This meant that sparks were sure to rise in 1858 when British warships along Cuban coasts began halting and searching all suspect craft, including those flying the American flag. Despite the approaching sectional split, this temporarily brought together almost all Americans. The Senate spoke for the country when it trumpeted: "American vessels on the high seas, in times of peace, bearing the American flag, remain under the jurisdiction of the country to which they belong, and therefore any visitation, molestation, or detention of such vessels by force . . . on

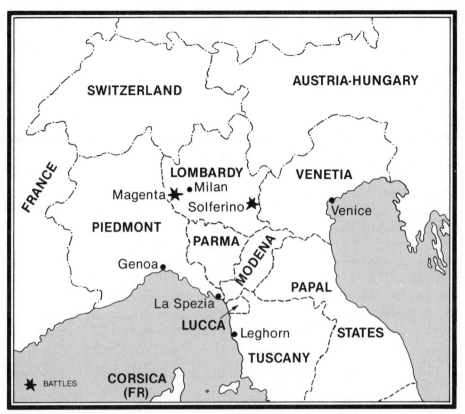

Northern Italy Before Italian Unification, 1870

the part of any foreign Power, is a derogation of the sovereignty of the United States."

Navy Secretary Isaac Toucey immediately combined the twelve warships of the Mediterranean and Home Squadrons and positioned them off Cuba to resist by force any British efforts to halt and board the nation's merchantmen. In his *Report* for 1858 Toucey explained the legal justification for such stringent orders to his officers: ". . . the deck of an American vessel [is] on the same footing with American soil, the invasion of which under foreign authority is to be as strenuously resisted in the one case as the other."

Commodores Elie A. F. Lavallette and James M. McIntosh's combined armada swept down upon Cuba and probed its shores and adjacent seas. Somewhat to their surprise, it did not take long to discover that their nation's merchant marine was no longer being plagued by British boarding parties, so there were no Anglo-American fireworks whatever. Any such potentiality had been avoided by an abrupt British about-face. In June, aware of how vehemently Washington was reacting against its practices, London had advised the Royal Navy commodore in the Caribbean to suspend visitations. This had been determined by the unanimous opinion of the "law officers of the Crown" that the right of search did not legally exist.

Over the next four years even suspected American slavers escaped harassment by British men-of-war. In 1862, however, in response to the stronger anti-slavery sentiments throughout the Union, by treaty Washington gave the right of visitation or search to the Royal Navy, in that way sounding the death knell, by and large, for slave-carrying by Americans. But in 1858 the decision of the administration to amass most of its public vessels and send them south to protect American commerce had helped to persuade London that the country was in earnest about these violations of its national sovereignty. President Buchanan was happy that "no collision took place" between the two navies, and Toucey complacently summarized the outcome of his decision to dispatch his warships to Cuba: "The result proved the wisdom of the measure." True enough, his use of the navy had added eye-catching italics to American protests.[10]

The War of Italian Unification, 1860–1861
Commander James S. Palmer at Palermo and Naples, 1860, and Commander Charles H. Bell at Messina, 1861

Italian patriots, rebuffed in their attempts to unify their peninsula in 1848, suffered another setback in 1860–1861. Sardinian Premier Camillo di Cavour's efforts to gain French help toward that end managed to liberate Lombardy but not Venetia from Austria. But Giuseppi Garibaldi, a longtime revolutionary, changed everything. Secretly supported by Cavour, he organized one of the most productive filibustering expeditions in history. Between May and September 1860 he led his 1,000 "Red Shirt" volunteers from southern France to Sicily, where recruits flocked to his standard; took Palermo; crossed over into Italy proper; and sent the King of the Two Sicilies into flight when he marched into Naples. By the next spring the Kingdom of Italy had been proclaimed under Victor Emmanuel of Sardinia, Garibaldi having gracefully stepped aside to avoid dissension. Even so, Italian unity was only partial, for Venetia and the Papal States were not yet included. The former was to be acquired in 1866, but in 1860 the French emperor stationed a garrison in Rome to keep Pius IX in power. The Papal States remained outside Italian jurisdiction until 1870, when the French defeat by Prussia resulted in the recall of the garrison and enabled Victor Emmanuel to take over all of them except Vatican City itself, and Rome became his new capital.

The American navy was relatively inconspicuous while these stirring events were taking place. Commander James S. Palmer in the sloop *Iroquois* anchored at Palermo shortly after Garibaldi's dramatic landing in May. Although he sympathized with the insurgents, he had refused to compromise American neutrality when asked for direct assistance in the landing. He redeemed himself in November, however, while Victor Emmanuel was entering Naples: his *Iroquois* was the only foreign warship in the harbor to return the salutes of the king's fleet gun for gun. Commander Charles H. Bell in the sloop *Richmond* did no more than to safeguard Americans and act as a general peacekeeper at Messina, in Sicily, early in 1861. By April the sad news arrived that the Civil War had broken out, and almost all U.S. men-of-war were hurriedly recalled.[11]

Summary

Of all the U.S. naval officers active in Europe from 1816 to 1861, Gwinn, at Gaeta, Italy, in 1849, behaved the worst. His insubordinate decision to entertain the leaders of reaction officially could have seriously negated American neutrality. Chauncey, at Naples in 1816, could be deemed a failure, but since he had no orders to use force and was cognizant of strong British opposition, he may avoid blame. In the gray area between achievement and failure, Mercer and Engle turned out to be comparative ciphers in the Italian uprisings of the late 1840s, as did Palmer and Bell during the Italian drive for unification more than a decade later. At least they caused Washington no embarrassment. As for Long and Kossuth in 1851, the captain may have permitted his dislike for the Hungarian to spill over into disrespect, but since he was reflecting the opinion of his superiors, he emerged unscathed. The attempts of Lavallette and McIntosh to force British concessions with their combined squadrons in 1858 proved unnecessary, for London had voluntarily relinquished any right to halt and search suspected slavers under American colors in the Caribbean or elsewhere.

In the European sphere American naval accomplishments outweighed any frustrations. In 1818 Biddle followed his instructions to the letter, thereby contributing his bit to the final pro-American settlement of the Oregon dispute in 1846. Patterson and Perry, at Naples in 1832, listened to Nelson's appeal for naval support and cowed the Two Sicilies into a complete reversal of its previous refusal to meet its responsibilities in the spoliation claims. At Toulon in 1834 Ballard (although he could hardly have done otherwise) apologized with enough speed and substance to quell any ill effects that might have come from the incident. Perry was lucky enough in 1852 to find an equally pacifistic Royal Navy counterpart in the fisheries issue, and the two of them resolved that issue, as Shubrick in Canadian waters the following year could confirm. Ingraham, at Smyrna in 1851, was the right man in the right place under the right circumstances to tally an outstanding victory in the Koszta case. In short, U.S. naval officers abetted well their country's foreign policy in their encounters with Europeans from 1816 to 1861.

CHAPTER EIGHT

The Middle East

1820–1860

Commodore William Bainbridge in the Mediterranean, 1820–1821

If Barbary piracy had finally been eradicated by 1815, Turkey (the Ottoman Empire until 1922) remained a power of the first rank into the early nineteenth century. Yet the sultan and his bureaucracy could not respond effectively to the industrialism and other innovations that were sweeping through much of Europe and America. Moreover, he ruled a hodgepodge of nationalities, religions, languages, and cultures that sprawled from Austria to the Red Sea and beyond. As internal weaknesses sapped Turkish strength, external events speeded up its decline. Among these were the Greek rebellion of the 1820s, the decimation of its huge navy at Navarino in 1827, and the de facto independence of Egypt in the 1830s. The darkest shadow of all was cast by the Russian Bear, continuing its efforts to leap over the Turkish hurdle from the Black Sea into the Mediterranean. The sultan was given some relief when the Russians were sent into temporary retreat after their trouncing in the Crimean War, during 1854–1856.

Morocco and independent Greece occupied U.S. naval attention in the Middle East to a very minor extent during the two decades before the Civil War. But of all the nations in that part of the world, it was Turkey to which the navy gave most of its attention during the early nineteenth century. Its officers sought to ease the labors of American diplomats, a goal often achieved by the mere presence of warships offshore. After years of trying, several commodores finally succeeded in writing the first treaty between Washington and Constantinople in 1830, one of the more notable naval contributions to their country's foreign policy

Commodore William Bainbridge, as he trod the deck of his ship of the line *Columbus* during late April 1820, was delighted with his appointment as commodore of the Mediterranean Squadron. It offered him the opportunity to realize a dream that had haunted him for twenty years. In 1800 and 1801, while in the *George Washington* at Constantinople, he had agreed most heartily with Admiral Hussein Kutchuk, his influential Turkish friend, that formal diplomatic relations between their two nations would be mutually advantageous. Somehow Washington let slip the opportunity to establish those relations. Two decades later the United States had a burgeoning Turkish trade centered at the city of Smyrna. David Offley, a prosperous merchant there since 1808, told his government that the time was ripe for reaching an understanding. In his orders the secretary of the navy let Bainbridge know that a Turkish-American treaty took precedence over his other duties.

Before proceeding on that business Bainbridge conferred on important matters with Britons and Spaniards. At Gibraltar the dueling between American naval and British army officers had become so frequent and bloody that it threatened to get out of hand. Bainbridge and Gibraltar Governor Sir George Dom defused the crisis. The Briton cracked down on his hotheads, and the American kept his warships away from the Rock as much as possible until he found a substitute Mediterranean supply base. This he found in Mahon, on Minorca, one of the Spanish Balearic Islands. His timing was perfect: Spanish-American relations had been strained over the Floridas and other matters, but they warmed up after the signing of the Adams-Onís Transcontinental Treaty of 1819. The governor of Minorca affably permitted Bainbridge to set up a "duty-free deposit" for the squadron's stores; Mahon remained an American supply base for years.

Yet Bainbridge was unable to conclude a treaty opening additional Turkish ports to American enterprise and gaining most-favored-nation status for his country. It was partly his fault. He wanted to get a firman (official permission) from the Turks allowing him to sail to the capital in his flagship, as he had done by subterfuge in 1800. He asked Baron Gregory Stroganoff, Russian ambassador to Constantinople, for aid. Stroganoff was a poor choice, for the sultan still feared the age-old Russian desire to shatter his Turkish barrier which kept them from bursting into the Mediterranean. Hence Stroganoff's advocacy served only to ensure that no firman would be issued; the Turks explained that Europeans had regularly tried without success to have their warships pass through the Dardanelles, the Bosporus, and by the capital into the Black Sea, and that no exceptions could be made for Americans.

Bainbridge had been accompanied by Luther Bradish, a New York lawyer appointed by the Department of State as special envoy to the sultan's court. He dispatched Bradish and Charles Folsom, the latter's private secretary, to Smyrna. From there Bradish went on to Constantinople for treaty negotiations, and Folsom remained behind as U.S. commercial agent. The dispute over the firman hurt Bradish's capabilities during the months he remained in Constantinople after the departure of the *Columbus*, accomplishing nothing. The last vestige of hope for a Turkish-American pact vanished for the immediate future; early in 1821 the Greeks rose in rebellion against their Turkish masters, and the news evoked the strongest philhellenic sentiments in the United States, much to the resentment of the Turkish government. Even though Bainbridge could not end his diplomatic career on a triumphant note, he could reflect, when he debarked in Boston in July 1821, that few of his colleagues could match his achievements in this sphere.[1]

Commodores John Rodgers (the Elder) and William M. Crane at Turkey, 1825–1829

Following the abortive efforts of Bainbridge and Bradish, another start was made a few years later in reaching a Turkish-American accord. After receiving hints that the sultan was reconsidering his relations with the United States, Commodore John Rodgers (the Elder) in the *North Carolina* was instructed to gain most-favored-nation standing, American commercial entry into the Black Sea, and the right to appoint consuls to any city in the Turkish empire. In July 1826 he met twice with Husrev, the Capudan Pasha (admiral), off southern Greece, each man visiting the other's flagship. Lieutenant Samuel F. Du Pont, serving in the *North Carolina*, reported that Admiral Husrev was entirely captivated by the appearance and fire power of the handsome new ship of the line, saying that he had "never seen anything to compare with it." This commenced a Turkish fascination with U.S. naval craftmanship that lasted for decades. Husrev also told Rodgers that he had recommended to the sultan that he accept the American terms, although a reply might take some time—which it did.

Much of the Turkish delay was caused by internal turmoil and naval disaster. The janizaries, the sultan's personal guard since the mid-1300s, had degenerated into an unruly mob, worthless militarily. They refused to accept their master's dismissal in 1826 and were slaughtered by the thousands. While the Greek rebellion sputtered along, the European powers became increasingly concerned about its international repercussions. During 1827 British, French, and Russian efforts to persuade the Turks to grant Greek independence brought their warships to Navarino in southern Greece. There lay the massed Turkish fleet. Somehow everyone started firing, and when the day was over the sultan had lost no less than "5 ships of the line, 19 frigates, 26 sloops, 12 brigs, and 5 'fire vessels.'" Actually this worked to American advantage, for reconstruction of its shattered fleet became a major priority in Constantinople, and the U.S. Navy remained its model.

During the tenures of Rodgers and Commodore William M. Crane, disunity among the Greek rebels and the chaos resulting from sporadic Turkish campaigns against them had created an administrative no-man's-land in the eastern Mediterranean. Pseudoprivateers and pirates in the Aegean and adjacent waters began pouncing upon weak or unwary merchantmen to such an extent that Secretary of State Samuel L. Southard reported in 1826 that "Private letters . . . prove that piracies of the worst sort are daily increasing." The warships of both commodores busied themselves with trying to convoy American merchantmen and chasing corsairs at sea and ashore, to some effect. Perhaps the most celebrated fight took place in 1827 when Lieutenant Louis M. Goldsborough, leading a small detachment from the sloop *Porpoise*, boarded and captured a Greek-occupied former English brig at the cost of one American life. Yet the depredations continued. Southard mourned in 1828 that he had insufficient men-of-war either to convoy or police the lawless areas. Piracy was not ended in the eastern Mediterranean until the European navies joined in the hunt and relative peace arrived with the recognition of Greek independence in 1829.

Crane had assumed Mediterranean command a year earlier, and matters looked auspicious for him; the sultan's reply for which Rodgers had been waiting was promising. But when the commodore and Offley, the American merchant in Smyrna, dickered with the Turkish foreign minister, they could not countenance his demand for bribes in the form of warships and money before a treaty could be signed. The rupture became final after the Turk was unwilling to grant America tariff equality with the Europeans.[2]

Commodores James Biddle, Daniel T. Patterson, and Jesse D. Elliott at Smyrna and Constantinople, 1830–1835

In 1829 the new Jackson administration moved quickly to negotiate a Turkish treaty, eager to score diplomatic points against its predecessor, the Adams administration. To this end the usual commodore-consul tandem was increased to a three-man commission. Charles Rhind, a New

Yorker with commercial experience in the Middle East, was appointed to work with Biddle and Offley. Since the commodore's uniform kept him in the public eye and Offley was a local fixture, the comparatively unknown Rhind was sent ahead to Constantinople. His colleagues, growing increasingly impatient, were compelled to wait in Smyrna from early February to early May 1830. At first the Turkish foreign minister contended that the United States must pay somewhat higher tariffs than other countries; until that principle was accepted no American ships could trade in the Black Sea. Rhind spurned the dictum and negotiations were temporarily suspended. All along, foreign intrigue was at work. The British ambassador kept putting obstacles in the way of his leading maritime opponent, and the Anglophobic Russians supported the American competitor. Partly because of the influence of the tsar's ambassador, a new foreign minister took office who proved more conciliatory.

On 7 May Rhind was able to trumpet the news that his efforts were victorious. He sent to Biddle and Offley as the complete text of his treaty nine "public" articles granting the United States equality in tariffs, consular appointment entitlements, extraterritoriality, and a shipwreck convention. Biddle and Offley were irked about the other's charging ahead on his own without consulting them, but had to admit that basically the treaty met Washington's conditions. But once the two had journeyed from Smyrna to the capital to sign the agreement, their relations with Rhind nose-dived. Four days after their arrival and a few hours before the official ceremonies would commence, he informed them that he had also included a "secret" article in the treaty permitting the Turkish government to order the construction of warships of whatever number and whatever size it desired, and that contracts between the two governments would be drawn to that effect.

Paullin says that this concession was of "trifling importance," in that the sultan already enjoyed the right of ordering men-of-war from Washington. If he is technically correct, most assuredly neither the other commissioners nor most of their compatriots considered it to be of no consequence. Offley was outraged, and Biddle even more so, for Biddle viewed the covert provision as violating America's longstanding policy "to establish no relations other than commercial with the natives of Europe." Rhind exploded with "violence" at their objection, breaking off contact with Biddle except by letter. Even worse, both of his companions recognized that he was determined to keep for himself all the treaty credits. He defiantly declared that his own name on the document was all that was necessary, and he forbade the others "further interference in the matter."

Although resentful over this brush-off, Biddle and Offley put their heads together and concluded that should their signatures be lacking on the treaty, 11 years of off-again, on-again negotiations would have been wasted.

So both signed it, Biddle "with great repugnance." But they were able to exact their revenge when Rhind told them that he would personally carry the completed agreement back to Washington. Biddle replied with relish that instead it would be conveyed in the first homeward-bound vessel of his squadron. Rhind took such umbrage at this that he peevishly refused to sign his own treaty. Biddle and Offley were correct in surmising how American political leaders would assess the secret provision. Ex-President Adams spoke for many when he described it as "incompatible with the neutrality of the United States." Incredibly, in view of his passionate advocacy of the provision. Rhind soon shrugged it off as "of no importance in itself"; indeed, he said he had forgotten all about it. The Senate could hardly wait to get at the article and voted it down, 27 to 17, while accepting the "public" text, 42 to 1.

Three decades after Bainbridge and Hussein Kutchuk had started the process, in October 1831 ratifications of the first Turkish-American treaty were exchanged by the Turkish foreign minister and David Porter, who was the U.S. chargé d'affaires, having resigned his naval commission in 1826; he later became minister to the sultan. The Turks, despite the most-favored-nation provision in the treaty, commenced collecting higher tariffs on American commodities than those paid by the Europeans. Porter, however, soon righted this wrong. Although Rhind's secret article had been wiped out by the Senate, the United States informally helped Turkey rebuild its navy, which had been decimated at Navarino in the action narrated above. Porter managed to have Henry Eckford, America's master naval architect, appointed to the Turkish service. After Eckford's premature death, his disciple Foster Rhodes replaced him. As early as 1837 the sultan was provided with two frigates, two schooners, a corvette, and a brig, in addition to a steamboat and several cutters.

Part of the U.S. Mediterranean commander's routine was "to show the flag" at the major ports in his area, seldom with any discernible diplomatic impact. An exception, however, must be made for Commodore Daniel T. Patterson's tour of Turkish possessions from October 1833 through the next August. In the ship of the line *Delaware* he was received with great enthusiasm, both official and public, at Alexandria, Jaffa, and Smyrna. Porter was able to get him a firman so that he could visit Constantinople, where he enjoyed a private audience with the sultan. Patterson's display of naval pomp helped to cement Turkish-American relations, and British jaws may have clenched when the pasha at Beirut commented to the queen's consul there that "after the American, the English is the next best fleet at sea."

Commodore Elliott in the recently rebuilt *Constitution* occupied himself primarily with trying to follow through on U.S. consular suggestions that

Jesse Duncan Elliott
(Enoch Pratt Library)

a commercial understanding with Egypt might be attainable. That portion of the sultan's domains had been usurped by Mehmet (Mohammed) Ali, pasha at Alexandria for many years. Although he had supported his overlord against Greek rebels, his demand for a free hand in Egypt and Syria was refused. He defeated Turkish armies and established de facto independence. Elliott twice visited him; in 1837 he was accompanied by Lewis Cass, secretary of war in Jackson's cabinet, on a diplomatic fact-finding mission for the president. Nothing came of their discussions with Mehmet, however, for Washington had second thoughts as to whether Egypt could make legally acceptable treaties on its own.[3]

Commodore Charles W. Morgan, et al., at Morocco, Turkey, and Greece, 1842–1860

Although Morocco had usually been more restrained than other North African powers in its behavior toward the United States, Moroccan-American relations worsened in 1842. Thomas N. Carr, U.S. consul at Tangier, ever since his appointment had inundated the Department of State with complaints about his insufficient stipend, which had been depleted by the sultan's gift of two lions that he had to feed and house in the consulate at his own expense. Tiring of his jeremiads, Secretary Webster fired him late in 1841. When Carr tried to leave Morocco the next March, he was forcibly detained by order of Tangier's lieutenant-governor. The consul appealed for aid to Commodore Charles W. Morgan, who eventually managed to obtain the lieutenant-governor's dismissal, an official apology for the incident, and the honoring of his flag by a twenty-one-gun salute from the city's garrison. Abel P. Upshur, the navy secretary, complimented Morgan by writing, "The friendly relations between the two countries are now restored."

In Turkey, Dabney S. Carr (perhaps a relative of Thomas N.) had succeeded David Porter as U.S. minister. He discovered that the earlier anticipation of a booming American trade in the Black Sea had proved wildly optimistic: of the 6,286 merchant ships that traded there in 1843, two were American. Carr decided that a naval demonstration past Constantinople could ease the way for commercial expansion and the assignment of consuls in Black Sea ports. The Navy Department concurred, sending Commander Henry Henry in the sloop *Plymouth* for such purposes. It was a disastrous appointment. Once he had pulled into the capital during July 1844, he immediately quarreled with Carr and proved himself to be "loud and boisterous in conversation and rude and inhospitable to the Turks who visited his ship." He was quickly recalled. Considering what had been expected of him, the redundant Henry had been totally ineffective.

By the early 1850s American Protestant missionaries in the eastern Mediterranean were under assault. In the 1820s they had applauded the Greek rebels for apparently recapturing a portion of Islam for Christianity, only to discover that the priests of what was then called "the Greek Maronite Church" were much more zealous in defending their faith than the Moslem imams had been. George P. Marsh, U.S. minister to Turkey, commented that the Greek government was in "slavish submission to an ignorant, bigoted, and corrupt priesthood." For example: the Reverend Jonas King was briefly imprisoned in 1851 after being menaced by mobs, seeing his property destroyed, and regularly called into court on a variety of charges, sexual peccadilloes among them. During mid-1852 Marsh and Captain Silas H. Stringham in the *Cumberland* demanded redress but were thwarted in Athens by disingenuous and slippery evasions. They tried again the next year, but all that they could get was a nonbinding Greek promise of future reimbursement for King's property losses.

By this time the Crimean War, pitting Britain, France, Sardinia, and Turkey against Russia, was rapidly approaching, and Americans in the

Middle East were extremely pro-Turkish. According to James A. Field, Carroll Spence, the new American minister to Constantinople, argued that "the expansion of the Russian Empire was expansion of the area of despotism and that a triumph of the Greek Orthodox Church would mean the destruction of all other Christian sects in Turkey." Stringham, now commanding the *Saranac*, went along with Spence to meet the sultan in 1854, thanking him for offering sanctuary "to the exiled friends of Liberty," and hoping that the Crimean War would satisfy his "most sanguine expectations." Public opinion in the United States, however, was pro-Russian, primarily because of Anglophobia, coupled with sentiments of amity for the tsar. Although the secretary of the navy did not censure Stringham for his outward show of support for the Turks, Spence was reprimanded for that offense by the secretary of state.

The final pre–Civil War contribution to U.S. diplomacy in the Middle East by an American naval officer was that of Commodore Elie A. F. Lavallette, who had hastened back to the Mediterranean after patrolling against British searches off Cuba in mid-1858. By November he was attempting to ensure the punishment of men who had brutalized an American missionary and his family. Earlier that year five Arabs had swept down upon the home of Walter Dickson at Jaffa, wounding him, killing his son-in-law, and raping his wife and daughter. Four of them were soon apprehended by local authorities, but when Lavallette appeared, he found that their guilty verdicts had not been acted upon by the court, because the captives asserted that the atrocities had been committed by the missing fifth man. The commodore expostulated vigorously, demanding that an example be made of them. Perhaps the 40 guns leveled at Jaffa from his flagship, the new steam frigate *Wabash*, served as some kind of stimulant, for the four were sentenced to life imprisonment at hard labor. Secretary of the Navy Isaac Toucey forecast that this would have "a salutary effect upon the lawless tribes."

Lavallette then went on to Constantinople, where he was sumptuously entertained, but by this time the sultan was dependent on British and French support to ward off the rapidly augmenting Russian threat, so the longstanding American contributions to him in naval construction and advice soon lapsed, although relations between the two governments remained cordial.[4]

Summary

The 1830s proved to be the high-water mark in Turkish-American affinity. The preliminary cooperation between U.S. diplomats and Bainbridge, Rodgers, and Crane to bring the first treaty into being was completed satisfactorily by Biddle. Patterson topped off the resultant naval collaboration with his ostentatious display of American maritime prowess, and at least Elliott added no discordant note to mar the harmony between Washington and Constantinople. In later years before 1861, Americans were unable to maintain this high level in the Middle East. To be sure, Morgan swiftly and efficiently restored rapport with Morocco in 1842, and Lavallette moved effectively to arrange for the punishment of Dickson's assailants at Jaffa in 1858. Stringham was unable to right the wrongs done to Knight in 1853, and during the Crimean War he backed the wrong side in that conflict, at least in the opinion of his fellow-countrymen. Yet the irascible and irresponsible Henry was the only marplot who even temporarily disrupted Turkish-American relations. Considering the obstacles erected by Washington's early ambivalence about a pact with Constantinople, anti-American intrigues by the British and French, the inability or unwillingness of the Greeks to protect foreigners in their midst, and the massive internal and external ailments of nineteenth-century Turkey, U.S. naval officers contributed reasonably well toward the realization of their nation's foreign-policy aims in the Middle East.

CHAPTER NINE

China

1819–1860

Like all other foreigners, the first Americans arriving at Canton in the 1780s found that they were considered "barbarians" by the Chinese; the term meant "not yet Sinicized." The nearby Asian tributary states were more enlightened barbarians, for they had adopted Chinese-style governments and cultures. Europeans and Americans, however, were so unlike the Chinese that they could never become Sinicized. Barbarians they were and barbarians they would remain, while China pursued its serene course, undefiled by contamination from abroad.

This innate inferiority took both political and economic forms. Peking was the capital of no nation state such as those in the West. All foreigners must recognize that China was "the Middle Kingdom," suspended between heaven and earth, below the one but above the other. For that reason its emperor enjoyed suzerainty over all other rulers. Therefore the Chinese refused even to consider the concept of equality in foreign relations. All trade with the Middle Kingdom must be conducted at the southern port of Canton alone, and that through the medium of the *co-hong*, an organization of a dozen or so Chinese mercantile houses that had been granted imperial monopolies in foreign commerce. Western businessmen there usually found their enterprises most lucrative, but at the price of considerable social and political inferiority. Furthermore, they remained unprotected against any whims of China's rulers, for their governments had no treaties with Peking guaranteeing their lives, property, or rights of trade or residence. But until the Opium War the alien community in Canton, the English excepted, wished no intrusions, diplomatic or naval, from home authorities. Americans and others feared that this meddling might bring about the one thing that they dreaded the most—a Chinese trade embargo. American naval-officer diplomacy in China down to 1860 may be conveniently divided into five periods: (1) Early activities, 1819–1836; (2) the Opium War and its aftermath, 1839–1843; (3) American Treaty of Wanghia negotiations, 1844–1846; (4) pre-Arrow (or Second Opium) War, 1849–1855; (5) The Arrow (or Second Opium) War, 1856–1860.

Early Activities, 1819–1836
Captain John D. Henley at Canton, et al., 1819–1820

Captain John D. Henley commanded the first U.S. man-of-war to sail to China. In 1819 he was told to proceed in the frigate *Congress* "upon important service for the protection of commerce of the United States in the Indian and China Seas." On 3 November he arrived at Lintin Island, close to Portuguese Macao and some 60 miles south of Canton. His arrival led to prompt and outspoken apprehension among Chinese officials about the appearance of a foreign warship in the Pearl River estuary. The acting viceroy (the functionary primarily responsible for conducting external relations) told Henley to depart at once and instructed his underlings—in a text forwarded to the captain—"to keep a strict watch on the said vessel and not to allow her to approach the inner waters." But Henley, after conversing with the U.S. consul at Canton, realized that this peremptory order to leave was an empty formality, and disregarded it. After experiencing obstructionism when he tried to buy "bread, spirits, etc.," Henley boldly sailed the *Congress* up to the entrance of the Boca Tigris, the northernmost point legally open to foreign men-of-war. This move brought about the desired result: the supplies he needed before leaving soon arrived.

Despite his provocations when he defied orders to sail and approached Canton itself, Henley had restrained whatever combativeness he may have felt, in part because of the spirit of his instructions and in part because of the advice given him by American residents. Their caveat was simple: Do nothing that might incite Chinese displeasure and retaliation in the form of severing all trade with Americans. The *Congress* came into Hampton Roads, Virginia, late in May 1821, Henley's mission well accomplished.[1]

Commander William B. Finch at Canton, et al., 1830

More than a decade later Commander William B. Finch was the next U.S. officer to test Chinese diplomatic temperatures. Commanding the *Vincennes* in the first round-the-world cruise of an American warship, he came to China in January 1830 and remained something over two weeks. Navy Department documentation consists of a single letter that Finch wrote to the secretary, which gives some insight into the changing thought processes of contemporary American merchants in the Far East. He enclosed messages from that community that somewhat watered down the previous insistence to Henley that no naval activity be undertaken lest it provoke the Chinese into banning trade with Americans. Now merchants in Canton asked for an annual visit by a U.S. public vessel. Naval appearances, they concluded, would be valuable to them if their commanders would show "the same deference toward the customs of China, and conciliatory disposition as exhibited by yourself." Pleased with this testimonial to his good work, Finch departed for Manila, and was in Washington early that June.[2]

Captain John Downes, et al., at Canton, 1832–1836

The next sojourns of U.S. naval officers to China had little diplomatic significance. Moreover, the first three stopped there only incidentally in going to or from major responsibilities elsewhere. The letters to the department from Captain John Downes in 1832, Commander David Geisinger in 1833, and Commander John Aulick in 1835 agreed that American merchants were being permitted to conduct their business without hindrance. But they deserve this brief mention, since the arrival of any foreign warships without permission affronted Chinese authorities and might have caused trouble.

A change in the navy's Far Eastern policy accompanied the advent of "Commodore" (technically still a captain) Edmund Kennedy, who headed a squadron from his flagship, the sloop *Peacock*. The department had finally agreed with Finch that frequent visits of American men-of-war would be beneficial. This decision was considerably reinforced by Special Envoy Edmund Roberts, who wrote the first U.S. treaties with Siam and Muscat. He advised that a permanent naval establishment should be stationed there. This was done in 1835 with the de facto creation of the East India Squadron, made official six years later.[3]

The Opium War and Its Aftermath, 1839–1843

Commodore George C. Read at Canton, et al., 1839

While American officers in the Far East were carrying on their somewhat desultory and timid diplomacy, it remained for the Royal Navy to pry open China's closed door. London had found it intolerable that the emperor was unwilling to negotiate on terms of equality. Missions to write treaties had been sent to China in vain in 1793 and 1816. After a third failure in the early 1830s, the British settled back to await the first op-

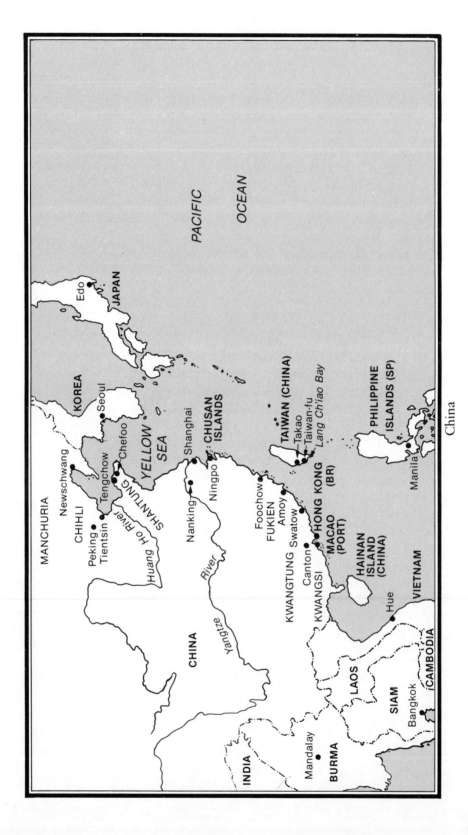

China

portunity to compel Peking by force to sign a pact giving them the rights of trade and residence there.

Opium proved to be the key that opened London's way. While all the Western maritime states were concerned in this dirty, illegal, but remunerative business, the British were by far the most successful. Their exports of opium to China, from their extensive poppy fields in eastern India, surged from a mere 200 "chests" (133 pounds) in 1775 to 40,000 in 1839.

The Ch'ing emperor was aghast at the damage wrought to his country by this British-dominated traffic, which was depleting China's monetary reserves, corrupting its officials, and debauching its people. In 1839 he sent Lin Tse-hsü to Canton as imperial commissioner with orders to stamp out the business. After demanding without success that all opium in the city be turned over to him for destruction, Lin blockaded the Western settlement.

The terror of those trapped there was eased in April 1839 by the arrival of Commodore George C. Read in the USS *Columbia*, on his way home after chastising Sumatrans for assaulting an American merchantman. Some 20,000 chests of British opium, worth $12,000,000, were surrendered to Lin, who promptly destroyed it. He then lifted the blockade, allowing the English to flee, most of them to an anchorage at nearby Hong Kong Island. Americans, however, stayed behind, hoping to profit by taking over the opium market, at least temporarily. They begged Read to remain in China, and because a Sino-British war appeared probable, to cooperate with the Royal Navy in compelling Peking to sign treaties guaranteeing their protection. But the commodore was unauthorized by his government to enter into any kind of diplomatic discussions with the Chinese, so he could do little for the next few months other than to watch events unfold. Early that August Read pleaded that illness of his crew required his immediate departure, and he sailed for the United States, much to the resentment of his compatriots.[4]

Commodore Lawrence Kearny at Canton, et al., 1842–1843

British outrage over the destruction of their opium was enhanced by other disputes with Commissioner Lin. Fighting commenced that autumn and continued off and on for about two and a half years. Despite its name, the Opium War was carried on mainly to compel China to accept Western entry and eventual dominance rather than to collect damages for ruined narcotics. The English had little trouble in pulverizing China's archaic defenses. Canton had to ransom itself to avoid city-leveling bombardments. Meanwhile the Royal Navy was moving leisurely up the coast, picking off whatever ports it wished, and when a squadron moved into the Yangtze River in August 1842, China surrendered.

The ensuing Treaty of Nanking (and a supplementary agreement signed at the Bogue Forts the next year) ceded Hong Kong Island to Britain; opened Canton, Amoy, Foochow, Ningpo, and Shanghai as "treaty ports" where English commerce and residence were permitted; extracted a large indemnity from China; and ended the *co-hong* system. A modified form of "extrality" (extraterritorial jurisdiction) was established, whereby the British were allowed to set up consular courts in the treaty ports to try under English law their nationals accused of crimes committed there. Finally, the British were given most-favored-nation status, under which any privileges, such as lower tariffs, that China extended to any other most-favored nation would automatically be bestowed upon them as well. Such was the situation that confronted Commodore Lawrence Kearny during his tenure in the Far East.

During 1841 the East India Squadron was formally in existence. Commodore Lawrence Kearny, a seasoned professional and one of the best U.S. naval diplomats, was selected by the secretary as its first official commodore. For his China tour he was given the frigate *Constellation* and the sloop *Boston*, and ordered to oversee American interests in East Asia, maintain a strict neutrality vis-à-vis the Opium War antagonists, and try to earn greater Chinese friendship by proceeding against opium smugglers operating under the protection of the U.S. flag. He reached Macao late in March 1842, just as the war was beginning to wind down.

Kearny's most conspicuous accomplishment during his fourteen months in East Asia was to establish harmonious relations with Ch'i Kung, the major Chinese bureaucrat in Canton. The commodore was deeply worried about the recently completed Treaty of Nanking, fearing that it might lead to the British monopolizing foreign trade in China, and asked Ch'i Kung to grant the United States most-favored-nation status. The Chinese replied, "Decidedly it shall not be permitted that the American merchants shall not come to have merely a dry stick [that their commercial interests should be ignored]." This diplomatic doubletalk committed him to nothing, of course, but its congeniality was appreciated, and this informal promise was put into effect in the Sino-American Treaty of Wanghia two years later.

An examination of his letters to the secretary of the navy reveals that Kearny recognized that his diplomatic achievement was well short of earthshaking. Throughout, he had kept in mind that he was without authorization to negotiate meaningfully with the Chinese. He knew that he was no "minister plenipotentiary and minister extraordinary," clothed with the power of the president to write a treaty. Nor did he consider that his little two-ship squadron was worth anything as a naval threat to

Lawrence Kearny
(Official U.S. Navy Photo)

force concessions from a China that had just faced the massed fire power
of the Royal Navy.

Two other matters came to a head shortly before Kearny's departure
from the Far East in May 1843. He persuaded Ch'i Kung to promise to
pay damages for an assault upon an American boat and for a mob attack

on the foreign settlement in Canton that had resulted in the sack of an American warehouse. He fared less well in his efforts to stop his fellow-countrymen from opium-running. He issued a proclamation against it, but Americans in that business paid no attention to him, since they knew that no U.S. law forbade it. To be sure, Kearny did seize the *Ariel*, an opium-carrier that had just landed her cargo at Amoy, but this was because he thought that she had no right to fly the American flag. Indeed, the *Ariel* was released after she had proved the legality of her U.S. registry.

In toto, Kearny merits approbation. He had kept Washington fully informed about developments in China. He had urged successfully that an accredited envoy should be sent there at the first opportunity, empowered to put his own informal agreement about most-favored-nation standing into treaty form. With Ch'i Kung he had conducted his transactions with dignified aplomb, meriting the Chinese's complimentary description of him as one who "manages affairs with a clear understanding, profound wisdom, and great justice."[5]

Treaty of Wanghia (Wanghsia) Negotiations, 1844–1846
Commodore Foxhall A. Parker and Lieutenant Edward G. Tilton at Canton, et al., 1844

Soon after Kearny's return President John Tyler received congressional appropriations for a treaty-making mission to China, and chose Caleb Cushing, an ex-congressman from Massachusetts, as his man. Eventually the envoy made his way to India, where he joined Commodore Foxhall A. Parker's squadron, and he came into Macao in the *Brandywine* during February 1844. Unable to go to Peking as ordered, Cushing sensibly agreed to the Chinese alternative of a meeting in south China early in July. It is hard to evaluate the navy's contribution to these first contacts, for Cushing seldom mentions Parker in his correspondence with the Department of State, and the commodore adds little in his few letters to the Navy Department.

At least Parker and Lieutenant Edward G. Tilton contributed something to the mission's success. In June numerous Chinese trespassed on the grounds of the American "factory" just outside Canton's walls. When they refused to leave, a melee broke out, during which one Chinese was killed. Aware that an uprising might ensue, Parker sent forces to rescue his compatriots trapped in their settlement, but that proved unnecessary. Tilton had already brought the *St. Louis* to the spot where the Chinese still remained. He sent boat detachments ashore and there they stayed until the crowd finally dispersed.

Cushing and Parker finally met Ch'i-ying, Chinese emissary at the Nanking negotiations in 1842, at Wanghia, a temple just outside of Macao, where the three signed the first Sino-American pact on 3 July. In it the United States received most-favored-nation standing, thereby automatically gaining the rights of domicile and commerce first won by Royal Navy guns. Cushing achieved a privilege on his own. At Wanghia he procured extrality for Americans in civil as well as criminal cases, a provision quickly adopted by the British. China also promised to protect Americans except those engaged in illegal activities. Furthermore, U.S. naval officers henceforth could communicate with Chinese officials "in terms of equality and courtesy." His work having been done satisfactorily, Cushing left for home in August. Parker remained, and shortly prior to his departure early in December, Ch'i-ying informed him that the treaty had been endorsed by the emperor and his Grand Council.[6]

Commodore James Biddle at Canton, et al., 1845–1846

Cushing's efforts were hailed in Washington: Mrs. Tyler exulted that "The Chinese Treaty is accomplished—Hurrah! . . . I thought the President would go off in an ecstasy a minute ago with the pleasant news." But of course no treaty is operative until it is ratified. Navy Secretary George Bancroft chose Biddle to command the East India Squadron and, as his major responsibility, to transport to China Commissioner Alexander H. Everett, a former diplomat. In the flagship *Columbus* and her escort the *Vincennes*, they arrived in Rio, where Everett was so ill that he reluctantly authorized Biddle to replace him as "Acting Commissioner," not only to exchange Wanghia ratifications, but to set up a U.S. legation at Canton and consulates, if advisable, at the four other treaty ports. The commodore sped on to China and dropped anchor at Lintin Island on Christmas Day.

In less than 24 hours he was in Canton, for haste was essential. According to the agreement of 1844, ratifications must be concluded within 18 months. Acutely aware of this limitation, when the same Ch'i-ying who had negotiated with the British and Cushing suggested that the ceremonies be set for a lucky day in the Chinese calendar early in January 1846, Biddle counter-proposed that they settle the matter before the end of the year. On 31 December the commodore; Dr. Peter Parker, interpreter and sometime acting commissioner; the U.S. consul at Canton; his officers; and some other Americans met Ch'i-ying and his entourage at a palatial mansion owned by a wealthy Chinese near the city. The *Chinese Repository* noted what followed:

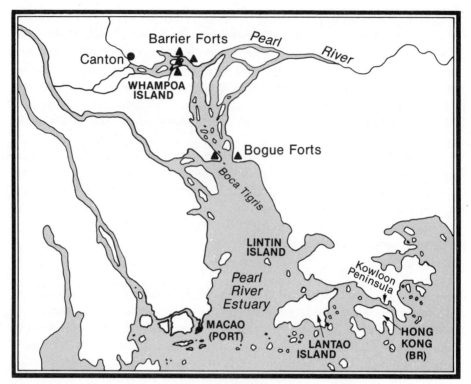

Canton Environs

> After the parties had passed the compliments usual when meeting on such occasions, the two copies of the treaty . . . were exchanged in due form, commodore Biddle, acting commissioner, presenting that from Washington to Kiying [sic], who in turn delivered that from Peking, the whole party standing. . . . This closed the business of the day. . . . At about 5:00 the party sat down to dinner—one of those rich entertainments that have been so often described by visitors. It was in good style, in every way suited to the occasion.

Biddle dashed off copies of the ratified pact to Washington, via an American merchantman. Ch'i-ying, however, had no easy solution in wording his report to Peking. He knew only too well that his country's outmoded military and naval forces were helpless before the armed superiority of the West. But he also had to recognize that the xenophobes in the imperial court were still deluding themselves into thinking that their Middle Kingdom remained the dominant entity on earth. Even though Wanghia carried a clear provision that renegotiation of the treaty could take place, he lied, telling the emperor what he thought he wanted to hear: Biddle "had been extremely grateful for Heavenly favor and would maintain the treaty forever without any other proposals whatever."

Although his major chore had been quickly accomplished, the commodore was not idle during his remaining months in China. After selecting the building that would house the U.S. legation, he took the *Columbus* north along the coast. His cruise was designed to add new consulates to the original one in Canton, dating back to 1790. He looked into the treaty ports of Amoy, Foochow, and Ningpo, but concluded that American trade was so moribund that resident consulates there were unjustifiable. He did, however, appoint the first U.S. consul at Shanghai, for that burgeoning commercial entrepôt, closest of the five to the seat of imperial power, was rapidly forging ahead to rival Hong Kong as a Western bastion in China.

Meanwhile, Biddle was demonstrating a sincerity and at least a partial sense of China's weighty problems, an attitude recognized and appreciated by its officials. They must have learned that in a commercial dispute between a leading American merchant and Shing-ho, a Chinese businessman, the commodore ruled against his fellow countryman. Moreover, he took upon himself to advise Ch'i-ying and other imperial diplomats about the perils they faced from the imperialistic Europeans. Biddle demonstrated some Anglophobia when the British occupied the strategic Chusan Islands off the mouth of the Yangtze River. He claimed that they would hold them until China paid in full the $21,000,000 indemnity assessed at Nanking in 1842, despite Peking's meeting the first three installments and expressing willingness to pay the concluding fourth. Biddle thought that the British were using a financial excuse as a "mere pretext for retaining possession of the islands," but was proved wrong when the Chusans were evacuated. Indeed, he soon lined up with the English in the Canton entry question, in which the Chinese claimed that foreigners were permitted only in Canton's suburbs. When Ch'i-ying acceded to pressure and opened the walled city itself to the British, rioting swept through it. Concluding that Western solidarity must take precedence over everything else, Biddle brought the *Columbus* and *Vincennes* to join two Royal Navy frigates outside Canton, and the crisis ebbed, at least for a time.

Despite this pro-British move, Biddle remained free with his counsel to Ch'i-ying. His Chinese friend readily accepted his suggestion that China's first priority must be the modernization of its army and navy. But he could get nowhere when he urged that the emperor should permit Western emissaries to reside in Peking so that they could keep an eye on one another. Should one of them, Biddle said, attempt any sort of "aggrandizement or conquest against China," they could notify their respective governments in Europe or America; ensuing diplomatic coercion could compel the offender to desist. Ch'i-ying told him that it could not be done, for it was "contrary to the laws of the empire."

As the commodore sailed for Japan early that July, he could reflect that his work had gone well in China. Age was venerated by the Chinese, and his 62 years were to his benefit. The coldness, reserve, and snobbishness that made him disliked by some of his naval colleagues were traits shared by Ch'i-ying and his associates. Barbarian and naval officer though he might be, he at least approximated the Chinese ideal of the gentleman-scholar.[7]

Pre-Arrow (or Second Opium) War, 1849–1855
Lieutenant George H. Preble, et al., at Canton, 1849–1855

Two chronic local problems, piracy and the coolie trade, briefly affected American relations with both China and Great Britain. Piracy was a thriving enterprise along China's eastern and southern shores, where whole fleets of heavily armed junks and barges hid in wait for the weak or unwary merchantman, attacks that Ch'ing officials were helpless to stop. Responding to the anguished appeals of Western businessmen, the first effective countermeasures against piracy began to be taken. Naturally it was the puissant Royal Navy, rich in steam warships, that took the lead, with the occasional cooperation of the Americans.

In 1849 Captain David Geisinger in the sloop *Preble* cooperated with the Royal Navy. He and the British captured 57 junks and burned two pirate bases. During the autumn of 1855 Captain William J. McCluney in the frigate *Powhatan* and the British killed hundreds of sea marauders off Amoy. A little later Commander John Pope took the sloop *Vandalia* on a similar mission with similar results, taking time to overawe local officials at Amoy who were trying to whittle away the treaty rights of the American consul there. In 1854 Lieutenant Preble's activities in the chartered Chinese steamer *Queen* were most impressive. He and the Royal Navy, moving against islands near Hong Kong, smashed pirate bases and annihilated scores of junks.

The U.S. Navy had only a tangential association with the Chinese coolie trade, carrying contract laborers to plantations of Peru and Cuba in particular. It was a dirty business, for most of the coolies had been recruited by deception and coercion, and they often mutinied once they realized what was happening to them.

The case of the *Robert Bowne* caused a short-lived Sino-American controversy. Captain Leslie Bryson, en route from Amoy to California in 1852, began hauling batches of his 410 coolies topside and cutting off their queues, ostensibly for reasons of cleanliness. This was an intolerable insult to a Chinese male; the loss of his queue for whatever reason de-personalized him and made him outcast from even his own family. The infuriated passengers rose, hacked Bryson to pieces, and killed some of the crew, while sparing others needed to operate the ship. When the *Robert Bowne* piled up on a Ryukyuan reef, most of the mutineers went ashore. The American survivors recaptured the vessel and returned to Amoy, where they evoked an Anglo-American response. The British warship *Lily* sailed first to the Ryukyus, bombarded the coolies, and arrested some of them. Commander William S. Walker soon arrived there in the *Saratoga*, and after capturing the remaining 46 coolies, picked up the *Lily*'s contingent in Hong Kong and turned to Acting U.S. Commissioner Dr. Peter Parker for help in their disposal.

After some thought, Parker decided that, although he could claim American jurisdiction under extrality, the evidence against 17 of the mutineers was so airtight that he might as well let the Chinese handle it. To his incredulous rage, the two officials deciding the matter ignored the testimony of American and Chinese prosecution witnesses, declared that Bryson was "tyrannical beyond doubt," and found the accused not guilty. Parker fumed and protested, but the best that he could do was to have another trial. At the second one evidence from Chinese but not Americans was admitted, and almost all of the prisoners were liberated.

One U.S. landing in China emanated from the coolie business. In August 1859 the Shanghai populace were inflamed by reports that Chinese were being kidnaped and taken on board a French vessel probably bound for Peru or Cuba. The American consul and merchants persuaded Captain William C. Nicholson in the *Mississippi* to send sailors and marines ashore in Shanghai to overawe any potential rioters. The task was done handily.

American officers were hamstrung throughout the 1850s by a lack of pertinent legislation, for the U.S. attorney general held that the anti-slave-trade laws did not apply, since coolies were paid wages, no matter how minuscule. In 1862 "An Act to Prohibit the 'Coolie Trade' by American Citizens" was passed, but its loopholes made real enforcement difficult. The problem faded into insignificance when the traffic in Chinese markedly declined in the mid-1870s.[8]

Commodores John Aulick and Matthew C. Perry at Canton, et al.,
1853–1854

Widespread Chinese rebellions exploded in the wake of the Opium War. The Ch'ing dynasty seemed to have lost "the Mandate of Heaven," a charmingly pragmatic concept that if harmony prevailed and matters throughout the empire went reasonably well, the emperor enjoyed the cosmic favor and deserved to rule. But the ignominious defeat by the British, the imposition of heavy new taxes to pay for the indemnity owed to the victors, and a series of massive floods late in the 1840s all demonstrated that chaos had triumphed and the Manchus had lost the mandate. Indeed, one of the major historical mysteries is how that battered dynasty managed to stagger on for another 70 years before being toppled in 1912.

The Taiping Rebellion was by far the most menacing of these uprisings. Hung Hsiu-chüan, a young Chinese in the south, had broken down mentally after failing the imperial examinations that opened the way into the imperial bureaucracy. While convalescing, he received a smattering of instruction from an American Baptist missionary and incorporated some Christianity into his new philosophy. Millions disaffected with the Ch'ing flocked to his standard, attracted by one or another of the reforms he advocated: a communally based economy, land redistribution to the peasants, monotheism, women's rights, anti-foreignism, and fervent opposition to the opium traffic. By 1853 Hung's armies had swarmed out of the south into the central Yangtze Valley and seized Nanking as their capital, where he proclaimed his new rule, called in Chinese "T'ai P'ing T'ien-kuo," or "The Heavenly Dynasty of Great Peace." One of Hung's generals struck far to the north, almost as far as Tientsin, gateway to Peking, before being repelled in 1855. Had he taken the capital, almost certainly the Ch'ing would have fallen, but his failure eventually doomed the uprising. Nevertheless, Taiping-inspired disorders continued to convulse the country. Not until 1864 were imperial armies able to capture Nanking. When Nanking fell, Hung killed himself, and the Taiping Rebellion was finally over. The usual estimate is that between 20 and 30 million Chinese died, directly or indirectly because of it, during that terrible decade and a half.

Initially many Westerners, Protestant missionaries in particular, had been attracted by the Christian-like trappings of the Taiping beliefs, but they were soon dissuaded by Hung's assertion that he was the son of God and the brother of Jesus Christ. Catholics had always opposed Hung, because of his original Protestant affiliations. Furthermore, European and American diplomats quickly discovered that, if anything, the hostility and xenophobia of the Taipings was even more pronounced than that of the Manchus. Eventually a consensus was reached that it would be more advantageous for the West to manipulate the weak and discredited Ch'ing rule than to try to cope with anti-foreign reformers wearing the mantle of successful revolutionaries.

An insurrection that took place along the south and east coast was the most frightening for Europeans and Americans, for it centered in the two main areas of their penetration into China. It was fomented by the Triads and their local affiliates, the Red Turbans in Canton and the Small Swords in Shanghai. The Triads were among the most prominent of the secret societies that had long been a feature of Chinese culture. Their roots stretched back to the seventeenth century, when they had been the stout champions of the tottering Ming dynasty, then in the process of being overthrown by the Manchus. Since then their motto had been "Revere the Ming; Oust the Ch'ing." For a time the Taipings and Triads attempted to cooperate against Peking, and had they been able to cement a real alliance, it seems likely that the Ch'ing would have been obliterated. But the Taipings could not tolerate the ancient ritualistic practices and the reactionary Confucian beliefs of the Triads, so they went their separate ways.

It was against this background of Chinese internal paroxysms that Humphrey Marshall, U.S. commissioner to China, would clash with Commodores John Aulick and Matthew C. Perry, and that Commander John Kelly would bring about the first American armed intervention in China, anti-piratical and coolie-trade operations excepted.

Aulick must have thought that his appointment as commodore of the East India Squadron to lead the American naval expedition to open Japan would terminate his 42 years in the navy with a burst of glory. But hardly had he reached China early in 1852 than everything fell apart for him. The secretary had become angry with him for exceeding his orders in a disciplinary case and behaving discourteously to American and Brazilian officials in Rio. Not only was he relieved of command but forced to remain in China until his replacement arrived. For more than a year the outraged Aulick, bereft of his Japanese opportunity, was isolated and impotent, while his disposition curdled.

Hence he was in no mood to ingratiate himself with the new American commissioner to China. Humphrey Marshall was an irascible and arrogant Kentuckian, a former soldier and congressman, who based himself at Hong Kong. Britain, he was soon convinced, was fishing in the turbulent waters of Chinese civil wars in calculated efforts to gain superiority there. He told Washington that "China is like a lamb before the shearers, as easy a conquest as the provinces of India." Only a strong central government in Peking could check British machinations, he thought, and recommended to the administration that the United States actively support the Ch'ing dynasty against the Taipings and all other rebels. Wishing to investigate the situation to the north, in effect he ordered Aulick to take him there in a U.S. warship. The commodore curtly reminded him that naval officers, not diplomats, assign men-of-war, and turned him down. The stranded commissioner was left fuming with impatience until his adversary was gone.

In April 1853 Matthew C. Perry appeared and clashed with Marshall at once. The latter wanted a strong naval force stationed at Shanghai to protect Americans from any ripple effects of the Taiping or Triad rebellions. Perry would leave behind only a sloop, and when he returned from his first Japanese sojourn in July, once more sparks flew. Marshall insisted that a naval vessel guard every treaty port, but Perry scoffed at the demand, maintaining that he would not become the Western policeman dabbling in China's internal affairs. Basic, of course, to the commodore's stand was his determination that nothing must impede his opening of Japan. Perry won hands down, and the discredited commissioner was quickly called home. Once the commodore had written his Japanese treaty, he became the soul of friendly cooperation with Marshall's successor, Robert McLane, allowing him to use the *Susquehanna* practically as his private yacht. Although there is something a bit ludicrous about the spats between Marshall and Aulick and Perry, they demonstrated the difficulty of reaching a consensus in foreign policy while navy and State Department personnel were so unresponsive to one another.[9]

Commander John Kelly at Shanghai, 1854

Shanghai was the scene of violent diplomacy in the form of the first U.S. armed intervention in China. That treaty port had thrived as the northernmost city open to Westerners and the one closest to the Chinese power center. By 1853 several hundred Westerners resided in a foreign settlement located just outside the walled Chinese city. Although the Taiping Rebellion was nearing its crescendo, the "Small Sword Society," an offshoot of the Triads, posed the chief threat to Shanghai. This menace might have been anticipated since May, when Amoy had fallen temporarily to what one British merchant correctly called "members of the short-knife society (same as Triad society)." Shanghai's turn came early in September when a mere 600 Small Swords pulled off successfully a combined land-and-sea assault upon the Chinese walled city. An army loyal to the Ch'ing quickly appeared but lacked the will to attack. The result was stalemate: the Small Swords behind the walls, the Ch'ing forces encamped outside the city, and the frightened Western community caught between them.

During March 1854 Ch'ing naval forces were trying to besiege the rebels; two of their ships had been purchased from the British and retained their remarkably un-Chinese names: The *Sir Herbert Compton* and the *Clown*. Troops swarmed aboard an American-owned boat, ripped down the flag, carried her six Chinese sailors back to the *Compton,* and restrained them by the somewhat Draconian method of tying their queues around the mainmast. Commander John Kelly in the sloop *Plymouth* (acting in Perry's stead as the ranking U.S. naval officer in China) immediately sent Lieutenant Robert Guest with a small detachment to rescue the Chinese. When the Americans arrived, resistance was threatened, but Guest seized the *Compton*'s acting captain, put a pistol to his head, and told him that "at the first shot fired I would blow his brains out." This permitted the lieutenant to depart unscathed with his liberated Chinese. Kelly further humiliated the Ch'ing by compelling the *Compton,* before all the other ships of their blockading fleet, to honor the American flag with a 21-gun salute. From abroad Perry commended to the Navy Department the "energetic and gallant" conduct of Kelly and Guest.

A few weeks later the imperial army moved its camp to Shanghai's new race course, just to the west of the foreign settlement. On 3 April several Britons were attacked in the vicinity, and some English marines who had rushed to their aid were driven away. That night members of the Western community, terrified of a Ch'ing assault upon them, gathered under the leadership of the British consul, Rutherford Alcock (later Sir Rutherford, minister to China and Japan); U.S. consul Robert Murphy; Royal Navy Captain James O'Callahan; and Kelly, his American counterpart. They were not lacking in audacity, for convinced that the best defense was a stout offense, they decided to attack the imperial camp, although they could muster only a few hundred men to oppose perhaps 10,000 Chinese soldiers. On the 4th Alcock and Murphy, going through the motions of negotiating with the Ch'ing military leader, demanded that by 3:00 P.M. the camp by the race course be evacuated. This was a manifest impossibility, for their ultimatum was not delivered until 2:30.

A little army of 250 Englishmen and 150 Americans gathered from the *Plymouth* and two British warships, as well as civilians from merchantmen and the foreign settlement, commenced their advance at 4:00. When they reached the race course the Americans looped to the left and ran into trouble. Confronted by a creek too wide and swift for fording, they could only mill about while the Ch'ing troops poured shot at them. The British were luckier: they found a bridge to the right and battled through their antagonists to rescue the Americans. But the probable turning point came when more and more of the Small Swords raced out from behind their walls and fell upon the Ch'ing, who fled from the scene, allowing their camp to be destroyed the next day. Anglo-American casualties were 2 Britons dead and 4 wounded and 2 Americans dead and 5 wounded. The records do not tell the number of Small Swords who perished, but estimate that about 300 Ch'ing died.

This encounter is officially called "the Battle of Muddy Flat," an odd name, since all concerned agree that 4 April was a beautiful clear day and participant William Wetmore mentions that bullets threw up "jets of dust." Two sources claim that a British sailor stepped into a soft, wet spot by the creek, thereby giving rise to the original name of "the Battle of Muddy Foot," and that the later alteration came from either a typographical error or a preference for some sort of geographical nomenclature. Yet a modern Chinese scholar says that the imperial camp was enclosed by high and thick walls of turf and mud, and that contemporary usage called the area within a "muddy flat."

Meanwhile, Anglo-American policy toward the imperialist–Small Sword confrontation was reversing itself, and both nations started opposing the rebels. They left the main work to the French, whose hatred of the Taipings rubbed off upon all forms of Chinese insurgency and who energetically assisted the Ch'ing in clamping a total blockade of Shanghai's walled city. The next February most of the starving Small Swords managed to break out of the city and escape, although 250 who surrendered to the French were turned over to their enemies for decapitation.

Alcock, O'Callahan, Murphy, and Kelly were praised by their diplomatic and naval superiors, but the fact was that Americans had joined Englishmen in participating in a Chinese civil war and, moreover, had moved against a regime recognized by both of their governments. They had another choice available. On 4 April Ch'ing forces might have been given a reasonable length of time to move their camp, and Western civilians could have been advised to stay away from the race course until that had been done. Instead, Murphy had joined with Alcock in delivering an ultimatum the terms of which could not possibly have been met. One sympathizes with the imperial general Chi-erh-chang-a when he complained:

> You did not consider that in removing the camp, there was first the necessity of selecting a place and then getting new tents for the shelter of the soldiers. Such business cannot be done in one or two hours on any account. . . . You drove away those good soldiers who had committed no bad acts, and their hearts are not pleased. . . . The difficulties of my position cannot be expressed by words.

American involvement at Muddy Flat was based upon the assumption that the Ch'ing army was planning to storm the foreign settlement. There was no evidence to support that conclusion, except assertions by interested parties attempting to justify their impetuosity. All in all, the U.S. Navy at Shanghai in 1854 did little to promote its country's foreign policy.[10]

The Arrow (or Second Opium) War, 1856–1860
Commodore James Armstrong and Commander Andrew H. Foote
at Canton, 1856

Another clash between China and the West was probably inevitable, for both interpreted differently the meaning of the Opium War and its resultant treaties. Britain, France, the United States (and soon Russia) became increasingly insistent that new agreements must be signed with China, opening additional treaty ports to foreign commerce and residence, granting Christian proselyting privileges, and permission for Western diplomats to live in Peking. Furthermore, the timing for war was right for the Europeans; after 1850 the emperor had his hands more than full with the Taiping and other rebels. The Chinese, to the contrary, considered the pacts of 1842–1844 as mere extensions of their venerable tributary system, marking not commencements but terminations, and even rollbacks wherever possible. The incident for which London was waiting occurred late in 1856 when the British-registered ship *Arrow* was seized by the Ch'ing navy. Yeh Ming-chen, "Imperial Commissioner and Governor-General of Kwangtung and Kwangsi Provinces," was the "Viceroy" responsible for dealing with the West. He released the *Arrow* and expressed regrets for her apprehension, but was unwilling to provide the abject apology required by the British. Hostilities broke out in which Paris joined; the French had ached to avenge the torture and judicial murder of a French priest some time before. By October the Arrow War was under way.

Initial action was concentrated at Canton, which the British occupied briefly but soon relinquished, for they lacked sufficient troops to garrison the city. Simultaneously Americans were intervening in China, this time to destroy the Barrier Forts, Canton's main defenses. The Arrow War then quieted down for many months, because reinforcements from England had to be sidetracked during 1857 to quell the Sepoy Rebellion in India. Early the next year the strengthened British stormed Canton and arrested Yeh, who soon died in exile.

The focus then swung to the north. During the spring, British, French, Russian, and American envoys accompanied an Anglo-French fleet, which, after neutralizing Chinese forts at Taku, sailed up the Pei-ho River to Tientsin, close to the capital. China sued for peace, and the forthcoming treaties of Tientsin with the four Western powers gave foreign diplomats the right to reside in Peking, opened ten new treaty ports, condoned Christian proselyting, and rewarded the two victors with monetary indemnities. Ratifications were supposed to be exchanged within a year, but the emperor procrastinated. To compel Chinese compliance a largely British gunboat flotilla attempted to smash through the secretly rejuvenated defenses at Taku in June 1859. Instead, China won its only major nine-teenth-century victory over the West, sinking four English warships with extremely heavy casualties. Yet there was little jubilation in Peking over this triumph, for even the most xenophobic Chinese knew that the English and French would soon be back, stronger than ever.

Sure enough, a year later an irresistible force of over a hundred men-of-war and 17,000 troops returned to Taku, took the Chinese forts from the rear, marched north through Tientsin to Peking, and sacked the capital mercilessly. Some members of a British diplomatic mission were tortured to death by the Chinese. In retaliation, about 200 or so palaces, temples, and pavilions comprising the emperor's summer palace near the city were burned. At the so-called Protocol of Peking, the British took Kowloon Peninsula across from Hong Kong Island, and heavy indemnities were awarded London and Paris. The four treaties of Tientsin were ratified, and the Russians, by separate agreements reached in 1858 and 1860, were given without firing a shot almost 400,000 square miles of Chinese ter-ritory, north of the Amur and east of the Ussori Rivers. What the Chinese would call "the unequal treaty system" had been fully implanted.

Even before the Arrow War had broken out, Washington had called upon East India Squadron Commodore James Armstrong to maintain the strictest neutrality should Anglo-Chinese hostilities ensue. This he did, although it proved to be a herculean task in the face of strong Chinese provocation and repeated British efforts to inveigle him into cooperative action with them. When the Royal Navy moved against Canton during October and November 1856, two vessels flying the American flag trav-eling along the Pearl River to the foreign settlements outside the walled city were fired upon from the Barrier Forts. These forts were four structures of massive granite walls, mounting heavy artillery, located about halfway along the river near Whampoa Island and Canton. Armstrong vehemently protested these outrages to Viceroy Yeh Ming-ch'en, who did no more than to urge him to evacuate all Americans from the area, since Chinese soldiers could not distinguish between the Union Jack and the Stars and Stripes. While Armstrong pondered his next move, British Admiral Sir Michael Seymour attacked. He stormed the Barrier Forts, but left them relatively intact, smashed a hole in Canton's walls, and looted Yeh's pal-ace. Scandalously, the U.S. consuls at Canton and Hong Kong accom-panied the invaders into the city, the one to help sack the viceroy's palace, the other to allow a U.S. sailor to wave an American flag atop the wall while the British were pouring in, an act promptly condemned by Arm-strong and Commander Andrew H. Foote.

The commodore was ailing during this interim, having to remain on his deep-draft frigate, the *San Jacinto*, and turned naval operations over to Foote. Armstrong decided that Yeh's advice was sound: he decided to remove all Americans from Canton. On 15 November he dispatched Foote in a ship's launch to attend to that matter, but as he neared the Chinese strongholds, shots rang out, despite the waving of a large American flag. On the following day a sailor was killed by a Chinese projectile while his boat was sounding the channel close to the forts. The incensed Armstrong ordered Foote to assail the defenses with the shallow-draft sloops *Portsmouth* and *Levant*. Even though the *Levant* went aground, the *Portsmouth* went on alone to hammer the strongest Chinese position. The sloop knocked out the opposing guns with a well-directed barrage, despite being hulled six times. But on the 17th the *Portsmouth*'s grounding canceled further action until the 20th, when Foote rained shells on the north-bank fort closest to Whampoa, sent ashore 300 men, who captured it, and turned its cannon on a south-shore fort. That evening about 3,000 Chinese soldiers fell upon the Americans but were easily driven away. On the 21st, south-bank redoubts were taken and an island fortress was knocked out. The last position fell on the 22nd. Over the next fortnight all the huge granite edifices were razed stone by stone, a strenuous task for Foote's exhausted sailors and marines.

The Americans had fought splendidly. Their seven-day offensive had stormed four major forts and some lesser defenses, and captured almost 200 guns, at a cost of 7 dead and 29 wounded; Chinese mortalities were estimated at 250. Foote's practically flawless operation won the plaudits of Admiral Seymour: "During their protracted and arduous service, the American officers and men displayed their accustomed gallantry and energy."

If Foote the combatant deserves congratulations, so too does Armstrong the diplomat. Although Dr. Peter Parker, recently appointed U.S. commissioner to China, had just returned to Hong Kong from the north, it was Armstrong who determined American policy at this time. On the 17th he had been approached by the governor of Hong Kong, who asked him to cooperate with the British against the Chinese, but he refused, stressing that he must not compromise his country's neutrality. Three days later the governor tried again, accentuating that Yeh was incorrigible and that only the two nations acting together could force him into better behavior. The commodore once more demurred, pointing out that all he wished to do was to "redress the injuries offered our flag and countrymen." On the 24th Admiral Seymour suggested joint Anglo-American naval movements to clear the Pearl River's banks of Chinese fortifications and keep them clear, but Armstrong repeated that he would act alone.

While Foote was assaulting the Barrier Forts and the British were trying to lure the United States into the Arrow War, Armstrong was keeping in touch with Yeh. Finally the viceroy bent a little when he wrote the Commodore: "There is no matter of strife between our two countries. Henceforth, let the fashion of the flag which the American ships employ be clearly defined or made known, and inform me what it is beforehand. This will be verification or proof of the friendly relations between our Countries." Even though this letter contained not a word of apology for what had been done, and no more than a tepid promise of future accommodation, Armstrong decided to accept it, explaining to Parker:

> I do not see how there is any necessity for further correspondence with the imperial commissioner relative to the affair of the forts. They have been destroyed as a punishment for the assault upon our boat, and if nothing more was done than this we are at least on an equal footing. As you will see by the last letter of Yee [sic], however, there is an intimation that the United States flag will be respected for the future, and until this is shown to be incorrect by some other act, I would prefer to let matters remain as they are.

Subsequent events in south China attested to the accuracy of the commodore's perceptions. Americans were soon withdrawn from Canton, obviating any more shots at their ships. China and the United States remained at peace, albeit a shaky one. Because Yeh never once referred to the American annihilation of his city's most essential defenses, the court in Peking knew nothing about it until told of it by the Chinese governor-general of the Shanghai area. Even then it was considered only some sort of a British plot or lie. Certainly Ch'ing bureaucrats understood that the U.S. Navy's bellicosity at Canton concerned only the specific question of the Barrier Forts and marked no significant alteration in American neutrality. The Hsien-feng emperor wrote to Yeh that he believed that the United States had no quarrel with his realm, and that "intelligent people" should be sent to explain to American officials in China that he viewed the British as foes, but that the Americans, if not friends, at least were not enemies.

Surely Armstrong had shown himself to be a naval diplomat par excellence in this instance. Four American ships, two of the navy itself, had been fired upon, and Yeh could or would give no assurance that such hostility might not become chronic. Only then did Armstrong send Foote against the offending positions, under carefully limited instructions. Resisting the temptation to simplify his immediate task by accepting the British aid so freely offered, he continued to act independently so that his country's neutrality would not be irretrievably compromised. All the while the Barrier Forts were being stormed and destroyed, he maintained contact with Yeh. Once he received a quasi-pledge of future rectitude, he accepted it, calling off further operations. Perhaps the lesson for his American descendants taught by James Armstrong at Canton in 1856 is that if intervention by force should become imperative, one should decide exactly what limited objectives might be achieved and whether they were worth the risk involved; announce what was being done and why; do it; and then, if possible, resume normal relations, behaving as though the episode from start to finish had been abnormal.[11]

Commodore James Armstrong and Formosa (Taiwan), 1856–1857

Although Armstrong had behaved impeccably in the Barrier Forts affair, he shone less brightly in his collaboration with Commissioner Parker in a capricious imperialistic scheme to take Formosa. That offshore island was titularly Chinese, although Ch'ing occupation and influence affected only parts of its west coast; the east and south remained the haunts of local aborigines. Parker's interest there had been sparked by his knowledge that Commodore Perry, in 1854, had considered it "a splendid island" upon which an American "settlement" should be established. Furthermore, the commissioner had received enthusiastic reports from American entrepreneurs trading in Formosa about its abundant supplies of coal, camphor, and other products. Irked by his difficulty in reaching satisfactory agreements with the viceroy, during December Parker suggested to Washington that the United States join offensively with the English and French. The three nations could compel Yeh to consent to a French occupation of Korea, a British seizure of the Chusan Islands, and an American takeover of Formosa, although the latter should be considered only as a "last resort."

Parker met with Armstrong a couple of months later to discuss the topic. He reported to Secretary of State Marcy that he and the commodore had agreed on four points: (1) An American acquisition of Formosa would be "justified" by "international law." (2) Existing "claims and grievances" against China were acute enough to "amply justify reprisals." (3) The island would be a "most desirable" and "valuable" addition to America. (4) But "the present force" of the U.S. Navy made it "impracticable . . . to execute the measure." Hence additional warships should be dispatched at once to the Far East. A little later Armstrong supported Parker's implausible aspirations by sending a marine captain to Formosa to use an already established American trading post at the city of Tainan as "an official residence." This would "legitimate a prior American foothold" should the government seek "future reprisals and occupancy." Luckily for Armstrong, the scheme proved fruitless, and the American flag never floated over Formosa.

For Parker, however, his Formosan policy added up to diplomatic suicide. Marcy tore into his "last resort" letter, asserting that the phrase meant war, that the situation in China certainly did not call for such extreme measures, and that the president had no war-making powers under the constitution. The commissioner was soon recalled in disgrace. As the historian Tyler Dennett commented, "Much reading in international law since the eye doctor became the diplomat had made Dr. Parker a little mad."[12]

Commodore Josiah Tattnall at Taku, 1859–1860

The Hsien-feng emperor kept delaying ratification of the Western-dictated treaties of Tientsin, hoping that some miracle might enable him to wriggle out of their distasteful obligations. But by the spring of 1859 he glumly accepted the inevitable and invited the representatives of the four powers to have their pacts ratified in Peking. John E. Ward, of Georgia, with the new title of minister to China, and East India Squadron Commodore Josiah Tattnall, of the same state, proceeded to Taku. Since Tattnall's flagship, the *Powhatan,* drew too much water for shoal operations off the Pei-ho's mouth, they chartered the *Toeywan,* a small Chinese steamer, and joined the 21-ship Anglo-French armada there, under the command of British Admiral James Hope.

The emperor had refused to allow the Western fleet to proceed upriver past the Chinese fortifications at Taku, offering instead the use of an alternate route a few miles north at Pei-t'ang, a village on another branch of the Pei-ho. But the British and French envoys, convinced that this was simply a further example of Chinese evasion and procrastination, insisted on Taku, ordering Hope to clear their way. None of them realized that the able General Seng-ko-lin-ch'in (the British sailors called him "Sam Collinson") had so massively reinforced his defenses that an English engineer called them "the best of the kind I ever heard of."

On 24 June, Ward and Tattnall in the *Toeywan* were reconnoitering the mouth of the river when they ran aground just where the mud flats at low tide met the deep channel; there was a real danger that the vessel might turn turtle and founder. Hope sent over a couple of gunboats to see if his assistance was required. The Americans thanked him but declined his offer. Toward evening the *Toeywan* was refloated by shifts in the wind and tide. But Tattnall considered that he had a debt of honor to repay.

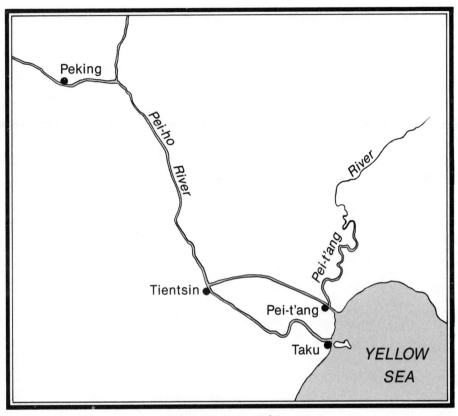

Taku, Tientsin, Peking

The next day Hope led his gunboats, nine British and one French, up the channel, which was only 200 yards wide at low water, protected by a barrier of iron posts, an unfinished steel cable, a huge boom of heavy logs chained together, and two rafts. Although there were others, the major redoubt was the "Great South Fort" on the left bank, mounting some 50 pieces of heavy artillery, all focused upon the exact spot through which the attacking ships must pass. Suddenly "a terrible fire of very heavy guns opened with fatal skill," concentrated on Hope's flagship, and within a few minutes 39 of the 41 men aboard were either killed or wounded, the admiral among the wounded. He was taken to a second gunboat and hit again, before being removed to a third, where he lay "constantly fainting from loss of blood." Before that day was over he was in his fourth, and Tattnall remarked that it was "unprecedented" in naval warfare for a commander to have three flagships shot out from under him.

At this juncture, with wind and river conditions such that no British reinforcements could be brought up, Hope sent an officer to the *Toeywan*, where Ward and Tattnall were watching the slaughter with horrified astonishment. The commodore responded to the Briton's "silent appeal" as he kept his eyes moving back and forth from the immobilized reserves to the *Cormorant,* Hope's latest flagship. With Ward's consent but also with his admonition not to engage in hostilities, Tattnall used the *Toeywan* to tow the reinforcements into battle. He returned to his anchorage but almost at once decided to visit Hope and thank him for his "chivalrous conduct" of the day before. Ward agreed but once more urged him to remain neutral. Just as Tattnall reached the *Cormorant,* his launch was sunk and one sailor was killed, but the commodore managed to clamber aboard. According to his official report to the Navy Department, he consoled the stricken admiral and "after about ten minutes" returned to the *Toeywan* in a British vessel.

Tattnall's errors of commission and omission are impressive. He lied about the duration of his stay in the *Cormorant.* One contemporary account says that he remained there "nearly an hour" and another "an hour and a half." He failed to admit that he had ignored Ward's counsel that he stay aloof from participation. Quite the contrary: when he came on deck he saw that almost no Englishmen remained physically able to operate their cannon. He said to his sailors, "Meanwhile, my good fellows, you might man that gun forward until the boat is ready." The supposedly nonbelligerent Americans then proceeded to hammer the Great South Fort for either sixty or ninety minutes. Finally, the commodore neglected to mention the famous comment he made when he moved to help the British: "Blood is thicker than water." Undoubtedly he said it; four separate eyewitness accounts quote that statement. One also noted that he had said that "he'd be damned if he'd stand by and see white men butchered before his eyes. No, sir, old Tattnall isn't that kind, sir. This is the cause of humanity." At the very least, such sentiments would not be out of character in a mid-nineteenth-century American from a slave state.

Tattnall's last breach of neutrality occurred late the same night. Hope compounded his series of dreadful errors by ordering an after-dark assault across extensive mud flats to storm the Great South Fort. The Americans hauled 600 British marines to the channel's edge. Barely one-tenth were able to wade through the mire to reach the walls, only to find out that they had forgotten to bring scaling ladders. Eventually the survivors had to fight their way back to the channel. Fifty per cent of the attackers were casualties. The final tally on that awful 25 June was 89 dead and 345 wounded, roughly 40 percent of Hope's command. Little wonder that one

Josiah Tattnall
(U.S. Naval Academy Museum)

Crimean War veteran who participated compared fighting the Chinese at Taku to battling the Russians: "Talk of Balaclava! I was there and this is much worse. I had rather go three times to Balaclava!"

A Boston newspaper's summary of what Ward and Tattnall had done on the Pei-ho was typical of many others. Their gallantry and humanitarianism were lauded, but their unneutral intervention "can hardly be thought creditable to their sound judgment and discretion" and had "endangered our relations with a nation with whom we are and ought to be at peace." Perhaps only the British response to his interjection saved Tattnall from a court-martial and suspension for exceeding his orders. In London the Palmerston ministry effusively commended him to Washington, and the usually anti-American press in both Britain and China heaped accolades upon him. Some time later the Navy Department gave him a lukewarm endorsement, but more significantly, neither the secretary nor the president even mentioned the happenings on the Pei-ho in his annual report for 1859.

The "blood is thicker than water" episode also had direct diplomatic repercussions, for the Chinese court knew how Tattnall had worked against them, Seng-ko-lin-ch'in having reported the details. When Ward was invited to come to Peking during the summer of 1860 so that ratifications of the Sino-American Treaty of Tientsin might be exchanged, the Hsien-feng emperor inflicted some harrowing conditions upon him, partly in retaliation for what Tattnall had done. He and his entourage were compelled to travel to the capital in hot, uncomfortable wooden carts, and although lavishly accommodated and fed, were at first placed under virtual house arrest and forbidden to meet the Russian minister to Peking. Worst of all, Ward was informed that he must perform the kowtow, a number of ritualistic prostrations, before the throne. He of course refused to degrade himself. He was then asked if he would at least kneel, but he intoned that he restricted his genuflections to "God and woman." The Chinese tried to persuade him that "The Emperor is the same as God," ignoring, no doubt, as some incomprehensible Western imbecility Ward's mention of the second recipient of his ceremonious respect. His defiance prevented further negotiations in Peking, although a little later at Pei-t'ang, on the coast, he was permitted to exchange Tientsin ratifications with the Chinese.[13]

Summary

The early naval sojourns in China of Henley, Finch, Downes, Geisinger, and Aulick, from 1819 to 1836, featured their shrugging off the feeble attempts of imperial officials to control their movements and departure dates; at least they did nothing to depart from their government's foreign policy in the Far East. The urgings of Kennedy in 1836, Read three years later, and especially Kearny in 1842 were instrumental in the creation of the East India Squadron, the navy's diplomatic arm. Although Foxhall Parker's contributions to Cushing's Treaty of Wanghia in 1844 are problematical, at least he and Tilton kept Sino-American disturbances from rupturing. Biddle, two years later, was a model of naval decorum in forming his amicable relations with Ch'ing emissaries, and he did well in founding the first American legation at Canton, as well as the new consulate in Shanghai. Yet when an uprising in Canton menaced the Western community there, he dispensed with his Anglophobia long enough to stand shoulder-to-shoulder with the British until calm had been restored.

The efforts of Preble and other officers against piracy did what the Chinese themselves could not accomplish—they at least partially stemmed this flourishing business. American naval officers, however, could do little to terminate American participation in the coolie trade, for they were hogtied by the lack of U.S. laws against that traffic until after 1860. Aulick's and Perry's tiffs with Marshall highlighted the difficulty of composing a harmonious American program in the Far East when commodore and commissioner were castigating rather than cooperating with one another.

The three American armed interventions in China from 1854 to 1859 would seem to add up to a plus and two minuses in the naval diplomatic annals. Kelly at Shanghai and Tattnall at Taku overreacted and acted against their government's desires; the latter's intrusion against Seng-ko-lin-ch'in hampered Ward's ratification of the Treaty of Tientsin. So too had Armstrong intervened at Canton, but his provocation had been so strong and his retaliation so well thought out and self-contained that he merits special praise. Hence his Formosan policy may be excused as an aberration. Save for sporadic movements against pirates, and a brief landing at Shanghai in 1859 by Captain William S. Nicolson in the *Mississippi*, to put down a local disturbance, the U.S. Navy did not roil Sino-American relations until after 1865.

CHAPTER TEN

Japan

1815–1860

The remarkable Japanese, in the sharpest contrast to the Chinese, had long demonstrated an ability to select from foreigners the things they wanted and then shape them to fit their own needs. For example, they installed China's administrative system featuring a strong emperor, but by the late 1100s had altered it significantly. The Japanese emperor was relegated to impotence, residing in the cultural center of Kyoto, where he remained a virtual palace prisoner, occupying himself with religious and symbolic duties. Real power, military and civil, was given to the shogun in Edo (later Tokyo), a "generalissimo," whose dynasty (the shogunate) was hereditary, and whose bureaucracy was called the *bakufu*. This odd political division prevailed until 1867. It took years before Americans recognized this distinction; as late as the 1850s Washington's notes were always addressed to "The Emperor."

Portuguese Jesuit missionaries were the first Westerners to visit Japan. During the half-century after the 1540s, they converted perhaps 300,000 to Catholicism, most of them in the extreme southwest. By the early 1600s the new Tokugawa shogunate had won supreme power, over strong opposition from the great nobles (daimyo) in southern Honshu and Kyushu, the very areas that were the most Christianized. The shoguns feared that their still dangerous adversaries might rise to topple them, calling upon Europeans for naval, military, and financial aid, abetted by a potential

Catholic fifth column. To avert this possibility the Tokugawas started a brutal series of intermittent persecutions, while expelling foreign missionaries. By 1638 almost all Japanese Christians had been exterminated. The one Asian people that had welcomed the advent of the Europeans and their religion became the one to expel them the most savagely and thoroughly.

For the next 215 years Japan retreated into the most extreme form of isolationism. Alien vessels approaching those islands were rebuffed and sometimes fired upon. Emigration was forbidden, and local shipping was restricted to fishing boats or coastal traders. Japan's only view of the outside world was at Deshima, a small island in Nagasaki Harbor, where the nonproselyting Dutch were allowed to maintain a trading post. But a few Japanese learned Dutch and were kept informed about current world conditions. One may imagine the shock with which they greeted the news that China had been humiliated by the British in the Opium War.

As Sino-Western relations increased, American whalers and other ships taking the great circle route from California to Canton had to pass along the forbidden and forbidding shores of Japan unable to buy essential supplies and aware that sometimes shipwrecked crews were treated harshly by their unwilling hosts.

Prior to the American Civil War, U.S. naval officers concerned themselves with Japan on six separate occasions. The first two were instances of wishful thinking only, for the first remained on paper and the second had to be canceled. In 1846 and 1849 U.S. men-of-war actually went to Japan. The first visit was at Edo for the purpose of collecting information, although its commander endured some embarrassment. The second managed to rescue some imprisoned American whalemen. Neither, however, made a chip in Japan's wall of isolationism. It was, of course, the famous expedition of 1853–1854 that made the breach, for it coincided with a decision in Edo that the country must begin looking outward. An incident in 1860, while minor, was much appreciated for its assistance in enabling Japan's infant navy to make its first long cruise.

Captain David Porter and Japan, 1815

The Treaty of Ghent naturally resulted in massive layoffs of U.S. Navy personnel, men and officers alike. Flushed with enthusiasm over his recent voyage to the Pacific, Captain David Porter turned his active mind to an attempt to compensate for the peacetime consequences and add to his own glory. In October 1815 he wrote to President Madison suggesting that he command an expedition around Cape Horn to join an overland expedition in Oregon, and thus strengthen the national claim to that tract.

But his main point was to open up Japan. He stressed what an accomplishment it would be for the citizens of a country "of only forty years standing to beat down their rooted prejudices—to secure to ourselves a valuable trade, and make that people known to the world." He revealed his real motivation, however, in his closing words: "The world is at peace. . . . We have ships . . . [and] officers who will require employment."

Some earlier historians, Charles O. Paullin among them, have stated that the president ignored Porter's proposition. Not so. Madison set about implementing it by ordering Commodores Oliver H. Perry and Charles Morris to serve in Porter's squadron, and as late as mid-1816 Morris was enjoined to "prepare for a cruise to the Pacific." But the plan fell through, partly because of Perry's refusal to accept a subordinate position, and largely because of a temporary spasm of unpleasantness with Spain. The ships earmarked for Porter's cruise were sent instead to the Caribbean. Although he overstates his case, a modern historian has argued that subsequent American interest in Japan "developed from the idea which the proposal of 1815 initiated." The matter then lapsed until the early 1830s.[1]

Commander David Geisinger, Captain Edmund P. Kennedy, and Japan, 1832–1836

Special envoy Edmund Roberts (in the lowly official status of a navy clerk) was instructed by President Jackson in 1832 to sail with Commander David Geisinger in the *Peacock* to sign whatever treaties he could with countries in western, southeastern, and eastern Asia. Specifically, he was told to be "very careful in obtaining information regarding Japan—the means of opening communication with it, and the present value of its trade with the Dutch and Chinese." He was also told that, although a separate expedition might be sent to that nation, "if you find the prospect favorable, you may fill up one of the letters of credence with the proper title of the Emperor, and present yourself there for the purpose of opening a trade." But while being brushed off by the Sinified court of Cochin China (South Vietnam), Roberts and Geisinger concluded that heading for China and Japan would be a waste of time. Instead they signed pacts with Siam (Thailand) and Arabian Muscat (Oman) and returned home.

Japan was even more heavily emphasized in 1835 when the president sent Roberts back in the *Peacock* to exchange ratifications with the two signatories, this time under Captain Edmund P. Kennedy. They should carry to that nation a letter from Jackson to the emperor, accompanied by presents, among them "a gold watch with a heavy gold chain eight feet long . . . a shotgun . . . and ten Merino sheep of the finest wool." But after they executed their duties in Muscat and Siam, Roberts died in China

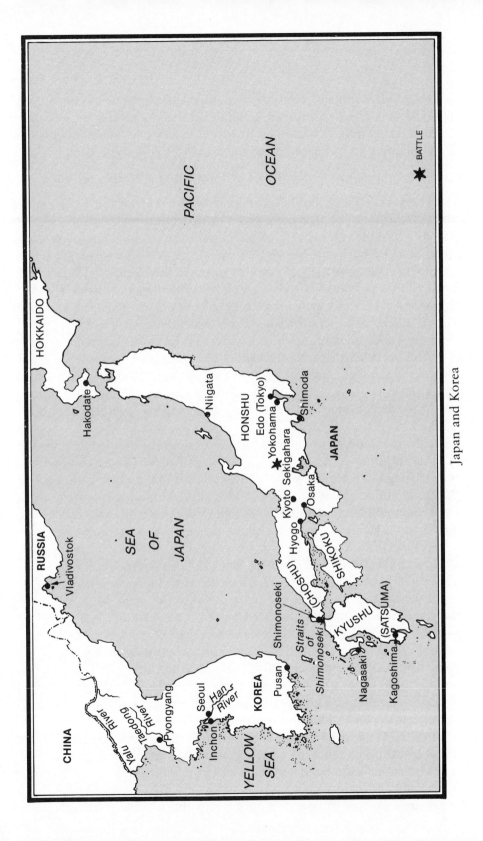

Japan and Korea

in mid-1836. Kennedy, aware that he lacked the proper diplomatic credentials for a Japanese mission, abandoned the project. As in the case of Porter's suggestion, it was undoubtedly just as well. Japan was resolute in maintaining its treasured isolationism.[2]

Commodore James Biddle at Edo (Tokyo) Harbor, 1846

Commodore James Biddle's orders from the secretary in 1845 explain what he did in Japan, for there could be no confusing their meaning. He was to "take the utmost care to ascertain if the ports of Japan are accessible," but he must not behave "in such a manner as to excite a hostile feeling or distrust of the Government of the United States." Therefore his mission was restricted to fact-finding and must be pacifistic. These instructions contrasted with those to be given Perry in 1852, for their emphasis was different. To be sure, Perry was advised to be friendly while using "every argument and means of persuasion for a reciprocal arrangement" about returning stranded sailors. Should he fail, however, he should inform the Japanese that if they subsequently inflicted any "cruelty" upon American castaways, "they will be severely chastised." This distinction, I feel, has escaped many contemporary and modern commentators about Biddle's alleged weakness.

As the commodore approached his destination he decided to ignore the Japanese injunction that all foreign vessels must come to the southwestern port of Nagasaki. He knew that power resided in the capital and that any of his communications delivered at Nagasaki would require many weeks for a response. When the *Columbus* and *Vincennes* came into Edo's lower harbor on 21 July, a Japanese minor official accepted Biddle's letter to "the Emperor." A week later a frosty reply arrived: only unimportant trade with the Dutch and China is permitted; no other country, including the United States, can engage in commerce with Japan, because exclusion of foreigners has long been its policy; it will do no good to try again, for the same response will be received; and in conclusion: "we have to say that the Emperor positively refuses the permission you desire. He earnestly advises you to depart immediately, and to consult your own safety by not appearing again on our coast." Biddle accepted this rebuff with equanimity, saying that his nation wanted a trade treaty with Japan only if mutually acceptable. He had now found out that Edo would sign no such agreement, so he would leave as soon as possible.

Meanwhile an incident had taken place that brought considerable criticism upon the commodore. The Japanese had asked him to accept the response to his note personally in a nearby junk. Biddle described what happened: "At the moment I was stepping aboard a Japanese on the deck of the junk gave me a blow or a push which threw me back into the ship's boat." Shaken, he demanded that the Japanese officers arrest the offender, and returned to the *Columbus* in a state of such fury that one of his sailors described him as "the hottest little old man I ever saw. He stamped into his cabin in great rage, and I thought at one time that he was going to open up his batteries on them." An officer thought so too. But since Japanese authorities had hurriedly followed him to the *Columbus* to apologize and pledge that the offender would be "severely punished," he relented. After pointing out to them "the enormity of the outrage" and how much they owed to his "forbearance," he agreed to turn the matter over to "the laws of Japan." On the 29th the two U.S. warships headed for Hawaii.

Negative reactions to his "forbearance" erupted. A missionary to China pointed out in 1850 that Biddle had been *"struck with much violence by a sailor"* and did nothing. A rumor circulated in the Ryukyu Islands that the "American chief" had accepted in Edo "an insult offered with impunity." Commander James Glynn, in Nagasaki during 1849, thought that his predecessor's meekness had been "very unfavorable to the interests of the United States." Without mentioning his name, Perry used the Biddle incident to reinforce his determination never to place himself in such a position. Yet Biddle had his staunch defenders. Two of his officers concurred that the commodore's "friendly disposition" showed the difference between Americans and Europeans and was useful for Perry eight years later. Charles O. Paullin thought that "Biddle's amiable and judicious relations with the Japanese officials gave them a favorable impression of the strength, candor, and justice of the great Western republic."

It has to be granted that Biddle erred in judgment when he went unprotected to the Japanese junk; had he remained in his ship he would have escaped embarrassment. But the nature of his orders should not be forgotten. If he had overreacted to what was after all a minor incident, he could well have caused in Edo "a hostile feeling or distrust" of his government and people. He could have expected later censure in Washington, and the possibility that the relatively smooth course of Japanese-American relations would have been much more difficult and progress certainly delayed. Perhaps the comment that Secretary Bancroft jotted in the margin of one of Biddle's letters to him may be accepted as a satisfactory conclusion: "His prudent and judicious conduct at Yedo merits the strong approbation of the Department."[3]

Commander James Glynn at Nagasaki, 1849

By the late 1840s it was common knowledge in the Far East that a few sailors who had either deserted from or been shipwrecked in American whalers within Japanese waters were incarcerated in Nagasaki. The prisoners later avowed that they had been looked upon as spies and treated so savagely that one man had committed suicide, yet there is evidence that they had been insolent to their captors and had repeatedly attempted to escape. Probably the only thing that saved their lives was the intervention of the Dutch superintendent of the trading post at Nagasaki.

In 1849 East India Squadron Commodore David Geisinger told Commander James Glynn to sail to Nagasaki in the sloop *Preble* and try to bring about their release to him. Should he fail, he was to proceed to Edo and present his case to the *bakufu* in a "firm, temperate, and respectful" manner. On 17 April Glynn dropped anchor off Nagasaki's forts. Consternation swept the city, 6,000 soldiers were mustered, and defensive repairs were commenced in the forts. The commander adopted an air of cold disdain and demanded that the prisoners be given to him at once. Thanks in part to continued Dutch support, 14 whalemen boarded the *Preble* on the 27th and were carried away to Hong Kong.

Samuel Eliot Morison, in his *Old Bruin*, uses Glynn's accomplishment as a scourge to belabor Biddle, contrasting the former's tenacious resolve with the latter's "soft stuff" and "palsy-walsy approach." He goes on to say that Glynn "promised to open gunfire" on Nagasaki should he be refused the prisoners. This is total nonsense. Paullin, in his *Diplomatic Negotiations*, devotes five pages to the verbatim exchange between the commander and the Japanese bureaucrats. What he actually said to them was quite otherwise: "I will . . . report to my government that you decline complying with my demand for the release of the men." It is incomprehensible how a historian of Morison's caliber could construe this into a threat to bombard a city in a country with which the United States was at peace. Indeed Glynn's orders were that if he failed at Nagasaki he was to sail to Edo and present his arguments there "in a conciliatory but firm manner." Had he disregarded his instructions and opened fire, he would have deserved to be cashiered from the service. In short, Glynn had been given a particular chore and performed it creditably. But so too had Biddle in amassing information and avoiding any clash, as directed by his government.[4]

Commodore Matthew C. Perry in Japan, the Ryukyus, and the Bonins,
1853–1854

The Japanese expedition had been long in prospect, and once Perry became commodore he urged successfully that he be given some of the more modern and powerful steamers and the title of "Minister Plenipotentiary and Envoy Extraordinary" so that he might act for the president in treaty-making. In late November 1852 he sailed in the *Mississippi*, and came into Hong Kong early in April. After bickering with and routing Commissioner Humphrey Marshall, as narrated above, he put to sea on 26 May 1853.

His first port of call was Naha, the capital of Okinawa, in the Ryukyu Islands (called then the "Lew-chews"); he remained there until 9 June. He utilized his sojourn as a dress rehearsal of the circumlocutions and procrastinations that he knew were practiced in the diplomacy of that area. Nominally independent, the Okinawans were militarily impotent and could offer little to withstand Perry, beyond protestations, isolation of its people from American contacts, and pleas that he depart. Perry paid no attention to them, explored the island's interior, and, over horrified protests, entered the royal palace. He eyed the strategic location of Naha as a possible American base, for he was interested in procuring U.S. territorial establishments in the Far East to offset at least partially the British possessions at Hong Kong and Singapore. He next proceeded to the almost unpopulated site of Port Lloyd, in the Bonin Archipelago, on an island near Iwo Jima, of World War II fame. From 14 to 18 June he looked over this tiny settlement as a potential acquisition, for it was closer to the whaling grounds than Naha.

After a short stay in the Ryukyus, Perry's four-ship squadron entered Edo's lower bay on 8 July. Dismay among the local populace was immediately observable: boats scurried about helter-skelter and troops began hurriedly assembling. Perry promptly informed the Japanese that he would deal with their highest authorities near the capital and with no one else. During the first few days he remained out of sight, conduct that led one of his biographers to call him "Lord of the Remote Interior." Mingled with his imperious behavior, however, was his care in letting the Japanese know that at present his only purpose was to deliver the president's letter to the emperor, after which he would give them time to consider a response. But if they would not accept the letter, he would "consider his country insulted, and will not hold himself accountable for the consequences."

At this time the *bakufu* was frozen into relative inertia. The shogun, ineffective at best, was deathly ill—he died between Perry's two visits. Nevertheless, his top-level councilors could not overlook the fact that their obsolete defenses could be turned into rubble by American firepower, with a potentially catastrophic loss of face for the shogunate. So they decided that Fillmore's message must be accepted. On the 13th two of their members agreed to hold the proper ceremonies for its delivery the next day at a small village near the town of Uraga. That morning Perry and his officers, in full martial regalia, accompanied by 250 sailors and marines, went ashore. Tension was high, for the Americans were outnumbered some twenty to one by Japanese troops, but tranquility was broken only by salutes fired by both sides. The meeting ended after Perry had read the missive to the *bakufu*'s representatives and stated that he would soon depart but would come back the next spring with a larger armada for their answer.

On the 17th he led his squadron away from Japan for Naha, where he rested for a few days. During this interim he sent one of his ships to reconnoiter the Bonins further. By 7 August he was in Hong Kong, the first part of his mission well accomplished by his combination of hauteur and conciliation. As Morison points out, he was using the same tactics that he had found successful at Naples 21 years before—appearing with force, presenting in effect an ultimatum, giving the other side time for reflection, and showing up later with a more impressive fleet.

Perry had left the *bakufu* to pick its way through a thicket of unappetizing choices. Councilor Abe Masahiro (who had written the inflexible message to Biddle seven years before) was aware of the power vacuum at the top of his government, with a new and untried shogun just installed. So he decided that the responsibility for handling Perry must be apportioned among as many as possible. He even asked the emperor for his advice, much to the latter's delighted astonishment, for no such request had been made within memory. More to the point, Abe sent questionnaires to scores of the daimyo, asking whether they thought the Americans should be welcomed. A handful were willing to do so with some enthusiasm; a militant wing advocated resistance. But the middle ground, represented by Abe, won the day, although its purpose was no more than to buy time to buttress their defenses. A treaty would be signed protecting stranded sailors and providing two places where American ships could purchase necessities, but no commercial agreement would be tolerated.

Back in China, Perry, by the end of the year, learned that a Russian fleet was nosing about Japan, and determined not to await the spring before returning to those islands. First he made a quick stopover at Naha, where he chided the Okinawans for their unfriendly attitude toward Americans, sent an officer once more to Port Lloyd in the Bonins, who went so far as to put up a plaque claiming it for the United States (although nothing ever came of it), and went back to Hong Kong. He was happy to see that his reinforcements and supplies had arrived, including the powerful frigate *Powhatan*, and on 14 January 1854 he sailed for Japan. After once again reminding the badgered Okinawans of his expectations, he pulled into an anchorage some 20 miles south of Edo on 13 February.

Over the next three weeks the commodore endured tiresome negotiations about where the treaty should be signed, but finally Kanagawa, a

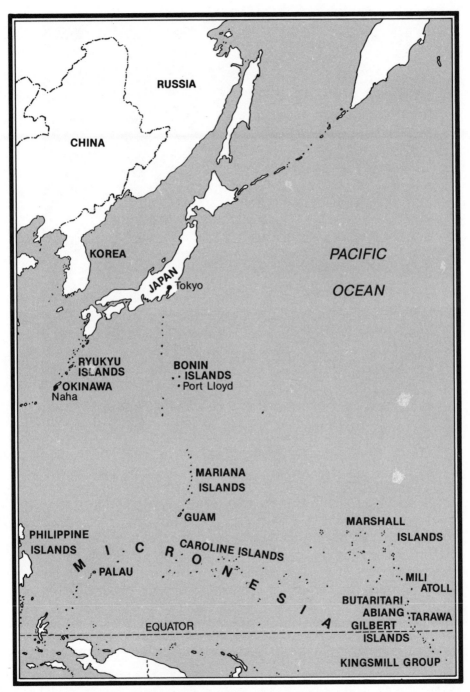

The Western North Pacific Ocean

Matthew Calbraith Perry
(Official U.S. Navy Photo)

village near Yokohama, was selected. During this interim presents and entertainments were exchanged.

On 27 March Perry invited the Japanese delegation to a banquet in his flagship, during which his guests partook of champagne, punch, and whisky to such an extent that one of the tipsy envoys threw his arms around the commodore's neck, crushing his epaulets, and cried, "Japan and America, all the same heart!" One of his officers asked the imperturbable Perry how he could tolerate such an effusion, and he replied, "Oh! if they will only sign the Treaty he may kiss me!"

The shogun's emissaries, in addition to letting Perry know that they would agree to provide for shipwrecked American mariners and would grant most-favored-nation status, confirmed that they would allow basic supplies to be bought by American whalers and merchantmen in two ports—hence the popular name of "The Wood and Water Treaty." Hakodate on the southern tip of Hokkaido, the northernmost home island, and Shimoda on the Izu Peninsula well to the south of Edo were selected. Perry later visited both sites, and while Hakodate was of considerable usefulness, picturesque but out-of-the-way Shimoda was almost completely isolated from the rest of Japan. But when Perry broached the idea of a commercial pact, the Japanese were firmly opposed, claiming that their nation was self-sufficient and wished no export trade. They cleverly emphasized that the nurture of castaways was one thing, but "Commerce has to do with profits, but has it anything to do with human life?" The commodore thought that over and conceded the point.

On the 18th the final deliberations took place at Kanagawa. Perry, having surrendered on a trade pact, became subtle himself when he persuaded his hosts that resident consuls should be posted in each country. The Japanese asserted that the agreement on consuls pertained only to commerce, but Perry said that its purpose was to have someone in authority on hand to mediate the disputes between visitors and natives that were sure to arise, and he won the argument. He was satisfied to obtain the provision about consuls as an entering wedge, correctly surmising that this Japanese concession would soon result in a trade agreement. On 31 March the Treaty of Kanagawa was signed, with both sides trying to outdo the other in lavish displays of pomp and color. Ratifications would be exchanged in February 1855.

Perry spent most of June relaxing at Shimoda before leaving Japan for Naha on the 28th. By this time the Okinawans had learned about Kanagawa and realized that they had no hope of avoiding a similar imposition. The Treaty of Naha, signed on 11 July, contained no commercial arrangement and further mirrored the Japanese pact in its provisions for the treatment of stranded Americans and the right of U.S. shippers to buy supplies. Late in July Perry was back in Hong Kong.

During his last few weeks in the Far East, his major difficulty concerned the North Pacific Surveying Expedition, under Commodore Cadwalader Ringgold, with Lieutenant John Rodgers as second in command. The five-ship squadron had been sent around South Africa in 1853, anticipating Perry's success. In order for Americans to use effectively and safely any ports that he might open, Japanese shores and waters must be surveyed and sounded. In China Ringgold and Rodgers were soon at sword's-points over policy, with the sickly commodore's behavior becoming increasingly erratic. Rodgers announced that his superior was insane and assumed command. Perry looked into the matter and was appalled at the expedition's demoralization from disease and liquor. He appointed a board of physicians to examine Ringgold, accepted their dubious verdict of lunacy, and confirmed Rodgers's appointment in August. The new commander provided one small contribution to his country's external relations. That November he moored the *Vincennes* at Naha, Okinawa, to buy water, wood, and foodstuffs, but the Okinawans ignored their treaty stipulations that they must provide such supplies. They wailed that "if they furnished the wood we demanded it would take every stick on the island, that none would be left for them to cook their food, that they would all die of starvation," with Okinawa finally becoming "one vast sepulcher." Since the lieutenant had seen "fifty times" the amount he needed lying around the city, he landed about 100 men and a cannon and marched them to the palace "to scare them into propriety and truth." The next day all requirements were met with alacrity, and the *Vincennes* departed a little later.

Otherwise the members of Rodgers's expedition passed their time surveying Shimoda, Hakodate, and the Japanese coast in general before performing the same duty as far north as the Bering Sea. Funds exhausted, Rodgers disbanded his fleet at San Francisco in October 1856. As for Perry, complacently aware of how his triumph would be hailed at home, he left China on 11 September and was in New York on 11 January 1855.[5]

Lieutenant John M. Brooke, Uraga to San Francisco, 1860

A sequel to the Ringgold-Rodgers Expedition (1853–1856) occurred four years later. Lieutenant John M. Brooke, who had been along on that voyage, was selected by the department to ascertain the best trans-Pacific route to the Far East. Sailing in the minuscule schooner USS *Fenimore Cooper*, he worked around Hawaii and the Mariana Islands, stopped off at Hong Kong, and proceeded to the Ryukyus and Japan. During August 1859 his ship was swamped in a storm at Yokohama, stranding him and his crew. That autumn East India Squadron Commodore Josiah Tattnall offered them passage home in the *Powhatan*, which was carrying the first Japanese delegation to visit America. But those proud people, most self-conscious about their delegation's being transported in a foreign vessel, insisted that one of their own men-of-war must also make the passage. The *bakufu* asked that Brooke and a few other American seamen come along on the Japanese vessel, aware that the inexperience of its officers and men would make a safe voyage unlikely. Tattnall gave his permission, and the lieutenant, a draftsman, and nine sailors were detached for the assignment. In February 1860 the *Kanrin Maru*, a 10-gun former Dutch steamboat of less than 300 tons, set out from Uraga with the eleven

Americans and about a hundred Japanese, some of whom would later rise to the highest levels in their navy.

It was an unforgettable crossing. Beset by foul weather most of the way, with the distance to be traversed requiring the use of sails for all but three days, the American contingent at first had to perform the essential duties practically alone. Several of the Japanese officers were immobilized by seasickness, and the others needed further training before they could be of much help. An exception was Nakahama Manjiro, who when 14 years old had been shipwrecked off his coast, saved by an American whaler, and taken to Massachusetts before finally making his way home via California. He quickly picked up the necessary seamanship, particularly in navigation.

Brooke was horrified at such Japanese practices as keeping fires going continually for their never-ending bowls of rice, smoking below, sneaking nips of sake, and demonstrating a churlish unwillingness to stand watch or handle the sails; at one point he agonized that "all is confusion." But he gradually turned things around by his ability to walk a line between compliance with their dangerous nautical habits on the one side and an overreaction to them on the other that might have offended their strong sense of personal honor. By the time they came into San Francisco on 17 March, 37 days out of Uraga (having beaten the *Powhatan,* which had detoured into Honolulu for supplies), he was able to conclude that the Japanese would become "excellent sea officers." So grateful were his companions for his efficiency and encouragement of them that one of their highest-ranking officers brought Brooke to his cabin, which held a chest said to contain $80,000 in gold, and invited him to take as much of it as he wished, but as a naval officer he had to decline. A final evaluation of his contribution to the success of the *Kanrin Maru* is easy: With no American on board, the ship retraced her route without untoward incident, arriving home early in July.[6]

Summary

The navy's contribution to the establishment of American relations with previously seclusive Japan was limited. Prior to 1850 it is likely that only the British had the martial sinews to compel Edo to accept diplomatic relations, as they had with Peking. Americans could have done nothing to reach that end until the Japanese had concluded that their long-cherished isolationism had outlived its usefulness. The Japanese would have to assume that their ability to accept and alter foreign importations, so often demonstrated, would permit them to do what the Chinese could not—westernize and industrialize. Hence Porter's grandiose plan of 1815, admirable though it may have appeared in concept, was no more than shadow-boxing. Had Roberts remained alive and gone to Japan, his expulsion would have been assured. Even Perry, effective though he was in his synthesis of pressure and mollification, very probably would have toiled in vain had he stopped off there during the 1840s, as indicated by the experiences of Biddle and Glynn. They followed their instructions meticulously, but any opportunities to do more were obviated, because they appeared before the *bakufu* had commenced to change its collective mind and started to inch into the mid-nineteenth-century world. To state the obvious, Brooke would never have been able to contribute his bit toward cross-Pacific amity had not Japan begun purchasing ocean-going warships abroad. Of the last four Perry deserves the highest ranking, for by history's pragmatic standards his approach was the one that achieved the breakthrough, but commendations for the others are also in order. As for the North Pacific Expedition's contribution, that of Rodgers at Okinawa was perhaps more amusing than meaningful.

CHAPTER ◆ ELEVEN

The Indian Ocean and Southeast Asia

1832–1853

The Indian Ocean is the third largest ocean, almost as big as the Atlantic. The territories around its rim, an enormous sweep from East Africa past India and Southeast Asia all the way to Australia, contained a potpourri of administrative systems. Those in which the American naval presence was felt before 1861 had one feature in common with Latin America, Europe, the Middle East, China, Japan, and Hawaii: unlike West Africa and most of the Pacific islands, all were governed by some kind of recognizable centralized authority. On the ocean's western shores lay Moslem Muscat in Arabia, the island of Zanzibar in the center, and far to the south independent Joanna in the Comoro Archipelago near huge Madagascar. To the north the British already held India effectively and were taking initial steps toward the annexation of Burma. Farther east and south lay self-governing Siam (Thailand); Laos; Cambodia; and a Vietnam composed of Tonkin, Annam, and Cochin China—all still free, although French encroachments were under way. The Dutch were in the central part of what is now Indonesia, the British were infiltrating into Malaya, there were two British enclaves in Borneo, and the Spanish ruled the Philippines.

Where European colonial rule was firmly entrenched, as in India, any U.S. naval interventions were out of bounds, for controversies there would be settled between Washington and London. But in self-governing areas or places claimed as colonies but whose outlying regions were not well policed, as in the Dutch East Indies, openings existed for American naval officers to contribute, one way or another, to their nation's external affairs. During these years the navy was active, both hostilely and peacefully in Sumatra, Cochin China (southern Vietnam), Siam, Muscat, lower East Africa's Joanna, Madagascar, North Borneo, Annam (central Vietnam), Siam again, and Dutch Java.

Sumatra, 1832, 1839
Captain John Downes at Kuala Batu, et al., 1832

The "pepper coast," in extreme northwestern Sumatra, was the scene of the first U.S. naval intrusion into the Indian Ocean, as well as the first American armed intervention in Asia on an official basis. This area was ostensibly ruled by the Sultan of Atjeh ("Achin" or "Acheen" in contemporary nomenclature), but something of an administrative vacuum existed there. Although he could not enforce his authority upon his unruly Malay subjects, who acted as they wished, usually as pirates, he was potent enough to keep his realm free. Since the Anglo-Dutch Treaty of 1824, the British had withdrawn entirely from the East Indies to concentrate upon Malaya and the booming new city of Singapore. The Dutch, still reeling from their disastrous naval losses in the Napoleonic Wars, were content to restrict their effective control to southern Sumatra, adjacent to their administrative center at Batavia (Djakarta), Java, leaving Atjeh alone.

If the foreign political impact upon northern Sumatra was nonexistent, there certainly was an economic influence. The world's finest pepper was grown there, and United States carriers had predominated in that trade since the first Salem ship stumbled upon that coast in the 1790s and brought home a cargo sold at a 700-percent profit. The rush was on from that brash Massachusetts port, turning Salem into the pepper capital of the world until the 1850s. Before 1830 Atjehnese-American relations were generally cordial, although a couple of pepper ships had had to ward off attacks. But steep price declines created growing tensions between buyers and sellers, accompanied by an increase in piracy. This was a well-organized Malayan industry, centered in several towns along the northwest coast.

In February 1831 the Salem vessel *Friendship* pulled into the settlement called Kuala Batu (Americanized to "Quallah Battoo" and other variations). Captain Charles M. Endicott, with some of his crew, went ashore to haggle over pepper prices. Meanwhile the mate stupidly permitted armed Malays aboard who killed or wounded six Americans and took possession of the ship. Endicott, seeing the commotion from the beach, escaped with the remainder of his men, rowed to the nearby town of Muki, enlisted the support of three Salem shipmasters, and with their people returned to recapture the *Friendship*. He found that the assailants had disappeared along with trade goods, opium, and specie valued at over $40,000. News of this event aroused some excitement in the United States, taking political form in the person of Senator Nathaniel Silsbee of Massachusetts, a part owner of the *Friendship*. He received a sympathetic reception from President Jackson, always on the *qui vive* for insults to his flag. Naval retaliation was promptly ordered.

Navy Secretary Levi Woodbury dispatched Captain John Downes in the *Potomac* to proceed via the Cape of Good Hope to Kuala Batu, where he must question Malays and Americans alike as to whether Endicott's account had been accurate. If it was, he should demand property restitution and punishment of the guilty. Only after local rulers had "delayed beyond a reasonable time" in complying with his stipulations could he assail "the forts and dwellings near the scene of aggression."

By the time Downes reached his destination he had decided to ignore Woodbury's scenario. In Cape Town he had conversed with Britons and Dutchmen who apparently persuaded him that the Malays were totally treacherous, and concluded that rather than holding prior discussions with anybody, he would disguise his frigate as a Dutch merchantman and strike at Kuala Batu without warning. He justified this decision by writing to the department: "No demand of satisfaction was made previous to my attack; because I was satisfied, from the knowledge I already had of the character of the people, that no such demand would be answered, except only by refusal."

Early on the morning of the 6th Downes sent ashore 282 sailors and marines. They picked off, one by one, four of the five forts defending the town, burned them to the ground, and killed "nearly all" of the Malays inside. American casualties amounted to 2 killed and 11 wounded; those of the Kuala Batuans were estimated at about 100 killed and many more wounded, among them women and children. The next day Downes brought in the *Potomac* to lob a few broadsides into the remaining fortress, after which a white flag was raised. He informed the chastened Malays that since he could get no recompense for the *Friendship*'s losses nor find those responsible for the outrage, it would suffice that they recognize that any such recurrence would inevitably bring down upon them America's "martial thunder." He stressed to them that his country, unlike Britain or the Netherlands, had no colonial ambitions, concerning itself only with the maintenance of peaceful trade. He then leisurely sailed along the pepper coast. He later told the secretary that the Malays had expressed "their

John Downes

friendly disposition toward the Americans and their desire to obtain our friendship." He did not return to the United States until May 1834.

Long before his homecoming, his summary punishment of Kuala Batu had become a political football in Washington. The news of it arrived in July 1832, about the same time that Jackson, the Democrat, had vetoed the bill rechartering the Second Bank of the United States, thereby infuriating his opponents, soon to call themselves Whigs. They seized upon the Sumatran occurrence to embarrass the president. The matter of Downes's behavior and its consequences came up in Congress, but the House bandied the issue about for some time and settled nothing one way or the other.

It was different in Washington's journalistic circles, however. The strongly anti-Jackson *Daily National Intelligencer*, smarting over the loss of government printing contracts to the *Globe*, the pro-administration organ, led off with an argument remarkably prescient of a similar controversy that would rock Americans some 140 years later. After remarking that its editors wished that "there had been a parley before a fight," it honed in upon the war-making powers spelled out in the Constitution:

> However undoubted be the right of the *Government* to punish the Malays by indiscriminant war, we are not certain of the right of the *Executive* in this particular. To *Congress* belongs the right "to declare war." . . . But if the President can direct expeditions with fire and sword against the Malays, we do not see why he may not have the power to do the same in reference to any other power or people. Under this construction, it appears to us, what has been considered a very important provision of the Constitution may in time become a mere nullity.

The *Globe*, of course, leaped to Jackson's side, tearing into the *Intelligencer*'s "new and extraordinary doctrine" that an act of Congress would be required before the president could order the punishment of pirates "who had been preying upon our commerce and murdering our citizens." The *Intelligencer* curtly replied that the *Globe*'s editors were "ignorant of the public law," and there the matter rested.

This journalistic brouhaha was intensely discomfiting to the administration. Jackson and Woodbury knew that Downes had disobeyed his instructions, but by no means could they admit that publicly. Instead, the president described the Kuala Batuans as "a band of lawless pirates" who needed such "chastisements as would deter them from like aggressions," with the result that both respect for the American flag and safety for American merchantmen had been enhanced. Woodbury did no more than parrot his instructions to Downes, omitting entirely whether or not he had carried them out, before jumping to his conclusion that the *Potomac*'s bombardment had forced the Malays into "acknowledgements of past errors, and promises of future forebearance from like offenses."

But in a private letter the secretary let the captain know how he and Jackson really viewed the timing and nature of his assault: "The President regrets that you were not able, before attacking the Malays . . . to obtain . . . fuller information of the particulars of the outrage on the *Friendship*." Downes should also have waited until his demand for "restitution and indemnity" had been refused. The beleaguered captain answered as best he could: the Malays were treacherous pirates, he could not have recovered the purloined property, and he thought that the government wanted him to act with vigor. Thanks to the administration's aversion to the publicity sure to attend a trial, Downes escaped a court-martial, but for all practical purposes his brilliant naval career was over. Before his death in 1854 he held a number of shore assignments, only once being offered a sea command, which he felt compelled to decline. His last position was that of "lighthouse inspector."

The case of Downes at Kuala Batu did not die in the 1830s. From it the *National Intelligencer* raised the point of the president's right to send the American navy into action without a congressional declaration of war, as prescribed in the Constitution. During the late 1960s and early 1970s, Americans debated heatedly the same issue, as well as the question of governmental duplicity. Jackson and Woodbury had carefully concealed their true opinion that Downes had overreacted lest it furnish political ammunition for their adversaries. Several modern American administrations engaged in hiding evidence and even outright lying about the real situation in Indochina to retain public support. And above all, each was concerned with the major point: to what extent and for how long may a president commit his nation to hostilities without a congressional declaration that they exist?[1]

Commodore George C. Read at Kuala Batu, et al., 1838–1839

Greater cohesion will come to this narration through temporarily ignoring chronology. A discussion here of the two cruises between 1833 and 1836 in which Commander David Geisinger and Captain Edmund P. Kennedy carried Edmund Roberts on his diplomatic mission to Cochin China, Siam, and Muscat would interrupt the continuity of the American naval assaults on the pepper coast. Furthermore, Roberts was instructed to negotiate trade treaties, quite unlike the punitive expeditions of Downes and Read; hence they should follow rather than precede those of 1838–1839.

To confirm the affirmations of Downes, Jackson, and Woodbury that the excessive punishment of Kuala Batu had made the pepper coast safe for Americans, the department sent Commodore George C. Read with the *Columbia* and *John Adams* to cruise around the world on a commerce-protecting mission, with special attention to Sumatra. After sailing in May 1838, the commodore learned in Colombo, Ceylon (Sri Lanka), early in December that another atrocity against Americans had occurred in Kuala Batu the previous August and sped there, pulling in on the 22nd.

The rajahs of that town and of Muki and Susu had plotted together to seize Salem Captain Charles F. Wilkins's ship *Eclipse*. While some of his men were ashore loading pepper, Wilkins foolishly allowed a certain Libee Usu ("Oosoo") and other Malays to retain their arms when they boarded his ship. He paid for his indiscretion with his life, crying "I am stabbed!" when Usu plunged his kris into him; the ship's boy was also killed, but the others of the crew either leaped overboard or climbed into the rigging. After looting the vessel of goods valued at approximately $20,000, the Malays departed. The Americans on the beach appealed to the rajah of

George C. Read
(Naval Historical Center)

Trabangan, who saved his settlement by accompanying the survivors back to their ship to rescue the others. Meanwhile, Usu's loot had been apportioned among the three towns.

In contrast to Downes, Read was in no hurry. On the 22nd and 23rd he sent Commander Thomas W. Wyman, of the *John Adams*, protected by armed detachments, to demand from the Kuala Batuans that "the pirate and the property said to have been conveyed with him" be surrendered, but only excuses were forthcoming. By the 24th the commodore decided that the Malays were merely stalling, so on Christmas Day the two warships moved in to let loose "round shot and a few strands of grape" at the ramshackle forts reconstructed since Downes had leveled them. After half an hour a white flag was waved. Read, concluding that he had made his point, spared the rest of the town from destruction.

He then went on to Muki, chief motivator of the conspiracy against the *Eclipse*, and met the same unwillingness to comply with his ultimatum: either hand over the guilty and their spoils or face demolition. On 1 January 1839 broadsides flattened what weak defenses Muki possessed, and Wyman landed 320 men from both ships, spiked all the town's guns, and applied the torch to everything that remained standing, all without resistance. Not an American had been touched and evidently only one Malayan perished, the inhabitants having been granted ample time to head for the bush before the cannon spoke out.

Read's last Sumatran stop was at Susu, as culpable as Muki, and he had planned to inflict upon it "a moderate castigation." But generously deciding that magnanimity would better serve his country's long-range interests, on the 4th he accepted the Susuans' explanation that they had really tried to meet his requirements but Usu—"that bad man"—had fled. Instead of further hostile operations, the commodore negotiated with several rajahs from Susu and Kuala Batu, wringing from them assurances always to spare American merchantmen, warn them of impending attacks, and turn over at once assailants and their loot. Business done, Read took his little squadron to conduct pre–Opium War diplomacy in China before ending his cruise in June 1840.

When Read's letter particularizing his Sumatran campaign arrived in the United States in the spring of 1839, it was received with nothing approximating the furore attending Downes's report. Press coverage was scanty but generally favorable. The *Intelligencer* and *Globe* printed the official correspondence without editorial comment, ignoring the constitutional question of what war-making powers the president possessed, which had so preoccupied them in 1832. Governmental approbation of Read's conduct was both immediate and lasting. Secretary James K. Paulding's *Report* for 1839 summarized it well: "Having vainly sought redress by the restoration of the plundered property and the surrender of the murderers, he inflicted a severe and merited chastisement of the barbarians." While Downes's immoderation wrecked his career, Read's continued to flourish, with later squadron commands in Africa and the Mediterranean. He was a rear admiral on the retired list when he died in 1862.

In the last analysis, however, the results of 1832 and 1838–1839 were about the same, neither officer having been able to guarantee security off Sumatra for American pepper-carriers. Downes's well-advertised pacification lasted only six years before the *Eclipse* was taken. Read's relative compassion brought little more. Granting that no American merchantman

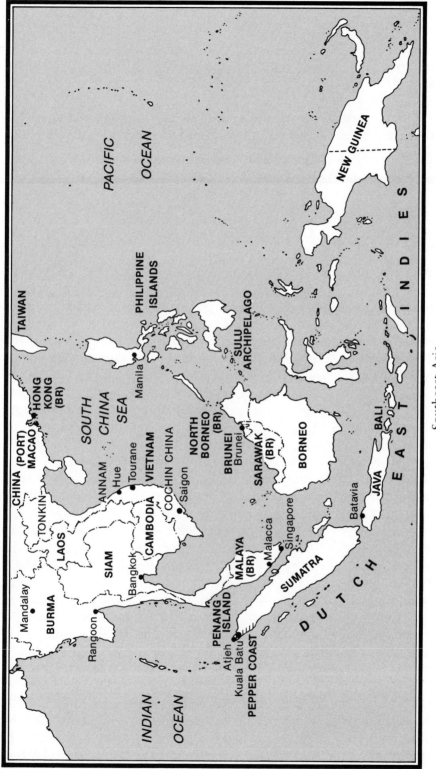

Southeast Asia

was ever again captured along the pepper coast, attempts to do so were made in 1843, 1845 (twice), 1846, and 1850. By mid-century the Sumatran pepper trade was languishing, Salem's contacts there dwindled into insignificance, and American relations with modern Indonesia remained inconsequential until it became independent in 1949.[2]

Cochin China, Siam, and Muscat, 1833–1836
Commander David Geisinger at Saigon, Bangkok, and Muscat, 1833–1834

Following Downes's return, Secretary of the Navy Levi Woodbury received appropriations for "a sufficient force to visit occasionally the Indian and China Seas." He used this occasion to appoint Edmund Roberts, of Portsmouth, N.H., his relative by marriage, a special agent to write treaties with Cochin China, Siam, and Muscat. Roberts, a merchant with previous experience in the Indian Ocean, was given the title of "secretary to the Commander" and the unimpressive salary of $1,500 per year. Woodbury specified that his agent should be considered a "gentleman," but at first he was given no cabin and had to sleep on the gun deck of Commander David Geisinger's *Peacock*. Perhaps that is why Geisinger's name appears so seldom in Roberts's subsequent book, *Embassy to the Eastern Courts*. Moreover, the commander was anything but informative about his companion in the three letters he wrote to the department en route, so their precise relationship is hard to fathom. After sailing in the *Peacock* from Boston early in 1832, they reached Cochin China on 1 January 1833.

At this time Vietnam, long a tributary of China, was composed of Tonkin in the north and Cochin China in the south, connected by the central strip of Annam, whose emperor ruled the country from Hué, at least formally. Vietnam's governments were authoritarian, deliberately modeled on that of Peking; most of its people were Buddhist. The initial European influence came from French missionaries, starting in the 1600s. After prolonged internal and external disorders, the nation was unified by the Emperor Gia Long, 1802–1820. Under his rule the priests were given a relatively free hand and converted a few hundred thousand to Catholicism. But Ming Mang, his successor, who ruled in 1820–1840, was a devout Buddhist and tried to drive this foreign religion from his domains. Indeed, only six months after the *Peacock*'s departure, he had a French missionary slowly strangled at his capital; perhaps it is fortunate for the Americans that they came into Saigon rather than Hué.

It turned out that nothing could be accomplished in Cochin China, but at least Roberts was presented with an opportunity to demonstrate his ingenuity. His reluctant hosts refused to believe the American explanation that titles of nobility did not exist in their society. So Roberts bestowed a number upon himself on the spot. He commenced by calling out all the counties of New Hampshire while the scribe moaned over his insuperable task of putting the sounds of "Merrimac" and "Rockingham" into Vietnamese characters. On the next day he started to reel off the names of the cities of his native state, but the transcriber threw down his pen, wailing that he was too ill to continue, thus ending the farce. All negotiations terminated when Roberts found out that to be received he would have to perform the degrading kowtow before the court. When they sailed away in mid-February, Geisinger's only comment was "I regret to say that it [the mission] was not crowned with the success it deserved."

Conditions were much more benign at Siam, also a Chinese tributary country but, like Vietnam, able to act with almost complete independence. The Thais, age-old enemies of the Vietnamese and Burmese, had managed to stabilize their government under the Rama dynasty. Luckily for Roberts and Geisinger the court at Bangkok was considerably less xenophobic than those of Vietnam and China and less isolationist than that of Japan. In 1826 Siam had signed a limited commercial agreement with Great Britain, thereby setting a precedent that could be easily followed. The Americans were housed in a palatial residence and sumptuously entertained during their six-week sojourn. Shortly before they left in April, Roberts was able to sign the first U.S. treaty with an Asian nation. American commodities could enter without duties and were free from competing with government-controlled monopolies. But most-favored-nation status was not spelled out, nor was there any provision for resident consuls (Washington did not send one there until the mid-1850s). Geisinger informed Woodbury about his companion's work with a single sentence: he had "brought to a conclusion a Commercial Treaty with the King of Siam."

The *Peacock* then plowed through the Indian Ocean to Muscat, in Arabia. Salem traders had long been busy there, and Said bin Sultan, an old friend of Roberts who ruled both Muscat and Zanzibar, off central East Africa, awaited their arrival. By this time American interest concentrated on Zanzibar, rich in cotton and spices. It took only three days to agree with the sultan on treaty terms. Roberts won import duties of no more than five per cent, most-favored-nation rights, and extrality, whereby U.S. consular courts would try Americans for crimes committed in the Sultan's realms. Geisinger outdid himself in restraint by omitting altogether any commentary on Roberts's diplomatic triumphs. The *Peacock* was in New York by late May 1834.

Roberts's achievements were greeted in the United States with what might be called a thundering silence. Although Jackson did bring to the Senate's attention the need to accept both treaties—which was speedily done—he chose to ignore them in his December message of that year. The press seems to have paid no attention to the foreign-relations aspects of the *Peacock*'s cruise, reporting only that her voyage had ended; *Niles' Weekly Register* devoted one sentence to the subject.[3]

Commodore Edmund P. Kennedy at Muscat, et al., 1835–1836

Mahlon Dickerson, the new secretary of the navy, sent out Roberts to exchange ratifications with Siam and Muscat, to try once more in Cochin China, and endeavor to pry open Japan a bit. In late April Roberts left again in the *Peacock*, pleased that his former $1,500 salary had been raised to $4,400. Commodore Edmund P. Kennedy was equally happy that he could fly the East India Squadron's broad pennant as its first official commodore.

As the *Peacock* neared Muscat she piled atop a coral reef, because of Kennedy's incorrect chart. Roberts volunteered to get aid from the sultan in a four-day rowboat ordeal that proved to have been unnecessary, for her crew kedged the *Peacock* afloat by themselves. While makeshift repairs were being made, ratifications were exchanged, with appropriate ceremonies.

After heartfelt thanks to the Sultan, Kennedy and Roberts were able to steer their leaky vessel to Bombay, where the *Enterprise* waited and a sizable British dockyard was made available to them. A month later they departed for Bangkok, and during mid-April had to endure elaborate rites before putting the Siamese treaty into effect. Its constantly sweltering humidity was enervating enough; much worse were the cholera and dysentery that raged through the complements of both warships. Roberts was among those stricken—one wonders how much his rowboat ordeal had sapped his resistance. The Americans were able to pass a convalescent period at Dutch Batavia, from which Kennedy finally wrote to the department in February 1836, but since he reported only about squadron matters, it remains a mystery how he and Roberts apportioned their responsibilities. The still-ailing envoy insisted upon going to Cochin China, but after eight days off its coast had to admit that he was too ill to conduct any negotiations. Both vessels sailed to Macao, where Roberts died on 12 June. Kennedy pondered for a time whether he should go alone to Japan, but even though he had asked his government for the necessary diplomatic credentials "in the event of an accident to Roberts," nothing had been done. Correctly deciding that a Japanese visit would be useless, he ended his cruise at Hampton Roads, Virginia, in October 1837, having traveled there by way of Hawaii, Peru, and Brazil.[4]

Comoros Islands, 1841, 1851
Commodore Lawrence Kearny at Joanna, 1841

Joanna (Anjouan) is one of the four major islands making up the Comoro Archipelago in the channel between Africa's Mozambique and the huge island of Madagascar (Malagasy Republic) to the east. It lay athwart the direct route of American ships destined for Zanzibar or Arabia after rounding the Cape of Good Hope, and it was a rendezvous for New England whalers needing to buy supplies during the pre–U.S. Civil War era. Joanna was ruled by King Selim, who was free enough from foreign control to have on his own two confrontations with the American navy; the first was merely disappointing, the second humiliating to him.

In 1841 Commodore Lawrence Kearny was on his way in the frigate *Constellation* to perform his diplomatic functions in China during the Opium War. While he was moored at Joanna, Selim gave him a letter addressed to the president of the United States begging for American "powder, muskets, and lead" to use in a civil war. Kearny's reply shows his hope that diplomatic language might avoid an angry reaction to his refusal: "The United States are friendly to all nations, and being at peace with them all . . . the Government does not permit its officers to interfere in foreign wars. . . . And the undersigned hopes His Majesty will believe that this principle so just in itself will explain why arms and munitions of war are withheld." Whether the commodore's soothing words would be effective remained to be seen.[5]

Commander William Pearson at Joanna, 1851

Selim was mollified not at all by Kearny's explanation and commenced systematically harassing American whalers who called at Joanna to buy necessities. They protested so vehemently to Washington about their treatment that Commander William Pearson in the sloop *Dale* was sent to the Comoros to end that behavior. After coming into Joanna on 4 August, he quickly confirmed Selim's hostility and sent the king an ultimatum the next day to either forfeit $20,000 or face attack. All that was promised was $500 in cash and a like amount in "bullocks and trinkets." Irked by this response, on the morning of the 6th Dale briefly shelled the town. In part because he had given advance warning of the bombardment, no one at sea or ashore was even touched.

Nonetheless, Selim had had enough. He told Pearson that his poverty was so dire that the utmost that he could provide would be $1,000 and 30 head of cattle, and he admitted that he was "very sorry that he had done wrong, and faithfully promised not to do so in the future." Pearson accepted these terms but added that a formal understanding with his country must be written. On the 15th what might be called the "Pearson-Selim Treaty" was signed, granting American citizens the right of persons and property to move safely in Joanna, giving most-favored-nation status to the United States, and carrying a loaded final proviso: in case of disputes between "natives" and Americans, "the matter is to be referred to the U.S. Government which shall act as it may judge proper." U.S. naval power was, of course, the motivator behind this odd form of arbitration, in which one party makes the final determination on a controversial issue. Apparently this agreement was lasting, for never again did the American navy have to visit the Comoros with offensive intent.[6]

North Borneo, Annam (Vietnam), and Siam, 1845–1851
Captain John Percival at Borneo and Annam, 1845

The venerable frigate *Constitution* was extraordinary and so was her commander, Captain John Percival, during her only round-the-world cruise. "Mad Jack" (as he called himself) in his mid-sixties was a naval legend, the subject of many stories, some of them true, but during this voyage his impetuosity would ruin his naval career. The department's orders for his global jaunt were vague; he should look after American commercial interests throughout, with special emphasis on the East Indies.

Leaving New York in May 1844, the famous frigate sailed to Rio, East Africa, and Singapore, among other stops, before arriving at Brunei in April 1845. This tiny state in northern Borneo was in the British sphere, the Dutch having already staked out their claim to the southern part of the island. The sultan of Brunei, grateful for the military and naval aid of the Englishman James (later "Sir James") Brooke, had recently rewarded him with the coastal strip called Sarawak. This enabled "the White Rajah" to found a Brooke dynasty that ruled that area until the mid-twentieth century. One of Percival's officers attempted to talk the sultan into granting "an open & fair trade for our Merchant Vessels," but received the discouraging reply that the British had been given "the exclusive right of trade in Borneo Proper . . . and that Mr. Brooke was *now* the English Rajah of Borneo Proper & that nothing could be done without reference to him."

If he had to be inactive in Borneo, Percival's pendulum swung too far toward hyperactivity in Vietnam. By May he had come into Tourane (Danang), in Annam, the seaport for the emperor's nearby capital at Hué. There his frustration and failure would presage what happened to the United States in the same locale a century and a quarter later. At first all seemed well. On the 14th a party of high-ranking Annamese nobles was entertained in the *Constitution*, amid an air of amiability on both sides. But as the delegation was leaving, its interpreter handed Percival a note, whispering that his life was forfeit should he be discovered. It was addressed to the commanding French admiral in East Asia and signed by Dominique Lefevre. This Catholic bishop appealed for the hastiest rescue possible to save himself and twelve Vietnamese Catholics who were all "under the sentence of immediate death." He had first come to Vietnam in 1835, and until his death over forty years later he was repeatedly arrested, tried, and sentenced to exile or death, either escaped or was pardoned, and infiltrated the country once more. He was lucky that the Annamese emperors of the 1840s were in a bind. Although they were antiforeign and anti-Christian, they had to curtail the severity of their persecutions lest the imperialistic French use any atrocities as excuses for territorial acquisitions, which soon occurred anyway in the first steps along the road to an all-French Indochina.

Percival at once started to mount a rescue mission, apparently with the support of his officers. Lieutenant John B. Dale wrote in his diary, "Here was an opportunity of a rescue from this semi-barbarous nation. It was enough to know that a fellow Christian was in danger of his life. Humanity was to be our warrant [rather] than the law of nations." On that same day Percival strode along a line of armed Americans stretching through Tourane all the way from the dock to the home of the leading local official and issued an ultimatum to him: the French cleric must be handed over to him within 24 hours; he added that he would hold hostages until that had been done. If the Annamese defied him he would turn the city's three forts into rubble and confiscate all the shipping in the harbor. Without opposition the Americans seized as hostages three nobles and two of their attendants and marched them back to the *Constitution*.

When the stipulated time had passed without compliance, Percival captured three nearby warships without difficulty; when these junks tried to escape upriver a few days later, they were hunted down and some Vietnamese were killed, evidently most by drowning. Meanwhile Percival turned conciliatory and liberated his hostages, but still there was no response from Tourane. On the 24th letters were delivered to the ship saying that the priest would be set free once the junks were returned, which was done but without effect. Communications ceased the next day after Percival announced that he was departing for Canton and would report this outrage to the French, who would undoubtedly retaliate viciously. The Annamese coldly responded that he could threaten as he wished but they would accept no further insulting words from him. By this time Vietnamese warships had collected, the forts were being strengthened, and it was clear

John Percival
(U.S. Naval Institute)

even to Percival that his solitary eighteenth-century frigate was helpless offensively. Sixteen wasted days after his arrival, the beaten captain sailed away. As for Lefevre, he was soon turned over to the commander of a French man-of-war.

Although Percival had been motivated by an admirable humanitarianism, nonetheless at Tourane he had demonstrated how naval diplomacy should not be conducted. Had he carefully thought through his objectives, he should have realized that the Vietnamese had to do practically nothing to render his ultimatum ridiculous. They could easily afford to let the days slip by until disease, depleted supplies, or other responsibilities to be met would drive away the Americans. Retired Commander Tyrone G. Martin, in his biography of "Old Ironsides," sums up the matter as a professional naval officer. Lieutenant Dale had written in his diary about the experience that "it seems, I must say, to have shown a sad want of 'sound discretion,' in commencing an affair of this kind, without carrying it through to a successful issue." After quoting Dale, Martin's entire comment is this: "Prophetic words."

Percival tried to justify his Vietnamese aggression by telling the secretary, "The motives which influenced me were humane; exerted in the cause of suffering humanity, to aid the subject of a Nation long in amity with the United States." Furious that violence had been perpetrated in an area presumed wide open for additional American trade, Secretary George Bancroft ripped into Percival's actions, jotting on the margin of the captain's explanatory letter: "The Department wholly disapproves the conduct of Captain Percival as not warranted either by the demands of the Bishop or by the Law of Nations." When Special Agent Joseph Balestier visited Tourane five years later, he carried with him a letter from President Zachary Taylor addressed to "the Emperor of Anam [sic]," disavowing Percival's "act of hostility, offering to make amends on being satisfied of the truth of the complaint [Balestier having reported that he had received word from 'the King' protesting the deaths and injuries inflicted by the Americans]." The apology was, however, ignored. The *Constitution* made her way back to Boston late in September 1846. Not surprisingly, this was "Mad Jack's" last active duty.[7]

Commodore Philip Voorhees at Cochin China, Siam, and Borneo, 1850–1851

Commodore Philip Voorhees and Special Agent Joseph Balestier antagonized each other almost from the beginning. The new commodore of the East India Squadron has already enlivened these pages by his mishandling of the *Sancala* affair in Argentina in 1844. Balestier, a former U.S. consul in Southeast Asia, was selected by the Department of State as a "Special Agent and Envoy" to that part of the world. Unhappily, these two opinionated individuals, with conflicting objectives, managed to make their expected collaboration impossible. To the commodore, Balestier was "unnecessarily fastidious" and "singularly strange, unreasonable, irritable & captious—so as to make it a most painful and anxious time for me." Voorhees was so uncooperative in Siam that Balestier wrote that he became "an outcast from my ship and abandoned by her, the result of which was to me neglect, affront, and indignities." Their priorities were disparate as well. Voorhees had to spend almost all his tour as commodore in furnishing transportation for the ungrateful envoy at the expense of meeting other fleet responsibilities. Balestier occupied himself exclusively with his diplomatic assignments, appearing oblivious to such essential matters as shipboard health and safety.

Secretary of State Webster's instructions to his envoy were that he should extend regrets to the Annamese for what Percival had done at Tourane in 1845 and see if a commercial agreement could be realized with them; rewrite the treaty of 1832 with Siam; and try to reach understandings in Brunei and Sarawak. All of the envoy's transportation was to be in Voorhees's flagship.

In Tourane during late February Balestier and Voorhees delivered the president's letter of apology for Percival's behavior, but the Annamese construed some of its remarks as threatening, to which Balestier reacted with obvious anger. In mid-March the Americans headed for Siam, their Vietnamese mission stillborn. Equal frustration met them in Bangkok. The commodore refused to approach the city in the *Plymouth* because of a cholera epidemic, so Balestier had to go in alone, with a fleet of Thai barges. He and resident American missionaries met with the king's council to assert that Roberts's treaty had been violated by "farmed out" monopolistic grants to selected noblemen who set their prices high enough to eliminate American competition. The Thais insisted that there was no need to revise the 1832 understanding. Balestier rose from his chair, denounced the proceedings, and abruptly departed, defeated once again.

The envoy asserted that the entire blame for his Siamese failure must be placed squarely on the commodore. The missionaries who had been with him agreed: "That the unfortunate circumstance of your being unattended here, has much to do in bringing about these humiliating indignities, we cannot doubt. It has been said to us by Siamese officials, as a reason for their course of conduct, 'that our own government has thrown you away, and why should they show you respect!' " Voorhees was equally positive that the real reason for the fiasco lay in Balestier's tactlessness, irritability, and impatience.

The two men, evidently no longer on speaking terms, next went to Borneo during late May and June. In Brunei Balestier enjoyed his only tour de force. Its sultan welcomed him with a "royal reception" and was agreeable to a trade treaty with the United States. Although Brooke was in England, recuperating from an ailment, he had reversed his earlier opposition to foreign competition, leaving word in Sarawak that he had no objection to such a pact. It was signed on 23 June and was typical of mid-nineteenth-century commercial accords. Americans were granted residential and business liberties, most-favored-nation status, and extraterritoriality. Ratifications were finally exchanged three years later.

The final example of Voorhees-Balestier unpleasantness occurred when the former refused to have his flagship carry the latter on his proposed five-month voyage through the Dutch East Indies, adding the dour comment that it would be "a cruise of observation and not to negotiate treaties." He offered instead the sloop *Marion*, under Commander William L. Glendy. Balestier indignantly refused and by late 1851 was back in Washington. Voorhees sealed his own fate by bringing the *Plymouth* home without authorization, pleading that he and his men were "debilitated" after so long a time "under a nearly vertical sun." Secretary William A. Graham castigated him for his disobedience to orders. Never again would Voorhees command an American fighting ship.[8]

Commander George A. Magruder at Java, 1853

The final pre-1861 U.S. naval activity on the rim of the Indian Ocean could hardly be called an activity. Commodore James Aulick, in China, had learned that an American was in trouble in Dutch Java. Walter M. Gibson, master of the merchant vessel *Flirt*, while drunk, had promised to aid a local sultan in rebellion against the Dutch; worse, he had put that information into a letter that fell into official hands. He and his men were arrested and held for trial. Aulick dispatched Commander George A. Magruder in the *St. Mary's* to inquire into the case. The Dutch colonial bureaucrats were pleasant enough, saying that the crew had been freed for lack of evidence. But Gibson, damned by his own handwriting, was imprisoned. Unfortunately he could not be tried soon, for the pertinent witnesses were in the back country, fighting against the rebellious sultan. Before leaving, all Magruder could do was to ensure that the prisoner's conditions were as tolerable as possible; luckily for the accused he was later able to escape. Gibson's case found the navy completely helpless, but it was scarcely the commander's fault.[9]

Summary

U.S. naval officers have labored more productively elsewhere than in Southeast Asia and the Indian Ocean during 1832–1851. Read, at Sumatra in 1838–1839, was faithful to his orders, acted prudently, and delivered a merciful castigation to the towns along the pepper coast, although further attacks were made upon American merchantmen in those waters. As for Geisinger, Kennedy, and Roberts, the later experiences of Percival and Voorhees demonstrated that at the time no accord could be reached with the Vietnamese. Furthermore, their treaties with Siam and Muscat turned out to be insignificant in themselves, for the patterns of

American trade with those places changed very little after the adoption of the treaties. Probably their most significant contribution was to help bring into being the East India Squadron. The efforts of Roberts and his two naval colleagues blazed a trail for the more substantial diplomatic accomplishments of Cushing in China and Perry in Japan. Insofar as Joanna is concerned, Kearny, in 1841, was unable to provide arms for King Selim but tried to ward off any ensuing resentment by the tactful wording of his refusal. Even if anti-Americanism was evident over the next decade, Pearson's little lesson brought about a treaty with Joanna that, dictated at cannon's mouth though it was, ensured safety thereafter for American carriers along the Mozambique Channel.

These small victories, however, must be weighed against the defeats of 1832, 1845, and 1850. Downes recognized no need for negotiation, inflicted an excessively harsh castigation on Kuala Batu, and paid for his behavior in suffering the disapproval of his superiors. In his thoughtless haste to save a foreign cleric, Percival put himself in a position guaranteeing that the Annamese could humiliate him. Although a treaty with Borneo was written, the results of the 1850 mission were unhappy. Balestier's prickly personality, Voorhees's unwillingness to follow the well-defined directives from two departments of his government, and especially the inability of each to comprehend the problems of the other soured American relations with Annam and Siam. In consequence the sea-going careers of all three officers were rightly terminated. Unlike them, Magruder found that conditions in Java were beyond his control, and his failure had no unpleasant results for his service or his nation.

CHAPTER TWELVE

Hawaii

1826–1851

Although an integral part of Oceania, the Hawaiian Archipelago should be discussed separately, for American influences there were much greater than in any other Pacific islands. Even before the arrival of the first U.S. man-of-war in 1826, Hawaii had been unified by the Kamehameha dynasty, which would endure until the late nineteenth century. Americans dominated religion, economics, and politics there more than in other areas of Polynesia, Micronesia, or Melanesia, where British and French dominance was gaining strength or where the white impact was relatively nonexistent. The early advent of American missionaries had resulted in a Hawaiian people thoroughly Christianized and reasonably literate, with some New England traits, both attractive and ugly, imposed upon them. American merchants, seamen, whalemen, and land speculators also swarmed into Honolulu and the other ports.

Politically, Hawaii by mid-century had been recognized as a sovereign entity by the international community. It had a Western-type government in Honolulu under a written constitution, with a royal bureaucracy that included a foreign minister who aided the king in writing treaties with the leading European nations and the United States. During the Kamehameha era Americans sometimes held important administrative positions; admonitions or advice from Washington's resident ministers were listened to most carefully and usually heeded. Throughout Polynesia other islands were being swallowed up, New Zealand by the British, and the Tuamotus, Societies, and Marquesas by the French; but European threats to annex Hawaii eventually amounted to nothing.

In the pre–Civil War decades the activities of American naval officers in Hawaii were responses to several different challenges. During the 1820s they focused upon the chronic dispute between New England missionaries and their commercial and whaling rivals for domination of the native dynasty; compelled the Hawaiians to admit to the amount of debt that they owed to foreigners, primarily from the sandalwood trade; and wrote Honolulu's first "treaty." Toleration of Catholics and the rights of foreign landholders concerned other officers in the 1830s. European threats against Hawaiian independence came to a head early in the next decade, especially the British-induced crisis of 1843, witnessed by two American commanders. A decided ebb in naval activities followed in those islands, for resident U.S. ministers saw to it that officers who sojourned at Honolulu from 1846 to 1851 did not have the freedom of action enjoyed by their predecessors.

American Commanders at Honolulu, 1826–1829
Lieutenant John Percival, 1826

Although probably reached by earlier anonymous Spaniards, the Hawaiian (or "Sandwich") Islands came into world awareness in 1778 when Captain James Cook discovered them during his third voyage to the Pacific. The Polynesian population, estimated at 300,000, was socially striated. Each of the major islands tended to be ruled by a theoretically absolute "king" and his "chiefs," who governed the great mass of the commoners. A system of kapus (tabus, taboos, etc.) imposed from above characterized their religion. Politically, Hawaii ("the big island"), Oahu, Maui, and Kauai had been independent until the late eighteenth century, when Hawaii's King Kamehameha I went out from his "big island" to conquer all of the archipelago save Kauai, which was annexed by Hawaii shortly after his death in 1819. This "Napoleon of the Pacific" established the Kamehameha dynasty, which maintained an independent Hawaiian monarchy until the late nineteenth century. Foreigners, Americans for the most part, showed up during the founder's reign, eager to exploit the huge sandalwood forests for the China trade. Fur traders and whalers from Nantucket and New Bedford soon began using Lahaina on Maui and Honolulu on Oahu as rendezvous.

Calvinistic Protestantism also entered the Hawaiian picture. Animated by the proselyting success of the London Missionary Society in Tahiti, the American Board of Commissioners for Foreign Missions sent out to Honolulu its first ordained ministers. When they arrived there in 1820, conversions were easy because of an incredible stroke of luck. The year before, the new young King Kamehameha II (Lilolilo) and the dowager queens had decided that their complicated latticework of *kapus* had broken down and ordered its abolition, an order that in general was obeyed, idols being smashed and *kapus* violated. The result was a religious void, which the Reverend Hiram Bingham and his fellows were delighted to fill. Enjoying royal favor, they attempted with some success to transform South Sea culture into a social as well as a religious replica of their native New England. They provided the Hawaiians with their first written language and set up an educational system that pretty well wiped out illiteracy. Perhaps less admirably, they prescribed heavy clothing and cold-resistant houses, and they rigidly enforced obedience to Sabbath restrictions and a stern code of sexual repression. By the mid-1820s the resident whites had split into two blocs, each vying for Polynesian support. The missionaries held the greater power, but they were opposed by the traders, who resented Bingham's revealing to the Hawaiians that they were being cheated in commercial transactions. Sailors and whalers were also irate at religious interference with their customary diversions ashore.

Up to this time no U.S. warship had ever showed up at the islands. The remedy for this deficiency came from the American merchants there, who appealed to the Navy Department to provide some security for the national commerce in the Pacific. Their concern had been accentuated by the mutiny aboard the whaler *Globe* early in 1824. After murdering four officers, the mutineers sailed the ship to Mili atoll in the Marshall Islands; there some of the nonmutineers managed to cut her cables and escape in the vessel, coming into Valparaiso to tell their sad story. Secretary Samuel Southard ordered Isaac Hull, commodore of the Pacific Squadron, to detach one of his men-of-war to find the mutineers and bring them back for punishment. Hull's man was also to call at Hawaii and find out how its government viewed the United States in comparison to other countries and whether Americans were treated as well as Europeans. Lieutenant John Percival— whose later misadventures in Vietnam have been narrated above—drew the assignment and took the schooner *Dolphin* on the hunt, which ended somewhat anticlimactically. Only two Americans had survived on Mili to be rescued, both innocent of complicity in the mutiny, the rest having been killed by the atoll's Micronesian inhabitants.

When Percival sailed past Diamond Head in mid-January, one situation in Hawaii irked him, namely the fact that all Western navies had to deal with their sailors' sexual frustrations. In some ports circumstances might compel all shore leaves to be cancelled, and no man-of-war could permit

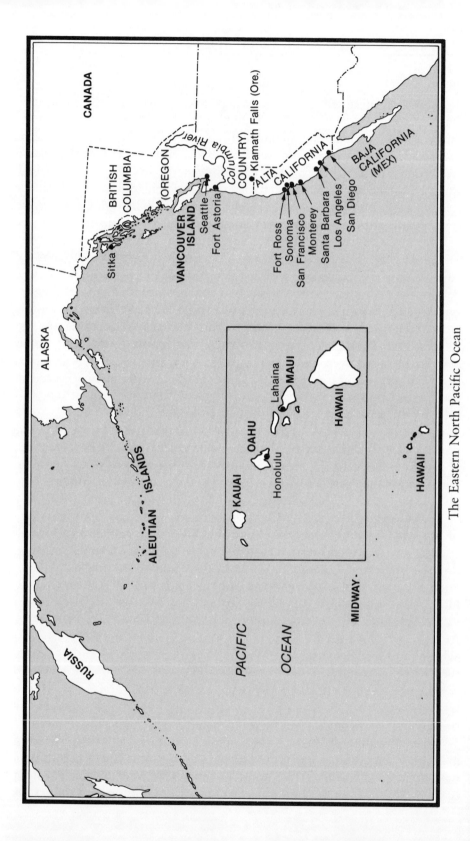

The Eastern North Pacific Ocean

more than a minority of its people to be away at any one time. Therefore, warships often had local prostitutes rowed out to them. Even the very proper Commodore James Biddle admitted that he allowed this privilege, explaining why with the utmost delicacy: "It is an evil which is tolerated as a preventive of greater evils." A taxidermist on the later Wilkes expedition, with a breezy disregard for Noah Webster's *Blue-Backed Speller*, described the typical scene less exquisitely: "Nerley all day the Ship has been filled with Yellow *Hores* . . . these Loos Ladyes of Pleasure." The *Dolphin*'s sailors who were permitted to go into Honolulu could easily gratify their lust, and some of the officers took "temporary wives," apparently including both Percival and Lieutenant Hiram Paulding, his second in command. During Bingham's campaign against "lewdness" a missionary-sponsored *kapu* on women's visiting ships was applied to the *Dolphin*. Once Percival learned that this restriction had been lifted a short time before during the stopover of HMS *Blonde*, commanded by Lord George Byron (a cousin of the poet), he concluded that his country's honor had been tainted. He called at the palace to complain about the *kapu* to Kamehameha I's widow and co-regent for the recently orphaned little King Kamehameha III. He demonstrated his respect for Hawaiian royalty when she said that the tabu on providing women was made by God. According to the historian Lina McKee (Maloney), he leveled a finger at her and roared, "You lie, you damned old bitch! Mr. Bingham governs you!" Brooding about his men's forced celibacy, he told Paulding "that the sailors would serve the missionaries right if they should pull down their houses."

Violence detonated on Sunday, 26 February. Some 25 men were sent ashore from the schooner and passed enough hours in Honolulu's grogshops to decide to act on their own. Reinforced by whalemen, the combined mob smashed some windows and furniture at the house of a prominent chief where Bingham was conducting a service. Fearing for the safety of his wife and child, the missionary ran home but found himself locked out. He was insulted and roughed up by the sailors, although a counterattack by Hawaiian Christians saved him from injury. Just then Percival, livid with rage, racing up with two midshipmen, shouted at his men, "I'll teach you to disgrace us!" and laid about furiously with a cane. The rioters were tied up and carried back to the *Dolphin*; the next day a number of them received 24 lashes. But Percival still kept his eye on his main concern. While apologizing to Bingham and assuring him that all damages would be paid for, he insisted that "the tabu must come off" and that he would not leave Hawaii until it was. He concluded that he would rather have his "hands cut off than to have it said that Lord Byron was allowed a privilege greater than was allowed to me." A few days later an apprehensive Hawaiian government removed the objectionable ban, permitting the *Dolphin*'s people, who had been kept on board since the riot, "an enjoyment they have always been in participation of" in other ports, as Percival clumsily put it in a letter to captains of all other vessels in the harbor advocating that no shore leaves be granted. The chief historian of Wilkes's cruise writes that "emptying the two mission schools, the girls poured out in a steady stream" while "the happy ship was in port."

During his three-month sojourn in Honolulu, Percival found an opportunity to make another enemy by engaging in a hand-to-hand brawl with Alfred P. Edwards, an American trader who had quarreled with him over a salvage matter and had even accused him of stealing a mattress from Edwards's ship. The trader, floored by Percival in the fracas, sought legal counsel to bring his adversary to a mainland court for "Assault and Battery." Nor had Bingham been idle. When the *Dolphin* finally stood out from Hawaii in May, he dubbed her "the mischief-making man-of-war" and settled down to inform the missionary press about the many delinquencies of her commander.

When Percival finally returned to the United States, he discovered that the accusations against him from Honolulu had been well aired. Bingham's account of his efforts to enforce the *kapu* and of the subsequent violence directed against him had found a sympathetic audience in the religious magazines and newspapers. The *Missionary Herald* pontificated:

> It is proper, in our view, that the Christian public, both in Europe and America, should know that the persons and lives of the Sandwich Island missionaries are exposed eminently to the violence of nominal Christians, who oppose, with the bitter spirit of persecution, the laudable efforts of the chiefs to suppress the crimes and vices of the country; in obedience to the requirements of the word of God.

During May 1828 the Navy Department brought Percival before a three-man court of inquiry in Boston on charges of "unofficerlike and ungentlemanly conduct" for his scuffle with Edwards, interference with attempts to promote morality in the islands, and moral turpitude as an individual. After testimony recorded on scores of handwritten pages, the verdict held that insufficient grounds existed to justify a court-martial. Percival was not so lucky in a civil court, whose judges found for Edwards, assessing damages of $100. The administration handled the Bingham-Percival confrontation gingerly, obviously hoping that it would soon be forgotten. The president said nothing about it, but Secretary Southard tore into his officer in a private letter, informing him that Adams "has not been able to approve the whole of your conduct" because of Percival's lack of "prudence, decorum of language and manners, and . . . caution."

The activities of Percival at Hawaii may be assessed as only one contributing to his country's diplomatic aspirations while the others hampered them. Between his personal clashes he had taken the opportunity to negotiate with the king and his major chiefs, who "acknowledged the debts due to American citizens, to be Government debts," a decision brought about "by the exertions of Lieut. Percival." Otherwise, the fact that Hawaiian-American relations were generally friendly during most of the nineteenth century was surely not due to any warmth and light spread by that mercurial and choleric officer, but to his more tolerant, discreet, and diplomatic naval successors.[1]

Commander Thomas a. C. Jones, 1826–1827

Percival's call at Hawaii had been incidental to his main purpose of chasing down the *Globe*'s mutineers, but Commander Thomas a. C. Jones was specifically sent there. The U.S. commercial agent in Honolulu had asked Commodore Hull, commanding the navy in the South Pacific, to start safeguarding the burgeoning and valuable American trade in the Pacific, help merchants collect the debts owed them by Hawaiian chiefs, and do something about the many derelict sailors who for one reason or another had been abandoned in the islands. He described the latter as "a race of savages and lawless outcasts . . . naked and destitute, lost to every sense of justice, honor, and integrity." Jones left Peru during the late spring of 1826 in the sloop *Peacock*, and after looking into the Marquesas and Tahiti, moored at Honolulu in mid-October.

He did little during the early part of his stay, leisurely investigating the general situation. Eventually he found himself involved in the missionary-trader division, which had recently widened. The commercial interests, spearheaded by the British consul, accused Bingham and his colleagues of trying to create a theocratic and censorious dictatorship over the islands, a charge which the missionary naturally denied. The disputants asked Jones to decide the truth. The ensuing trial, he said, resulted in "The most perfect, full, complete, and triumphant victory for the missionaries," but this conflict remained to mar Hawaiian tranquility.

Turning to his prescribed duties, Jones called upon the king and chiefs to settle their "longstanding debts" to American merchants by funding them through public taxation. He told them that this had to be done at once, for the United States had "the *will*, as well as the power to enforce [compliance] when other, and more pacifistic measures are disregarded."

The Hawaiian government passed an act for that purpose, and somewhere between $120,000 and $160,000 was collected, some of whom paid in sandalwood, others in "Spanish dollars."

Shortly before Christmas Jones chalked up his most significant accomplishment. He talked the court into signing with him seven "articles of arrangement," Hawaii's first international agreement, usually referred to as a treaty. His act was audacious, for Washington had endowed him with no treaty-making powers. The two nations agreed that peace and amity should prevail between them, granted most-favored-nation status to both, set conditions for shipwreck salvage, and itemized terms for the relief of marooned seamen.

Jones's treaty raises a thought-provoking question of international law. It was never sent to the Senate for agreement, and since it was not ratified, it was legally void. Why the American government did not accept it is problematical; perhaps the commander's unauthorized donning of a diplomatic mantle caused resentment. But Jones still merits plaudits for it. Hawaii considered it binding for many years; so did most Americans at home and in the islands.

It is clear that when the *Peacock* sailed away early in January 1827, Jones had outclassed Percival completely. Jones's efforts to collect the amounts owed American traders earned their endorsement, and the missionaries were unstinting in their admiration for him. Bingham said that the people called Jones "the kind-eyed chief," perhaps the last appellation that he could think of to describe Percival.[2]

Commander William B. Finch, 1829

During mid-October Commander William B. Finch swept into Honolulu harbor in the sloop *Vincennes* bearing presents for the royal family and some extremely complimentary letters from the president and secretary of the navy about Hawaii's progress. Although he persuaded the king to add $48,000 to his debt, most of his efforts were devoted to the religious question. Soon the merchants became aware of his tilt and protested to the secretary of state about this "missionary visit," arguing that warships coming to the islands should be for "the protection of commerce and industry, and not for the purpose of aiding . . . the establishment of creeds or the enforcing of any religious doctrine on an ignorant and unsuspecting people." Finch concluded his report to the department about his stay with a rhetorical question. "Suppose that undue power is exercised by either . . . merchants or missionaries over the government of the Sandwich Islands; from which source will come either the greatest good or the least evil ensue? I certainly think from the missionaries."[3]

Captains John Downes and Edmund P. Kennedy and Commodore
George C. Read, 1832–1839

When Captain John Downes in the *Potomac* dropped anchor in Hawaii on his way home in the summer of 1832 from Sumatra and China, he had to involve himself in a religious conflict, but this time a different one. By 1829 two Catholic priests, one a French subject, had converted a few Polynesians, much to the indignation of the Protestant clergy and its allies among the chiefs. Two years later the Catholic faith was outlawed, the priests were exiled, and some Hawaiian converts imprisoned at hard labor. This posed for the royal government an international threat not to be taken lightly. The French were the self-proclaimed global protectors of Catholicism and apt to intervene in its behalf wherever it suffered persecution, as they had in Vietnam.

Although Bingham referred to Downes as "courteous" and offering "very polite attentions" to him and his colleagues, he knew that he was dealing with no Jones or Finch. The captain threw his weight against bigotry, recommended repeal of anti-Catholic legislation, and told the king that "all civilized nations were in favor of free toleration of religion." He also expressed opposition to the restrictive rule of the missionaries, criticized their imposition of morality by edict, and stated that the Ten Commandments should not be the only basis of law. Ever alert to the happiness of his crew, he urged that they be permitted to buy liquor ashore. After he left in mid-October his advice was in general followed. Catholicism was legally permitted, its enslaved converts freed, and the prohibitory acts repealed. The result, according to Bingham, was "an obvious increase of drunkenness, gambling, and debauchery." Although the missionaries and the reform-minded chiefs made further attempts to outlaw both priests and saloons, with one brief exception they failed.

Early in January 1835 Americans in Hawaii, concerned over the legal status of foreign landholding there, asked the government to send a man-of-war "to settle the affairs of this country." Captain Edmund P. Kennedy, with the *Peacock* and *Enterprise*, was available for that assignment, for he was en route to the United States after his cruise in connection with Roberts's second diplomatic tour. After arriving in late September 1836, the captain held meetings with Hawaiian authorities about the landholding question early the next month for four straight days, three of them attended by the king. They discussed in particular whether foreigners could transfer land. Kamehameha III, while conceding that the development of tracts by "industrious" aliens might be advantageous to his country, insisted that if he "yielded the right of transfer," all his territory could eventually be lost to his jurisdiction, and his royal title would be worthless. Kennedy maintained that such privileges had been clearly implied in Jones's treaty of 1826, but the king, supported by many of his leading chiefs, demurred, probably reflecting Bingham's advice. The squadron departed in October, mission unfulfilled.

Commodore George C. Read brought the *Columbia* to Hawaii in October 1839 on his way home from Kuala Batu and Canton, soon to find himself entangled in the smoldering contention about Catholicism in the islands. The American missionaries, frightened as always by the continual growls from French naval officers, asked Read to hold a court of inquiry in his ship to determine whether they had any responsibility for the royal strictures against the priests and their flock. When he refused on the ground that it was not a U.S. navy matter, the Protestant clergymen appealed for support from the king, who stoutly defended them. That the commodore disagreed with his subordinates is shown by their collective letter supporting the missionaries, signed by all the officers save their commander.[4]

Commander John C. Long and Commodore Lawrence Kearny, 1843

The Kamehameha dynasty could only shakily maintain Hawaiian independence in the face of dangers from abroad. Four nations—Russia, Great Britain, France, and the United States—had the greatest interest in the islands. Of these, the menace from the tsar evaporated the most thoroughly. Alexandr Baranov, manager of the Russian-American Company, centered at Sitka, Alaska, labored to draw a commercial triangle to implement Alaska's fur trade and shipbuilding. In 1812 he received Spanish permission to establish a base at "Fort Ross" north of San Francisco to use as a breadbasket, and Russia held it until 1842. He hoped that Hawaii, with its tropical produce, would become the third point. Dr. Georg Anton Sheffer, a German employee of the company, tried in 1817 to construct a fort at Honolulu and when driven away went to Kauai. Its king allowed him to raise the Russian flag and erect a stone fortification. But Kamehameha I heard about it and exerted so much pressure on that island's government that Sheffer was expelled, thereby ending Baranov's dream of a Russian empire in the Pacific.

Well before Sheffer's failure, the British concerned themselves with Hawaii, and until the mid-1820s they remained the predominant foreigners. During 1794 British Captain George Vancouver actually annexed the islands, although London paid no attention to him. Even after Americans had achieved social and commercial supremacy, the British remained a weighty factor in insular affairs. Only six weeks after Kennedy had left in 1836 Lord Edward Russell in HMS *Acteon*, exhibiting a "wholly dictatorial" air, told Kamehameha III that he would bombard Honolulu unless the king accepted a treaty granting British subjects better residential and property rights. Unable to defend himself, the king signed such a pact. Once more, however, the English government remained inert, concluding that an agreement with "the petty chief of a distant and almost unknown archipelago" could amount to nothing.

As mentioned above, during this period the French were preoccupied with their championship of Catholicism in the Pacific. Captain Abel Du Petit-Thouars compelled the Hawaiians in 1837 to grant his countrymen privileges similar to those won for the British by Russell. Two years later a more serious emergency was sparked by Captain Cyril P. T. Laplace, who avowed that unless his demands were met, particularly one guaranteeing equal treatment of Catholics and Protestants, he would open immediate hostilities. Again, the Hawaiians had to bow, endorsing his dictated terms.

Before midcentury the United States had become the dominant foreign influence in the islands. The authority of American missionaries was still very much felt, and the economic success of their compatriots was even more pronounced. By October 1844, 373 American whalers valued at over $18,000,000 had stopped off at Honolulu, Lahaina, and other ports during that year. Nonetheless, this dominance by no means led Washington to accept recommendations that it annex the islands. Compared to Britain and France the country was still relatively weak in naval strength, and the appropriation of noncontiguous lands was contrary to contemporary national policy. Hence the United States satisfied itself with safeguarding Hawaii from European colonization. The unwillingness of the three to see the islands fall into the hands of either of the other two was probably why Hawaii's independence was so long maintained.

All this was prelude to the closest call Hawaiian self-government had before the islands were annexed by the United States in 1898. This was a direct outgrowth of the European expansionism in the Pacific that moved into high gear during the early 1840s. Britain made the Polynesian Maoris of New Zealand subjects of the queen in 1840 and two years later ripped Hong Kong Island away from China. At about the same time, the French took the Marquesas Islands as a colony and set up protectorates over Tahiti and most of the other Society Islands. Hawaii, crossroads of the Pacific, with as yet generally undeveloped agricultural potentials, would have been a savory tidbit for either power. There is a modicum of evidence that the arbitrary behavior of an Englishman in 1843 was calculated to forestall French occupation.

Rear Admiral Richard Thomas, commanding the Royal Navy from his base at Valparaiso, learned of recent Hawaiian anti-British activities, in particular the expropriation of property owned by the former British consul. He made an unfortunate choice when he sent Lord George Paulet in HMS *Carysfort* to look into these allegations. That officer was evaluated by the U.S. commercial agent in Honolulu as a "young man of whose intellectual capacities very little can be said." Paulet sailed into Honolulu early in February, and after a week collecting information dropped his bombshell. Putting his frigate into fighting trim, he announced his intention of leveling her guns at the royal palace unless his terms were met. As usual, the king could only surrender, bitterly mourning that he was now "a dead man," his "ruin" assured. Paulet personally annexed the entire archipelago, imposing a sizable punitive indemnity on its government. On the 25th a "deed of cession" was read, the Union Jack went up as the Hawaiian standard fluttered down, a 21-gun salute was fired, and the *Carysfort*'s band played "God Save the Queen."

A few days after Paulet had arrived, Commander John C. Long showed up in the *Boston*, to add no spangles to his navy's mantle during his brief stay. Naturally he would not fight Paulet over the matter of another country's annexation. But he must have known that Washington would not approve of a peremptory British takeover of a place where American interests were so important. Incredibly, he did nothing beyond offering the *Boston* as a sanctuary for Americans the night before the threatened English attack. As his successor noted in a letter to his commercial agent, "I am not aware of any protest or remonstrance" coming from him.

Commodore Lawrence Kearny in the *Constellation* was an American officer of different mettle from Long. He docked in Honolulu four and a half months after British rule had commenced. Although he never considered starting any offensive, he soon let Paulet know how he and his nation viewed the present situation. On 11 July he had his note to King Kamehameha III published: "And whereas the United States' interests and those of their citizens resident in the aforesaid Hawaiian Islands, are deeply involved in the seizure of His Majesty's government. . . . Now, therefore, let it be known that I solemnly protest against every act and measure in the premises." He next made a point of receiving the king and his entourage aboard his ship, with the Hawaiian flag flying over her, and letting loose a royal salute.

Paulet had reported his doings to Admiral Thomas in Valparaiso. Recognizing the extent to which his subordinate had overreached himself, Thomas set sail for Hawaii "to remedy, if possible, whatever might be prejudicial to British interests," and brought his flagship *Dublin* into Honolulu on 25 July. He closeted himself with the king, who assured him that Britons would receive absolute parity in treatment with other foreigners. This done, Thomas on his own initiative aborted Paulet's takeover; later he is said to have looked upon his behavior with "high disapprobation." On the 31st the Hawaiian flag was raised again, and the admiral read his "Declaration" that "he does not accept the Provisional Cession of the Hawaiian Islands ... but considers His Majesty Kamehameha III the legitimate King of those Islands." Today Thomas Square in Honolulu commemorates his generous abnegation. The admiral's government eventually endorsed his restoration and by late 1844 Britain, France, and the United States agreed to respect Hawaiian independence. As for Kearny, he was delighted with the British renouncement and early in August sailed for California.[5]

Commodore Robert F. Stockton, et al., 1846–1851

U.S. naval officers were much more peripheral in Hawaiian-American diplomatic relations during 1846–1851 than their predecessors during 1826–1843. Therefore their experiences need comparatively little commentary. The main reason for this change was that in 1843 and thereafter U.S. resident ministers stationed at Honolulu carried much more authority than consuls or commercial agents. As a result naval commanders tended to follow ministerial advice rather than initiating policy on their own.

Commodore Robert F. Stockton in the *Congress*, who stopped off at Honolulu in March and April, is mentioned only in the Navy Secretary's *Report* for that year, and merely as delivering Alexander Ten Eyck, the U.S. minister. Captain John "Mad Jack" Percival, of 1826 notoriety, returned to Hawaii late in 1846 near the end of his round-the-world cruise in the *Constitution*. The only eye-catching aspect of his visit is that one of his officers pointed to Pearl Harbor as an incomparable naval position. Commodore James Biddle in the *Columbus* arrived en route from Japan to California about the same time to warn King Kamehameha III that in any dispute between him and U.S. Minister Ten Eyck, Washington "would be slow to believe that he, and not His Majesty's Government, were to blame." Here Biddle's usual perception of others deserted him. Ten Eyck was anything but a facile diplomat, offending the Hawaiians by his rude and disrespectful attempts to force upon them a treaty they considered unfair. Secretary of State James Buchanan sent him a stinging rebuke and soon recalled him. His replacement did better: he signed a trade pact in 1849 that was ratified the same year. This was Honolulu's first bona fide treaty, and the U.S. Navy had nothing directly to do with it.

Another storm from France—"that perennial disturber of Hawaiian peace"—blew over the islands in August 1849. At the behest of the French consul in Honolulu, Admiral Legoarant de Tromelin brought two warships into the harbor and issued a ten-point ultimatum, but the king refused to agree to it. The admiral's servicemen at once seized the royal yacht, occupied all the government buildings, dismantled the harbor fort, throwing its powder into the ocean, and created havoc. Conferences between the king and admiral were ineffective, and the French huffily departed early that September, thereby breaking diplomatic relations. The Hawaiian government protested the incident to Great Britain and the United States, and Paris soon disavowed the behavior of the impetuous Tromelin. Since no U.S. warships were in Hawaiian waters during the occupation, obviously the navy played no part in this incident.

It is essential, however, as background for a close approach of Franco-American hostilities in 1851. That February a French commissioner materialized in the man-of-war *Sérieuse* to dictate Tromelin's exactions. Panic ensued, for it seemed to Hawaiians that the long-feared French conquest was at hand. A few days later Commander William H. Gardner showed up in the sloop *Vandalia*, to become a much more effective diplomat than most of his predecessors. He and the U.S. minister secretly and unofficially agreed that if circumstances required it, the *Vandalia* would open fire on the *Sérieuse*. Luckily the French commissioner proved to be more moderate than his admiral, accepting the Hawaiian suggestion that the dispute should be shifted to Paris for solution on a higher level. After watching the French weigh anchor in March, Gardner left a few days later. For the rest of the decade there is no evidence that the American navy had anything significant to do with Hawaiian diplomacy.[6]

Summary

U.S. naval activities in Hawaii during the pre-1861 era range from the productive to the inept, but in toto their influence strengthened the American position in the islands and helped pave the way for eventual union. John Percival, however, in 1826, sent this relationship into reverse with his defiance of the missionaries' attempt to bring a stricter code of sexual morality to the people. Amusingly, Ralph Kuykendall, whose three-volume *The Hawaiian Kingdom* runs well over a thousand pages, replete with picayune detail, is still so offended by Percival that he says in a footnote, "It seems unnecessary to go into detail about this phase of Hawaiian history." A few months later Thomas a. C. Jones more than repaired the damage, strongly supporting Bingham and his fellows. Of greater essence, he signed the first Hawaiian-American "treaty." Although unratified, its stipulations were generally followed by both countries for more than the next twenty years. If William B. Finch swung too far to the religious side, three years later John Downes corrected his bias by supporting the business community. The latter's advocacy of religious toleration in persuading the king to relax his anti-Catholic measures obviated for the time any French seizure of the archipelago. Edmund P. Kennedy may have failed to get American landholding rights legalized, but it made little difference, for they were soon granted.

When Lord Paulet in 1843 was personally annexing Hawaii, the responses of two U.S. officers were in utter contrast. The indolent and unperceptive John C. Long observed the British takeover without protest, but a few months later Lawrence Kearny let that arrogant Englishman know that his act would face unrelenting American opposition. Once again he showed himself to be a naval diplomat of the first water, as he had just demonstrated in China. The sojourns of Robert F. Stockton, Percival, and James Biddle had comparatively few after-effects. The French, however, must have surmised, while watching Gardner putting the *Vandalia* into battle conditions, that he might fight. In all probability this helped them decide to abandon their hold. The American navy would reappear in Hawaii in the post–Civil War years.

CHAPTER THIRTEEN

The Pacific Islands Other than Hawaii

1826–1858

B efore the U.S. Civil War the navy was busy in Pacific islands outside of Hawaii and in West Africa, locales far apart geographically but similar insofar as the diplomacy of American naval officers is concerned. In these areas the conduct of international relations was generally different from that in other quarters of the globe. Elsewhere some sort of recognized government existed, although they varied widely. Many, resembling that of the United States, had by the mid-nineteenth century a formalized system of external affairs: foreign ministers or secretaries acting as conduits for the exchange of communication beween the top executives of Europe, Latin America, Hawaii, and to a lesser extent those of the Barbary States, Muscat, Turkey, and a handful of others. To be sure, their stability oscillated between that of rock-solid Britain at one extreme to the tottery regimes south of the Rio Grande, shaken by internal disorders, on the other.

Many governmental structures in Southeast and East Asia, such as in Siam and Vietnam, were modeled on that of China: absolutist and hierarchical in form, smugly certain of their cultural superiority to anything offered to them by what they deemed the crude and rapacious West. Hence foreign relations could not be conducted with most of them on terms of equality, at least until European firepower forced China and its vassal states to reconsider. Other regimes were adamantly opposed to any outside intercourse whatever, except on the narrowest terms: Japan and Korea, so deliberately withdrawn into isolation that Europe and America would have no official relations with them until the 1850s and 1860s. But all of these had a central governmental authority with which to negotiate.

Conditions were different in some other parts of the world: West Africa and the not-yet-colonized Pacific archipelagos beyond Hawaii. Tribalism was the general rule in both, so that usually no single individual or group had domination enough over all to speak for all in intercourse with the outside. These governments were not recognized officially by the West, having neither a foreign office nor diplomatic representation abroad. Except for a consul here and there, typically preoccupied with his own economic affairs, no European or American foreign-service people were stationed in areas marked by such tribal disunity. To be sure, several kingdoms along West Africa's coast had a reasonably effective central government, but only Lagos reached a diplomatic agreement (1854) with the United States.

Elsewhere U.S. naval commanders tended to work in concert with Department of State employees, and if a resident minister in particular was on hand, their freedom of action was somewhat curtailed. But in the Pacific and West Africa, much greater leeway was open to them, either to write treaties or to launch disciplinary expeditions. They busied themselves in both pursuits. American naval officers concluded nine treaties with tribal chieftains in the Pacific from 1839 to 1858 and four in West Africa from 1823 to 1855. How well these agreements were observed is indicated by the hostile U.S. naval landings—nine in the Pacific and four in West Africa.

Commanders Thomas C. Jones and William B. Finch at Tahiti, 1826, 1829

Hawaii was the cynosure of American attention in the Pacific prior to 1861 and would become the only nineteenth-century possession there except for unpopulated Navassa Island, acquired in 1858, Midway Island in 1867, the Philippines and Guam in 1898, and eastern Samoa a year later. But other island groups in that endless expanse of water also commanded the national interest, mainly other parts of Polynesia such as Tahiti, in the Societies, and New Zealand, although Melanesian Fiji received much attention and the Micronesian Gilberts a little. Books, magazine articles, and newspaper items by eyewitnesses in the Pacific were a continuing source of fascination at home. They were filled with missionary reports, accounts of mercantile adventures, and derring-do stories narrated by whalers, all of which titillated their readers, especially if they told of gory cannibal banquets or hinted at bizarre sexual customs. Backed by

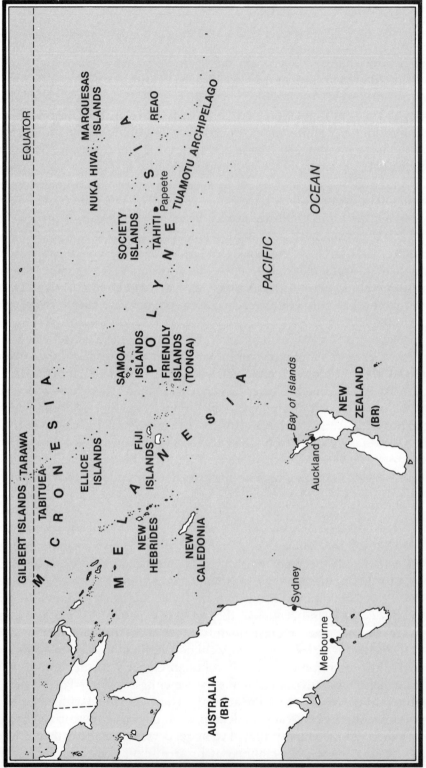

The South Pacific Ocean

such public absorption, navy secretaries were willing to send their warships into the Pacific wherever Americans congregated.

Captain David Porter in the *Essex*, during 1813 and 1814, was the first U.S. officer to have influence in this area, and his destruction of the British whaling industry and his attempt to annex Nuka Hiva Island in the Marquesas have already been described. But he set only one example to be followed by his naval colleagues who later turned Cape Horn or the Cape of Good Hope. One authority noted that "the government did adopt one of the precedents that Porter set by implicitly recognizing the use of naval ships as an arm of executive authority, and it did not hesitate to use them throughout Polynesia during the next two decades [and more]." No other officer imitated his imperialistic activity, except for a couple of feeble ventures in that direction in the Far East during the 1850s. Porter was also the only one who operated there under wartime requirements; naval duties are of course quite different in peacetime.

Although there were three earlier voyages through the central Pacific, most U.S. diplomatic (and punitive) actions there grew out of Charles Wilkes's "Great United States Exploring Expedition" during 1840 and 1841; those of the next decade were in effect follow-ups to it. Officers of the American, British, and French navies watched one another's operations carefully but—as in the contemporary Far East—were apt to band together against "the lesser breeds." One happy result was an opportunity for a conspicuous act of American humanitarianism in 1845.

U.S. naval visits to Tahiti, most important of the Society Islands, may be recounted with great brevity. Thanks to the work of clerics from the London Missionary Society, by the 1820s Tahitians were well Christianized and reasonably well educated. When Commander Thomas C. Jones tarried at Papeete in the *Peacock* from October through December 1826, he was assured of an amiable reception. The island was ruled by the teenaged Queen Pomare I, and even if she admitted that she was "young and inexperienced," her behavior was sophisticated. The two outdid one another in exchanging courtesies. In a letter written three years later to President Jackson, she recalled that Jones had "Treated us with great kindness." In return, the commander had no trouble in persuading her to accept responsibility "for the friendly reception of American ships and traders."

Equal cordiality attended the sojourn of Commander William B. Finch in the *Vincennes* during September 1829. The only ripple of anxiety for the queen was caused by the sudden roar of the ship's guns in a salute to her. She wrote the president in the letter mentioned above that Finch's "kindness to us has also been great," concluding, "We are always glad to see American vessels at Tahiti. . . . Continue to sail your vessels without suspicion." But European influences in Tahiti kept on growing to such an extent that this amicable association with the charming young Pomare marked the end as well as the beginning of meaningful American seafaring diplomacy in the Society Islands.[1]

Commander John Aulick at Savai'i Island, Samoa, 1835

The Samoans were closely akin in language and customs to their fellow Polynesians in Hawaii, Tahiti, and New Zealand. They inhabited the South Pacific archipelago originally called by European discoverers "the Navigator Islands" because of the uncanny ability of their inhabitants to sail vast distances in outrigger canoes to pinpoint eight or ten square miles of land in hundreds of thousands of square miles of ocean. Like most of Polynesia they were divided into many tribes, and warfare between them was constant; occasionally their ferocity spilled over against white intruders.

The department selected Commander John Aulick to cruise among the islands, with special orders to visit Fiji and others of the more remote archipelagos. Starting in July 1835 he peeped into Tonga before proceeding to Fiji, but heard that Fiji's coral reefs were intimidating. A British trader in Tonga told him, "I have no hesitation in saying that it is the worst navigation in the world." Aulick explained to the secretary that without a smaller vessel to guide him, he dared not go on alone, and he canceled his plans. It was a wise decision. A year later HMS *Sulphur*, cruising through those islands, went aground no less than 52 times.

While in Tonga he also learned that recently two boats from the American merchantman *William Penn* had been cut out and some of her people killed at Savai'i Island in Samoa. En route he decided to substitute fighting for diplomacy, although he had no mandate from the department to appoint himself a one-man prosecutor, judge, and jury. He followed to the letter John Downes's assault on Kuala Batu in Sumatra three years before. He crept up on the Savai'i town responsible for what he called "the diabolical outrage" on the *William Penn*, and the next morning sent off an 80-man landing party. Enough time had elapsed, however, for all its inhabitants to flee, including "the chief who led the murderous gang." The sailors vented their frustration by following the commander's orders "to set fire to the town and destroy it." Once again an American naval officer had ignored his orders and overreached himself, but this time no expression of displeasure was forthcoming from the secretary.[2]

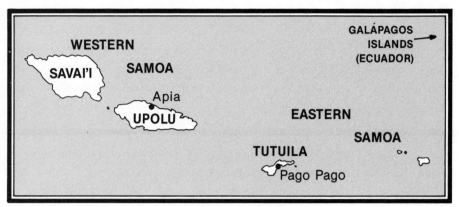

The Samoan Islands

Lieutenants Charles Wilkes and William L. Hudson at the Tuamotus, Samoa, and New Zealand, 1839–1840

After reviewing the 14-year history of the Wilkes Expedition prior to its departure, one is astonished that it ever got under way at all. Its genesis came through the promotional work of President Adams and many others, but political backbiting, clashes between officers and scientists, rivalries within the navy, and the sloth of Secretary Mahlon Dickerson combined to delay its preparation. Worst of all, some high-ranking officers would not serve and others were passed over. Command finally passed to Charles Wilkes, a mere lieutenant. He was sometimes jeeringly referred to as "Commodore-Lieutenant," yet he was a capable surveyor, having directed the navy's Department of Charts and Instruments. Furthermore, he was an indefatigible worker, driving everyone mercilessly, including himself. He was, however, vain, arbitrary, humorless, sadistic to his sailors, and quick-tempered, so that he quarreled with superiors, equals, and underlings alike. His unwarranted removal of the Confederate envoys from the British steamer *Trent* late in 1861 would earn him notoriety as the U.S. naval officer who came closest to taking his country into a war on his own.

And yet, for all his glaring personal deficiencies, Wilkes was the man for the job. In a voyage lasting almost four years he nagged and coerced his people into significant accomplishments in chart-making and scientific fact-finding. As for his diplomatic endeavors, he alternated between completing the usual informal treaties characteristic of the area and inflicting stern punitive measures against wrong-doers, the latter in spite of the secretary's caution that "the expedition is not for conquest but discovery.

Its objects are all peaceful. They are to extend the empire of Commerce and Science."

The squadron left New York in mid-August 1838. The sloops *Vincennes* (under Wilkes) and *Peacock* (under Lieutenant William L. Hudson, his second in command) were accompanied by four other vessels—soon only two, for one was lost turning Cape Horn and another was sent home. So much time was spent in South America and off Antarctica that the expedition did not reach the South Pacific until a year later. Reao Island, in the Tuamotus (Paumotus), in mid-August 1839 furnished a portent of things to come. Its inhabitants threatened a scientist trying to land, and Wilkes wounded some Polynesians with small shot from his "fowling piece." Proceeding to Apia, on Upolu Island, during October, after a short stay at Tahiti the month before, the Americans met with Samoan chiefs and prevailed upon them to sign a pact applicable to the entire archipelago. It guaranteed the safety of all foreigners who obeyed the local laws, permitted minimal port duties and pilotage charges, called for the detention of deserters, and compelled the surrender of those committing crimes against visitors. Wilkes also appointed the first U.S. consul to Apia, although the post was not filled for three years. On a more discordant note, attempts to arrest Chief Opotuno (Oportuno), noted throughout Samoa for his hatred of the white interlopers, came to nought.

After brief calls at Sydney and Hawaii during that year, in March 1840 Wilkes brought the *Vincennes* to meet the gun-brig *Porpoise* and the little former New York ferryboat *Flying Fish* at New Zealand. Its two sizable islands were inhabited by Polynesian Maoris, well-known for proficiency in both warfare and cannibalism. British influence there was already predominant. Anglican missionaries had shown up as early as 1814 and eventually Christianized the people, a triumph of determination, for it took them ten years to make their first convert. In a Hawaii-like scenario, they were opposed by fellow Englishmen more interested in commerce and landholding than in religion. While whites vied for influence, the Maoris became armed with muskets, making their constant tribal feuds increasingly bloody. This violence allowed the British settlers to call for their government's intervention.

While politically impotent, the U.S. presence in New Zealand was paramount economically. By the early 1800s American sealers and whalers started to congregate at the Bay of Islands, well above Auckland in the extreme north. Soon that locality was celebrated as "the happy hunting ground for runaway convicts [from Australia], deserters from vessels, sealers, and bay whalers, many of whom served to vary the menu and provide new vitamins for the Maoris."

Wilkes had missed by only a few weeks one of the most momentous events in the annals of New Zealand. In February 1840 British officials assembled over 500 Maori chiefs to sign the Treaty of Waitangi at the Bay of Islands. New Zealand was formally annexed to the queen's empire; in return the Maoris were assured permanent possession of their lands, a commitment that turned out to be as well-honored as similar pledges by contemporary U.S. Army officers to Amerindian tribes. Wilkes conversed at length about this development with James R. Clendon, the American consul, who had been most prominent in the Waitangi negotiations. This supposed representative of American interests was a British subject heavily engaged in land speculation, to which he was selfishly addicted. The combination of the British occupation and Clendon's treacherous disregard of his consular duties was ruinous to Americans in New Zealand. Their land titles were voided, traders were hamstrung by exorbitant port duties and oppressively high tariffs, and whalers were forbidden to do business in the territorial waters of the islands. Wilkes was curiously quiet about these distressing events. Perhaps he thought that the British stranglehold was too imposing, for he refers to Clendon with guarded compliments in his *Autobiography*. He did, however, recommend to Washington that only U.S. citizens should hold diplomatic appointments abroad.[3]

Lieutenants Charles Wilkes and William L. Hudson at Fiji, 1840

The expedition next ventured into the jagged coral reefs and dangerous shoals of Fiji to face more than maritime perils. The archipelago's 300-odd "Cannibal Islands" were populated by Melanesians, darker-skinned and even more unbridled than the Polynesians, presenting "a spectacle of mingled hideousness and ferocity," with their elaborate tattoos, human bones through the nose, and what Kipling would call " 'ayrick 'eads of 'air." During mid-May at Levuka, on an island just off Viti Levu, largest of the Fijis, Wilkes brought together many chiefs and concluded with them a treaty like the one that he had signed with the Samoans a short while before.

Whites often called the Melanesians treacherous, but if they were they met their match in Lieutenant Hudson. In June Wilkes was informed that Vendovi (Veindovi), brother of the king of Rewa on Viti Levu, had been responsible for the massacre of the American merchantman *Charles Doggett*'s crew in 1834. Hudson, dispatched to Rewa, lured the royal family aboard the *Peacock* and held them as hostages until Vendovi surrendered himself. When he did so the next morning, explaining that his murderous act was no more than following "Feegee custom," Hudson's solution was novel. The chief would not be executed but would be taken to the United

States and after proper instruction returned to let his fellows know that "to kill a white person, was the very worst thing that a Feegee could do." Unfortunately for the moral lesson anticipated, Vendovi, whose dignified bearing and calm acceptance of his strange fate had impressed officers and men alike, died just after reaching New York in June 1842.

One of the expedition's launches went up on a reef in July while surveying at Solevu, off the southwestern coast of Vauna Levu, the second largest island. Although her crew was spared, the Fijians seized the boat. Wilkes was sailing under departmental orders that he should not "commit any act of hostility, unless in self-defense, or to protect or secure the property of those under your command," but he decided that these circumstances justified retaliation. He and Hudson took the *Flying Fish* and ten boats to Solevu and recovered the stolen launch but not the personal belongings of her sailors, which Wilkes estimated most generously at $1,000. While the Fijians made for the bush, the Americans torched their empty town. Some of the officers thought that such a theft did not merit so vehement a response, but Wilkes defended himself: "The infliction of the punishment I deemed necessary; it was efficiently and promptly done, and without the sacrifice of any lives, taught the savages a salutory lesson." Unfortunately for the Melanesians, this "salutory lesson" was repeatedly expounded. One miscreant Fijian village had the dismal honor of being destroyed three times, once by the Americans, once by the British, and once by the French.

A much more serious incident occurred at the small island of Malolo, off western Viti Levu, later that month. Midshipman Joseph A. Underwood considered himself particularly well endowed to be an envoy to the Fijians because he knew a few words of their language. Worse, he had already disregarded Wilkes's standing order that constant vigilance must be maintained against surprise attacks. With nine sailors and Midshipman Wilkes Henry, the commander's nephew and the only son of his widowed sister, Underwood went ashore and seized an armed boy as a hostage. Nearby in a boat, Midshipman James Alden was watching the scene, and shortly after noticing that Underwood's boat had grounded, was startled by the outburst of violence. By the time he and his men came in to drive away the assailants, a grisly sight awaited them. The islanders, furious at the hostage-taking, had gathered menacingly and waded in the moment that the boy managed to escape. The two officers, acting as a rear guard for the headlong flight of their sailors, fought valiantly, and killed three Fijians before they fell under a rain of club blows. Both died almost immediately. American rage and horror were enhanced by the sight of their bodies partially stripped for a victory dinner. A graphic account of the disaster was written by sailor Joseph G. Clark, who survived after days in a coma from head injuries and a spear thrust through the face that left his upper lip dangling to his chin.

Alden, his clothes drenched with the blood of his stricken comrades, reached the *Flying Fish*, shouting to Wilkes, "Great God, Sir, Underwood and Henry are murdered! We have been attacked by natives and both are dead!" For once the commander's serene self-assurance was shattered. According to Clark he fainted, and after being revived, "cried and moaned in the most piteous and melancholy manner." His grief was soon replaced by a craving for vengeance; he vowed to "inflict the punishment it merited . . . not by burning towns alone, but in the blood of the plotters and actors of the massacre." Sualib and Arro, Malolo's only two settlements, were the natural focuses of his wrath. Lieutenant Cadwalader Ringgold and some 70 sailors and marines were sent to assault the first; Wilkes and the rest were to storm the second. The only combat was at Sualib, where opposition was initially fierce. For a quarter-hour the battle went on and a few Fijians were killed before an American rocket glanced into a thatched roof and wildfired to the rest; resistance ended with the dazed survivors in full retreat. The obliteration of the town had been achieved at the cost of a few Americans wounded, only one seriously, whereas fifty or so Fijians were slain. When Ringgold's victors crossed the island to Arro, they found that Wilkes's force had already leveled it. Meanwhile, boats under Lieutenant George F. Emmons cut off some Fijian canoes and inflicted many casualties. At Sualib the next morning a line of over 40 men and women approached Wilkes on their hands and knees, "groaning and sighing in the most piteous and supplicating manner." After they had sworn that the murderers of Underwood and Henry were dead and had begged for clemency, he levied a fine upon them of 3,000 coconuts, plus a few pigs and yams, to reprovision his fleet. Two more weeks of surveying amid a tense watchfulness ensued before the expedition, all four vessels, left "the Cannibal Islands" without regret for other destinations. In his December 1841 *Report* Secretary of the Navy Abel P. Upshur congratulated the commander for his "severe chastisement" and went on to express the hope that it would "probably deter them from similar outrages in future." In 1842 Wilkes was cleared by a court-martial of charges brought by some of his officers that he had maltreated the Fijians.[4]

Lieutenant William L. Hudson at Samoa and the Gilberts, 1841, and Lieutenant Charles Wilkes at Sulu, 1842

During the autumn of 1840 the expedition spent much time at Hawaii, where Wilkes remained impervious to local suggestions that Jones's treaty of 1826 be revised. Early the next year Hudson took the *Peacock* and

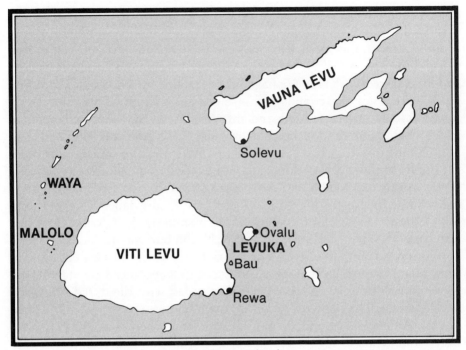

The Fijian Islands

Flying Fish to Samoa. Poor Samoa! One authority on the islands summarizes its sad record of nineteenth-century relations with the West:

> It is a story of native revolutions and civil wars, often instigated by intriguing foreign adventurers; of vainglorious, jealous consuls, who hoisted their flags on the islands and schemed to secure commercial and political influence for their respective nations; of blustering, impetuous naval commanders who shelled and burned native villages; of quarrelling officials and shouting patriots who almost precipitated an armed international clash on a major scale. It is an account of numerous conferences, treaties, and agreements that finally resulted in the partition of the islands between Germany and the United States [in 1899].

Although usually calm and much kinder to his sailors than Wilkes, in Samoa Hudson fit the pattern of a "a blustering, impetuous" naval commander. At Savai'i Island early in February 1841, he found out that an American sailor had recently been killed at the town of Saluafata. He informed its chief that the treaty signed with Wilkes a year and a half before required him to hand over the murderer, but he was told that the culprit was under the protection of a chief more powerful than he and he could do nothing about fulfilling his obligation. Without further ado Hudson moved both of his warships close to Saluafata and hammered that now abandoned settlement with grape and round shot, the latter with considerable effect. Shore parties set afire forty or fifty huts and went on to duplicate their work at two nearby hamlets. Next two officers were assigned to track down the anti-white Opotuno but they failed utterly, as their colleagues had in 1839. They began to realize that another capture through artifice, like that of Vendovi, would ensure that in the future the Samoan chiefs would dare not trust them and effective understandings would be much more difficult to achieve. The combination of unrelenting tension and occasional frustration suddenly seemed to one American officer "silly, and . . . fraught with Nothing but Evil," a description that fits Hudson's actions in Samoa.

The two men-of-war then passed through the Polynesian Ellice Islands, well to the northwest, where they narrowly avoided a battle with native canoes, and approached the Kingsmill Group, in the southern Gilbert Islands. They were now in Micronesia, inhabited by a people lighter in color than the Melanesians and rivaling any other Pacific islanders in martial valor. Most were almost completely naked, the men bearded and armor-clad, the young women "decidedly pretty and their gestures alarmingly provocative." Early in April at the town of Utiroa, on Tabituea (Drummond's Island at the time), the Micronesians jostled some Americans while others were being enticed by the girls to follow them. Sailor John Anderson, apparently led away, was never to be seen again. On the morning of the 9th, with the *Flying Fish* standing by to lend support, 87 men from the *Peacock* climbed into their boats and started for Utiroa's beach five miles away, defended by several hundred warriors. Small-arms fire began cutting the Micronesians down, but they maintained their position until the boats grounded; then they retreated behind coconut palms to watch their 300 dwellings burn. Anderson was the only American casualty, but some 20 Gilbert Islanders were cut down, most of them killed. This was the *Peacock*'s last skirmish. The following July she became one of the hundreds of ships victimized during the nineteenth century in Oregon by the Columbia River's vicious shoals, although Hudson and his crew were rescued by the *Flying Fish*.

After calling at Hawaii, the *Vincennes*, *Porpoise*, *Flying Fish*, and *Oregon* (a brig bought in the Pacific Northwest to replace the *Peacock*) halted at Manila and soon set out for the United States. Early in February 1842 at the Sulu Archipelago, between the main Philippine Islands and Borneo, Wilkes performed his final diplomatic chore as the expedition's leader. He concluded a treaty with Sultan Mohammed Damaliel Kisand at Jolo, on Sulu, the group's largest island, giving Americans commercial rights and providing for the succor of marooned seamen. Wilkes thought that the agreement was worthwhile, for the islands housed nests of corsairs who for centuries had darted out to loot merchantmen. He optimistically concluded that his pact would "soon put an end to all the dangers to be apprehended" from Sulu pirates. The battered *Flying Fish* had to be sold at Singapore. The three remaining ships arrived at New York on 2 June 1842 to meet new kinds of challenges from litigation, scientific squabbles, and publication difficulties. All of these tribulations made little difference to Wilkes, for nothing could disturb his tranquil evaluation that his every act during the long cruise had been faultless.[5]

New Zealand, 1845
Captain Isaac McKeever at Kororareka, Bay of Islands, 1845

After the unpleasantness generated by the Wilkes expedition, with its casualty count, smoldering embers, and wailing villagers, Captain Isaac McKeever's disinterested and benevolent behavior was a happy exception. On the way home on a global cruise in the sloop *St. Louis*, he appeared at the Bay of Islands on 3 March. A quick appraisal of local situations revealed to him that the town of Kororareka (Russell at the time) was "in a state of great commotion from a threatened attack upon the British authorities by the Natives."

Solemn promises to the Maoris in the Treaty of Waitangi about the sanctity of their lands had been quickly broken by voracious white "Land Sharks," and popular resentment soon flared into active hostilities. Their leader was Honi Heke, a Maori chief. He had won his spurs as a skillful battler in tribal conflicts, and was also noted for honesty, magnanimity, and a patriotic devotion to the interests of his people. In March he assembled a force of several hundred and moved on Kororareka. Prospects for the resident British were dire; only Lieutenant George Philpots's little warship *Hazard* was on hand to lend support to the few soldiers defending the "Flagstaff Block House," a total "entirely inadequate to the protection of . . . wives, children, and property." McKeever went ashore, met Honi Heke and other chiefs, and received from them "a pledge of safety to the innocent women and children of the Europeans," which would be scrupulously observed. By the 7th the *St. Louis* was opened as a haven for the more panicky settlers, who started swarming aboard. Four days later Honi Heke brilliantly feinted his enemies out of position, captured the Block House, and blew up its magazine; its garrison fled to ships in the harbor. At this juncture Philpots begged McKeever to land "150 men" to help save the day, but the American insisted on maintaining neutrality. He did, however, send in his unarmed sailors on repeated trips under Maori gunfire to rescue noncombatants.

Isaac McKeever
(U.S. Naval Academy Museum)

During the 13th Honi Heke's men poured into Kororareka, burning everything but the Catholic mission and "some American warehouses," while every European made for the waterfront, some going to the *Hazard*, some to an English whaler, but most to the *St. Louis*. The next day McKeever left for Auckland, his sloop jampacked with 133 refugees, dropped them off two days later, and went back to Kororareka. Once again the Maori leaders renewed their assurance to him that American property would be protected. This enabled the *St. Louis*, her errand of mercy completed, to depart for the United States on 4 April, reaching Hampton Roads early that September.

The British showered the American commander with well-deserved compliments. Robert Fitz Roy, the colony's governor, said that although McKeever "could not interfere hostily . . . he sent his unarmed boats and went himself under frequent fire to succor the women and children and convey them safely to his frigate [sic]." Secretary of the Navy George

Bancroft agreed with the governor, if less extravagantly: "At the Bay of Islands Captain McKeever in the *St. Louis* had the happiness to render valuable service to the inhabitants of an infant British settlement." Honi Heke soon was overwhelmed, but in recognition of his admirable personal qualities, he suffered no lasting penalties, dying a devout Christian in 1850.[6]

Fiji, 1851–1858

Commanders Thomas Petigru and George A. Magruder at Lauthala, 1851

By midcentury Fiji was full of foreigners primarily engaged in whaling, sandalwood-cutting, collecting *beches de mer* (sea slugs), and speculating in land. The presence of many Americans necessitated the appointment of a U.S. consul at Lauthala, in southeastern Veti Levu. It was located in the domains of Chief Thakombau (Cakobau), ruler from the islet of Bau of the strongest tribal aggregation in the entire archipelago. Through incessant warfare this "Napoleon of Feejee" had enlarged his control over so many nearby areas that he called himself the "Tui Viti" (king) of all the islands. The title was accurate in that he was the most potent ruler; false because many parts of Fiji were partially or wholly independent of him. Foreigners who had lost possessions or the relatives of those slain found it much to their advantage to hold Thakombau responsible for any outrages committed, thereby making collection of damages potentially easier.

John B. Williams, consul at Lauthala from 1845, led this movement for the most personal reasons. His claims against the Fijians date from 4 July 1849. He habitually celebrated Independence Day by borrowing a ship's gun and firing salutes. This time some flaming wadding landed on the consulate roof and spread throughout the structure, destroying everything except what was rescued by Fijians rushing to the scene. They took their salvage to the beach and that night stole many of the items. From this opera bouffe until his death in 1860, Williams bombarded Washington with a never-ending barrage of letters trying to collect payment, which he originally set at $4,500. Through such exertions he was able to turn the U.S. Navy Department into a collection agency for himself and other American claimants.

Responding to the consul's pleas, the secretary sent Commander Thomas Petigru in the sloop *Falmouth* to Lauthala. When the ship arrived there late in February 1851, it was the first visit by an American man-of-war since Wilkes had left a decade before. Williams promptly made the commander his ally. Together they sought to persuade Thakombau that as the "Tui Viti" he was personally liable for the total American claims, amounting to $17,000, with that of Williams taking precedence.

Four months later Commander George A. Magruder entered the picture in the sloop *St. Mary*'s to behave in a considerably more impartial manner than his colleague. He conversed about the debt owed to Americans, not with Williams alone, but also with Thakombau and his English missionary interpreter and adviser. Magruder noticed that the consul's claim had mysteriously jumped some $500 and contained property already returned to him. Furthermore, he found a number of his land transactions highly questionable. Before the commander had time to confirm his suspicions, however, other responsibilities compelled a quick departure. He left behind a two-man commission to decide upon the rights and wrongs of the matter, but it could reach no agreement. The issue then slumbered for a few years.[7]

Commander Edward B. Boutwell and Captain Theodorus Bailey at Rewa, et al., 1855

During the four years after Magruder's leave-taking, Consul Williams kept on pressing his demands that the Navy Department direct another warship to reinforce his claims against Thakombau. Meanwhile, continuing Fijian disorders kept raising the debts owed there to U.S. citizens. The town of Levuka, on Ovalu Island east of Viti Levu, was assailed by invaders from Rewa, near Bau, who burned it in 1853 and again a year later; American property was torched. Early in 1855 the same people also burned Williams's new U.S. consulate, at nearby Laucala. In other locales two American ships had been looted, and two Americans were severely beaten at Namuka Island before their liberation by a friendly chief. Williams eventually became so desperate that he wrote to newspaper editors in Sydney, asking them to start beating the drum for the dispatch of a British man-of-war to eradicate Thakombau's headquarters at Bau, which he thought could be accomplished "while one smoked a cigar."

In 1855 the secretary told Pacific Squadron Commodore William Mervine to attend to these accumulating Fijian problems. Selecting Commander Edward B. Boutwell in the sloop *John Adams* for the task, Mervine instructed him "to demand and insist upon reparation for wrongs, committed upon the property of American Citizens." He added, however, a cautionary note that Boutwell must not take for granted that "all the allegations against the supposed offenders were true simply because claimants have filed their statements at the State Department." Boutwell absorbed the first order but shrugged off the second.

In mid-September the *John Adams* reached Rewa, where Boutwell fined its chiefs $12,000, to be paid in commodities, for the burning of the American consulate. Late in the month he commenced chastising the inhabitants of tiny islands near Bau, describing to Mervine his activities against these "robbers and murderers" inside Thakombau's jurisdiction. His movements are hard to follow, for some of the place names he used have disappeared, according to the authoritative *Geographical Handbook of the Fijian Islands*. As best may be discerned, on the 28th he burned the hamlet of Navoa, where he assumed the two Americans had been manhandled; unfortunately what he destroyed belonged to the very chief who had rescued the two. The next day he left the town of Vutia "in ashes," because two of its leaders had promised to kill Williams after the warship departed. On the 30th, while hunting without success for anti-Americans, he destroyed a settlement he called "Lassa-lassa" but this time at the price of one of his men dead and two others wounded.

Arson completed, Boutwell spent his remaining month at Fiji on what he thought, with breathtaking disregard for the truth, to be diplomacy. Dismissing the two-man commission set up by Magruder, he airily stated, "I shall . . . decide these matters myself, without the assistance of a board of arbitration." He lined up behind Williams a hundred percent, accepting without demurrer the consul's claim, increased from some $5,000 to $15,000, while the total owed to Americans soared to $30,000, partly because of compounded interest. Thakombau was absent but Boutwell assembled the lesser chiefs and compelled them to admit "the justice of John B. Williams' claim and also that of the other American citizens" and to promise they would meet the entire obligation within a year. He brusquely informed his listeners that his time in Fiji was short and urged "the authorities of Bau to act quickly and not compel me to go after the so-called Tui Viti . . . for my powder is quick." He disregarded one chief's assurance that much of the destruction had been wrought by those beyond Thakombau's control. Throughout he treated the missionary supporters of the Fijians with a mixture of contempt and neglect.

A gleam of hope for the beleaguered Thakombau came with Captain Theodorus Bailey's arrival in the *St. Mary's* early in October, for he outranked Boutwell. Bailey became influenced by the missionaries, who persuaded him that Boutwell's conduct had been dictatorial and unfair. He chided him for his "deviations from your instructions," in particular his refusal to heed Fijian arguments, for "they should be heard before a final decision." He suggested the importance of a demonstration "to an uncivilized people, in a transition state from the worst cannibalism to Christianity, that civilized nations are just as well as formidable." Boutwell equivocated by proposing that Bailey handle the matter himself. This was a meaningless recommendation, for he knew that his superior would be called away in a few days by duties elsewhere. Unquestionably Bailey, while recognizing that the bona fide claims of Americans must be met, would have come to a much less menacing and more impartial decision than Boutwell.

After watching the *St. Mary's* drop below the horizon, the implacable commander deviated not at all from his preset course. He appointed as the only arbiters two of his officers from the *John Adams*, who barred any pro-Fijian testimony. Following a week's deliberation, on the 19th they reached their decision. Now Thakombau's bottom line was a debt of $45,000, an unbelievable jump of $15,000 over Boutwell's own assessment less than a month before. Of this, Williams was awarded another $3,000, bringing the total to $18,000. The commander's only justification of these startling increases was that Bailey's "interference" had made his work more difficult and that payment to the claimants had been further delayed.

Thakombau was promptly brought to the ship and presented with the bill, which he was told would have to be paid in installments over the next two years. Should he fail to meet that deadline, he must resign his leadership of Bau and present himself for judgment to the next American man-of-war that called. This was no mean threat, for Thakombau had known Vendovi and well recalled what had happened to him. On 23 October he put his mark on the document. Two missionaries aided the Fijian in writing a formal protest about Boutwell's treatment of him to the U.S. consul at Sydney. Thakombau swore that Boutwell had warned him that if he failed to sign the paper he would be taken "away to America. I was then afraid and signed the document under fear." Naturally his allegation was vehemently denied by the commander, the consul, and other Americans, some of whom were financially interested. The Fiji chief was not far off the mark when he characterized what had been done to him as "unrighteous, tyrannical, unwarrantable, and unworthy of the Government of America."

The *John Adams* weighed anchor on 4 November. An Australian newspaper sarcastically congratulated Boutwell for his accomplishments at Fiji: "A naval representative of the model republic has been doing a little in the true Greytown [Nicaragua] style among the Fijians. It were a pity that the chivalric proceedings of this most gallant commander should pass unnoticed." In 1859 Boutwell himself blew to pieces his rationale for his bullying conduct. Although everything he had done to ruin Thakombau had been based upon his premise that he was the real Tui Viti of all Fiji, he admitted that he was not. Why, then, had he acted as he had? He had "held the chief of Bau responsible for the payment of money due American citizens . . . because he was the greatest robber."[8]

Commander Arthur Sinclair at Levuka and Lieutenant Charles H. B. Caldwell at Waya Is., 1858

The sloop *Vandalia*, in 1858, was the next U.S. naval vessel to approach Fiji. Before going on to Bau for further discussions about Thakombau's unpaid American debt, Commander Arthur Sinclair received some grim tidings. Two American sailors had recently been taken from their merchantman and eaten at Waya Island, west of Viti Levu and north of Malolo, which had been devastated by the Wilkes expedition 18 years before. The commander turned the retaliatory mission over to Lieutenant Charles H. B. Caldwell. The *Vandalia* was too deep-drafted to hazard the myriad reefs north of the main island, but the trading schooner *Mechanic* was available. She was chartered and given to the lieutenant and about 50 men. Waya was a sobering sight. It was no coral atoll but a highly mountainous island, studded "with deep ravines," with two peaks rising as high as 1,800 feet. The Lomati cannibals were to be feared; even among their fellow Fijians they were notorious for pugnacity and relentless savagery. In keeping with that reputation was their chief's reply to Caldwell's demand for the murderers: "we have killed the two white men . . . and eaten them. . . . Come, Papillangi [whites], our fires are lighted, our ovens are hot. . . . Come."

Caldwell's tactics were superb. On both the ascent and the descent to their lofty village, he used adjacent ridges to outflank some 300 Lomatis massed to ward off the expected frontal assault on them. Nonetheless, the fighting was intense. Amid "yells and screams" the Fijians resisted with "fire arms, stones thrown from slings, short heavy clubs hurled with great force, and a flight of arrows. . . . Our men returned the assault with a steady and rapid discharge of their rifles, and after a severe action of twenty or thirty minutes repulsed them with heavy loss." The Americans burned "over 115 huts" before marching back to their schooner. Astonishingly only 6 Americans had been wounded, but evidently about 50 Lomatis were casualties, among them 14 dead, including the two chiefs responsible for killing the two Americans. Considering the obstacles in his way, Caldwell had directed the most impressive U.S. armed campaign in the nineteenth-century South Pacific.

Meanwhile, Commander Sinclair had gone on to Levuka, on Bau. The Tui Viti must have been filled with consternation at the sight of the American flag, remembering Vendovi's abduction and Boutwell's assurance that the next U.S. naval commander in Fiji might do just the same to him. Although Thakombau's personal safety was temporarily guaranteed, Sinclair told him that the American claims must be paid with either "cash or blood." On 8 October another treaty was forced on the chief, holding him accountable for $45,000 due within a year.

Knowing that he could not possibly meet that deadline, Thakombau offered to cede all of Fiji to the queen. He and the English consul, William T. Pritchard, made an agreement that in return for 200,000 acres and the Tui Viti's promise to accept the "guidance" and "counsels" of resident British officials, London would pay the $45,000 owed to the American claimants. After lengthy deliberation, however, the cession was refused. This meant that the muddied complexities of Fijian-American relations arising from Williams's incendiary salute on 4 July 1849 would remain unresolved until after 1865.[9]

Summary

Analysis of U.S. naval actions prior to 1861 in the islands south of Hawaii, including retributory landings and treaty-making, shows that the officers ranged from fairly good to terrible. Wilkes's firing of birdshot against the Polynesians in the Tuamotus during 1839 left no observable legacy. The amiable relations in the 1820s between Jones and Finch and the young Tahitian queen amounted to little more, for the Society Islands were in the process of being annexed by the French and rapidly passed beyond the orbit of American interests.

The story darkened when U.S. warships infiltrated Samoa and the Gilbert Islands. Officers there sometimes failed to distinguish between group punishment for what individuals had done and discipline for on-the-spot offenses. In 1835 Aulick burned a town on Savai'i Island for the crime of an absent chieftain, thereby setting a course too often followed in Samoa and elsewhere. Saluafata, also on Savai'i, was put to the torch by Hudson in 1841, because its chief had no power to find and arrest the person responsible for the death of two sailors. Yet naval retaliation seemed justified when officers and men were killed by islanders while surveying or stopping over for supplies and information. When in 1841 one of his sailors was spirited away and undoubtedly slain at Utiroa in the Gilberts, Hudson had every right to destroy the settlement and kill some of its defenders.

The ugliest episodes took place at Fiji, probably because its inhabitants were the most feral and unyielding of all the South Sea islanders, traits enhanced by Western abhorrence of their cannibalism. Although Underwood erred in seizing a hostage, the slaying of two officers by Fijians at

Malolo in 1841 was so much of an overreaction that Wilkes may be excused for his ruthless eradication of Sualib and Arro, while contemplating with pleasure the villagers suing for peace on their knees. A case can be made for Sinclair's sending a detachment against the Lomati cannibals, in the light of their nasty reputation among the other Fijians, the revolting nature of their offense, and their chief's expressions of sheer delight at the prospect of giving battle to that master tactician Caldwell.

These, unfortunately, are the only reprisals that appear to have been warranted in Fiji. The underhanded arrest of Vendovi by Hudson at Rewa in 1840 was clearly under ex post facto law. The captive explained that when he had killed Americans six years before he had been following the customs of his people, who regularly slew uninvited visitors. Reprehensible though his deed was in Western eyes, no treaty pronouncing such behavior criminal had yet been made. At Solevu in the same year, Wilkes left a township in flames because of the stealing of a launch, which was recovered intact, and of the personal effects of American sailors. This response was considered so questionable by some of his officers that Wilkes was court-martialed for it, although he was acquitted.

In telling of these retaliations, either the perpetrators themelves or secretaries of the navy always ended their accounts with statements such as: "This taught the savages a lesson they will not soon forget." Nonsense!— at least in their assumption that punishment guaranteed future good conduct. Such belligerent societies could shrug off a few casualties, and thatched-roof huts and belongings lost when villages were burned could be rebuilt or replaced usually within days. The only sure consequence, especially among the Fijians, was their smoldering hatred for Americans and a fierce anticipation of vengeance that would not be permanently quelled until those islands were acquired by the British in 1874.

As for friendlier activities, Wilkes brought together chiefs in both Samoa and Fiji in 1840 to draw up diplomatic arrangements, and did the same with the sultan of Sulu a year and a half later. Ostensibly these treaties protected Americans and their property; persons considered guilty of anti-American outrages were to be handed over to U.S. naval officers for judgment. They may have provided some legitimization for later punishment, but their impact was negligible. Since the governments of these islanders south of Hawaii were so weak, no assembly of leaders, to say nothing of any single individual, could speak for all. Little wonder that the treaties were so often broken.

In Fiji the dismal U.S. naval record was generated in the main by the American claimants, Consul Williams in particular. Undoubtedly many of the debts accumulated by Thakombau were genuine and required payment. But once Williams made Petigru, Boutwell, and Sinclair his advocates, these assessments climbed from $17,000 in 1851 to $45,000 in a mere four years; that of Williams from $4,500 to over $18,000 by 1858. Magruder and Bailey may have recognized the basic partisanship of their colleagues who permitted no testimony opposing the American claimants from either Fijians or their missionary supporters, but they gave themselves no time to reverse the process.

The brightest U.S. naval light shone in New Zealand, probably because the British and their Royal Army and Navy had already entrenched themselves there. If Wilkes stood by while the English-born U.S. consul Clendon arranged for the nullification of American economic interests in the Bay of Islands, McKeever proved the best of all. At Kororareka in 1845 he threaded his way between rescuing Europeans and successfully advised Honi Heke and his Maoris to take a merciful course, while at the same time preserving the neutrality that his government demanded. Too bad that he was the exception among American naval officers in the South Pacific during 1826–1858.

CHAPTER FOURTEEN

West Africa

1820–1861

Observations made in regard to American naval diplomacy in the early and mid-nineteenth century at the beginning of the last chapter about the Pacific Islands outside of Hawaii also apply to West Africa. To be sure, south along its shores from Dakar in modern Senegal, there were some effectively centralized governments, often governed by bona fide rulers, sometimes called "kings," such as in Benin, Dahomey, and the Ashanti Confederation in what is now Ghana. A few European enclaves also dotted the coast, like British Sierra Leone and Portugese Angola. They are beyond the scope of this inquiry, for no U.S. officers either conducted negotiations with or punished them, with the exceptions of Mayo's treaty with Lagos in 1854 and Brett's landing at Kissembo, Angola, in 1860. Elsewhere a tribalism akin to that in the Pacific prevailed. Sometimes a local headman would elevate himself to royal status with no right to do so. For example, documentation refers to one commander's clashing in 1844 with "King" Ben Krako, who was no more than the chief of a Fishmen's tribal faction. Consequently the American navy generally was active in areas without Western-like machinery for conducting foreign relations.

Its officers in West Africa were indeed "the United States on the firing line," for during almost all the years before 1861 they were the nation's only official representatives there. No Department of State personnel were assigned anywhere along the entire coast north of Cape Town until U.S. consuls began appearing late in the 1850s, and Washington's first minister was the man posted to Liberia in 1863.

The slave trade was the determinant of American naval actions in Africa; only that from its west coast to the Western Hemisphere deserves attention here. To be sure, there was a sizable Arab-directed traffic in blacks from East Africa to the Moslem Middle East, but that area was a Royal Navy responsibility; apparently the U.S. Navy had no part in it. Europeans and Americans alike participated in the trans-Atlantic procurement of slaves for the U.S. South, Cuba, other West Indian islands, and Brazil in particular. They depended for their supplies on a latticework of local rulers, active deep in the interior to capture the slaves needed and transport them to their "barracoons" (holding sheds) on the beach, there to await the slave ship. Reliable information about the number concerned is lacking, but no one questions that it was enormous, certainly in the many millions. Some students of the subject estimate that perhaps as many blacks migrated to the Americas as whites from its commencement in the late 1400s to the abolition of the slave trade in the early 1800s, although the first was entirely compulsory and the second largely voluntary, indentured servants excepted. No amelioration could be realized until the illegal smuggling of slaves was quashed and no termination until slavery itself was eradicated.

While the American naval presence in West Africa was almost continuous in the four decades after 1820, the navy was especially active in protecting the national commerce and fighting the slave trade during 1820–1823, 1844–1845, 1850–1851, 1853–1855, 1860, and 1861.

Captain Edward Trenchard, et al., off Sierra Leone and Liberia, 1820–1823

During 1807 the United States had joined other countries in banning its nationals from participation in the slave trade from West Africa to the American South, the Caribbean islands, and Brazil, for it was generally agreed that conditions for those trapped in the so-called "Middle Passage" were intolerable. Yet this commendable law remained a dead letter. The naval weakness of the Jefferson and Madison administrations ensured that anything in that connection would remain in limbo until after the Treaty of Ghent. In 1819 and 1820 naval strength had increased enough to permit Congress to pass not only acts against piracy but legislation to "suppress the slave trade," appropriating $100,000 for those purposes.

By that time the American Colonization Society had been organized to send back to their African homelands black freedmen, who were popular nowhere in the country. The A.C.S. attracted strong support from such luminaries as President James Monroe and John Marshall, chief justice of the United States, who were convinced that blacks could never attain true equality with whites in the United States. By concerning itself with the 200,000-plus freedmen and women, it ducked the more pressing problem of the roughly million and a half slaves, for that was becoming a sectional tinderbox. Indeed, the vast majority of liberated blacks were thoroughly Americanized; to them Africa was only an ancestral memory, and they begged the A.C.S. to spend its money on their education instead. Nonetheless, a few were willing to migrate, so the navy was told to transport them across the Atlantic and to help the new "colony" to establish itself, all the while hunting down slavers.

In February 1820 Captain Edward Trenchard, with Lieutenant Matthew C. Perry as second in command, sailed east in the corvette *Cyane*, accompanied by the Society's ship *Elizabeth* with 88 settlers. Their destination was Freetown, capital of Sierra Leone, a British colony set up in West Africa to provide a home for blacks rescued by the Royal Navy from slave ships. Governor Sir George McCarty would not permit the American immigrants to remain there, so Trenchard had to leave them temporarily at Sherbro, an island to the south, which quickly proved to be pestilential. He then went on to Cape Mensurado (later Morovia), a far healthier site than Sherbro. There he made plans for the eventual purchase of the necessary territory from local "kings." During her cruise the *Cyane* had halted and investigated a number of suspected slavers, most of them obviously American-owned, although some were under Spanish registry, and thus immune from confiscation. Two, however, without such protection, were destroyed after their cargoes had been liberated in Sierra Leone. The *Cyane* then retraced her crossing, arriving home late in 1820.

The next July Perry took the schooner *Shark*, his first command, to Freetown. He found there the Sherbro colonists, who had abandoned that disease-ridden island, only to be further decimated by a host of new ailments. A second U.S. warship carried the survivors to Cape Mensurado, where they soon faced another danger. Local tribesmen, angry about American interference with their prosperous share in the slave trade, were preparing to attack the settlement. By that time the Reverend Jehudi Ashmun, now regarded as the founder of Liberia, had disembarked with a few more expatriates sent out by the A.C.S. His appearance was providential, for even though a mere 28 of his people were physically able to join in the fight, they beat off the assault. As for Perry, he had been chasing down a few likely slavers, among them two French vessels, unquestionably guilty, but "reluctantly" he had to let them go. He soon departed from Africa and reached Norfolk in December 1821.

Captain Robert T. Spence, who had succeeded Trenchard in command of the *Cyane*, had also been energetic. His major contribtion was to strengthen protection for Ashmun's frightened people, since local rulers were avowing that they "never had any intention of selling" Cape Mensurado, for they had been "ignorant of the paper they had signed." Within two weeks during the spring of 1823, he, his crew, and some hired workers constructed a Martello tower, which he described as "a circular massive work of stone," 112 feet in diameter, 8 feet thick, and 10 feet high. This tower, he assured the secretary, had caused a marvelous transformation in the "powerful chiefs" from truculence to their present "amiable and conciliatory conduct."

When Spence wrote about the "paper" that the rulers wanted to repudiate, he was calling attention to Lieutenant Robert F. Stockton's recent success. Commanding the 12-gun sloop *Alligator* and operating under ambiguous orders from the department that he interpreted as enabling him to buy territory, he had set out for Africa in September 1821 with Dr. Eli Ayres, the A.C.S. agent, as his companion. While en route on 5 November, they had an unpleasant surprise. Somewhere off the Madeira Islands a vessel later identified as the Portugese warship *Marianna Flora*, of about the same size and armaments as the *Alligator*, sent up a distress signal. When the Americans approached on what was supposedly an errand of mercy, they were greeted with a volley from the other ship's guns "in a most outrageous and piratical manner," according to Lieutenant Joel Abbot, second in command. The battle went on for the next hour and a half before the *Marianna Flora* surrendered; no casualty count for either side is recorded. Abbot was sent over to the captive, arrested the 29 men on board, and brought her into Boston. Any dreams of prize money, however, vanished for the *Alligator*'s people. The Portugese captain denied any piratical intent, stressing that he had acted under the impression "that she was a privateer." A court accepted his version and the ship and all her crew were liberated. With circumstances so muddled, evidently neither Washington nor Lisbon decided upon any diplomatic follow-through.

When Stockton and Ayres reached Freetown, they harkened to Governor McCarty's recommendation that Cape Mensurado and adjoining tracts would be well suited for the society's permanent establishment. During December they went to the cape and met with regional tribal authorities, headed by one "King Peter." Arguing that it would bring great

West-Central and Southern Africa

riches to him and his people, they received his reluctant consent to sell the land in question. But he soon reneged on his pledge, persuaded to do so by an unnamed mulatto slave trader, who stressed that anything done to keep the U.S. Navy in the vicinity would ruin their mutually lucrative business in "black gold."

On the day that the agreement was to be signed, Stockton and Ayres had to penetrate several miles into the interior before they could find Peter. He, other chiefs, and 500 glowering tribesmen confronted the Americans. When the mulatto began stirring up their bloodlust, Stockton decided at once that audacity was his only escape, and in "an overpowering voice" shouted for silence. He whipped out two pistols, handed one to Ayres telling him to shoot the slave trader if he uttered another word, and, thrusting the other against Peter's head, reiterated the advantages the local blacks would get from the agreement. At that moment the clouds parted, bathing the lieutenant in sunlight, which was interpreted by the tribesmen as a divine intervention. Resistance collapsed, and on 15 December Stockton was able to purchase not only Cape Mensurado but also a coastal tract 140 miles long and 40 miles deep, thereby establishing the basic territory of what became an independent Liberia. The Americans paid for this generous cession with rum and a variety of trade goods such as muskets, beads, iron articles, umbrellas, and mirrors. These gifts were not exactly shining examples of magnanimity, for their total value was "less than $300."

Stockton had also been carrying out his antislaver mission. He nabbed four vessels and, convinced that they were really Americans with a status no higher than that of pirates, sent them into New York. Since he had ignored the fact that they were under French registry, he had sparked a brief Franco-American controversy that made a few days unpleasant for Secretary of State Adams and President Monroe. As described by Adams, both men had to confess to the French minister that Stockton had erred, for the department's orders had been to apprehend only vessels with American papers, and they "very much regretted" his "mistake." Yet the lieutenant was never punished, and a later U.S. circuit court decision agreed with him that slave-carrying was the same as piracy and therefore was outlawed by all nations. The claims of the French owners for damages caused by Stockton's seizures were denied.[1]

Commodore Matthew C. Perry off Liberia and the Ivory Coast, 1844–1845

Following its spate of accomplishments from 1820 to 1823, the navy's diplomatic activities along the slave coasts of Africa wallowed in the doldrums for the next two decades. In 1824 the department informed Commodore David Porter, battling corsairs in the Caribbean, that the range of his West India Squadron was being extended by several thousands of miles; he was henceforth commanding "U.S. Naval Forces, West Indies, Gulf of Mexico, and Coast of Africa." He was told to send one of his schooners to attend to the wants of America's African "colony," returning on "the usual track of the Slave Ships." With their major responsibilities focused upon nearby waters, commodores paid little attention to their trans-Atlantic obligations. Although U.S. warships appeared in West Africa on an average of about one a year, their stays were unproductive. As one historian notes, "These visits degenerated to little more than perfunctory stops undertaken to satisfy the demands of the Colonization Society and to fulfull the promises of the Naval Secretary that an American man-of-war would occasionally visit the African coast."

After 1815 Royal Navy efforts to investigate suspected slavers flying U.S. colors usually came to nought in the face of American governmental resistance. The Anglo-American Webster-Ashburton Treaty of 1842 had promised to solve the matter. Both countries pledged to maintain squadrons of no less than 80 guns to operate against the slave trade; the Americans would search vessels flying their flag, the British the rest.

The roseate expectation that this commitment would resolve the difficulty was soon darkened. It was not so much that American officers of the new West African Squadron were derelict in their duty as that most of the naval secretaries during the ensuing years were pro-Southern. Their bias was reflected in their exhortations to their commodores that anti-slave-trade operations were distinctly secondary to their promotion of American commerce in West Africa. Furthermore, they furnished too many deep-drafted sailers and too few small, fast steamboats. Necessities for the U.S. squadron were no closer to their field of patrol than Porto Praia in the Portugese Cape Verde Islands. As the slave trade steadily moved south, the distances involved increased to such an extent that one American man-of-war spent no less then 40 percent of a 15-month tour going back and forth. Repeated requests by naval officers that store ships be stationed close to the slave-trade routes were ignored. Finally, officers and men alike hated West African assignments, characterized by a hot and humid climate, the monotony of idleness, a lack of shore leave, and lethal diseases.

The statistics are revealing. Washington annually dispatched about four or five warships, usually under canvas, and sometimes mounting fewer than 80 guns. London sent down an average of 19, carrying almost 150 guns, with most of them shallow-draft steamers and sloops, ideal for their tasks. The British soon discovered that American deficiencies made cooperative endeavors a hindrance, and they increasingly patrolled alone.

The performance of Commodore Matthew C. Perry, first commodore of the Africa Squadron (1843–1845), showed that he realized that the promotion of trade took precedence over slaver-hunting. Secretary of the Navy Abel P. Upshur, although urging that slave ships be apprehended, emphasized that the squadron's "paramount duty" was rather the protection and augmentation of American commerce. Morison, in his *Old Bruin*, fails to note how carefully Perry restricted his responsibilities. In two years his four ships took precisely one outlaw vessel, and she contained no black cargo.

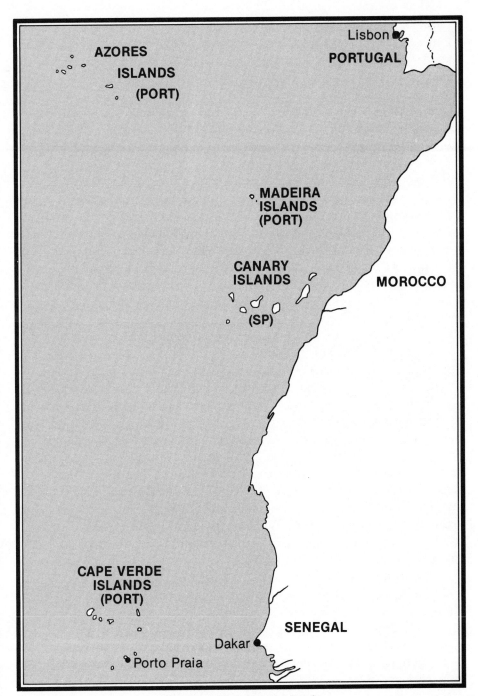

The Eastern Atlantic Islands

Instead Perry concentrated on other activities. He sent one of his sloops to investigate the status of U.S. trade with West Africa, and recommended that American tobacco, weapons, and hardware could be profitably exchanged for African gold dust and palm oil. He passed most of his time protecting American citizens by bringing peace to the area, a task he assumed on his own. Arriving at Monrovia early in August 1844, he changed his flagship from the *Saratoga* to the *Macedonian* and proceeded to eastern Liberia, where the American Colonization Society had established a settlement called "Maryland in Africa," from the society's branch in Maryland, directed by the effective mulatto John B. Russworm. He and his colonists were threatened by the so-called Fishmen in the nearby village of Sino, who felt that the advent of the American blacks had interfered with the money they had been making as middlemen in the slave trade. Their menace was no joke; they had recently killed two sailors from an American merchantman. Perry landed at Sino with an armed escort and held discussions with them. After listening to their side of the question he concluded that although their murders had been reprehensible, the white men had been the original aggressors. While presents were being exchanged, Perry told the Fishmen that any crime against Americans would be severely punished but that commanders of U.S. naval vessels would do the same to any Africans who injured them.

That December the expedition went on to the western border of what is now the Ivory Coast. Other Fishmen there had tortured the captain of the Salem merchantman *Mary Carver*, slain him and his crew, and looted the ship. Since Perry was sure that resident chiefs were responsible for the atrocity, he was in anything but a conciliatory mood when he met them at a spot called Little Berebee. He blew up after hearing a number of palpable lies told by their leader, "King" Ben Krako, and called on the marines to arrest him. On their approach Krako's interpreter panicked and fled, only to be shot dead. What next occurred paints a comical mental picture in retrospect, although it most certainly was not amusing to the commodore at the time. When Krako took off for the woods, Perry grabbed his long robe. The austere, reserved, and status-conscious "Old Bruin" bounced along the ground behind him for some yards before the fleeing "king" was mortally wounded. Ben Krako was carried to the flagship and soon died there. Meanwhile general shooting had broken out, and the Fishmen dashed into the bush, leaving their village to be burned.

The next day at adjacent Grand Berebee, local chiefs protested their innocence in the *Mary Carver* affair and professed their delight that Krako, a "very bad man," was gone. They signed with Perry the "Treaty of Grand Berebee," pledging that they would treat American traders and missionaries well. The commodore wrote to the secretary that his efforts had proven to the natives that crimes would be repaid with interest, and that his "friendly demonstrations" would show the Fishmen and others that the United States "greatly prefers a pacifistic intercourse with all nations, however insignificant, to one of strife." The squadron moved up and down the coast for many months without further meaningful incident, and Perry was back in New York by April 1845.[2]

Commander Andrew H. Foote off West Africa, 1850–1851

Commodore Perry's abstinence from hunting slave-traders was accentuated by Commander Andrew H. Foote during his eighteen-month cruise in the brig *Perry* back and forth between Liberia and Angola, with stopovers for provisions, recuperation, and relaxation at Porto Praia and St. Helena. To Foote his voyage was important enough for him to devote much space to it in his book on Americans in Africa. When one scans his account, however, it becomes palpable that his accomplishments were meager. Apparently the squadron under Francis H. Gregory captured only one slaver, and she was taken by another one of the commodore's warships. But the 24-vessel British squadron apprehended several suspects flying the American flag, and much of Foote's tour was occupied in friendly correspondence with British naval officers as to whether the captive ships had the right to display those colors. If not, the British kept them; if they did, they were turned over for eventual trial in U.S. courts. It is not that Foote was unenthusiastic about his task, for he was an ardent foe of slavery in all its forms. It is rather that U.S. naval officers were virtually helpless to affect the slave trade under the restraints laid down by Washington.[3]

Commodore Isaac Mayo at Liberia, Nigeria, et al., 1853–1855

In March 1853 Commodore Isaac Mayo sailed in the *Constitution* for Monrovia, Liberia. He had the honor of commanding the most famous American man-of-war on her last active duty. His two-year cruise in her demonstrated how well Upshur's orders to Perry a decade before had taken hold. Like "Old Bruin" he could interpret them to mean that he had a free hand to help the national trade by bringing peace to the slave coast; the tactics he used were on his own initiative. Slaver-catching, however, was once more subordinated to the promotion of American commercial opportunities. In general, Mayo plodded along the path well worn by his predecessors. He apprehended exactly one suspected slaver, again without blacks aboard.

Mayo's most significant contribution to his country's commerce happened during the summer of 1854 in present-day Nigeria. He had learned that the British and French had been signing coastal agreements gaining palm-oil concessions, and he feared that Americans might be cut off from supplies of that valuable commodity. He met the king of Lagos in his flagship and "without making any pledge whatever," persuaded him to grant most-favored-nation standing to the United States, although for reasons unspecified in the documents, the treaty was never ratified.

As for peace-keeping, Mayo was told that a tribal war at Cape Palmas was disturbing law and order. In September 1853 he found that the bellicose slave-catching Barbos had been raiding the villages of the more pacifistic Grebos, but when he approached the aggressors they "rudely repelled my messenger and defied my power . . . using terms . . . equivalent to a declaration of war." On the following morning the commodore went toward their settlement with boats carrying 200 servicemen, and after "a few shells" had wounded two, the Barbos quickly surrendered. The next day the commodore called a "Grand Palaver" in the *Constitution* and engineered a Barbo-Grebo "treaty of peace," after which, he avowed, normal trade was resumed. Some months later Mayo managed to settle a quarrel between two other tribes near Cape Palmas prior to his return to the United States in June 1855.[4]

Commander Thomas W. Brent at Kissembo (Quisembo), Angola, 1860

Commander Thomas W. Brent's only direct connection with the slave trade was that he was on patrol against its carriers, so his success in peace-keeping off Angola should be stressed. The Portuguese had been there since the late 1500s, and primarily by furnishing slaves to Brazil, the colony prospered to some extent. Yet the Portuguese effectively occupied only Loanda and a few other ports. By the 1850s matters were worsening, in large part because of British coercion, which resulted in the gradual abolition of the slave trade after 1842 and of Angolan slavery after 1858. From 1854 to 1860 a new governor-general tried to reverse the colony's downward slide. Lacking naval and military power to push Angola's boundaries north to the Congo River's mouth, he concentrated instead on penetrating the interior behind his coastal enclaves. This decision, coupled with the imposition of a new tax on currency and trade goods, aroused the ire of the still potent inland tribes, who assaulted Portuguese outposts.

This dangerous situation came to a head in February 1860, when "Prince Nicolas," claimant to the throne of the Kongo tribe in northern Angola, was trapped by local blacks in Kissembo and "immediately shot and beheaded by the Natives" under the mistaken impression that he was a Portuguese collaborator. The governor-general dispatched some 300-400 soldiers to Kissembo. European and American inhabitants there were terrified at being caught in the middle of Portugese-black hostilities. Luckily for them, Brent in the sloop *Marion* was nearby and sped to Kissembo, where he joined the commander of a Royal Navy warship in cooperation with the governor-general to restore peace. Early in March he twice sent his sailors and marines ashore. Their presence discouraged the plans of the blacks to burn the waterfront buildings, and the detachment was soon withdrawn, Brent correctly surmising that the crisis was over. As Secretary of the Navy Isaac Toucey put it, "Commander Brent observed a strict neutrality throughout, his only object being the protection of American citizens." Over the next few years Portugal was able to retain Angola by withdrawing from much of the interior and the eventual imposition of stricter controls from Lisbon.[5]

Commodore William Inman off West Africa, 1859–1861

Commodore (technically "Flag Officer") William Inman finally demonstrated what an active and determined American naval officer could accomplish along African shores. He did this in the face of the department's continuous exhortations that such errands were secondary to the discovery of further national business opportunities. He managed to overcome foot-dragging by Secretary Toucey by locating store ships close to his cruising area and keeping his squadron at sea more constantly than those of his predecessors. From 1842 to 1861 U.S. patrollers took 24 slavers and freed 4,945 blacks. Inman was able to brag that his 11 and 2,793, respectively, during his short tenure amounted to almost half of these totals. Unfortunately this record has to be compared with the Royal Navy's record of 595 slave vessels apprehended and 45,612 bondsmen liberated during the same period. Furthermore, even with Inman's yeoman endeavors, the slave trade continued to flourish under the U.S. flag. The British consul in New York reported that from 1859 to 1861 no less than 170 slavers had deposited cargoes in Cuba alone. Of these, 117 were Americans, 74 from New York.[6]

Efforts to terminate the slave trade turned around in 1862. During that February the legislation of 1819–1820 making slave-trading as well as piracy a capital crime was enforced for the first time. Prior to that date complacent prosecutors and indifferent juries had refused to punish any captains so charged, although many of them were obviously guilty; that same month the execution of slaver Captain Nathaniel Gordon reversed the trend. More to the point, the Anglo-American treaty of 1862 at long last permitted English cruisers to stop and investigate all suspect ships, including those flying the American flag. In 1861 the U.S. African Squadron was called home, but even so, the immediate result of the treaty was startling. In all of 1862 not a single slaver left New York. Although occasional voyages for that purpose occurred before their markets were wiped out by the final abolition of slavery in Cuba and Brazil, the Anglo-American understanding sounded the death knell for that repulsive business.

Summary

African Squadron commodores during these years did their best work in pacification, despite no more than the tacit approval of the department. They were somewhat efficacious in enhancement of commerce, but did almost nothing to curtail the slave trade. Trenchard, Perry, Spence, and Stockton started the squadron's operations in whirlwind fashion by executing their singular task of assisting in the foundation of what became Liberia. Spence's Martello tower helped to save the A.C.S. colony at "Maryland" and Stockton triumphed in purchasing from unwilling tribal chiefs the land that provided Liberia with its basic boundaries. These successful activities, however, were followed by almost 20 years of naval visits that added up to window-dressing. On paper the Webster-Ashburton Treaty of 1842 promised much, with its bi-national patrols against slavers apparently hurdling the roadblock of American refusal to cede the right of search or visitation. But it soon proved barren, because of the repeated urgings of naval secretaries that U.S. warships should relegate cruising against slavers to well below the improvement of commercial opportunities.

Yet the pacification attempts of U.S. commodores merit approbation. Perry subdued the Fishmen near Cape Palmas and Mayo did the same when he terminated a Grebo-Barbo war, and both achieved their diplomatic goals by signing treaties with the tribes involved. As to the slavers, the obtuseness of Perry in the mid-1840s, as exemplified by his conclusion that no Americans were transporting human cargoes across the Atlantic, a response echoed to some extent by Mayo ten years later, was reversed by Inman, much to his credit. But able though his work had been, the end of the West African slave trade was brought about, not by U.S. naval officers, but by Royal Navy cruisers and by Anglo-American diplomats in 1862.

CHAPTER FIFTEEN

The U.S. Civil War

1861–1866

No more is required about Civil War circumstances than to stress two points. First, the Confederates knew that their best hope of establishing an independent republic would be through foreign intervention in the conflict on their side, particularly by Great Britain. Second, the navy contributed essentially to Union victory by enduring the excruciating boredom of blockade duty in sweltering heat or frigid storms, broken now and then by the exhilarating pursuit of a blockade-runner. Even more consequential, the navy picked off or immobilized the South's largest ports and provided cover and transportation for Northern armies penetrating the Confederacy along its rivers. But too much of its time had to be given to hunting down the handful of Southern commerce-raiders who were playing ducks and drakes with the Northern merchant marine. This was an area in which foreign relations could become an issue, especially when the raiders were holed up in neutral European or South American ports.

As far as the U.S. Navy's wartime activities are concerned, only four actions merit discussion: the abduction of Confederate envoys from a British ship off Cuba in November 1861; the shattering of Brazilian neutrality by the ramming and kidnaping of a Southern cruiser at Bahia in October 1864; the chasing of a Confederate ironclad off Spain and a brief crisis between Portugal and the United States in March 1865; and an

American warship's interference with Irish-American Fenian raids across the border into Canada in 1866 and 1870, which helped clear the rocky road of Anglo-American relations leading to the successful Treaty of Washington and the Geneva Arbitration of 1871–1872.

Some thought has been devoted to whether to include in this narrative anything about the hundreds of blockade-runners, especially British, intercepted and brought before the courts for adjudication by U.S. naval officers in 1861–1865, in particular the well-known cases of the *Springbok*, *Bermuda*, and *Peterhoff*. But Stuart L. Bernath's *Squall across the Atlantic: American Civil War Prize Cases and Diplomacy* (Berkeley, 1970) has convinced me that these cases were not part of American naval diplomacy but legal problems settled by civilians. Hence they have been omitted.

Captain Charles Wilkes off Cuba, 1861

If ever a decision taken on his own initiative by a naval officer could have the most dangerous diplomatic consequences, it was that of Captain Charles Wilkes late in the war's first year. He forcibly, if farcically, removed the Confederate emissaries James M. Mason and John Slidell from the British packet *Trent* and brought them to his *San Jacinto*. As a result the United States and Great Britain came closer to war than at any time since 1812. Had not the stand maintained by Wilkes and his myriads of jingoistic and short-sighted supporters eventually been disavowed by his government, the American union just might have come to an end. The British intervention that seemed to be the Confederacy's only realistic chance to make secession permanent is precisely what the captain's unauthorized act almost accomplished.

Wilkes had been in the public eye since his command of the U.S. Exploration Expedition from 1838 to 1842, when his impressive talents and equally impressive personal shortcomings became evident. After he had been given in effect an independent command early in the Civil War, a treasury official warned Secretary of State William H. Seward, "He will give us trouble. He has a superabundance of self-esteem and a deficiency of judgment. When he commanded the great exploring expedition he court-martialled [sic] nearly all his officers. He was right, everyone else was wrong." This prognostication received almost immediate confirmation.

While on patrol in his steam frigate the *San Jacinto*, Wilkes learned that Mason and Slidell, Confederate agents appointed to London and Paris, respectively, had gone through the Union blockade to Havana, en route to Europe. Wilkes spent some time poring over his law books and those owned by Robert W. Shufeldt, U.S. consul in Havana. Shufeldt agreed with Wilkes that one way or another the Confederates must be apprehended, reinforcing the captain's confidence that his interpretation of international law, as of everything else, was impeccable. Since written enemy communications were classified as contraband of war, and since Mason and Slidell undoubtedly recalled their oral instructions, they were "the embodiment of dispatches," and they and the ship that transported them were subject to seizure.

Knowing the route that the *Trent* would be sure to take, the *San Jacinto* lay in wait for her on 8 November. Two shots across the bow halted the English ship. Wilkes ordered that the Confederate emissaries be removed and a prize crew put aboard the *Trent* to take her into a Northern port for adjudication. Lieutenant Donald M. Fairfax and a small detachment were sent over in a boat. Although its consequences could have been monumental, what ensued approached slapstick.

Fairfax was brought before James Moir, the *Trent*'s captain, who coldly protested the interception of his unarmed vessel in open water. The lieutenant asked for Mason, Slidell, and their two secretaries, George Eustis and J. M. McFarland. He had already recognized two of the four standing in the crowd that had gathered to watch the confrontation. Slidell informed Fairfax that they were under the protection of the Union Jack and that they could only be removed by coercion. Richard Williams, a retired British naval commander, clad in his old uniform, chose this moment to push forward, bellowing that he represented the queen's government, and denounce this "illegal act, an act in violation of international law, an act, indeed, of wanton piracy!" Fairfax ignored him and repeated his request for the four Confederates. At this juncture Mrs. Slidell said that Wilkes was "doing the very thing the South was hoping for—something to arouse England. . . . Really Captain Wilkes is playing into our hands." Mason politely suggested that she keep her mouth shut.

After the arrival of a second boat full of marines sent over from the *San Jacinto*, the sound of shattering glass and a woman's scream startled everyone. It turned out that Slidell was trying to escape through his stateroom window (to where?). Mason proclaimed that he would resist any arrest, but after Fairfax had told his men, "Gentlemen, lay your hands on Mr. Mason," his bravado vanished. Slidell informed the lieutenant that "considerable force" would be required for his apprehension, but offered no resistance. Much comment was aroused on both sides of the Atlantic by the next episode. Miss Rosina Slidell, an attractive seventeen-year-old, slapped Fairfax across the face, it was reported, and according to the oratorical Williams she was saved from a fate worse than death at the

Charles Wilkes
(U.S. Naval Institute)

approach of the slavering Yankees only by his standing in front of them shouting "Back! you damned cowardly poltroons!" Apparently the truth is that while she was reproaching Fairfax for his behavior, a roll of the ship caused her to steady herself by putting a hand on the lieutenant's shoulder. Without further ado the four men and their luggage were transferred to the *San Jacinto*, where they lived in Wilkes's cabin and shared their meals with him until being imprisoned at Fort Warren in Boston Harbor.

Wilkes must have been puzzled as he watched the British steamer head out to sea, rather than toward a Union port for adjudication, but accepted Fairfax's decision to let her go. It should be noted that the captain could have overruled him and gone after the *Trent*, so Wilkes has to be accountable. The point is important, for by seizing the men and not the ship, according to the international law of that day, he put the Union clearly in the wrong. Whether British public opinion would have realized the distinction is, however, another matter.

The extent of Northern despondency during mid-November 1861 must be understood to explain the hysterical jubilation that followed the arrest of Mason and Slidell. The war had gone contrary to Union expectations. Save for picking off four ports, the major clash had resulted, not in a triumphant campaign "On to Richmond" (a press cliché) and a Confederate surrender, but in the Union rout at the First Battle of Bull Run in July, which made Lincoln's army a laughing-stock throughout Europe. Nothing much better had occurred until Wilkes's bold act electrified the North.

Cities showered him with acclaim, the *New York Times* wanted to "consecrate another Fourth of July to him," the House of Representatives voted him a gold medal, President Lincoln voiced his thorough approval, and Secretary of the Navy Gideon Welles, in a message that he soon wished he had deposited in a trash can, said that the seizure of Mason and Slidell was "marked by intelligence, ability, and firmness and has the emphatic approval of the department." So unanimous was Northern enthusiasm in the immediate afterglow of the event that for a time it appeared politically impossible to release the Confederates, no matter how high the stakes if they were not.

When the British heard about the *Trent* affair, they instantly exploded in national wrath. Queen Victoria thought that the Union had "behaved scandalously," Prime Minister Lord Palmerston ("Lord Pumicestone") told his colleagues, "You may stand for this, but damned if I will!," Foreign Secretary Lord Russell concluded that "it looks like war," and the London *Times* editorialized that Wilkes's "swagger and ferocity" marked him as "an ideal Yankee." Charles Francis Adams, U.S. minister to Britain, gloomily prepared to close his legation in London, and his son Henry, later the famous autobiographer, called those who applauded Wilkes "a set of bloody fools!" The Palmerston ministry forbade the export of munitions, put its armament factories on wartime schedules, and started sending some 8,000 soldiers toward Canada.

Much attention has since been directed at the state of transatlantic communications late in 1861. The cable from Ireland to Newfoundland, which had operated briefly during 1858, had soon broken and was not again in service until 1867. Hence some weeks elapsed before the Union public knew about Britain's bellicose reaction to the *Trent* affair, and Englishmen remained unaware that Wilkes was being hailed throughout the North as one of the country's greatest heroes. It is certainly possible that had the underwater telegraph been available to make known at once to each public the response of the other to the crisis, cooler heads in both nations would not have been able to control the lurch of each toward war.

Luckily there were peacemakers in the top government echelons of both Washington and London. Lincoln soon regretted his earlier enthusiasm for Wilkes, recognizing the possibility of disastrous fallout from the captain's action, although he also had to weigh domestic political implications carefully. Adams, who had never approved of the seizure, kept doggedly trying to douse the conflagration. But it was Seward in particular who earned his nation's thanks at this time and added to his laurels as one of the finest secretaries of state. He was no expert in international law, but he rapidly concluded that the American case could hardly be flimsier. He was sure that Wilkes had enough justifiable suspicions about the *Trent* and her Confederate passengers to bring her into a Union port for search and judicial decision. Yet when Wilkes removed four men from a vessel that he allowed to proceed, he was engaging in what could accurately be called impressment, which had been practiced by the Royal Navy against American sailors from 1793 to 1812. Seward decided that the captives would have to be liberated, but in view of the Captain's continued popularity, not until political circumstances would allow such a move.

British leaders were also inclined to avoid war if permitted to by public opinion. Despite their chronic anti-Americanism, neither Palmerston nor Russell wanted to involve their country in the fratricidal conflict in the United States. They had to face the fact that their Canadian defenses were woefully weak, and they feared a French stab in the back should they move west, for Paris was expanding and modernizing its navy.

Nevertheless, Palmerston, though in agony from a savage attack of his gout, cooperated with Russell in sending a stiff note to Washington. It demanded the prompt release of the prisoners and an apology for the wrong committed, and carried an intimation that London believed that Wilkes had been officially ordered to seize the Southern emissaries. Written in such a tone as to make it most unlikely that the Lincoln administration could have complied with its terms, it made hostilities a distinct possibility. Prince Consort Albert, husband of the queen, was mortally ill that November; he would be dead in a little more than a fortnight. But he roused his flagging energies enough to make a last major contribution to the welfare of his adopted country. He moderated the wording in the Palmerston-Russell dispatch, sending it on to Washington without the intimation that the British government thought Wilkes had been instructed to apprehend Mason and Slidell. Moreover, private letters from Russell to Lord Lyons, the pro-Union British minister to the United States, were circulated among Northern leaders to emphasize that London wished to remain aloof from the war, if its national honor was not compromised.

The crisis began to dissipate. By mid-December Adams was able to tell Palmerston and Russell that the Union wanted a compromise solution. Seward came away from a Christmas Day cabinet meeting to notify the British that the captured Confederates would be released and that Wilkes had erred in his interpretation of international law. But the wily secretary of state managed at the same time to diffuse much of the pro-Wilkes ardor among his fellow countrymen. He cleverly concealed what had been a Union surrender by congratulating the British upon finally, after all the years, admitting that President Madison had been correct in his castigation of impressment. While unhappy Southerners realized that their high hopes for British intervention on their side were being frustrated, Mason and Slidell went on to Europe, where their labors were futile. If anything, the English attitude toward the Confederate representatives in their midst cooled after the *Trent* crisis.

And what of Wilkes? His later wartime career was anticlimactic. He could accomplish nothing in several special assignments, incurring the lasting enmity of Secretary Welles. He was even court-martialed, receiving a short suspension, although in 1866 he was appointed a rear admiral on the retired list. At least he may be given a top grade for inflexibility. From the moment that he decided to intercept the *Trent*, he knew for the rest of his life that he had been right in every detail. Years later he was still basking in the warmth of his 1861 cheers, writing in his *Autobiography* that his proper and heroic deed could have brought an end of the war:

> Mr Seward was a very coward in this whole business. . . . What if war did ensue. . . . It is my firm conviction that the . . . Southern States would have made a common cause in the affair from the scurvy manner and broken faith of the English Govt towards them at that time; it would have opened the way for a reconciliation . . . and the leaders of the Confederacy would have seized the opportunity to have entered into terms with the Northern States as they had become aware of the utter uselessness of prolonging the fight and misunderstanding.

Two points in this farrago of nonsense should be stressed. First, even without British entry into the war against the Union, the Confederacy was able to fight on for three and a half years after the *Trent* crisis. Second, there is no evidence that it even crossed Wilkes's mind that British intervention in the Civil War would have been calamitous for the United States. In his singular obtuseness he did not comprehend that a basic Confederate policy was to speed English participation in the conflict by any means possible as the surest guarantee of Southern independence, for every indicator shows that it would have been greeted with rapture in Richmond. The *Trent* affair illuminates the necessity for the maintenance of civilian political and diplomatic control over military professionals, lest a later Charles Wilkes plunge his country into a needless war.[1]

Commander Napoleon Collins at Bahia, Brazil, 1864

Charles Wilkes may have misinterpreted international law in the *Trent* affair, but there was at least a possible argument about the legal issues concerned. Not so the behavior of Commander Napoleon Collins when in the neutral harbor of Bahia (Salvador) he rammed the Confederate cruiser *Florida* with his frigate *Wachusett*, accepted her surrender, and with the Brazilian fort guns ablaze and warships giving chase, towed his quarry out to sea and eventually to the United States. Collins did not merely break international law, he pulverized it. But since what he had done was secretly desired by Union diplomatic personnel, including the secretary of state himself, he not only survived a court-martial verdict dismissing him from the service, but was promoted to captain within fifteen months and eventually to rear admiral.

As the skies gradually brightened for the North over the last two years of the Civil War, elation in the country's seaports was tempered by the continual arrival of news that yet another Yankee merchantman had fallen victim to a Confederate raider; losses finally totaled over 200 vessels. Maritime insurance rates soared to such a level that another 800 ships had to be sold to foreigners, for only under other banners would they be spared by the Southern predators. The impact was devastating for the postwar American merchant marine, which never recovered from its 1861–1865 ravishing. The successes of the Confederate raiders, however, had little effect on the result of the war itself, for Secretary Welles applied almost all the Navy's strength to the blockade and to cooperative endeavors with the Army. The best that he would do to quell the howls of anguish arising from the seaboard was to scatter a handful of men-of-war around the world on the lookout for the *Alabama*, *Florida*, *Shenandoah*, and other Southern cruisers.

Early in the war the *Florida* (originally the *Oreto*) had been built in England for the Confederacy. A law passed in 1819 forbidding the construction or sale of men-of-war for a belligerent during periods of British neutrality proved to be most inadequate. Reasonable suspicion was not enough for the government to seize a questionable vessel. London had to prove that she was equipped as a warship; if it could not, costly lawsuits would follow from her owners. This legislation enabled the *Florida*, without armaments aboard, to sail unimpeded for the Bahamas, where she picked up guns and other necessities from a waiting supply ship. She then commenced her two-year voyage in which she destroyed Union merchantmen at a rate second only to that of the *Alabama*.

For some weeks Collins in the *Wachusett* had been on the prowl for the *Florida*. Requiring supplies, he dropped anchor at Bahia on 26 September. On 4 October his quarry steamed into that port for provisions. Confederate Captain Charles M. Morris soon realized that he had stumbled upon his stalker, but consoled himself that his safety from Collins should be guaranteed by his location well within Brazil's territorial limits. Morris, who had no intention of attacking the *Wachusett*, relaxed when A. J. da Silva Gomez, president of Bahia State, told him that Thomas F. Wilson, the resident U.S. consul, had vouched for the security of the *Florida* while in port. Convinced that his command was in no danger, the captain took half his crew ashore, leaving Lieutenant Thomas K. Porter in charge, with only about 70 sailors.

Collins at first refused to breach Brazilian neutrality, but reconsidered in the face of passionate assurances from Wilson and his own officers that it was now or never. Rather than jeopardize shipping in the harbor, they decided to ram and sink the Confederate. At 3:00 A.M. on the 7th the *Wachusett* slipped past nearby Brazilian men-of-war and about a half-hour later rammed the *Florida*. Lieutenant Porter described the result: "She smashed us abreast the mizzenmast, broke it into three pieces, crushed in the bulwarks, knocked the quarter boat in on deck, jammed the wheel, carried away the mainyard, and started the beams for about thirty feet forward." To the surprise of the *Wachusett*'s people, the stricken Confederate did not sink, since she had taken a glancing rather than a direct blow. With a damaged vessel, unloaded guns, and only half of her normal complement, Porter had no option except surrender. Cables were attached from her conqueror and the *Florida* was towed safely out to open water, unhampered by fire from Bahia's forts and the ineffective pursuit by Brazilian warships.

Responding to the frantic protests of Morris, stranded ashore during the fracas, Brazil called Washington's attention to an action that "involves a manifest violation of the territorial jurisdiction of the Empire and an offense to its honor and sovereignty." Well before receiving the Brazilian protest, Seward had been pondering how to handle the matter. Since the United States had been so clearly in the wrong, under international law the *Florida* would have to be sent back to Brazil, probably soon to be released, once again to harry Northern commerce. Seward is said to have suggested a solution to the problem during a conversation with Admiral David Dixon Porter:

"I wish she was at the bottom of the sea!"

"Do you mean it?"

"I do, from my soul."

"It shall be done."

At Newport News, Virginia, on 25 November, it happened that the *Florida*, already "leaking badly," was run into and sunk. A resultant court of inquiry carrying Porter's endorsement concluded:

> It is proven that the army transport *Alliance*, in getting underway, drifted across the bow of the *Florida* and did her some injury, causing increased leakage to the vessel. At this time the wind was high and there was considerable sea running. There is nothing to show that the collision was designed, or that it was anything more than one of the common accidents which occur in a crowded roadstead.

Possibly so, but its timely resolution of a Union dilemma at the very least strains the bounds of coincidence to the limit.

Such a dramatic event as the seizure of the Confederate raider naturally aroused worldwide journalistic comment. Southern, Brazilian, and European newspapers ripped into Collins and his country. A British service magazine spoke for most foreign publications when it said, "The chivalrous commander of the *Wachusett* . . . boards the *Florida* in the harbor of Rio [sic], and carries her off as a prize and the New York press applauds the deed as a glorious triumph." Most Northern papers did echo the sentiments of Welles, who noted in his *Diary* that Brazil had "given refuge and aid to the robbers whom she does not recognize as a government . . . and permitted these plundering marauders to get supplies and to refit in her ports, and almost makes her harbors the base of operations."

When the Brazilian protest finally crossed his desk, Seward quickly replied to it. He admitted that "the President will disavow and regret the proceedings at Bahia," Collins would be court-martialed, and Consul Williams dismissed. Except, of course, for the unhappy accident to the *Florida* at Newport News, she would have been returned to Bahia. While technically correct, the secretary's reference to Collins worked out quite differently from what the Brazilians might have anticipated. In the spring of 1865 a court-martial charged Collins with "Violating the territorial jurisdiction of a neutral government." Collins admitted his guilt, offering as his only excuse that he had acted "for the Public Good." He was sentenced to be cashiered from the service, a verdict which could not go into effect without the approval of the secretary of the navy. It may be considered a little odd that Collins was promoted to captain while still under suspension and that two months later Welles overturned the court's verdict, restoring him to active duty.

The records suggest that Collins had every reason to anticipate the utmost leniency for his Bahian aggression. He wrote Welles that he and his officers had met with J. Watson Webb, U.S. minister to Brazil, at Rio and learned that Webb had issued instructions to the commanders of all U.S. warships "to attack any of the rebel cruisers in any of the ports of Brazil, or to run them down . . . and that he Webb would make it all right with Brazil."

The finale of the *Florida* incident occurred in July 1866. Commander Homer C. Blake in the USS *Nipsic* came into Bahia to inform its provincial president that his country wished to atone for what Collins had done. At noon on the 23rd, the American flag was lowered from the masthead, the Brazilian ensign raised, a 21-gun salute thundered out, and the generally amicable relations between the two nations were restored, to the satisfaction of both.

What lesson about American naval diplomacy did Napoleon Collins teach in Brazil during 1864? The answer is simple. When a naval officer correctly surmises that in wartime his government will surreptitiously excuse an action that will help achieve victory, he may disregard the niceties of international law. But the astute professional must also understand that in peacetime, when the stakes are so much lower, the same behavior would probably result in a prompt notice from the department that he should commence earning his living in the hay, grain, and feed business, or some other civilian occupation. Most assuredly he, unlike Collins, would not attain eventual promotion to the highest rank in the Navy.[2]

Captains Thomas T. Craven and Henry Walke at El Ferrol, Spain, and Lisbon, Portugal, 1865

Union officials in western Europe early in 1865 learned with trepidation that the Confederacy was about to put into commission a new heavily armed and armored raider, equipped with a ram, "pointed with iron or steel, and projecting under water 25 feet." Clearly she could sink practically every Northern warship. Built for the South at Bordeaux, she came temporarily under the French and Danish flags before being named the CSS *Stonewall* and placed under the command of Captain Thomas J. Page, who had won notoriety in *Water Witch* in Paraguay a decade before. Supplied by a British ship off Brittany with officers, cannons, and ammunition, during February 1865 she had to come into El Ferrol, in extreme northwestern Spain, for repairs.

Horatio J. Perry, U.S. minister to Madrid, alerted Union personnel to the peril the *Stonewall* posed, but the only warships available to oppose her were Captain Thomas T. Craven's *Niagara* and the even weaker *Sacramento*, under Captain Henry Walke. Both vessels were unarmored and comparatively slow wooden steam frigates, and only some of their arms were the more modern, powerful, and accurate rifled guns. All too aware of his predicament, Craven had no choice but to go after the *Stonewall*, and he moored the *Niagara* at La Coruna, eight miles from his enemy. Because of engine trouble, the *Sacramento* could not join him until early March. Meanwhile, Perry had been bombarding A. Benavides, the Spanish foreign minister, with demands that the *Stonewall* be forced to evacuate El Ferrol, stressing without success that international law permitted no belligerent vessel more than a 24-hour stopover in a neutral port. The Spaniard held that he lacked naval strength to compel her to leave.

While Craven at La Coruna awaited the coming of the *Sacramento*, he had plenty of time to consider his future, and it appeared bleak. His two ships might outgun the enemy 21 to 3 but that made no difference. He wrote Perry, "The *Stonewall* is a very formidable vessel, about 175 feet long, brig-rigged, and completely clothed in iron plates of five inches in thickness . . . [mounting a] casemated Armstrong 300-pounder rifled gun . . . and two 120-pounder rifled guns. . . . If as fast as reputed to be in smooth water, she ought to be more than a match for three such ships as the *Niagara*." He thought that his only chance would be "in rough water," where "we might possibly be able to put an end to her career." Captain Walke added that her 13-knot speed was considerably faster than that of either Union warship. Complicating Craven's dilemma were his own personal characteristics. A little earlier Welles had jotted in his *Diary* that he was "a little timid and inert by nature," adding a week later that "his constant doubts and misgivings impair his usefulness."

Learning that the Confederate cruiser was about to depart, Craven brought his two ships over to El Ferrol on 21 March and for the next two days kept watch. The *Niagara*'s log of the 24th laconically described what happened on that day: "The rebel ram *Stonewall* went to sea . . . [and] we made preparations for getting under way." But Craven filled in this bare outline in a letter to Perry the next day:

> On yesterday morning, the weather being remarkably calm and the sea perfectly smooth, [the *Stonewall*] again made her appearance, and with feelings that no one can appreciate, I was obliged to undergo the deep humiliation of knowing that she was there, steaming back and forth, flaunting her flags and waiting for me to go out to the attack.
>
> *I dared not do it.* The condition of the sea was such that it would have been perfect madness for me to go out. We could not possibly have inflicted the slightest injury upon her, and should have exposed ourselves to almost instant destruction—a one-sided combat which I do not consider myself called upon to engage in.

Before going on to conclude the story of the *Stonewall* and what happened to Craven three days later at Lisbon, it would be well to narrate what transpired because of his unwillingness to fight. Certainly the Navy Department could not overlook the behavior of an officer who, during a war, had not taken advantage of an opportunity to give battle to the enemy, no matter what the odds against him. Early the next November Craven's court-martial convened, presided over by Vice Admiral David Glasgow Farragut himself, to try him for "Failing to do his utmost to overtake and capture or destroy a vessel which it was his duty to encounter." The judges even strengthened the indictment by changing the wording to "the imperative duty of the accused to join battle with the *Stonewall*." He was found guilty but given the ludicrous sentence of suspension from active duty "on leave pay for two years."

The secretary was appalled at this decision, pointing out that Craven had been convicted of an offense that might have required the death penalty. Instead the officer had been given a sentence that amounted to a two-year paid holiday. He ruled that "It is therefore impossible for the Department to gather from the action of the court whether the accused is guilty or not." Throwing up his hands, he set aside the verdict and released Craven from arrest. Probably Welles correctly surmised that the sentence was the papering over of an irreconcilable split between the judges voting for his acquittal and those voting for his conviction. He attributed the compromise to Farragut's "kind and generous heart." The fact that the war was over may have caused the court to conclude that such "craven" behavior could now be overlooked, although there is nothing in the evidence to support this hypothesis. Finally, that the navy probably considered that the captain really had no viable option other than to let such a potent adversary depart unmolested is reinforced by the fact that he was promoted to rear admiral the next year.

To return to March 1865: The *Niagara* and *Sacramento* followed the *Stonewall* out of El Ferrol on the 25th and reached Lisbon two days later to find Page's ship at anchor, but she stood out to sea a few hours later, again without hindrance. James E. Harvey, the resident Union minister, was miffed when the Portuguese government informed him that the Southern ram must leave immediately but that the Northern warships must remain behind for another 24 hours so there would be no naval battle in front of the capital. A few hours after Page had steamed away, Craven moved the *Niagara* to a new anchorage on the Tagus. The commander of the fort at Belem, across that river from Lisbon, suddenly opened fire on her, obviously thinking that she was prematurely giving chase to the *Stonewall*. The *Niagara* came about at once, dipping her flag in the recognized international signal that compliance was under way. But the Portuguese did not let up, firing nine projectiles in all and hitting the ship three times, although luckily no one aboard was injured. Craven was astonished at "this gross outrage" but kept his own guns silent. Harvey dispatched at once an angry protest to Lisbon's foreign minister, asserting that if the fire had been returned, "a state of actual war would have been inaugurated." He demanded a prompt disavowal of the act and "the most exemplary punishment" of the officer responsible. The foreign minister praised Craven's forbearance, apologized for the incident, and said that the guilty man had already been dismissed. The crisis died away as quickly as it had begun.

These occurrences in Spain and Portugal wrote finis to the practice of foreign governments of permitting the construction, and departure of, and granting of port privileges to, Confederate raiders moving against Union shipping. To Washington these activities ignored the fact that the ships belonged to an entity recognized only as a belligerent but not as a sovereign nation by any country on earth. The *New York Times* spoke for the Northern consensus: "Spain and Portugal should be made to feel promptly and effectually that the time has gone when the United States vessels of war can be put upon a level with foreign built rebel craft that lie skulking in neutral ports to prey upon our commerce." The end of the Civil War, however, made such issues academic.[3]

Commander Andrew Bryson off Buffalo, N.Y., and Fort Erie, Ontario, 1866

Although they happened well after Appomattox, the Fenian invasions of Canada, one actual and the other only attempted, were so thoroughly motivated by Civil War issues that they deserve inclusion here rather than in chronological order. The semisecret society called the Fenian Brotherhood (from *fēne*, an old Celtic word for the Irish) was founded in New York during the late 1850s and soon gained adherents on both sides of the Atlantic. Dedicated to freeing Ireland from English rule, its members concluded that the only way such liberation could be attained was by invading Canada, the only London-owned place close to American bases, and hitting the British so hard there that they would be pressured into granting Irish independence.

The Fenians, led by former Union General Thomas W. Sweeny, were optimistic by the end of the war, for they expected to prosper from the stormy state of Anglo-American relations. Not only Irish-Americans but the public as a whole was vocally Anglophobic. London was unwilling either to apologize or pay damages for the crippling of the Union merchant marine by the Confederate cruisers purchased or built in England. Moreover, Northerners recalled the Canadian sympathy for the South that had allowed Confederates to operate openly from Montreal and other cities, even to the point of standing aside when Southern agents crossed the border to sack St. Albans, Vermont, in 1864. Buoyed by this favorable climate, many Irish veterans of the Union army, tired of inaction or unemployed, flocked to the green banner, and money for the Fenians poured in from many cities, New York in particular.

In late May 1866 several thousand recruits had collected in northern New York and Vermont; those assembled at Buffalo were crucial. On 1 June over a thousand Fenians, under Colonel John O'Neill, crammed themselves into small craft, crossed the narrow Niagara River to Fort Erie, Ontario, advanced a short way inland, and forced some Canadian militia to retreat in what is known as "The Battle of Limestone Ridge." Learning that about 1,400 troops, some of them British regulars, were hurrying toward them, O'Neill and his men scurried back to Fort Erie, where they drove off a few Canadian defenders. Total casualties in the two skirmishes amounted to approximately 80. By the morning of the 3rd, only about 700 remained, primarily because of desertions, so they were sent back into their boats, evacuating Canada, to plan for another incursion along with several thousand Fenians left behind in Buffalo.

Just as they were under way, catastrophe struck. At the worst possible moment Commander Andrew Bryson's iron-hulled warship *Michigan*, attended by two chartered tugboats, steamed across their escape route. O'Neill and his entire contingent were trapped and loaded into the three vessels. Two days later Bryson was able to notify the department, "I think I can take care of the Niagara River," in that way preventing further violations of his nation's antifilibustering legislation. At least in part for his work against the Fenians, the commander was promoted to captain within two months.

Because of his need for Irish-American political support, President Andrew Johnson hesitated a few days before issuing a proclamation denouncing the raid from Buffalo as illicit and warning citizens that participation in such incursions would be penalized. Meanwhile O'Neill and Sweeney were taken into temporary custody, and about 7,000 destitute Fenians were sent home at Washington's expense. Johnson's manifesto, coupled with Bryson's decisive naval intervention and army reinforcements, helped to prevent any real acrimony between Washington and London over the episode of 1866. An attempted Fenian incursion from Buffalo four years later, easily quashed, was overlooked.

Two results of this Irish-American filibustering ensued. Canadians felt that the United States should never have permitted the invasions to happen, and some burgeoning support for American annexation diminished. The British had captured a few Fenians and threatened them with deportation to penal colonies or worse. Washington of course objected, and London gave in. In 1870 the Royal Navy's traditional practice of impressing British-born Americans came to an end when the British admitted that persons of Irish parentage born in America or naturalized were truly citizens of the United States.[4]

Summary

The four incidents of the navy's influence on the government's foreign relations during the American Civil War and its immediate sequel might compose a hypothetical mountain range consisting of a Himalaya, an Appalachian, and two foothills in that chronological order. Wilkes, in the case of the *Trent*, towers above every other naval officer of the span between 1798 and 1883, in that his behavior could so easily have brought on the third Anglo-American war. Its outcome could well have led to the permanent dissolution of the United States into two quarreling entities, with the European powers playing off one against the other, to the lasting disadvantage of both. Indeed, had Wilkes been directing his government, transatlantic hostilities would have been inevitable. He never wavered in his irrational confidence that a British attack on the Union blockade would bring Southerners stampeding to the Stars and Stripes, though all evidence shows that nothing would have pleased them more.

Even though many other American officers have violated the territorial rights of foreign nations, none could match the degree to which Collins did it when he abducted the *Florida* from Bahia harbor, although circumstances enabled him to avoid condemnation for it. Craven's experiences in Spain and Portugal were no more than the proverbial tempests in teapots, for there was little if any likelihood that they could escalate into breaks in relations between the United States and those countries. Timely though Bryson's appearance was, it must be admitted that the Fenian cause was doomed with or without his intervention.

These instances of naval influence on foreign relations may be said to have been wrapped up in a tidy package consisting of the Anglo-American Treaty of Washington in 1871 and the Arbitration Tribunal at Geneva a year later. In them Great Britain admitted responsibility for the direct costs inflicted by the Confederate commerce raiders and paid the United States $15,500,000. This ensured in a satisfactory and relatively inexpensive manner that an unforgiving Washington would not unleash American cruisers to swoop down upon the English merchant marine while the British were engaged in a future conflict. It also marked the conclusion of the navy's wartime effect on U.S. diplomacy during the period covered in this work. But that is only part of the story. America's foreign relations down to 1883 would continue to be affected by the navy.

CHAPTER SIXTEEN

The Post–U.S. Civil War Period 1865–1883

Latin America 1866–1881

When Grant was accepting Lee's surrender at Appomattox, the Union strength at sea was a match for almost any navy in the world, perhaps even the Royal Navy itself. Having started in 1861 with 69 vessels in commission and 7,500 officers and men, it had swollen to 626 vessels, of which 65 were ironclads among 160 steamers, serviced by a personnel of 51,500. The war-weary nation faced the immediate challenge of restoring its unity, and it neither required nor wanted such a gigantic sea arm. Moreover, the country was following its usual tradition of rapid demobilization at the end of every conflict. Still, the cutback of the post-1865 Navy was exceptional. By 1881 the department had less than 50 obsolete vessels, not one of which was adequately gunned, powered, and protected. A mere 6,000 men were on the roster, the fewest since the mid-1830s. In 1877 the admiral commanding the squadron was compelled to patrol the eastern Pacific from Nome to the Straits of Magellan with three antique sloops and a store ship.

The national postwar turn inward was primarily responsible for all this. After 1865 the country, while trying to reunite once more, was also developing its industrial base, and opening the West by expanding its agriculture, mining, and transportation there. What happened to American foreign trade on the one hand and its carrying commerce on the other was extraordinary: the first soared while the second was collapsing. By

1900 U.S. imports were three and exports nine times their 1865 levels, but concurrently the percentage of them carried in American bottoms declined from 66.5 in 1860 to 9.3 forty years later. This process could have been reversed, but Washington stood aside while the fall continued, doing no more than granting some mail contracts to shipping concerns. In stark contrast, the government lavished financial support on the western railroads, heavily subsidizing them with huge land grants and, in the case of the transcontinental line, paying it for every mile of track laid.

As a result the navy ranked low in national priorities. To most Americans that seemed logical. Unlike the British and French, Americans had no distant colonies to defend, and U.S. efforts to acquire bases in such places as the Dominican Republic, Hawaii, and Samoa came to nought. Oceans stretching 3,000 miles to the east and 7,000 to the west seemed to be ample protection from any assailant. The war scares of the mid-1860s had been soothed by the withdrawal of the French from Mexico in 1867 and the triumphant Anglo-American diplomacy of 1871 and 1872. These factors meant that until the early 1880s appropriations for the Navy Department were kept at bare-bone levels, while the repeated warnings and pleadings of successive secretaries were pigeon-holed by congressional committees. The craze for naval economies commencing in the late 1860s was furthered by the long cyclical depression of the 1870s, evoking cries of national poverty.

As if these trends were not enervating enough, the navy itself contributed to its semidemise. Top-ranking officers dragged their heels when called upon to modernize, for they were sentimentally—and with some justification—attached to the wood-and-canvas service in which their careers had flourished. They remained dubious about the efficacy of the revolutions in engineering, armaments, and gunnery that were sweeping through other navies, preferring to wait until these foreign innovations proved themselves. Hence departmental economy won the day. Orders were issued that every U.S. warship, steamers included, must be sail-equipped. Commanders who turned on their engines had to report that fact with red ink in their ship's log; if they exceeded their coal quota, they might have to make up the difference out of their own pocket.

Some of the secretaries during this forlorn period were political hacks, ignorant of their new responsibilities, although many earlier appointees to that position had managed to overcome their previous lack of maritime knowledge or experience and had served capably. Still, it is eye-opening that many Americans appeared to have believed the undoubtedly apocryphal story that when first boarding one of his ships Navy Secretary Richard W. Thompson is said to have exclaimed, "Why the derned thing is hollow!" George M. Robeson, secretary from 1869 to 1877, was one of President Grant's many unfortunate selections. He used departmental budgets for graft-ridden repairs; cost overruns during his tenure sometimes exceeded the original monetary outlay for constructing a vessel. He was probably lucky to escape a penitentiary sentence.

Able, up-to-date young lieutenants and commanders, already incensed about the suffocating weight of the senior brass that blocked their promotions for years, felt a deep humiliation over the state of their profession. The floating curiosities they directed were often visited abroad by British or French officers. Their guests might have politely tried to conceal their astonishment, but their amused commiseration was all too obvious.

The nation escaped the perils that might have resulted from its naval weakness. It maintained a neutral course, with ease avoiding entanglement in the Franco-Prussian War and others, and fortunately settled without hostilities dangerous disputes with Spain in 1873 and Chile in the early 1880s. Opponents of strength at sea proved to be correct in their prediction that at the time a potent American navy would be an expensive and unnecessary luxury. That America avoided war, however, was luck. Or perhaps the venerable bromide about God's having a special affection for sailors, drunks, and the United States of America did apply in the postwar period.

By the 1880s public opinion was beginning to reconsider the advisability of permitting these glaring naval infirmities to continue. The depression of the previous decade was finally over and the economy took off, with foreign trade among the gainers. Stirrings of the expansionism that would culminate in the imperialism of the late 1890s were being felt. The doleful and minatory yearly messages of the navy secretaries were being reinforced by the persuasive articles written by officers appearing in the new *United States Naval Institute Proceedings*. Captain Alfred T. Mahan's effective arguments that seapower is an essential conduit to national greatness were just around the corner. This groundswell started tentatively in 1883, when Secretary William E. Chandler managed to wheedle funds out of Congress for the construction of the "ABCD" ships, the cruisers *Atlanta*, *Boston*, and *Chicago* and the dispatch boat *Dolphin*. This was the first step along the path of the American naval renaissance, followed by the "Great White Fleet" a little later, and eventually a seagoing force large and modern enough to brush aside Spain in 1898 and enforce the gunboat diplomacy of the Roosevelt, Taft, and Wilson administrations.

Given the post-1865 condition of the navy, it may be deemed remarkable that it was able to contribute anything to diplomacy; after all, force and the threat to use it are a component of conducting effective foreign relations. It did make such a contribution, however, especially in Latin America and the Far East, but on a considerably smaller scale than in the pre–Civil War years. For instance, the years from 1840 to 1860 witnessed almost 90 separate instances in which the navy influenced external relations. But from 1863 to 1883 there were only about 40. Chronology has to move aside in the case of the U.S. Navy in Japan. Its interventions of 1863 and 1864 are much more comprehensible as part of the civil wars in that nation than inclusion in the American equivalent, 1861–1865.

Latin America, 1866–1881

The woeful political, economic, and social situations plaguing Latin America from 1866 to 1881 duplicated the agonies that region had suffered since winning its independence from Spain and Portugal almost a half-century before. Violence periodically broke out here and there: sometimes in civil wars, sometimes by hostilities among Latin-American nations or by Mexicans against France or by South Americans against Spain. As always resident Americans could not avoid being caught up in them, and as always they clamored for naval protection. U.S. officers scurried about, appeared where breakdowns in stability occurred, and in their rescue missions often brought about confrontations with the governments concerned, Latin American or European, or both. At other times they acted— or tried to act—as peacemakers.

There were four areas of contention in which the blue-water service affected Washington's external relations: (1) Mexico: the aftermath of Maximilian's imperial collapse (1867–1877); (2) the Caribbean: the Dominican Republic (1866–1870) and Cuba (1869–1877); (3) the lower east coast of South America: the War of the Triple Alliance—Argentina, Brazil, and Uruguay against Paraguay (1866–1868); (4) the west coast of South America: Spain against Chile, Peru, Bolivia, and Ecuador (1866), and the War of the Pacific: Chile against Peru and Bolivia (1879–1881). Considering how often the navy was busy in Central America during the 1840s and 1850s, it is surprising how greatly its activities were reduced after 1865. Captain Andrew W. Johnson went ashore from the *Lackawanna* at Matamoros, Mexico, in 1876, and there were four such landings in Central America: Master Thomas Nelson went ashore from the *Penobscot* at Nicaragua in 1868, and there were three short occupations at Panama—by Captain Edward Middleton in the *St. Mary's* in 1865, by Admiral Charles Steedman in the *Pensacola* and *Tuscarora*, and by Admiral John J. Almy in the *Benicia* and *Pensacola*, the latter two in 1873.

Admiral Charles H. Davis sent marines from the *Guerrière* into Montevideo for three weeks in 1868.

Although Milton Offutt, in his *The Protection of Citizens Abroad*, gives extended treatment to those incidents, and they are mentioned in David Cooney's *Chronology of the United States Navy, 1775–1965*, as well as Jack Sweetman's *American Naval History: An Illustrated Chronology*, the opinion here is that they deserve no more than this listing. All were in response to appeals for aid from governments in power during brief periods of local disorders, and their diplomatic results were negligible.[1]

Mexico, 1866–1877
Commander Francis A. Roe at Vera Cruz, 1867

Although Juarez's Anticlericals emerged victorious in the War of the Reform (1857–1861), more trouble for their beleaguered country loomed ahead. Unable to pay European creditors, Mexico was blockaded in 1862 by the French, British, and Spanish navies, but the latter two withdrew after the Emperor Napoleon III revealed his plans. Backed by Clericals on both sides of the Atlantic, he sent his army to topple the Mexican republic, and by 1864 he had installed a puppet regime under the Austrian Archduke Maximilian as his handpicked emperor. For the Lincoln-Johnson administrations this was a most blatant violation of the Monroe Doctrine, but after the Civil War the United States was not disposed to start another sanguinary conflict. Although Washington kept pressure on Napoleon III to withdraw, its admonitions were expressed circumspectly. French difficulties became the final determinants, particularly their inability to crush Mexican resistance, soaring costs for the occupation army, and heightened opposition from Anticlericals at home. In 1867 the French pulled out, and the gallant but deluded Maximilian remained behind, to be shot by a firing squad. Yet Mexico remained in turmoil through the late 1870s.

The U.S. Navy entered this picture only four times during the period ending in 1883. One officer took a famous Union general on a futile diplomatic mission in 1866. At Vera Cruz the next year another tried but failed to save Maximilian's life, although he adroitly isolated Santa Anna. A third destroyed the pirate ship *Forward* at San Blas in 1870. The fourth rescued an American consul from prison at Acapulco in 1877.

Captain John Alden at Vera Cruz, et al., 1866

Late in 1866 the Johnson administration decided to send a mission to confer with Juarez, who was clearly emerging triumphant in his struggle against Maximilian and the French. This was done partly to ensure an orderly transfer of power from the empire to the republic, so that Americans in Mexico might not be endangered, and partly because of American domestic politics. Since General Ulysses S. Grant had moved into the enemy Radical Republican camp, the president tried to get rid of him for a time. When he refused to go, General William T. Sherman volunteered to take his place. Accompanied by an ineffective Ohio congressman, he sailed to Vera Cruz and other nearby Mexican ports with Captain John Alden in the *Susquehanna*. The mission became an exercise in frustration. Juarez remained far to the north, and Sherman soon announced, "I have not the remotest idea of riding on mule back 1,000 miles" to meet him, and came home. The congressman remained a few futile days longer and followed suit. Gideon Welles jeered from the Navy Department that "the whole turns out to be a *faux pas*, a miserable bungling piece of business." Documentation does not reveal to what extent Alden may have contributed to this result.[2]

Commander Francis A. Roe at Vera Cruz, 1867

As the summer of 1867 neared, almost everyone recognized that the defeat of Maximilian and his French-sponsored empire was only a matter of time, for he had been trapped by superior forces at Queretaro. In early June the tidings that he had been captured arrived at Vera Cruz, a city still held by an imperial garrison against a besieging republican army. The harbor was filled with foreign warships—French, British, Spanish, Austrian, and the American gunboat *Tacony* under Commander Francis A. Roe. The United States may have stood solidly behind the rebels and their cause, but Washington added its voice to those rising in Europe asking Juarez to spare the life of the stupid but gallant emperor. Roe became the medium of this message. As early as May he had written Juarez, suggesting that should the Austrian be captured, "he might be pleased, through a spirit of clemency and also of friendship for the United States, to spare his life." With the news that the emperor would go on trial, he redoubled his efforts, working hand-in-glove with a British naval officer and the consuls of both countries to bring about the surrender of Vera Cruz to the republicans in return for Maximilian's safe-conduct pass to an Austrian man-of-war. But Juarez was obdurate about making an example of foreign usurpers, and had him executed. Even though he had failed, Roe was thanked by the Austrian naval commandant for "your exquisite kindness towards me, and your noble feelings in the disastrous days of Maximilian's murder."

Although he had failed in this task, the commander helped Mexico avoid yet another onset of the disease that might be called "Santanismo";

had Santa Anna succeeded in his plot, it would have been the twelfth time that the chameleon-like dictator had inflicted his rule upon his unlucky nation. Just as the final efforts to bring about the surrender of Vera Cruz to the *Juaristas* were climaxing, on 3 June the American mail steamer *Virginia*, carrying Antonio Lopez de Santa Anna, came into the harbor. Always intriguing to come back into power, since his last ouster from Mexico City in 1855 he had been in exile, living in Cuba, Venezuela, the Danish West Indies, and for the last year New York City. There he persuaded some naive optimists to loan him money for another Mexican escapade, with which he enlisted a few American volunteers and bought some munitions. For a day or two after his arrival, Santa Anna, unable to go ashore, received visitors who apprised him of current events in Mexico. He offered himself as a middle-of-the-road alternative to the liberal Anticlericals of Juarez and the defeated Clericals of Maximilian. Roe became involved after being informed that Santa Anna was representing himself as "under the protection of the United States," acting as an agent for President Johnson and the American government. Realizing that these allegations could only be outright lies, Roe went to the *Virginia* to confront Santa Anna. There are conflicting accounts as to whether he treated the Mexican courteously or not, but he kept him on the ship as long as he thought necessary.

During this interim the Anglo-American exertions to arrange a peaceful accession of the republicans in Vera Cruz came into fruition. Since this meant that Santa Anna could no longer make trouble there, Roe permitted him to sail wherever he pleased in the *Virginia*, provided that it was outside Mexico's territorial limits. Instead, the erstwhile dictator proceeded to Sisal in the Yucatán, where he was arrested. Although acquitted of treason, he was sentenced to an eight-year exile. In 1872 Santa Anna returned to Mexico, old, poverty-stricken, and almost forgotten, and he died there four years later.

The navy secretary was lavish with his compliments of Roe for the way he had handled his assignment: "Commander Roe is entitled to commendation for the discretion and zeal which he manifested. To his good judgment, in concert with that of our consul, the surrender of Vera Cruz without disaster or bloodshed is attributed."[3]

Commander William W. Low and Lieutenant Willard H. Brownson off Mexico's West Coast, 1870

After the departure of the French and Maximilian's death, Benito Juarez was restored to power. But tranquility remained far off: by 1870 rivals began appearing among those who had won the victory, among them one General Placido de Vega. He tried to set up a private state from his headquarters at Mazatlán and with his failure disappeared from the story. But that May 170 pirates acting in Vega's name seized the former gunboat *Forward* and late that month fell upon Guaymas, and after extorting a reported $100,000 in cash and thrice that amount in "arms and merchandise" from the foreign businessmen in the town, left the same day.

Commander William W. Low in the steam sloop *Mohican* was at Mazatlán when he heard about the pirate vessel and immediately went south along the coast toward San Blas on the lookout for her. In mid-June he located the *Forward* 40 miles up a river too shallow for the *Mohican* to navigate, so he sent 79 men in six boats under Lieutenant Willard H. Brownson upstream to capture her. Although they had no trouble in seizing the ship, they discovered that the main body of her crew was ashore with four guns. The pirates opened fire on the Americans, killed a petty officer, and wounded three men. Outnumbered and with no artillery, Brownson sensibly set fire to the *Forward* and escaped downriver to rejoin the *Mohican* the next day.

Two points might be made about this incident. After so many instances of ill will between Mexicans and Americans, often punctuated by violence, this was a case of the most amicable carrying out of a friendly neighbor's request. Yet at the same time it spotlighted the weakness of nineteenth-century Mexico's political infrastructure, which made it so hard for that nation to protect itself externally or unify internally. This latter point was pounced upon by the *New York Times* in editorializing about the case of the *Forward*. "The spectacle of a Government so impotent that it cannot protect its chief ports from the attacks of a privateer mounting one or two guns [four], and whose merchants are compelled to invoke the aid of a foreign Power to prevent their utter spoliation is one which custom has enabled us to regard without astonishment but whose continuance is nevertheless one of the most striking anomalies of the North American continent."[4]

Admiral Alexander Murray at Acapulco, 1877

Early in 1877 the Department of State was notified that its resident consul at Acapulco—identified in the documentation no better than as "Mr. Sutter"—was in trouble with the law. He was being held, although in relative comfort and without maltreatment, after brawling with a caller at his consulate and slightly wounding him with a pistol bullet. Admiral Alexander Murray, commanding the North Pacific Station from his flagship *Pensacola*, was sent there to inquire into the matter. Thanks at least in part to Murray's persuasiveness, Sutter was soon acquitted on the ground of self-defense, and the *Pensacola* was honored with a seven-gun salute.[5]

The Caribbean, 1866–1873
Admiral David D. Porter at the Dominican Republic, 1866–1867

Considerable postwar American attention was directed at the Dominican Republic (Santo Domingo), which shared the island of Hispaniola with Haiti to the west, smaller but more populous. It had been ruled by Haiti until successfully rebelling in 1844. Two years later Lieutenant David Dixon Porter was sent there to decide whether circumstances justified recognition of the new republic, a visit described earlier in this book. During the 1850s the living conditions of the Dominicans worsened, the consequent discontent culminating in a vicious civil war between followers of Buenaventura Baez and those of Pedro Santana. Although later Baez would be a staunch backer of the United States, at the time he was strongly anti-American, to such an extent that Commodore John M. McIntosh in the *Colorado* was able to use his Dominican enemies to engineer him out of office in 1858. By the end of the decade the situation in that country had become intolerable.

In 1860 the pro-Spanish Santana opened negotiations with Madrid, suggesting that its former colony be readmitted to the Spanish empire. Seeing that the outbreak of the U.S. fratricide would bar any effective American opposition based upon the Monroe Doctrine, the Spaniards did just that, and they ruled the former republic from 1861 to 1865. The experiment amounted to unmitigated disaster for most concerned. Promises of better Dominican economic development were ignored, the oppressive hand of military and religious tyranny fell on its people, and carpetbaggers from Madrid seized the top governmental jobs for themselves. By 1863 the back country had risen against the occupiers, resistance heightened, and eventually some 10,000 Spanish soldiers perished from illness or Dominican bullets. The death of the disillusioned Santana in 1865 helped impel Spain to abandon the entire project. Unbelievably, Baez, who had spent the years of Spanish dominance in European luxury under a generous allowance from Madrid while his countrymen suffered, was nonetheless able to become president of the Dominican Republic on the heels of the Spanish withdrawal. By this time he had become an unusual patriot: he kept trying to give his nation away to any great power that might accept it, especially the United States.

Learning that the Andrew Johnson administration was interested in the possibility of setting up a naval base at Samaná Bay on the northern coast, early in 1866 Baez welcomed Frederick Seward, son of the secretary of state, on that errand. Later the same year the younger Seward returned to Santo Domingo for treaty negotiations to that end, accompanied by

David Dixon Porter, 1813–1891
(Official U.S. Navy Photo)

Admiral Porter. As his father put it, "It is not to be doubted that his great experience in foreign countries and especially his familiarity with the region you are about to visit will be found useful towards the purpose of your mission." The two envoys could offer the Dominicans as much as $2,000,000, half in cash, half in arms, payable on the exchange of ratifications granting the United States sovereignty over Samaná Bay. Finally, Americans must have the right to fortify that area.

Even though José Maria Cabrál had ousted Baez in May 1866, when Seward and Porter appeared the next January he seemed equally eager to reach an agreement. According to the admiral, Cabrál and his colleagues listened to the American propositions "with the greatest courtesy," but discussions were stalemated by a provision in the new Dominican constitution forbidding even any temporary foreign occupation of the national territory. Cabrál counterproposed that Americans and Dominicans "hold joint sovereignty" over Samaná. Negotiations collapsed when Seward replied that this "would be contrary to the established policy of the United States to avoid entangling alliances." Porter, whose "judgment, tact, and thorough knowledge of the country and the people" were praised by the secretary of state, commented with humorous exaggeration when he left, "When . . . we departed, tears stood in the eyes of the [Cabrál] administration at the thought of so much specie being carried away which ought to have belonged to them." In May 1867 Johnson sounded the knell of the naval base during his term when he reported "with much regret that the Government of Dominica has not . . . decided to negotiate with the United States for a cession or lease . . . of Samaná to be occupied as a naval station, a consummation of which it is conceived would be altogether beneficial" to both countries. Everyone settled back to await the new administration.[6]

Admiral Charles H. Poor, et al., off the Dominican Republic and Haiti, 1869–1870

Ulysses S. Grant came into office aspiring to outdo Johnson in the Caribbean. He would not be satisfied with Samaná, for he wished to annex the entire Dominican Republic. Unfortunately for his hopes, Hamilton Fish, his astute secretary of state, had a single major foreign-policy aim in that area. He would labor to make sure that the United States would remain aloof from any involvement in the Cuban rebellion against Spain in 1868, which would flicker on and off for a decade. Grant wanted to recognize the Cubans as belligerents, but Fish was able to talk him out of it, sure that any such move would result in a serious crisis with Spain. Fish accomplished this in part by offering little public objection to the President's obsession about Dominican annexation.

Meanwhile, in Santo Domingo Cabrál's presidency ended in January 1868, when he was toppled by local rivals. During the next May none other than Buenaventura Baez took over that position once more. He wanted to sell his nation to the United States, for both his own benefit and personal survival. In addition to Grant, he picked up support from shady American entrepreneurs, eager to exploit Dominican resources, and from expansionistic naval officers.

In mid-1869 the president sent to Santo Domingo General Orville E. Babcock, later to be implicated in the Whisky Ring scandal. He closeted himself with Baez and his foreign minister. In return for a down payment of $150,000 and $1,500,000 more once formal annexation had been completed, the Dominicans asked Babcock to "use all his influence with members of Congress to popularize the idea" of annexation. Once the general even raised the American flag at Samaná.

That summer Grant decided to use the navy to investigate internal Dominican conditions, hoping that the information might fuel his expansionistic plans, and sent to the republic Commander Thomas O. Selfridge in the *Nipsic*, who was soon discouraged by Dominican "political intrigue, poverty, and a general air of instability," becoming a foe of annexation. Grant was privately furious with him, but since Selfridge's observations were unpublished, his negative conclusion remained hidden in the White House.

About the same time Baez was menaced by an alliance against him by Cabrál and General Gregorio Luperón, a Haitian black fearful that union with the United States might endanger the liberty of his own people. After failing to invade the Dominican Republic, Luperón sent to sea his little armed steamer *Telegrafo*, which attacked shipping along the Hispaniola coast. Baez called this action "piratical" and dispatched two steamers after her. The *Telegrafo* was soon cornered and, in the act of slipping away, fired some shots that "grazed" a New York merchantman. The secretary of the navy ordered Commander Elias K. Owen in the *Seminole* to capture the marauder, saying that she had been "interfering with American commerce and sailing upon the high seas without legal authority." Owen was unsuccessful in his quest but Commander Walter W. Queen in the *Tuscarora* did it for him, chasing the *Telegrafo* into the British West Indian island of Tortola, where Luperón eventually had to sell her.

In January 1870 the situation suddenly worsened for Americans hoping to annex the republic. The pro-Baez Haitian president Sylvain Salnave was toppled and shot by the pro-Luperón Nissage-Saget, who assumed that office himself. Grant's reaction was pronounced. He told Admiral Poor in his flagship the *Powhatan* to use his seven men-of-war in any manner necessary to let the Haitians understand that the United States would tolerate no opposition to Baez. The admiral soon massed his command off the capital and informed Saget that "any interference or attack therefore by vessels under the Haytien [sic] or any other Flag upon Dominicans . . . will be considered an act of hostility to the Flag of the United States, and will provoke hostility in return." This energetic verbal barrage, coupled with the U.S. blockade, drove both the Haitians and rebel Dominicans into temporary inactivity, although only for a short time. Meanwhile in Santo Domingo Baez engineered a plebiscite on the issue and announced its result as a somewhat dubious vote of 15,169 in favor of American annexation and 11 against.

Nevertheless, insurmountable difficulties were looming ahead for President Grant's expansionistic aspirations. The American public refused to become excited by the idea of an American Dominican Republic. Apparently the purchase of Alaska in 1867 was deemed sufficient territorial acquisition for the time being. Furthermore, the failure to buy the Danish West Indies (St. Thomas, St. Croix, and St. John) in the same year perhaps set a precedent against acquisitions in the Caribbean. At home Reconstruction was under way, with all the problems implicit in turning slaves into freedmen; the idea of bringing into their country many more blacks and mulattoes was evidently anything but enticing to most white Americans.

The use of the navy for territorial aggrandizement was particularly counterproductive, for it brought about a terminal backlash. Charles Sumner, powerful chairman of the Senate's Foreign Relations Committee, announced that he was "shocked" by what Poor and his subordinates had been doing. Historian Allan Nevins summarizes well the senator's reaction, which helped to thwart the president's intent: "It seemed to others, as to him, that the President's use of the Navy to threaten Haiti came dangerously close to levying war, and as such was unconstitutional. After all, if Baez needed our gunboats to remain in power, what was he but our puppet? And what were we doing but forcing upon a weak people the sacrifice of their sovereignty?" Sumner castigated the proposal in his famous speech called "Naboth's Vineyard," a reference to the Biblical story. Legislation annexing the Dominican Republic died in the Senate on 30 June 1870, 28 pro and 28 con, a vote far short of the two-thirds necessary for acceptance. Grant's high-handed employment of his naval arm was a mistake that amounted to a *coup de grace* for his pet project.[7]

Cuba, 1869–1873
Admiral Henry H. Hoff at Santiago, 1869

Cuba and Puerto Rico were the only portions of Spain's far-flung American empire that failed to gain independence during the Latin-American wars of liberation (c. 1810 to 1825). Yet many Cubans remained unhappy about their continued attachment to the mother country and raised the standard of revolt late in 1868. Despite widespread guerrilla activities the insurgents failed to break away. The ten-year civil war ended in the so-called "Peace of Zanjón," with little more for the rebels than vague Spanish promises of internal reforms and somewhat expanded local autonomy.

The uprising's success depended upon U.S. intervention, and at first American public opinion was enthusiastically behind it, backing a potent and vocal Cuban junta in New York City. Both volunteers and materiel of war for the insurgents were regularly sent in chartered steamers, infuriating Madrid and its Cuban allies. The pro-rebel President Grant was appalled by the savagery with which the Spaniards sought to crush them. In 1869 he actually signed a proclamation recognizing the Cubans as belligerents, giving them the right to borrow money and purchase warships. Had it been put into effect, a Spanish-American war would have loomed as a distinct possibility.

Luckily for peace, Hamilton Fish was secretary of state. He too detested the oppression and intolerance used against the rebels, but thought they should not be granted belligerent status while they had "no capital, no properly organized government, no tax system, no stable army under properly commissioned officers, no ports, no realm." He persuaded the president to put aside his proclamation, a decision for which he was later thankful. As the years passed, the American people lost their enthusiasm for the insurgents and Fish saw his peaceful endeavors prevail.

During the ten-year war the attention of the U.S. Navy was attracted by two incidents in which its fellow-citizens were executed by Spanish officials in Cuba. An admiral investigated the killing of two Americans in 1869. The second occasion, in which a commander intervened, was the shooting of 53 persons, many of them U.S. citizens, from the ostensibly American-owned ship *Virginius* in 1873.

Among the several vessels leased by the rebels in the United States and sent to Cuba with men and ammunition was the schooner *Grapeshot*, out of New York, supposedly bound for Jamaica, during April 1869. This enterprise was sure to be chancy when she neared Cuba, for in the preceding month the Spanish captain-general in Havana had proclaimed that any ships suspected with reason of aiding the insurrectionists and taken in Cuban waters or even on the nearby high seas would be considered pirate craft and those on board would be summarily shot. Fish called in the Spanish minister to Washington and berated him so thoroughly that this harsh pronouncement was soon withdrawn, but not in time to save two Americans from a Spanish firing squad.

Charles Speakman, who had a wife and small son in Indiana, and Albert Wyeth, a young Pennsylvanian, appeared to be innocent victims of circumstance and Spanish injustice. They bought tickets for Jamaica, and when the worried pair watched fifty Cubans come aboard in New York, they were relieved by the assurance of the *Grapeshot*'s captain that he had no intention of approaching Cuba. But the Cubans seized control of the vessel, went ashore near the eastern city of Santiago, and forced the two Americans to accompany them inland. Speakman and Wyeth escaped as soon as they could and turned themselves over to the Spaniards. Evidently they were given no opportunity to prove their innocence by information easily obtainable from the *Grapeshot* or their business correspondence in Jamaica. Over the heated protests of E. G. Smith, the U.S. vice-consul in Santiago, they were shot on the morning of 21 June.

This is a heartrending and tragic story, but it may not be true, at least insofar as Wyeth is concerned. Without mentioning Speakman, the *New York Times* wrote about the execution of Wyeth, claiming that he had been close to Cuban rebels in New York, had been going to that island to war upon the Spaniards, and had even carried a letter of introduction to a rebel leader, hoping to serve him as a staff officer. If the story is true, his execution by a firing squad was no atrocity at all.

Hoff, commanding the North Atlantic Squadron, went to Santiago in the *Contoocook*, accompanied by the *Albany*, to look into the matter. During July he met with Spanish and American officials. He enclosed in his report to the department a letter from the U.S. vice-consul verifying Speakman's innocence. He himself was sure that the two had been "cruelly murdered" by cowardly bureaucrats who had caved in to the demands for vengeance from the reactionary civilian "Volunteers." Whatever the truth, particularly in regard to Wyeth, Secretary Robeson, in his annual report, complimented Hoff: he had taken "measures for the better protection of American citizens and interests. He executed this duty with promptness and discretion; his reports have been made the basis for negotiations for redress: and since this timely show of power no further aggressions are reported."[8]

Commander William B. Cushing at Santiago, 1873

The affair of the steamer *Virginius*, which resulted in the hasty execution of 53 men, many of them American citizens, was much more serious than the crisis of 1869, for Madrid and Washington hovered on the brink of war because of it. Ostensibly owned by an American, this decrepit former Southern blockade-runner was really the property of Cuban rebels in New York. By late 1873 she had already made several voyages to the island landing filibusters and their arms for service with the insurgents. On her last trip she sailed from Jamaica with a complement of 52 officers and men (most of them Americans and Britons) and 103 passengers (the majority of whom were Cubans). On 31 October she was intercepted off Santiago by the Spanish man-of-war *Tornado* and brought into the city the next day.

General Juan M. Burriel, an ardent reactionary, was in charge there. Urged on by the pro-Spanish Cuban "Volunteers," he proceeded to act solely on his own, without awaiting instructions from Havana. Four who had been previously convicted, upon mere identification were shot on 4 November. Over the strenuous objections of Vice-Consul Smith and the resident British consul, drumhead courts-martial were raced through without permitting any legal defense for the accused. On the 7th and 8th Joseph Fry, captain of the *Virginius*, and 48 others were killed. One onlooker asserted that the condemned had been lined up against a wall and "the Spanish butchers" poured a volley into them and finished off the wounded, who "lay writhing in agony." The toll would have unquestionably been higher had it not been for the Royal Navy. Captain Lambton Lorraine in HMS *Niobe* heard of the first executions, raced to Santiago from Jamaica, demanded an interview with Burriel, and told him point-blank that further killings would result in his bombardment of the city.

The U.S. Navy entered the proceedings when Commander William B. Cushing arrived from Panama in the *Wyoming* on the 16th. He walked uninvited into Burriel's office, refused his outstretched hand, and curtly informed him, "If you intend to shoot any more of the *Virginius* prisoners, you had better first have the women and children removed from Santiago as I shall bombard the town." Meanwhile the secretary had been concentrating in Cuban waters what strength the post–Civil War navy possessed.

Despite the clamor in some American newspapers that hostilities should be commenced at once in retaliation for the bloodshed, Fish opted for peace. Outraged though he was by Burriel's savagery, he looked upon the *Virginius* affair as no adequate reason to go to war. He knew that responsible officials in both Havana and Madrid were shocked by what had happened. Furthermore, Minister to Washington Admiral José Polo de Bernabe, an accomplished diplomat, was dedicated to the maintenance of Spanish-American friendship. After protracted negotiations a compromise was worked out. Once Fish understood that the *Virginius*, as Cuban-owned, had no right to fly the U.S. standard, he decided against requiring the Spanish to salute the American flag. In return, the ship and her survivors were turned over to the navy, Burriel was to be punished (actually he was later promoted to major-general), and eventually Madrid paid $80,000 to the kin of the slain. The case ended when the unseaworthy *Virginius* foundered off Cape Hatteras en route to New York. Cushing may be lauded for the icy reserve with which he let Burriel know the unpleasant consequences should he continue killing Americans. But despite the commander's good work, in the last analysis it was the Royal rather than the U.S. Navy that saved those not yet shot by the Spaniards.[9]

The Lower East Coast of South America, 1866–1868
Admiral Sylvanus Godon, et al., and Paraguay, 1866–1868

Carlos Antonio López, president of Paraguay, who had been involved with the U.S. Navy in 1855 and 1859, died in 1862 and was succeeded by Francisco Solano López, his eldest son, who had had some European education. A madness that included a titanic Napoleonic complex made him see himself as the conqueror of lower South America, and for that purpose he raised an army largely composed of Guarani Indians, peerless hand-to-hand fighters. Exploiting border disputes and ignoring the huge preponderance of strength that would be thrown against him, Lopez declared war on Argentina and Brazil in 1864 and against Uruguay a year later. This was officially called the War of the Triple Alliance or, more simply, "the Paraguayan War."

Its five-year duration may be separated into three periods. In 1864–1865 fighting occurred in Argentina's Corrientes and Brazil's Matto Grosso, provinces in which initial López victories were nullified. In 1866–1868 warfare was concentrated along the Paraná and Paraguay Rivers, ending with the fall of Humaitá Fortress and Asunción. By 1868 López had gone mad and was imprisoning, torturing, and murdering thousands as he tried to track down one nonexistent plot after another. In 1868–1870, his guerrilla campaigns convulsed the back country beyond his capital, ending with his death and Paraguay's surrender. The consequences of this conflict for that little nation were so dire as to defy exaggeration. Apparently about nine-tenths of its males 15 years old and older were killed or died of disease.

The American navy became part of this somber story when its officers engaged in a longstanding controversy with Charles A. Washburn over first delivering him to his ministerial duties at Asunción in 1866 and then rescuing him from the capital two years later. The battle finally moved from South America to Washington, ending inconclusively and with no luster shed upon either the naval or the foreign service.

Washburn had first come to Paraguay in 1862. He conducted his diplomacy well, while maintaining a good personal relationship with López. Back in South America in October 1866 following a long home leave, he was foiled in his attempts to reach Asunción, most of the time fuming helplessly in Buenos Aires. Some of his rage was directed at the Argentine and Brazilian leaders, for he was sure that they feared that his arrival would hearten the resistance of López and his people. Much of his choler, however, was directed at Admiral Sylvanus Godon in the *Guerrière*. When they first met at Rio, each apparently formed a quick aversion to the other.

Washburn demanded the prestige and protection of a U.S. warship for his journey to Paraguay but Godon equivocated, claiming that he lacked any such instructions from the department. Some six weeks later when they again conferred, Washburn found "greatly to my chagrin" that the admiral, by refusing to give him any transportation whatever, "seemed insensible to the scandal and contempt that his conduct was bringing upon the naval service." This standoff was mirrored in Washington, where the secretaries of state and the navy each supported his own man. Seward insisted that Godon help Washburn get to Asunción in any way possible; Welles noted in his *Diary* that the minister had been "inexcusably wrong." The U.S. ministers in Buenos Aires and Rio finally induced the allies to ease their blockade, and early in November Washburn reached the capital in Commander Pierce Crosby's *Shamokin*.

Although López effusively welcomed Washburn, their mutual bonhomie was short-lived. In 1867 and 1868 Paraguay was a far different country than the one the minister had left early in 1865. As one authority writes, "The war had spread and intensified. Industry was paralyzed. Human and financial costs were mounting. Liberties were suppressed. López's rule grew more tyrannical." Yet for the most part Washburn retained the dictator's friendship until the appearance of Major James Manlove, a former Confederate. He arrived uninvited at Asunción with an arcane plan to have allied merchantmen hunted down by a fleet of Paraguayan privateers. López concluded that he must be some sort of hostile agent and was infuriated when Washburn tried to protect him. Eventually Manlove was arrested and shot.

The enmity between the president and the minister became total during February 1868. After Fort Humaitá had fallen and allied warships were approaching the capital, López ordered the evacuation of the city. Washburn refused to leave, and since his was the only legation, some 50 foreigners of many nationalities flocked to him for the safety of themselves and their possessions. When López demanded the surrender of the American Porter C. Bliss and the Englishman George R. Masterson, whom he charged with operating against him, Washburn not only turned him down but appointed both men to his legation staff, thereby conferring diplomatic immunity on them. This convinced the paranoid president that Washburn must be his chief enemy. He put to torture several persons who were close friends of Washburn, starting with his own brother-in-law. Naturally they soon screamed what he wanted to hear—that the U.S. minister was plotting to have him overthrown and killed. By this time Washburn realized that he and his family were in real danger of their lives and applied to López for permission to depart.

Admiral Charles H. Davis had recently replaced Godon as head of the South Atlantic Squadron, and from his flagship the *Guerrière* he sent Lieutenant Commander William A. Kirkland's gunboat *Wasp* to rescue the Washburn party. Late in August he came to Asunción and talked with the dictator, bluffing magnificently, laughing at López's suspicions, telling him that the minister was a close friend of President Grant and that should he be harmed six American floating batteries would pulverize Asunción. He then anchored near the city to await Washburn and his people.

On 10 September the legation was vacated but while the fugitives were leaving, Lopez had Bliss and Masterson seized, although they managed to survive and make it back to the United States. By the 20th Washburn was safe in Buenos Aires, at first praising Kirkland for his "firmness and good judgment" but soon turning against his rescuer, calling him a López apologist. He also ripped into Admiral Davis, describing him in his book as "utterly wanting in that tact or quality that carries with it obedience without assuming the appearance of authority. Incapable of organization, his time was devoted to trifling details, which so engaged his attention that matters of grave importance were neglected."

The controversy ended inconclusively in Washington. A House committee looked into the affair, a majority censuring Godon for not helping Washburn to reach Asunción, and reading "a lecture to naval officers for failing to cooperate with diplomatic officers." A minority held that the minister had been "imprudent" in quarreling with López and that neither Godon nor Davis should be held accountable for any offense.

In this incident no one merited kudos. Washburn revealed himself as insufferable—conceited, arrogant, and highly irritable. The behavior of Godon and Davis ranged across a gamut from intransigence on one extreme to vacillation on the other; an authority on the subject calls them "insolent and overbearing, with hardly enough discretion to scrub a deck." U.S. naval diplomacy has seen better days.[10]

Spain vs. Chile and Peru, 1866
Commodore John Rodgers at Valparaiso, 1866

It might be imagined that mid-nineteenth-century Spain, beset with mammoth internal problems, would have the intelligence to avoid non-essential escapades abroad, but it certainly did not. Indeed, during the 1860s that nation's former American colonies had reason to think that Madrid was aspiring to reestablish its old empire, especially when it reabsorbed the Dominican Republic (1861–1865). Not satisfied with this dabbling in relatively nearby Atlantic waters, Spain embarked upon even more quixotic adventures in the Pacific. Off Callao its sizable fleet demanded payment of a dubious and highly inflated claim, holding the guano-rich Chinchas until the resentful Peruvians paid the sum required. But when the Chileans answered Spanish aggression by declaring war, Peru, Bolivia, and Ecuador followed suit. Madrid's armada, however, was potent enough to assault first Chile and then Peru early in 1866; an American officer almost intervened in behalf of the Chileans when the Spaniards announced that they would shell Valparaiso.

Commodore John Rodgers, commanding the U.S. squadron in the Pacific from his flagship the *Monadnock*, steamed late in March to Valparaiso to protect American interests during the expected Spanish attack. After conversing with U.S. minister Hugh J. Kilpatrick, he began leaning toward a course that could have started Spanish-American hostilities had he carried it out. Both Americans found it hard to think of the toll in lives and property that might be inflicted when the Spanish admiral announced that on the 31st he would commence shelling Valparaiso. Rodgers decided that to prevent it he would attack the Spanish fleet. In a remarkable letter to Secretary Welles he admitted that his instructions could not have been more explicit: he must at all times "observe a strict neutrality" between the combatants. But he went on to justify the violation of his orders that he planned: neutrals "might interpose with force, if necessary, to keep the operations of belligerents at least within the law for the protection of neutral persons and neutral property."

Rodgers also called upon Joseph G. Denham, the British admiral commanding three strong warships, "who informed [me] that he intended to prevent any sudden bombardment" of Valparaiso "and would suffer it only after ample notice." Rodgers mulled over this information and on the next day told the Englishman that he "would go as much further as he [the admiral] chose." But on the 30th, as one American officer observed, "somehow or other the English Admiral broke our agreement." Evidently Denham had concluded that a four-day warning prior to opening fire was "ample notice." Rodgers was unwilling to act alone, nor did Kilpatrick so advise, and the minister was later praised by Secretary Seward for realizing that it was "not your duty . . . to instruct Commodore Rodgers to resist the bombardment by force."

Therefore the English and American ships stood by on the 31st while the Spanish armada carried out a three-hour hammering. Although its guns ostensibly aimed at public buildings, private property was demolished as well, and the total damage was estimated at about $15,000,000. Yet at least enough warning had been given to permit the Chileans to flee from their city, as proven by the total casualty count of a mere six or so.

Welles, the day that he read Rodgers's letter about the potential violation of his orders, wrote no more in his *Diary* than that he considered the bombardment of Valparaiso "a brutal and barbarous proceeding on the part of Spain." He ignored the commodore's account of his contemplated behavior, probably because, in the last analysis, Rodgers had not disobeyed his orders. He did refer to the subject in his *Report* for 1866: "it became his [Rodgers's] duty, even while endeavoring to mitigate the harsh severities of war, to maintain a strict neutrality. . . . The officers of other neutral powers having declined to unite in any decided steps to protect the city, no alternative remained for him to pursue . . . than that which he adopted."

While Rodgers may be lauded for the humanitarianism that impelled him to consider an action which his government would be sure to disavow, he was fortunate to escape professional ruin. Had he, even with British cooperation, assailed the Spanish fleet, he could have plunged his nation into an unwanted war. Had he done so and somehow peace had prevailed between Washington and Madrid, it is hard to see how Rodgers could have avoided a court-martial, a conviction, and if extremely lucky, a long suspension from the service without pay. Instead, he was promoted to rear admiral three years later.[11]

To conclude the war: After battering Valparaiso, the Spanish squadron moved against Callao to punish the Peruvians, unaware that some powerful modern artillery had recently arrived there and had already been installed. When the assailants moved in to shell the city, the hail of fire in return was sufficient to damage all seven Spanish men-of-war and inflict about 200 casualties. Even though the Peruvians lost many times as many, the Spaniards had had enough. Shortly thereafter they departed for home, having accomplished nothing except for arousing continuing Latin-American resentment. Repeated efforts by Secretaries of State Seward and Fish finally arranged an armistice in 1871, although it was not until 1886 that Spain finally signed treaties officially ending its war against the South American countries.

The War of the Pacific, 1879–1883
Admirals C. R. Perry Rodgers and George B. Balch off Valparaiso and Callao, 1879–1881

During the mid-nineteenth century Peru, Bolivia, and Chile found that their possession of the richest contemporary natural fertilizers were at the same time their chief source of income and their major cause of war. Peru not only thrived from its guano deposits on the Chincha and Lobos Islands but shared with its Andean neighbors the valuable nitrate beds in what is now northern Chile. Politically and militarily Peru and Bolivia were allies, with their largely Indian populations ruled by small white or mestizo upper classes. They were opposed by overwhelmingly homogeneous Chile, settled by European immigrants. By the late 1870s quarrels over Bolivia's right to tax Chilean nitrate exports passing through its ports led to Santiago's occupation of the disputed area, and Bolivia declared war in February 1879. Two months later its "entangling alliance" with Bolivia pulled a reluctant Peru into the conflict, Lima correctly fearing that its more antiquated forces at sea and ashore would be outclassed by those of the Chileans.

One Latin-American scholar divides this War of the Pacific into four phases. The first consisted of Chile's retention of Bolivia's entire coastline, an offensive that practically knocked that country out of the contest. The second featured naval action. The Peruvian ironclad *Huascar* accomplished maritime miracles for five months against a more potent opposition before being tracked down and sunk; Santiago retained control of the seas thereafter. In the third phase Chilean troops swarmed over Peru's southern provinces and by mid-1880 inflicted enormous economic damage on the enemy by capturing his nitrate deposits. Early in 1881, the fourth saw 30,000 Chileans land near Lima and storm Peru's capital, enabling them to impose a victor's peace two years later.

Throughout the war diplomatic maneuverings of three American administrations clouded rather than clarified issues. In general Washington carried on a pro-Peruvian policy. This was exemplified by President Chester A. Arthur in December 1882: "It is greatly to be deplored that Chile seems resolved to exact such rigorous conditions of peace and indisposed to submit to arbitration the terms of an amicable settlement. No peace is likely to be lasting that is not sufficiently equitable and just to command the approval of other nations." Arthur was correct about Santiago's "rigorous conditions." During October 1883 the Treaty of Ancón and supplemental agreements dictated by the victors added up to catastrophe for the losers. Bolivia was permanently deprived of its entire coastline, becoming a land-locked country. Peru, in addition to its loss of the nitrate-rich southern areas, for a short time literally almost disintegrated as a nation.

From 1879 to 1881 there were several instances of navy diplomacy, marked by policy disagreements between American ministers accredited to the warring capitals and admirals commanding the "Pacific Station." Clearly the officers outmatched the diplomats in efficiency and dedication to their national principles, especially in promoting the neutrality and non-involvement that served their country well.

Shortly after the war began, the Chilean navy blockaded the Peruvian nitrate port of Iquique. Admiral C. R. Perry Rodgers proceeded there in the *Pensacola*, his flagship, to review the situation. He ordered his squadron's commanders to do their "utmost to protect the lawful interests of our countrymen" but at the same time they must "observe the most careful neutrality toward the powers now at war." Although he and his officers tended to admire the Chileans for their élan and efficiency, in general his admonitions were heeded by his naval colleagues throughout the War of the Pacific.

Rodgers personally took charge in two specific instances. When the Chileans briefly lifted their blockade of Iquique, he warned an American company that was considering sending its nitrate ships there to stay away, for the blockade could be legally reimposed without warning, as it soon was. While the Peruvian *Huascar* was briefly terrorizing enemy merchantmen, the admiral learned that Chilean vessels were flying the Stars and Stripes, having been granted that permission by the U.S. consul at Valparaiso—illegally, he surmised. Although he was tempted to halt and search these vessels of such dubious registry, he notified Washington that instead he would let future prize courts settle the legitimacy of the American flag-carriers, a decision for which he was praised by the Navy Department.

From the *Pensacola* Admiral George B. Balch, who succeeded Rodgers in 1881, had to grapple with the serious problems caused by Secretary of State James G. Blaine's incredible appointment of the hot-tempered and irresponsible Stephen A. Hurlbut as minister to Lima, who quickly became a noisy advocate of the Peruvians. He even went so far as to tell a Chilean admiral that the United States might not recognize Chile's right to acquire any Peruvian territory whatsoever, no matter how sweeping its victory in the war. When the story became public the anti-American reaction of the Chileans was heightened.

Late in 1881 Balch learned that Hurlbut had told the Peruvians that his country would support them in future treaty negotiations with Santiago. In return, land was to be ceded for a U.S. naval coaling station at Chimbote, some 200 miles up the coast from Callao. In two letters to Washington, Balch tore into Hurlbut's behavior, emphasizing that the Navy Department, not the State Department, must decide on any locations for naval establishments. He also said that he doubted very much whether Peru, once the war was over, would ever surrender part of its territory to the United States. Blaine agreed with the admiral and castigated his minister, but that worthy managed to retain his post until his death early in 1882. Balch tried to allay Chilean rage by sending one of his captains to make what explanations he could to Santiago, but resentment about American interference remained strong.

Over the next two years the navy kept to its ships while American diplomats continued in vain their attempts to deny Chile the full measure of its military and naval triumphs. It seems that, if anything, they exacerbated the situation, intensifying Chilean ruthlessness toward downtrodden Peru and Bolivia, as reflected in the Treaty of Ancón's draconic terms. From 1879 to the end of the conflict, U.S. naval officers served better their nation's desire to maintain neutrality, as well as avoiding the embarrassing gaffes committed by the diplomats. Rodgers and especially Balch earned a "Well done."[12]

Summary

At first glance it might appear that American naval diplomacy from 1866 to 1881 had been unimpressive, but perhaps upon reflection that judgment should be reversed. It has to be admitted that Admirals Godon and Davis, in their relations with Washburn, brought little credit to themselves. Admirals Porter and Poor could not accomplish what the Johnson and Grant administrations hoped to achieve in the Dominican Republic; Admiral Hoff and Commander Cushing sprang into action after Americans had been killed in Cuba; and Admiral John Rodgers came close to provoking a most unnecessary war with Spain. But Commanders Roe and Low earned plaudits in Mexico; Washburn was both delivered to and taken away from Paraguay, and the only casualty would seem to be the U.S. minister's disposition; the failure of Porter and Poor was due to nothing they had done but to domestic American decisions over which they had no control; the intervention of Hoff worked to keep Americans from being murdered in Cuba for four years, and Cushing's similar action in the *Virginius* affair helped to save them for a longer period; and John Rodgers's unwise decision does not count, since "almost's" are not entered into the permanent record. In the War of the Pacific C. R. Perry Rodgers behaved with circumspection, and Balch stands out for his attempts to compensate for the pro-Peruvian tendencies of Minister Hurlbut.

CHAPTER SEVENTEEN

The Far East

1866–1871

As in the case of Latin America, the efforts of America's sea arm in the Far East, few though they were, were important enough to justify a separate chapter. In China the Western countries, satisfied for the time being with their second round of treaties signed in 1858, chose not to duplicate their earlier aggressions. This decision naturally led to fewer naval interventions. The battered Ch'ing dynasty seemed to be pulling itself together in a promising reform movement, which collapsed by the end of the 1860s. With hindsight it can be perceived that its adherents never had much of a chance. The reformers could not overcome the opposition to meaningful change by the scholar-gentry class, embedded in the imperial bureaucracy.

Across the Yellow Sea the 1860s were a period of great turmoil for the Japanese, although it ended with their directions set toward the westernization and modernization that would soon raise them to great-power status. The anti-Tokugawa leaders of the extreme southwest at first warmed themselves in the xenophobic fires that killed Westerners and burned their buildings, resulting in European and American naval retaliations. By the mid-1860s, however, the opposition managed to persuade the foreign nations that all this had been the fault of the shogun's *bakufu*. Capitalizing to some degree on Western arms and advice, by the late 1860s they waged a bloody civil war and toppled the shogunate.

For the first time Korea comes within the purview of U.S. naval diplomacy. That reclusive monarchy had rivaled the Japanese in its fierce insistence upon isolating itself from outside contamination. The Western countries, preoccupied in East Asia with China and Japan, did not get around to forcing Korea open until the 1860s. The French in 1866 and the Americans in 1871 fought short battles there but could accomplish nothing diplomatically. Korea was able to go its own way in withstanding more open relations with the outside world until compelled to sign treaties with Japan in 1876 and the United States during 1882–1883.

There were nine instances of American naval diplomacy in the Far East from 1863 to 1871, three each in China, Japan, and Korea—less than half as many as with China and Japan alone during the 20 years before 1861, reflecting to what extent American naval intervention had ebbed since the Civil War.

China, 1866–1868

Commander Robert W. Shufeldt and Lieutenant Commander Chester Hatfield off Canton, et al., 1866, 1868

The piracy that had ravaged the China coast in the 1850s was still a cause for concern a decade later. Secretary Welles urged American cooperation with China and Great Britain to stem the danger: "Rear Admiral [Henry H.] Bell has been fully authorized to act in concert with . . . other nations on that station in the suppression of piratical depredations." It was, however, a British undertaking throughout. The Royal Navy in the Far East had between 34 and 38 warships; the U.S. Navy's new Asiatic Squadron had three to five (the earlier East India equivalent had gone out of existence because of Civil War needs).

Only two American activities in this sphere are worth mentioning. Commander Robert W. Shufeldt, cruising in the *Wachusett* off the Canton-Macao-Hong Kong triangle, was discouraged by the immensity of his assignment and shaken by the killing and looting aboard the Boston ship *Lubra*. He told Bell that as long as piracy remained "the natural companion" of the opium trade, only the application of a "huge naval force" could end the piracy. Even the powerful Royal Navy lacked sufficient warships for that purpose.

In May 1868 Lieutenant Commander Chester Hatfield in the little four-gun *Unadilla* sailed against corsairs busy along China's extreme southwestern shores. His chief contribution was burning two abandoned junks and cooperating with a British gunboat in assailing pirates at sea and ashore. By the 1870s piracy had markedly declined, but the China coast remained a chancy place for merchantmen of all nations for years to come.[1]

Commander Robert Townsend at Newshwang (Yinkow), Pengchow (Penglai), and Amoy, 1866

While primarily engaged in hunting down pirates, the navy landed forces three times to protect its citizens. U.S. Consul Francis P. Knight, at Newschwang, in southern Manchuria, had been badly wounded there by Chinese xenophobes calling themselves "Sword Racks." Commander Robert Townsend brought the *Wachusett* to that port, hunted down some of the Sword Racks, turned them over to local officials, and took them back to his ship after their torture-induced confessions that they had assaulted Knight. Following threats by culprits still at large that they would kill an American for every one of their comrades executed, he kept his captives until Ch'ing authorities pledged that they would protect Americans, provided the prisoners were turned over to them for judgment, which was done. Lieutenant John W. "Jack" Philip was very likely correct when he forecast in his *Diary* that doubtless they would be "released as soon as we sail."

At Pengchow on the Shantung Peninsula, Townsend learned that some local Chinese had been "desecrating American graves, tearing down houses, and declaring that they would not allow 'foreign devils' to live in the city any longer." The commander required Pengchow's bureaucrats to arrest the guilty, only to find the next day that every one of them, fearing Peking's wrath should they affiliate too closely with the Americans, had fled to nearby Chefoo (Yentai). When a search there could not unearth them, Philip vowed that "John Chinaman will have to pay dearly for the trick that he plays on us," but he was merely gasconading. The *Wachusett* steamed south to Amoy, where her sailors and marines quelled local unrest that was imperilling their fellow countrymen. There the cruise ended.[2]

Admiral Henry H. Bell at Formosa (Taiwan), 1867

Among those engaged in shipping along the China coast, the shores of Formosa (Taiwan) were recognized as something of a graveyard for merchantmen. Between 1850 and 1869, 32 vessels piled upon its rocky shores, of which 16 were looted and three had all their survivors massacred. The perpetrators had nothing to fear from any official reprisals, for the island's extreme south and east were administrative no-man's-lands. Legally Formosa was part of China, an extension of Fukien Province, but even in the partially controlled west coast, Chinese authority ended some 20 miles north of its southernmost tip. The rest of the island remained in the hands of the aboriginal tribesmen.

In March 1867 the American bark *Rover*, sailing north from Swatow, China, was sunk when storm-driven onto a reef just off Taiwan's southern promontory. Her people managed to row ashore in boats at Lang Ch'iao Bay; all were slain by the "Koaluts," part of a loose coalition under "Tok-e-tok, chief of the eighteen tribes." A Chinese sailor escaped to Taiwan-fu (Tainan) and told his harrowing story to British Consul Charles Carroll and Commander George D. Broad. In the sloop HMS *Cormorant* they sailed south at once to investigate the atrocity. But when 37 sailors tried to go ashore at Lang Ch'iao, they were met by a steady rattle of fire from the heavy undergrowth. The British warship lobbed a few shells into the bush and returned to Taiwan-fu. Broad explained that he had called off his little expedition because it would have been folly "to risk the lives of his men in pursuit of an invisible enemy in a jungle, where every advantage would have been on their side."

Since no U.S. diplomat was stationed at Formosa, that island was part of the Amoy consul's responsibilities. He was Charles W. LeGendre, a French-born, twice-wounded Union general who would later hold important government positions in Japan and Korea. After receiving the endorsement of the governor of Fukien Province, he quickly sailed with Commander John G. Febiger in the gunboat *Ashuelot* to offer assistance to Chinese officials at Taiwan-fu in retaliating for the *Rover* atrocity. He was rebuffed with the explanation that they would do nothing, for the Koaluts and other aborigines were "savages . . . like Monkeys. . . . Their territory is not on our Maps, they do not obey our laws." The Americans went back to Amoy after looking into Lang Ch'iao, but with a gunboat's limited personnel they realized that a landing might be suicidal. Both Febiger and LeGendre reported their findings to Admiral Henry H. Bell, Asiatic Squadron commandant, laying much stress upon the formidable terrain around the bay and asserting that any invaders would find penetration inland extremely difficult and could accomplish nothing purposeful. Bell undoubtedly read their letters but he might as well have used them to light a cigar, for he ignored what they said.

When the news of the *Rover* reached Washington, Seward instructed Bell through Anson Burlingame, U.S. minister in Peking, only to investigate the disaster. If any hostile response was necessary it must be through cooperation with Chinese officials. But the admiral shrugged off this directive and never even attempted to discuss the situation with them. Furthermore, he disregarded the experiences and recommendations of Febiger and LeGendre, acting throughout as if he were unaware that his two compatriots had already visited the exact locale into which he would soon intrude. They could have quickly joined him at Shanghai, but he issued no such invitations.

On 7 June the impetuous Bell headed for Takao, Formosa, in his flagship, the "screw sloop" *Hartford*, accompanied by the corvette *Wyoming*, en route picking up British guides and interpreters. On the morning of the 13th, the Americans reached Lang Ch'iao, and at once it became obvious that any invasion would be resisted, Bell reporting that "the savages" were assembling "on cleared hills about two miles distant." He divided his 181 men into two prongs that were supposed to rendezvous atop the same crests where the Koaluts had been observed, closing a pincers movement on them.

Each detachment plunged into an inferno of discomfort. One officer wrote that his contingent had to begin a "very . . . circuitous, and toilsome" march through "rocks, bushes, dense jungle, and rugged ravines which afforded facility and shelter to the savages, and gave us no hope of getting at them." As the two columns wound slowly toward one another, the tropical sun exacted its toll. In their official reports, officers referred to the temperature and humidity as "killing," "burning," "oppressive," and "scorching." In the early afternoon Lieutenant Commander Alexander S. Mackenzie was shot from ambush, the only American to die that day. The landing parties finally reunited on the hills and straggled back to their ships. The *Hartford*'s surgeon listed 15 "sunstruck" casualties. The *Hartford* and *Wyoming* arrived in Shanghai the next day.

On either tactical or strategic grounds, Bell's incursion into Formosa was ill-conceived and poorly handled. His tactical planning was askew from the start. LeGendre and Febiger had warned him about the practically impenetrable terrain, and high temperatures had to be expected in southern Formosa during June. Even if his two columns had reunited and occupied some ground for a day or two, what could they have accomplished? They could have done no more than kill a handful of Koaluts and burn a few isolated huts that would have been rebuilt at once, for there was no settlement there, not even the tiniest village. Bell told the Navy Department that "sailors are not adapted to that kind of warfare against a skillful enemy, and they should be fitted for it only by a lengthy experience," but he had already disregarded his own intelligent observation. Rather than the censure he deserved, Secretary Welles, in his *Annual Report* for 1867, did no more than to paraphrase the admiral's apologia for his inept campaign. One reason that I have criticized Bell is that I visited the exact spot of his invasion a few years ago. The environs of Lang Ch'iao Bay lack any natural feature that might aid an attack force, and one cannot imagine a much more hopeless terrain for the successful completion of a pincers movement.

Strategically Bell's mission was also programmed for failure. It should have been clear to him that his only prospect for success was to combine naval and diplomatic actions with those of the Chinese, but he approached no Ch'ing authorities, bulling ahead on his own. In the *Dictionary of American Biography* he is described as an officer "distinguished by high technical skill." Although this summary is well deserved because of his brilliant Civil War career, it is not for what he did at Lang Ch'iao Bay.

The local reporter for the *New York Times* made a point that might have somewhat exonerated the admiral had he shown any awareness of it: "an occasional war-like demonstration" such as his would force the Chinese government to move into the vacuum in southernmost Formosa lest the United States or some other power do it for them. But nowhere in Bell's extensive explanations of why he tried and failed at Lang Ch'iao is there the slightest indication that this sensible argument even occurred to him, so he must be evaluated on his own rationalizations.

It remained for LeGendre the diplomat to settle matters satisfactorily. He received in Amoy a letter from the Chinese authorities in Formosa full of excuses for not moving against the Koaluts, placidly stating that the *Rover* murders had taken place beyond "the limits of our jurisdiction." LeGendre was so infuriated by this disavowal that he dashed off a 14-page reply, emphasizing that if China forfeited by neglect its domination of the extreme south, the Western nations or Japan might control it for them. He forecast that this could lead to foreign annexation of part or even all of Formosa. He then persuaded the governor of Fukien Province to instruct his underlings at Taiwan-fu to cooperate with him; he even provided a steamer to take him there, a service which, LeGendre grumbled, "my admiral had refused."

In September, LeGendre, accompanied by British interpreters and some Chinese soldiers, spent a month hacking a road of sorts through the thick underbrush before reaching Lang Ch'iao. On 10 October he met Tok-e-tok. The chief justified his people's aggressions by explaining that foreigners had killed a number of Koaluts 50 years before and that since then they had feared and hated all interlopers. LeGendre promised that they would not be punished for their *Rover* murders but instead would be protected from future hostile landing parties. This cleared the way for the oral understanding called the "Legendre–Tok-e-tok Treaty." The Koaluts pledged that shipwrecked sailors, provided that they identified themselves as peaceful castaways, would be escorted to safety. To conclude his productive work, the consul induced the Chinese to construct a temporary fort and later a lighthouse at the Bay. This brought the area for the first time under reasonably effective Chinese control.

It is easy to assess the relative effectiveness of LeGendre and Bell—the diplomat outclassed the sailor. LeGendre proved himself to be both perceptive and persistent. Although his natural truculence sometimes seemed on the verge of exploding, he kept it under control. He maintained a steady pressure on the Chinese, maneuvering them adroitly to his and their mutual advantage, and his discussions with the Koaluts averted another *Rover* tragedy. In 1869 he again met with Tok-e-tok, whose brother asked that the verbal agreement of two years before be put into written form. LeGendre was surprised at the sophistication of the request but was happy to comply. In 1870 the value of the treaty was underscored when refugee Chinese seamen were helped to safety by the same tribesmen who had treated the *Rover*'s complement so ferociously.

Chinese officials were required to take a much more active part in a place that they had not even been aware that they owned, if for no other reason than to fill the hiatus revealed by the *Rover* episode and its aftermath. They were persuaded by LeGendre to pacify the Lang Ch'iao area, thereby helping to ensure that atrocities would not again be committed upon foreign sailors, which might lead to additional punitive expeditions, which if for temporary purposes at first, might have hardened into permanent occupancy. The Chinese had little to do with the LeGendre–Tok-e-tok Treaty, but it was accomplished under their general sponsorship. In short, the events before, during, and after 13 July 1867 enabled China to expand its hold over Formosa and to keep it for almost a generation before the Japanese would snatch it away in 1895.[3]

Japan, 1863–1869
Commander David McDougal at Shimonoseki, 1863

In 1858 Townsend Harris, U.S. consul-general in Shimoda, led the way in forcing on Japan treaties with the major Western powers like those already imposed upon China. Their effect was to ravage the Japanese society and economy. A wild inflation saw the cost of rice, the nation's food staple, rocket more than a thousand percent from 1860 to 1867. Practically everyone was hurt, and many became convinced that the coming of Europeans and Americans had caused their woes. By 1859 the movement called *sonno-joi* and its slogan "Revere the emperor and expel the barbarians" began menacing the Tokugawas. The shoguns were powerless to protect foreigners, and something of a reign of terror commenced. Russians, Frenchmen, Dutchmen, Britons, Americans, and their Japanese employees were murdered; the British and American legations were burned. The most notorious outrage occurred near Yokohama in 1862. Charles L. Richardson, an Englishman, refused to dismount from his horse while the entourage of the daimyo of Satsuma province was passing. For that discourtesy his throat was cut. An infuriated London imposed "penalties" of £100,000 on the *bakufu* for its failure to safeguard English subjects, and £25,000 on Satsuma for Richardson's murder.

In early 1863 the *sonno-joi* faction pressured the shogun into promising to expel the foreigners by late June, although Westerners had made clear that they would stay in Japan. The rattled *bakufu* tried to placate the British by paying the £100,000 required, an act more than offset by the Choshu daimyo's defiance. He closed his strategic Strait of Shimonoseki between Honshu and Kyushu, blocking the major route to China, and commenced firing on Western merchantmen attempting to pass through it, thereby evoking U.S., Dutch, and French reprisals. A little later a British fleet under Admiral Augustus L. Kuper assailed Kagoshima, the capital of Satsuma in Kyushu, but the battle was inconclusive.

A momentous development in Japanese history took place late in 1863: the coming of Anglo-Satsuma friendship. After the £25,000 indemnity for the murder of Richardson had been paid, the British agreed to help that daimyo purchase warships. Satsuma had belatedly recognized that the best policy for Japan was to learn from the foreigner so that one day it would be strong enough to expel him. This was later passed on to Choshu and other great nobles: to support the emperor and topple the shogunate. Meanwhile, however, the Strait of Shimonoseki remained sealed until the summer of 1864, when a Western armada opened it, while pulverizing Choshu's resistance.

Somewhat incredibly, Satsuma and Choshu, whose attacks on Europeans and Americans had exposed the *bakufu*'s inability to maintain law and order, soon managed to persuade the West that the anti-foreign movement had really been the fault of the shogun, not theirs. With outside backing the Satsuma-Choshu armies, joined by those of other anti-Tokugawa daimyo, seized the imperial palace at Kyoto and announced the restoration of the emperor's authority. Despite *bakufu* counterattacks, the shogunate's cause was doomed with the fall of Edo, and the last shogun abdicated late in 1867. The way was open for the so-called "Meiji Restoration" to usher Japan into the modern world.

Three U.S. naval interventions during the 1860s deserve attention. Two were at Shimonoseki in 1863 and 1864. The first was brilliant tactically but failed to reopen the strait. In the second a sizable European fleet easily did that, with the United States contributing a bare minimum of naval cooperation. The third, from 1867 to 1869, featured some pacifistic and diplomatic success by the officer in command amid the throes of the emperor-shogun civil war.

The events concerning Commander David McDougal started when the *Pembroke*, a little American steamer, was the first to feel Choshu's wrath. On 25 June she approached Shimonoseki and anchored off the town, not daring to hazard the swirling waters of the strait in the dark. Soon two ships of Choshu's navy opened up on her and inflicted minor damage to her rigging before she fled to China by an alternate route. Robert H. Pruyn, U.S. minister to Japan, talked about the matter with McDougal, whose new eight-gun corvette *Wyoming* was the only American steam warship in the Far East. The commander sailed at once to annihilate or capture Choshu's offending vessels.

On 16 July, after keeping the *Wyoming* hugging the shores to avoid detection, McDougal darted into Shimonoseki, where a four-gun steamer, a ten-gun brig, and a four-gun bark guarded the town. According to McDougal's official report the corvette "at pistol shot range" left the brig "settling by the stern," the bark suffering "serious damage," and the steamer sinking after one of his projectiles had exploded in her boilers. He then doubled back to the east, battering shore fortifications all the while, and inflicting severe punishment on Shimonoseki, as the Japanese admitted. After an hour and ten minutes of nonstop action, McDougal steamed away with 5 dead and 6 wounded against about a hundred Choshu casualties. This cool performance of duty stands in contrast to bumbling European naval campaigns at the same time and place. A Dutch warship was driven away from Shimonoseki heavily damaged. A French admiral bragged that he had hammered that town but his claim is simply ludicrous; neither of his vessels came closer to the strait than two miles.

Although McDougal's work as a naval officer was lauded by the Navy Department, much comment in the American press was negative. A Boston paper saw no advantage to the nation in fighting Japan while the Civil War raged and wished that the assault had never occurred. Ingenious and daring as McDougal's operation was, it made no difference whatsoever diplomatically. Choshu ignored the savage mauling of his capital and remained as defiant as ever, keeping the strait closed for the next 14 months.[4]

Lieutenant Frederick Pearson at Shimonoseki, 1864

By this time Western patience with both Choshu and the *bakufu* had run its course; there was general agreement that the Strait of Shimonoseki must be forced open. For that purpose Admiral Kuper, who had attacked

Satsuma's Kagoshima the year before, commanded nine British, four Dutch, and three French warships. U.S. minister Pruyn and the European envoys alike thought that American participation in the expedition was essential to demonstrate to the Japanese the degree of Western unanimity that existed. Unfortunately the *Wyoming* had been called away on other business. The only U.S. man-of-war remaining in the Far East was the obsolete sailing sloop *Jamestown*, under Captain Cicero Price, which could not possibly keep up with the fast European steamers. Indignantly turning down a British offer to tow his ship into action, Price chartered the *Ta-kiang*, an American steamboat of only 600 tons, taking from the *Jamestown* one "Parrot gun or howitzer" for her armament, with Lieutenant Frederick Pearson and 50 men composing her personnel. The lieutenant was warned that his flimsy little craft was not designed for battle and that he must restrict himself to such duties as "towing boats, landing men, and receiving the wounded on board."

On the afternoon of 5 September, the Western fleet began pounding Shimonoseki, and within an hour four of Choshu's coastal batteries had been silenced, Kuper noting that "the *Ta-kiang* also fired several shots from her Parrot gun, doing good service." During the next day almost 2,000 European sailors overran the town's remaining defenses and then easily beat back a last-ditch onslaught by Choshu's soldiers. This ended hostilities, with European casualties only 12 killed and 60 wounded; not an American had been touched. Over the next few days some of the injured were brought to the *Ta-kiang* and taken to Yokohama.

The most incongruous aspect of the American role in the attack is the astonishing degree to which the British lavished accolades upon Pearson for action that, it must be admitted, contributed almost nothing to the Western victory. Kuper wrote him two separate notes shortly after the battle about his "efficient assistance," "courtesy," and "ready acquiescence to orders." The lords of the Admiralty in London officially notified Washington of their appreciation of Pearson's "ready cooperation," referring to him as a "gallant officer." To compound the farce, a little later he was knighted! This caused a problem, for section 9 of the U.S. Constitution forbids anyone holding an "office" in the government to accept any "Title" from any "King, Prince, or foreign state," unless Congress should consent. In 1875 a special act was passed enabling "Sir Frederick Pearson" to become the only knight on the American naval roster.

Although Pruyn and Secretary of State Seward praised the Lieutenant, Secretary of the Navy Welles was highly contemptuous of the affair, writing in his *Diary* that although they had done nothing to deserve it,

Britain was "extolling our men who were mere spectators, and even gave honor to our officers [sic], who rendered no service." He also blasted Pruyn, lamenting that because he had permitted Pearson to participate, "we have joined in the fight" and "become involved in an English and French war with Japan, although the Japanese have no quarrel with us." Perhaps Welles was too harsh. Granting the basic unimportance of what Pearson had done at Shimonoseki, it may well have shaken the Japanese to observe that even in the midst of a terrible U.S. civil war, the Americans had stood shoulder to shoulder with the Europeans in a demonstration of Western unity. They finally had to realize that even vestiges of their former isolationism would no longer be tolerated by the outside world.[5]

Admiral Stephen C. Rowan at Hyogo (Kobe), Yokohama, and Hakodate, 1867–1869

As Japan slid closer to all-out war between the pro- and anti-Tokugawa forces, the U.S. Navy became much less belligerent later in the 1860s than before. For example, a powerful Western armada gathered off Hyogo on the Inland Sea during November 1865 to compel the Japanese to accept treaty revisions much to the latter's disadvantage. But A. C. L. Portman, the chargé d'affaires temporarily directing American policy in Japan, made no effort to emulate Pruyn's decision that his nation must be represented in joint action with the Europeans by some kind of warship, even one as unimpressive as the *Ta-kiang*. Instead, he contented himself with watching the bloodless proceedings from a British man-of-war.

Admiral Stephen C. Rowan arrived in Japan late in 1867. His tenure as commander of the Asiatic Squadron was marked by his ability to work in tandem with Robert B. Van Valkenburg, the new U.S. minister. Late that year the Japanese internal conflict began to reach a crescendo. In January 1868, near Osaka, a Satsuma-Choshu army loyal to the emperor routed troops supporting the Tokugawas. On the 31st Van Valkenburg acceded to the shogun's request for sanctuary in the USS *Iroquois*, stationed off the city. He and his party stayed aboard for a couple of hours before being taken off by a ship of his own navy. With the collapse of the *bakufu* in Osaka, the entire Western community fled to nearby Hyogo, where the shogun was temporarily in residence.

A few days later soldiers of a Satsuma-Choshu daimyo fell upon foreigners on Hyogo's beach, wounding a sailor from the *Oneida*, Rowan's flagship. Americans, Britons, and Frenchmen raced to the local customhouse and defended themselves until relief detachments sent by Rowan and European commanders drove the assailants away. About the same time men from other American warships at Nagasaki, Yokohama, and Niigata landed to keep order.

When Japan's civil conflict spread toward Edo (just being renamed Tokyo), the U.S. Navy kept an eye on events. Matters were considerably complicated for Rowan and Van Valkenburg by the appearance of the *Stonewall*, the same Confederate armed ram that had humiliated Craven in Europe in 1865. She had been bought and paid for by the *bakufu* in a transaction supported by Seward, but she was also claimed by the increasingly victorious supporters of the imperial cause. The Americans came to the wise decision to hold the *Stonewall* until the course of the war had been settled. She did not appear at Yokohama until the spring of 1869, when she became the first unit of the emperor's armored fleet.

A potentially nasty situation had arisen the previous September. Two midshipmen from the *Oneida* and four French junior officers were behaving obstreperously enough in Hyogo's red-light district to attract the attention of the police, who beat them and were fired upon. Luckily no one was hit, much to Rowan's relief. Had a Japanese policeman been killed, he would have had no alternative save turning over the guilty American for execution.

By February 1869 the emperor's adherents had swept to victory throughout Honshu, but a naval detachment still supporting the shogun offered last-ditch resistance at Hakodate, in the northernmost home island of Hokkaido. Rowan dispatched three ships of his squadron there to protect the national commerce and to offer succor to Americans who might be in danger. By June the imperial navy finally triumphed, and when opposition to the emperor collapsed, peace returned to troubled Japan. Once the fighting stopped, so too did most of the U.S. Navy's responsibilities in that quarter.

The last years of the *Stonewall*, the most peripatetic warship in history, are worth a brief comment. Once the Confederates learned that the Civil War was over, the ship was abandoned in Havana to Spanish colonial authorities. Later in 1865 she was turned over to the United States before being sold to the *bakufu* for $400,000. After the Japanese internal hostilities had ended, the erstwhile *Stonewall* became first the *Kotetsu* and then the *Adsuma*. Some years later she was "sold to a fishing company"; one wonders what such a concern could do with an obsolete armored ram. At one time or another that ship was either under the flag or at least the control of France, Denmark, the Confederacy, Spain, the United States, and Japan, undoubtedly a record unmatched by any other man-of-war.[6]

Korea, 1866–1871

Commander Robert W. Shufeldt off the Taedong River, 1867

Korea's astonishing record of having been ruled by only three dynasties from 670 to 1910—Silla, Koryo (hence the name), and Yi—might have denoted tranquility, but was far from it. Tumult at home, and invasions that bloodied the peninsula, occurred almost constantly. Very early the Chinese had exported much of their culture and religion south of the Yalu River; during most of its history Korea was Peking's tributary state, even through terrible assaults by the Mongols (mid-1200s), Japanese (1590s), and Manchus (1627–1639). Meanwhile Chinese and Japanese pirates devastated its coasts. Shattered by these disasters, the country withdrew into a self-imposed isolation, earning its nickname of "the Hermit Kingdom," maintaining only ritualistic ties with China and minimal economic contacts with that empire and Japan.

The first Western influences arrived there with the infiltration of French Catholic priests, who by 1860 had won an estimated 18,000 Korean converts. Meanwhile the court in Seoul was watching with concern the European humiliations of China and American assistance to the Japanese in their emergence from seclusion. In 1864, the *Taewon'gun*, the able, ruthless, and foreign-hating father of the young King Kojong, became his regent. Positive that he could keep the outside world at bay if he crushed his Catholic minority, he started by killing nine French clerics and some Koreans. French Admiral Pierre Gustave Rose soon took several warships and 600 men to Kangwha Island, near Seoul, early in 1866, but his efforts to capture a fort there were repulsed with heavy losses, and he had to creep back to China in disgrace.

Two weeks prior to the French fiasco the American merchantman *General Sherman*, with Western officers and a largely Chinese crew, went up the Taedong River toward Pyongyang, today the capital of North Korea, but her terrified Chinese pilot left the ship. In an act of unbelievable rashness and stupidity the pilotless *Sherman* continued up an uncharted river into a most xenophobic nation. Surely those aboard should have seen that their only chance for survival was to adopt a conciliatory course. Instead, they behaved with the utmost aggression.

As they neared Pyongyang they kidnaped a high Korean official who came to question them, although he later escaped. As the *Sherman* dropped anchor outside the city, her return flight downriver was suddenly blocked by a sandbar when the level of the previously rain-swollen Taedong dropped. According to Korean accounts her people fired into a crowd on shore, killing 5 and wounding 7. The local governor ordered the vessel's destruction. Despite stout resistance, the *Sherman* was soon set afire, and every intruder was either incinerated, drowned, clubbed to death, or beheaded. The defeat of both French and Americans naturally convinced the *Taewon'gun* that his policy of defiance was correct.

In China the news of this Korean victory caused general bewilderment. Shortly before, those in the American ship *Surprise*, which had been wrecked on the Korean western coast, were treated kindly and escorted to safety. Actually the difference between the two episodes was explained to Admiral Rose by Kangwha's governor: "Officials in our country are ordered to receive . . . those who happen to drift to our boundaries, and to treat them as if they were old friends. . . . But if there be those who infiltrate our land, . . . deceive our people, and corrupt our customs, we . . . have a law for them. Whenever they are found they are punished severely."

In January 1867 Commander Robert W. Shufeldt turned the *Wachusett* toward Korea to investigate the *Sherman* case. He managed to persuade a fisherman to deliver a letter to the *Taewon'gun* declaring his nonbelligerent intent, asking that any *Sherman* survivors be given him, and wondering about the disparate treatment meted out to those in that ship compared to the *Surprise*'s crew. Fearful of being trapped by a Korean winter, Shufeldt left before the *Taewon'gun*'s reply arrived, so no American would read it until over a year later. The key result of the commander's brief stay was to kindle in him an abiding interest in the "Hermit Kingdom" that would lead him to sign its first treaty with the West in 1882.[7]

Commander John C. Febiger off the Taedong River, 1868

In April 1868 Admiral Stephen C. Rowan, Bell's replacement, ordered Commander John C. Febiger in the corvette *Shenandoah* to Korea. He was to probe into the matter of the *Sherman*, with a new directive that he take estuarial and topographical surveys of the Taedong River and its environs, surely a hostile act. When he arrived there a minor functionary gave him the *Taewon'gun*'s letter that had missed Shufeldt, explaining that all the *Sherman*'s personnel were dead, having met their grim fate through their own calculated atrocities. This told the Korean side of the story so ably that Shufeldt later called it "statesmanlike in its character" and said it bore "intrinsic evidence of the truth." Before heading back to China in mid-May, Febiger passed a few weeks working his way about 25 miles up the Taedong, sounding and surveying as he went, and later repeated the same duties around the river's mouth. While he was in the interior one of his boats was fired upon from a Korean fort. Although he did not retaliate, he felt that an apology was due for this affront to the American flag. Rowan, in Yokohama, agreed and informed the secretary

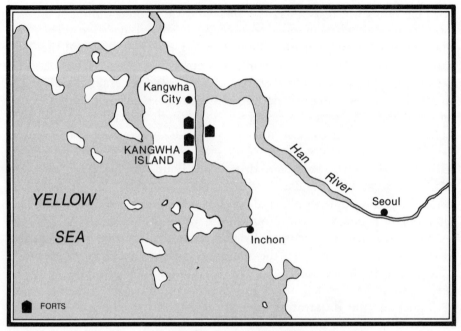

Kangwha Environs—1871

that he wanted to send an expedition there to avenge the insult. Until Japanese affairs were quiet, however, he could not move in that direction. Since the emperor-shogun battle continued well into 1869, he had to stay where he was.[8]

Rear Admiral John Rodgers at Kangwha Island, 1871

For two years after Febiger's sojourn in Korea, little happened to help establish relations between that country and the United States. By 1870 Washington finally got around to preparing for the settlement of scores with the *Taewon'gun*. Rear Admiral John Rodgers and the diplomat Frederick F. Low, U.S. minister to China, were chosen to conduct their differing responsibilities jointly and told to sign at least a shipwreck convention and if possible a trade treaty with Korea. Ominous forebodings made both men pessimistic. Low admitted that he was not "sanguine" about the likelihood of any diplomatic achievements, and Rodgers was well aware that a stronger French force had been repelled in the very area into which he must go.

The Korean reply to Low's missive asserted that a shipwreck treaty was unnecessary, because "the rescuing and forwarding home" of those stranded were "provided by existing laws." In regard to a trade agreement, "our people are very poor" and their habits are "sparing and plain, the workmanship rude and poor, and we have not a single article worthy of commerce with foreign nations." Disheartened by these initial frustrations, nonetheless the two Americans had to plod ahead with their preparations.

By May 1871 a motley fleet had been assembled that reflected the navy's post-1865 doldrums. It consisted of the frigate *Colorado* as flagship, the twin corvettes *Alaska* and *Benicia*, and the gunboats *Monocacy* and *Palos*. Although the fleet might look impressive on paper, mounting 85 guns and carrying 1240 men, the three larger vessels drew too much water to dare the vicious currents and eddies set in motion during Korean high tides; they were to serve only as transports and store ships. This meant that the United States, with a pair of gunboats, four steam launches, and a score of ship's boats, was trying to force into submission a country determined to retain its isolation.

On 1 June the gunboats and launches, under the direction of Commander Homer C. Blake in the *Palos*, were surveying and sounding the strait, which was defended by four forts at Kangwha, all reinforced since the French assault five years before. Three bastions were on that island and one on the mainland. Located on a bend in the strait, Kwangsong, or "the citadel," farthest to the north, was the most powerful of the four. After passing the silent first fortification, Blake's ships were fired upon in a barrage that a U.S. officer called more concentrated than any he had endured in the Civil War. But their defective cannon, usually fixed to aim at a single spot, damaged no American vessel and wounded only one sailor. The gunboats answered in kind, battering the Korean positions effectively. Just when victory seemed assured, the *Monocacy* went aground, ripping herself open to such an extent that it took all day to repair and refloat her, requiring the detachment to return to the flagship. The developments on that day were to be pivotal. Both American emissaries decided that Seoul must apologize for what Rodgers called a "sudden and treacherous assault." They issued to the Koreans an ultimatum giving them ten days to comply or face the consequences. What had commenced as a treaty-making expedition had now expanded into a punitive force as well, a dichotomy that would defeat the objectives of both.

Over the 10th and 11th the gunboats, launches, and twenty-two boats carrying 651 sailors and marines, again under Blake's command, moved against Kangwha. Brisk cannonading followed by landings drove the defenders from three forts, but the fiercest combat occurred at Kwangsong citadel, perched atop a 150-foot hill and protected by some "Tiger Hunters" from the Yalu River area. Howitzers were laboriously hauled up and

John Rodgers the Younger, 1812–1882
(Official U.S. Navy Photo)

down ravines, and once in place joined the *Monocacy* in pounding the fortress and cutting off any Korean reinforcements. Blake's assailants charged up to Kwangsong, and Lieutenant Hugh W. McKee was the first to scale the wall, but he was killed by "a musket ball in the groin and a spear-jab in the side." According to an American participant, "The conflict inside was of the most desperate character; our men fought, some with their cutlasses, others with muskets and carbines, using them as clubs; the Koreans with spears, swords, stones, and even threw dust to blind us." The carnage at the citadel went on until nearly all the 300-odd defenders had either died in action, committed suicide, or were too badly wounded to kill themselves. Only 3 Americans perished and 10 were wounded, a remarkably light count that may be attributed in large part to the archaic quality of Korean weapons, for some of their handguns dated back to the 1500s. The efficacy and zeal with which the assault on Kangwha was carried gave the Americans some reason for pride in an otherwise dismal experience.

The expedition returned to its Inchon mooring on the 12th, and everyone passed a monotonous three weeks while Low and Rodgers waited for Korean acquiescence to their demands, knowing all along that they would not yield. On 3 July the expedition gave up and steamed back to China, mission unfulfilled.

All this left a legacy of burning Korean resentment. The day after the citadel fell, Low received a letter written by a Korean general accusing the Americans of committing murder, theft, and arson, asking, "When was such unsparing and implacable savagery ever exceeded? . . . Not only will every urchin in our kingdom spit at and curse you" but the rest of the world "will indignantly sympathize with us." Young King Kojong doubted whether there could ever be peace between "the dogs and the lambs." Believing that, although he might have lost a skirmish, the American departure signified that he had won the campaign, the *Taewon'gun* erected several steles around the country reading, "There are only two choices when the Western Barbarians invade—fight or surrender. Those who favor friendly relations with them are betrayers of their own country. I hereby warn our descendants thus unto ten thousand generations."

Resentment was not a Korean monopoly; Rodgers ached to visit retribution upon those who had humiliated him. Low wanted a second expedition dispatched to smash those Korean "barriers that stand in the way of intercourse," but the Grant administration washed its hands of the matter. Secretary of the Navy George M. Robeson appended 38 pages of documents about the campaign to his *Report* for 1871. One looks in vain for Rodgers's request to try again. The Korean question faded away for the United States for over ten years.

Quite likely American public opinion, as reflected in the press, contributed to this hands-off attitude. The martial abilities and courage displayed by the sailors and marines on Kangwha were lauded, but the expedition's diplomacy was denounced. A few papers called for another round in what one named "Our Little War with the Heathen," but most dissented, forecasting another failure. Two in New York summarized the basic fault behind the Low-Rodgers fiasco—too much for one purpose, too little for another. The *Times* put it in capsule form: "In Corea we have blundered between . . . two policies." The *Herald* elaborated most perceptively on the same theme: "Our wiseacres evidently could not make up their minds whether the expedition was to accomplish its avowed purpose by force or by diplomacy. They, therefore, sent a force altogether too large for the delivery of a message of peace and altogether too small for the effectual prosecution of a war." A mission that cannot decide whether it is an agency of amiable diplomacy or a naval assault team and tries to be both at the same time is earmarked for miscarriage. Such was the Rodgers-Low incursion and such was its destiny.[9]

Summary

The American navy gets low grades for its activities in China and Korea after 1865, but a higher mark for those in Japan. In China, Shufeldt and Hatfield, operating in a squadron of approximately one-seventh as many ships as that of the Royal Navy, could only play a secondary role to the British in campaigns against pirates. Townsend, in the northern environs, was hamstrung by the Chinese's refusal to cooperate with him in protecting American citizens. Although Bell's defeat when he landed in Formosa amounted to little in itself, he demonstrated impulsiveness and incompetence, in the main by his refusal to work with Chinese authorities. By adept diplomacy LeGendre prodded those officials into filling a vacuum by establishing their control over southern Taiwan.

As for Japan, McDougal was given a chance in 1863 to demonstrate his sterling qualities as a combat officer at Shimonoseki, even though his derring-do had no diplomatic impact whatever. "Sir Frederick" Pearson's contribution to Western victory at the same place a year later was *opéra bouffe*, but his show of American solidarity with the Europeans may well have helped nudge the Japanese toward emulation of the West rather than opposition to it. Finally, Rowan earns praise for cooperating so efficiently with Minister Van Valkenburg in maintaining a difficult neutrality between the pro- and anti-imperial elements later in the decade. Rather than the bellicosity of his predecessors, Rowan's contribution had been largely pacifistic, abetting Van Valkenburg's attempts to avoid entanglements while doing his best to help restore Japanese tranquility.

In Korea circumstances allowed Shufeldt and Febiger to be no more than observers of events beyond their control. Despite the competence of their offensive campaign at Kangwha Island, the inability of Rodgers the sailor and Low the diplomat to recognize their dual and conflicting policies—to punish while simultaneously trying to conciliate the Koreans enough to bring them to a conference table—could only guarantee frustration and damage the American image in the Far East.

CHAPTER EIGHTEEN

The Rest of the World

1866–1882

The generalization previously made applies even more accurately for the postwar than the prewar period: American naval initiatives in Europe and the Middle East from 1865 to 1883 were much more restricted than elsewhere. For all the recurrent turmoil in their internal and external affairs, systematized governments existed there with which the United States carried on normal diplomatic relations. The presence of American ministers and consuls in residence throughout this area meant that opportunities for independent naval responses to crises were much less numerous than in parts more chaotically ruled. European and Middle Eastern countries were also connected by telegraphic networks, allowing U.S. diplomats to pass along Washington's orders very rapidly via the Atlantic cable to warship commanders. In contrast, even the Far East had no telegraphic connections beyond Western Asia and North Africa until 1871, when for the first time Europeans could wire China and Japan via Russian Vladivostok. The far-flung Pacific Islands were without cable service during the entire period covered in this work. Hence U.S. naval officers were as much on their own there as earlier in the century.

In addition, the postwar ebbing of American sea power until a slow recovery began in the mid-1880s necessitated a cautious response to foreign confrontations. As late as the Chilean-American crisis of 1891, the Benjamin Harrison administration had to face the fact that Santiago's one heavily armed and armored new cruiser could have sent every American warship to the bottom. Finally, after the spate of wars of the 1850s and 1860s had ended with the Franco-Prussian conflict of 1870–1871, a generation of comparative peace prevailed, not to be broken until the turn of the twentieth century. Hostilities that did break out were localized without other nations being pulled in.

During this time only two American diplomatic actions affected relations with European nations; three with those in the Middle East; four with Hawaii; and three with other islands in the Pacific, two in Fiji and one in Samoa. Until the cruise of Commodore Robert W. Shufeldt in 1879 and 1880, there were no U.S. naval episodes worthy of even the briefest mention in Africa, the Indian Ocean, or Southeast Asia.

Europe, 1867–1873
Captain George F. Emmons at Sitka, Alaska, 1867

The taking of Russian North America was a noteworthy occasion in the history of the United States, for it marked the first time that this nation had annexed noncontiguous territory on the continent. Accounts of the Alaskan Purchase are so numerous and well-researched that there is no need to include here details of Seward's treaty with Russian minister Edouard de Stoeckl, hurriedly signed during the early morning of 30 March 1867; its rapid acceptance by the Senate; and the long delay in payment, due to the House's failure to appropriate the stipulated $7,200,000 until July 1868. The navy was of course the conduit for bringing into actuality expansion into nonadjacent areas or those overseas. Therefore at least the essential facts of the Alaskan Purchase deserve some slight attention.

Hoping to disarm critics of his purchase with a fait accompli, Seward hastened to have appropriate ceremonies held in Sitka (former New Archangel) well before the tsar had seen a dollar of what he was owed. He called upon the army to provide a transport for 250 soldiers and the navy to furnish three men-of-war, the aged sailer *Jamestown* as a store ship and the gunboats *Resaca* and *Ossipee*, both under the command of Captain George F. Emmons in the latter. The captain was to carry there the two commissioners, General Lovell Rousseau for the United States and a Russian diplomat. They came into Sitka on the morning of 18 October and rushed through the rituals of exchange that same afternoon. Americans and Russians gathered around the town's flagpole, among them Governor Dimitrii Matsutov and his young wife, both bitterly opposed to the transfer. The double-eagle flag of the Romanovs was supposed to come down gracefully, but it stuck so tenaciously that a man had to be sent up to cut it down. All this was punctuated by the sobs of Mariia Matsutov, who fainted and fell to the ground just before the American flag was raised. Emmons, in his long report to the Department of his visit, omitted these colorful details, concentrating instead on the bad weather encountered and the severity of Rousseau's seasickness. Once the Stars and Stripes floated over Sitka, Seward was able to ask his opponents if, unlike him, they were accustomed to pulling down the American flag.[1]

Admiral A. Ludlow Case and Captain Clark H. Wells off Spain, 1873

The only other relevant U.S. naval diplomacy in Europe during the post-1865 era posed a problem frequently encountered by navy secretaries: a commanding officer's recognition that neutrality must be maintained and a subordinate colleague's permitting his enthusiasm for one side to challenge this policy.

In 1873 yet another uprising took place in Spain, revolution-wracked through much of the nineteenth century. The basic division dated back to the Bourbon king's decision in 1823 to push aside his brother Don Carlos in order to seat his daughter Isabella on the throne. Starting in the mid-1830s conservative elements gathered behind Carlos (hence "Carlists") to fight against the somewhat more liberal backers of the queen in recurring insurrections usually marked by atrocities. In 1868 Isabella was deposed and replaced by a short-lived and ineffective royal successor. Early in 1873 he in turn was toppled and the first Spanish republic proclaimed, against which the Carlists continued to battle. During this tumult Admiral A. Ludlow Case in the *Wabash* and Captain Clark H. Wells in the *Shenandoah* found themselves at cross-purposes.

That summer Case sent Wells from the eastern Mediterranean to southern Spain after Madrid had called upon all navies to recognize that ships supplying Carlists were pirates. His subordinate overreacted in his partisanship for the republicans. After hearing that a rebel vessel was levying tribute on ports along the coast, Wells sailed for Cadiz, where he first sent in provisions and then brought aboard the *Shenandoah* republican officers besieged ashore. Case recognized that these actions were contrary to Washington's aims and reminded Wells, "Our mission abroad . . . is one of peace, and our policy is to take no part in any European troubles or complications." The department agreed, reprimanded the captain, and terminated this instance of an unauthorized intervention by one of its officers.[2]

The Middle East, 1866–1882

Admirals Louis M. Goldsborough and David G. Farragut off Crete, 1866–1869

The ailing Turkish empire was in one way or another the epicenter of the storms swirling around the Middle East in the late nineteenth century. The decaying authority of the sultan offered continuous opportunities for trouble to be caused by dissident minorities inside his shrinking domains; by ambitious subordinates in outlying areas, eager to substitute their rule for his; and by the Russians, avid to gain entry into the warm sea through Constantinople.

Turkish-American relations were generally cordial until the mid-1860s, for Constantinople had been supportive of Washington during the Civil War. But tensions were created late in the decade by the outbreak of a rebellion in Crete, from the sultan's viewpoint continued by mainland Greek support for the Greeks in that island. The ardently philhellenic U.S. minister to Turkey, endowed with the felicitous name of E. Joy Morris, attempted to get the navy to safeguard American-chartered supply ships heading for the island. This aroused the ire of Secretary Robeson, who objected to Morris's efforts "to induce our naval officers to break through neutrality and interfere with this insurrection."

While the State Department was tilting toward intervention, Admiral Louis M. Goldsborough in the *Colorado* remained "correctly neutral and unenthusiastic," delaying for months sending ships to evacuate those who wished to flee from Crete. When he finally acceded in 1867 and sent the *Canandaigua* and *Swatara* on such errands of mercy, he insisted that no one could board either vessel without the consent of the Turks. Both ships were turned away without passengers when the local pasha "peremptorily refused to grant permission." Admiral David G. Farragut in the *Franklin* emulated Goldsborough in caution in 1868–1869. Any possibility of a Turkish-American clash was obviated when the British and French pressured the Greeks into cutting off supplies to Crete and the rebellion collapsed.[3]

Admiral John L. Worden and Tripoli (Libya), 1875

In the early 1870s the French-born Michel Vidal, a former U.S. congressman living in Tripoli as the American consul, urged the acquisition of a U.S. naval base at Cyrenaica (eastern Libya) to interfere with the local slave trade. This much displeased the sultan's pasha in Tripoli, who profited from the flow of blacks passing through from mid-Africa to Constantinople, and vowed to rid himself of his abolitionist opponent. In the summer of 1875 Vidal tussled with Turkish sailors at his home, assaulting them without reason according to the Turks, protecting his despatch book according to Vidal. The consul telegraphed Admiral John L. Worden in the *Franklin* at Southampton, England, about his treatment. Too far away to go himself, the admiral sent the *Congress* and *Hartford* to provide some naval muscle for Vidal. The pasha, with his people panicking and American cannon frowning on him, surrendered. The humiliated Turk was compelled to march in full regalia to the consulate to offer his abject apologies. Lieutenant Commander Robley D. Evans in the *Congress*, watching the proceedings, was disgusted with Vidal's vindictiveness. After the pasha had figuratively said that "he ate dirt in the presence of the offended," the consul demanded that "the dirt should actually be eaten," but the commanding officer "put an end to the business." Yet Vidal's jubilation was short-lived. The State Department had already undercut him by publishing some of his earlier recommendations that a naval base be acquired in Cyrenaica, and he was soon recalled.

Although several U.S. warships gathered in the eastern Mediterranean during the Russo-Turkish War of 1877–1878 to evacuate Americans if necessary, nothing of diplomatic significance transpired. In 1879 the decrepit *Wyoming* became the first U.S. man-of-war to cruise in the Black Sea, but the only result was to pinpoint the alarming collapse of American sea power after 1865. A travesty of a fighting ship, with leaky boilers and guns reportedly inoperable, she crawled around to several Russian and Turkish ports at her top speed of six knots.[4]

Admiral James W. A. Nicholson at Alexandria, Egypt, 1882

In 1879, Ismail, the reform-minded but spendthrift khedive (Turkish viceroy) of Egypt, was deposed by the sultan in favor of his son Tewfik. Nationalistic Egyptian officers, spearheaded by Colonel Ahmed Arabi, continued to despair about Western encroachments upon their country. In the spring of 1882 Arabi formed a new ministry and commenced reinforcing Alexandria's fortifications, after which foreign warships gathered offshore. In mid-June riots swept through the city in which some 50 aliens were killed, setting in motion a mass exodus of Europeans and Americans. Admiral James W. A. Nicholson in his flagship *Lancaster* sent in the smaller *Galena*, and she, along with a chartered merchantman, rescued about 300 persons, most of them American but many of them foreigners without naval protection of their own. Outside efforts to defuse the approaching explosion failed because of British opposition, and London's minister in Cairo announced on 10 July that a bombardment of Alexandria would start on the morrow. His American counterpart was sure that the desire of the English to take over Egypt and the Suez Canal, linchpin in their vital route to India and the Far East, was the reason for their intransigence.

With the warships of eight other nations observing, prolonged Royal Navy battering compelled Arabi to withdraw his army from the city. For some reason the British admiral dispatched no landing parties, and Alexandria lay undefended while dangerous conflagrations broke out. Tewfik asked Nicholson to help fight fires and prevent looting. The admiral accommodated him at once; he sent in from the *Lancaster* and two lesser men-of-war about 150 men, who acted as combined firemen and police officers; order was soon restored. Once the British occupation force came ashore, the Americans were able to return to their ships. Two months later Arabi's army was routed at Tel el-Kebir, near Cairo, allowing the British to occupy the capital and commence their "temporary" rule of Egypt, which lasted in one form or another until 1956.

Navy Secretary William E. Chandler summarized well his admiral's conduct in Egypt: "The timely arrival of the vessels gave protection to the American consulate and to American citizens and interests, and also afforded a refuge for our own fugitives and for the fugitives of other nations. . . . The action at this juncture of Admiral Nicholson was judicious and humane, and met the approval of the department." It would be hard to refute the secretary's conclusion.[5]

Hawaii, 1867–1875

Captain William Reynolds at Honolulu and Midway Atoll, 1867–1868

The news of Appomattox cast a pall over the economic prospects of the Hawaiian kingdom. The Civil War had spawned soaring sugar prices; exports of that product in 1865 were ten times those of 1860. When prices slumped over the next couple of years, a number of planters went bankrupt, and those still operating begged King Kamehameha IV for relief. They wanted a reciprocity treaty with the United States that would open that huge market free of tariffs for their tropical crops. The royal government concurred, and General Edward M. McCook, the new U.S. minister to Honolulu, was equally in favor of such an agreement. In May 1867 he and the Hawaiian foreign minister signed a treaty to that effect.

A major opponent of reciprocity lurked offshore, however, in the person of Captain William Reynolds, commanding the *Lackawanna*. A worse choice for that time and place could hardly have been found, for the king and his advisers considered him personally objectionable. Reynolds knew Hawaii well, having lived there from 1852 to 1861, and was outspoken against McCook's treaty, for he wanted American annexation of the islands and feared that reciprocity might delay it.

The *Lackawanna* had been ordered to remain in Hawaii until further notice, "to guard the interests of your government most faithfully." Honolulu notified Washington that it could not tolerate the permanent stationing of a foreign warship in its waters, and the treaty could not be ratified while she was there. In his correspondence with the department, Reynolds was scathing in his remarks about the Hawaiian authorities, asserting that their demands for his withdrawal were only "a silly and frivolous pretext . . . to trifle with the Government of the United States"; in short, "a piece of chicanery and humbug." Luckily for the treaty's prospects, he was called away for two months on other business, during which the king approved the reciprocity understanding.

Rear Admiral Henry K. Thatcher had told Reynolds to take possession of remote Midway, today classified as part of the Hawaiian archipelago. There is no reason to believe that the ceremonies on 28 August were impressive, for the atoll was uninhabited. This acquisition is, nonetheless, of some historical interest. The almost simultaneous purchase of Alaska marked the addition of the first noncontiguous territory in North America. Except for Navassa, the tiny guano island near Haiti taken in 1858, Midway became the first overseas U.S. possession.

Much to the annoyance of the Hawaiians, the *Lackawanna* was back in their waters early in October and remained until May 1868, despite continued remonstrances. When Reynolds was finally recalled, Welles wrote in his *Diary* that all the captain had accomplished was to aggravate "a spirit of mischief among those islands." Yet Reynolds's opinion temporarily prevailed over that of McCook and the Hawaiians, for American opposition to reciprocity was too strong. Its defeat was due in part to those who resented the potential loss of tariff revenues, in part to others who agreed with Reynolds that the adoption of the pact would possibly thwart U.S. annexation of the archipelago. For three years the treaty was tabled by committees, and when the Senate finally voted on it in June 1870, the bare majority for it fell well short of the two-thirds essential for adoption.[6]

Admiral Alexander M. Pennock at Honolulu, 1873

Despite its defeat, the Hawaiian-American reciprocity issue failed to die. Exports of sugar languished during the early 1870s, and again planters began beating their drums for a tariff-free understanding. The death of King Kamehameha V in 1872 left two claimants to the throne: the top-ranking chief Prince William Charles Lunalilo and Prince David Kalakaua. The pro-annexationist U.S. Minister Henry A. Peirce asked Washington to station a man-of-war off Honolulu "*as soon as possible*" and keep it "in those waters constantly"; Admiral Alexander M. Pennock in the *California* arrived there two weeks later. Lunalilo was elected, much to popular acclaim.

The relatively pro-American new king set to work for reciprocity by adding an enticement. He implied that Washington might be able to lease or buy Pearl Harbor, by far the best natural site for a naval base in the North Pacific. The ploy backfired. Many Polynesian Hawaiians feared that the alienation of Pearl Harbor would be the opening wedge for their loss of independence, a stand strongly backed by the pro-British advocates in the islands. The issue was settled by Secretary of State Fish, who informed Peirce that although Hawaii might one day become American, "for the present the government has no *arriere pensée* [ulterior motive]" in that direction. Along with annexationist hopes, the reciprocity question faded into the background.[7]

Commanders George E. Belknap and Joseph S. Skerrett at Honolulu, 1874

The next Hawaiian crisis affecting the U.S. Navy grew out of the approaching end of Lunalilo's reign, for tuberculosis had been added to the ravages of his chronic addiction to alcohol; he died early in February after ruling for less than 13 months. There were once again two rivals to succeed to the throne: Prince David Kalakaua and Queen Emma, the widow of Kamehameha IV, known as a backer of British interests. Peirce, strongly behind Kalakaua, was sure that his man would be selected but was equally positive that Emma's advocates would not accept this verdict without violent protest. He prepared for the expected emergency by warning the commanders of the three foreign warships in the harbor—Commander George E. Belknap in the *Tuscarora*, Commander Joseph S. Skerrett in the *Portsmouth*, and the captain of HMS *Tenedos*—that in all probability their services would be required to keep or restore order in Honolulu.

In mid-February the Hawaiian legislature convened in the city's courthouse and chose Kalakaua by better than a six-to-one margin, after which the enraged devotees of Emma stormed the building, attacking those who had voted for the victor, killing one and injuring others. Within ten minutes 150 Americans and 70 Britons dashed ashore in their boats, to put to flight the rioters "like rats out of a burning barn." In a little over a week the servicemen were back in their vessels. Well before, Peirce had visited the defeated queen, begging her to call upon her supporters to accept the verdict, and she had complied at once. The general satisfaction in Washington about this denouement was reflected by Secretary Robeson, who "highly commended" the naval operations, adding that official thanks for them had been received from Hawaiian authorities.[8]

Admiral John J. Almy at Honolulu, 1874–1875

Once Kalakaua was firmly in power, Hawaiian-American relations improved. Admiral John J. Almy may have contributed a bit to this development, for unlike Reynolds he was a great favorite of the king and his top functionaries. From his flagship, the *Pensacola*, he kept his total of five warships rotating in and out of Honolulu without protest from the royal government. It must be admitted, however, that the main duty of officers under the admiral's direction was to serve as passenger-liner captains. The *Benicia* carried Kalakaua, his party, and Minister Peirce to San Francisco in November 1874, and the king returned in the *Pensacola* the next February.

The primary result of Kalakaua's warmly greeted nation-wide tour of the United States was to bring into being the Hawaiian-American reciprocity treaty, signed in January 1875, that established practically free trade between the two countries. Senators liked its proviso that Honolulu would never dispose of any of its land or grant special privileges to any nation other than the United States. Trade between the two flourished to such an extent as to fulfill Peirce's prophecy that reciprocity "would bind these islands to the United States with hoops of steel." In 1887 the navy received its base at Pearl Harbor, another step on the way to an American Hawaii. All the islands were annexed in 1898.[9]

Other Islands of the Pacific, 1867–1881
Captain Fabius Stanley at Levuka, 1867

Except for Hawaii, the only archipelagos that caught the American naval eye after 1865 were Fiji and Samoa, those earlier twin hotbeds of violence. The intricacies and occasional hostile landings of the 1850s that marked the navy at Fiji had revolved in large part around the claims of Consul John B. Williams and other Americans, the details of which have been described before. Sinclair in 1858 had forced Thakombau, the self-designated king of all the islands, to admit that he owed $45,000 to the interested parties. But nothing happened for the next nine years; more pressing Civil War exigencies could spare no warship for a debt-collecting cruise to the Southwest Pacific, and the neglect continued after 1865. The Department finally ordered Captain Fabius Stanley in the *Tuscarora* to Levuka for that purpose, warning him to commit no hostile acts while there. He managed to stay inside the bounds of the latter instruction, but just barely. According to Fiji's leading historian, he called Thakombau aboard his vessel to be "browbeaten" during a "stormy interview" in which the captain "threatened to shell the township—indeed he took up a position to do so."

The Fijian was given no option other than to sign a treaty in June 1867 (which proved abortive), promising that he would meet the amount required, which Stanley had calculated at precisely $43,516.18, although he generously forgave $20,000 in accumulated interest. Payment was to be divided into four equal installments, commencing the next May. Should Thakombau default, three small islands in his domain would be ceded to the United States for sale in order to settle the claims.[10]

Commander William T. Truxtun at Levuka, 1869

By no means could Thakombau meet the financial terms dictated by Stanley, and the department had to dispatch Commander William T. Truxtun in the *Jamestown* to Fiji under orders to settle the matter of the claims once and for all. During his stay there in October and November, he managed to complete his assignment. He set up a court of inquiry composed of himself as president, two of his officers, and two resident U.S. citizens, one of them a claimant. The judges ruled that all such debts incurred by Thakombau before 1859 were valid and must be paid, with one exception. The sum owed to the estate of Consul Williams (he had died in 1860) was nullified, for a search of the Levuka consulate records could find no explanation of how a total of $5,000 in 1851 had swollen to almost $20,000 by 1868. Truxtun also took the occasion to denounce Boutwell for his tendency in 1855 "to harass and annoy the old King. . . . it is making us appear contemptible in the eyes of all Foreign nations, and causes these half civilized people to regard us with feelings not akin to love."

Thakombau finally met his obligations, thanks to the Polynesia Company, organized by Australian investors. The king was so eager to rid himself of this onus that he made his mark on a contract by which the company would pay the American claimants $42,248. In return the investors were awarded 200,000 scattered acres within which they could make laws, set up courts, collect customs duties, enjoy a banking monopoly over all of Fiji, and buy additional land. But London refused to countenance the agreement, and the investors had to sign a second contract with Thakombau, voiding most of the sweeping governmental and monopolistic powers granted them in the first. Within a year the Americans collected their claims, but the Polynesia Company failed to make money and soon went bankrupt.

After Fiji became a British colony in 1874, American interests there, economic and strategic, dwindled to practically nothing, ending the need for further U.S. naval visits of diplomatic consequence.[11]

Truxtun at the Gilbert Islands, 1870

That spring Truxtun took the *Jamestown* north to the far-flung Gilbert archipelago. In May he collected eight chiefs from Abaiang, Tarawa, and Butaritari (Makin) islands and persuaded them to make their marks on a treaty with him. Victims of shipwrecks were to be cared for until a rescuing vessel appeared, and the rights of missionaries and merchants to ply their trades guaranteed, but the latter two must first obtain permission from the insular authorities. This agreement seems to have been honored.[12]

Commander Richard W. Meade, Jr., at Pago Pago, 1872; and Captains Ralph Chandler and James H. Gillis at Apia, 1879, 1881

By the late 1860s Samoa was well on its way to becoming the international plaything that it would be for the remainder of the century. German, British, and American planters and traders, clustered about their own consuls, were elbowing one another in efforts to take advantage of local tribal wars in order to dominate the islands. William H. Webb, an American entrepreneur and land speculator, set up a mail-carrying steamship company to connect San Francisco with Sydney and Auckland via Honolulu. The distance between Hawaii and Britain's Australasian colonies was so great that a Samoan port was deemed essential for coaling and repairs. Washington learned of the report of Webb's agent describing Pago Pago, on Tutuila Island, as the "most perfect land-locked harbor that exists in the Pacific Ocean," and that the entire island was a "garden spot," ideal for planters.

Admiral John A. Winslow, commanding the Pacific Station from Honolulu, talked about Samoa with Minister Henry A. Peirce, who thought it "very important that the Navigator [Samoan] Islands should be under American control—ruling through native authorities." Commander Richard W. Meade, Jr., in the *Narragansett* was selected to start this process. He wrote Secretary Robeson that he would survey Pago Pago and choose a spot for a coaling depot, adding, "I think some kind of a treaty with the native chiefs will be necessary to frustrate foreign influence." He came into Pago Pago in February 1872, staying there for about a month. On the 17th Meade signed a pact with Mauga, the most prominent chief in the area, giving the United States "the exclusive privilege of establishing in the said harbor . . . a naval station." In exchange, Mauga and his people were to enjoy "the friendship and *protection* . . . of the United States [emphasis added]."

Although the *New York Times* headlined, "Our New Possession: The Navigator Islands Part of the United States," rocks and shoals lay ahead for Meade's work. Could a treaty signed by the individual Mauga bind other chiefs? International objections were highlighted by the rapid appearance of the German consul at Apia in Pago Pago to protest the exclusiveness of the agreement. Nonetheless, Robeson, Fish, and Grant all praised Meade's "great judgment and skill" and sent his treaty to the Senate, only to have it tabled by the Foreign Relations Committee; it never even came to a vote. In addition to the other doubts as to its validity, some senators worried that Meade's use of the word "protection" might result in entanglements with Britons and Germans, both deeply concerned about the islands and both possessing strong navies.

Little energy need be expended on the remaining two American naval visits to Samoa. In July 1879 Captain Ralph Chandler in the *Lackawanna* showed up while a tribal clash was going on between one faction backed by the Germans and English and another considered more pro-American. Chiefs of the first were welcomed aboard the ship but given no salute; a salute was extended to representatives of the friendlier tribe a few hours later. Resentment over this slight caused a fear that disorders might become widespread. British and American naval and diplomatic personnel hurriedly convened and persuaded Chandler to salute the aggrieved party, an act that satisfied everyone.

Two years later Captain James H. Gillis in the same ship tried to halt a civil war while promoting American interests. Under the direction of the U.S. consul his British and German counterparts were brought to the *Lackawanna*, where they agreed on one chief as "king" of the whole archipelago, but conditions remained volatile.[13]

The Samoans themselves in 1878 had sent Chief La Mamea to Washington. Although he could not persuade the Rutherford B. Hayes administration to guarantee the security of his people, he was able to sign an agreement considerably watered down from Meade's promise of "protection." In it the United States would have the right, if not the exclusive privilege, of using Pago Pago as a naval base, while America would use its "good offices" to help the islanders settle their controversies with "any other Governments." This was Samoa's first treaty, to be soon followed by others with Britain and Germany. In 1889 a joint tripartite rule of the concerned powers lasted for a turbulent decade. After London withdrew, following Berlin's grant of compensatory land in Africa, the archipelago was divided in 1899 between the other two. Germany gained the western islands, centered at Apia, and the United States the eastern, with their capital at Pago Pago. New Zealand acquired the former as a League of Nations mandate in 1919, and in 1962 they became the independent country of Western Samoa. At this writing, the eastern islands form what is still an unincorporated and unorganized territory of the United States.

Summary

Although the navy's influence on the nation's international relations over these sixteen years was considerably less than during earlier times, something new happened and several familiar patterns were repeated. Except for Navassa, never before 1867 had the United States gone beyond its borders to annex territory, as it did in buying Alaska and taking Midway atoll. Although a generation would have to pass before American imperialism came into full flower, the United States for better or worse had taken its first steps along a road leading to the imperialistic acquisitions of 1898 and later.

Handling an issue that had plagued officers from the beginning, Case, in Spain, and Goldsborough and Farragut, in Crete, had to dissipate the pro-rebel sympathies of U.S. diplomats or naval subordinates in order to maintain a proper neutrality in civil wars. During the British bombardment of Alexandria, Nicholson apparently conducted himself impeccably in his peace-keeping operations. As before, maritime force was used or threatened in this period. This aggressiveness was commendable in Belknap's and Skerrett's bloodless dispersal of rioters in Honolulu; considerably less so when Worden's warships leveled their guns at Tripoli to back an unworthy U.S. consul, and when Stanley moved to shell Levuka to compel Thakombau's acceptance of an unfair treaty. Pennock and Almy, in Hawaii, may have made a small contribution to the establishment of an American naval base at Pearl Harbor, but their function was primarily to supply transportation for Hawaiian royalty.

As for diplomacy involving neither neutrality nor compulsion, Reynolds, with his outspoken advocacy of Hawaiian annexation, deliberately did what he could to delay for years a reciprocity treaty with the United States, so essential to Honolulu. Truxtun's approach in Fiji was much superior to that of Stanley, but he was lucky that the Polynesia Company appeared at the right moment to pay the American claimants. His "treaty" with the Gilbert islanders appears productive. Finally, Meade reached accords with the Samoans by persuasive arguments rather than coercion. Even though the Senate refused to accept his treaty, as Joan I. Brookes has emphasized, both Americans and Samoans behaved as if it were binding until La Mamea's formal agreement in 1878. Minister to Honolulu Peirce saw an analogy between Meade at Samoa and Thomas a. C. Jones at Hawaii in 1826. Both treaties likewise remained unratified, but all concerned apparently abided by them until they were replaced by formal pacts.

CHAPTER NINETEEN

Commodore Robert W. Shufeldt

1879–1883

From West Africa to the Far East, 1879–1880, and the First U.S. Treaty with Korea, 1880–1883

For a study of the U.S. navy from its constitutional beginning in 1798, the later career of Commodore Robert W. Shufeldt forms a natural termination. His long voyage in the *Ticonderoga* in 1878–1880 took him first around Africa, along the northern rim of the Indian Ocean, and through Southeast Asia, bringing these areas back into these pages for the first time since the pre–Civil War period. He ended his cruise in China and Japan, laying the foundation for the first American treaty with Korea, signed in 1882 and ratified the next year. It also marks the end of significant contributions by U.S. naval officers to the country's foreign relations, for Shufeldt's basically one-man show would seldom if at all be duplicated by his later colleagues. Although collaborations between naval officers and diplomats had been frequent since the formation of an independent Navy Department in 1798, with continued advances in communications, decisions were made, by and large, not by warship commanders but by State Department representatives abroad or in Washington. Finally, just after the Korean treaty was being considered and adopted, initial planning and construction of a more modern navy were under way, a renewal that kept on accelerating. By the 1890s the nation's diplomacy could be conducted from an increasingly strong-navy position, certainly in contrast to that necessitated by the service's decline after 1865.

Shufeldt, chief of the navy's Bureau of Recruiting and Equipment from 1875 to 1878, was in a position to start improving what he and practically every other officer saw as the deplorable condition of their service. If Admiral David Dixon Porter had exaggerated in 1869 when he wailed to Shufeldt, "The Navy is all gone!" he would have been closer to the truth a decade later. The commodore, through his cordial and almost daily meetings with Navy Secretary Richard W. Thompson, was able to execute some of his ideas on launching a naval renaissance.

The key, as Shufeldt viewed it, was the revival of the pre–Civil War naval-commercial alliance, which had been accomplished without federal aid, this time to be federally subsidized. Ever since 1865 Americans had concentrated their attention on internal expansion and development, while their merchant marine lolled in depression and the country's overseas carrying trade slumped ever lower. He published an influential letter originally written to a member of the House Naval Affairs Committee under the title *The Relation of the Navy to the Commerce of the United States*. In it he emphasized that foreign trade was essential both as a measure of national greatness and as a consumer of industrial and agricultural overproduction. The means to achieve a healthy foreign trade would be the building of a fleet of governmentally subsidized, fast, armed, steel-constructed, and mail-carrying steamers; in peacetime they would protect commerce, but they would have been built to allow rapid conversion to warships once hostilities broke out. They would, of course, require American-controlled coaling stations and repair facilities abroad. He called upon history to support his recommendations. The navy–merchant marine partnership before 1861 had been "linked to every act which made the nation great" when it acted for the "aggrandizement of American commerce."

Shufeldt also held that the navy, despite its current decrepitude, would be essential in aiding the country to develop markets outside Europe, where expansion was unlikely, because of intense competition. Instead, new ones in the less highly industrialized parts of the world should be discovered and utilized. Abolish the European (formerly Mediterranean) Squadron and send its components elsewhere, he urged, for it caused national humiliation. From their well-armored and armed warships, European officers gazed with wondering contempt and veiled smiles at the relatively unprotected American anachronisms, still carrying smooth-bore guns, as they plodded back and forth from Gibraltar to Constantinople, welcoming aboard local dignitaries for what Shufeldt called "gala fo'c's'le frolics." An officer reported that service in the Mediterranean made one "a member of a perpetual yachting party."

Trade should be encouraged with non-European countries, which could become part of the American commercial empire. Much of Latin America could be pulled into place by a canal through Mexico's Isthmus of Tehuantepec, dug and owned by America, and Shufeldt doggedly continued to advocate that project well after it became clear that any such canal would go through Nicaragua or Panama. He believed that up-to-date warships must eventually be provided to promote the country's commercial opportunities in Africa, the Indian Ocean, Southeast Asia, and East Asia. But until such ships became available, even outmoded American men-of-war could furnish valuable service in far-flung underdeveloped areas.

From Liberia to South Africa, January–September 1879

On 7 December 1878 Shufeldt sailed from Norfolk in the *Ticonderoga*, a sizable 11-gun, wooden warship, constructed early in the Civil War. Captain Bartlett J. Cromwell was her commander; there is no evidence that he made any diplomatic contribution whatever. The commodore's instructions from Thompson, although mentioning a few specific places to be visited, were couched in generalities, leaving much to the commodore's judgment. He should go to the "unfrequented ports of Africa, Asia, the islands of the Persian Ocean, and adjacent seas . . . with a view to the encouragement and extension of American Commerce."

Liberia was the cynosure of Shufeldt's attention, for he looked upon it as "the garden spot of Africa." With its long coastline and supposed easy entry into the interior, it would "become of the greatest commercial importance to the United States" as a large consumer of American exports. Most important, he planned to base his subsidized steamship fleet there. Although Liberia had once been considered an "American colony," Washington had not even recognized it as an independent nation until 1847, having left it in abeyance for the 20 years since the American Colonization Society had landed black freedmen there. By the late 1870s Liberia had become embroiled in two controversies—to the northwest over its boundary with British Sierra Leone and to the southeast over its jurisdiction over Grebo tribesmen, adjacent to what would become the Ivory Coast.

On 15 January the *Ticonderoga* docked at Freeport, capital of Sierra Leone, and Shufeldt began a most boring and frustrating three-month stay. He quickly discovered that the area in question, a small coastal

Robert W. Shufeldt
(Official U.S. Navy Photo)

enclave, had been forcibly taken by a former Liberian president. Hence the British held all the trumps and would neither accept Shufeldt as a mediator in the dispute nor make any concessions to the Liberians. Three years after the *Ticonderoga*'s departure, troops from Sierra Leone recaptured the enclave, accompanied by menacing flourishes by the Royal Navy. The commodore also looked into the other controversy, in which Grebo tribal leaders were denying Monrovia's jurisdiction over them, shrugging off both American and Liberian appeals to accept its rule. Eventually

Grebo lands were annexed by French soldiers from the Ivory Coast. Since Liberia was central to Shufeldt's plan, his initial West African experience was a severe blow to his grandiose concept of a steamship network to promote American trade.

In May he put into the small Spanish island of Fernando Po (Bioko), south of modern Nigeria and west of Cameroon, hoping to use it as a substitute for Liberia. He thought of recommending that his government buy it, perhaps a simple matter, for it existed primarily as a prison colony. But he realized that America's noncolonization policy would make such a purchase most unlikely, so he fell back to advocating that a site for a naval coaling station might be leased there. But his idea of a leasehold at Fernando Po was given short shrift in Washington.

As the commander set out toward the Congo River's mouth, he had little hope of achieving anything, for he knew that Belgium's King Leopold II was on his way to setting up the infamous "Congo Free State," his personal possession, based upon merciless exploitation of African workers. He sent an officer up the Congo to check on a story that a tribal chief had assaulted Americans from a merchantman, but his errand was futile. Shufeldt quickly left the river, expressing to the secretary his angry disapproval of Leopold's policies. The *Ticonderoga* soon left for the distant island of St. Helena, in the mid-Atlantic, where most of the ship's fever victims were cured.

Shufeldt arrived in southern Africa early in August and found a situation different from those in sites already visited. The British had taken it from the Dutch in 1815, but within two decades many white Afrikaners (Boers) of Dutch, German, and French descent had trekked well to the north, eventually setting up Transvaal and the Orange Free State as their independent republics. Abandoning his usual Anglophobia, Shufeldt became convinced that the British, the representatives of uplift and modernization, would finally prevail over the Afrikaners, "surly in their immense farms— never learning and never forgetting anything—the political control of the country will pass out of their hands." As for the blacks, their fate would be that of the Amerindians—"extermination." In any case the commander could forecast that European domination was so thoroughly implanted that any economic opportunities for Americans were vanishing.[1]

From Madagascar (Malagasy Republic) through the Comoro Islands, and Zanzibar, September–October 1879

After leaving Cape Town for islands off southeastern Africa, Shufeldt was entering an area where France, not Britain, was the leading expansionist. Time did not permit him to visit the more thickly settled northeastern part of Madagascar. Hova tribesmen there, from their capital of Tananarive, claimed sovereignty over all of that island but controlled only the east coast. Shufeldt went instead to the southwestern shore. He persuaded himself that the Hovas had no jurisdiction over the Sakalava and other tribes around Tullear Bay. Although he was aware that a U.S. consul had made a treaty with the Hovas in 1867 granting Americans most-favored-nation status and extrality, he decided that new understandings had to be drawn up along the western coast. He negotiated shipwreck conventions with several tribes and in one of them inserted the right to set up and maintain a U.S. coaling station at Tullear, but that proviso was ignored by the department.

At this point Shufeldt wrote the secretary an important evaluation of such treaties. The pacts with the Sakalavas and others, he continued, were not treaties at all but "simply agreements in writing, by virtue of which our people can be protected against the violence of a turbulent, savage, and often drunken population which acknowledges no other authority than the chiefs whose signatures we have obtained."

The commander's lodestar was, as always, the promotion of American commercial opportunities. Believing that his nation's $300,000 annual trade with the Hova-controlled eastern ports was unlikely to increase, he thought that his "treaties" would open western shores to American enterprise for the first time. It was not to be. First, he was undercut by W. W. Robinson, U.S. consul at Tananarive's seaport, an ardent Hova supporter, who in 1881 signed a new treaty granting that tribe rule over the entire island. Second, steadily increasing pressure brought all of Madagascar under French rule in the mid-1890s.

Shufeldt's next port of call was at Joanna (Anjouan), in the Comoros Islands, a few hundred miles northwest of Madagascar, which had been visited by American officers in 1841 and 1851. During his few days there early in October, he signed a comprehensive treaty with Sultan Abdallah gaining practically everything that nineteenth-century Americans desired in such remote areas: most-favored-nation status, residential and commercial rights, protection of shipwrecked sailors, and extrality. He forwarded his agreement with some enthusiasm to Washington, and the Hayes administration passed it along to the Senate, where, for unknown reasons, it was never accepted. The day after the treaty was concluded, in a letter to the White House Abdallah asked Hayes to take Joanna as a United States protectorate, because the Europeans might "soon be annexing this Island whether I wish it or not." Indeed, one of the Comoros had been seized by France as early as 1841. Soon, however, the sultan's

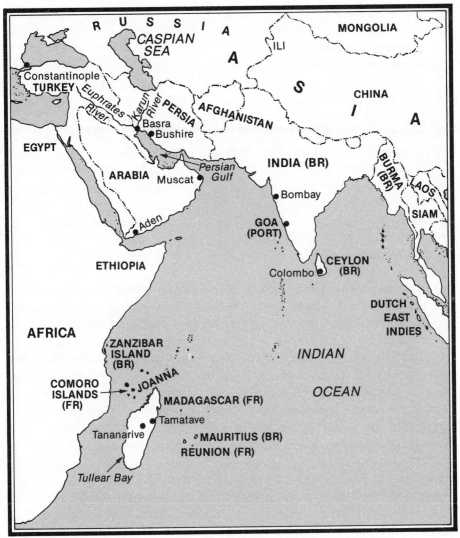

Indian Ocean Environs

letter was gathering dust in a government archive. In any case, the commodore was trying to stop a whirlwind; in 1886 Joanna became a French protectorate.

When Shufeldt arrived at Zanzibar on 9 October, he had moved from a sphere where the French power was felt to the great swathe from East Africa to Australia where the British predominated. Through the remainder of his cruise he pondered and worried about this supremacy, for as the historian Kenneth J. Hagan says, "As the British Empire grew, American commerce shrank."

Zanzibar was an assigned stop for the *Ticonderoga*. Secretary of State William M. Evarts wanted the commodore to investigate rumors that its sultan was discriminating against American trade and to ascertain whether the U.S. treaty of 1833 with Muscat-Zanzibar was still in effect. While being sumptuously regaled by Said (Sayid) Barghash, Shufeldt found during his two-week sojourn there that the terms of the 1833 treaty were being carried out satisfactorily. Barghash imitated Abdullah by asking that a letter be forwarded to President Hayes. Although he did not need official American protection, he requested that U.S. warships appear more often in East African waters to counter European machinations. Shufeldt was in complete accord with him, noting in a personal missive, "What a shame it is to keep a fleet at Nice, & send three [war]ships to Zanzibar in thirty years."

In addition to his own visit, he was alluding to the brief stopover of Captain Edmund P. Kennedy en route to Muscat in the *Peacock* during 1835; since that visit was for supplies only, it had no diplomatic significance. In 1851 James Aulick in the *Susquehanna*, on his way to his humiliating tour as commodore of the East India Squadron, made short visits to Joanna and Zanzibar, where, according to Robert E. Johnson, he had been "called on to settle controversies between local authorities and American merchants," doing so "to the satisfaction of all." Aulick also reestablished the recently vacated American consulate at Zanzibar.

As he prepared to leave, Shufeldt was despondent about the island's future, feeling sure it would become a British protectorate. Although American trade with Zanzibar had thrived 75 years before, by 1879 it was barely one-tenth that of the British. The commodore was on target; in 1890 the sultan went under the queen's protection and the death knell was sounded for U.S. commercial aspirations in East Africa.

From Aden to the Philippines, November 1879–March 1880

Shufeldt next went ashore at British Aden in southern Arabia for a few days early in November. He was impressed by its growing commercial and strategic value, close to the Suez Canal's terminus, but his expectations of increased sales of American cotton goods there were never fulfilled. After a tiresome passage the *Ticonderoga* came into Arabian Muscat, at the mouth of the Persian Gulf. It had steadily fallen in economic importance behind Zanzibar, its former partner. Sultan Seyyid Turki was controlled politically by the resident English consul, supported by a Royal

Navy gunboat stationed in the harbor. During December Shufeldt spent three unpleasant weeks at the top of the Persian Gulf, most of the time at Bushire and Basra, Iran. Even though they had no territorial possessions in the Gulf, the ubiquitous British were there, seizing most of the area's trade. Almost always throughout his cruise, Shufeldt lamented the paucity of U.S. diplomatic representation in most of the places where he called. For instance, no American official lived closer to the Persian Gulf than Constantinople. He pressed his argument to his government that wherever a consul and his flag resided, trade would be attracted. An American minister and consul were sent to Tehran in 1883, but State Department records show no nineteenth-century Persian Gulf consulates.

Stepping onto Indian soil at Bombay late in December, Shufeldt's disposition was not sweetened by the chilliness and aloofness with which British officialdom greeted him. During his two weeks there he struck back as best he could by writing at length to the Department about India, where, he thought, the British could rule only as long as the Royal Navy could keep imperial communications and supply lines intact. He was sure that in the long run Hindus and Moslems could be "neither grateful nor loyal" to their European masters. He hoped that one day American exports might "overshadow the Indian Empire even in its own markets." But for that purpose a revitalized U.S. steam and iron navy was mandatory. He asked the navy secretary, "Do we really mean 'to extend American influence' or are we to continue to play the role long ago assigned to us in China—of No. 2 Englishmen?"

Shufeldt decided that the press of other responsibilities cancelled prospective stopovers at Burma and Siam, so the *Ticonderoga* steamed all the way from Bombay to North Borneo, weighing anchor there late in February 1880. Secretary of State William M. Evarts had asked him to see if the U.S.-Brunei Treaty of 1850 had been broken when a British concern had bought or leased property belonging to an American company in that tiny enclave. Shufeldt sent one of his officers to meet with Brunei's sultan, who admitted that the transaction had taken place but had not realized that it had any relevance to the American treaty. The commodore called this example of "perfidious Albion" to Washington's attention, but apparently his letter was filed and forgotten.

The Philippines were the commodore's last stop on the way to Japan and China. In Manila during mid-March he surveyed the economic and political landscapes of that longtime Spanish colony. He thought that further diplomatic pressure on Spain, a "non-manufacturing country," could draw additional Filipino customers to American dry-goods counters; therefore U.S. consulates should be spotted among the islands, but Washington never followed through on his recommendation. When he headed for more tolerable climates, Shufeldt probably sighed with relief to escape the constant heat that had attended him for the past several months.[2]

From Japan to Korea and China, April–September 1880

When the *Ticonderoga* sliced into East Asian waters, Shufeldt kept before himself the light that had guided him from the beginning of the cruise—the need to usher in the American "Empire of the Seas." Korea was the only maritime country not yet opened to foreign intercourse, minimal trade with China and Japan excepted, and at the very least a shipwreck convention would have to be written. The rebuffs to the French and the Americans administered by the *Taewon'gun* a few years before had enhanced his authority, but the isolation of the "Hermit Kingdom" was drawing to a close; first the Japanese, then the Americans, and finally the other Western powers knocked at the door. After a surveying party had been fired upon in 1875, Tokyo imposed upon Korea the Treaty of Kangwha, gaining residential and commercial rights in three ports. Moreover, its opening sentence said that "Korea, being a self-governing nation, enjoys equality with Japan." This contradicted China's stand on the matter: "Chosen [Korea], being a dependent state of the Chinese Empire," was in effect a "vassal" of Peking, even though it had long conducted itself independently in domestic and foreign affairs. Shufeldt would try to take advantage of this discrepancy.

His orders from the department told him to go to Korea, explain away the Rodgers-Low assault of 1871 (which he easily did), and use "a moderate and conciliatory course" that might open "the ports of that country to American commerce." Hoping to use the diplomatic pressure exerted by the U.S. minister to China on Japan to expedite the matter, Shufeldt came into Nagasaki on 15 April and met obstructionism from both Tokyo and Seoul. The Japanese evinced no desire to add a new rival in East Asia and did little to help. Although the *Taewon'gun* had fallen from power, he and his xenophobic adherents were a force still potent, and the Koreans sent back the commodore's letter asking for a meeting there unopened, for it had named the country "Great Corai [sic]," rather than the correct title of "Great Chosen."

Shufeldt's despondency over this dash of ice water evaporated when he was invited to confer with Li Hung-chang, practically the de facto ruler of China under the Dowager Empress Tzu-hsi, the superintendent of trade for the ports of north China, and governor-general of Chihli Province, where Peking was located. Li was worried about the rising Japanese influence in Korea and told the commodore that he "would use his influence

. . . in behalf of the government of the United States" to promote a Korean-American treaty. Heartened by this influential backing, Shufeldt left for home in September, and the *Ticonderoga* entered San Francisco Bay "two years, more than fifty ports of call, and 36,000 miles after she cleared Cape Henry."[3]

Shufeldt's Korean Treaty, March–December 1881

Once in Washington, the commodore rang his own bell for a quick return to the Far East so that the momentum provided by Li Hung-chang would not be dissipated. James G. Blaine, President James A. Garfield's secretary of state, swung solidly behind him. Under the title of "naval attaché" to the U.S. legation in Peking, Shufeldt crossed the Pacific by private transportation, coming into Shanghai in June.

During July he met twice with Li, who had finally written Seoul urging that treaty negotiations with the Americans should commence. The Chinese recommended that Shufeldt wait in China for a reply, which might well take three months to arrive, considering the glacial pace of most Far Eastern negotiations. While almost three months inched past, the American was despondent about the lack of information and instructions from Washington. This silence was understandable, for Garfield had been shot on 2 July and did not succumb until 19 September. The transfer of power to the new Chester A. Arthur administration caused the resignation of Blaine in favor of Frederick T. Freylinghuysen in the State Department, and William E. Chandler became secretary of the navy. Shufeldt knew all this, but it was small comfort to him, since mail from the United States contained nothing of substance. Not until 15 December did Li inform him that a Korean answer had arrived, expressing a willingness to sign an American treaty. Shufeldt telegraphed this welcome information to Washington, implying that he should be named commissioner for that purpose. Blaine, just before his retirement, had already given him that honor, along with new instructions about what the treaty should contain, but the dispatch did not reach him until January. Had the commodore known about that letter he probably would not have committed an indiscretion that would come back to haunt him.

Shufeldt's Korean Treaty, January 1882–May 1883

Resentful about what he considered the cat-and-mouse game that the Chinese and Koreans were playing with him, around the beginning of the new year Shufeldt expressed opinions that he should have kept to himself. He sent an "open letter" (i.e., it could be published) to California Senator Aaron A. Sargent (a Sinophobe of the first water, who would use some of its statements to help him push through the Chinese Exclusion Act of 1882), who sent it to the press on 20 March. Secretary of State Freylinghuysen accurately characterized it as "extraordinary . . . brutal in its frankness." Shufeldt described Peking's military and political systems as archaic and corrupt. Since the Chinese possessed "an ineradicable hatred" of all foreigners and were impervious to reason, in dealing with them *"force"* must be used. American policy toward China should be *"purely selfish . . .* disregarding the fallacious idea of inter-national friendship." Governor-General Li, although "the absolute and despotic ruler of 400,000,000 of people," was under the sway of the Empress Tzu-hsi, "an ignorant, capricious, and immoral woman." Only the final decision of the Chinese and Koreans that a Washington-Seoul agreement would be beneficial to them enabled Shufeldt to hurdle the barrier thrown up by his own impetuosity.

The commodore was heartened by Freylinghuysen's telegram when he read it on the 7th. About two weeks later he perused Blaine's November letter enclosing President Arthur's authorization of him as commissioner to write a Korean treaty. The gist of its instructions emphasized that a shipwreck convention had to be the sine qua non of any agreement but that the United States would be happy "If the government of Corea (or Chosen) is willing to open its ports to our commerce as China and Japan have done." Shufeldt was warned not to resort to "force or to entreat such an action."

By mid-March it was clear that the U.S. treaty with Korea would be under Chinese auspices. Although Li did keep in touch with Kim Yun-sik, the Korean emissary, he so isolated him in China that Shufeldt never even met him. For the next several weeks, until early May, the commodore and the governor-general conversed, and during that period the treaty was endangered by a Sino-American controversy over delineating the precise relationship between Peking and Seoul. Li insisted that a proviso must be included in the treaty admitting that "Korea is a vassal state of China," even though it had "always enjoyed autonomy in both its internal and external affairs." This was completely unacceptable to Shufeldt, for it clouded the nature of any formal U.S. understanding with Korea. How could a sovereign nation complete a pact specifying equality with one characterized as a "vassal" of another country? Moreover, Li's qualification could well be interpreted as making the United States and China co-guarantors of Korean independence; Shufeldt pointed out that that would never be accepted by the Senate. After several drafts had passed back and forth, Li finally surrendered to the American's arguments, and an ostensible compromise was hammered out. The treaty itself would ignore completely the Chinese-Korean connection, but King Kojong of Korea would append to it a letter admitting his nation's dependency on China. Shufeldt cheerfully accepted this condition, correctly surmising that such a statement, not a part of the treaty, would be meaningless.

On 4 May Shufeldt went to Cheefoo (Tantai) and boarded the *Swatara*, a steam sloop provided by Admiral John M. B. Clitz, Asiatic Squadron commodore. Four days later he sailed for Korea and arrived off Inchon on the 12th. Li's influence on the entire affair was demonstrated by the presence of a leading Chinese diplomat and three Chinese warships. A Japanese man-of-war was also on hand, suggesting to Shufeldt that Tokyo now regretted its lack of cooperation with him in 1880. The ceremonies attending the signing of the pact were time-consuming and anticlimactic. Banquets, entertainments, and exchanges of presents occupied more than a week. On the 22nd the treaty was formally concluded with the signing of six copies in English and Chinese. Its terms, with one minor exception, were identical to those agreed upon by Li and Shufeldt in China, and King Kojong sent along with the text two letters to President Arthur. By the 26th the commodore was in Shanghai.

The fourteen articles of the first Korean-American pact, filling six printed pages, established the following: the reciprocal appointments of diplomatic personnel, a shipwreck convention, extrality, limitations on tariffs, prohibition of the opium traffic, and most-favored-nation status. Two points were unusual. Article I carried this ambiguous wording: "If other powers deal unjustly or oppressively with either Government, the other will exert their good offices . . . to bring about an amicable arrangement, thus showing their friendly feelings." This might be construed as an American pledge to keep Korea free, but certainly Washington never moved in any such direction. The other unusual provision was that, unlike earlier Western treaties in the Far East, this said nothing about Christian proselyting rights, an omission calculated evidently to allay opposition from the *Taewon'gun*'s anti-foreign supporters.

The U.S. Senate received the treaty in July, but its Committee on Foreign Relations did not report on it favorably until 9 January 1883; it was accepted on the same day, and ratifications were exchanged during May. Over the next few years, Britain, Germany, Italy, Russia, France, and Austria-Hungary modeled their agreements with Korea on that of Shufeldt.

The commodore thought that this accomplishment was the acme of his life's work. He wrote some time later, "I am very glad for the sake of our country that we were the pioneers in accomplishing the feat of bringing the last of the exclusive countries within the pale of Western Civilization." A naval colleague told him, "The making of the treaty will place you in history beside Perry, and when your detractors will have been long forgotten your name will still shine brighter than ever." It was not to be. Perhaps for every thousand Americans who have at least a vague awareness that Perry opened up Japan, one might realize that Shufeldt opened up Korea. Perry had been able to work independently and was backed by a powerful fleet composed of some of America's best and most modern warships. Shufeldt was compelled to appear in Korea with a single unimpressive vessel, and that in the shadow of Chinese warships. Nor could there be much of a comparison between contributing to the emergence of Japan, destined to be a great power, and doing the same for the relatively insignificant "Hermit Kingdom," pawn as it was of its more potent neighbors.

This difference was spotlighted by the way the press handled the agreements of 1854 and 1882. Although Shufeldt's work was by no means overlooked, its press coverage had no comparison with the lengthy articles and laudatory editorials that hailed Perry. Frederick T. Drake, Shufeldt's biographer, summarizes the difference: "There was no vote of thanks from a grateful Congress, no award of expenses to publish his manuscript of the cruise of the *Ticonderoga*, no plaudits from the press." Drake's last phrase is a little misleading. Most American newspapers told about Shufeldt's treaty, many of them with the full text, and some published verbatim his letter to Sargent. In early July 1882 the *New York Times* lauded him in a somewhat tongue-in-cheek editorial, but praise it was, nonetheless:

> Commodore R. W. SHUFELDT has been recalled from duty in China and Corea. It may be said that he comes home under a cloud. This is a pity, because he has served his country faithfully and well. . . . To say that SHUFELDT is the man to whom more than any other this great victory over Oriental exclusiveness is due is to give the gallant Commodore only his due meed of praise. . . . The letter . . . to Sargent revealed the hollowness and unsavoriness of Oriental diplomacy, ridiculed the emptiness of the Chinese military and naval establishment, and gave a graphic picture of the espionage, theft, and promiscuous black-mailing that prevail in the Chinese Government from the bottom to the top. . . . The letter was as interesting as a fairy tale and as real as the multiplication table. But it reached China at last and made the imperial dragon very mad. So Commodore SHUFELDT was recalled.

The effect of the Sargent letter continued to haunt him during the days of his rest in California that autumn. He had longed to command the Asiatic Squadron as Clitz's successor. Instead Secretary Chandler curtly rejected his appointment. A friend on the House Naval Affairs Committee told Shufeldt that it was because of "the letter you wrote to Sargent attacking the Chinese Government and which the Chinese representation here object to . . . as coming from an officer attached to the American Legation in China." Responding in October to a California newspaper account that said "his notorious letter was not intended for publication and that Sargent violated confidence in printing it," the commodore denied the allegation to Sargent: "I have never said publicly or privately that you had violated my confidence in publishing my letter. . . . It was marked an 'open letter' & . . . you had the right to so use it—Nevertheless it was not intended for that purpose. . . . I have suffered from it more than any other act of my life. . . . I have been summarily recalled from China & my Corean work to a great extent nullified."

In addition to refusing him the command of the Asiatic Squadron, the Arthur administration cold-shouldered him for the next few months. The president devoted considerable space to the Korean Treaty in his annual message of 4 December 1883, but did not mention Shufeldt. *Foreign Relations of the United States* for 1883 has ten pages of documentation on that subject; no correspondence of the commodore appears. His undiplomatic comments to Sargent seem to have been only part of the reason for this frigid treatment. Freylinghuysen evidently regarded him as Blaine's man and hoped to have the treaty concluded by John R. Young, an Arthur appointee just named minister to China. According to Paullin, Young "could not conceal his profound disappointment" on learning that his rival had already accomplished that task.

Although the harm done to his diplomatic reputation was irrevocable, Shufeldt overestimated the damage caused him by the Sargent letter. The treaty process continued on its way to a successful conclusion despite it. Li obviously knew its contents, including the unflattering references to him and the empress. Yet evidently he alluded to it only once, permitting the American to explain it away on a technicality. Nor did it ruin Shufeldt's naval career. Washington's negative attitude toward him abruptly changed for the better. He was promoted to rear admiral and presided over the influential Naval Advisory Board from 1882 until his retirement early in 1884.

Summary

If one were using a diplomatic scorecard for Shufeldt's actual accomplishments during his cruise from West Africa into the Far East (1879–1880), he would have to give the commodore a string of zeros. He was unable to deal satisfactorily with either of Liberia's disputes with the British or the Grebo tribes. No U.S. coaling station at Fernando Po ever came into being. Nothing that he could do would stop his nation's commerce from being squeezed out of the Congo and South Africa. The commodore's plan to open Madagascar's west coast to American trade by treaties with the Sakalava chiefs was frustrated; any prospects for a base at Tullear Bay terminated at the same time. His single most impressive diplomatic victory was his Washington-approved treaty with Sultan Abdallah of Joanna, but the Senate pigeon-holed it, and a U.S. protectorate in the Comoro Islands was never seriously considered. He was able to ensure that the 1833 pact with Muscat-Zanzibar was still applicable in 1879, but he could not ward off the British tentacles reaching out for Zanzibar. London was so thoroughly in charge from Aden through India that no effort of his could halt the trend toward the decline rather than the advancement of American trade in the Indian Ocean. Everything that he did to promote his country's commerce in North Borneo and the Spanish Philippines turned out to be equally sterile.

Shufeldt often asserted that his basic aim was to open new opportunities for American trade in areas where it was relatively insignificant. This could be realized only through a naval renaissance. That in turn was dependent upon a merchant marine revived to an approximation of its magnitude during the 1850s, when it was successfully challenging that of Britain in global competition. He was sure that the "Mistress of the Seas" had attained its supremacy, not merely by the fire-power of its navy, but by its essential supplement—a fleet of swift modern liners in its peacetime carrying trade. In emergencies the steamers were ready to be used as troop transports and supply ships, and some were convertible to Royal Navy auxiliaries.

Instead, every square foot of the African continent, except for Liberia and Ethiopia, fell under European occupancy—the final step was Italy's wrenching Libya away from Turkey in 1911—and the figures tell what happened. Drake erred in his conclusion about Shufeldt's voyage: "Africa became the subject of considerable debate in the country, but the fruit of Shufeldt's enterprises were not gathered until after the 1890s." He should have checked the U.S. Bureau of Census's *Historical Statistics of the United States* (1975) and its *Statistical Abstract of the United States* (1985; 1983 is the last year included). He would have found that when the commodore started trying to change the patterns of American overseas trade in 1879, of total American exports and reexports, amounting to $712,000,000, those to Europe were $594,000,000 (73%), those to Africa $5,000,000 (about 0.1%). Later figures were as follows:

U.S. EXPORTS AND REEXPORTS

	To Europe	To Africa
1900	75%	0.1%
1913	60%	0.7%
1939	41%	4.0%
1983	29%	4.0%

In short, while the proportion of U.S. exports to Europe declined sharply, those to Latin America, the Middle East, and the Far East soared. But in over a century, those to Africa, where Shufeldt hoped to create new customers for American goods, had merely moved from the totally to the relatively insignificant.[4]

As a naval strategist the commodore scores better. To be sure, he concluded that in peacetime the navy should restrict itself to protecting the nation's commerce abroad and its shores at home, becoming wartime raiders against the enemy's merchant marine. Mahan and his followers, however, opted for sea power that would match European armadas. Shufeldt's chief service came from his official reports, publications, and correspondence, departmental and private, that kept the Navy in both the official and the public eye. As president of the Naval Advisory Board in 1882–1884, he cooperated admirably with Secretary William E. Chandler to start out along the road leading to a modern sea arm through appropriations for the "ABCD" ships. Perhaps an adequate, if lukewarm, summary of Shufeldt's work in 1879–1880 is that considering the staggering odds against him, he accomplished about as much as anyone else could have done.

In the last analysis, trends more international than American in the Far East, denied Shufeldt the accolades he deserved. In China and Korea, as well as in the areas he visited during the earlier portions of the *Ticonderoga*'s cruise, he tried bravely and vainly to check the onrushing tides of history. In aiding Korea to emerge from behind its centuries-old walls, he ensured that it would be regarded, at least for a while, as an independent state rather than China's minion, and his treaty marked the path that the European nations would follow. When the widely heralded pact brought off by Perry in 1854 and the comparatively ignored agreement of 1882 are compared, one finds that Shufeldt gained much more substantial benefits for his country than did Perry in his "Wood and Water Treaty," in which Americans received only permission to get supplies, a shipwreck convention, and most-favored-nation standing.

For a time Li Hung-chang looked upon the U.S.-Korean treaty as a Chinese triumph, for by it "Japan's aggression" would be checked, but events dictated otherwise. Any lingering traces of Chinese control over the peninsula evaporated in the wake of the Sino-Japanese War of 1894–1895, opening the way for Russia to become the roadblock against Japan's drive for hegemony over Korea. By the time of the tsar's defeat in 1905, Korean reformers belatedly awoke to an awareness that they had escaped other potential masters only to fall to Japan's ruthless imperialists, who crushed any resistance and took over the nation completely in 1910.

Shufeldt, who died on 7 November 1895, lived long enough to know about the establishment of Japan's protectorate over the country he had aided, but at least he was spared awareness of Korea's 40-year-long obliteration as an independent entity. Nor could he realize on his deathbed that never again would an American naval officer be officially empowered to affect United States foreign policy so directly as he.

CHAPTER TWENTY

Recapitulation

The categories of the diplomatic activities performed by U.S. naval officers in 1798–1883 were the following: (1) protection and enhancement of commerce; (2) making war; (3) peacetime aggression; (4) treaty-making or negotiating; (5) nonbelligerent diplomacy; (6) affiliation; (7) humanitarianism; (8) expansionism.

These categories are by no means exclusive. A single naval visit shows four. When Commodore George C. Read in the frigate *Columbia* and the sloop *John Adams* spent a few days in northwestern Sumatra over New Year's, 1838–1839, retaliating for an assault upon a Salem pepper ship, he was primarily a commerce protector, trying to ensure that similar outrages would not recur. But first he sent an officer ashore to discuss the matter with local officials, becoming a nonbelligerent diplomatic activist. Failing to receive satisfactory explanations or apologies, he shelled and burned two small towns in an act of peacetime aggression. He finished by signing informal agreements with nearby rajahs, who pledged amity for Americans in the future; thus he engaged in treaty-making.

1. Protection and enhancement of commerce: Almost every secretary of the navy from 1798 to 1883 hammered home this activity as the naval officer's primary responsibility. Nearly all the other activities somehow affected this dominant priority. This activity was more common in the early nineteenth century than later, reaching its height during the Latin American rebellions against Spain, especially in southwestern South America and the Caribbean. Rebel and Royalist alike announced without adequate warning patently illicit blockades against one another and granted licenses to scores of privateersmen who often became pirates. By the 1840s, however, foreign conflicts that might have endangered American shipping were conducted more or less in accordance with current international law. The stronger maritime power announced its blockade well before it took effect, and Anglo-American offensives practically eradicated the privateersman-pirate. The statistics are revealing. About half of the officer activities constituting protection of commerce occurred during the quarter-century from about 1810 to 1835. In the 1850s, the most active decade for American naval diplomacy, only six were of this kind.

2. *Making war*: Since the United States was at at war for only 17 of the 85 years covered in this work, warriors appear less often than their bellicose colleagues when peace reigned. Yet exigencies during official hostilities sometimes permitted them to take drastic actions that would have been sure to bring down upon them strong departmental disapproval and punishment had they occurred in more tranquil times.

3. *Peacetime aggression*: During the 68 years in which the nation was at peace, naval officers sometimes behaved in ways similar to war-makers. Resorting to coercion, they either shot their guns to achieve their objectives or, keeping them silent, gained much the same result by intimidation. Yet they always had to be aware that the secretary's peacetime instructions invariably warned them that amicable relations must be maintained with all other nations and if there were conflicts between other countries, the officers must practice the strictest neutrality. This would surely apply to nations with which the United States had formal diplomatic relations, although the Navy Department tended to shrug off punitive expeditions in Pacific islands (Hawaii and existing European colonies excepted) or along the shores of West Africa.

4. *Treaty-making or negotiation*: Officers engaged in this activity were seldom appointed to accomplish that purpose in solitary splendor. Perry in Japan in 1853–1854 and Shufeldt in Korea in the early 1880s were the most conspicuous examples of those who were. More frequently they were ordered to cooperate with an accompanying presidentially appointed agent or a resident U.S. minister abroad. Occasionally officer-directed negotiations that failed at the time resulted later in a signed and ratified pact, after conditions that had militated against success changed for the

better. Often an officer wrote a so-called "treaty" with tribal chieftains in remote locales where no American diplomatic representatives were stationed.

5. *Nonbelligerent diplomacy*: This is something of a catchall for the peacetime actions of officers affecting their nation's external relations that do not naturally fall into one of the other categories. In the earliest years they had to bear tribute to North Africa. Later, without coercion or even a show of it, they labored to maintain American neutrality when wars erupted overseas, dickered with local functionaries over whether their sailors and marines should be sent ashore to quell assaults on law and order, argued for the release of confiscated merchant ships, or tried to rescue their fellow countrymen in danger or in captivity. From time to time an officer would be sent on fact-finding voyages, scientific or otherwise; to carry a U.S. minister to his appointed capital; or to earn the gratitude and friendship of foreign dignitaries by providing them with transportation in an American man-of-war.

6. *Affiliation*: Commanders, during their cruises, almost always talked with the U.S. ministers at their ports of call; if none was available, at least with the American consul. The only such associations mentioned in this book are those very few that led to collaboration, with some sort of diplomatic consequence. Often the implementation of Washington's foreign policies was promoted or frustrated by the personal chemistry between naval officers and diplomatic appointees or special envoys of the president.

7. *Humanitarianism*: With so much unpleasantness in the conduct of naval diplomacy, it is refreshing to contemplate the many benevolent naval officers. Sometimes they were ordered by the department to perform humanitarian duties. More often they did so on their own initiative, responding to emergencies by saving castaways, carrying to safety noncombatants trapped by hostile outbreaks, or going ashore at ports to end insurrections or riots. If they landed at the invitation of local authorities and completed their tasks without bloodshed, and if there were no diplomatic sequels of note, they were humanitarians. Furthermore, a few of those officers already described as peacetime aggressors deserve inclusion here, provided that their original motive was clearly humanitarian, even though unforeseen events compelled them to resort to force.

8. *Expansionism*: Knowing that their nation wished no noncontiguous or overseas possessions, few officers acted to acquire distant naval bases or colonies. Indeed, while discussing this subject with tribal leaders, U.S. commanders often pointed out how differently Washington viewed expansionism than did London or Paris. Therefore, unlike the Europeans,

Americans would not use agreements as opening wedges for conquest. There were some exceptions: the occupation of Midway Island in the Pacific, unimportant until 1941, and Navassa in the Caribbean, of no use whatever; the inept presidential attempts to procure a base in or to annex the Dominican Republic in 1866–1870; and the purchase of Alaska in 1867. The last of these, however, emerged at least in part from a desire to accommodate the Russians, who wanted to rid themselves of a possession too expensive to administer and impossible to defend. So the generalization holds: those officers who urged expansion abroad either were reprimanded by the Navy Department for going against Washington's opposition (until 1898) to raising the flag over noncontiguous lands or saw their recommendations ignored.

Statistics show the close relationship between American economic, political, and diplomatic trends, on one hand, and the contribution of U.S. naval officers to their country's foreign relations, on the other.

TABLE 1

DIPLOMATIC ACTIVITIES OF U.S. NAVAL OFFICERS, 1798–1883, BY DECADES

	Number	Percentage
1798–1809	30	6
1810–1819	56	11
1820–1829	54	11
1830–1839	62	12
1840–1849	66	13
1850–1860	135	27
1861–1869	67	13
1870–1883	34	7
Total	504	100

Table 1 shows the number of diplomatic activities performed by American naval officers during each decade from 1798 to 1883. Three of these periods are a bit longer than a decade: 1798–1809, the first years of the constitutional navy; 1850–1860, in order to include the last pre–Civil War year; and 1870–1883, when postwar American trends, particularly economic, became irreversible, negatively affecting the navy and reducing diplomatic opportunities for its officers.

In the first period, 1798–1809, the U.S. was warring with France and Tripoli, and fewer than half of the service's activities were peacetime pursuits. During the four decades ending in 1849—despite the War of 1812, the Algerian hostilities, and the Mexican War—the nation was usually at peace, and officers could concentrate upon such diplomatic activities as commerce-protection and other categories. The American carrying trade steadily increased during these years, but this growth was not fully reflected in naval diplomacy until the 1850s. Then the country's imports and exports soared, until by 1860 the United States was seriously challenging British overseas commercial supremacy in goods carried in its own merchantmen. The navy followed suit; in 1850–1860 there were no fewer than 135 contributions of officers to U.S. foreign policy, over twice as many as during any similar period from 1798 to 1883. In the 1860s the numbers remained about the same as those in 1810–1849, for the momentum established by the booming 1850s continued. But by the 1870s the American merchant marine was in the process of collapse, paralleled by the navy's decline in power and influence. The reduced number of naval diplomatic actions is striking. In the 14 years from 1870 to 1883—Shufeldt's cruises excepted—they were a mere 34, fewer than in any such period since 1809. The naval renaissance achieved by the late 1890s arose from new political, strategic, and diplomatic additions to the perennial economic considerations.

TABLE 2
DIPLOMATIC ACTIVITIES OF U.S. NAVAL OFFICERS,
1798–1883, BY GEOGRAPHICAL AREA

	Number	Percentage
Latin America	70	26
West Indies and Caribbean	48	18
Far East	46	17
Middle East	27	9
Pacific Islands other than Hawaii	24	9
Europe	20	7
Hawaiian Islands	17	6
Indian Ocean and Southeast Asia	13	4
West Africa	11	4
Total	276*	100

*The discrepancy between the 276 total here and the 504 in tables 1 and 3 occurs because table 2 merely locates activities, whereas the others give the several functions that may be performed in a single diplomatic activity.

The geographical statistics given in table 2 reflect the nation's strategic situation. The nineteenth-century United States, guarded by thousands of watery miles to the east and west, was quite invulnerable to invasions from the European, African, or Asian mainlands, or from the Pacific islands. Bases near America would be essential for any successful intrusion.

By about 1825 the French were gone from Haiti; they and the Spaniards from Louisiana; and the Spaniards from the Floridas, Mexico, and Central and South America. The insignificant Russian establishment in Alaska posed no threat. After 1815 the British, while powerful in Europe and on the high seas, were weak militarily in Canada. Furthermore, the Anglo-American tendency to settle crises without war negated the likelihood of any intrusion from the north, to say nothing about one from the tiny English colonies in the Caribbean.

Danger to the United States loomed only from the south. But Spain had more than enough trouble retaining the Cuban and Puerto Rican remnants of its former American empire and was unlikely even to consider a strike against the northern neighbor. Events from 1836 to 1848 demonstrated that an invasion from Mexico was chimerical. This security, however, would be challenged should a powerful European nation, France in particular, seize bases in the Spanish islands, Mexico, Central America, or South America's northeastern coast. The president and Secretary of State Adams saw this with the utmost clarity. Their Monroe Doctrine (1823) declared that the Western Hemisphere was out of bounds for further European colonization, although it was never invoked south of Colombia and Venezuela.

The fears expressed in the doctrine were realized in 1864 when Napoleon III sent the French army to topple the Mexican Republic and forcibly install the Austrian Maximilian as his puppet emperor, and they lasted until the army withdrew and Maximilian was executed in 1867. These events brought the doctrine, previously ignored or seized upon by special-interest groups such as pro-slavery expansionists, into general acceptance by the American people as the strongest plank in their diplomatic platform. Christian Science Founder Mary Baker Eddy even elevated it to divine status when she said that she believed truly in only three things: "the U.S. Constitution, the laws of God, and the Monroe Doctrine." American naval officers, the "cutting edge" of diplomacy, usually acted in accordance with the principles of the doctrine, though almost never mentioning it by name.

At first glance the geographical statistics appear to contradict this conclusion. There were more instances of U.S. naval diplomacy outside than inside the Western Hemisphere, 146 to 126. But such actions outside the Americas were less important, for many of them were no more than punitive expeditions in West Africa, Southeast Asia, and the South Pacific. To the contrary, those happening in the Americas tended to be more menacing to the country's peace and security than those elsewhere.

Only Silas Ingraham's ultimatum to the Austrians when he rescued Martin Koszta at Smyrna in 1853 and the possibility that the United States might be enticed into joining the British and French in the Arrow War against China in 1856–1860 compare in intensity and significance with those occurring on this side of the Atlantic. With Mexico there was one declared war and a number of near misses, such as Thomas a. C. Jones's seizure of Monterey, California, in 1842. The adroit diplomacy of James Biddle and his successors helped prevent a rupture with Spain during the Chilean-Peruvian revolts against Madrid in 1818–1825. Similar exertions were required to avert official hostilities between the two nations until John Rodgers the younger reconsidered opening fire on the Spanish fleet off Valparaiso in 1866, and tempers flared over the *Virginius* episode in 1873. Anglo-American confrontations in the Americas peaked during 1861, when mutual fury over the *Trent* affair required peacemakers in Washington and London to work overtime to avert the catastrophe that the errant zeal of Charles Wilkes almost caused. So although there were fewer than half as many diplomatic actions by the U.S. navy in the Western Hemisphere as in the rest of the world, they highlight the special relationship of the United States with its fellow-American countries to the south.

The diplomatic activities of U.S. naval officers are evaluated in table 3. The largest number of these were peacetime aggressions; officers used their batteries, or at least threatened to, in order to achieve their government's foreign-policy aims. Next came nonbelligerent diplomatic activities apart from negotiation of treaties. Humanitarian actions, affiliations with civilian diplomats, and treaty-making or negotiating were numerically about the same. There were fewer activities in protection and enhancement of commerce per se, especially frequent during the early years. War-making and expansionism occurred so seldom as to be relatively insignificant.

The evaluations in this table make no claim to scientific accuracy; they are my subjective judgments alone. Another scholar using the same sources might disagree with some of my appraisals, especially in the "mixed-results" listing, but probably not with many of them.

Of all the U.S. naval officers' diplomatic activities described in this work, a majority have been rated successful, or at least partially so. It may therefore be concluded that in return for the prestige, power, and financial security bestowed by their government upon them, the "Gold Braid" of the old navy amply repaid the United States by promoting its foreign-policy objectives.

TABLE 3
DIPLOMATIC ACTIVITIES OF U.S. NAVAL OFFICERS, 1798–1883, EVALUATED

	Successful		Mixed Results		Unsuccessful		Total	
	Number	Percentage	Number	Percentage	Number	Percentage	Number	Percentage
1. Protection and enhancement of commerce*	30	11	7	6	8	7	45	9
2. Making war	13	5	3	3	9	8	25	5
3. Peacetime aggression	94	33	22	20	18	16	134	27
4. Treaty-making or negotiating	19	7	17	15	25	22	61	12
5. Nonbelligerent diplomatic activities	33	12	35	32	16	14	84	17
6. Affiliation	41	14	9	8	18	16	68	13
7. Humanitarianism	50	18	8	8	4	4	62	12
8. Expansionism	2	0	9	8	14	13	25	5
Total	282	100	110	100	112	100	504	100

*As stressed in the text, many actions listed in categories 2–8 contributed to category 1, the protection and enhancement of commerce.

Chronology

Diplomatic Activities of U.S. Naval Officers, 1798–1883

1798–1809

1798, Oct.–Jan. 1799	Lt. William Bainbridge in *Retaliation* at Guadeloupe.	WIC
1798, Nov.	Capt. Isaac Phillips in *Baltimore* off Cuba.	WIC
1799, Feb.–Apr.	Capt. Henry Geddes in *Sophia* at Algiers, Tunis, and Tripoli.	ME
1799, Nov.–Apr. 1800	Comdr. William Bainbridge in *Norfolk* at Haiti.	WIC
1800, Feb.–March	Capt. Christopher R. Perry in *General Greene*, et al., off Jacmel, Haiti.	WIC
1800, Sept.–Jan. 1801	Capt. William Bainbridge in *George Washington* at Algiers and Constantinople, Turkey.	ME
1801, July–March 1802	Commo. Richard Dale in *President* and Tripoli.	ME
1802, March–Aug. 1803	Commo. Richard Morris in *Chesapeake* off Tripoli and at Tunis.	ME
1803, Aug.–Oct.	Commo. Edward Preble in *Constitution* at Tangier, Morocco.	ME
1803, Oct.–Aug. 1804	Commo. Edward Preble in *Constitution* at Tripoli.	ME
1803, Oct.–June 1805	Capt. William Bainbridge in *Philadelphia* at Tripoli.	ME
1804, Sept.–May 1805	Commo. Samuel Barron in *Constitution* at Tripoli.	ME
1805, June	Lt. James Lawrence in *Gunboat #6* off Cádiz, Spain.	EUR
1805, June–Aug.	Commo. John Rodgers in *Constitution* at Tripoli and Tunis.	ME
1807, June	Commo. James Barron in *Chesapeake* off Virginia Capes.	EUR
1808, July–June 1810	Comdr. David Porter with gunboats off Gulf Coast.	WIC

1810–1819

1810, June	Lt. John Trippe in *Vixen* off Bahama Is.	WIC

1811, Aug.	Commo. John Rodgers in *President* off Virginia Capes.	WIC
1812, March	Capt. Hugh Campbell with gunboats at Amelia Is., Florida.	WIC
1812, Dec.–Jan. 1813	Commo. William Bainbridge in *Constitution* and James Lawrence in *Hornet* at Bahia, Brazil.	LA
1813, March	Capt. David Porter in *Essex* at Valparaiso, Chile.	LA
1813, March	Capt. David Porter in *Essex* off Peru.	LA
1813, July	Capt. David Porter in *Essex* at Galápagos Is.	OPI
1813, Oct.–Dec.	Capt. David Porter in *Essex* at Nuka Hiva, Marquesas Is.	OPI
1814, March	Capt. David Porter in *Essex* at Valparaiso.	LA
1815, June–July	Commo. Stephen Decatur in *Guerrière*, et al., at Algiers, Tunis, Tripoli.	ME
1815, Aug.–Sept.	Commo. William Bainbridge in *Independence* at Algiers, Tunis, and Tripoli.	ME
1815, Nov.	Capt. David Porter and Japan.	FE
1816, July	Sailing Masters Jared Loomis and James R. Barrett in gunboats at Ft. Apalachicola, Florida.	WIC
1816, Aug.	Lt. Thomas B. Cunningham in *Firebrand* off Vera Cruz, Mexico.	LA
1816, Dec.	Commo. Isaac Chauncey in *Washington* at Naples, Italy.	ME
1817, Jan.–Jan. 1819	Capt. James Biddle in *Ontario* at Valparaiso and Callao, Peru.	LA
1817, July–Aug.	Capt. Charles Morris in *Congress* at Haiti.	WIC
1817, Dec.	Capt. John D. Henley in gunboats at Amelia Is., Florida.	WIC
1818, May–Aug.	Comdr. George R. Read in *Hornet* at Haiti.	WIC
1818, Aug.	Capt. James Biddle in *Ontario* at Ft. Astoria, Oregon.	EUR
1818, Oct.	Capt. Arthur Sinclair in *Congress* at Rio de Janeiro, Brazil.	LA

1819, Feb.–March 1821	Capt. John Downes in *Macedonian* at Valparaiso and Callao.	LA
1819, Apr.–Feb. 1820	Capt. Edward Trenchard in *Cyane* off Liberia.	WA
1819, Aug.	Capt. Oliver H. Perry in *Nonsuch* at Venezuela.	WIC
1819, Nov.–Feb. 1820	Lt. John R. Madison in *Lynx* at Galveston, Texas.	LA
1819, Nov.–March 1820	Lt. Lawrence Kearny in *Enterprise* at Galveston.	LA
1819, Nov.–Sept. 1820	Capt. John D. Henley in *Congress* at Canton, et al., China.	FE

1820–1829

1820, Sept.	Commo. William Bainbridge in *Independence* at Constantinople.	ME
1821, March–Apr. 1822	Capt. Charles Ridgely in *Constellation* at Valparaiso and Callao.	LA
1821, July–Dec.	Lt. Matthew C. Perry in *Shark* off Sierra Leone and Liberia.	WA
1821, Nov.	Lt. Robert F. Stockton in *Alligator* off Madeira Is.	EUR
1821, Dec.–July 1823	Lt. Robert F. Stockton in *Alligator* off Sierra Leone and Liberia.	WA
1822, Apr.–Apr. 1824	Commo. Charles Stewart in *Franklin* at Valparaiso and Callao.	LA
1822, Apr.–July, Nov.–Apr. 1823	Commo. James Biddle in *Macedonian* in Caribbean.	WIC
1823, Mar.–Oct. 1824, Feb.–June, Oct.–Feb. 1825	Commo. David Porter in *John Adams* in Caribbean.	WIC
1823, March–June	Capt. Robert T. Spence in *Cyane* off Sierra Leone and Liberia.	WA
1824, Apr.–Sept. 1826	Commo. Isaac Hull in *United States* at Valparaiso and Callao.	LA
1825, Feb.–Nov. 1826	Commo. Lewis Warrington in *Constellation* in Caribbean.	WIC
1825, July–July 1827	Commo. John Rodgers in *North Carolina* and Turkey.	ME

1826, Jan.–May	Lt. John Percival in *Dolphin* at Honolulu, Hawaii.	HAW
1826, Aug.	Comdr. Thomas a. C. Jones in *Peacock* at Tahiti.	OPI
1826, Oct.–Jan. 1827	Comdr. Thomas a. C. Jones in *Peacock* at Honolulu.	HAW
1826, Nov.–Oct. 1828	Commo. James Biddle in *Macedonian* and Capt. Jesse D. Elliott in *Cyane* off Uruguay.	LA
1826, Dec.–July 1828	Capt. Charles Ridgely and Comdr. George Budd in *Natchez* at Key West.	LA
1827, Feb.–March 1828	Commo. Thomas a. C. Jones in *Peacock* at Valparaiso and Callao.	LA
1828, Dec.	Comdr. Daniel Turner and Lt. Josiah Tattnall in *Erie* at Swedish St. Barts.	LA
1828, Dec.–Oct. 1829	Commo. William W. Crane in *Java* and Turkey.	ME
1829, Sept.	Comdr. William B. Finch in *Vincennes* at Tahiti.	OPI
1829, Oct.–Nov.	Comdr. William B. Finch in *Vincennes* at Honolulu.	HAW
1829, Nov.–Jan. 1830	Lt. Jesse D. Elliott in *Peacock* and Comdr. David Conner in *Erie* at Vera Cruz and Sisal, Mexico.	LA

1830–1835

1830, Jan.	Comdr. William B. Finch in *Vincennes* at Canton, et al.	FE
1830, May–June	Commo. James Biddle in *Java* at Smyrna and Constantinople.	ME
1831, Apr.	Capt. John D. Sloat in *St. Louis* and Commo. Charles C. B. Thompson in *Guerrière* at Callao.	LA
1831, Dec.–Jan. 1832	Comdr. Silas Duncan in *Lexington* and Capt. George W. Rodgers in *Enterprise* at Falkland Is.	LA
1832, Feb.	Capt. John Downes in *Potomac* at Kuala Batu, et al., Sumatra.	IOSEA

1832, May	Capt. John Downes in *Potomac* at Canton, et al.	FE
1832, June	Lt. Jesse D. Elliott in *Fairfield* at Tampico, Mexico.	LA
1832, July–Oct.	Commo. Daniel T. Patterson and Comdr. Matthew C. Perry in *Brandywine,* et al., at Naples.	EUR
1832, Aug.	Capt. John Downes in *Potomac* at Honolulu.	HAW
1832, Aug.	Lt. Josiah Tattnall in *Grampus* at Tampico and off Matamoros, Mexico.	LA
1833, Jan.–Dec.	Comdr. David Geisinger in *Peacock* at Cochin China, Siam, and Muscat.	IOSEA
1833, Feb.	Comdr. David Geisinger in *Peacock* and Japan.	FE
1833, Oct.	Capt. M. T. Woolsey in *Lexington* at Buenos Aires, Argentina.	LA
1833, Oct.–Aug. 1834	Commo. Daniel T. Patterson in *Delaware* at Constantinople.	ME
1834, May	Commo. Henry E. Ballard in *United States* at Toulon, France.	EUR
1835, Jan.–March 1839	Commos. Alexander Wadsworth in *Brandywine* and Henry E. Ballard in *North Carolina* at Callao.	LA
1835, Sept.–Apr. 1836	Comdr. Edmund Kennedy in *Peacock* at Muscat and Siam.	IOSEA
1835, Nov.	Comdr. John Aulick in *Vincennes* at Savai'i Is., Samoa.	OPI

1836–1839

1836, Jan.	Comdr. John Aulick in *Vincennes* at Canton, et al.	FE
1836, May	Commo. Alexander J. Dallas in *Constellation* at Tampico.	LA
1836, May–June	Capt. Edmund Kennedy in *Peacock* at Canton, et al.	FE
1836, June	Capt. Edmund Kennedy in *Peacock* and Japan.	FE

1836, Sept.–Oct.	Capt. Edmund Kennedy in *Peacock* at Honolulu.	HAW
1836, Oct.–Oct. 1837	Commo. Jesse D. Elliott in *Constitution* and Egypt.	ME
1836, Oct.	Comdr. William Mervine in *Natchez* at Vera Cruz.	LA
1837, Jan.	Commo. Alexander J. Dallas and Comdr. Bladen Dulany in *Boston* along Texas coast.	LA
1837, Feb.	Lt. Josiah Tattnall in *Pioneer* at Vera Cruz.	LA
1837, Apr.	Comdr. William Mervine in *Natchez* off Matamoros.	LA
1838, Dec.–Jan. 1839	Capt. George C. Read in *Columbia* at Kuala Batu, et al., Sumatra.	IOSEA
1838, Dec.–March 1839	Commo. John B. Nicholson in *Independence* off Montevideo, Uruguay.	LA
1839, Apr.–Aug.	Capt. George C. Read in *Columbia* at Canton, et al.	FE
1839, July	Lts. Thomas R. Gedney and Richard W. Meade in *Washington* off Long Is.	WIC
1839, Aug.	Lt. Charles Wilkes in *Vincennes* at Tuamotu Is.	OPI
1839, Aug.	Lt. Charles Wilkes in *Vincennes* at Apia, Samoa.	OPI
1839, Oct.	Capt. George C. Read in *Columbia* at Honolulu.	HAW

1840–1844

1840, March	Lt. Charles Wilkes in *Flying Fish* and *Porpoise* at Bay of Islands, New Zealand.	OPI
1840, June	Comdr. French Forrest in *St. Louis* at Monterey, Mexico.	LA
1840, May–July	Lts. Charles Wilkes and William L. Hudson in *Peacock,* et al., at Vitu Levi and Vauna Leva, Fiji Is.	OPI

1841, Feb.	Lt. William L. Hudson in *Peacock* and *Flying Fish* at Savai'i Is., Samoa.	OPI
1841, Apr.	Lt. William L. Hudson in *Peacock* and *Flying Fish* at Gilbert Is.	OPI
1841, Aug.	Commo. Lawrence Kearny in *Constellation* at Joanna, Comoros Is.	IOSEA
1842, Feb.	Lt. Charles Wilkes in *Vincennes* at Sulu Archipelago, Philippine Is.	OPI
1842, March–Oct. 1843, Jan.–March	Commo. Lawrence Kearny in *Constellation* at Canton, et al.	FE
1842, June–July	Commo. Charles M. Morgan in *Fairfield* at Tangier, Morocco.	ME
1842, Oct.–March 1843	Commo. Thomas a. C. Jones in *United States* and *Cyane* at Monterey.	LA
1843, Feb.	Comdr. John C. Long in *Boston* at Honolulu.	HAW
1843, March–Dec.	Capt. Matthew C. Perry in *Saratoga* and *Macedonian* at Liberia and Ivory Coast.	WA
1843, July	Commo. Lawrence Kearny in *Constellation* at Honolulu.	HAW
1844, Feb.–Dec.	Capt. Foxhall A. Parker in *Brandywine* and Lt. Edward G. Tilton in *St. Louis* at Canton, et al.	FE
1844, July	Comdr. Henry Henry in *Plymouth* at Constantinople.	ME
1844, Sept.–Oct.	Captain Philip Voorhees in *Congress* off Montevideo.	LA

1845–1849

1845, Jan.–Dec.	Comdr. Garrett J. Pendergast in *Boston* off Buenos Aires.	LA
1845, Apr.	Capt. John Percival in *Constitution* at Brunei, Borneo.	IOSEA
1845, May	Capt. John Percival in *Constitution* at Tourane, Annam.	IOSEA
1845, May	Capt. Isaac McKeever in *St. Louis* at Kororeka, Bay of Islands, New Zealand.	OPI

1845, Sept.	Comdr. Daniel Turner in *Raritan* at Rio de Janeiro.	LA
1845, Oct.–Apr. 1846	Lt. Archibald H. Gillespie (USMC) at Monterey and Klamath Falls, Oregon.	LA
1845, Dec.–July 1846	Commo. James Biddle in *Columbus* and *Vincennes* at Canton, Shanghai, et al.	FE
1846, March–Apr.	Capt. Robert F. Stockton in *Congress* at Honolulu.	HAW
1846, May–July	Lt. David D. Porter in *Porpoise* at Santo Domingo.	LA
1846, June–July	Comdr. Alexander S. Mackenzie at Havana.	LA
1846, July	Commo. James Biddle in *Columbus* and *Vincennes* at Edo, Japan.	FE
1846, July–March 1847	Commos. John D. Sloat in *Savannah* and Robert F. Stockton in *Congress* at Monterey, et al.	LA
1846, Sept.	Commo. James Biddle in *Columbus* at Honolulu.	HAW
1846, Oct.–June 1848	Commos. David Conner and Matthew C. Perry in *Mississippi*, et al., off Yucatán peninsula.	LA
1846, Oct.–Dec.	Lt. Alonzo B. Davis in *Saranac* and Commo. Lawrence Rousseau in *Columbia* at Rio de Janeiro.	LA
1846, Nov.–Dec.	Capt. John Percival in *Constitution* at Honolulu.	HAW
1846, Dec.–Feb. 1848	Commos. James Biddle in *Columbus*, William B. Shubrick in *Independence*, and Thomas a. C. Jones in *Ohio* at Monterey, et al.	LA
1848, March	Commo. George C. Read in *United States* at Genoa, Italy.	EUR
1849, Apr.	Comdr. James Glynn in *Preble* at Nagasaki, Japan.	FE
1849, June–Sept.	Commo. John Gwinn in *Constitution* at Naples and Palermo, Italy.	EUR
1849, Oct.	Capt. David Geisiner in *Plymouth* at Canton, et al.	FE

1850, Jan.–June 1851	Comdr. Andrew H. Foote in *Perry* off West Africa.	WA
1850, Feb.–July	Capt. Philip Voorhees in *Plymouth* at Cochin China and off Siam and Brunei, Borneo.	IOSEA
1850, May	Lt. John Rodgers in *Petrel* at Key West, Florida.	WIC
1850, June	Comdr. Victor M. Randolph in *Albany* off Havana.	WIC
1850, June–July	Capt. Josiah Tattnall in *Saranac* off Havana.	WIC
1850, June–Aug.	Capts. Charles Morris in *Vixen* and Isaac McKeever in *Congress* at Yucatán.	WIC
1851, Feb.–March	Comdr. Thomas Petigru in *Falmouth* at Lauthala, Fiji.	OPI
1851, Feb.–Apr.	Comdr. William H. Gardner in *Vandalia* at Honolulu.	HAW
1851, June	Comdr. George A. Magruder in *St. Mary's* at Lauthala, Fiji.	OPI
1851, Aug.	Comdr. William Pearson in *Dale* at Joanna, Comoros Is.	IOSEA
1851, Aug.–Oct.	Comdr. Charles T. Platt in *Albany* and Capt. Foxhall A. Parker in *Saranac* at Havana.	WIC
1851, Sept.–Oct.	Capt. John C. Long in *Mississippi*, Constantinople to Gibraltar.	WIC
1851, Sept.–Oct.	Capt. John Aulick in *Susquehanna* at Comoros and Zanzibar.	IOSEA
1851, Nov.–Jan. 1852	Capt. Foxhall A. Parker in *Saranac* and *Albany* at Greytown, Nicaragua.	WIC
1852, Feb.–March 1853	Commo. John Aulick in *Susquehanna* at Canton, et al.	FE
1852, Feb., Sept.	Captain Isaac McKeever in *Jamestown* at Buenos Aires.	LA
1852, Apr.–May 1853	Commo. Silas H. Stringham in *Cumberland* at Athens and Constantinople.	ME

1852, May	Lt. William S. Walker in *Saratoga* at Ryukyu Is.	FE
1852, July–Sept.	Commo. Matthew C. Perry in *Mississippi* off eastern Canada.	EUR
1852, Sept.	Capt. Charles S. McCauley in *Raritan* off Lobos Is, Peru.	LA
1853, March–May	Comdr. George N. Hollins in *Cyane* at Greytown, Nicaragua.	WIC
1853, Apr.–May, July– Feb. 1854; 1854, July–Sept.	Commo. Matthew C. Perry in *Susquehanna* at Canton, et al.	FE
1853, May–July; 1854, July	Commo. Matthew C. Perry in *Susquehanna* at Ryukyu and Bonin Is.	FE
1853, June–July	Comdr. Duncan N. Ingraham in *St. Louis* at Smyrna, Turkey.	EUR
1853, July	Commo. Matthew C. Perry in *Susquehanna* at Edo.	FE
1853, July	Comdr. George A. Magruder in *St. Mary's* at Batavia, Java.	IOSEA
1853, Aug.–Sept. 1854	Commo. Isaac Mayo in *Constitution* at Liberia.	WA
1853, Aug.–Sept.	Commo. William B. Shubrick in *Princeton* off eastern Canada.	EUR

1854–1856

1854, Jan.	Comdr. Thomas A. Dornin in *Portsmouth* at Enseñada, et al., Mexico	LA
1854, Feb.–July	Commo. Matthew C. Perry in *Powhatan* at Edo, et al.	FE
1854, March	Comdr. William F. Lynch in *Germantown* at Falkland Is.	LA
1854, Apr.	Comdr. Theodorus Bailey in *St. Mary's* at Chincha Is, Peru.	LA
1854, Apr.	Comdr. John Kelly in *Plymouth* at Shanghai.	FE
1854, July	Comdr. George N. Hollins in *Cyane* at Greytown, Nicaragua.	WIC
1854, Oct.	Lt. George H. Preble in *Queen* at Canton, et al.	FE

1854, Nov.	Lt. John Rodgers in *Vincennes* at Ryukyu Is.	FE
1855, Apr.	Lts. Thomas J. Page and William Jeffers in *Water Witch* at Asunción, et al., Paraguay.	LA
1855, May	Commo. Hiram Paulding in *Susquehanna* at Greytown, Nicaragua.	WIC
1855, May–June	Commo. Charles S. McCauley in *San Jacinto* off Havana.	WIC
1855, Sept.–Nov.	Capt. William J. McCluney in *Powhatan* off Amoy.	FE
1855, Sept.–Oct.	Comdr. Edward B. Boutwell in *John Adams* at Rewa, et al., Fiji.	OPI
1855, Oct.	Comdr. Theodorus Bailey in *St. Mary's* at Rewa, et al., Fiji.	OPI
1855, Oct.	Comdr. Thomas R. Rootes in *Vandalia* at Manila, Philippine Is.	FE
1855, Nov.	Comdr. William F. Lynch in *Germantown* at Montevideo.	LA
1855, Dec.–Feb. 1856	Capt. John Pope in *Vandalia* at Amoy, China.	FE
1856, May–Sept.	Capt. Theodorus Bailey in *St. Mary's* at Panama.	WIC
1856, May–Sept.	Commo. William Mervine in *Independence* at Panama.	WIC
1856, Nov.–Dec.	Commo. James Armstrong in *San Jacinto* and Comdr. Andrew H. Foote in *Portsmouth* and *Levant* at Canton.	FE
1856, Nov.–March 1857	Commo. John Armstrong in *San Jacinto* and Formosa (Taiwan).	FE

1857–1860

1857, Feb.–May	Comdr. Charles H. Davis in *St. Mary's* at Rivas, Nicaragua.	WIC
1857, Nov.	Comdr. Frederick Chatard in *Saratoga* at Greytown, Nicaragua.	WIC
1857, Dec.	Commo. Hiram Paulding in *Wabash* at Greytown, Nicaragua.	WIC

1858, Jan.	Capt. French Forrest in *St. Lawrence* and *Falmouth* at Montevideo.	LA
1858, Apr.	Lt. John J. Almy in *Fulton* at Tampico.	LA
1858, May–June	Commos. Elie A. F. LaVallette and James M. McIntosh in combined Home and Mediterranean Squadrons off Cuba.	EUR
1858, June	Commo. John M. McIntosh in *Colorado* at Dominican Republic.	WIC
1858, Aug.	Comdr. Thomas Turner in *Saratoga* off Haiti.	WIC
1858, Oct.–Dec.	Commo. Elie A. F. LaVallette in *Wabash* at Jaffa and Constantinople.	ME
1858, Oct.	Comdr. John A. B. Dahlgren in *Portsmouth* at Tampico and Vera Cruz.	LA
1858, Oct.	Comdr. Arthur Sinclair in *Vandalia* at Levuka and Lt. Charles H. B. Caldwell in *Mechanic* at Waya Is., Fiji.	OPI
1859, Jan.	Comdr. Charles H. Davis in *St. Mary's* at Guaymas and Mazatlán, Mexico.	LA
1859, Jan.–Feb.	Commo. William M. Shubrick in *Sabine,* et al., and Asunción.	LA
1859, March–Sept. 1861	Commo. William M. Inman in *San Jacinto* off Liberia, et al.	WA
1859, June	Commo. Josiah Tattnall in *Powhatan* and *Toeywan* at Taku.	FE
1859, Aug.	Capt. William C. Nicholson in *Mississippi* at Shanghai.	FE
1860, Feb.–March	Lt. John M. Brooke in *Kanrin Maru,* Uraga to San Francisco.	FE
1860, March	Capt. Joseph R. Jarvis in *Savannah* and Comdr. Thomas Turner in *Saratoga* at Antón Lizardo, Mexico.	LA
1860, March	Comdr. Thomas W. Brent in *Marion* at Kissembo, Angola.	WA
1860, May–Nov.	Comdr. James S. Palmer in *Iroquois* at Palermo and Naples.	EUR

1860, Aug.–Sept.	Comdr. Charles H. Poor in *St. Louis* at Rio Hacha, Colombia.	WIC
1860, Sept.–Oct.	Commo. John D. Montgomery in *Lancaster* and Comdr. William D. Porter in *St. Mary's* at Panama.	WIC
1860, Nov.–Feb. 1861	Capt. Charles H. Bell in *Richmond* at Messina, Italy.	EUR

1861–1866

1861, Nov.–Dec.	Capt. Charles Wilkes in *San Jacinto* off Cuba.	EUR
1863, July	Comdr. David McDougal in *Wyoming* at Shimonoseki, Japan.	FE
1864, Sept.	Lt. Frederick Pearson in *Takiang* at Shimonoseki.	FE
1864, Oct.	Comdr. Napoleon Collins in *Wachusett* at Bahia, Brazil.	LA
1865, Feb.–March	Capts. Thomas T. Craven in *Niagara* and Henry Walke in *Sacramento* at El Ferrol, Spain, and Lisbon, Portugal.	EUR
1865, Feb.–March	Capt. Edward Middleton in *St. Mary's* at Panama.	WIC
1866, March	Commo. John Rodgers in *Monadnock* at Valparaiso.	LA
1866, May–June	Comdr. Robert Townsend in *Wachusett* at Newschwang, Tengchow, and Amoy.	FE
1866, June	Capt. Andrew Bryson in *Michigan* off Buffalo, N.Y., and Fort Erie, Ontario.	EUR
1866, July	Comdr. Homer C. Blake in *Nipsic* at Bahia.	LA
1866, Aug.	Comdr. Robert W. Shufeldt in *Wachusett* off Canton, et al.	FE
1866, Aug.–Jan. 1869	Adms. Louis M. Goldsborough in *Colorado* and David G. Farragut in *Ticonderoga* off Crete and at Constantinople.	ME

1866, Oct.–Dec.	Adm. Sylvanus W. Godon in *Guerrière* at Rio de Janeiro.	LA
1866, Oct.	Comdr. Pierce Crosby in *Shamokin* at Asunción.	LA
1866, Nov.–Dec.	Capt. John Alden in *Susquehanna* at Vera Cruz, et al.	LA
1866, Dec.–Jan. 1867	Adm. David D. Porter at Santo Domingo, Dominican Republic.	WIC

1867–1872

1867, Jan.–Feb.	Comdr. Robert W. Shufeldt in *Wachusett* off Taedong River, Korea.	FE
1867, Feb.–Aug., Oct.–May 1868	Capt. William Reynolds in *Lackawanna* at Honolulu.	HAW
1867, June	Capt. Fabius Stanley in *Tuscarora* at Levuka, Fiji.	OPI
1867, June	Comdr. Francis A. Roe in *Tacony* at Vera Cruz.	LA
1867, June	Adm. Henry H. Bell in *Hartford* at Formosa (Taiwan).	FE
1867, Aug.	Capt. William Reynolds in *Lackawanna* at Midway Atoll.	HAW
1867, Oct.	Capt. George F. Emmons in *Ossipee* at Sitka, Alaska.	EUR
1868, Jan.–Feb. 1869	Adm. Stephen C. Rowan in *Oneida*, et al. off Hyogo, et al., Japan.	FE
1868, Feb.	Adm. Charles H. Davis in *Guerrière* at Montevideo.	LA
1868, Apr.	Master Thomas Nelson in *Penobscot* at Greytown, Nicaragua.	WIC
1868, May	Lt. Comdr. Chester Hatfield in *Unadilla* off Hainan Is., China.	FE
1868, July	Comdr. John Febiger in *Shenandoah* off Taedong River.	FE
1868, Aug.	Lt. Comdr. William A. Kirkland in *Wasp* at Asunción.	LA
1868, Sept.	Adm. Charles H. Davis in *Guerrière* at Rio de Janeiro.	LA

1869, June	Comdr. Thomas O. Selfridge in *Nipsic* at Dominican Republic.	WIC
1869, July	Comdr. Elias K. Owen in *Seminole* off Dominican Republic.	WIC
1869, July	Comdr. Walter W. Queen in *Tuscarora* off Dominican Republic.	WIC
1869, July	Adm. Henry H. Hoff in *Contoocook* and *Albany* at Santiago, Cuba.	WIC
1869, Oct.	Comdr. William T. Truxtun in *Jamestown* at Levuka, Fiji.	OPI
1870, Jan.–March	Adm. Charles H. Poor in *Powhatan*, et al., off Dominican Republic.	WIC
1870, May	Comdr. William T. Truxtun in *Jamestown* at Gilbert Is.	OPI
1870, June	Comdr. William N. Low and Lt. Willard H. Brownson in *Mohican* off Mazatlán and San Blas, Mexico.	LA
1871, June	Adm. John Rodgers in *Colorado*, et al., at Kangwha Is., Korea.	FE
1872, Feb.–March	Comdr. Richard W. Meade, Jr. in *Narrangansett* at Pago Pago, Samoa.	OPI

1873–1883

1873, Jan.	Adm. Alexander H. Pennock in *California* and *Benicia* at Honolulu.	HAW
1873, May	Adm. Charles Steedman in *Pensacola* and *Tuscarora* at Panama.	WIC
1873, June	Comdr. Byron Wilson in *Yantic* at Zanzibar.	IOSEA
1873, July–Sept.	Adm. A. Ludlow Case in *Wabash* and Capt. Clark H. Wells in *Shenandoah* off Spain.	EUR
1873, Sept.–Oct.	Adm. John J. Almy in *Benicia* and *Pensacola* at Panama.	WIC
1873, Nov.	Comdr. William B. Cushing in *Wyoming* at Santiago, Cuba.	WIC
1874, Feb.	Comdrs. George E. Belknap in *Tuscarora* and Joseph S. Skerrett in *Portsmouth* at Honolulu.	HAW

1874, Nov.–Feb. 1875	Adm. John J. Almy in *California,* et al., at Honolulu.	HAW
1875, Aug.	Adm. John L. Worden in *Franklin* and Tripoli.	ME
1876, May	Comdr. Andrew W. Johnson in *Lackawanna* at Matamoros.	LA
1877, May	Adm. Alexander Murray in *Pensacola* at Acapulco, Mexico.	LA
1879, Feb.–Nov. 1880	Capt. Bartlett J. Cromwell in *Ticonderoga* from West Africa–Far East.	WA–FE
1879, Feb.–April	Commo. Robert W. Shufeldt in *Ticonderoga* at Liberia–South Africa.	WA
1879, Feb.–Dec. 1881	Adms. C. R. Perry Rodgers and George E. Balch in *Pensacola,* et al., at Callao.	LA
1879, June–July	Capt. Ralph M. Chandler in *Lackawanna* at Apia, Fiji.	OPI
1879, Sept.–March 1880	Commo. Robert W. Shufeldt in *Ticonderoga* from Madagascar through Philippines.	IOSEA
1880, April–Sept.	Commo. Robert W. Shufeldt in *Ticonderoga* in Far East.	FE
1881, March–Dec.	Commo. Robert W. Shufeldt in private transportation at Tientsin, China.	FE
1881, Nov.–Dec.	Capt. James H. Gillis in *Lackawanna* at Apia, Samoa.	OPI
1882, May–July 1883	Commo. Robert W. Shufeldt in *Swatara* at Inchon, Korea, and aftermath.	FE
1882, July	Adm. James W. Nicholson in *Lancaster* at Alexandria, Egypt.	ME

Notes

How much personal research to do for this book has been a major problem, with over 500 separate instances of U.S. naval-officer diplomacy. I have tried to solve this problem by a rule-of-thumb procedure. Some of the more celebrated episodes in this field have had entire books devoted to them, such as Wilkes' conduct in the *Trent* affair (1861); Ingraham's rescue of Martin Koszta (1853); M. C. Perry's opening of Japan (1853–1854); and the activities of American commodores in southwestern South America during the Chilean and Peruvian wars of rebellion against Spain (1818–1828). Others, if less well known, still have received extensive coverage in biographies, monographs, and articles. In such cases it would have been ridiculous for me to attempt to duplicate or better the efforts of scholars who may have spent years of research on their topic. Hence I have accepted their findings, selecting from their sources those that I considered unusually helpful to my own treatment.

I found little, however, upon which to build an account of many other naval diplomatic activities. Sometimes only a short paragraph or even a mere sentence referred to them. When faced with a dearth of information, I have occasionally gone to manuscript collections, those that I have used in my three published naval biographies and other works. But usually I have been satisfied to amplify my knowledge by consulting the microfilmed Navy and State Department correspondence at the National Archives, as well as published documentation.

Both the publisher and I had originally planned to provide a full bibliography listing the manuscripts, source works, monographs, biographies, newspapers and magazines, unpublished doctoral dissertations, and articles used in this work. But such a bibliography would have had to contain some 600 to 700 individual items and would have swollen the book to an unmanageable size. Therefore we have decided to list only the most important works, which are located below in the "Abbreviations Used in the Notes." Scholars will be able to find what they need in them.

As for the organization of the notes, when a single work is basic to a diplomatic activity, usually a monograph, but sometimes a biography, or even an article, I have placed that first in an entry. Otherwise, I lead off with "primary" sources—correspondence both unpublished and published, eyewitness accounts, and newspapers, for I agree with the observation that newspapers provide "the first draft of history." "Secondary" sources follow, typically with books first and articles last. I have dispensed with this organization when only a very few references to an episode have been unearthed.

Abbreviations Used in the Notes

AH   *American Heritage*, N.Y., N.Y.

AMW   James A. Field, Jr., *America and the Mediterranean World, 1776–1886* (Princeton, Princeton University Press, 1969).

AN   *American Neptune*, Salem, Mass.

ASHS   Clayton R. Barrow, Jr., ed., *America Spreads Her Sails: U.S. Sea Power in the Nineteenth Century* (Annapolis, Naval Institute Press, 1973).

ASP   *American State Papers: Documents Legislative and Executive, 1789–1838*, 38 vols. (Washington, Gales and Seaton, 1832–1861).

BDP   DFL, *Nothing Too Daring: A Biography of Commodore David Porter, 1780–1843* (Annapolis, United States Naval Institute, 1970).

BJB   DFL, *Sailor-Diplomat: A Biography of Commodore James Biddle, 1783–1848* (Boston, Northeastern University Press, 1983).

BW   USND, *Naval Documents Related to the United States Wars with the Barbary Powers: Naval Operations, Including Diplomatic Backgrounds, 1785–1807*, 6 vols. (Washington, Government Printing Office, 1939–1944).

BWB   DFL, *Ready to Hazard: A Biography of Commodore William Bainbridge, 1774–1833* (Hanover, N.H., and London, University Press of New England, 1981).

CAPL   USND, Letters received by the SN from captains ("Captains' Letters"), 1807–61, 1865–83, M 125, 410 rolls, NA.

CMPP   James D. Richardson, ed., *A Compilation of the Messages and Papers of the Presidents, 1789–1897,* 10 vols. (Washington, Published by Authority of Congress, 1899).

COML USND, Letters received by the SN from commanders ("Masters Commandant" through 1837, thereafter "Commanders' Letters"), 1804–86, M 147, 121 rolls, NA.

CSS U.S. Congress, Congressional Series (such entries as "27th, 2nd" refer to "27th Congress, 2nd Session"), especially for the SN's annual reports, 1823–1883.

DAB *Dictionary of American Biography,* 22 vols. (N.Y., Charles Scribner's Sons, 1928–1944).

DCUS-ILAN William R. Manning, ed., *Diplomatic Correspondence of the United States concerning the Independence of the Latin American Nations,* 3 vols. (N.Y., Oxford University Press, 1925).

DCUS-IAA William R. Manning, ed., *Diplomatic Correspondence of the United States: Inter-American Affairs, 1831–1860,* 12 vols. (Washington, Carnegie Endowment for International Peace, 1932–1939).

DDP David Dixon Porter, USN.

DFL David F. Long, author of this work.

DGW Gideon Welles, *The Diary of Gideon Welles,* ed. by John T. Morse, Jr. (Boston, Houghton Mifflin, 1911).

DIL John B. Moore, ed., *Digest of International Law, as Embodied in Diplomatic Discussions, Treaties, and Other International Agreements, International Awards, the Decisions of Municipal Courts, and the Writings of Jurists, and Especially in Documents, Published and Unpublished, Issued by Presidents and Secretaries of State of the United States, the Opinions of the Attorneys-General, and the Decisions of Courts, Federal, and State,* 8 vols. (Washington, Government Printing Office, 1906).

DNANO Charles O. Paullin, *Diplomatic Negotiations of American Naval Officers, 1778–1883* (Baltimore, Johns Hopkins University Press, 1912).

DNI *Daily National Intelligencer* (Washington, D.C.)

DP David Porter, USN.

EAAFR Henry R. Wriston, *Executive Agents in American Foreign Relations* (Baltimore, Johns Hopkins University Press, 1929).

ESRWS Frederick C. Drake, *The Empire of the Seas: A Biography of Rear Admiral Robert Wilson Shufeldt, USN* (Honolulu, University of Hawaii Press, 1984).

FCS   Robert E. Johnson, *Far China Station: The U.S. Navy in Asian Waters, 1800–1895* (Annapolis, Naval Institute Press, 1979).

FRUS   USDS, *Foreign Relations of the United States, 1861–1883, 1894—* for Hawaii only—(Washington, D.C., Government Printing Office, usually issued annually).

HAHR   *Hispanic American Historical Review* (Durham, N.C.).

HR   U.S. House of Representatives.

IDNR   Edward B. Billingsley, *In Defense of Neutral Rights: The United States Navy and the Wars of Independence in Chile and Peru* (Chapel Hill, N.C., University of North Carolina Press, 1967).

JB   James Biddle, USN.

JQAM   John Quincy Adams, *Memoirs of John Quincy Adams, Comprising Portions of His Diary from 1795 to 1848*, ed. by Charles Francis Adams, 12 vols. (Philadelphia, J. B. Lippincott, 1872).

LC   Library of Congress, Washington, D.C.

MW   K. Jack Bauer, *The Mexican War, 1846–1848* (N.Y. and London, Macmillan, 1974).

NA   National Archives, Washington, D.C.

NASP   *New American State Papers, Naval Affairs, 1789–1860*, ed. by K. Jack Bauer, 16 vols. (Wilmington, Scholarly Resources, Del., 1981).

NWR   *Niles' Weekly Register,* Baltimore (the title sometimes varies slightly).

NYT   *New York Times,* N.Y., N.Y.

OBMCP   Samuel E. Morison, *"Old Bruin": Commodore Matthew Calbraith Perry, 1794–1858* (Boston and Toronto, Little Brown, 1967).

ORUCN   USND, *Official Records of the Union and Confederate Navies in the War of the Rebellion,* 30 vols. (Washington, Government Printing Office, 1894–1914).

PCA   Milton Offutt, *Protection of Citizens Abroad by the Armed Forces of the United States* (Baltimore, Johns Hopkins University Press, 1928).

PHR   *Pacific Historical Review* (Los Angeles).

QW   USND, *Naval Documents Related to the Quasi-War between the United States and France,* 7 vols. (Washington, Government Printing Office, 1935–1938).

SEN   U.S. Senate.

SL   USND, Letters received by the SN from commanders of squadrons ("Squadron Letters"), 1841–86, M 89, 294 rolls, NA.

SN   Secretary of the navy.

SNL   Letters sent by the SN to officers ("Officers, Ships of War"), 1798–1868, M 149, 86 rolls, NA.

SS   Secretary of state.

TIAUS   Hunter Miller, David, ed., *Treaties and Other International Acts of the United States of America,* 8 vols. (Washington, Government Printing Office, 1931–1948).

TRCH   Robert E. Johnson, *Thence round Cape Horn: The Story of the United States Naval Forces on Pacific Station, 1818–1923* (Annapolis, United States Naval Institute, 1963).

USCH 1 Jules Davids, ed., *American Diplomatic and Public Papers: The United States and China: Series 1: The Treaty System and the Taiping Rebellion, 1842–1860,* 21 vols. (Wilmington, Del., Scholarly Resources, 1973).

USCH 2 Ibid. *Series 2: The United States, China, and Imperial Rivalries, 1861–1893,* 18 vols. (ibid., 1979).

USDS   U.S. Department of State.

USN   U.S. Navy.

USND   U.S. Navy Department.

USNIP   *United States Naval Institute Proceedings* (Annapolis, Md.).

USSDOM Charles A. Tansill, *The United States and Santo Domingo, 1798–1873: A Chapter in Caribbean Diplomacy* (Baltimore, Johns Hopkins University Press, 1938).

WB   William Bainbridge, USN.

Introduction

1.   Treaty-making powers of a naval officer. Gerhardt von Glahn, *Law among Nations: An Introduction to Public International Law,* 4th ed. (N.Y., Macmillan, 1981), 483; *PCA,* 5; William T. Mallison, letter to me, 25 January 1982; Harold D. Langley, letter to me, 4 November 1981; and Kenneth J. Hagan, *American Gunboat Diplomacy and the Old Navy, 1877–1889* (Westport, Conn., Greenwood Press, 1973), 80.

2.   Naval vis-à-vis civilian diplomats. Glenn Tucker, *Dawn like Thunder: The Barbary Wars and the Birth of the United States Navy* (Indianapolis, Dodd, Mead, 1963), 135; Frank M. Harris, "The Navy and the Diplomatic Frontier," *USNIP*, vol. 62 (1936), 473–474; *DNANO*, 7, 9; William N. Still, Jr., *American Sea Power in the Old World: The United States Navy in European and Near Eastern Waters, 1865–1917* (Westport, Conn., Greenwood Press, 1980), 9; Peter Karsten, *The Naval Aristocracy: Mahan's Messmates and the Emergence of Modern American Navalism* (N.Y. and London, Free Press, 1972), 172; Leland P. Lovette, *Naval Customs, Traditions, and Usage,* 4th ed. (Annapolis, USNI, 1959), 372 (for John Paul Jones); James E. Merrill, "The Asiatic Squadron, 1835–1907," *AN*, vol. 29 (April 1969), 109; and *DIL*, vol. 7, 615–617.

3.   Naval responsibilities. SN Upshur's *Report, 1842, CSS,* 27th, 3rd, *HR 1*, vol. 1, *Serial 413*, 541; SN Welles's *Report, 1865,* ibid., 39th, 1st, *HR 1*, vol. 5, *Serial 1243*, xv; and *NRW*, vol. 31 (25 Sept. 1826), 63.

4.   The communications revolution and the "old" and "new" navies. *TRCH*, 9–10; *DNI*, 14 Jan. 1843, 2/6; H. S. Knapp, "The Naval Officer in Diplomacy," *USNIP*, vol. 73 (1927), 312; G. B. Vroom, "The Place of Naval Officers in International Affairs," ibid., vol. 47 (1921), 698; Still, 11–12; and *EAAFR*, 174.

Chapter 1

1.   Bainbridge, et al. *BWB*, 23–33. Primary: *QW*, vol. 2, 122–125, 219, 395–398; *Columbian Centinel* (Boston), *Philadelphia Gazette,* and *Aurora* (Philadelphia), Jan.–March 1799, passim. Secondary: Thomas Harris, *The Life and Services of Commodore William Bainbridge, United States Navy* (Philadelphia, Carey Lea and Blanchard, 1837), 24–33; Henry A. S. Dearborn, *The Life of William Bainbridge, Esq., of the United States Navy,* ed. by James Barnes (Princeton, Princeton University Press, 1931), 7–8; and Alfred T. Mahan, *The Influence of Sea Power on the French Revolution and Empire* (Boston, Little, Brown, 1893), 72–75.

2.   Phillips. Primary: *QW*, vol. 2, 26–43. Secondary: Leonard F. Guttridge and Jay D. Smith, *The Commodores* (N.Y., et al., Harper & Row, 1969), 37–39; Gardner W. Allen, *Our Naval War with France* (Boston, Houghton Mifflin, 1909), 76–79; Jack Sweetman, *American Naval History: An Illustrated Chronology of the U.S. Navy and Marine Corps, 1775–Present* (Annapolis, Naval Institute Press, 1984), 24; and Michael A. Palmer, "The Dismission of Capt. Isaac Phillips," *AN*, vol. 45 (Spring 1985), 94–104.

3.   Perry, et al. Primary: *QW*, vol. 5, 260–463, passim, especially 310; and scattered references in *Columbian Centinel* and *Philadelphia Gazette,* Feb.–June 1799. Secondary: *BWB*, 36–39; Rayford W. Logan, *The United States and Haiti, 1776–1891* (Chapel Hill, University of North Carolina Press, 1941), 102–111; Ludwell L. Montague, *Haiti and the United States, 1714–1938* (Durham, N.C., Duke University Press, 1940), 36–41; *USSDOM*, 70–75; and Allen, 115–116.

4.   (A) Geddes. Primary: *BW*, vol. 1, 307–312, 318–319. Secondary: Glenn Tucker, *Dawn like Thunder: The Barbary Wars and the Birth of the U.S. Navy*

(Indianapolis and N.Y., Dodd, Mead, 1963), 110, 117–121, 125–126. (B) Bainbridge. *BWB*, 40–54, based partly on *BW*, vol. 1, passim; *Boston Gazette* and Philadelphia's *Aurora* and *Gazette of the United States,* Dec. 1800–April 1801, passim; Tucker, 30–31; and *AMW*, 114–117.

5. Dale. Primary: *BW*, vols. 1–2, passim. Secondary: Tucker, 132–149; *DNANO*, 60–62; and Ray W. Irvin, *The Diplomatic Relations of the United States with the Barbary Powers, 1776–1816* (Chapel Hill, University of North Carolina Press, 1931), 108–109. I may claim some familiarity with the Tripolitan War in general and the loss of the *Philadelphia* in particular, for all three subjects of my naval biographies were captured by the Bashaw: *BDP*, 22–32; *BWB*, 67–103; and *BJB*, 19–27, based largely on *BW*, vols. 3–6, passim, and private papers.

6. Morris. *BW*, vols. 2–3, passim; Tucker, 171–187; and *DNANO*, 63–68.

7. Preble and the *Philadelphia*'s people. *BDP*, 22–31; *BWB*, 69–102; and *BJB*, 19–27. Primary: *BW*, vols. 2–6, passim (note especially the scattered references to eyewitness Dr. Jonathan Cowdery's *Journal*); and William Ray, *Horrors of Slavery, or, American Tars in Tripoli* (Troy, N.Y., Oliver Lyon, 1808), 69, 79–81, 116–117. For reactions to the *Philadelphia*'s loss, Boston, N.Y., and Philadelphia newspapers, 20–28 March 1804. Also, *DP*, *WB*, and *JB* private correspondence. Secondary: Tucker, 189–304; *DNANO*, 71–82; Guttridge and Smith, 83–100; and Allan R. Millett, *Semper Fidelis: The History of the United States Marine Corps* (N.Y. and London, Macmillan, 1980), 44–45.

8. Samuel Barron. *BW*, vols. 4–6, passim; Tucker, 312–423; and *DNANO*, 82–86.

9. (A) Algerian War and the WB-Decatur relationship. Primary: *BWB*, based in part on CAPL, rolls 42–43, passim; and SNL, roll 12, passim; WB papers at New-York Historical Society; Rodgers Family Papers at ibid.; and Rodgers family papers, Rodgers-Meigs-Macomb family papers at LC. Boston's *Columbian Centinel* and *Independent Chronicle,* and Philadelphia's *Poulson*'s, June–Nov. 1815, passim. Secondary: Tucker, 447–465; Guttridge and Smith, 269–283; *DNANO,* 108–109; and Roy F. Nichols, *Advance Agents of American Destiny* (Philadelphia, University of Pennsylvania Press, 1956, repr. Westport, Conn., Greenwood Press, 1980), 108–121. (B) Chauncey. CAPL, roll 52, passim; *DNANO*, 119–120; and Nichols, 121–125.

Chapter 2

1. James Barron. Primary: *BW*, vol. 6, 540–570; *ASP, Class 1, Foreign Relations,* vol. 3, 6–23; and *Proceedings of the General Court Martial Convened for the Trial of Commodore James Barron* (Washington, Jacob Gideon, Jr., 1822), passim. Secondary: William O. Stevens, *An Affair of Honor: The Biography of Commodore James Barron* (Baltimore, Chesapeake Historical Society, 1969); Charles B. Gross, Jr., *The Chesapeake: The Biography of a Ship* (Chesapeake, Va., Norfolk County Historical Society, 1968); John M. Emmerson, comp., *The*

Chesapeake Affair of 1807 (Portsmouth, Va., privately printed, 1954); and Edwin M. Gaines, " 'Outrageous Encounter!' The *Chesapeake-Leopard* Affair of 1807" (unpublished Ph.D. dissertation, University of Virginia, 1960), all passim. Also, *BWB*, 109–112; *BDP*, 37–39; Leonard F. Guttridge and Jay D. Smith, *The Commodores* (N.Y., et al., Harper & Row, 1969), 125–133; Alfred T. Mahan, *Sea Power in Its Relation to the War of 1812*, 2 vols. (Boston, Little, Brown, 1903), vol. 1, 245–252; and Bradford Perkins, *Prologue to War: England and the United States, 1805–1812* (Berkeley and Los Angeles, University of California Press, 1963), 140, 147, 190–197, 354–355.

2.   Many of the naval histories that are eloquent on the *Chesapeake-Leopard* and *President-Little Belt* are silent about the *Vixen-Moselle*. Primary: Trippe to SN, 30 June 1810, USND, Letters received by the SN from officers below the rank of commander ("Officers' Letters"), M 148, roll 7; SN to Trippe, 20 July 1810, SNL, M 149, roll 9; *New Hampshire Patriot* (Concord), 7 Aug. 1810, 2/3–4; and *Times* (London), 2, 4 Sept. 1810, 3/1, 3/2. Secondary: Glenn Tucker, *Dawn like Thunder: The Barbary Wars and the Birth of the U.S. Navy* (Indianapolis and N.Y., Dodd, Mead, 1963), 301–302; Guttridge and Smith, 175–176; and "John Trippe," *DAB*, vol. 18, 645.

3.   Rodgers. Primary: *ASP, Class 1, Foreign Relations*, vol. 3, 471–500. Secondary: Henry Adams, *History of the United States of America during the Administrations of Thomas Jefferson and James Madison*, 9 vols. (London and N.Y., Charles Scribner's Sons, 1892), vol. 3, 26–45; Guttridge and Smith, 176–177; Mahan, vol. 1, 256–259; and Perkins, 272–273.

4.   Bainbridge in Brazil. Primary: CAPL, rolls 25–26, passim; SNL, roll 10, passim; USDS, Despatches from U.S. ministers to Brazil, M 121, roll 2, passim; and USDS, Consular despatches, St. Salvador (Bahia), T 432, rolls 1–2, passim; all at NA. Except for my *BWB*, 145–148, there seems no secondary account of this confrontation.

5.   For easy reference I have broken down the following notes on DP's cruise in the *Essex* according to chronological topics rather than retaining the primary-secondary division. *Nereyda, BDP*, 91; and DP, *Journal of a Cruise Made to the Pacific Ocean by Captain David Porter in the United States Frigate Essex, in the Years 1812, 1813, and 1814*, 2 vols., 2nd ed. (N.Y., Wiley & Halstead, 1822), vol. 1, 108–111.

6.   Galápagos. *BDP*, 91–108; and DP *Journal*, 117–227. (A) British reaction. *Times* (London), July 1814, passim; and William James's anti-American diatribe, *The Naval History of Great Britain from the Declaration of War by France, in February 1793, to the Accession of George IV, in January 1820*, 6 vols. (London, Harding, Lepard, 1826), vol. 6, 420. (B) American reaction. *NWR*, vols. 4–5, Aug. 1813–Jan. 1814, passim; Thomas H. Benton, *Thirty Years' View, or, a History of the Workings of the American Government for Thirty Years, from 1820–1850*, 2 vols. (N.Y., D. Appleton, 1854), vol. 2, 498; Theodore Roosevelt, *The Naval War of 1812*, 7th ed. (N.Y. and London, G. P. Putnam's Sons, 1898), 165; and C. S. Forester, *The Age of Fighting Sail: The Story of the Naval War of 1812* (Garden City, N.Y., Doubleday, 1956), 203–204.

7. (A) Marquesas. *BDP*, 109–137; and DP, *Journal*, vol. 2, 5–177. (B) Polynesian backgrounds. Robert C. Suggs, *The Hidden Worlds of Polynesia: The Chronicle of an Archaeological Expedition to Nuka Hiva in the Marquesas Islands* (N.Y., Harcourt, Brace & World, 1962), 31–57; and Ralph Linton, "Marquesan Culture," in Abram Kardiner, *The Individual and His Society* (N.Y., Columbia University Press, 1939), 150–158; Charles L. Lewis, *David Glasgow Farragut: Admiral in the Making* (Annapolis, U.S. Naval Institute, 1941), 84–88, 324, nn. 5, 18. (C) British reaction. *Quarterly Review* (London), vol. 13 (July 1815), 353–372. (D) American reaction. Boston's *Columbian Centinel* and *Independent Chronicle*, and *Salem Gazette*, 13–19 July 1814, passim.

8. (A) Loss of the *Essex. BDP*, 142–162; DP, *Journal*, vol. 2, Appendix, 233–256; and DP to SN, 4 April, 3 July 1814, CAPL, rolls 37, 38. (B) Hillyar. Hillyar to British Admiralty, 13 April, 26 June 1814, Captain's in-letters, Admiralty, 1/1950; HMS *Phoebe* Journal, Feb.–May 1814, passim, Admiralty 51/2675, both at Public Record Office, London; and Hillyar's *Official Report, Morning Chronicle* (London), 6 July 1814. (C) British reaction. *Times* (London), July 1814, passim; and James, vol. 6, 420–422. (D) American reaction. *Columbian Centinel, Independent Chronicle,* and *Salem Gazette*, 13–19 July 1814; Lewis, 91–106, Roosevelt, 291–310, and Forester, 205–210.

Chapter 3

1. Porter at West Florida. *BDP*, 43–50. This account is based largely on DP to SN, COML, roll 4; and SN to DP, SNL, roll 8, both 1808, passim.

2. Matthews. Primary: *CMPP*, vol. 1, 507–508; and *NWR*, vol. 2 (11 April 1812), 93–94. Secondary: Rembert W. Patrick, *Florida Fiasco: Rampant Rebels on the Georgia-Florida Boundaries, 1810–1815* (Athens, University of Georgia Press, 1954), 83–122; Wanjohi Waciuma, *Intervention in the Spanish Floridas, 1801–1813: A Study in Jeffersonian Foreign Policy* (Boston, Branden Press, 1976), 242–295; Virginia D. Peters, *The Florida Wars* (Hamden, Conn., Archon Books, 1979), 36–40; William T. Cash, *The Story of Florida* (N.Y., American Historical Society, 1938), 214–216; R. K. Wyllis, "The East Florida Revolution," *HAHR*, vol. 9 (1929), 428–437; and Thomas P. Abernethy, "Florida and the Spanish Frontier, 1811–1819," in Lucius P. Ellsworth, et al., eds., *The Americanization of the Gulf Coast, 1803–1850* (Pensacola, Historic Pensacola Preservation Board, 1972), 90–96.

3. Loomis and Barrett. Primary: Loomis to Patterson, 13 Aug. 1816, *ASP, Class 1, Foreign Relations,* vol. 4, 559–560; Patterson to SN, 16 Aug. 1816, *NASP*, vol. 2, 27–33; *DNI*, 18 Sept. 1816, 3/1–2; and 15 Nov. 1819, 2/1–2; and *NWR*, vol. 11 (14 Sept. 1816), 38. Secondary: Peters, 17–26; Cash, 228, 231–235; George F. Fairbanks, *History of Florida* (Philadelphia, Lippincott, 1871), 263–266; Hubert B. Fuller, *The Purchase of Florida: Its History and Diplomacy* (Cleveland, Burrows Brothers, 1906), 227–231; Frank D. Owsley, Jr., *The Struggle for the Gulf Borderlands* (Gainesville, University of Florida Press,

1981), 183–184; and James W. Silver, *Edmund Pendleton Gaines: Frontier General* (Baton Rouge, Louisiana State University Press, 1949), 60–64.

4. Henley. Primary: SN to Henley, 6 Feb. 1818) (2 letters), SNL, roll 13; Henley to SN, 30 Dec. 1817, CAPL, roll 56; *NWR*, vol. 13 (24 Jan. 1818), 348–352; *DNI*, 22 Dec. 1817, 2/3; 10, 14 Jan. 1818, 2/3, 2/4; *Times* (London), 26 Dec. 1817, 2/1; 4 Feb. 1818, 2/1; *CMPP*, vol. 2, 23–25; and *DIL*, vol. 2, 406–408. Secondary: Cash, 40; Abernethy, 112–117; Carlos C. Calkins, "The Repression of Piracy in the West Indies," *USNIP*, vol. 37 (1911), 1213–1214; and Richard G. Lowe, "American Seizure of Amelia Island," *Florida Historical Quarterly*, vol. 45 (1966), 18–36.

5. Morris. Primary: *NWR*, vol. 13 (15 Sept. 1817), 47; Secondary: *USSDOM*, 112–116; Ludwell L. Montague, *Haiti and the United States, 1714–1938* (Durham, N.C., Duke University Press, 1940), 48–49; and Rayford W. Logan, *The Diplomatic Relations between the United States and Haiti, 1776–1891* (Chapel Hill, University of North Carolina Press, 1941), 188–190. Read. Primary: Read to SN, 8 May, 15 June 1818, COML, roll 7; *NWR*, vol. 13 (14 May, 13 June 1818), 4, 263–264. Secondary: *USSDOM*, 116–119; Montague, 48–49, 59, n. 47; and *EAAFR*, 432.

6. Perry. Primary: Maury D. Baker, ed., "The Voyage of the U.S. Schooner *Nonsuch* up the Orinoco: Journal of the Perry Mission to South America," *HAHR*, vol. 30 (Nov. 1950), 480–498; *NWR*, vol. 15 (2 Oct. 1819), 71–72; *DNI*, 28, 30 Sept. 1819, 3/2, 2/5. Secondary: Alexander S. Mackenzie, *Life of Oliver Hazard Perry*, 2 vols. (N.Y., Harper & Bros., 1840), vol. 2, 184–225; Richard Dillon, *We Have Met the Enemy: Oliver Hazard Perry: Wilderness Commodore* (N.Y., McGraw-Hill, 1978), 213–220; and Arthur P. Whitaker, *The United States and the Independence of Latin America, 1800–1830* (Baltimore, Johns Hopkins University Press, 1941), 289–292.

7. Madison and Kearny. Primary: *NWR*, vol. 17 (5 Feb. 1820), 395–396. Secondary: George F. Emmons, *The Navy of the United States, from Its Commencement, 1775–1853* (Washington, Gideon & Co., 1853), 76–79; Calkins, 1208–1209; Louis N. Feipel, "The United States Navy and Mexico, 1821–1914," *USNIP*, vol. 41 (1915), 34; and "Lawrence Kearny," *DAB*, vol. 10, 540–541 (although the destruction of Galveston is misdated "early 1821"). Oddly, neither *DNI*, Feb.–April 1820, nor *NWR*, vol. 19 (1820) mentions Kearny's good work.

8. (A) Biddle. *BJB*, 93–111. Primary: Letters between JB and SN, 1822–1823, CAPL, rolls 78–80; SNL, roll 13, both passim; and *ASP*, Class 6, *Naval Affairs*, vol. 1, 804–806. Much of BJB was based upon three manuscript collections: JB papers, Andalusia (the Biddle family estate near Philadelphia), vol. 3; letters between JB and Thomas Cadwalader, Cadwalader Collection, Historical Society of Pennsylvania; and the Samuel F. DuPont letters, Winterthur Collection, Eleutherian Mills Historical Society, Greenville, Del., all passim. (B) JB in Cuba. Philip J. Foner, *A History of Cuba and Its Relations with the United States*, 2 vols. (N.Y., International Publishers, 1962, 1963), vol. 1, 140–141; and *JQAM*, vol. 6, 70–74. (C) JB, yellow fever, and aftermath. Primary: Midshipman Charles Gauntt's *Macedonian Journal*, 21 March–20 June 1822, LC; *Columbian Centinel*

(Boston), 17 Aug. 1822, 4/2; *NWR*, vol. 24 (19 April), 98; and (20 April 1823), 128. Secondary: David McCullogh, *The Path between the Seas: The Creation of the Panama Canal* (N.Y., Simon & Schuster, 1977), 140; Charles L. Lewis, *David Glasgow Farragut: Admiral in the Making* (Annapolis, U.S. Naval Institute, 1941), 163; and Leonard F. Guttridge and Jay D. Smith, *The Commodores* (N.Y., et al, Harper & Row, 1969), 301–302.

9. Porter. *BDP*, 207–255; *BJB*, 126–131; and *BWB*, 289–292. Primary: CAPL, rolls 85–89; and SNL, roll 15, 1823–1824, both passim. DP papers in the DDP papers, LC, is the main manuscript collection. DP's apologia for his Fajardo invasion is in his *An Exposition of the Facts and Circumstances Which Justified the Expedition to Foxardo* (Washington, Davis & Force, 1825), passim. For Presidents Monroe and JQA's agreement that DP must be punished, see Monroe, "Rough Notes," 18 July 1825; James Monroe papers, vol. 24, LC; and *JQAM*, vols. 6–7, passim, buttressed by Adams's "Diary" and "Rubbish III," at the Massachusetts Historical Society, Boston. DP's trials: *Minutes of the Proceedings of the Court of Inquiry and Court Martial in Relation to Captain David Porter Convened at Washington, D.C. on Thursday, the Seventh of July, A.D. 1825* (Washington, Davis & Force, 1825), passim. Also, *DNI* and *NWR*, July–Sept. 1825, passim. Secondary: DDP, *Memoir of Commodore David Porter of the United States Navy* (Albany, N.Y., J. Munsell, 1875), 271–296; Archibald D. Turnbull, *Commodore David Porter, 1780–1843* (N.Y. and London, The Century Co., 1929), 256–280; Richard S. West, Jr., *The Second Admiral: A Life of David Dixon Porter, 1813–1893* (N.Y., Coward-McCann, 1937), 16–17; Lewis, 150–153; Gardner W. Allen, *Our Navy and the West Indian Pirates* (Salem, Mass., Essex Institute, 1929), 28–71; and Michael Birkner, "The Foxardo Affair Revisited: Porter, Pirates, and the Problem of Civilian Authority in the Early Republic," *AN*, vol. 42 (July 1982), 165–178.

10. Warrington. Primary: Warrington-SN letters, CAPL, rolls 95–99, 101–106; SNL's *Report, 1825, ASP, Naval Affairs*, vol. 2, 93–94; and ibid., *1826*, CSS, 19th, 2nd, *HR 2*, vol. 1, *Serial 148*, 7. Anglo-American correspondence, *NASP*, vol. 5, 14–17. Adams's quote, *CMPP*, vol. 2, 309–310; and *NWR*, vol. 29 (17 Sept.), 36–37; (1 Oct.), 65; and (15 Oct. 1825), 100. Secondary: Richard Wheeler, *In Pirate Waters* (N.Y., Crowell, 1969), 167–171; Allen, 83–87; Calkins, 1237–1238; and Caspar F. Goodrich, "Our Navy and the West Indian Pirates, 1814–1825," *USNIP*, vol. 43 (1917), 2023–2025.

11. Cunningham. Primary: *CMPP*, vol. 1, 575; *DNI*, 8, 9, 10, 14 Oct. 1816, 2/1, 3/2, 3/2, 3/1; and *NWR*, vol. 11 (14 Dec. 1816), 255. Secondary: The only reference I could find was John Frost, *Book of the Navy* (N.Y., D. Appleton, 1843), 344.

12. (A) Porter's privateers. My research on DP in Mexico was much helped by Robert W. Bidwell's first-rate unpublished Ph.D. dissertation, "The First Mexican Navy, 1821–1830" (University of Virginia, 1960), passim. Primary: DP–Joel R. Poinsett correspondence, Gilpin collection, Historical Society of Pennsylvania, passim; USDS, Despatches from U.S. ministers in Mexico, M 97, rolls 3–4, passim; and *JQAM*, vol. 7, 229, 269. (B) Budd. *ASP, Naval Affairs*, vol.

4, 236–238. Secondary: William R. Manning, *Diplomatic Relations between the United States and Mexico* (Baltimore, Johns Hopkins University Press, 1916), 270–275; DDP, *Memoir*, 351–384; and Feipel, 35–36.

13. Elliott and Conner. Primary: *NWR*, vol. 37 (26 Sept.), 70; (28 Nov. 1829), 215. Secondary: Ranco Flores Caballero, *Counterrevolution: The Role of the Spaniards in the Independence of Mexico* (Lincoln, University of Nebraska Press, 1974), 135–150; and Michael C. Meyer and William L. Sherman, *Course of Mexican History* (N.Y., Oxford University Press, 1979), 319–322.

14. (A) Porter and Latin American independence, 1813, 1814, *BDP*, 144, 162–163. Primary: DP *Journal* (see chapter 2, n. 5 for full citation), vol. 1, 106–115; vol. 2, 144, 162–163. Secondary: J. Fred Rippy, *Joel R. Poinsett: Versatile American* (Durham, N.C., Duke University Press, 1935), 40–49; Joseph F. Straub, "José Miguel Carrera" (unpublished Ph.D. dissertation, University of Illinois, 1953), 86–90; and John C. Pine, "The Role of United States Special Agents in the Development of a Spanish American Policy, 1810–1822" (unpublished Ph.D. dissertation, University of Colorado, 1955), 183–185. (B) Porter and later Latin American independence. *BDP*, 189–202. Primary: Joel R. Poinsett Papers, Historical Society of Pennsylvania; *JQAM*, vol. 4, 444–445, 515–516; *DCUS-ILAN*, vol. 1, 42–45, 49, 74; vol. 2, 554; and *DIL*, vol. 1, 81–92. Secondary: Laura Bornholdt, *Baltimore and Early Pan-Americanism: A Study in the Background of the Monroe Doctrine* (Northampton, Mass., Smith College Studies in History, 1949), 34, 61–104; and Straub, 117–156.

15. (A) Biddle. *BJB*, 63–75; 80–81. Primary: USND, Confidential letters sent by the SN to officers, 1813–1822, 1840, and 1843–1879, NA; CAPL, rolls 56–60, passim; JB, "Journal Kept by James Biddle on the *Ontario*, 4 Oct. 1817–22 March 1819," M 902, roll 1, passim, NA; David Conner, "Journal of the *Ontario*, James Biddle, Esq., Master Commandant [Captain], by Her First Lieutenant, David Conner, U.S.N., 4 Oct. 1817–20 Feb. 1819," Franklin D. Roosevelt Library; and Jeremy Robinson, "Diary, 1818–1819," Peter Forbes collection, LC. Secondary: I acknowledge my debt to *IDNR*. In my research for *BJB* I was able to check thoroughly the accuracy of Billington's first 75 pages about JB in lower South America. In general I found that his research had been exhaustive and his conclusions judicious. Hence, I have not the slightest compunction about basing most of my description of JB's successors—Downes, Ridgely, Stewart, and Hull—upon this excellent monograph. *TRCH* is also well worth reading, but Johnson is able to devote only 38 pages to 1818–1825, compared to *IDNR*'s 209. (B) Cochrane. Thomas, Lord Cochrane, *Narration of Services in the Liberation of Chili (sic), Peru, and Brazil from Spanish and Portuguese Domination*, 2 vols. (London, James Ridgway, 1859), vol. 2, 29–34; and Christopher Lloyd, *Lord Cochrane: Seaman—Radical—Liberator: A Life of Thomas, Lord Cochrane, 10th Earl of Dundonald* (London, Longmans, Green, 1947), 143–147.

16. Downes. *IDNR*, 76–120. Primary: CAPL, rolls 60–70, passim; SNL, rolls 13–14, passim; *DCUS-ILAN*, vol. 2, passim; John Downes, "Narrative of a Cruise Made by the United States Frigate *Macedonian*, John Downes, Esq., Commander," NA; Charles J. Deblois, "Private Journal Kept on Board the U.S.

Frigate *Macedonian*, 1818–1819," NA; Charles Gauntt, "Private Remarks of Lieutenant Chas. Gauntt, of the U.S. Ship *Macedonian*, Made during a Cruise in the Pacific Ocean in the Years 1818, 19, 20, 21," NA; and Cochrane, vol. 2, 83–94. Secondary: Lloyd, 147–154; and *TRCH*, 17–26.

17. Ridgely. *IDNR*, 121–147. Primary: CAPL, rolls 70–78, passim; SNL, roll 14, passim; Charles G. Ridgely, "Journal of Charles G. Ridgely, Captain in the U.S. Navy, from 18 May 1815 till 30 March 1821 [actually July 1821]," NA; *DCUS-ILAN*, vols. 2–3, passim; and Gerald S. Graham and R. A. Humphreys, eds., *The Navy and South America, 1807–1823: Correspondence of the Commanders-in-Chief of the South American Station* (Oxford, U.K., Clarendon Press; N.Y., Oxford University Press, 1962), passim. Secondary: *TRCH*, 27–29.

18. Stewart. *IDNR* has two chapters: 8 on his cruise, 148–173, and 9 on his court-martial, 174–193. Primary: CAPL, rolls 78–87, passim; SNL, rolls 14–15, passim; *DCUS-ILAN*, vol. 3, passim; "The Log of the *Franklin*, 31 July 1821–14 Sept. 1824," NA; Lieutenant Thomas S. Hammersly, "Journal Kept on Board the United States Ship *Franklin* of 74 Guns, Charles Stewart, Esq., Commander," LC; USND, Records of the office of the judge advocate general (navy), Record Group 125, Records of general courts-martial and courts of inquiry, 1799–1867, NA. Most of these records are reprinted in a far more accessible form in *ASP, Naval Affairs,* vol. 2, 487–610. Secondary: *TRCH*, 29–35.

19. Hull. *IDNR*, 194–201, but the definitive study is Linda M. Maloney, *Captain from Connecticut: The Life and Naval Times of Isaac Hull* (Boston, Northeastern University Press, 1986), 364–412. Primary: CAPL, rolls 86–98, passim; SNL, rolls 15–16, passim; and *DCUS-ILAN*, vol. 3, passim. Secondary: *TRCH*, 35–38; and T. Ray Shurbutt, "Chile, Peru, and the U.S. Pacific Squadron, 1823–1850," Craig L. Symonds, et al., eds., *New Aspects of Naval History: Selected Papers Presented at the Fourth Naval History Symposium, United States Naval Academy, 25–26 October 1979* (Annapolis, Naval Institute Press, 1981), 202–204.

20. Jones. Only one letter refers to his Peruvian difficulties: Jones to SN, 17 March 1828, CAPL, roll 124. Also, Maloney, 410–411; and *TRCH*, 39–40.

Chapter 4

1. Elliott. Primary: Robertson to SS, 9 June 1832, USDS, Consular despatches, Tampico, M 304, roll 1, NA. Secondary: Louis N. Feipel, "The United States Navy and Mexico, 1821–1914," *USNIP*, vol. 41 (1915), 38–39.

2. Tattnall. Primary: Tattnall-Elliott letters, 11, 20 Sept. 1832, USND, Letters received by the SN from officers below the rank of commander, M 148, roll 78, NA; *DNI*, 3, 10 Sept. 1832, 3/5, 3/1; and *NWR*, vol. 43 (15 Sept.), 42; (6 Oct. 1832), 82–83. Secondary: Charles C. Jones, Jr., *The Life and Services of Commodore Josiah Tattnall* (Savannah, Morning News, 1878), 38–39; and Feipel, 38.

3. Dallas. Primary: *DCUS-IAA*, vol. 8, *Mexico, 1831–1848*, 81; *NWR*, vol. 51 (25 Feb. 1837), 410; and HR *Foreign Relations Committee Report*, 21

Feb. 1837, in *DNI*, 27 Feb. 1837, 3/1. Secondary: Feipel's account, 39–40, is obviously based upon the latter, for his wording is often the same.

4.   Mervine. Primary: HR *Report* in *DNI*, 27 Feb. 1837; *DCUS-IAA*, vol. 8, 79–82; and Jackson's *Proclamation*, 6 Feb. 1837, *CMPP*, vol. 3, 278–279. Secondary: Feipel, 40–42.

5.   Dallas. Primary: *DCUS-IAA*, vol. 8, 81, 469–470; and *NWR*, vol. 51 (17 Sept. 1837), 33. Feipel ignores this incident.

6.   Tattnall. Primary: Antonio Lopez de Santa Anna, *The Autobiography of Santa Anna*, ed. by Ann F. Crawford (Austin, Pemberton Press, 1967), passim; and *NWR*, vol. 52 (8 April 1838), 93. Secondary: C. G. Jones, Jr., 43–46; Oakah L. Jones, *Santa Anna* (N.Y., Twayne Publishers, 1968), 74–75; Willfrid H. Callcott, *Santa Anna: The Enigma Who Was Mexico* (Norman, Oklahoma University Press, 1931), 150–151; M. K. Wisehart, *Sam Houston: American Giant* (Washington, Robert B. Luce, 1962), 281–285; and Feipel, 42–43.

7.   Mervine. Primary: *NASP*, vol. 2, 39–41. For *Urrea* correspondence, *CSS*, 25th, 2nd, *HR 75*, vol. 3, *Serial 322*, 1–46; *DCUS-IAA*, vol. 8, 423; *NWR*, vol. 52 (13 May–10 June 1837); and *DNI*, 12–31 May 1837, both passim. Secondary: Feipel, 43; and K. Jack Bauer, "The U.S. Navy and Texas Independence," *Military Affairs*, vol. 34 (April 1970), 44–48.

8.   Forrest. Primary: SN Upshur's *Report, 1841*, *CSS*, 27th, 2nd, *SEN 1*, vol. 1, *Serial 395*, 368; and *NWR* vol. 58 (8 Aug. 1841), 354. Secondary: Hubert H. Bancroft, *The Works of Hubert H. Bancroft*, 39 vols. (San Francisco, The History Co., through 1886; A. L. Bancroft, 1887–1890), vol. 21, *History of California*, 6–13; Andrew F. Rolle, *California: A History*, 2nd ed. (N.Y., Thomas Y. Crowell, 1969), 160–165; Robert G. Cleland, *A History of California: The American Period* (N.Y., Macmillan, 1922), 191–192; and David Lavender, *California: Land of New Beginnings* (N.Y., et al., Harper & Row, 1972), 118–119. Feipel's account, 44, is based so closely on Upshur's *Report* as to approach plagiarism.

9.   Jones. Few episodes in U.S. naval diplomacy have received more attention than this. Primary: *CSS*, 27th, 3rd, *HR 166*, vol. 5, *Serial 422*, 1–115 (SN Upshur's *Report, 1843*, in this *Serial* does not mention Monterey; his only reference to the occurrence was this: "On the 24th of January Commodore Jones was recalled."); Charles R. Anderson, ed., *Journal of a Cruise to the Pacific Ocean, 1842–1844, in the Frigate United States* (Durham, N.C., Duke University Press, 1937), appendix B, 78–102; Richard H. Maxwell, *Visit to Monterey*, ed. by John H. Kemble (Los Angeles, G. Dawson, 1955), 17–27; Samuel R. Franklin, *Memories of a Rear-Admiral Who Has Served for More than Half a Century in the Navy of the United States* (N.Y. and London, Harper & Bros., 1898), 48–51; *DNI*, Jan. 1843, and *NWR*, vol. 63 (21 Jan.–13 May 1843), both passim. Secondary: George C. Rives, *The United States and Mexico, 1821–1848*, 2 vols. (N.Y., Charles Scribner's Sons, 1913), vol. 1, 516–523; Bancroft, 298–329; Neal Harlow, *California Conquered: War and Peace on the Pacific, 1846–1850* (Berkeley, et al., University of California Press, 1982), 3–13; Cleland, 148–152; *TRCH*, 62–66; David M. Pletcher, *Diplomacy of Annexation: Texas, Oregon,*

and the Mexican War (Columbia, University of Missouri Press, 1973), 100–101; George M. Brooke, Jr., "The Vest Pocket War of Commodore Jones," *PHR*, vol. 31 (Aug. 1962), 217–233; G. G. Hatheway, "Commodore Jones's War," *History Today*, vol. 16 (March 1966), 194–201; Gilbert Workman, "A Forgotten Fire-brand: Commodore Thomas C. Jones," *USNIP*, vol. 94 (Sept. 1968), 79–87; Frank W. Gapp, "The 'Capture' of Monterey in 1842," ibid., vol. 105 (March 1979), 46–54; and Feipel, 45–49.

    10.   Gillespie. Primary: James K. Polk, *The Diary of a President, 1845–1849*, ed. by Allan Nevins (London, et al., Longmans, Green, 1952), 22; and George P. Hammond, ed., *The Larkin Papers, Personal, Business, and Official Correspondence of Thomas O. Larkin, Merchant and U.S. Consul in California*, 11 vols. (Berkeley, University of California Press, 1951–1968), vol. 4, passim. Secondary: Allan Nevins, *Frémont: Pathmarker of the West* (N.Y. and London, D. Appleton, 1939), 22, 237–249; *MW*, 186–187; and Harlow, 77–84.

    11.   Mackenzie. Primary: Polk, *Diary*, 5–53. Secondary: Jesse L. Reeves, *American Diplomacy under Tyler and Polk* (Baltimore, Johns Hopkins University Press, 1907), 299–307; Callcott, 231–236; O. L. Jones, 104–107; Rives, 232–237; Pletcher, 444–449; and *MW*, 76–77.

    12.   Biddle, et al. Primary: USND, Pacific SL, rolls 32–34, passim; Stockton to JB, 17, 25 March 1847, JB papers, Andalusia, vol. 13; Benajah Tichnor, "Journal, 1845–1848, on Board the *Columbus* on a Voyage from New York to the East Indies," 4 Jan. 1847, 195–197, Benajah Tichnor Collection, Yale University. Secondary: *MW*, 164–172; Harlow, 116–278; *TRCH*, 77–79, 89, 91; Nevins, *Frémont*, 305–311.

    13.   Conner and M. C. Perry. Primary: *NASP*, vol. 2, 191–204; vol. 5, 94–95, 196–203. Secondary: Frederick Merk, *The Monroe Doctrine and American Expansionism, 1843–1849* (N.Y., Knopf, 1966), 198–232; *OBMCP*, 202–203, 243–249; Dorothy Graebner, *Crisis Diplomacy: A History of U.S. Intervention Policies and Practices* (Washington, Public Affairs Press, 1959), 81–82; Pletcher, 568–571, 574–575; and *MW*, 109–110, 338–339.

    14.   Dornin. Primary: Dornin to SN, 15 Feb.–20 March 1854, COML, roll 46, passim (for Walker); ibid., 22 May 1854, ibid. (for Mazatlán prisoners); SN Dobbin's *Report, 1854, CSS*, 33rd, 2nd, *HR 1*, vol. 1, *Serial 778*, 389–390; and *DCUS-IAA*, vol. 9, *Mexico, 1848–1860*, 158, 162–163, 719–737, 1170–1173. Secondary: Albert Z. Carr, *The World and William Walker* (N.Y., et al., Harper & Row, 1963), 73–91; Joseph A. Stout, *The Liberators: Filibustering Expeditions into Mexico, 1848–1862, and the Last Thrust of Manifest Destiny* (Los Angeles, Westernlore Press, 1973), 80–101; and Feipel, 1193–1194.

    15.   Almy. Primary: Almy to SN, 13, 23 April 1858, USND, Letters received by the SN from officers below the rank of commander, M 148, roll 250. Secondary: Feipel, 1194. The *NYT* ignored the story.

    16.   Dahlgren. Primary: Dahlgren's letters, Madeleine Dahlgren, *Memoir of John A. Dahlgren, Rear-Admiral, United States Navy, by His Widow* (N.Y., C. L. Webster, 1891), 214–217. Secondary: Feipel, 1995. Again, the *NYT* was silent.

    17.   Davis. Primary: Davis to SN, 1 Oct. 1858–30 June 1859, COML, rolls

59–61, passim; and SN Toucey's *Report, 1859, CSS*, 36th, 1st, *SEN 2*, vol. 2, *Serial 1025*, 1146. Secondary: Feipel, 1996.

18. Jarvis and Turner. Primary: *CSS*, 36th, 1st, *SEN 29*, vol. 9, *Serial 1031*, 1–13; *NASP*, vol. 2, 261–267; *DCUS-IAA*, vol. 9, 1169–1172; SN Toucey's *Report, 1860, CSS*, 36th, 1st, *SEN 1*, vol. 3, *Serial 1080*, 12; *DIL*, vol. 2, 893–895; and *NYT*, 21 March–2 April 1860, passim. Secondary: Charles A. Smart, *Viva Juarez! A Biography* (Philadelphia and N.Y., Lippincott, 1963, repr. Westport, Conn., Greenwood Press, 1975, 205–219); Ralph Roeder, *Juarez and His Mexico*, 2 vols. (N.Y., Viking, 1947), vol. 1, 221–222; Bancroft, *Works*, vol. 13, *History of Mexico, 1824–1861*, 776–779; and Feipel, 1996–1997.

Chapter 5

1. Gedney and Meade. Primary: *The Basic Afro-American Library*, sel. by Charles L. Holte, *The Amistad Case: The Most Celebrated Slave Mutiny of the Nineteenth Century* (N.Y. and London, Johnson Reprint Co., 1968), passim. U.S. Congress, 26th, 1st, *HR 185, Africans Taken in the Amistad*, 1–69, added later, 1–6; *DNI* and *NWR*, many articles and editorials, 1839–1841, both passim. Secondary: Christopher Martin, *The Amistad Affair* (London, et al., Abelard-Schuman, 1970), passim; and William A. Owens, *Black Mutiny: The Revolt on the Schooner Amistad* (Philadelphia and Boston, J. Day Co., 1953), passim.

2. Rodgers, et al. Primary: SN Graham's *Report, 1850, CSS*, 31st, 2nd, *HR 1*, vol. 1, *Serial 595*, 193. Secondary: Robert C. Caldwell, *The Lopez Expeditions to Cuba, 1848–1851* (Princeton, Princeton University Press, 1915), 57–78; Robert E. Johnson, *Rear-Admiral John Rodgers, 1812–1882* (Annapolis, U.S. Naval Institute, 1967), 91–92; French E. Chadwick, *The Relations of the United States and Spain: Diplomatic* (N.Y., Scribner's, 1909), 230–246; Philip S. Foner, *A History of Cuba and Its Relations with the United States*, 2 vols. (N.Y., International Publishers, 1962, 1963), vol. 2, 45–55; Basil Rauch, *American Interest in Cuba, 1848–1855* (N.Y., Columbia University Press, 1948), 128–135; Charles R. Jones, Jr., *The Life and Services of Commodore Josiah Tattnall* (Savannah, Morning News, 1878), 67–70; Paolo E. Coletta, *The American Naval Heritage in Brief* (Washington, University Press of America, 1978), 131–133; and Louis N. Feipel, "The Navy and Filibustering in the Fifties," *USNIP*, vol. 44 (1918), 1009–1027.

3. Platt and Parker. Primary: SN Graham's *Report, 1851, CSS*, 32nd, 1st, *HR 2*, vol. 2, *Serial 612*, 1; Fillmore's *Message, 1851, CMPP*, vol. 5, 113–115; *NASP*, vol. 2, 137–138; *CSS*, 32nd, 1st, *HR 19*, vol. 3, *Serial 637* (on American prisoners in Spain), passim; and Charles S. Stewart, *Brazil and La Plata: The Personal Record of a Cruise* (N.Y., G. P. Putnam, 1856), 38–41. Secondary: Caldwell, 83–113; Chadwick, 236–241; Foner, 55–60; Rauch, 154–165; and Paolo E. Coletta, *American Secretaries of the Navy*, 2 vols. (Annapolis, Naval Institute Press, 1980), vol. 1, 253–254.

4. McCauley. Primary: SN Dobbin's *Report, 1855, CSS*, 34th, 1st. *HR 1*,

vol. 1, *Serial 842*, 4; Buchanan's *Message, 1857, CMPP*, vol. 5, 445; *DIL*, vol. 2, 890–891; and *NYT*, 15 March, 10 April 1855, 4/5, 4/1, 8/1.

5.   Parker. Primary: *DCUS-IAA*, vol. 7, *Great Britain, 1832–1860*, 73–84, 444–449; *CSS*, 32nd, 1st, *SEN 30*, vol. 7, *Serial 618*, 1–9; *NASP*, vol. 2, 208–211; and *NYT*, 2 Dec. 1851, 2/1, 3/1. Secondary: Charles H. Brown, *Agents of Manifest Destiny: The Lives and Times of The Filibusters* (Chapel Hill, University of North Carolina Press, 1980), 245–246; Lester D. Langley, *Struggles for the American Caribbean: United States–Europe Rivalry in the Gulf-Caribbean, 1776–1904* (Athens, University of Georgia Press, 1976), 100; and Mario Rodriguez, "The *Prometheus* and the Clayton-Bulwer Treaty," *Journal of Modern History*, vol. 36 (Sept. 1976), 260–278, especially 264–269.

6.   Hollins, 1853. Primary: SN Dobbin's *Report, 1853, CSS*, 33rd, 1st, *HR 1*, vol. 1, *Serial 712*, 297; *DCUS-IAA*, vol. 4, *Central America, 1851–1860*, 59–60, 113–114, 461–463, 963–964; and *NYT*, 2 April 1853, 3/1. Secondary: Roy F. Nichols, *Franklin Pierce: Young Hickory of the Granite Hills* (Philadelphia, University of Pennsylvania Press, 261–262; and Mary W. Williams, *Anglo-American Isthmian Diplomacy, 1815–1915* (Washington, American Historical Association, 1916, repr. Gloucester, Mass., P. Smith, 1965), 171–173.

7.   Hollins, 1854. His derring-do at Greytown was attention-getting enough to evoke a tremendous amount of comment, contemporary and later. Primary: SN Dobbin's *Report* and Pierce's *Message*, both 1854, *CSS*, 33rd, 1st, *SEN 8*, vol. 4, *Serial 694*, ibid., *SEN 85*, vol. 12, *Serial 702*, 1–30; ibid., *HR 126*, vol. 16, *Serial 734*, 500–502; *DCUS-IAA*, vol. 7, 80–84, 108–109, 494–495, 500–502; *DIL*, vol. 2, 404–418; *NYT*, 29 July 1854, 4/1; and *Times* (London), n.d., in ibid., 28 Sept. 1854, 2/4. For a real oddity, George N. Hollins, "Autobiography of Commodore George Nicholas Hollins," *Maryland Historical Magazine*, vol. 34 (1939), 228–243. It contains nothing about Greytown; indeed, not a word concerning Hollins's life, 1821–1861. Secondary: Williams, 168–186 (including the London *Globe* quotation); Kenneth Bourne, *Britain and the Balance of Power in North America, 1815–1908* (Berkeley, University of California Press, 1967), 178–185; Nichols, 261–262; Brown, 247–250; Ivor D. Spencer, *The Victor and the Spoils: A Life of William L. Marcy* (Providence, Brown University Press, 1959), 264–268; *PCA*, 32–35; H. C. Allen, *Great Britain and the United States: A History of Anglo-American Relations, 1783–1952* (London, St. Martin's Press, 1954), 433–434; and Richard W. Van Alstyne, "Anglo-American Relations, 1853–1859," *AHR*, vol. 42 (1937), 491–500.

8.   Paulding, 1855. Primary: SN Dobbin's *Report, 1855, CSS*, 34th, 3rd, *SEN 5*, vol. 2, *Serial 876*, 405–406; and Jonathan Wheeler to SS, 4 June 1855, USDS, Despatches from U.S. ministers to Central America, Nicaragua, M 219, roll 10.

9.   Davis. Primary: SN Toucey's *Report, 1857, CSS*, 35th, 1st, *HR 1*, vol. 2, *Serial 942*, 575–576; William Walker, *The War in Nicaragua* (Mobile, S. H. Goetzel, 1860, repr. Detroit, B. Ethridge, 1972), 419–429—ending with Davis, May 1857; *DIL*, vol. 1, 140–144; and *NYT*, 28 May 1857, 1/5, 4/2. *DCUS-IAA*, vol. 4, *Central America, 1851–1860*, which devotes scores of pages to

Walker's career, does not even mention Davis. Secondary: Albert Z. Carr, *The World and William Walker* (N.Y., et al., Harper & Row, 1963), 218–221; Charles H. Davis, *Life of Charles Henry Davis; Rear Admiral, 1807–1877* (Boston and N.Y., Houghton Mifflin, 1909), 101–104; William O. Scroggs, *Filibusters and Financiers: The Story of William Walker and His Associates* (N.Y., Macmillan, 1916), 292–303; Wheaton J. Lane, *Commodore Vanderbilt: An Epic of the Steam Age* (N.Y., A. A. Knopf, 1942), 113–131; Gerstle Mack, *The Land Divided: A History of the Panama Canal and Other Isthmian Canal Projects* (N.Y., A. A. Knopf, 1944), 196–199; Feipel, 1540–1545; Scroggs, "William Walker and the Steamship Corporation in Nicaragua," *AHR*, vol. 10 (July 1905), 806–811; and James A. Wood, "Expansionism as Diplomacy: The Career of Solon Borland," *The Americas,* vol. 40 (Jan. 1984), 399–415.

10. Paulding. Primary: *CSS*, 35th, 1st, *SEN 83,* vol. 13, *Serial 930,* 1–22 (dealing only with Walker's arrest, not his ensuing controversy with Paulding); Buchanan's *Message, 1858, CMPP,* vol. 5, 466–469; SM Toucey's *Report, 1858, CSS,* 35th, 2nd, *HR 1,* vol. 2, *Serial 1000,* 3; Rebecca Paulding Meade (Paulding's daughter), *Life of Hiram Paulding* (N.Y., Baker & Taylor, 1910), 180–200 (with his letters about this episode); *DCUS-IAA,* vol. 4, 963–964; and *NYT,* 28 Dec. 1857, 1/1–4, 4/2 (followed by numerous articles and editorials over the next several weeks). Secondary: Carr, 233–240; Brown, 411–419; Scroggs, *Filibusters,* 326–351; Robert E. May, *The Southern Dream of a Caribbean Empire, 1854–1861* (Baton Rouge, University of Louisiana Press, 1973), 112–117; and Feipel, 1837–1848, 2063–2074.

11. D. D. Porter. Primary: DDP, "Secret Mission to San Domingo," *North American Review,* vol. 128 (1879), 616–626. Secondary: *USSDOM,* 127–130; and *EAAFR,* 446–449.

12. Bailey and Mervine. There are so many skeins in the pattern of the U.S. Navy in Panama that subdivisions seem to be in order. (A) Watermelon Riot. Primary: *DCUS-IAA,* vol. 4, 392; *DIL,* vol. 3, 34–39 and 7, 109–111; and *NYT,* 30 April 1856, 1/6, 2/1–3, 4/1–2 (for the riot); 23 Sept. 1856, 1/5–6, 3/1–2 (for the complete Corwine *Report*). Secondary: Mack, 161–165; Hubert H. Bancroft, *The Works of Hubert H. Bancroft,* 39 vols. (San Francisco, The History Co., 1883–1886; A. L. Bancroft, 1887–1890), vol. 8, *Central America, 1801–1887,* 526–529; E. Taylor Parks, *Colombia and the United States, 1765–1934* (Durham, N.C., Duke University Press, 1935), 219–224; and Jean C. Niemeir, *The Panama Story* (Portland, Ore., Metropolitan Press, 1968), 65 (how the Panama City *Star and Herald* newspaper covered the riot). (B) Bailey's protests. *DCUS-IAA,* vol. 5, *Chile and Colombia,* 737, 741, 745; and Parks, 223. (C) Mervine and the tonnage issue. *DCUS-IAA,* vol. 5, 412, 780, 781*n,* 914–915; and Parks, 237–239. (D) September disorders. SN Dobbin's *Report, 1856, CSS,* 34th, 3rd, *SEN 5,* vol. 2, *Serial 876,* 405–406; *NYT,* 29 Sept. 1856, 2/3; Bancroft, 527–528; and *PCA,* 37–38. (E) Financial settlement. Pierce's *Message, 1856, CMPP,* vol. 5, 416; and Parks, 286–302.

13. Turner. Primary: Thomas Turner Letterbook, 1858–1860, Mss and Archives Division, N.Y. Public Library, 12–26, especially 25–26. Secondary: Roy

F. Nichols, *Advance Agents of American Destiny* (Philadelphia, University of Pennsylvania Press, 1956), 187–189, 207–209; Ludwell L. Montague, *Haiti and the United States, 1714–1938* (Durham, N.C., Duke University Press, 1940), 61–65; Rayford W. Logan, *The United States and Haiti, 1776–1891* (Chapel Hill, University of North Carolina Press, 1941), 361–362; *USSDOM*, 206–207; and Nichols, "Navassa: A Forgotten Acquisition," *AHR*, vol. 38 (1933), 505–510.

14. Poor. Poor to SN, 21 Aug., 24 Sept. 1860, COML, roll 65; and SN Toucey's *Report, 1860, CSS*, 36th, 2nd, *SEN 1*, vol. 3, *Serial 1080*, 11–12.

15. Montgomery and W. D. Porter. Primary: Ibid., 15; and *NYT*, 8, 16, 24 Oct. 1860, 4/1, 4/3, 4/1. Secondary: *TRCH*, 110–111; *PCA*, 42; and J. Reuben Clark, "The Right to Protect Citizens in Foreign Countries by Landing Forces of the United States," *Memorandum of 5 October 1912*, by the Solicitor (Washington, Government Printing Office, 1912), 62–63. The latter two do no more than quote or closely paraphrase Toucey's *Report*, ignoring altogether the Anglo-American clash.

Chapter 6

1. Sinclair. Primary: Henry M. Brackenridge, *A Voyage to South America, Performed by the Order of the American Government in the Years 1817 and 1818 in the Frigate Congress*, 2 vols. (London, privately printed, 1820), vol. 1, 156–164; *DNI*, 29 April; 5, 29 May 1818, 3/2, 3/1–2, 2/3; and *NWR*, vol. 14 (2 May 1818), 168. Secondary: Lawrence F. Hill, *Diplomatic Relations between the United States and Brazil* (Durham, N.C., Duke University Press, 1932), 10–11.

2. Elliott and Biddle. *BJB*, 131–138. Primary: Samuel L. Southard letter book to officers, 19 May 1826–1 Nov. 1828, passim, New-York Historical Society; CAPL, roll 100, passim (located for some reason in what the NA calls "Letters from Captain Isaac Hull, 19 Jan.–10 Dec. 1826, and Captain James Biddle, 16 Aug.–17 Dec. 1826"; also CAPL, rolls 117–120, passim. Brazilian-Argentine War. *CSS*, 20th, 1st, *HR 281*, vol. 7, *Serial 175*, 1–282; USDS, Despatches from U.S. ministers to Argentina, roll 4, passim, NA; *JQAM*, vol. 7, 385, 500; and *NWR*, vol. 31 (25 Sept., 9 Oct. 1826), 63–64, 128. Secondary: John Street, [José Gervasio] *Artigas and the Emancipation of Uruguay* (Cambridge, U.K., Cambridge University Press, 1959), 346–349; Hill, 44–45; Harold F. Peterson, *Argentina and the United States, 1810–1964* (Albany, N.Y., State University of New York, University Publishers, 1964), 88–92; Henry S. Ferns, *Britain and Argentina in the Nineteenth Century* (N.Y., 1960, Oxford University Press), 155–194; John H. Hahn, "Brazil and the Rio de la Plata, 1808–1829," (unpublished Ph.D. dissertation, University of Texas, 1967), 425–428; and Donald W. Giffin, "The American Navy at Work on the Brazil Station," *AN*, vol. 19 (Oct. 1959), 239–256.

3. Turner and Tattnall, 1828. Primary: USDS, Thomas M. Harrison to

Mayor, 5 Dec. 1828; 2 Feb. 1829, Consular despatches, St. Barts, M 72, roll 2; and *NWR*, vol. 35 (10 Jan. 1829), 323. Secondary: Charles C. Jones, Jr., *The Life and Services of Josiah Tattnall* (Savannah, Morning News, 1878), 30–33.

4.   Mayo. Primary: Mayo to SN, 23 Oct. 1837, COML, roll 21; William Hunter to SS, 12, 22 Feb., 7 March, USDS, Despatches from U.S. ministers to Brazil, rolls 12–13, NA. Secondary: Hill, 79–80.

5.   Turner, 1845. Primary: *DIL*, vol. 2, 4–5; *DNI*, 24 April 1845, 3/2–3; and *NWR*, vol. 68 (12 April 1845), 84–85. Secondary: Hill, 139–140.

6.   Davis. Primary: *DCUS-IAA*, vol. 2, *Bolivia and Brazil*, 140–153, 358–365; *DNI*, 18 Jan. 1847, 4/1; and *NWR*, vol. 71 (23 Jan. 1847), 336. Secondary: Hill, 95–105; Barton H. Wise, *The Life of Henry A. Wise of Virginia, 1806–1876, by His Grandson, the Late Barton H. Wise* (N.Y. and London, Macmillan, 1899), 118–119; and Giffin, 247–248.

7.   Much has been published about Duncan, and because of the Anglo-Argentine combat in 1982, more is sure to follow. Primary: SN Woodbury's *Report, 1831, CSS,* 22nd, 1st, *HR 1,* vol. 1, *Serial 216,* 37; ibid., *1833,* ibid., 22nd, 2nd, *HR 2,* vol. 1, *Serial 233,* 42; Jackson's *Messages, 1831, CMPP,* vol. 2, 553, *1833,* ibid., vol. 3, 27; *DCUS-IAA,* vol. 1, *Argentina,* 778; and *NWR,* vol. 42 (12 May 1832), 205–206. Secondary: Julius Goebel, *The Struggle for the Falklands: A Study in Legal and Diplomatic History* (New Haven, Yale University Press, 1927), 436–459; M. D. B. Cawkell, D. H. Maling, and E. M. Cawkell, *The Falkland Islands* (London, Macmillan, 1960), 38–43, 51, 100–101; Peterson, 101–117; Ferns, 224–233; John W. White, *Argentina: The Life Story of a Nation* (N.Y., Viking, 1943), 274–277; William W. Robertson, *Hispanic-American Relations with the United States* (N.Y., Oxford University Press, 1923), 170–175; Charles E. Martin, *The Policy of the United States as Regards Intervention* (N.Y., Columbia University Studies in History, Economics, and Public Law, 1921), 124–127; John M. Belohlavek, *"Let the Eagle Soar!" The Foreign Policy of Andrew Jackson* (Lincoln and London, University of Nebraska Press, 1985), 162–173; P. D. Dickens, "The Falkland Islands Dispute between the United States and Argentina," *HAHR,* vol. 9 (Oct. 1976), 17–21; Robert Greenhow, "The Falkland Islands: A Memoir: Descriptive, Historical, and Political," *The Merchant's Magazine and Commercial Review,* vol. 6 (Feb. 1842), 139–151; and Craig E. Klafter, "United States Involvement in the Falkland Island Crisis of 1831–1833," *Journal of the Early Republic,* vol. 4 (winter 1984), 395–420.

8.   Lynch. Primary: *DIL,* vol. 1, 888–889; and *NYT,* 23 May 1854, 8/1. Secondary: Dickens, 486; and *Time* (19 April 1982), 39.

9.   Primary: *DCUS-IAA,* 201–202, 206–207; and *NWR,* vol. 56 (2 March, 25 May, 15 June, 10 Aug. 1839), 1, 294, 42, 370. Secondary: John C. Cady, *Foreign Intervention in the Rio de la Plata, 1838–1850: A Study of French, British, and American Policy in Relation to the Dictator Juan Manuel Rosas* (Philadelphia, University of Pennsylvania Press, 1929), 56–61; Peterson, 124–127; John Lynch, *Argentine Dictator: Juan Manuel de Rosas* (Oxford, U.K., Clarendon Press, 1981), 266–269; Ricardo Levine, *A History of Argentina,* trans.

and ed. by William S. Robertson (Chapel Hill, University of North Carolina Press, 1937), 424–425; and Robertson, 144–145.

10. Voorhees. Primary: *DCUS-IAA*, 27–29, 237–251, 262–268, 302–303; *DIL*, vol. 1, 178–182; *DNI*, 11 Dec. 1844; 12 Sept., 6 Oct. 1845, 3/4, 3/3, 3/1; and *NWR*, vol. 67 (4 Dec. 1844), vol. 68 (22 March, 26 April, 14 June, 16 Aug., 23 Aug. 1845), 225–226, 36, 117, 227–228, 372, 403; and vol. 69 (13 Dec. 1845), 217. Secondary: K. Jack Bauer, "The *Sancala* Affair: Captain Voorhees Seizes an Argentine Squadron," *AN*, vol. 29 (July 1968), 174–186; and Peterson, 129–131.

11. Pendergast. Primary: *DNI*, 12 Sept., 6 Oct. 1845, 3/3, 3/1; and *NWR*, vol. 69 (6 Sept., 20 Sept., 1 Oct. 1845), 18, 48, 83. Secondary: Caleb Cushing, "English and French Intervention in the Rio de la Plata," *United States Magazine and Democratic Review*, vol. 18 (March 1846), 163–184; and Peterson, 135–137.

12. Page and Jeffers. Basic is Thomas O. Flickema, "The United States and Paraguay, 1845–1860: Misunderstanding, Miscalculation, and Misconduct," Ph.D. dissertation, Wayne State University, 1966 (Ann Arbor, Mich., University Microfilms, 1976), 152–183. Primary: *DCUS-IAA*, vol. 10, *Netherlands, Paraguay, Peru*, 154–160; SN Dobbin's *Report, 1855, CSS*, 74th, 1st and 2nd, *HR 1*, vol. 1, *Serial 842*, 4–5; Thomas J. Page, *La Plata: The Argentine Confederation and Paraguay* (N.Y., Harper, 1859), 301–317; Charles A. Washburn, *History of Paraguay: With Notes of Personal Observations, and Reminiscences of Diplomacy under Difficulties*, 2 vols. (Boston, Lee and Shepard, 1871), vol. 1, 362–376; and *NYT*, 12 Jan., 12 April, 14 May, 25 May 1855, 5/1, 1/4–5, 2/4, 1/4. Secondary: Vincent Ponko, Jr., *Ships, Seas, and Scientists: U.S. Naval Explorations in the Nineteenth Century* (Annapolis, Naval Institute Press, 1974), 164–173; Peterson, 165–170; Philip Raine, *Paraguay* (New Brunswick, N.J., Scarecrow Press, 1956), 128–132; John H. Williams, *The Rise and Fall of the Paraguayan Republic, 1860–1870* (Austin, University of Texas Press, 1979), 158–168; Harris G. Warren, *Paraguay* (Norman, University of Oklahoma Press, 1949), 190–195; Robertson, 335–338; Daniel Ammen, *The Old Navy and the New* (Philadelphia, J. B. Lippincott, 1891), 269; John F. Harrington, "Science and Politics," *HAHR*, vol. 3 (May 1955), 192–201; Flickema, "The Settlement of the Paraguayan-American Controversy of 1859: A Reappraisal," *The Americas*, vol. 25 (July 1968), 51–54; O. P. Fitzgerald, "Profit and Adventure in Paraguay," in *ASHS*, 70–79; Clare V. McKanna, "The *Water Witch* Incident," *AN*, vol. 31 (Jan. 1971), 7–18; and John H. Williams, "The Wake of the *Water Witch*," *USNIP*, Supplement, March 1985), 14–19.

13. Shubrick. Basic here too is Flickema's Ph.D. dissertation, 178–183, 241–246; and his "Settlement," 57–69. Primary: *DCUS-IAA*, vol. 10, 38–46, 184–204, 205–211, especially 209–211; Pierce's *Message, 1859, CMPP*, vol. 5, 560; SN Toucey's *Reports, 1858, 1859, CSS*, 35th, 2nd, *HR 1*, vol. 2, *Serial 1000*, 5; and ibid., 36th, 1st, *SEN 2*, vol. 2, *Serial 1025*, 1137–1138; *TIAUS*, vol. 8, 210–257; and Washburn, vol. 1, 377–385; *DIL*, vol. 7, 110–111; and *NYT*, 12 Oct. 1858, 5 April 1859, 4/2–3, 4/4. Secondary: Peterson, 172–179; Warren, 195–

196; Raine, 132–134; *EAAFR,* 667–670; Fitzgerald, 75–79; and Susan F. Cooper, "Rear Admiral William Branford Shubrick," *Harper's New Monthly Magazine,* vol. 53 (Aug. 1876), 406.

14. (A) Woolsey. David Cooney, *Chronology of the United States Navy, 1775–1965* (N.Y., Watts, 1965), 54. (B) McKeever. Ibid., 69; Lynch, ibid., 72; and *PCA,* 36–37. (C) Forrest. Cooney, 39–40.

15. Sloat and Thompson. Primary: *ASP, Naval Affairs,* vol. 3, 125–128; and *NWR,* vol. 41 (1 Oct. 1831), 95–96. Secondary: Clements R. Markham, *A History of Peru* (Chicago, Sergel, 1892; repr. Westport, Conn., Greenwood Press, 1968), 294–295, 326–328, 362; and Frederick A. Pike, *The Modern History of Peru* (N.Y. and Washington, Praeger, 1967), 69–75.

16. Wadsworth and Ballard. Primary: *DCUS-IAA,* vol. 10, 131–134, 146–147, 151–153, 326–327, 419–421; and *NWR,* vol. 52 (12 April 1837), vol. 54 (18 Aug.), vol. 55 (6 Oct. 1838), vol. 56 (18 May 1839), 19, 389, 82, 178. Secondary: *TRCH,* 49–50; Luis A. Galdames, *A History of Chile,* trans. and ed. by Isaac J. Cox (Chapel Hill, University of North Carolina Press, 1941), 266–272; Pike, 79–83; and David A. Werlich, *Peru: A Short History* (Carbondale and Edwardsville, Southern Illinois University Press, 1979), 139–141.

17. McCauley. Primary: *DCUS-IAA,* vol. 10, 613–614, 636–637, 642–643, 660–662; *DIL,* vol. 1, 575; and *NYT,* 9 Oct., 13, 20 Nov. 1852, 1/5, 1/4, 1/3–4. Secondary: Roy F. Nichols, *Advance Agents of American Destiny* (Philadelphia, University of Pennsylvania Press, 1956), 162–170; and Robertson, 169–170.

18. Bailey. SN Dobbin's *Report, 1854, CSS,* 33rd, 2nd, *HR 1,* vol. 1, *Serial 778,* 390; and USDS, J. R. Clay to SS, 25 Aug.; 12 Sept. 1854; Diplomatic despatches from U.S. ministers to Peru, T 52, roll 11, NA.

Chapter 7

1. Chauncey. Primary: *ASP, Foreign Affairs,* vol. 3, 583–584; and *Times* (London), 30 Aug., 18 Sept. 1816, 2/4, 2/4. Secondary: Howard R. Marraro, *Diplomatic Relations between the United States and the Kingdom of the Two Sicilies,* 2 vols. (N.Y., S. F. Vanni, 1951–1953), vol. 1, 18–20, 89–164; Paul C. Perrota, *The Claims of the United States against the Kingdom of Naples* (Washington, Catholic University of America, 1926), 9–40; and *AMW,* 107–108.

2. Patterson and Perry. Primary: USND, Box VD, Government relationships (domestic and foreign), diplomatic negotiations, treaties, etc. (1782–1871), Folder, negotiations with Neapolitan government by Commodore James Biddle and Commodore Patterson, NA, passim; *TIAUS,* vol. 3, 711–721; and *NWR,* vol. 42 (19 May), vol. 43 (15 Dec. 1832), 210, 250. Secondary: *OBMCP,* 121–123; Thomas H. Benton, *Thirty Years' View; or, a History of the Workings of the American Government for Thirty Years, from 1820 to 1850,* 2 vols. (N.Y., D. Appleton, 1854–1856), vol. 1, 604; and Marraro, 20–21, 201–337.

3. Biddle. *BJB,* 75–80. Primary: "Journal Kept by James Biddle in the *Ontario,* 4 Oct. 1817–22 March 1819," USND, roll M 902, NA, 12–15. Sec-

ondary: Barry M. Gough, *The Royal Navy and the Northwest Coast of North America* (Vancouver, University of British Columbia Press, 1971), 125–126; Joseph Schafer, "The British Attitude toward the Oregon Question," *AHR*, vol. 16 (1911), 282; Frederick Merk, "The Genesis of the Oregon Question," *Mississippi Valley Historical Review*, vol. 36 (March 1950), 606–611; Frederick W. Longstaff and W. Kaye Lamb, "The Royal Navy on the Northwest Coast, 1813–1850," *British Columbia Historical Review*, vol. 9 (1945), 3–4; and Katherine B. Judson, "The British Side in the Restoration of Fort Astoria," *Oregon Historical Quarterly*, vol. 20 (1919), 309.

4. Ballard. Primary: *ASP, Naval Affairs,* vol. 4, 564–565; and *DIL,* vol. 2, 369. Secondary: Robert V. Remini, *Andrew Jackson and the Course of American Democracy, 1833–1845* (N.Y., Harper & Row, 1984), 201–218, 230–236, 274–292; Elizabeth B. White, *American Opinion of France from Lafayette to Poincaré* (N.Y., A. A. Knopf, 1927), 94–109; and John M. Belohlavek, *"Let the Eagle Soar!" The Foreign Policy of Andrew Jackson* (Lincoln and London, University of Nebraska Press, 1985), 102–126.

5. Gwinn, et al., *AMW,* 216–25; Howard R. Marraro, *American Opinion of the Unification of Italy, 1846–1861* (N.Y., Columbia University Press, 1932), 55–58; and Tyrone G. Martin, *A Most Fortunate Ship: A Narrative History of "Old Ironsides"* (Chester, Conn., Globe Pequot Press, 1980), 247–250.

6. Long. Primary: *CSS,* 32nd, 1st, *HR 78,* vol. 6, *Serial 641,* 1–58; and *NYT,* 10 Jan., 21 Feb. 1852, 4/2, 4/1. Secondary: John H. Comlos, *Louis Kossuth in America, 1851–1852* (Buffalo, East European Institute, 1979), 33–39; Donald S. Spencer, *Louis Kossuth and Young America: A Study of Sectionalism and Foreign Policy* (Columbia, University of Missouri Press, 1977), 1–5; Istvan Deak, *Lawful Revolution: Louis Kossuth and the Hungarians, 1848–1849* (N.Y., Columbia University Press, 1979, 342; and *AMW,* 228–234.

7. Ingraham. Andor Klay, *Daring Diplomacy: The Case of the First American Ultimatum* (Minneapolis, University of Minnesota Press, 1957), passim, especially 52–97. Primary: SN Dobbin's *Report, 1853, CSS,* 33rd, 1st, *HR 1,* vol. 1, *Serial 712,* 299; Pierce's *Message, 1853, CMPP,* vol. 5, 209–210; R. C. Parker, ed., "A Personal Narrative of the Koszta Affair," *USNIP,* vol. 53 (1927), 295–298; and *NYT,* 25 July–13 Aug., passim. Secondary: Ivor D. Spencer, *The Victor and the Spoils: A Life of William L. Marcy* (Providence, Brown University Press, 1959), 309–317; *AMW,* 234–237; William P. Langdon, "A Naval Incident in the Mediterranean, 1853," *Magazine of History,* vol. 14 (1911), 231–238; and Chester M. Colby, "Diplomacy of the Quarterdeck," *Journal of International Law,* vol. 8, (1914), 446.

8. Perry. Primary: William R. Manning, ed., *Diplomatic Correspondence of the United States, Canadian Relations, 1784–1860,* 4 vols. (Washington, Carnegie Endowment for International Peace, 1940–1945), vol. 4, 465–481; and Fillmore's *Message, 1852, CMPP,* vol. 5, 158. Secondary: *OBMCP,* 280–282.

9. Shubrick. Manning, ed., *Canadian Relations,* vol. 4, 523–528; and Shu-

brick to SN, 19 Sept. 1853, USND, Eastern SL, M 89, roll 113; and SN Dobbin's *Report, 1853*, 33rd, 1st, *HR 1*, vol. 1, *Serial 712*, 301.

10. Lavallette and McIntosh. Primary: *DCUS-IAA*, vol. 7, *Great Britain*, 188, 746–747; *CSS*, 35th, 1st, *SEN Reports*, vol. 2, *Serial 939*, 1–4; ibid., *HR 1*, vol. 13, *Serial 959*, 1–44; SN Toucey's *Report, 1858, CSS*, 35th, 2nd, *HR 1*, vol. 2, *Serial 1000*, 3–4; and Buchanan's *Message, 1858, CMPP*, vol. 5, 507. Secondary: Hugh B. Soulsby, "The Right of Search and the Slave Trade in Anglo-American Relations, 1814–1862," *Johns Hopkins University Studies in History and Political Science, Series 51, no. 2* (Baltimore, Johns Hopkins University Press, 1933), 159–176; and H. E. Landry, "Slavery and the Slave Trade in Atlantic Diplomacy," *Journal of Southern History*, vol. 27 (May 1961), 184–207.

11. Palmer and Bell. AMW, 301–305; and Marraro, 287–296. Several biographies of Garibaldi were consulted but they contain nothing about U.S. naval activities in connection with him.

Chapter 8

1. Bainbridge. *BWB*, 224–226, 247–261. Primary: WB to SN, CAPL, rolls 67–71, passim; SN to WB, SNL, roll 14, passim; and Luther Bradish papers, New-York Historical Society. Secondary: David H. Finnie, *Pioneers East: The Early American Experience in the Middle East* (Cambridge, Harvard University Press, 1967), 26–28, 50–52; *AMW*, 119–120; and *DNANO*, 132–133.

2. (A) Rodgers. Primary: *DNI*, 8 Sept. 1832, 2/4–6; and James M. Merrill, "Midshipman DuPont [sic] and the Cruise of the *North Carolina*, 1825–1827," *AN*, vol. 40 (July 1980), 22–23. Secondary: *BJB*, 155–156; *AMW*, 134–136; and Finnie, 54–57. (B) Greek and Turkish Backgrounds. Barbara Jelavich, *History of the Balkans*, 2 vols. (Cambridge, U.K., Cambridge University Press, 1983), vol. 1, *Eighteenth and Nineteenth Centuries*, 223–229; and Lord Kinross, *The Ottoman Centuries: The Rise and Fall of the Turkish Empire* (N.Y., Morrow, 1977), 441–450. (C) Crane. Primary: *JQAM*, vol. 8, 147–148. Secondary: *AMW*, 147–149; *DNANO*, 141–143; and *EAAFR*, 328–329. (D) Greek piracy. Primary: SN Southard's *Report, 1826, CSS*, 19th, 2nd, *HR 2*, vol. 1, *Serial 148*, 6; ibid., *1828*, 20th, 1st, *SEN 1*, vol. 1, *Serial 181*, 134; *ASP, Naval Affairs*, vol. 1, 732–733; and ibid., vol. 4, 175–177. Secondary: *AMW*, 127–128; *PCA*, 17–20; Douglas Dakin, *The Greek Struggle for Independence, 1821–1833* (Berkeley and Los Angeles, University of California Press, 1973), 220–230; Jack Sweetman, *American Naval History: An Illustrated Chronology* (Annapolis, Naval Institute Press, 1984), 43–44; and Edgar S. Maclay, *History of the United States Navy*, 2 vols. (N.Y., D. Appleton, 1894), vol. 2, 124–125.

3. (A) Biddle. *BJB*, 212–233. Primary: *TIAUS*, vol. 3, 541–598. Secondary: *BDP*, 289–291; Finnie, 57–63; and *AMW*, 150–151. (B) Eckford and Rhodes. Finnie, 149–152; and *AMW*, 152–153, 166–167. (C) Patterson. Finnie, 260–261; and *AMW*, 192–194. (D) Elliott. Finnie, 261–262; *AMW*, 194–196; Tyrone G. Martin, *A Most Fortunate Ship: A Narrative History of "Old Ironsides"*

(Chester, Conn., Globe-Pequot Press, 1980), 209–212; and John M. Belohlavek, *"Let the Eagle Soar!" The Foreign Policy of Andrew Jackson* (Lincoln and London, University of Nebraska Press, 1985), 135–138.

4. (A) Morgan. Primary: *CSS*, 27th, 3rd, *HR 22*, vol. 2, *Serial 419*, 1–5; and *NWR*, vol. 62 (13 Aug.), vol. 63 (26 Oct., 31 Dec. 1842, 11 Feb. 1843), 129, 276–277, 369–370, 372. Secondary: Luella J. Hall, *The United States and Morocco, 1776–1956* (Metuchen, N.J., Scarecrow Press, 1971), 112–119. (B) Henry. *AMW*, 197–198. (C) Stringham. Ibid., 243–245. (D) Lavallette. Primary: SN Toucey's *Report, 1859, CSS*, 36th, 1st, *SEN 2*, vol. 2, *Serial 1025*, 1147; and USDS, S. Williams to SS, 24 Oct. 1858, Consular despatches, Constantinople, T 194, roll 6. Secondary: *AMW*, 255, 292.

Chapter 9

1. Henley. Primary: Henley to SN, 5, 13, 19 Nov., 26 Dec. 1819, CAPL, roll 65. Secondary: *DNANO*, 167–182; Tyler Dennett, *Americans in Eastern Asia: A Critical Study of the United States with Reference to China, Japan, and Korea in the Nineteenth Century* (N.Y., Barnes & Noble, 1931, repr. ibid., 1963), 78–80; *FCS*, 4–5; E. Mowbray Tate, "American Merchant and Naval Contacts with China, 1784–1850," *AN*, vol. 31 (July 1971), 181–182; and G. B. Vroom, "The Place of Naval Officers in International Relations," *USNIP*, vol. 47 (1921), 694–695.

2. Finch. Primary: Finch to SN, 14 Jan. 1830, COML, roll 15. Secondary: *DNANO*, 184–185; *FCS*, 5; Tate, 181–182; and Curtis T. Henson, Jr., *Commissioners and Commodores: The East India Squadron and American Diplomacy in China* (University, University of Alabama Press, 1982), 13.

3. (A) Downes. Primary: *ASP, Naval Affairs*, vol. 4, 153; Downes to SN, 2 June 1832 (two letters), CAPL, roll 171; Jeremiah M. Reynolds, *Voyage of the United States Frigate Potomac under the Command of Commodore John Downes, during the Circumnavigation of the Globe, in the Years, 1831, 1832, 1833, and 1834* (N.Y., Harper, 1835), 340–343; Francis Warriner, *Cruise of the United States Frigate Potomac round the World, during the Years 1831–34, Embracing the Attack on Quallah Battoo, etc.* (N.Y., Leavitt, Lord, and Boston, Crocker & Brewster, 1835), 206–207; and *Canton* (China) *Register*, 23 June 1832. Secondary: Tate, 182–183. (B) Geisinger. Edmund Roberts, *Embassy to the Eastern Courts of Cochin-China, Siam, and Muscat in the U.S. Sloop-of-War Peacock, David Geisinger, Commander, during the Years 1832–3–4* (N.Y., Harper, 1837), 431–432; *FCS*, 6–7; and Henson, 14. (C) Aulick. Aulick to SN, 6 Jan. 1836, COML, roll 21; Henson, 20; and *FCS*, 11. (D) Kennedy. SN to Kennedy, 26 Jan., 24 Feb., 2 April 1835, SNL, roll 23; William S. Ruschenberger, *Voyage Around the World; Including an Embassy to Muscat and Siam, in 1835, 1836, and 1837* (Philadelphia, Carey Lea & Blanchard, 1838), 53–70; and *FCS*, 15–16.

4. Read. Secondary: Henson, 26–27; *FCS*, 20–22; *DNANO*, 188–190;

Tate, 184–185; and Charles O. Paullin, "Early Voyages of American Naval Vessels to the Orient," *USNIP*, vol. 36 (1910), 1081–1083.

5. Kearny. By far the best and most convenient collection of U.S. naval, ministerial, and consular (as well as Chinese and European) correspondence is *USCH 1 (Series 1, 1842–1860)* and *USCH 2 (Series 2, 1861–1893)*. Primary: *USCH 1, vol. 1, Kearny and Cushing Missions,* xxi–142; Earl Swisher, ed., *China's Management of the American Barbarians: A Study in Sino-American Relations, 1841–1861, with Documents* (New Haven, Yale University Press, 1953), 101–129; and *Chinese Repository* (Canton), vol. 12 (April 1843), 225. Secondary: Carroll S. Alden, *Lawrence Kearny: Sailor-Diplomat* (Princeton, Princeton University Press, 1936), 164–186; John K. Fairbank, *Trade and Diplomacy on the China Coast, 1842–1854* (Cambridge, Mass., Harvard University Press, 1953), 195–199; Dennett, 108–111; Henson, 33–35; *FCS*, 23–32; Thomas Kearny, "Commodore Lawrence Kearny and the Open Door and Most Favored Nation Policy in China in 1842 and 1843," *Proceedings of the New Jersey Historical Society*, vol. 50 (1932), 162–190; and T. F. Tsiang, "The Tsiang Documents, and Note in Reply [to Thomas Kearny]," *Chinese Social and Political Science Review*, vol. 16 (1935), 75–109.

6. Parker and Tilton. Primary: *USCH 1*, vol. 1, 147–339; vol. 2, ibid., 3–317. Secondary: Claude M. Fuess, *The Life of Caleb Cushing*, 2 vols. (N.Y., Harcourt, Brace & Co., 1923), vol. 1, 402–454; Henson, 46–47; *FCS*, 31–35; *DNANO*, 205–211; Te-kong Kong, *United States Diplomacy in China, 1844–1860* (Seattle, University of Washington Press, 1964), 3–5, 44–54; Paullin, "Early Voyages," 1091–1096; and Tate, 185–187.

7. Biddle. *BJB*, 192–207. Primary: *USCH, 1*, vol. 2, 321–382; JB to SN, 1 Aug. 1845–3 July 1846, East India SL, roll 3; "Smooth Log of the United States Ship *Columbus,* Thos [sic] W. Wyman, Bearing the Broad Pennant of Commodore James Biddle," 25 Dec. 1845–7 July 1846, JB papers, Andalusia (the Biddle family mansion near Philadelphia), vols. 9–11, passim; "Log Book of the U.S. Ship *Vincennes,* Captain Hiram Paulding," USND, appendix D, vol. 13, no. 78, 4 June 1845–27 June 1846, NA; Benajah Tichnor, "Journal, 1845–1848, on Board the *Columbus* on a Voyage from New York to the East Indies," 30 June 1845–27 June 1846, Benajah Tichnor collection, Yale University; and *Chinese Repository*, vol. 14 (Dec. 1845), 500–501. Secondary: Henson, 60–66; *FCS*, 37–40; *DNANO*, 211–213; and Tate, 187–189.

8. (A) Preble, et al., and piracy. Primary: Geisinger to SN, 25 Oct. 1849, in James B. Merrill, "The Asiatic Squadron, 1835–1907," *AN*, vol. 29 (April 1969), 111, n. 26; Abbot to SN, 24 Nov. 1854, USND, East India SL, roll 9; and SN Dobbin's *Report, 1855, CSS*, 34th, 1st and 2nd, *HR 1*, vol. 1, *Serial 842*, 7. Secondary: Grace E. Fox, *British Admirals and Chinese Pirates, 1832–1869* (London, Kegan Paul, 1940; repr. Westport, Conn., Greenwood Press, 1973), 123–125, 128; *FCS*, 47; Henson, 115; and Tate, 188–189. (B) Walker and the coolie trade. Primary: *USCH, 1*, vol. 17, *Coolie Trade and Chinese Emigration,* 345–351. Secondary: Hosea B. Morse, *International Relations of the Chinese Empire*, 2 vols. (London, Longmans, Green, 1910–1918), vol. 2,

163–176; Gunther Barth, *Bitter Strength: A History of the Chinese in the United States* (Cambridge, Mass., Harvard University Press, 1964), 66–71; Henson, 83–84; *FCS*, 53–54; and *PCA*, 41.

9. Aulick and Perry. Primary: *USCH, 1,* vol. 4, *Marshall Mission,* 13–20; 30–44, 50–52, 246–255. Secondary: *OBMCP,* 272–273, 344–345; Henson, 86–88; *FCS,* 50–53, 61–62; Tong, 120–122; and Chester A. Bain, "Commodore Matthew Perry, Humphrey Marshall, and the Taiping Rebellion," *Far Eastern Quarterly,* vol. 10 (May 1951), 258–270.

10. Kelly. Primary: *USCH, 1,* vol. 7, *Taiping Rebellion,* 127–206; Great Britain, Parliament, House of Commons Sessional Papers, 1854, vol. 72, no. 1792, *Correspondence respecting the Attack on the Foreign Settlements at Shanghai* (London, Her Majesty's Stationery Office, 1853), 13–18; and eyewitness William S. Wetmore, *Recollections of Life in the Far East* (Shanghai, *North China Herald* Office, 1894), 9–11. Secondary: Henson, 92, 108; *FCS*, 73–74, 408–409; and George E. Paulsen, "Under the Starry Banner at Muddy Flat, Shanghai, 1854," *AN*, vol. 30 (July 1970), 155–166.

11. Armstrong and Foote. DFL, "A Case for Intervention: Armstrong, Foote, and the Destruction of the Barrier Forts, Canton, China, 1856," in *New Aspects of Naval History: Selected Papers Presented at the Fourth Naval History Symposium, United States Naval Academy, 25–26 Oct. 1979,* Craig L. Symonds, et al., eds. (Annapolis, Naval Institute Press, 1981), 220–237. Primary: *USCH, 1,* vol. 13, *Arrow War,* 290–340; Great Britain, Sessional papers, 1857, vol. 12, no. 2163, *Papers Relating to Her Majesty's Naval Forces at Canton,* 95–100, 120–121, 177; and David Bonner-Smith and E. W. R. Lumby, eds., *The Second China War, 1856–1860* (London, Printed for the Navy Records Society, 1954), 2–4, 50, 114, 129, 144–145. Secondary: Henson, 128–136; *FCS*, 82–91; and Tong, 184–188.

12. Armstrong, Parker, and Formosa. Primary: *USCH, 1,* vol. 12, *Formosa,* 256–272. Secondary: Sophia S. Yen, *Taiwan in China's Foreign Relations, 1836–1874* (Hamden, Conn., Shoestring Press, 1965), 48–73; Ta-tuan Ch'en, et al., *The Chinese World Order: Traditional China's Foreign Relations,* John K. Fairbank, ed. (Cambridge, Mass., Harvard University Press, 1968), 257–275; Edward V. Gulick, *Peter Parker and the Opening of China* (Cambridge, Mass., Harvard University Press, 1977), 191–193; Henson, 138–139; Tong, 194–195; *OBMCP,* 425, 438–439; Thomas R. Cox, "Harbingers of Change: American Merchants and the Formosa Annexation Scheme," *PHR,* vol. 42 (May 1973), 163–184; and Harold D. Langley, "Gideon Nye and the Formosa Annexation Scheme," *PHR,* vol. 34 (Nov. 1965), 397–420.

13. Ward and Tattnall. Primary: *USCH, 1,* vol. 16, *Ward Mission,* 84–96, although for once this generally superb compilation falls short, containing only a single letter from Ward and none from Tattnall; *CSS,* 36th, 1st, *SEN 30,* vol. 10, 321, 579, 587, 594–599; Tattnall to SN, 4 July 1859, USND, East India SL, roll 13; Swisher, 566, 567, 560; Great Britain, Sessional Papers, 1860, vol. 69, no. 2857, *Correspondence with Mr. Bruce, Her Majesty's Envoy Extraordinary and Minister Plenipotentiary in China,* 14, 16–18, 37, 39; Bonner-Smith and

Lumby, 391–401; Edgar S. Maclay, *Reminiscences of the Old Navy* (N.Y. and London, Longmans, Green, 1898), 68–87; and *NYT*, 13 Oct. 1859, 4/3–4. Secondary: Charles C. Jones, Jr., *Life and Services of Commodore Josiah Tattnall* (Savannah, Morning News, 1878), 104–108; Gerald S. Graham, *The China Station: War and Diplomacy, 1830–1860* (Oxford, U.K., Oxford University Press, 1978), 368–380; John F. Cady, *The Roots of French Imperialism in Eastern Asia* (Ithaca, N.Y., Cornell University Press, 1954), 225–228; Henson, 165–167; *FCS*, 102–105; and Tong, 261–265.

Chapter 10

1. Porter. *BDP*, 173–174. Primary: DP to SN, 12, 21 Feb. 1815, CAPL, roll 42; and Charles Morris, *Autobiography* (Boston, A. Williams & Co., 1880), 75–76. Secondary: Alexander S. Mackenzie, *The Life of Commodore Oliver Hazard Perry*, 2 vols. (N.Y., Harper & Bros., 1840), vol. 2, 101–102; *DNANO*, 220–221; Arthur B. Cole, "Captain David Porter's Proposed Expedition to the Pacific and Japan, 1815," *PHR*, vol. 9 (1940), 61–65; and Frederick Merk, "The Genesis of the Oregon Question," *Mississippi Valley Historical Review*, vol. 36 (March 1950), 593.

2. Geisinger and Kennedy. *DIL*, vol. 5, 733–734; *DNANO*, 221–222; and *EAAFR*, 338–339.

3. Biddle. *BJB*, 209–219. Primary: SN to JB, 22 May 1845, "Cruise of the *Colimbia* [sic] and *Vincennes* to the Coast[s] of China, Inida [sic], and [the] East India Islands," USND, subject file 00, box 3, 1845, NA; JB to SN, 31 July 1845, East India SL, roll 3; Benajah Tichnor, 28 July 1846, "Journal, 1846–1848, on Board the *Columbus*, on a Voyage from New York to the East Indies," Benajah Tichnor collection, Yale University; *American and Gazette* (Philadelphia), 2 Feb. 1850, 3/1–2, in JB papers, box "Letters Received by James Biddle," folder "Commodore James Biddle Correspondence," Andalusia; and eyewitness Daniel Ammen, *The Old Navy and the New* (Philadelphia, J. B. Lippincott, 1891), 140–141. Secondary: *OBMCP*, 265–266, 322; *DNANO*, 222–232; *FCS*, 40–43; Merrill J. Bartlett, "Commodore James Biddle and the First Naval Mission to Japan, 1845 [sic]–1846," *AN*, vol. 61 (Jan. 1981), 32; and Edward S. Burton, "Commodore James Biddle's Failure to Enter Japan in 1846," *Independent Magazine*, vol. 59 (31 Aug. 1905), 502.

4. Glynn. Primary: *CSS*, 31st, 1st, *HR 84*, vol. 10, *Serial 579*, 1–44. Secondary: *DNANO*, 233–243; *BJB*, 218–219; *OBMCP*, *FCS*, 45–46; and Richard A. von Doenhoff, "Biddle, Perry, and Japan," *USNIP*, vol. 92 (Nov. 1966), 78–87.

5. Perry. (A) Ryukyus and Bonins. *OBMCP*, 300–317, 339–340, 398–399. Primary: *TIAUS*, vol. 6, 743–744, 750–786. Secondary: *DNANO* 257–259, 280; Vincent Ponko, Jr., *Ships, Seas, and Scientists: U.S. Naval Explorations and Discoveries in the Nineteenth Century* (Annapolis, Naval Institute Press, 1974), 142–145; and Earl Swisher, "Commodore Perry's Imperialism in Relation to America's Present-Day Position in the Pacific," *PHR*, vol. 16 (Feb. 1947), 30–

40. (B) Japan. *OBMCP*, 317–340, 357–397, 400–402. Primary: *TIAUS*, vol. 6, 436–442, 470–472, 490–666; and SN Dobbin's *Report, 1854*, CSS, 33rd, 2nd, *HR 1*, vol. 1, *Serial 778*, 387–388. Secondary: *DNANO*, 259–269, 271–280; *FCS*, 63–64, 68–72; and Ponko, 145–147, 149–157. (C) Japanese viewpoints. W. G. Beasley, *The Meiji Restoration* (Stanford, Stanford University Press, 1972), 78–99; and Kamikawa Hikomatsu, *Japan-America Relations in the Meiji-Taisho Era* (Tokyo, Pan-Pacific Press, 1958), 9–20. (D) Ringgold-Rodgers. *OBMCP*, 397–398. Primary: Allan B. Cole, ed., *Yankee Surveyors in the Shogun's Seas: Records of the United States Surveying Expedition to the North Pacific Ocean, 1853–1856* (Princeton, Princeton University Press, 1947, repr., Westport, Conn., Greenwood Press, 1968), 4–19. Secondary: Robert E. Johnson, *Rear Admiral John Rodgers, 1812–1882* (Annapolis, U.S. Naval Institute, 1967), 108–119; Ponko, 209–230; and Gordon K. Harrington, "The Ringgold Incident: A Matter of Judgment," in *ASHS*, 110–111.

6. Brooke. Primary: *NYT*, 17 April 1860, 3/5–6. Secondary: Masao Miyoshi, *As We Saw Them: The First Japanese to the United States* (Berkeley, et al., University of California Press, 1860), 25, 40–41, 145; George M. Brooke, Jr., "The Voyage of the *Kanrin Maru*, 1860: An Episode in American Naval Diplomacy," *AN*, vol. 30 (July 1960), 198–208; Cole, *Yankee Surveyors*, 19–25; and ibid., "Japan's First Embassy to the United States, 1860," *Pacific Northwest Quarterly*, vol. 32 (1947), 140–141.

Chapter 11

1. Downes. DFL, " 'Martial Thunder': The First Official American Armed Intervention in Asia," *PHR*, vol. 42 (May 1973), 143–162. Primary: Downes to SN, 17 Feb. 1832, CAPL, roll 167; SN to Downes, 16 July 1832, SNL, roll 21, p. 59; SN Woodbury's *Report, 1832*, CSS, 22nd, 2nd, *HR 2*, vol. 1, *Serial 233*, 42; *CMPP*, vol. 2, 596; Charles M. Endicott, "Narrative of Piracy and Plunder of the Ship *Friendship*," (Salem, Mass., Historical Collections of the Essex Institute, 1859), vol. 1, 15–32; Midshipman Levi Lincoln's diary, "Cruise of the U.S. Frigate *Potomac* . . . 26 August 1831 to 17 Feb. 1832," New York Public Library; Jeremiah N. Reynolds, *Voyage of the United States Frigate Potomac in 1831, 1832, 1833, and 1834* (N.Y., Harper, 1835), 95–124; Francis Warriner, *Cruise of the U.S. Frigate Potomac round the World, 1831–1834* (N.Y., Leavitt, Lord, and Boston, Crocker and Brewster, 1835), 71–113; and *DNI* and *Globe* (Washington), 10–17 July 1832, passim. Secondary: Edgar S. Maclay, "An Early 'Globe-Circling' Cruise," *USNIP*, vol. 36 (1910), 481–500; Charles O. Paullin, "Early Voyages of American Naval Vessels to the Orient," ibid., 707–716; John F. Campbell, "Pepper, Pirates, and Grapeshot," *AN*, vol. 21 (Oct. 1961), 293–296, 302; and John H. Belohlavek, "Andrew Jackson and the Malayan Pirates: A Question of Diplomacy and Politics," *Tennessee Historical Quarterly*, vol. 36 (1977), 19–29; updated by his *"Let the Eagle Soar!" The Foreign Policy of Andrew Jackson* (Lincoln and London, University of Nebraska Press, 1985), 152–162.

2. Read. Primary: Read to SN, 12 Jan.; CAPL, roll 249; ibid., 5 Feb., ibid., roll 250; and ibid., 11 April 1839, ibid., roll 252; SN Dickerson's *Report, 1839*, CSS, 26th, 1st, *SEN 1*, vol. 1, *Serial 354*, 522; Joshua N. Henshaw, *Around the World: A Narrative of a Voyage in the East India Squadron under Commodore George C. Read*, 2 vols. (N.Y. and Boston, 1840), vol. 1, 51–64; Fitch W. Taylor, *A Voyage round the World, and Visits to Various Foreign Countries, in the United States Frigate Columbia*, 5th ed. (New Haven, H. Mansfield, and N.Y., D. Appleton, 1846), vol. 1, 301–315; William M. Murrell, *Cruise of the Frigate Columbia around the World, under the Command of Commodore George C. Read, in 1838, 1839, and 1840* (Boston, B. B. Mussey, 1840), 101–112; and *DNI* and *Globe*, 28–30 May, passim. Secondary: DFL, " 'Martial Thunder,' " 160–162; Campbell, 296–302; and Paullin, "Early Voyages," 1081–1083.

3. Geisinger. (A) Cochin China. Primary: Edmund Roberts, *Embassy to the Eastern Courts of Cochin-China, Siam, and Muscat in the U.S. Sloop-of-War Peacock, David Geisinger, Commander, during the Years 1832–3–4* (N.Y., Harper, 1837), 171–226; Geisinger to SN, 6 July 1833, COML, roll 10; Jackson to Senate, 30 May 1834, CMPP, vol. 3, 53; *TIAUS*, vol. 3, 755–778; NWR, vol. 46 (31 May 1834), 218. Secondary: Belohlavek, 162–173; Stanley Karnow, *Vietnam: A History* (N.Y., Viking, 1983), 55–68; John F. Cady, *Southeast Asia: Its Historical Development* (N.Y. et al., McGraw-Hill, 1964), 409–411; FCS, 7–8; EAAFR 636–639; Tyler Dennett, *Americans in Eastern Asia: A Critical Study of the United States with Reference to China, Japan, and Korea in the 19th Century* (N.Y., Barnes & Noble, 1931, repr. ibid., 1963), 128–134; and Paullin, "Early Voyages," 717–718. (B) Siam. Primary: Roberts, 227–318; and Geisinger to SN, 28 July 1833, COML, roll 10. Secondary: Cady, 336–339; FCS, 7–8; and Paullin, 718–720. (C) Muscat. Primary: Roberts, 342–363; and Geisinger to SN, 5 Dec. 1833, COML, roll 10. Secondary: Ian Skeet, *Muscat and Oman: The End of an Era* (London, Faber & Faber, 1974), 45–52; David Finnie, *Pioneers East: The Early American Experience in the Middle East* (Cambridge, Mass., Harvard University Press, 1967), 245–248; and Paullin, 720–721.

4. Kennedy. (A) Muscat. Primary: Kennedy to SN, 11 Feb. 1836, CAPL, roll 212; *TIAUS*, vol. 3, 796–810; William S. W. Ruschenberger, *A Voyage Round the World, Including Embassy to Muscat and Siam in 1835–37* (Philadelphia, Carey Lea and Blanchard, 1838), 53–70; NWR, vol. 50 (19 March), 44; and ibid. (28 May 1836), 229. Secondary: Belohlavek, 173–176; Finnie, 245–248 (although he errs in placing the grounding of the *Peacock* under Geisinger rather than Kennedy); FCS, 11–14; and Paullin, 722–723. (B) Siam. Ruschenberger, 324–336; FCS, 14–15; and Paullin, 723–724. (C) Cochin China. Ruschenberger, 359–364; and FCS, 15.

5. Kearny. Kearny to Selim (Sultan of Joanna), ? August 1841, in Carroll S. Alden, *Lawrence Kearny: Sailor-Diplomat* (Princeton, Princeton University Press, 1936), 126–128.

6. Pearson. Primary: Pearson to SN, 15 August 1851, COML, roll 42 (the treaty text is included); and *DIL*, vol. 7, 112. Secondary: Peter Karsten, *The Naval Aristocracy: Mahan's Messmates and the Emergence of Modern American*

Navalism (N.Y., Free Press, 1972), 165–166; and Harry A. Ellsworth, *One Hundred Eighty Landings of the United States Marines, 1800–1934* (Washington, Marine Corps, 1934), 106–107.

7. Percival. (A) Sumatra. *NWR*, vol. 68 (21 May 1845), 193–194; and Tyrone G. Martin, *A Most Fortunate Ship: A Narrative History of "Old Ironsides"* (Chester, Conn., Globe-Pequot Press, 1980), 232–233. (B) Borneo: Martin, 233–235; Cady, 435–441; Nicholas Tarling, *Britain, the Brookes, and Brunei* (Kuala Lumpur, et al., Oxford University Press, 1971), 65–75; and ibid., *The Burthen, the Risk, and the Glory: A Biography of Sir James Brooke* (Kuala Lumpur et al., Oxford University Press, 1982), 95–108. (C) Annam. Primary: Percival to SN, 21 June, 26 July 1845, CAPL, roll 321; Balestier to SS, 25 Nov. 1851, *NASP*, vol. 3, 397; and Benjamin F. Stevens, "Around the World in the U.S. Frigate *Constitution* in the Days of Old or Wooden Ships," the *United Service*, vol. 5 (May 1905), 596–597. Secondary: Martin, 235–239; Cady, 411–415; Karnow, 69–70; and *FCS*, 36–37.

8. Voorhees. (A) Annam. *NASP*, vol. 3, 399–403; Tarling, *Britain*, 71–72; and *FCS*, 47–48. (B) Siam. *NASP*, 379–388, 403–412; and *EAAFR*, 344–346. (C) Borneo. Primary: *NASP*, 412–415; *TIAUS*, vol. 5, 826–843; and *NYT*, 22 July 1854, 1/4. Secondary: Cady, 340–341; and *EAAFR*, 658–659.

9. Magruder. *FCS*, 55–56.

Chapter 12

1. Percival. Primary: SN Southard's *Report, 1827*, CSS, 20th, 1st, *Sen 1*, vol. 1, *Serial 163*, 206; USND, Records of the office of the judge advocate general (Navy), Record Group 125, Records of courts-martial and courts of inquiry of the Navy Department, M 273, vol. 23, #531, passim; Hiram Bingham, *A Residence of Twenty-Nine Years in the Sandwich Islands*, 3rd ed. (Hartford, H. Huntington, 1849), 283–289; Hiram Paulding, *Journal of a Cruise of the United States Schooner Dolphin among the Islands of the Pacific Ocean* (N.Y., G. and C. and H. Carvill, 1831), 225–226; *TIAUS*, vol. 3, 269–281; *NWR*, vol. 31 (30 Dec. 1826), 283; vol. 32 (30 June 1827), 292; vol. 35 (29 Nov. 1828), 224; *DNI*, 12 Nov. 1828, 2/3–4; *Missionary Herald*, vol. 22 (Dec. 1826), 370. Secondary: Linda M. Maloney, *The Captain from Connecticut: The Life and Naval Times of Isaac Hull* (Boston, Northeastern University Press, 1986), 376–377, 397, 403–404, 409–412; W. Patrick Strauss, *Americans in Polynesia, 1783–1842* (East Lansing, Michigan State University Press, 1963), 43–83; Ralph S. Kuykendall, *The Hawaiian Kingdom*, 3 vols. (Honolulu, University of Hawaii Press, 1947–1953), vol. 1, *Foundation and Transformation, 1778–1854*, 91, 122–123; Harold W. Bradley, *The American Frontier in Hawaii: The Pioneers, 1789–1843* (Stanford and London, Stanford University Press, 1944), 104, 178–180; Rebecca Paulding Meade, *Life of Hiram Paulding, Rear Admiral* (N.Y., Baker & Taylor, 1910), 334–339; Linda McKee (Maloney), "Mad Jack and the Missionaries," *AH*, vol. 22 (April 1971), 30–37, 85–87; John P. Wagner, "San-

dalwood Bonanza," in *ASHS*, 51–54; and Allan Westcott, "Captain 'Mad Jack' Percival," *USNIP*, vol. 61 (1935), 315–316.

2.   Jones. Primary: Bingham, 301–303. Secondary: Kuykendall, 91–92, 98–99, 137, 143–144; Bradley, 106–110; *DNANO*, 339–341; *TRCH*, 38–39; Strauss, 86–88; Rufus Anderson, *History of the Sandwich Islands Mission* (Boston, Congregational Publishing Co., 1870), 72–73; William Stanton, *The Great United States Exploring Expedition of 1838–1842* (Berkeley et al., University of California Press, 1975), 222, 224; and Gilbert Workman, "Forgotten Firebrand [Thomas a. C. Jones]," *USNIP*, vol. 94 (Sept. 1968), 80.

3.   Finch. Primary: Bingham, 354–360; and Charles S. Stewart, *Visit to the South Seas in the U.S. Ship Vincennes, during the Years 1829 and 1830*, 2 vols. (N.Y., J. P. Haven, 1831), vol. 2, 249–254, 268–280. Secondary: Kuykendall, 97, 121, 435–436; Bradley, 113, 193–195; *DNANO*, 340–341; *TRCH*, 40–41; Strauss, 88–90; and Albert P. Taylor, "The American Navy in Hawaii," *USNIP*, vol. 53 (1927), 911–912.

4.   A. Downes. Primary: Bingham, 444–445; Francis Warriner, *Cruise of the United States Frigate Potomac round the World, During the Years 1831–1834* (N.Y., Leavitt, Lord, and Boston, Crocker and Brewster, 1835), 233–238; and Herman F. Krafft, "Commodore John Downes: From His Official Correspondence," *USNIP*, vol. 54 (1928), 54. Secondary: Kuykendall, 143–144; Bradley, 282–283, 287; *DNANO*, 343; Strauss, 90–91; and Taylor, 912. (B) Kennedy. Primary: William S. W. Ruschenberger, *A Voyage round the World, Including Embassy to Muscat and Siam in 1835–'37* (Philadelphia, Carey Lea and Blanchard, 1838), 492–502. Bingham does not mention Kennedy. Secondary: Kuykendall, 144–146; Bradley, 110, 180–181; Strauss, 92–93; and Taylor, 913–914. (C) Read. Strauss, 93–95; and Taylor, 912–913.

5.   Long and Kearny. Primary: *FRUS, 1894*, Appendix 2, 45–66; *NASP*, vol. 3, 130–137; *DIL*, vol. 7, 478–479; *NWR*, vol. 65 (12 Oct. 1943), 128; (2 Dec. 1843), 211. Secondary: Carroll S. Alden, *Lawrence Kearny: Sailor-Diplomat* (Princeton, Princeton University Press, 1936), 187–204; Kuykendall, 212–221; Bradley, 420–441; *DNANO*, 343–344; *TRCH*, 66–67; Jean I. Brookes, *International Rivalry in the Pacific Ocean, 1800–1875* (Berkeley, University of California Press, 1941, repr. N.Y., Russell & Russell, 1972), 131–137; and Taylor, 914–916.

6.   (A) Stockton. SN Mason's *Report, 1846*, CSS, 29th, 2nd, *HR 4*, vol. 1, *Serial 497*, 379. There are no letters from Stockton about Hawaii, April–June 1846, in CAPL, rolls 330–331. (B) Percival. Tyrone G. Martin, *A Most Fortunate Ship: A Narrative History of "Old Ironsides"* (Chester, Conn., Globe-Pequot Press, 1980), 242–243. (C) Biddle. Kuykendall, 378–379; Stevens, 21–22, 48–49; and especially *BJB*, 312–313, based largely on Benajah Tichnor, "Journal, 1845–48 on Board the *Columbus* on a Voyage from New York to the East Indies," 27–28 Sept. 1846, Benajah Tichnor collection, Yale University. (D) Gardner. Primary: *FRUS, 1894*, 70–78; and *DIL*, vol. 7, 480–482. Secondary: Kuykendall, 388–405; and Stevens, 62–63.

Chapter 13

1. (A) Jones. Primary: SN Southard's *Report, 1827*, CSS, 20th, 1st, *SEN 1*, vol. 1, *Serial 163*, 206; *TIAUS*, vol. 3, 249–260; and Charles S. Stewart, *Visit to the South Seas in the U.S. Ship Vincennes, during the Years 1829 and 1830*, 2 vols. (N.Y., J. P. Haven, 1831), vol. 2, 27–52. Secondary: Patrick Strauss, *Americans in Polynesia, 1783–1842* (East Lansing, Michigan State University Press, 1963), 88; *TRCH*, 39; Charles L. Lewis, "Our Navy in the Pacific and Far East Long Ago," *USNIP*, vol. 69 (1943), 860; and Gilbert Workman, "A Forgotten Firebrand [Jones], ibid., vol. 94 (Sept. 1968), 80. (B) Finch. Strauss, 89–90; C. Hartly Grattan, *The United States and the Southwest Pacific* (Cambridge, Mass., Harvard University Press, 1961), 90–91; *DNANO*, 345; *TRCH*, 40–41; and Lewis, 860.

2. Aulick. Primary: Aulick to SN, 19 Sept. 1835, COML, roll 20; 1 Jan. 1836, roll 21; and *NWR*, vol. 50 (19 March, 28 May 1836), 44, 229. Secondary: Strauss, 91–92; William Stanton, *The Great United States Exploring Expedition of 1838–1842* (Berkeley et al., University of California Press, 1975), 195; Lewis, 860; Charles O. Paullin, "Early Voyages of American Naval Vessels to the Orient," *USNIP*, vol. 36 (1910), 724–734; and E. Mowbray Tate, "Navy Justice in the Pacific: A Pattern of Precedents," *AN*, vol. 35 (Jan. 1975), 22–23.

3. Primary and secondary materials in re the Wilkes expedition are overwhelming. Primary: USND, Record Group 37, Records of the hydrographic office, United States Exploration Expedition under the command of Lieutenant Charles Wilkes, 1836–1842, M 75, 27 rolls, passim. Secondary: Stanton, passim; David B. Tyler, *The Wilkes Expedition: The First United States Exploration Expedition, 1838–1842* (Philadelphia, American Philosophical Society, 1968), passim; and Daniel M. Henderson, *The Hidden Coasts: A Biography of Admiral Charles Wilkes* (N.Y., Sloane, 1953, repr. Westport, Conn., Greenwood Press, 1969), 156–174. (A) Wilkes and Hudson at Tuamotus and Samoa. Primary: Charles Wilkes, *Narrative of the United States Exploration Expedition during the Years 1839, 1840, 1841, 1842*, 5 vols. (Philadelphia, Lea and Blanchard, 1845), vol. 1, 434–435; and *TIAUS*, vol. 4, 241–256. Secondary: Stanton, 116–120; and Joseph W. Ellison, *Opening and Penetration of Foreign Influences in Samoa to 1880* (Corvallis, Oregon State University Press, 1938), 144. (B) Wilkes at New Zealand. Primary: Charles Wilkes, *Autobiography of Rear Admiral Charles Wilkes, 1798–1877*, William J. Morgan et al, eds. (Washington, Naval Historical Division, 1978), 450–451; and ibid., *Narration*, vol. 2, 397–400. Secondary: Tyler, 154–156; Strauss, 28–29, 101–104, 128; Jean I. Brookes, *International Rivalry in the Pacific Ocean, 1800–1875* (Berkeley, University of California Press, 1941; repr., N.Y., Russell & Russell, 1972), 102–103; Osgood Hardy and Glenn S. Dumke, *A History of the Pacific Area in Modern Times* (Boston et al., Houghton Mifflin, 1949), 158–160.

4. Wilkes and Hudson at Fiji. Primary: Wilkes, *Autobiography*, 469–472; ibid., *Narration*, vol. 3, 273–303; SN Upshur's *Report, 1841*, CSS, 27th, 2nd, *SEN 1*, vol. 1, *Serial 395*, 370–371; *TIAUS*, vol. 4, 275–285; Joseph G. Clark,

Lights and Shadows of a Sailor's Life: As Exemplified in Fifteen Years' Service (Boston, B. B. Mussey, 1848), 144–145, 154–157; George M. Colvocorresses, *Four Years in a Government Exploring Expedition*, 5th ed. (N.Y., M. B. Fairchild, 1855), 157–173; Charles Erskine, *Twenty Years Before the Mast* (Philadelphia, George W. Jacobs, 1896), 172–181; and *NWR*, vol. 59 (13, 20 Feb. 1841), 374, 386–387. Secondary: Stanton, 205–215; Tyler, 157–182; Robert A. Derrick, *A History of Fiji*, 2 vols. (Suva, Fiji, Government Press, 1946), vol. 1, 91–92; Harry A. Ellsworth, *One Hundred Eighty Landings of the United States Marines, 1800–1934* (Washington, Marine Corps, 1934), 77–80; Strauss, 128–138; Tate, 24–25; and Mark R. Perry, "American Activities in the Fiji Islands, 1844–1874," (M.A. dissertation, University of New Hampshire, 1969—done under my direction), 8–9.

5. (A) Hudson at Samoa and Gilberts. Primary: Wilkes, *Narrative*, vol. 5, 32–34, 59–64. Secondary: Stanton, 237–238, 240–245; Tyler, 266–272, 274–279; Ellsworth, 144–146; and Ellison, 9–10. (B) Wilkes at Oregon. Geoffrey S. Smith, "Charles Wilkes: The Naval Officer as Explorer and Diplomat," James C. Bradford, ed., *Captains of the Old Steam Navy: Makers of the American Naval Tradition, 1840–1880* (Annapolis, Naval Institute Press, 1986), 73–76. (C) Wilkes at Sulu. Primary: Wilkes, *Narrative*, vol. 5, 357–358, 532; and *TIAUS*, vol. 4, 349–361. Secondary: Tyler, 353–356; James F. Warren, *The Sulu Zone, 1768–1898: The Dynamics of External Trade, Slavery, and Ethnicity in the Transformation of a Southeast Asian Maritime State* (Singapore, Singapore University Press, 1981), 51; Nicholas Tarling, *Sulu and Sabah: A Study of British Policy towards the Philippines and North Borneo from the Late Eighteenth Century* (Kuala Lumpur, et al., Oxford University Press, 1978), 58; W. Cameron Forbes, *The Philippine Islands*, 2 vols. (Boston, Houghton Mifflin, 1928), vol. 2, 8n3; and *DNANO*, 345–346.

6. McKeever. The basic work is Edwin N. McClellan, "Honi Heke's War of 1845 in New Zealand," *USNIP*, vol. 51 (1925), 1459–1468. Primary: SN Bancroft's *Report, 1845, CSS*, 29th, 1st, *SEN 1*, vol. 1, *Serial 470*, 645; and *NWR*, vol. 68 (2 August 1845), 338. Secondary: Tom Gibson, *The Maori Wars: The British Army in New Zealand, 1840–1872* (London, L. Cooper, 1974), 30–35; *FCS*, 35–36; and W. Patrick Strauss, "Pioneer American Diplomats in Polynesia, 1820–1840," *PHR*, vol. 31 (Feb. 1962), 26–29.

7. Petigru and Magruder. Primary: *TIAUS*, vol. 7, 292–295. Secondary: Derrick, vol. 1, 132–133; Stanley Brown, *Men from under the Sky: The Arrival of Westerners in Fiji* (Rutland, Vt., and Tokyo, C. E. Tuttle Co., 1973), 186–187; Perry, 13–16; and Captain G. W. Hope, RN, "Sketches of Polynesia—The Fijis," *Blackwood's Edinburgh Magazine*, American ed., vol. 55 (July 1869), 46.

8. Boutwell and Bailey. Primary: *CSS*, 34th, 1st, *HR 115*, vol. 12, *Serial 859*, 1–76; Boutwell's report to Mervine, 22 Dec. 1855, *NASP*, vol. 3, 164–170; SN Dobbin's *Report, 1856, CSS*, 34th, 3rd, *SEN 5*, vol. 2, *Serial 876*, 408; *TIAUS*, vol. 7, 283–292, 295–303; and Berthold Seemann, *Viti: An Account of a Government Mission to the Vitian or Fijian Islands in the Years 1860–61* (Cambridge, U.K., Macmillan, 1862), 106–108. Secondary: Derrick, vol. 1, 134–136; Brown,

113, 189–195, 199; Brookes, 232–237, 247–248; Ellsworth, 80–81; Ralph G. Ward, ed., *American Activities in the Central Pacific, 1790–1870*, 8 vols. (Ridgewood, N.J., Gregg Press, 1966–1967), vol. 2, 471–472; Tate, 25–27; Hope, 46–48; W. B. McIntyre, "Anglo-American Rivalry in the Pacific: The British Annexation of the Fiji Islands in 1874," *PHR*, vol. 29 (Nov. 1960), 362–365; and Perry, 27–41.

9. Sinclair and Caldwell. Primary: *TIAUS*, vol. 7, 307–311; and SN Toucey's *Report, 1859*, *CSS*, 36th, 1st, *SEN 2*, vol. 2, *Serial 1025*, 1145–1146. Secondary: Derrick, vol. 1, 138–139; Brown, 196–197; Ward, vol. 2, 482–483; Ellsworth, 81–82; W. B. Ammon, "Fijian Adventure," *USNIP*, vol. 63 (1927), 224–230; Francis X. Holbrook, "Come, Papillangi, Our Fires Are Lighted," in *ASHS*, 113–125; and Perry, 44–46.

Chapter 14

1. General background for West Africa and the international slave trade. Hugh B. Soulsby, "The Right of Search and the Slave Trade in Anglo-American Relations, 1814–1862," *Johns Hopkins University Studies in History and Political Science*, series 51, no. 2 (Baltimore, Johns Hopkins University Press, 1933); William E. B. DuBois, *The Suppression of the African Slave Trade to the United States of America, 1683–1870* (N.Y. and London, Longmans, Green, 1904); and Christopher Lloyd, *The [Royal] Navy and the Slave Trade: The Suppression of the African Slave Trade in the Nineteenth Century* (London, Longmans, Green, 1949), all passim. (A) Trenchard and Perry. Edgar S. Maclay, *Reminiscences of the Old Navy* (N.Y., G. P. Putnam's Sons, 1898), 8–24; *OBMCP*, 61–69; and Alan R. Booth, "The United States African Squadron, 1843–1861," *Boston University Papers in African History* (Boston, 1964), 80–84. (B) Perry in the *Shark*. *ASP, Naval Affairs*, vol. 1, 1098–1099; and *OBMCP*, 69–76. (C) Spence. *ASP*, vol. 1, 1100–1102; SN Southard's *Report, 1823*, *CSS*, 18th, 1st, *HR 2*, vol. 1, *Serial 93*, 112–113; and Andrew H. Foote, *Africa and the American Flag* (N.Y., D. Appleton, 1854), 128. (D) Stockton. Primary: *JQAM*, vol. 6, 28–31; and *DNI*, 28, 29 Jan. 1822, 2/1, 1/3. Secondary: Foote, 115–119; Samuel J. Bayard, *A Sketch of the Life of Robert F. Stockton: with an Appendix Comprising His Correspondence with the Navy Department respecting His Conquest of California* (N.Y., Denby & Jackson, 1856), 39–47; *DNANO*, 335–338; P. J. Staudenraus, *The African Colonization Movement, 1816–1865* (N.Y., Columbia University Press, 1961), 63–65; Marvin Duke, "The Navy Founds a Nation," *USNIP*, vol. 96 (Sept. 1970), 68–70; ibid., "Robert F. Stockton: Early U.S. Naval Activities in Africa," *Naval War College Review*, vol. 24 (May 1972), 86–94; Judd S. Harman, "Marriage of Convenience: The United States Navy in Africa, 1820–1847," *AN*, vol. 32 (Dec. 1972), 264–274; and Katherine Harris, *American and African Values: Liberia and West Africa* (Lanham, Md., University Press of America, 1985), 11–15.

2. Perry, 1844–1845. Primary: USND, Letter books of Commodore Matthew C. Perry, 1843–1845, M 206, 1 roll, passim, NA; *DNI*, 8 April 1844,

3/5; and *NWR*, vol. 66 (6 April 1844), 83. Secondary: *OBMCP*, 168–176; Foote, 232–239; *DNANO*, 359–361; Harry A. Ellsworth, *One Hundred Eighty Landings of United States Marines, 1800–1934* (Washington, Marine Corps, 1934), 3–7; Booth, 84, 86–88, 90–91; Harman, 269–273; Harris, 65–66; George E. Brooke, Jr., "The Role of the United States Navy in the Suppression of the African Slave Trade," *AN*, vol. 21 (Jan. 1961), 28–41; and Donald R. Wright, "Matthew Perry and the African Squadron," in *ASHS*, 80–89.

3. Foote. Foote, 253–368; and Brooke, 37.

4. Mayo. Primary: Mayo's correspondence with the SN, 1853–1855, USND, African SL, M 89, roll 107, passim; and *TIAUS*, vol. 6, 845–850. Secondary: Tyrone G. Martin, *A Most Fortunate Ship: A Narrative History of "Old Ironsides"* (Chester, Conn., Globe-Pequot Press, 1980), 253–263; and Booth, 91–9c.

5. Brent. For Angolan backgrounds, I am indebted to Douglas L. Wheeler, my colleague in the UNH History Department, and his unpublished Ph.D. dissertation, Boston University, 1963, "The Portuguese in Angola, 1836–1891," 169–188. This has been redone in a shorter form: Douglas L. Wheeler and René Pelissier, *Angola* (N.Y., et al., Praeger, 1971), 54–56, 87–89. Primary: Brent to Inman, 6 March 1860, African SL, roll 111; John C. Willis, U.S. commercial agent, to SS, 23 May 1860, USDS, Consular despatches, St. Paul de Loanda, F 430, roll 1, and SN Toucey's *Report, 1860, CSS*, 36th, 1st, *SEN 1*, vol. 3, *Serial 1080*, 14. Secondary: Ellsworth, 7; J. Reuben Clark, *The Right to Protect Citizens Abroad by Landing Forces of the United States, by the Solicitor* (Washington, Government Printing Office, 1912), 62; and *PCA*, 41–42. The latter two have used Toucey's *Report* almost to the extent of plagiarism.

6. (A) Inman. Inman's correspondence with the SN, 1859–1861, African SL, rolls 110–113; Booth, 96–113; and Brooke, 34–41. (B) Gordon. *NYT*, Feb. 1862; and *Times* (London), Feb.–March 1862, both passim.

Chapter 15

1. Wilkes. There is a huge mass of literature devoted to the *Trent* affair. Primary: for both naval and diplomatic correspondence, *ORUCN*, vol. 1, 129–202; Charles Wilkes, *Autobiography of Admiral Charles Wilkes*, William Morgan, et al., eds. (Washington, Naval Historical Division, 1978), 845–847. Secondary: Two modern monographs: Gordon H. Warren, *Fountain of Discontent: The Trent Affair and Freedom of the Seas* (Boston, Northeastern University Press, 1981); and Norman B. Ferris, *The Trent Affair: A Diplomatic Crisis* (Knoxville, University of Tennessee Press, 1977), both passim. Also, Daniel M. Henderson, *The Hidden Coast: A Biography of Admiral Charles Wilkes* (N.Y., Sloane, 1953), 237–247; Virgil C. Jones, *The Civil War at Sea*, 3 vols. (N.Y., Holt, Rinehart, & Winston, 1960–1962), vol. 1, 292–310; Frank T. Merli, *Great Britain and the Confederate Navy, 1861–1865* (Bloomington, Indiana University Press, 1970), 76–84; Glynden G. Van Deusen, *William Henry Seward* (N.Y., Oxford University Press, 1967), 308–317; Jay Monaghan, *Diplomat in Carpet Slippers: Abraham*

Lincoln Deals with Foreign Affairs (Indianapolis and N.Y., Dodd, Mead, 1945), 164–193; Allan Nevins, *The War for the Union*, vol. 1, *The Improvised War, 1861–1862* (N.Y., Charles Scribner's Sons, 1959), 383–393; Richard S. West, Jr., *Gideon Welles: Lincoln's Navy Department* (Indianapolis and N.Y., Bobbs-Merrill, 1943), 129–137; John Niven, *Gideon Welles: Lincoln's Secretary of the Navy* (N.Y., Oxford University Press, 1975), 444–447; Frederick C. Drake, "The Cuban Background to the *Trent* Affair," *Civil War History*, vol. 19 (March 1973), 29–49; and Geoffrey S. Smith, "Charles Wilkes and the Growth of American Naval Diplomacy," in Frank T. Merli and Theodore A. Wilson, eds., *Makers of American Diplomacy from Benjamin Franklin to Henry Kissinger*, 2 vols. (N.Y., Charles Scribner's Sons, 1974), vol. 1, 151–154. Neither *DGW* nor *DIL* has anything to say about the *Trent* and Wilkes's part in it.

2.   Collins. Primary: *ORUCN*, vol. 3, 264–294; *DGW*, vol. 2, 184–186; *DIL*, vol. 7, 1090; and *NYT*, 10 Nov. 1864, 4/2. Secondary: Frank L. Owsley, Jr., *The C.S.S. Florida: Her Building and Operation* (Philadelphia, University of Pennsylvania Press, 1965), 137–155; Edward D. Boykin, *Sea Devil of the Confederacy: The Story of the Florida and Her Captain, John Newland Maffitt* (N.Y., Funk and Wagnalls, 1959), 284–291; Jones, vol. 3, 302–309; Monaghan, 384–385; Owsley, "The Capture of the Florida," *AN*, vol. 32 (Jan. 1962), 45–54; and Benjamin F. Gilbert, "Confederate Warships off Brazil," ibid., vol. 25 (Oct. 1955), 287–302.

3.   Craven. Primary: *ORUCN*, vol. 3, 664–671; *FRUS, 1865*, for Spain, vol. 2, 473–524, 539–540, 569–579; for Portugal, vol. 3, 104–119; *DGW*, vol. 2, 261, 267, 392–393; vol. 3, 99, 513; "Autobiographical Sketch of Thomas Jefferson Page," submitted by P. S. Crenshaw, *USNIP*, vol. 49 (1923), 1678–1691; Thomas J. Page, "The Career of the Confederate Cruiser *Stonewall*," *Southern Historical Society Papers*, vol. 7 (1879), 263–280; and *NYT*, 13 April 1865, 4/4. Secondary: Monaghan, 407–408, 412, 423; and James M. Hyde, "Two *Stonewalls*, from a Seaside View," *Military Essays and Recollections: Papers Read before the Illinois Commandery, Military Order of the Loyal Legion of the United States*, 4 vols. (Chicago, 1891–1913), vol. 1, 453–476.

4.   Bryson. Primary: Bryson to SN, 3, 5 June 1866, COML, roll 85; and *FRUS, 1866*, vol. 1, 126–127. Secondary: Brian Jenkins, *Fenians and Anglo-American Relations during Reconstruction* (Ithaca, N.Y., Cornell University Press, 1969), 142–151, 305; Wilfried S. Neidhardt, *Fenianism in North America* (University Park, Pennsylvania State University Press, 1975), 62–71; William D'Arcy, *The Fenian Movement in the United States, 1858–1886* (N.Y., Catholic University of America Press, 1947), 180–181; and Martin B. Duberman, *Charles Francis Adams, 1807–1886* (Boston, Houghton Mifflin, 1961), 326–327.

Chapter 16

1.   Frank M. Bennett, *The Steam Navy of the United States: A History of the Steam Vessel of War in the U.S. Navy and of the Naval Engineering Corps* (Pittsburgh, W. F. Nicholson Press, 1896, repr. Westport, Conn., Greenwood

Press, 1972), passim; Tamara M. Melia, "David Dixon Porter: Fighting Sailor," James C. Bradford, ed., *Captains of the Old Steam Navy: Makers of the American Naval Tradition, 1840–1880* (Annapolis, Naval Institute Press, 1986), 227–249; Dean C. Allard, "Benjamin F. Isherwood: Father of the Modern Steam Navy," ibid., 301–322; Lance C. Buhl, "Maintaining 'An American Navy,' 1865–1889," Kenneth J. Hagan, ed., *In Peace and War: Interpretations of American Naval History, 1775–1978* (Westport, Conn., Greenwood Press, 1978), 145–173; Elting E. Morison, "Inventing a Modern Navy," *AH*, vol. 37 (June/July 1986), 81–96; Frederick C. Drake, *The Empire of the Seas: A Biography of Rear Admiral Robert Wilson Shufeldt, USN* (Honolulu, University of Hawaii Press, 1984), 151–172; and Edward L. Beach, *The United States Navy: 200 Years* (N.Y., Henry Holt and Co., 1986), 317–330. All the standard naval histories treat this topic, but the above are among the best and (save for Bennett) the most recent narratives.

2.   Alden. Primary: William T. Sherman, *Memoirs*, 2 vols. (N.Y., Appleton, vol. 2, 414–420. Secondary: Kathryn A. Hanna, *Napoleon III and Mexico: American Triumph over Monarchy* (Chapel Hill, University of North Carolina Press, 1971), 285–289; and Martin H. Hall, "The Campbell-Sherman Diplomatic Mission to Mexico," *Bulletin of the Historical and Philosophical Society of Ohio*, vol. 13 (Oct. 1955), 254–270.

3.   Roe. Primary: SN Welles's *Report, 1867, CSS*, 40th, 2nd, *HR 1*, vol. 4, *Serial 1327*, 10; and *NYT*, 24 June 1867, 5/1–2, 15 July 1867, 1/4–7. Secondary: Oakah L. Jones, Jr., *Santa Anna* (N.Y., Twayne, 1968), 145–147; Perry F. Martin, *Maximilian in Mexico: The Story of the French Intervention, 1861–1867* (London, Constable & Co., 1913), 148–149; and Louis N. Feipel, "The United States and Mexico, 1821–1914," *USNIP*, vol. 41 (1915), 1999–2001.

4.   Low and Brownson. Primary: Low correspondence, *FRUS, 1868–1869*, pt. 2, 802–803, 824–825; and *NYT*, 13 July 1870, 1/2–3, 6/4–5. Secondary: *PCA*, 53, 54, Feipel, *USNIP*, vol. 42 (1916), 176; Harry A. Ellsworth, *One Hundred Eighty Landings of the United States Marines* (Washington, Marine Corps, 1934), 114–115; and Willard H. Brownson, "The Pirate Ship *Forward*," in *ASHS*, 138–152.

5.   Murray. Feipel, vol. 42 (1916), 176, is the only source for this obscure incident.

6.   (A) McIntosh, 1858. *USSDOM*, 206–207. (B) D. D. Porter. Primary: DDP, "Secret Mission to Santo Domingo," *North American Review*, vol. 128 (1879), 627–630; Frederick W. Seward, *Reminiscences of a Wartime Statesman and Diplomat, 1830–1915* (N.Y. and London, Putnam, 1916), 344–356; and *DIL*, vol. 1, 598–600. Secondary: Sumner Welles, *Naboth's Vineyard: The Dominican Republic, 1844–1924*, 2 vols. (N.Y., Payson & Clarke, 1928), vol. 1, 322–333; Allan Nevins, *Hamilton Fish: The Inner History of the Grant Administration*, 2 vols. (N.Y., F. Ungar, 1936), vol. 1, 249–250; David Donald, *Charles Sumner and the Rights of Man* (N.Y., Knopf, 1970), 435–445; Ernest N. Paolino, *The Foundations of the American Empire: William Henry Seward and U.S. Foreign Policy* (Ithaca, N.Y., Cornell University Press, 1973), 118–125; *USSDOM*, 226–246; *EAAFR*, 671–673; Ludwell L. Montague, *Haiti and the United States*,

1714–1938 (Durham, N.C., Duke University Press, 1940), 91–93; and Rayford W. Logan, *Haiti and the Dominican Republic* (N.Y., Oxford University Press, 1968), 43–44.

7. Selfridge, et al. Primary: *CSS*, 41st, 3rd, *SEN 34*, vol. 1, *Serial 1440*, 1–38; SN Welles's *Report, 1868*, ibid., 40th, 3rd, *HR 79*, vol. 9, *Serial 1374*, xv; SN Robeson's *Report, 1869*, ibid., 41st, 2nd, *HR 1*, vol. 1, *Serial 1411*, 11; *DIL*, vol. 1, 278–280; and *FRUS, 1871–1872*, 566–572. Secondary: Sumner Welles, 359–408; Nevins, vol. 1, 249–278, 309–334, 363–371; *USSDOM*, 338–464; Logan, 45–47; Montague, 102–110; Selden Rodman, *Quisquaya: A History of the Dominican Republic* (Seattle, University of Washington Press, 1964), 85–87; and Paul B. Ryan, "The Old Navy and Santo Domingo: Pacification Patrols in the 19th Century," *Shipmate* (Feb. 1967), 305.

8. Hoff. Primary: Hoff to SN, 29 July 1869, North Atlantic SL, roll 276; A. E. Phillips to SS, 25 June 1869, USDS, Consular despatches, Santiago de Cuba, T 55, roll 6; SN Robeson's *Report, 1869*, 9; and *NYT*, 10, 14, 22 July 1869, 5/3, 1/7, 1/7. Secondary: Nevins, vol. 1, 180–189; Philip S. Foner, *A History of Cuba and Its Relations with the United States*, 2 vols. (N.Y., International Publishers, 1962, 1965), vol. 2, 184–275; Hugh Thomas, *Cuba: The Pursuit of Freedom* (N.Y., et al., Harper & Row, 1971), 245–270; Jaime Suchlicki, *Cuba from Columbus to Castro* (N.Y., Charles Scribner's Sons, 1974), 77–83; Lester D. Langley, *The Cuban Policy of the United States: A Brief History* (N.Y., Wiley, 1968), 55–73; and Charles E. Chapman, *A History of the Cuban Republic: A Study in Hispanic-American Politics* (N.Y., Macmillan, 1927), 63–67.

9. Cushing. The *Virginius* episode has been exhaustively analyzed. Richard H. Bradford, *The Virginius Affair* (Boulder, University of Colorado Press, 1980), passim. Primary: *FRUS, 1873*, vol. 1, 12–13 (for the Fish-Polo compromise); ibid., *1874*, vol. 1, 922–1117 (for the interminable correspondence connected with the case); Vice-consul E. G. Smith to SS, 13 Nov. 1873, USDS, Consular despatches, Santiago de Cuba, roll 7; *DIL*, vol. 2, 895–903; Charles W. Stewart, "William Barker Cushing," *USNIP*, vol. 38 (1912), 913–940 (for letters in re Cushing); and *NYT*, 10 Nov.–18 Dec. 1873, passim. Secondary: Nevins, vol. 2, 667–694; Chadwick, 314–357; Lawrence W. Allin. "The First Cubic War—the *Virginius* Affair," *AN*, vol. 38 (Oct. 1978), 233–248; Jim D. Hill, "Captain Joseph Fry of the S.S. *Virginius*," ibid., vol. 36 (April 1976), 88–100; Chester M. Colby, "Diplomacy of the Quarterdeck," *American Journal of International Law*, vol. 8 (1914), 458–460; and S. D. Lapham, "Commander Cushing and the *Virginius*," *Americana*, vol. 10 (1915), 903–905.

10. Godon, et al. Primary: *CSS*, 40th, 3rd, *HR 79*, vol. 9, *Serial 1374*, 1–95; SN Welles's *Report, 1868*, ibid., xvi–xvii; *DGW*, vol. 2, 491–492, 543; vol. 3, 427, 467, 513; Johnson's *Message, 1868*, *CMPP*, vol. 6, 685–686; Charles A. Washburn, *History of Paraguay; with Notes of Personal Observations and Reminiscences of Diplomacy under Difficulties*, 2 vols. (Boston, Lee & Shepard, 1871), vol. 2, 114–117, 435–463, 468–474, 476–485; *DIL*, vol. 2, 850; vol. 4, 559–563, 615–617; and *NYT*, Nov. 1869–May 1870, passim. Secondary: Harold F. Peterson, *Argentina and the United States, 1810–1974* (Albany, N.Y.,

State University of New York, University Publishers, 1964), 180–207; Harris G. Warren, *Paraguay: An Informal History* (Norman, University of Oklahoma Press, 1949), 248–260; William H. Koebel, *Paraguay* (London, T. F. Unwin, 1919), 191–207; Lawrence F. Hill. *Diplomatic Relations Between the United States and Brazil* (Durham, N.C., Duke University Press, 1932), 182–207; Charles E. Akers, *A History of South America, 1854–1904* (N.Y., E. P. Dutton, 1904), 130–186; and Richard C. Froelich, "The United States Navy and Diplomatic Relations with Brazil, 1822–1871" (unpublished Ph.D. dissertation, Kent State University, 1971), 479–512.

11. Rodgers. Primary: *FRUS, 1867*, pt. 2, 412–429 (for Rodgers's letters to an unnamed naval colleague); *NYT*, 3, 5 May 1866, 1/5, 8/1–2; SN Welles's *Report, 1866*, CSS, 39th, 2nd, *HR 1*, vol. 4, *Serial 1286*, 21; *DGW*, vol. 2, 495; and *DIL*, vol. 7, 354–359. Secondary: Robert E. Johnson, *Rear-Admiral John Rodgers, 1812–1882* (Annapolis, U.S. Naval Institute, 1967), 284–297; William C. Davis, *The Last Conquistadores: The Spanish Intervention in Peru and Chile, 1863–1866* (Athens, University of Georgia Press, 1950), 292–310, 311n.; W. S. Robertson, *Hispanic-American Relations with the United States* (N.Y., Oxford University Press, 1923), 147–149; Robert Marrett, *Peru* (N.Y. and Washington, Praeger, 1969), 112–113; Robert N. Burr, *By Reason or Force: Chile and the Balance of Power in South America, 1830–1905* (Berkeley, et al., University of California Press, 1965), 97–99; Akers, 326–327, 505–510; and James W. Cortada, "Diplomatic Rivalry Between Spain and the United States over Chile and Peru, 1864–1871," *Inter-American Economic Affairs*, vol. 27 (Spring 1974), 47–57.

12. C. R. P. Rodgers and Balch. Primary: Herbert A. Millington, *American Diplomacy and the War of the Pacific* (N.Y., Columbia University Press, 1948), passim (this monograph is based almost exclusively on USDS correspondence); USND, Pacific Station SL, rolls 66–68 (Rodgers), 69–71 (Balch), passim. Arthur's *Message, 1882*, CMPP, vol. 8, 130; and *DIL*, vol. 6, 34–45. Secondary: Markham, 387–426; Akers, 440–504; David M. Pletcher, *The Awkward Years: American Foreign Policy under Garfield and Arthur* (Columbia, University of Missouri Press, 1962), 40–51, 71–81, 89–101; David P. Werlich, *Peru: A Short History* (Carbondale and Edwardsville, Southern Illinois University Press, 1978), 106–119; Frederick B. Pike, *The History of Modern Peru* (N.Y. and Washington, Praeger, 1967), 142–149; Marrett, 112–117; J. Valerie Fifer, *Bolivia: Land, Location, and Politics since 1825* (Cambridge, U.K., Cambridge University Press, 1972), 61–63; and Lester D. Langley, "James Gillespie Blaine: The Ideologue as Diplomatist," Frank T. Merli and Theodore A. Wilson, eds., *Makers of American Diplomacy from Benjamin Franklin to Henry Kissinger*, 2 vols. (N.Y., Charles Scribner's Sons, 1974), vol. 1, 259–267. All of the above, however, suffer from an almost complete omission of the U.S. Navy's diplomatic contributions. This deficiency has been remedied by Kenneth J. Hagan, *American Gunboat Diplomacy and the Old Navy, 1877–1889* (Westport, Conn., Greenwood Press, 1973), 130–142.

Chapter 17

1. Shufeldt and Hatfield. Primary: Shufeldt to Bell, 3 Oct. 1866, in Bell to SN, 29 Oct. 1866, Asiatic SL, roll 1; and Hatfield to Rowan, 16 May 1868, ibid., roll 3. Secondary: *ESRWS*, 92–95; *FCS*, 129–130; and Grace E. Fox, *British Admirals and Chinese Pirates, 1832–1869* (London, Kegan, Paul, 1940; repr., Westport, Conn., Greenwood Press, 1973), 145, 175.

2. Townsend. Primary: Bell to SN, 10 Oct. 1866, Asiatic SL, roll 1; SN Welles's *Report, 1866, CSS,* 39th, 2nd, *HR 1,* vol. 4, *Serial 1286,* 15; and John W. Philip, *Life and Adventures of "Jack" Philip, Rear-Admiral, United States Navy* (N.Y., The Illustrated Navy, 1903), 21–29. Secondary: Harry A. Ellsworth, *One Hundred Eighty Landings of the United States Marines, 1800–1934* (Washington, Marine Corps, 1934), 28–29; E. Mowbray Tate, "Admiral Bell and the Asiatic Squadron, 1865–1868," *AN,* vol. 32 (April 1972), 126–127; and Charles G. Chadbourne III, "Sailors and Diplomats: U.S. Naval Operations in China, 1865–1877" (unpublished Ph.D. dissertation, University of Washington, 1976), 44–48.

3. Bell. Primary: *CSS,* 40th, 2nd, *SEN 52,* vol. 2, *Serial 1317,* 53–68 (naval documentation), ibid., 1–53 (diplomatic documentation); and Charles W. LeGendre, "Notes on Travel in Formosa," vol. 3, 152–174, Mss Division, LC. Secondary: George W. Carrington, *Foreigners in Formosa, 1841–1871* (San Francisco, Chinese Materials Center, 1977), 152–176; Ernest N. Paolino, *The Foundations of American Empire: William Henry Seward and U.S. Foreign Policy* (Ithaca, N.Y., Cornell University, Press, 1973), 166–169; *FCS,* 132–134; Tate, "Admiral Bell," 131–132; ibid., "Navy Justice in the Pacific: A Pattern of Precedent," *AN,* vol. 35 (Jan. 1976), 28–30; and Chadbourne, 53–82.

4. McDougal. Primary: McDougal to Welles, 27 April 1863, *ORUCN,* vol. 2, 58–59; SN Welles's *Report, 1863, CSS,* 38th, 1st, *HR 1,* vol. 4, xi; ibid., 43rd, 1st, *HR Reports,* vol. 3, no. 343, 1–5; and City of Shimonoseki archives, *The Battle of Bakkan* [Shimonoseki] *Strait* (Tokyo, 1971), 132–133 (trans. for me in Japan). Secondary: W. G. Beasley, *The Meiji Restoration* (Stanford, Stanford University Press, 1972), 198–207; Payson J. Treat, *Diplomatic Relations between the United States and Japan, 1853–1895,* 3 vols. (Stanford, Stanford University Press, 1932–1938), vol. 1, 184–213; *FCS,* 166–177; Hikomatsu Kamikawa, ed., *Japan-America Relations in the Meiji-Taisho Era* (Tokyo, Pan-Pacific Press, 1958), 45–47, 51–53; Benjamin F. Gilbert, "Lincoln's Far Eastern Navy," *Journal of the West,* vol. 8 (1969), 356–363; Frank E. Ross, "The American Naval Attack on Shimonoseki in 1863," *Chinese Social and Political Science Review,* vol. 18 (1934), 153–154; and William E. Griffis, "The 'Wyoming' in the Straits of Shimonoseki: The Story of a Very Brilliant Naval Action," *Century Illustrated Monthly Magazine,* vol. 43 (1892), 846.

5. Pearson. Primary: Pruyn to SS, 1 Oct. 1864, *FRUS,* vol. 3, 553; Pearson to Price, 11 Sept. 1864; Price to SN, 23 Sept. 1864, *ORUCN,* vol. 3, 203–204; *HR Reports,* vol. 3, no. 343, 1–5; Aizu Clan archivists, mss, Historical Institute, University of Tokyo, vol. 2083, 138–150 (trans. for me in Japan); *DGW,* vol.

2, 209–210; Lincoln's *Message, 1864, CMPP*, vol. 4, 245; and Great Britain, Parliament, House of Commons Sessional Papers, 1865, vol. 57, no. 3428, *Correspondence Respecting Affairs in Japan*, 30, 44–45, 86–87, 99–103, 109. Secondary: Grace E. Fox, *Great Britain and Japan, 1858–1883* (Oxford, U.K., Oxford University Press, 1969), 101, 112–115; Treat, vol. 1, 214–244; *FCS*, 120–123; and William E. Griffis, "Our Navy in Asiatic Waters," *Harper's Monthly Magazine*, vol. 97 (1898), 754.

6. Rowan. Primary: *CSS*, 40th, 2nd, *SEN 65*, vol. 2, *Serial 1317*, 2–3, 8–24; ibid., 41st, 2nd, *SEN 52*, vol. 2, *Serial 1406*, 1–10; Rowan to SN, Jan. 1868–Feb. 1869, Asiatic SL, rolls 253–254, passim; SN Welles's *Report, 1868, CSS*, 40th, 3rd, *HR 79*, vol. 9, *Serial 1374*, xii–xiii; and SN Robeson's *Report, 1869*, *CSS*, 41st, 1st, *HR 7*, vol. 1, *Serial 1411*, 11. Secondary: Paolino, 189–193; Treat, vol. 1, 309–310, 328–329; *FCS*, 140–145; Kamikawa, 68–69; and Charles O. Paullin, "Early Voyages of American Naval Vessels to the Orient," *USNIP*, vol. 36 (1910), 1141–1144.

7. Shufeldt. Primary: Van Valkenburg to SS, Sept.–Oct. 1866, *FRUS, 1867*, pt. 1, 414–417, 419–423, 426–427; Shufeldt to SN, Dec. 1866–Feb. 1867, Asiatic SL, passim; *USCH 2*, vol. 10, *Korea*, 6–82; and *Ilsongnok: The Daily Records concerning National Affairs*, multi-vols. (Seoul, 1872), vol. 8, July–Sept. 1866, passim (trans. for me in Korea). Secondary: John F. Cady, *The Roots of French Imperialism in Asia*, rev. ed. (Ithaca, N.Y., Cornell University Press, 1967), 278–279; and Lee Sun-keun, "Some Lesser Known Facts about the Taewon'gun and His Foreign Policy," *Korean Branch of the Royal Asiatic Society*, vol. 39 (1962), 27–32.

8. Febiger. Goldsborough to Febiger, 8 Feb. 1868; Febiger to Rowan, 19 May 1868; and Rowan to SN, 24 July 1868, Asiatic SL, roll 252.

9. Rodgers. Primary: Low to SS, April–June 1871, *FRUS, 1871–1872*, passim; Rodgers to SN, April–July 1871, Asiatic SL, rolls 256–257, passim; SN Robeson's *Report, 1871, CSS*, 42nd, 2nd, *HR 1*, vol. 4, *Serial 1507*, 277–311; *USCH 2, Korea*, 85–281; Grant's *Message, 1871, CMPP*, vol. 7, 146; *Ilsongnok*, vol. 8 (in re the 10–11 June attack), 8, 25 April 1871 (Korea's use of the lunar calendar explains the difference in dates), George R. Willis, *Story of Our Cruise in the U.S. Frigate Colorado, 1870–1872* (N.Y., n.p., 1873), 121–163; *NYT*, 17 Nov. 1871, 4/6; and N.Y. *Herald*, 22 Aug. 1871, 3/4. Secondary: Robert E. Johnson, *Rear-Admiral John Rodgers, 1812–1882* (Annapolis, U.S. Naval Institute, 1967), 308–333; *FCS*, 154–169; Lee Yur-bok, *Diplomatic Relations between the United States and Korea, 1866–1887* (N.Y., Humanities Press, 1970), 20–30; Albert Kastel and Andrew G. Nahn, "Our Little War against the Heathen," *AH*, vol. 19 (April 1968), 19–32, 72–75; and William M. Leary, Jr., "Our Other War in Korea," *USNIP*, vol. 94 (June 1968), 46–52.

Chapter 18

1. Emmons. Primary: *FRUS, 1867*, 388–408; ibid., *1868–1869*, pt. 1, 475; and Emmons to SN, 29 Oct. 1867, CAPL, roll 374. Secondary: Ernest N. Paolino,

The Foundations of American Empire: William Henry Seward and U.S. Foreign Policy (Ithaca, N.Y., Cornell University Press, 1967), 536–549; Hector Chevigny, *Russian America: The Great Alaskan Adventure, 1741–1867* (N.Y., Viking, 1965), 241–249; and Robert J. Jensen, *The Alaska Purchase and Russian-American Relations* (Seattle, University of Washington Press, 1975), 101–102.

2. Case and Wells. *AMW*, 332–333.

3. Goldsborough and Farragut. Primary: *FRUS, 1866*, pt. 2, 253–257; ibid., *1868–1869*, pt. 2, 110–112, 119, 120; and *DGW*, vol. 3, 139. Secondary: *AMW*, 318–323; and Arthur J. May, "Crete and the United States, 1866–1869," *Journal of Modern History*, vol. 16 (Dec. 1944), 286–293.

4. Worden. Primary: Robley D. Evans, *A Sailor's Log: Recollections of Forty Years of Naval Life* (N.Y., Appleton, 1903), 204–205. Secondary: *AMW*, 339–343, 377–378; and James A. Field, Jr., "A Scheme in Regard to Cyrenaica," *Mississippi Valley Historical Review*, vol. 44 (Dec. 1957), 445–468.

5. Nicholson. Primary: *CSS*, 47th, 1st, *HR Miscellaneous Documents 46*, vol. 12, *Serial 2046*, 1–6; Nicholson to SN, 14, 15 July 1882, European SL, roll 245; SN Chandler's *Report, 1882*, ibid., 47th, 2nd, *HR 1*, vol. 8, *Serial 2097*, 14; and *NYT*, 22, 1/2; 25 July, 4/4; 20 August 1882, 1/3–4. Secondary: *AMW*, 424–433; Lenoire C. Wright, *United States Policy toward Egypt, 1831–1914* (N.Y., Exposition Press, 1969), 112–131; and Peter Harrington, "Imperial Interest Protected," *Military History* (April 1987), 42–49.

6. Reynolds. Primary: Reynolds to SN, 29 July 1867, CAPL, roll 374; McCook to SS, July 1867–June 1868, USDS, Despatches from U.S. ministers in Hawaii, T 30, roll 12; and *DGW*, vol. 3, 322. Secondary: Ralph S. Kuykendall, *The Hawaiian Kingdom*, 3 vols. (Honolulu, University of Hawaii Press, 1947–1953), vol. 2, 207–228; Merze Tate, *Hawaii: Reciprocity or Annexation* (East Lansing, Michigan State University Press, 1968), 28–29; Jean I. Brookes, *International Rivalry in the Pacific Ocean, 1800–1875* (Berkeley, University of California Press, 1941, repr., N.Y., Russell & Russell, 1972), 276–281; and Glyndon G. Van Deusen, *William Henry Seward* (N.Y., Oxford University Press, 1967), 532–534.

7. Pennock. Kuykendall, vol. 2, 242–257; Tate, 30; and John Patterson, "The United States and Hawaiian Reciprocity, 1867–1870," *PHR*, vol. 7 (1938), 14–26.

8. Belknap and Skerrett. Primary: Belknap and Skerrett to SN, 19, 21 Feb. 1874, COML, roll 102; and SN Robeson's *Report, 1874*, CSS, 43rd, 2nd, *HR 1*, vol. 5, *Serial 1638*, 8. Secondary: Kuykendall, vol. 3, 10–11; Tate, 31–33; *PCA*, 62–64; and Albert P. Taylor, "The American Navy in Hawaii," *USNIP*, vol. 53 (1927), 919–921.

9. Almy. *DIL*, vol. 1, 485–486; Kuykendall, vol. 3, 17–45; and Tate, 33, 38–43.

10. Stanley. Primary: *TIAUS*, vol. 7, 314–318. Secondary: Robert A. Derrick, *A History of Fiji*, 2 vols. (Suva, Fiji, Government Press, 1957), vol. 1, 164–165, 177–183; Brookes, 304–307; Stanley Brown, *Men from under the Sky: The Arrival of Westerners in Fiji* (Rutland, Vt., and Tokyo, C. E. Tuttle Co.,

1973), 287; W. D. McIntyre, "Anglo-American Rivalry in the Pacific: The British Annexation of the Fiji Islands in 1874," *PHR*, vol. 29 (Nov. 1960), 366–368; and Mark R. Perry, "American Activities in the Fiji Islands, 1844–1874" (MA dissertation, UNH, 1969—done under my direction), 50–57.

11.   Truxtun at Fiji. Primary: *TIAUS*, vol. 7, 318–334. Secondary: Derrick, vol. 1, 177–183; Brookes, 317–324; Brown, 198–199; McIntyre, 368–369; and Perry, 59–66.

12.   Truxtun at Micronesia. "Agreement entered into by the Chiefs of the Islands of Apaiang, Tarawa, and Bu-tari-tari—Makin—[with Truxtun]," 19 May 1870, Ms Room, New-York Historical Society, N.Y., N.Y.; Peter Karsten, *The Naval Aristocracy: Mahan's Messmates and the Emergence of Modern American Navalism* (Riverside, N.J., Free Press, 1972), 146n 12.

13.   (A) Meade. Primary: Meade to SN, 21 Jan., 29 Feb. 1872, COML, roll 97; SN Robeson's *Report, 1872*, CSS, 42nd, 3rd, *HR 1*, vol. 4, *Serial 1562*, 13–14; *CMPP*, vol. 7, 168–169; and *NYT*, 1 June, 17 July 1872, 2/2, 5/4. Secondary: George H. Ryden, *The Foreign Policy of the United States in Relation to Samoa* (New Haven, Yale University Press, 1933), 56–74; Joseph W. Ellison, *Opening and Promotion of Foreign Influences in Samoa to 1880* (Corvallis, Ore., Oregon State University Press, 1938), 38–43; Sylvia Masterman, *Origins of International Rivalry in Samoa, 1845–1884* (Stanford, Stanford University Press, 1934), 110–115; Brookes, 322–323; Karsten, 170–172; Dorothy Graebner, *Crisis Diplomacy: A History of U.S. Intervention Policies and Practices* (Washington, Public Affairs Press, 1959), 90–91; *DNANO*, 350–352; and McIntyre, 375–376. (B) Chandler. Ellison, 103. (C) Gillis. Gillis to SN, 12 July 1881, CAPL, roll 401; and David M. Pletcher, *The Awkward Years: American Foreign Relations under Garfield and Arthur* (Columbia, University of Missouri Press, 1963), 127.

Chapter 19

The format of chapter notes used before is changed for this discussion of Shufeldt's cruise from West Africa through Southeast Asia (1879–1880) and his work in the Far East leading to the Korean treaty (1880–1883). In preparing his *Empire of the Seas: A Biography of Rear Admiral Robert W. Shufeldt, USN* (Honolulu, University of Hawaii Press, 1984), Frederick C. Drake has devoted much of the last fifteen years to revising his Ph.D. dissertation on Shufeldt (Cornell, 1970). This work spares the authors of such eclectic books as mine from listing "primary" sources; Drake's research in naval, diplomatic, and other areas has been exhaustive, and the results may be located in his voluminous chapter notes. Hence I feel that in general I need itemize only the secondary works (those of Hagan in particular) that I have used to amplify, simplify, or further qualify the points made by Drake.

1.   Africa. (A) Liberia. *ESRWS*, 167–200; Kenneth J. Hagan, *American Gunboat Diplomacy and the Old Navy, 1877–1889* (Westport, Conn., Greenwood Press, 1973), 35–41; ibid., "Alfred Thayer Mahan: Turning America Back to the Sea," in Frank T. Merli and Theodore A. Wilson, eds., *Makers of American*

Diplomacy from Benjamin Franklin to Henry Kissinger, 2 vols. (N.Y., Charles Scribner's Sons, 1974), vol. 1, 287–289; and David M. Pletcher, *The Awkward Years: American Foreign Relations under Garfield and Arthur* (Columbia, University of Missouri Press, 1962), 225–227. (B) Fernando Po and the Congo. *ESRWS*, 200–207; and Hagan, *Gunboat Diplomacy*, 69–77. (C) South Africa. *ESRWS*, 208–210; and Thomas J. Noer, "Commodore Robert W. Shufeldt and America's South African Strategy," *AN*, vol. 34 (April 1974), 81–88. For some reason Hagan has nothing to say about this visit. (D) Madagascar. *ESRWS*, 211–213; Hagan, *Gunboat Diplomacy*, 78–87; and Pletcher, 227–233. (E) Joanna, Comoros. *ESRWS*, 213–215; and Hagan, 87–93. (F) Zanzibar. *ESRWS*, 215–218; and *FCS*, 52.

2. Indian Ocean and Southeast Asia. (A) Aden. *ESRWS*, 219–220; and Hagan, 97–98. (B) Muscat. *ESRWS*, 220–221; and Hagan, 98–101. (C) Persian Gulf. *ESRWS*, 221–225; and Hagan, 101–104. (D) India. *ESRWS*, 225–227; and Hagan, 104–106. (E) Malaya, Borneo, and the Philippines. *ESRWS*, 227–232. Hagan does not discuss this leg of the voyage, except to explain why Shufeldt did not stop at Siam, 106–108.

3. (A) Shufeldt's treaty negotiations, 1880–1883. *USCH 2*, vol. 10, Korea, 99–191; C. I. Eugene Kim and Han-kyo Kim, *Korea and the Politics of Imperialism, 1876–1910* (Berkeley, University of California Press, 1967), 18–30; Michael Hunt, *The Making of a Special Relationship: The United States and China, to 1914* (N.Y., Columbia University Press, 1983), 125–132; Pletcher, 205–213; Milton Plesur, *America's Outward Thrust: Approaches to Foreign Affairs, 1865–1890* (De Kalb, Northern Illinois University Press, 1971), 220–225; *FCS*, 187–189; and Donald S. MacDonald, "The American Role in the Opening of Korea to the West," *Transactions of the Royal Asiatic Society: Korean Branch*, vol. 25 (1959), 51–58. (B) 1880. *ESRWS*, 233–256. Frederick F. Chien, *The Opening of Korea: A Study in Chinese Diplomacy, 1876–1885* (Hamden, Conn., Shoestring Press, 1967), 72–76; Martina Deuchler, *Confucian Gentlemen and Barbarian Envoys: The Opening of Korea, 1875–1885* (Seattle and London, University of Washington Press, 1977), 109–113; Lee Yur-bok, *Diplomatic Relations Between the United States and Korea, 1866–1887* (N.Y., Humanities Press, 1970), 30–38; and *DNANO*, 292–301. (C) 1881. *ERSWS*, 257–275; Chien, 76–86; Deuchler, 114–118; Lee, 38–39; and *DNANO*, 301–308. (D) 1882–1883. Arthur's *Message*, 1883, *FRUS*, 1883, vii–viii; correspondence, 241–250; *NYT*, 30 March, 6 June 1882, 2/6–7, 4/4–5; *ESRWS*, 276–311; Chien, 86–93; Deuchler, 118–122; Lee, 39–43; and *DNANO*, 308–328.

4. U.S. Bureau of Census, *Historical Statistics of the United States: Colonial to 1970*, pt. 2 (Washington, Government Printing Office, 1975), *Series U, Value of U.S. Exports and Reexports by Country of Destination, 1900*, 317–334; and ibid., *Statistical Abstract of the United States* (ibid., 1985), *Table 1466*, 816.

Index